Uncle John's
PERPETUALLY PLEASING
BATHROOM READER®

By the
Bathroom Readers'
Institute

Bathroom Readers' Press
Ashland, Oregon

OUR "REGULAR" READERS RAVE!

"The 'second' best use of paper in the bathroom!!"

— Ann I.

"I learn more on the throne than any other place in life. I promptly forget it, of course, but then there's always another Uncle John's Bathroom Reader. I put it up there with chocolate and WD-40 as one of life's necessities. Thanks, Uncle John."

— Robert G.

"When nature calls...let Uncle John answer."

— Melissa J.

"This book will never make me say 'uncle' on the 'John.'"

— Joe S.

"If I walk out of 'the John' still reading 'the John', does that make me weird or is that normal???"

— Lisandro G.

"Makes me look forward to enchilada night!"

— Neil K.

"Everything I know, I learned from a bathroom reader."

— James F.

"My brother calls me 'a veritable font of useless knowledge.' (He doesn't like losing at Trivial Pursuit.) I say no knowledge is useless."

— Toni H.

"Pure knowledge with a side of humor."

—Leo M.

UNCLE JOHN'S PERPETUALLY PLEASING
BATHROOM READER®

For information, write:
The Bathroom Readers' Institute,
P.O. Box 1117,
Ashland, OR 97520
www.bathroomreader.com

Cover illustration by Michael Brunsfeld
Cover design by Michael Brunsfeld and Sam Schuna

ISBN-13: 978-1-60710-903-7 / ISBN-10: 1-60710-903-4

Library of Congress Cataloging-in-Publication Data
Uncle John's perpetually pleasing bathroom reader.
    pages cm
ISBN 978-1-60710-903-7 (pbk.)
1. American wit and humor. 2. Curiosities and wonders.
PN6165.U53755 2013
081.02'07—dc23
                            2013012388

Printed in Canada
First Printing
1 2 3 4 5 6 7 8   17 16 15 14 13

THANK YOU!

The Bathroom Readers' Institute sincerely thanks the people
whose advice and assistance made this book possible.

Gordon Javna

John Dollison

Jay Newman

Brian Boone

Kim Griswell

Trina Janssen

Thom Little

Michael Brunsfeld

Sam Schuna

Angela Kern

Jack Mingo

Megan Todd

Brandon Hartley

Eleanor Pierce

Sam Javna

Jahnna and Malcolm

Rich Wallace

Jolly Jeff Cheek

Jill Bellrose

Joan M. Kyzer

JoAnn Padgett

Melinda Allman

Aaron Guzman

Ginger, Jennifer,
and Mana

Lilian the Great

Blake Mitchum

Monica Maestas

Maggie Javna

Peter Norton

Brandon Walker

The Marx Brothers

Media Masters

Publishers Group West

W.C. Fields

Raincoast Books

Thomas Crapper

*   *   *

"They say they can make fuel from horse manure. Now I don't know
if your car will be able to get thirty miles to the gallon, but it's sure
gonna put a stop to siphoning."   —**Billie Holliday**

CONTENTS

Because the BRI understands your reading needs, we've
divided the contents by length as well as subject.

Short—a quick read

Medium—2 to 3 pages

Long—for those extended visits, when something
a little more involved is required

* Extended—for those leg-numbing experiences

BATHROOM LORE
Short

Our Kind of Christmas
  Story.............................. 231

Medium

Natural Gas Report................. 54

The Purloined Potties........... 183

Toilet Tech 381

Uncle John's Stall of Fame...... 68

Uncle John's Stall of
  Shame............................. 419

Long

Stall of Fame: Mr. Toilet 267

A MOVING EXPERIENCE
Short

Blue Juice & Landing Lips...... 82

Odd NASCAR Sponsors...... 188

Bubbas & Barber Poles.......... 351

Medium

Road Warriors 61

Just Plane Weird: Bathroom
  Edition 163

The Ford Model K? 339

Long

The Lincoln Highway........... 410

AMERICANA
Short

$2 Bills.................................... 50

Medium

Breakin' Up Is Hard to Do...... 63

Long

The Other Wars Between
  the States......................... 503

*Honest Abe's Family Tree ... 471

BUSINE$$
Short

That's All We Sell 53

Why Didn't I Think of
  That?............................... 274

Medium

"Naturally" Beautiful............. 177

Timeline of Tiffany's.............. 386

Long

Microsoft Millionares............ 155

CANADIANA
Short

As Heard in Canada 245

ATM Vs. ABM 383

Medium

Weird Canada 96

Generic Canada 342

CREATURE FEATURE
Medium

Odd New Animals 44

Cool Critters 359

Mind Your Beeswax! 129

Freaky Frogs........................... 202

Animals in the News 483

Long

What an Animal!.................. 424

7 Fictional Cockroaches 516

Animals Famous for
15 Minutes........................ 520

FADS & FLOPS
Short

Egg-on-a-Stick 15

VCR Bored Games................ 232

Medium

Fake Lobster & Pineapple
Salads................................ 57

1-900-Rip-Off.......................... 83

Tasteless Toys 152

Let's Play Tiddlywinks! 292

Tech-No 349

FOOD & DRINK
Short

Candy Bits............................... 16

Yellow Snow............................ 89

Old-Timey Pies..................... 189

Diner Lingo 227

Curious Crisps 311

Medium

Regional Sandwiches 121

What Do You Want on Your
Hot Dog?........................... 261

The Life of Pies 325

Cooking With Roadkill 31

'Possum À La Road 300

Long

You Don't Know Legumes! ... 405

Eat Today, Gone Tomorrow... 451

FORGOTTEN HISTORY
Short

It Happened in '63 230

Razzle Dazzle Camo.............. 378

Medium

Prohibition Follies................. 205

"We Are Not Amused" 85

The Man Who Hated
Gravity.............................. 131

Man Vs. Gravity Pt. II 438

Long

The Year Without a
Summer............................. 499

*The Explorers...................... 463

GOING, GOING, GONE
Short

The Last Laugh: Epitaphs 98

Famous Last Words 369

Medium

First In Death 218

Buried Alive: a *Die*-Witness
Account 327

The Matthew Wall Awards..... 23

Dead Celebrities
(Who Weren't)................ 185

More Matthew Wall
Awards 356

Long
How to Tell if You're Dead.... 493

GOVERN-MENTAL
Short
Poli-Talks 90
Comedian-in-Chief............... 329
Medium
According to a Government
  Study................................ 27
Take Me to Your Leader.......... 80
Presidential Firsts 119
The Politically Correct
  Quiz................................. 166
The Golden Fleece Awards... 225
Political Firsts........................ 255
Take Me to Your Leader........ 422
According to a Government
  Study.............................. 486
Long
America's Secret Plan to
  Nuke the Moon 305

INTERNATIONAL AFFAIRS
Short
Baby in a Box 321
Medium
Where the Wild Things
  Rule.................................. 295
Ba-Su! Ba-Su! 215
Long
Dustbin of History: a New
  Germany In Texas 286
*A New Germany in Texas,
  Part II.............................. 445
*Dustbin of History:
  Champ Ferguson.............. 507

IT'S A BLUNDERFUL LIFE
Short
Text 911! Text 911! 14
Beat the Press........................ 482
Anarchy in the E.R. 497
Medium
Oops!.. 17
Don't Eat the Money! 175
Flaming Oopses..................... 246
Lame Excuses 366

HOW TO DO STUFF
Medium
How to Grow a
  "Bee Beard"........................ 29
Never Step In…..................... 251
Flash Photography................. 337
How to Enbalm a Dead
  Body................................ 149
The Proper Stance 460

LAW & ORDER
Short
Looney Laws........................... 285
Medium
Scam I Am 213
Dumb Crooks 352
Keystone Kops....................... 116
Long
*An Arresting History of the
  Police Car 477

LIFE IS STRANGE
Short
Crappy Products.................... 154
That's Amore?........................ 250
The Rest of the Story............ 398

Medium

It's a Weird, Weird World 71

Little Things Mean a Lot 123

Class Acts 143

Amazing Luck 309

Lucky Finds 179

Ironic, Isn't It? 271

MOUTHING OFF
Short

Drucker's Business 39

Kanye the Nucleus 56

You Can Do It! 105

Funny Tweets 192

Worst. Page. Ever. 201

Ode to Beer 236

Funny Ladies 263

Action Jacksons 320

MOVIES
Medium

Men in Black, Starring
    David Schwimmer 94

Unmade Sequels 113

Dirty Disney 127

Ghost Directors 253

Die Hard, Starring
    Frank Sinatra 469

An Alan Smithee Film 136

Long

Not-Your-Ordinary Film
    Festival 456

That Movie Really *Did*
    Stink 389

ORIGINS
Medium

Random Origins 21

The Swat Team 75

Founding Fathers 103

First Persons 134

Founding Fathers 344

MYTHS & LEGENDS
Short

Legends of the Rose 42

Medium

Urban Legends 193

Myth-Conceptions 241

"My Crazy Neighbor Said
    That Jackie Did It!" 354

If the Shoe Fits… 233

POP SCIENCE
Short

Know Your Ice 159

Powered by Pee 468

Medium

Paper Airplane
    Aeronautics 108

According to the Latest
    Research 322

Full Metal Jacket 513

Long

Please Touch the Exhibits 373

Aw, Shoot! 314

DNA Mystery: Her Kids
    Are Not Hers! 331

*All About Seashells 528

POP-POURRI
Short

You're My Inspiration 13

Making Scents 106

Uncle John's Page of Lists 115

The Cost of War 162

Uncle John's Page of Lists..... 297
You're My Inspiration 377
Medium
Ask the Experts....................... 51
Adult Summer Camps 171
Simple Math Tricks............... 195
Ask the Experts..................... 303
Simple Math Tricks.............. 346

PUBLIC LIVES
Short
Celebrity Rumors 336
Medium
Four Famous Firstborns........... 40
Stage Name Stories............... 139
A Good Impression............... 209
Family Secrets 228
"I Vant to Be Alone!" 403
Big Stars 77
The Strange Fate of Benito
    Mussolini, Jr. 99
Winners…and Losers............ 222
The Ghillie and the
    Munshi............................. 370
Long
Son of a Boche?..................... 237

SONG & DANCE
Short
Meet Paul Bearer................... 319
Medium
The British Are Coming! 59
Who's Jude 168
The British Are Coming!,
    Part II............................... 211
Pop Music Firsts 265
Second Time Around........... 363

The British Are Coming!,
    Part III............................. 395
"Weird"ed Out 258
Stage Name Origins............. 416
Long
Russian Rib Rock 441
The British Are Coming!,
    Part IV 524

SPORTS
Short
Shoeshines &
    Walkout Bouts.................. 43
Dumb Jocks 362
Tomato Cans & Sunday
    Punches........................... 498
Medium
Forgotten Sports Stars........... 125
Ballpark Eats 160
Name Changers.................... 248
Sports Conspiracy
    Theories........................... 280
Life After Baseball 435

TECHNO
Short
Quotes.com 26
The Meaning of Li-Fi........... 279
Medium
iPod, iPhone, iSmell 47
Dumb Crooks: Tech
    Edition 431
Long
Dustbin of History:
    the Pager......................... 399

THE BODY ECLECTIC
Short
Fitness Fads 365

Lose Weight Now! 397
Medium
Your #1 News Source 66
Old Drug, New Tricks 277
Long
Going Toe-to-Toe 488

THE PRINTED WORD
Short
Flubbed Headlines................... 34
Flubbed Headlines................ 434
Medium
Once Upon a Time… 173
Frightroom Reader 243
Long
Is it Shakespeare…
    or *Fake*speare? 197

TV OR NOT TV
Short
This Is *Jeopardy!* 107
Unseen Game Shows 330
This Is *Jeopardy!*, Pt. 2........... 394
Medium
Late Night No-Shows 35
Grounded TV Pilots.............. 190
Spun-Out Spinoffs 275
Jim Rockford's Answering
    Machine.......................... 298
Talk Nerdy to Me.................. 312
30 Rock…
    Starring Jon Hamm 379
Geraldo Vs. the Skinheads ... 145

WATCH YOUR LANGUAGE
Short
War Words 20
Carney Slang.......................... 148
Hi, My Name Is * 324

Medium
This Page Is Okay 37
Keep Calm and Carry On 73
Familiar Phrases 87
Un-Bee-Lievable................... 207

UNDERWEAR
Short
Special Underwear................ 170
Medium
High-Tech Underwear............ 91
Underwear in the News 428

WORDPLAY
Short
Let Me Write Sign—I Good
    Speak English 19
Bob Rock Rocks!................... 102
Give Me a Sign! 182
Riddle Me This 257
My Other T-Shirt Is a Tux 264
Prison Lingo 294
Warning Labels 348
Misfit Toys............................. 455
Medium
Sniglets.................................. 141
B-10 and Robbed 220
UJPORAD 283
"What a Handle that
    Ramo Obamacare"........... 384

YOU'RE MY HERO
Medium
Local Heroes 414
Nice Stories........................... 110
Long
The Man Who Sees with
    His Ears............................. 533

PLEASED TO SEE YOU!

HERE WE GO AGAIN.
It's our 26th Uncle John's Bathroom Reader!

If this is your first time taking the plunge with us, welcome. If you're an old friend, welcome back.

For the introduction to *Perpetually Pleasing*, rather than just tell you what's in the book, I thought we'd do something different and pull back the curtain to let you in on a few behind-the-scenes secrets.

One of the questions we get asked most often is: "Why don't you put an index in the book?" I think of *Uncle John's Bathroom Reader* as a treasure hunt. When you open the book, you should be able to turn to any page and discover a gem—a fact or a story or a cool quote—that will stick with you for the rest of your life. Sure, we could put an index in here, but that would take away from the fun of the hunt. Sometimes it's nice to wander without a map. And besides, putting an index in the back would mean ten or fifteen fewer pages of bathroom reading. (More maps, less treasure!)

Another question we get asked: "What's with your nutty table of contents? Why don't you make one with normal headings and chapters in order like every other book?" The answer is: "Normal" is overrated. Besides, we're not like every other book. And our table of contents is more like a rough guide—a way for you to see what's inside without spoiling the hunt. Put another way, the *Bathroom Reader* could be best described as a "digest." (I'd say more, but it's not polite to talk about digestion.)

Still another question: "Aren't you afraid you're going to run out of stuff to write about?" Of course we are! I mean...no! It's a big world, and we find new topics to write about every day. We could make *Bathroom Readers* for two lifetimes and only scratch the surface of all the things we want to cover. For example, we've been wanting to share the story of America's first freeway—the Lincoln Highway—for a decade and finally did in this book. And we're also pleased to bring you our long-gestating articles on the British Invasion, the

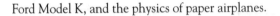

Ford Model K, and the physics of paper airplanes.

And we're always surprising ourselves with our new discoveries. Sometimes, while we're working on one topic, another one pops up. For example, there's an article in *Perpetually Pleasing* about a bizarre Russian fad called "Rib Rock" that we unearthed while researching the Cold War. Another big find for this year's book: The German attempt to start a colony in…Texas.

Finding great new topics is *our* treasure hunt. It seems like one of us at the BRI is always saying: "How have we never written about *that* before?" And here's the good news: By the time we're done with one book, we already have enough ideas to get going on next year's model.

One last question we hear a lot: "Do you have the best job in the world?" The answer is yes. I get to feed my obsession to collect weird information and then share it with you, our legion of loyal fans.

I'd love to tell you more about all the amazing stuff in *Perpetually Pleasing*, but that's for you to discover yourself. (Okay, just one more: A way that doctors used to test if someone was really dead was by twisting their nipples with metal clamps.) That little nugget—and thousands more—are awaiting you. So flip to the next page, or to any page, and start exploring! And as always…

Go with the Flow!

—Uncle John, the BRI staff, and Felix the Dog

YOU'RE MY INSPIRATION

It's always interesting to see where the architects of pop culture get their ideas. Some of these may surprise you.

THE WICKED WITCH OF THE WEST. Matilda Gage (1826–98) was an outspoken American feminist who frightened a lot of men, including her son-in-law—author L. Frank Baum. He borrowed the "scarier" aspects of her personality for the antagonist in his 1900 novel, *The Wonderful Wizard of Oz.*

THE ENERGIZER BUNNY. The rival Duracell battery company actually came up with the idea of a mechanical pink spokesrabbit in 1973. (One difference: no sunglasses.) But when Duracell failed to renew the Bunny's North American trademark, Energizer scooped it up and introduced their own version in 1989. Since then, the Duracell Bunny can only be used overseas.

"MRS. ROBINSON." When director Mike Nichols asked folk duo Simon & Garfunkel to write a song for 1967's *The Graduate*, Paul Simon dusted off an unfinished tune called "Mrs. Roosevelt," based on former First Lady Eleanor Roosevelt. For the film, Simon added some new lyrics and retitled it "Mrs. Robinson" after Anne Bancroft's character.

GRAMPA SIMPSON. When voice actor Dan Castellaneta was a kid, his sister often did a funny impression of old people, saying, "I'm a grandma! I'm a grandpa!" So when you hear Homer's dad yelling at clouds, that's Castellaneta impersonating his sister.

THE KOOL-AID MAN. Originally called the Pitcher Man, he was created in 1954 by ad man Marvin Plotts, who got the idea when his son drew a smiley face in a frosted window. (Oh yeah!)

DIRTY HARRY. Clint Eastwood's tough cop Harry Callahan was based on a real San Francisco detective—Dave Toschi, lead inspector of the Zodiac Killer case (Mark Ruffalo played him in 2007's *Zodiac*). Toschi was also the inspiration for the title character in Steve McQueen's *Bullitt*. California native George Lucas was a fan, too. Proof: In *Star Wars*, Luke Skywalker whines that he "was going to Toschi Station to pick up some power converters!"

A newborn piglet will double its weight in its first week of life. (Well, it does eat like a pig.)

TEXT 911! TEXT 911!

It stands to reason that as texting gets more popular, more people will end up in the emergency room with texting-related injuries. Here are some excerpts from actual emergency room reports.

"28-year-old male riding bicycle and texting on cell phone. Fell off onto face. Broken nose."

"23-year-old male leaving a bar texting on phone, tripped over friend's foot and fell; hit head on pavement, lacerating it."

"14-year-old female texting and walked into a closed glass sliding door. Strained wrist."

"43-year-old male texting on phone and driving. Front vehicle impact; hit a truck."

"12-year-old male in a tree texting on his cell phone. Fell out of tree. Laceration to face."

"Male, intoxicated, 29, texting on cell phone, fell out of wheelchair. Laceration to eyebrow."

"Male, 14, in parking lot standing on shopping cart and texting at same time, fell and hit head. Minor head injury."

"Patient, 15, was texting on his phone not paying attention and ran into a door. Bloody nose."

"Female, 53, tripped over curb while texting. Laceration to face."

"16-year-old male fell while on skateboard and texting at same time. Fractured hand."

"Female, 17, was walking and texting. Walked into a metal pole on street. Minor head injury, loss of consciousness."

"17-year-old male walking and texting; hit by car. Bruised leg."

"11-year-old female fell down steps while texting and wearing flip-flops. Ankle injury."

"12-year-old male was texting on cell phone and fell down six steps off of porch. Knee pain."

"Patient, 39, riding his bike while texting on cell phone and crashed the bike. Sustained a head injury. Had also been drinking alcohol."

"17-year-old female has been texting continuously for the last nine months according to Dad. Right wrist hurts."

What are "pluots" and "apriums"? Plum-apricot hybrids.

EGG-ON-A-STICK

Kitchen gadgets you didn't know you needed (because you probably don't).

Dog Dicer. It looks like an egg slicer. You place a hot dog in the tray and push down on the lid, and it cuts your dog into bite-sized pieces (which could also be done with a knife) to "reduce the risk of choking." Cost: $12.95

Hot Dog Toaster. Like an ordinary toaster, except the bread slots are replaced with two round holes for the hot dogs and two crescent-shaped holes for toasting the buns. Cost: $19.00

Better Bagger. Two plastic arms jutting up from a stand. Clip a bag to the arms; it holds the bag open for you. Cost: Ten bucks!

Bottle-Cap Buddy. This product promises to "keep those pesky bugs from spoiling your drink while you're outside." It's a plastic flip-top cap that goes on top of a soda bottle, replacing the cap that came with the bottle. How did you ever live without it? Cost: $13.99

Spinning Spaghetti Fork. "A thumb-activated button on the handle sets the prongs turning at 22 rpm, smoothly winding pasta into a mess-free mouthful, rather than fumbling awkwardly with a helper spoon or slurping up long noodles." Cost: $29.95 for two

Beer Hammer Bottle Opener. Replaces the claw on a standard claw hammer with a bottle opener. One way or another, somebody's getting hammered! Cost: $8.99

The RoboStir. Place this battery-powered device in any pot and its three "legs" rotate on silicone "feet" to stir your food while you do something else. Except that it says on the box, "Do not leave unattended." (You might want to try a spoon instead.) Cost: $9.99

Tabletop Cotton Candy Maker. For people who crave carnival food, but don't feel comfortable eating anything that's been touched by carnies. Cost: $69.95

Rollie EggMaster. Pour in eggs, and "Rollie" cooks them to a rubbery consistency, then pushes the cylindrical cooked eggs back up through the pour slot…on a stick, like an egg popsicle. Cost: $29.99

Babies are born with tastebuds on the inside of their cheeks. By adulthood they're gone.

CANDY BITS

The sweetest page in this book.

• Thanks to Halloween, the top five U.S. candy-selling days are all in October. Number one: the 28th.

• In ancient India, the Sanskrit word for a piece of crystallized sugar was *khanda*, which was later Anglicized to *candy*.

• One out of every five peanuts on Earth ends up in a chocolate bar.

• In 1925, Massachusetts chocolate salesman Robert Welch made a caramel lollipop on a stick, which he called the Papa Sucker. In 1932, the name was changed to Sugar Daddy.

• Sam Born, who invented the popular Easter candy, Peeps, was Jewish.

• In the two weeks leading up to Christmas, two billion candy canes will be sold.

• The world's hottest sweet: Vertigo Pepper Candy, made with *Bhut Jolokia*, also known as the ghost pepper. It ranks at 2 million Scoville units on the hotness scale. (Atomic Fireballs rank at 3,500.)

• Where can you find edamame-flavored Kit Kats? Japan.

• In 2001, a chocolate bar from Robert Scott's 1901 journey to the Antarctic was sold at auction. Price: $687.

• Every two and a half days, one billion M&M's are made.

• Candy Corn was once marketed under the name "Chicken Feed."

• According to the U.S. Census, the average American eats 25 pounds of candy per year.

• Hershey's Kisses were introduced in 1907, but the company was unable to trademark the name "Kiss" for decades because the courts ruled that "kiss" was a generic term for a small candy. Hershey's finally got the word trademarked in 2001.

• The world's oldest person, Jeanne Calment of France, lived to be 122 years old. Until she was 119, she ate nearly two pounds of chocolate every week. (Results not typical.)

OOPS!

*Everyone loves tales of outrageous blunders, especially
when they happen to someone else. So go ahead
and feel superior for a few minutes.*

NICE TRY, INDIANA JONES

In the middle of the night in April 2013, firefighters in Tucson, Arizona, were called to the scene of an unconscious man (unnamed in press reports) pinned under his SUV in his driveway. Rescuers had to lift the truck in order to free the man. When he came to at the hospital, he explained that he was trying to perform a late-night stunt. His plan was to put his SUV in reverse, jump out the back, and then lie down on the ground and let the vehicle roll over him. Then he would jump up, get in, and hit the brakes before it left the driveway. But he only made it as far as the "get under the SUV" part before the vehicle dragged him a few feet and then rolled to a stop directly on top of him. According to doctors (and Darwin), he's lucky to be alive.

STUMPED

"It is possible to actually love a tree. I *loved* those trees," said Carol Denny of Stroud Township, Pennsylvania, who had doted on her dear dogwoods for several years. That is, until she returned home one spring afternoon in 2013 to discover that all of them had been chopped down. Apparently, there was a mix-up between the power company, PPL Electric Utilities, and the tree removal company, Asplundh, which was only supposed to *trim* the trees away from the power lines. After Denny complained, PPL apologized, and Asplundh offered to give her a wooden birdhouse that she could "place on one of the stumps."

TOUGH DAY AT THE OFFICE

Aviva Investors, a London-based company with offices in several countries, employs more than 1,300 people. On Friday, April 19, 2013, they all received an e-mail informing them that they were fired: "Hand over company property and security passes before leaving the building...I would like to take this opportunity to thank you and wish you all the best for the future." As the 1,300 confused, angry workers were clearing out their desks and contemplating the future, another mass e-mail was sent informing them that they weren't getting fired—the e-mail was meant to go to one worker, but was accidentally sent to the entire staff. Management apologized for the confusion and told them all to get back to work.

AMPHIBIOUS ASSAULT

Three Japanese college students wanted to visit North Stradbroke Island, off the coast of Brisbane, Australia. When the GPS unit in their rental car instructed them to *drive* to the island, they followed the route to the water's edge...and kept driving into the bay. They had to make a quick escape before their car sank. The ordeal was witnessed by several people on a nearby ferry, which is how most travelers get to the island. "The GPS told us we could drive down there," a stunned 21-year-old Yuzu Noda told the *Brisbane Times*. "It kept saying it would navigate us to the road." The young tourists were uninjured, but the rental car was lost.

THE SQUEEZE

A 22-year-old college student named Courtney Malloy was walking around in Providence, Rhode Island, late one night in 2012 when she got stuck in an 8-inch gap between two buildings. Passersby heard her cries for help and called 9-1-1. When firefighters arrived, they found her a few feet above the ground in a horizontal position. Unable to reach her, the firefighters had to enter one of the buildings and take out a portion of the wall in order to free her. Malloy, who'd had a bit too much to drink that night, couldn't remember how she got there; witnesses had assumed she'd fallen from the roof of one of the buildings. However, when she woke up the next day, Malloy remembered what happened: She'd simply tried to take a "shortcut" between the two buildings. (She's thin—she wasn't *that* thin.)

*   *   *

"I'm trying to read a book on how to relax, but I keep falling asleep."

—Jim Loy

Since 1970, the width of a standard casket has grown from 22 inches to 26 inches.

LET ME WRITE SIGN—
I GOOD SPEAK ENGLISH

Actual signs, menu entries, and assorted notices from around the world.

At a religious site in Burma:
"Foot Wearing Prohibited"

In a Japanese bowling alley:
"Do you like bowling? Let's play bowling. Breaking down the pins and getting hot communication."

On a tank in a pet shop in China: "Letting Them Turtle"

In Saudi Arabia: "No slaughtering sheep at the beach"

At a shop in Thailand: "Mr. J's Condoms (Homemade). 20 Years Guarantee."

A street sign in Kerala, India: "GO SLOW: Accident Porn Area"

At the Great Wall of China: "If you have or brain disease, please ascend the Great Wall according to your capability."

Outside a restaurant in Thailand: "Our Food is Guaranteed to Not Cause Pregnancy."

In a clothing store in India: "The Proceeds gose to women who made all those Stuff."

On a menu in Cairo: "Half Gilled Chicken and Herpes"

On a package of chicken in China: "Former chicken"

In an Acapulco hotel: "The manager has personally passed all the water served here."

At a Beijing hair salon: "ASS Hair Salon"

In a Korean grocery store in Honolulu: "Please do not Taste a Food With Your Bear Hand."

On a restaurant menu in Paris: "Tomatoes, goat dung on toast, country ham, nuts"

In a hotel in Delhi, India: "Our dog is friendly. Please do not touch or pet him."

At an Istanbul souvenir stand: "Sorry We're Open"

Liquid oxygen is sky blue.

WAR WORDS

Some terms and phrases that were invented on the battlefield.

GRAPE. It first described a hooked weapon that 12th-century soldiers used to pierce armor and then yank it off the wearer. During peaceful times, it was used to pull fruit off vines. The words *grapple* and *grape* both come from the weapon.

TOXIC. Ancient Greek soldiers' bows were called *toxons*; a poison-smeared arrow was a *toxicon*, which led to the Latin verb *toxicare*, "to smear with poison."

FLAK. An abbreviation of *Flieger Abwehr Kanone*, a World War I German anti-aircraft gun. The word was used in WWII to describe bulletproof flak jackets worn by American airmen. In the 1960s, it became a term for verbal abuse, as in, "Don't give me any flak."

RANDOM. Comes from the German *rand*, meaning "outer limit." A soldier moving at top speed (on foot or by horse) would fire his weapon haphazardly. Where the shot came down was unpredictable. Soon anything unpredictable was described as *random*.

GARNISH. In Old French, a *garniss* was a warning that an attack was imminent, after which the castle would be quickly "dressed" with soldiers. *Garnish* entered Middle English, meaning "embellish," but didn't take on its culinary meaning "to embellish food" until the 17th century.

OVER THE TOP. When a WWI trench soldier attacked, he would literally go "over the top" of the trench, yelling loudly to scare the enemy. Later, any over-exaggerated behavior was considered "over the top."

HIGH AND LOW PROFILE. A product of the Cold War, when foreign sea vessels were designated "high profile" if they were battleships or carriers, and "low profile" if they were smaller boats or subs.

FRANK. This word for "honest" comes from the Francs, who wielded *francons* (javelins) in battle against other Germanic tribes. The Francs were known for being "free and open," which gave rise to the English word *frank* (1300s) and also to the country of France.

Country with the most circus performers: Russia, with over 15,000.

RANDOM ORIGINS

Once again, the BRI asks—and answers—the question:
Where does all this stuff come from?

MULTIPLEX MOVIE THEATERS

Nat Taylor owned the Elgin Theatre, a movie house in Ottawa, Canada. In late 1947, he opened another, smaller theater called the Little Elgin…right next-door, showing the same film that was at the Elgin. It wasn't until ten years later that he got the idea to show two *different* movies on the two screens. The concept worked, and by 1964, he'd opened two more twin-plexes in Montreal and Toronto. Around the same time, AMC Theatres president Stan Durwood got the idea of expanding a movie theater to two screens—doubling revenue without having to increase his staff. Still, both screens played the same movie. AMC debuted the first true multiplex in 1966 with a Kansas City theater playing four different movies on four different screens. Then AMC built a six-screen complex in Omaha in 1969. Multiplexes got bigger and bigger. In 1979, Nat Taylor opened the Cineplex in Toronto—the largest theater at the time—with 18 screens…and expanded it to 21 just two years later. In 1988, Kinepolis in Brussels, Belgium, topped that with 25 screens, and in 1996, the AMC Ontario Mills opened in California—it's got 30 screens.

INSTANT REPLAY

In the early 1960s, CBS hired young TV director Tony Verna, who had worked on the 1960 Olympics, to direct broadcasts of football games. Verna kept looking for ways to make timeouts, huddles, and other gaps in the action more compelling to TV audiences…and he found one: He'd videotape the game as it was being aired live, then rewind the tape to just before the beginning of the play to give viewers an "instant replay" of big moments in the game. Verna used the technique for the first time on December 7, 1963, for a broadcast of the Army-Navy football game in Philadelphia. Early video machines weighed 1,200 pounds and weren't exactly portable, and there were lots of glitches—cameras were usually trained on quarterbacks and didn't follow the action, for example. But Verna's technique did catch a one-yard touchdown play in the fourth

---

In blind "smell tests," mothers rated their own baby's diapers as the least smelly.

quarter. (As it was being replayed, commentator Lindsey Nelson said, "This is not live! Ladies and gentlemen, Army did not score again.") In 1965, ABC added slo-mo replay to its baseball broadcasts. In 1986, the NFL adopted the technology, allowing referees to use it to review and even overturn their own calls.

ELVIS IMPERSONATORS

Elvis Presley was so popular when he burst onto the music scene in the mid-1950s that impersonators sprung up almost immediately. The first person to ever publicly impersonate Presley's distinctive voice and hip-shaking moves was a 16-year-old named Jim Smith. (Presley was only 21 at the time.) In 1956, Smith did his Elvis act at dances and pageants in his hometown of Victoria, British Columbia, and became a local celebrity. Norm Pringle, the only DJ in town who played Presley's records, put Smith on his TV show, where he would lip-sync and pantomime playing the guitar to Presley songs. The first person to embody the common image of "Elvis impersonator"—the overweight, jumpsuit, Las Vegas-era Elvis— was comedian Andy Kaufman, who impersonated "late-period Elvis" while Elvis was still alive, as part of his live act in the mid-'70s.

STORAGE UNITS

Wherever people live, there has to be someplace for their stuff. In China, 6,000 years ago, people kept small belongings in clay pots, which were then stored in huge underground storage caves. In the 19th century, when wealthy Europeans set off on long voyages, they put their bankers in charge of their belongings. The bankers contracted with moving companies that stored the items in warehouses (basically stables without the animals in them). One of those moving companies, Bekins, opened a warehouse specifically for the storage of household goods and personal treasures in the 1850s, offering more security and a stronger roof to prevent rain damage. Storing things in movers' warehouses was the norm in the U.S. into the mid-20th century, when rented self-storage lockers came into being. In the 1960s, Russ Williams, a Texas oilman, needed someplace to store his oil field equipment when he went fishing, and his fishing gear when he went drilling for oil. Inspired by a row of tenant garages at an apartment building in Irving, Texas, he opened the A-1 U-Store-It U-Lock-It U-Carry-the-Key self-storage company in Odessa, Texas.

Nanomaterials are 10,000 times smaller than a human hair.

THE MATTHEW WALL AWARDS

Folks in the English village of Braughing have been observing October 2 as "Old Man's Day" for more than 500 years. Who's the old man? Matthew Wall. His claim to fame: He got a remarkable second chance at life. And it turns out he's not the only one.

WORST CAS(KET) SCENARIO

In the fall of 1571, a farmer named Matthew Wall fell ill on the eve of his wedding day and "died." His funeral was set for October 2, and at the appointed hour, the pallbearers arrived to carry the departed Wall to his final rest. As they made their way down Fleece Lane toward the churchyard, one of the pallbearers slipped on some wet leaves and sent the coffin crashing to the ground.

The person who dropped Wall must have been horrified by the blunder, but his horror surely was nothing compared to the shock that ensued when Wall, revived by the jolt, began pounding on the inside of the coffin and demanding to be let out.

BORN AGAIN

Whatever it was that caused Wall to become so ill, he soon got over it and made a full recovery. He married his sweetheart, fathered two sons, and lived another 24 years before dying of old age in 1595. Wall was so grateful for his deliverance (and for not being buried alive) that he celebrated October 2 as a second birthday for the rest of his life. When he died, he left instructions in his will that the celebrations continue and left some property and money to ensure that they would be.

Though he was saved by slippery leaves on Fleece Lane, for some reason, Wall requested that the lane be swept each year on October 2, and he arranged for a small payment to be made to the person doing the sweeping. Today, the local vicar is in charge of the effort, and each year receives £1 for his or her trouble. (The money goes into the church's poor box.) The actual sweeping is done by the schoolchildren of Braughing, some 60 to 70 in all, who meet

---

First known clock: Egyptian obelisks (3500 B.C.) acted as sundials.

the vicar at the top of Fleece Lane with brooms and brushes at the ready.

When the sweeping is finished, the group moves on to the churchyard where, as Wall requested, the church bells are rung as if for a funeral. The children gather around Wall's grave, prayers are said, and a song is sung. The church bells are rung a second time, this time in a celebratory way, just as they would be at a wedding. Then the children are given sweets and sent on their way. Everyone who has grown up in Braughing has a memory of participating in Old Man's Day. The tradition is so beloved that it is likely to continue for a long time to come.

WALL OF FAME

Matthew Wall isn't the only person to have revived after being given up for dead. Here are a few other people who lived to tell a similar tale—or didn't:

Honoree: Nicephorus Glycas, the Greek Orthodox Metropolitan (a bishop) of the island of Lesbos in 1896

Rest in Peace: In early 1896, Glycas, 80, took to his bed with what was assumed to be a terminal illness and was pronounced dead by his doctors several days later. Had he been an ordinary person, he would likely have been buried—alive—within 12 hours of the pronouncement of death. But because he was a metropolitan, he was dressed in his official vestments and propped up on a throne in the church, where he was to "sit" for three days and nights as mourners filed past his body to pay their respects.

Born Again: As the *London Echo* reported in March 1896, "On the second night of the 'exposition of the corpse,' the Metropolitan suddenly started up from his seat and stared round him with amazement and horror at all the panoply of death amidst which he had been seated. The priests were no less horrified when the 'dead' bishop demanded what they were doing with him. The old man had simply fallen into a death-like lethargy, which the incompetent doctors had hastily concluded to be death. He is now hale and hearty as can well be expected from an octogenarian."

Honoree: George Hayward, a farm boy in Moreton-in-Marsh, Gloucestershire, England, in the 1840s

Rest in Peace: Hayward was struck in the skull with a pitchfork while working on his parents' farm. His condition worsened, and a few days later he was pronounced dead. He was actually fully conscious, though immobilized and unable to communicate that he was still alive. Like John Macintyre (see the article on page 327), he remained completely alert as he was placed in his coffin and lowered into his grave. He could even hear the dirt hitting the lid of his coffin as the unknowing gravediggers buried him alive.

Born Again: Within hours of his funeral, Hayward's doctors began arguing over whether he'd really died from his injury or had in fact been killed by an infectious disease. Fearing an epidemic but not wanting to cause a panic, they secretly dug him up and were about to perform an autopsy when Hayward summoned enough strength to flutter his eyelids. The teenager made a full recovery and later moved to America, where he became a jeweler. He died at the age of 82.

Honoree: An unnamed German murderer, executed in the 1700s. His story was told in *The Newgate Calendar*, a book of famous and notorious criminal cases published in London in 1824.

Rest in Pieces: As was the case in other parts of Europe in the 18th century, the bodies of executed German criminals were given to medical schools for use as anatomical specimens. This particular "notorious malefactor" was taken directly from the gallows to a medical college to be dissected in front of a group of surgeons.

Born Again (Almost): As the criminal's body was being placed on the dissecting table, the lecturing surgeon, or "operator," detected signs of life. Noting this, he said to the surgeons:

> I am pretty certain, gentlemen, from the warmth of the subject, and the flexibility of the limbs, that by a proper degree of attention and care the vital heat would return, and life in consequence take place. But when it is considered what a rascal we should again have among us, that he was hanged for so cruel a murder, and that, should we restore him to life, he would probably kill somebody else: I say, gentlemen, all these things considered, it is my opinion that we had better proceed with the dissection.

The surgeons "nodded in accordance," the *Newgate Calendar* reports, "and the operator, on the signal, plunged his knife into the breast of the culprit, thereby at once precluding all dread of future assassinations—and all hopes of future repentance."

Only about one in four lightning strikes reach the ground—most are between clouds.

QUOTES.COM

We typed "What is the Internet?" into Google and got back 3.54 billion results in 0.23 seconds (really). Here are our favorite 13.

"The Internet is the nervous system of mother Earth…a living creature, linking up."
—**Dan Millman**

"The Internet is becoming the town square for the global village of tomorrow."
—**Bill Gates**

"Doing research on the Web is like using a library assembled piecemeal by pack rats and vandalized nightly."
—**Roger Ebert**

"Computers have made it really easy to rant. It's made everyone overly opinionated."
—**Scott Weiland**

"It is the greatest truth of our age: Information is not knowledge."
—**Caleb Carr**

"The Internet is a big distraction."
—**Ray Bradbury**

"Google can bring you 100,000 answers; a librarian can bring you back the right one."
—**Neil Gaiman**

"If television's a babysitter, the Internet is a drunk librarian who won't shut up."
—**Dorothy Gambrell**

"The Internet is the trailer park for the soul."
—**Marilyn Manson**

"Sometimes, the Internet can feel like a middle-school playground populated by brats in ski masks who name-call and taunt with the fake bravery of the anonymous. But sometimes—thank goodness—it's nicer than real life."
—**Susan Orlean**

"I have one major problem with the Internet: It's full of liars."
—**Johnny Rotten**

"The Internet has been a boon and a curse for teenagers."
—**J. K. Rowling**

"The seven marvels that best represent man's achievements over the last 2,000 years will be determined by Internet vote, so look for Howard Stern's *Private Parts* to come in No. 1."
—**Jon Stewart**

ACCORDING TO A GOVERNMENT STUDY

The federal government spends billions of dollars on research each year, and we have the moon landings, the Internet, fuel-efficient cars, and countless other benefits to show for it. But not every federally funded study passes the sniff test, as these examples from the 1970s and '80s show.

S**tudy:** "Social and Emotional Messages of Smiling: An Ethological Approach"

Purpose: To find out when and why bowlers, hockey fans, and pedestrians smile. It was part of a National Institute for Mental Health grant to study "Verbal and Nonverbal Cues in Detecting Deception." (Cost to taxpayers: $75,000)

Methodology: The researchers observed all three groups, and filmed the bowlers in secret. According to the authors, "An observer knelt on a platform among the pin-setting equipment at the end of the bowling alley behind the bowling pins and watched bowlers through binoculars as they finished through their roll."

Findings: 1) "Bowlers often smile when socially engaged, looking at and talking to others, but not necessarily after scoring a spare or a strike."

2) "Bowlers rarely smile while facing the pins but often smiled when facing their friends."

3) Hockey fans smiled "both when they were socially involved and after events favorable to their team."

4) Pedestrians "were much more likely to smile when talking but only slightly more likely to smile in response to nice weather than to unpleasant weather."

Study: Pigeonomics

Purpose: To test "the fundamental economic principles of supply and demand on pigeons." (Cost to taxpayers: $144,012)

Methodology: The pigeons were trained to "pay for their food" by pecking on a key. Different keys delivered different foods, and the "price" of each food was set by adjusting the number of pecks required and the quantity of food provided. Some foods were expensive (many pecks required for a little bit of food) and others were priced cheaply (just a peck or two delivered a lot of the food).

Findings: 1) "Changes in the relative price of these goods resulted in the birds substituting the lower-priced good just as humans would buy fewer apples when their price rose."

2) "Nonhuman workers (pigeons) are willing to trade off income for leisure if the price is right."

Study: "Environmental Determinants of Human Aggression"

Purpose: To test "if environmental determinants such as sexual arousal, humor, and empathy reduce human aggression in the form of horn honking" (Cost to taxpayers: $46,100)

Methodology: A researcher driving a car would stop at a red light at a predetermined Chicago intersection and wait for the light to turn green. When it did, the researcher would sit there for about 15 seconds. "The purpose was to determine when and how often the driver immediately behind would become impatient and aggressive enough to honk his horn." While this was happening, a young female researcher would walk past the stopped driver dressed in a "brief and revealing outfit" to test sexual arousal, wearing a clown mask to test humor, or hobbling on crutches with a bandaged leg to test empathy.

Findings: 1) "Empathy and humor as well as sexual arousal reduced the amount of horn honking."

2) "Not only did the male drivers smile at the briefly attired young lady and watch her walk down the street; but some whistled or made sexually oriented comments."

*   *   *

A COLD JOKE

A distraught man goes to his doctor and says, "Doc, there's a piece of lettuce sticking out of my butt!" The doctor asks him to drop his pants and examines him.

The man asks, "Doc, is it serious?!"

The doctor replies, "Sorry to tell you this, but it's just the tip of the iceberg."

Female hares can conceive a second litter of offspring while still pregnant with the first.

HOW TO GROW A "BEE BEARD"

Warning! Do not even THINK about doing this at home.

HONEY, I'M HOME
You've probably seen pictures of bee beards—brave and foolhardy people with their lower faces covered in insects, as if they're auditioning for some kind of entomologist-only version of ZZ Top. It's an old pastime among thrill-seeking bee fanciers. Ukrainian beekeeper Petro Prokopovych, the inventor of several beekeeping innovations still in use today, modeled the first bee beard in the 1830s. Demonstrating what he'd learned about bee-swarm behavior, Prokopovych placed a captive queen in a cage under his chin and released thousands of bees near his face. Sure enough, the bees went into their typical swarming behavior, bunching tightly around their queen, creating a "beard" that hung off his chin. Naturally, his stunt inspired imitators, and bee bearders soon became as popular in carnivals and freak shows as fat ladies, dog-faced boys, and wild men of Borneo.

THE STING
Making a bee beard isn't difficult, but it takes guts and a willingness to be stung a few times. Warning: This is NOT recommended for kids or anyone with an allergy or aversion to bee stings or any level of good sense…But, here's how it's done:

• Select a hive with easy-going bees willing to put up with your outrageous shenanigans without exacting too much revenge. (You must be experienced with bees to be able to identify this kind of hive.)

• Find the queen and lock her in a "queen cage"—a small wooden box with metal screening on one side that looks sort of like a homemade kazoo.

• For a lush, full beard, you need about 12,000 bees (three pounds). Box them up with the captive queen the day before, keep them in the dark, and feed them well. Spritzing them with sugar water is said to work pretty well for this. The intent is to calm them.

• When you're ready for the beard, tie the queen cage (screen facing out, not against your skin) under your chin. Protect your eyes with swim goggles. Bees will crawl everywhere, so cover your hair, button and secure your shirt, tuck your pants into your socks, put cotton loosely in your nostrils and ears, and put vaseline around your mouth and eyes.

• Remaining calm from this point on may seem counter-intuitive, but it is very, very important. Open the box and hold it against your chest so they can smell the queen. They will begin crawling up your neck to surround the queen's cage, hanging in bee garlands from your skin and each other.

• If all goes well, the worst that will happen is that you'll have to get used to the slightly electric sensation of thousands of bees gripping your skin with their barbed feet. Pose triumphantly for photos.

• While things are still going well, have your assistant untie the queen cage from your neck and place it inside the box you want the bees to return to.

• Standing over the box, jump up into the air and land hard. Do this only once and do it well. This will dislodge most of the bees onto your feet and the ground around your feet. (Aren't you glad you tucked your pants into your socks?) The befuddled bees will smell the queen and begin crawling toward and into the box. Any remaining bees can be gently brushed off with a bee brush. Eventually, all of them will make their way back to the box, ready to be transported home.

Final note: Hope for the best, but prepare for the worst. Odds are pretty good that you'll get a sting or two, even if you do it right. Experienced bearders sometimes misjudge the bees, the weather, or their own calmness and get stung dozens of times. Be prepared for medical emergencies and the potential of bees attacking civilians. Although they dread having to use them, pros keep two emergency tools handy: a sprayer filled with soapy water that can kill masses of bees…and an industrial shop vacuum to dispose of the evidence.

EXTREME BEARDING. As if a three-pound beard isn't impressive enough, there's a new trend in competitive bee bearding, in which the beard covers the bearder's entire body. World record: 87 pounds of bees (approximately 350,000 of them), set in 1998 by American Mark Biancaniello.

The metal gallium has a melting point of 85°F. It will melt in your hand.

COOKING WITH ROADKILL

Most of us simply keep on driving when we see a splattered 'possum on the side of the highway, but a peculiar few ask, "Why let all that free meat go to waste?"

CLEAR AND PHEASANT DANGER

One day in the 1950s, a 15-year-old British kid named Arthur Boyt found a dead pheasant on the ground while bicycling through a park near Windsor Castle. The creature piqued his curiosity, and he brought it home to show his mother. Mrs. Boyt responded in a way that might prompt a visit from a social worker today: She cooked the bird and told Arthur to eat it—not to teach him a lesson about the dangers of bringing home dead things, but because pheasants are game birds and good to eat.

Young Arthur happily ate the bird. Now in his seventies, he remembers the experience fondly. Boyt never lost his sense of wonder regarding the natural world: He became an entomologist, someone who studies bugs. And he never lost his taste for eating dead critters hit by cars, either. As he grew older and became philosophically opposed to hunting (cruel) and farm-raised meats (cruel and unhealthy), he obtained more and more of his meat on the road. The last time he purchased a piece of store-bought meat: 1976. All the creatures he's eaten since then—more than 5,000 animals in all—have been roadkill. Roast deer, spaghetti in hedgehog sauce, breast of barn owl, pheasant stew, pigeon pot pie, badger sandwiches (his favorite), you name it—if a car can hit it, Boyt has probably eaten it. He even eats rats, which he insists are delicious stewed. "People say rats carry disease, but I'd sooner eat a country rat than any raw meat you get served in restaurants," he told *The Times* of London in 2003.

IN THE STATES

Boyt isn't alone. In the United States, more than a dozen states allow the collecting of roadkill for food, and the number is growing. In 2011, Illinois Governor Pat Quinn vetoed a bill legalizing the

---

First Briton in space: Astronaut Helen Sharman (1991).

collecting of roadkill from the state's highways, fearing that people might themselves become roadkill while trying to drag critters off the asphalt. But the bill was so popular that the state legislature voted 87–28 to override the veto, and the bill is now law.

The rules regarding collecting roadkill vary. In some states, a permit is required; in others, carcasses may be collected only during hunting season. Reason: Officials want to discourage "bumper hunting"—deliberately running down game animals at times of the year when shooting them would be illegal. In Alaska, food banks, homeless shelters, and other charities get first dibs on meat from the more than 800 moose killed by cars and trains each year. (One adult moose yields as much as 700 pounds of meat.)

KIDS, DON'T FRY THIS AT HOME

If you're thinking about taking the plunge, it's important to know that handling and eating roadkill can kill you if you don't know what you're doing. Just because that tasty-looking raccoon died when it was hit by a car doesn't mean it didn't have rabies. If you're not experienced at handling wild game meat, it's not worth the risk. That being said, here are some safety tips from the pros:

• Know the animal and the parasites and diseases it suffers from. Know the visible signs of these maladies, so that you can distinguish healthy animals from sick ones.

• Wear goggles and thick rubber gloves when handling roadkill and preparing the meat for cooking. This is necessary to prevent blood (which may be disease-infected) from getting into your eyes and cuts in your skin. After working with the animal, thoroughly wash your hands and any blood-stained clothing immediately.

• Best time to look for roadkill: early in the morning. Many nocturnal animals are hit by cars when they come out at night, and road crews are unlikely to pick them up until the next day. Cooler temperatures after dark help prevent the meat from spoiling.

• Refrigerate raw meat immediately. Be sure to cook the meat to an internal temperature of at least 170° to kill bacteria.

• Only undamaged meat is edible, so look for animals killed by "clean hits," i.e., critters that were struck once, thrown to the side of the road by the impact, and not hit again. Animals that have been run over and squashed flat ("road pizza") are inedible.

Teflon was used in the first atomic bomb.

• Select only "fresh" roadkill—animals that have been hit by cars very recently. Evaluate them like fresh fish at the market. Is the animal's nose still moist? Are its eyes full and clear? Does it bleed bright red blood freely when you cut into its skin? These are signs of freshness. If it smells bad or rigor mortis has set in, leave it be.

• That's one school of thought, anyway. "I have consumed meat that was blown up, like horses on the Western Front (World War I)," Arthur Boyt told *The Times*. "If bodies are swollen, gasified, and green, they do taste different, but if you cook them thoroughly, you can still eat them. I have done it and had no repercussions."

SMORGASBROAD

So what do roadkill animals taste like? Here's a sampling:

Fox: Mild and salty, with little or no fat and a nice texture. (But it can make you burp.)

Rabbit: Bland.

Buffalo: High in protein, low in cholesterol, and half the calories and fat of beef, with a similar taste. Use in any beef recipe.

Swan: Unpleasant and muddy-tasting.

Ostrich: Tastes like venison and should be prepared as such. Best sautéed or grilled medium-rare.

Pheasant: A rich flavor similar to chicken, which is improved if the bird is refrigerated, unplucked, for three days.

Rat: A salty taste like ham or pork. Good in stir-fries.

Frog: Flavor and texture similar to chicken. Also good stir-fried.

Bear: A strong taste that can be improved by refrigerating the meat for 24 hours. Good in pot roasts and stews; prepare like beef.

Goose: Dark meat that tastes like roast beef.

Pigeon: Meat that's "dark, rich, tender, and succulent," and good roasted, broiled, braised (fried, then stewed), grilled or sautéed. Serve medium-rare, or the meat will taste like liver.

Hedgehog: Fatty, with an unpleasant taste.

Boar: Flavor ranges from mild to pungent, depending on the boar's age, diet, and the season of the year that it was hit by the car.

Ready to cook? See "'Possum À La Road" on page 300.

Top 3 baby names for boys in 2011: Jacob, Mason, William; girls: Sophia, Isabella, and Emma.

FLUBBED HEADLINES

Whether silly, naughty, or just plain bizarre—they're all real.

Planes forced to
land at airports

*Cows lose their jobs
as milk prices drop*

Sewage Spill Kills Fish,
but Water Safe to Drink

Study Shows Frequent Sex
Enhances Pregnancy Chances

**Top Secret Mission
to Launch Tuesday**

Laxative helps remove earwax

Local Children Are
Winners at Dog Show

*Tylenol Bottles: Hard to
Open for 30 Years*

Pirates sign up new hooker

*Hospitals Resort
to Hiring Doctors*

City unsure why
the sewer smells

**"We hate math," say 4 in 10
— a majority of Americans**

*Alton Attorney
Accidentally Sues Himself*

Fan gets kicked out of Kenny
Chesney concert for looking
too much like Kenny Chesney

Nutt faces sack

**Smoke alarms could be
disaster warning system**

Police Arrest Everyone
on February 22nd

Starvation Can Lead to
Health Hazards

**Animal Rights Group to
Hold Meeting at Steakhouse**

Good smell perplexes
New Yorkers

Bridges Help People
Cross Rivers

Miracle Cure Kills
Fifth Patient

Worker suffers leg pain
after crane drops
800-lb. ball on his head

You thought it was healthier? Think again—sherbet has more sugar than ice cream.

LATE NIGHT NO-SHOWS

There are only a handful of hosting jobs available in late-night TV.
Here are the stories of some big names who actually turned
down the chance to host their own late-night talk show.

LATE NIGHT WITH DANA CARVEY

When NBC's *Late Night With David Letterman* moved to CBS in 1993, NBC hired *Saturday Night Live* creator Lorne Michaels to develop a replacement show. The network told him he could hire anyone he wanted to host the show—and he had someone in mind—but they still made him extend the offer to a short-list of contenders. The list included former *SNL* star Dana Carvey, comedian Garry Shandling (who had just begun starring in *The Larry Sanders Show*, an HBO sitcom about a fictional late-night show), and future TV stars Drew Carey and Jon Stewart. But Michaels wanted 29-year-old Conan O'Brien (the world said, "Who?"), a writer on *The Simpsons* and *Saturday Night Live*, whose on-screen experience was made up entirely of one-line parts in *Saturday Night Live* sketches. Michaels ended up getting his way, and *Late Night with Conan O'Brien* ran from 1993 to 2009.

THE LATE SHOW STARRING HOWARD STERN

The very first show on the Fox Network upon its launch in 1986 was *The Late Show Starring Joan Rivers*. Getting Rivers was a coup for the tiny network—she was the guest host of *The Tonight Show* whenever Johnny Carson was on vacation. *The Late Show* was competitive with Carson for a few months, but by early 1987, the show was flailing in the ratings. Unbeknownst to Rivers, in April 1987, Fox executives met with radio shock-jock Howard Stern and filmed five test shows to serve as pilots for a late-night show to replace the Rivers show. Focus groups didn't like Stern or the show, so Fox scrapped the idea. However, they still fired Rivers in May 1987, and the show used guest hosts until it was cancelled for good in 1988.

THE DOLLY PARTON SHOW

When Johnny Carson retired in 1992, leaving late night open to competition for the first time in decades, Fox decided it was time to

---

What an ass! In 1785, King Charles III of Spain sent George Washington a donkey as a gift.

get back into late night. The network's first choice for host: beloved country singer and actress Dolly Parton. Executives approached Parton's agent, who immediately turned it down. Parton had soured on network TV after ABC cancelled her short-lived 1987 variety show, *Dolly*. Parton's manager had a suggestion, though: Chevy Chase. Fox liked the idea and hired Chase. That program, *The Chevy Chase Show*, aired for just five weeks in the fall of 1993. Fox hasn't had a late-night talk show since.

JON STEWART LIVE

By 2002, ABC was a distant third-place in late night. Its lineup consisted of the news show *Nightline* (11:00 p.m.–midnight) and Bill Maher's political-comedy panel show, *Politically Incorrect* (12:00–12:30). ABC was looking to seriously compete, so it cancelled *Politically Incorrect* and made an offer to Letterman to bring his show to ABC at 11:30, effectively cancelling *Nightline*. Letterman opted to stay at CBS. ABC then extended an offer to Jon Stewart, host of *The Daily Show* on Comedy Central. He, too, wanted to stay where he was, so ABC offered the slot to another Comedy Central personality: Jimmy Kimmel, a comedian hosting two shows on the network—the sketch-comedy program *The Man Show* and the game show *Win Ben Stein's Money*. ABC's *Jimmy Kimmel Live!* (it's actually taped) debuted in 2003 and has been running ever since.

THE TONIGHT SHOW WITH JERRY SEINFELD

NBC installed Conan O'Brien at *The Tonight Show* in June 2009, but by the end of the year, his ratings were terrible and NBC was already thinking of replacing him. In January 2010, the network famously forced out O'Brien and restored Jay Leno, who had been hosting a woefully received show in primetime. But before that switch, NBC was reportedly thinking about keeping Leno at 10:00 p.m. and replacing O'Brien with Jerry Seinfeld. NBC ultimately put Leno back on *Tonight*, of course, but one of the shows that replaced the 10:00 p.m. Jay Leno program was *The Marriage Ref*, a reality show produced by…Jerry Seinfeld.

*   *   *

"Theory is important…at least in theory."

—**Keith Martin, mathematician**

Who cleans all 16,100 windows on the Sears Tower? Six robotic window-washing machines.

THIS PAGE IS OKAY

*"Okay" is one of the most commonly used words
in the world. But who came up with it?*

WORLD WORD
Whether you spell it "okay," "o.k.," or "OK," it is so
universal in both its meaning and sound that linguists
say it's the most recognized word on the planet. (Second-most
recognized: Coke.) It's as close as anything we've got to a "universal
language."

But where the word actually came from is a bit of a mystery.
Here are a few theories of how it started—and because they all
developed in different parts of the world and spread, it's possible
that more than one or even all of them could be true.

• *Okay* is a derivative of the Old Scottish expression "och aye,"
which means "oh, yes."

• The Choctaw people (who once lived in modern-day Oklahoma)
had a word *oke*, which means "it is so."

• It comes from a Greek phrase, *ola kala*, which roughly translates
to "everything's good."

• Les Cayes is a port city in Haiti, and the center of the 18th-
century rum trade. *Aux cayes* (pronounced "oh-kay") means "from
Cayes" and was an expression used by French soldiers to describe
the rum they were shipping (or drinking).

• A Chicago baker named Orrin Kendall provided hardtack biscuits
to the Union Army during the Civil War and stamped his initials
into every one.

• It came from an abbreviation used by telegraph operators, short
for "open key," meaning "ready to receive."

THE OKAY CORRAL
But according to Columbia University linguistics professor Allen
Walker Read, those stories are just amazing coincidences, all of
which may have helped the word spread more quickly, but none are
the word's real origin. According to Read's research in the 1960s,
"OK" originated in Boston in the 1830s. Back then, comical

Unlike other birds, ducks molt their flight feathers all at once. They're flightless for weeks.

abbreviations and silly misspellings were a big fad among writers in New England newspapers. Boston newspapers typically featured satirical abbreviations like OFM ("our first men") to describe local hooligans, SP ("small potatoes") for matters of little importance, and NS ("nuff said"). Besides being funny, the abbreviations took up far less precious newspaper space than complete words. (Modern equivalent: texting the phrase "OMG.")

And then there was OW, which stood for "oll wright," a 19th-century equivalent to "all right." Oll wright didn't make it to the modern day. And neither did OW, because it was used interchangeably with another abbreviation—OK, which meant the same thing but was short for "oll korrect." The first known use of OK in print in this way dates to a March 1838 *Boston Morning Post* article by journalist Charles Gordon Greene (about a group called the Anti-Bell-Ringing Society).

VAN THE MAN

The rise of OK dovetailed with the presidency of Martin Van Buren. His nickname: Old Kinderhook, taken from the name of his birthplace in upstate New York. A group of supporters named itself after the initials of his nickname, calling themselves the OK Club.

The president's political opponents in the Whig party used the club's name against him during his failed reelection campaign. They came up with a variety of unflattering alternative meanings of OK to describe Van Buren and his lackluster 1837–41 term, such as "Out of Kash" and "Out of Kredit." Newspaper editors around the country followed suit, with variations like "Orfully Konfused" and "Often Kontradicts."

OKAY TODAY

By the time William Henry Harrison assumed the presidency from Van Buren in March 1841, OK was cemented in the public consciousness. As time went on, people forgot about the abbreviation/misspelling fad and where OK came from, leading to the rise of numerous theories like the ones listed earlier in this article.

Even with all that, we may never know the exact origin of the word, but we do know that you can say "okay" to another person almost anywhere in the world and be assured that regardless of their native language they'll know exactly what you mean.

If all 7.1 billion people on Earth stood on top of each other, they'd stand 6 million miles tall.

DRUCKER'S BUSINESS

Peter Drucker (1909–2005) was an author, professor, and one of the 20th century's most sought-after business consultants. Here's why.

"Whenever you see a successful business, someone once made a courageous decision."

"The moment people talk of 'implementing' instead of 'doing,' and of 'finalizing' instead of 'finishing,' the organization is already running a fever."

"Rank does not confer privilege or give power. It imposes responsibility."

"If you want something new, you have to stop doing something old."

"What's measured improves."

"Free enterprise cannot be justified as being good for business. It can be justified only as being good for society."

"Most of what we call management consists of making it difficult for people to get their work done."

"People who don't take risks generally make about two big mistakes a year. People who do take risks generally make about two big mistakes a year."

"There is nothing so useless as doing efficiently something that should not be done at all."

"The three most charismatic leaders in this century inflicted more suffering on the human race than almost any trio in history: Hitler, Stalin, and Mao. What matters is not the leader's charisma. What matters is the leader's mission."

"Management is doing things right; leadership is doing the right things."

"The most important thing in communication is to hear what isn't being said."

"Leadership is not magnetic personality. That can just as well be a glib tongue. It is not 'making friends and influencing people.' That is flattery. Leadership is lifting a person's vision to higher sights, raising a person's performance to a higher standard, building a personality beyond its normal limitations."

"The best way to predict your future is to create it."

FOUR FAMOUS FIRSTBORNS

*Most people, Uncle John included (so far), will live their
entire lives without ever making it into the record books.
These people were born into them.*

Baby: Gordon Campbell Kerr
Claim to Fame: First baby born on live television
Details: On December 2, 1952, NBC-TV filmed Lillian Kerr
as she gave birth at Denver's Colorado General Hospital, as part of
the network's "March of Medicine" program. A Caesarian delivery
kept the show on schedule, and while the procedure itself was too
graphic to broadcast, viewers watched doctors prepare for surgery,
listened to the unborn baby's heartbeat, and heard its cries as it drew
its first breath. Then they watched as the baby was brought into the
nursery and washed. Because fathers were typically not allowed in
delivery rooms in the 1950s, the 12 million viewers at home weren't
the only ones who witnessed the delivery via the tube: Proud papa
Sgt. John Kerr watched his son's birth on a TV in the waiting room.

Baby: Elena Nikolaeva-Tereshkova
Claim to Fame: First baby born to two astronaut parents
Details: In June 1963, Russian cosmonaut Valentina Tereshkova
became the first woman in space when she piloted *Vostok* 6 in
Earth orbit for just under three days, giving her more time in space
than all the American astronauts combined. Five months later,
she married Andriyan Nikolayev, pilot of the *Vostok 3* mission
(August 1962), and the only bachelor in the Soviet space program. Their daughter, Elena, was born on June 8, 1964. The couple
later divorced. Nikolayev died in 2004, but as of 2012, Valentina
Tereshkova, 75, is still alive and so is Elena, who's a physician and
practices medicine in Moscow.

Baby: Sean Oliver
Claim to Fame: First baby born live on the Internet
Details: As we told you in *Uncle John's Bathroom Reader Plunges into*

First U.S. president to host a fireworks display at the White House: John Adams.

History, on June 16, 1998, a woman identified only as "Elizabeth" gave birth to a baby boy at the Arnold Palmer Hospital for Children & Women in Orlando, Florida. The America's Health Network website broadcast the event over the World Wide Web. Among the viewers: Florida prosecutors, who recognized the mother as Elizabeth Ann Oliver, wanted in Orange County for passing bad checks. By the time the police arrived at the hospital, Oliver was gone, but two weeks later she surrendered to police. (The charges were later dropped because the statute of limitations had expired.)

Baby: A boy, identity unknown, born to the Quaker wife of a "wealthy merchant of Philadelphia" in 1884

Claim to Fame: First baby born by artificial insemination with the "assistance" of an anonymous donor father

Details: This baby owes its existence to something said in jest. When the merchant brought his wife to Philadelphia's Jefferson Medical College to find out why she couldn't get pregnant, the doctors discovered that the merchant himself was to blame. A sexually transmitted disease contracted during his youth had rendered him sterile. When the case was presented in class to some medical students, one of them joked that "the only solution of this problem was to call in the hired man." Hmm…Professor William Henry Pancoast promptly called the merchant's wife in for another "exam." Nineteenth-century medical ethics leaving something to be desired, he gave her chloroform and, while she was unconscious and without her or her husband's knowledge or consent, artificially inseminated her using a "contribution" from the best-looking member of the class. All witnesses were sworn to secrecy; the incident did not become public knowledge until one of the students present revealed it in a letter to a medical journal 25 years later:

> Neither the man nor the woman knew the nature of what had been done at the time, but subsequently the Professor repented of his action, and explained the whole matter to the husband. Strange as it may seem, the man was delighted with the idea, and conspired with the Professor in keeping from the lady the actual way by which her impregnation was brought about. That boy is now a businessman in the city of New York, and I have shaken hands with him in the past year.

LEGENDS OF THE ROSE

The rose appears in myths and legends around the world.

GREEK: Heartbroken after her lover Adonis was mauled by a wild boar, Aphrodite, the goddess of love, ran to him across a field of thorns. She cut her feet as she ran, and when Adonis died in her arms, her tears mixed with her blood and his. The liquids formed a new shape, and the first rose bloomed.

ARABIC: Nightingales weren't always songbirds. They croaked and chirped until one day a nightingale fell in love with a beautiful white rose. The bird's love for the rose caused it to sing for the first time. But when it pressed itself against the rose, the rose's thorn pierced his heart. Out of the drops of blood the first red roses grew.

CHRISTIAN: When God created roses and put them in the Garden of Eden, they didn't have thorns. But when Adam and Eve ate the forbidden fruit and were driven out of the garden, God gave roses thorns to serve as an eternal reminder of paradise lost.

HINDU: Brahma, the creator of the world, believed the lotus to be the best flower, while Vishnu, the protector of the world, thought the rose was best. Brahma had never actually seen a rose, so Vishnu showed him one. Brahma instantly saw the rose's superiority and thanked Vishnu by creating a bride for him, Lakshmi, made from 108 large rose petals and 1,008 small petals.

ROMAN: Cupid, the god of love, was stung by a bee and accidently shot an arrow into a garden of white roses. The arrow "stung" one of the rose bushes, and caused it to grow thorns. When Cupid's mother, Venus, walked into the rose garden she pricked her foot on a thorn, and her blood turned the roses red.

ANOTHER ROMAN LEGEND: Harpocrates, the god of silence, wanted to punish Venus, goddess of love, for her promiscuity. But he kept his mouth shut—he's the god of silence, after all—and Cupid thanked him with the gift of a rose. Roses became the symbol of silence, and were often painted on the walls and ceilings of Roman dining rooms to remind guests that anything said *sub rosa*—"under the roses"—during a meal did not leave the room.

In recorded history, the West Coast of the U.S. has never been hit by a hurricane.

SHOESHINES & WALKOUT BOUTS

Boxing lingo to make a palooka sound like he coulda been a contender.

Pitty-pats: Punches with no power that are used solely to rack up points in a round.

Mouse: A protruding bruise on a boxer's head.

Outside Fighter: A fighter who tries to keep a distance between himself and his opponent in order to throw long punches.

Walkout Bout: A minor fight that takes place after the main event, when many patrons are getting up and leaving. Also refers to any fight so boring that the crowd walks out.

Shoeshine: A flurry of quick punches, made with a vertical motion similar to polishing a shoe with a shoeshine cloth.

Queer Street: A fighter who's dazed and stumbling after too many punches to the head is said to be "on Queer Street."

No Count: When a knocked-down fighter gets up before the referee begins the ten count, making it unnecessary.

Twenty Count: If a fighter is physically knocked out of the ring, he gets a twenty count instead of the standard ten count to give him extra time to get back into the ring.

Palooka: A fighter with little or no skill.

Counterpuncher: A fighter who waits for his opponent to punch, then responds with a devastating counterpunch while the opponent's flank is exposed.

Clinching: "Hugging" an opponent to keep him from hitting you or to soften the impact of his blows.

Hitting on the Break: When the referee breaks apart two fighters who are clinching, they're supposed to take a full step back before resuming punching…but often don't.

Memorial Ten Count: Ringing the fight bell ten times before a fight in memory of a fighter who died recently.

First-known doctor (and engineer and architect): Imhotep, ancient Egypt (2650–2600 B.C.).

ODD NEW ANIMALS

Q: *What do whales say in secret whale language when they're hungry?*
A: *We could tell you, but then we'd have to krill you. Good joke!*
Okay, now check out these stories about bizarre animal
species, all discovered only in the last few years.

BURMESE SNUB-NOSED MONKEYS
Discovery: In early 2010, Swiss primatologist Thomas Geissman was shown the carcass of a monkey found in northern Burma. It appeared to be a species unknown to science. Geissman organized search teams, and over the course of the following year managed to get glimpses of a few living specimens. In January 2012, an automated camera got the only known photo of one of the creatures.

Why It's Odd: The Burmese snub-nosed monkey has mostly black fur, a pale pinkish face, prominent red lips, white ear tufts, and a line of white hairs along its chin. It also has, as its name suggests, a very tiny, almost non-existent, nose. There are many species of snub-nosed monkeys in Asia, but this one's nose is so stubby that it's essentially just two tear-drop-shaped nostrils in the center of its upturned face. According to locals (who, unlike scientists, have known about the species for some time), it's not hard to find the monkeys...when it's raining. Their unprotected nostrils collect water when it rains—causing them to sneeze. That's why, locals explained, Burmese snub-nosed monkeys prefer to wait out rains with their heads bent forward between their knees.

SQUID WORMS
Discovery: In 2007, marine biologists sent a remotely operated submarine down into the Celebes Sea, a marine basin situated between Indonesia and the Philippines. At a depth of about 1.7 miles, they suddenly saw something swimming through the water—and they'd never seen anything like it before. Over the course of several dives, the researchers were able to capture several of the strange creatures (the sub had a gentle suction device that pulled the animals into a collection chamber), and were able to study them closely.

Why It's Odd: The creatures were about four inches long and had long narrow bodies with a line of appendages on either side that the creature used to paddle through the water, making it look sort of like an underwater millipede. Ten long tentacles grew out from the creature's head, each as long as or longer than its body. Eight of the tentacles, the team discovered, were for breathing, and the other two were for snagging organic debris (food) floating in the water. The millipede-like legs turned out to be iridescent, bristly, almost winglike, which the creature used sort of like oars. The odd beast was finally determined to be an *annelid*, a type of marine worm (distantly related to earthworms), but it was so different from the thousands of known marine-worm species in the world that it was given an entirely new genus and species. And it had no eyes. Instead the "squid worm," as the researchers dubbed it, has six feathery sense organs on its head which it uses to "taste" its way around the water.

PINOCCHIO FROGS

Discovery: An international team of climate researchers was exploring the remote Foja Mountains on the island of New Guinea in 2008. "We were sitting around eating lunch," Smithsonian ornithologist Chris Milensky said later, when herpetologist Paul Oliver "looked down and there's this little frog on a rice sack, and he managed to grab the thing." It was a tiny green tree frog with very large eyes and one strange feature.

Why It's Odd: The frog had a very long skinny pointed nose that hung down over its mouth. And…it was inflatable. When the frog made one of its froggy calls—the long pointy nose filled with air and stood straight up. When the call ended, the nose deflated and hung down over the frog's mouth again. When it called again, up his nose went, and so on. For obvious reasons, the researchers dubbed their little friend the "Pinocchio frog." Further study found that only the males have the inflatable noses—but scientists still don't know why they have them. (For more weird frog species, hop over to page 202.)

KOLLASMOSOMA SENTUM

Discovery: German wasp expert Dr. Kees van Achterberg discovered this brand-new species of parasitic wasp in Spain in 2011.

Why It's Odd: *Kollasmosoma sentum* wasps reproduce by laying their eggs inside the bodies of living ants. When the eggs hatch, the larval wasps survive by eating the ants from the inside out. (Yum!) As bizarre as it may seem, that kind of behavior is actually pretty common in the parasitic wasp world. But these wasps were super fast. In 2012, Spanish biologist José María Gómez Durán was able to film the wasps, which only grow to about two millimeters in length—much smaller than the ants they terrorize—in super-slow motion as they performed their nasty business. The film shows a tiny female wasp fly up behind an unsuspecting ant, dart toward it, flip its backside toward the ant, and BAM! pierce the ant's tough exoskeleton with its *ovipositor* (its stinger/egg-depositor), depositing an egg inside the ant's abdomen. The wasp then flew away before the startled ant could even turn around. (If you watch the video—and you can on YouTube—you can almost hear the ants say, "What the H*LL was THAT?") So how fast are these wasps? Durán's super-slow-motion video showed that a wasp could deposit an egg inside an ant and be gone in less than 0.05 seconds.

PHALLOSTETHUS CUULONG

Discovery: This approximately one inch-long fish was first discovered by Japanese biologist Koichi Shibukawa, who caught one in the Mekong River Delta in Vietnam in July 2009.

Why It's Odd: *Phallostethus cuulong* fish have their reproductive organs on their heads. On the males, it's in the form of a complicated bit of anatomy known as a *priapium* that hangs down from just under the fish's mouth. The priapium has a pore through which the male fish emits sperm. (*Phallostethus* means "penis-chest.")

It Gets Odder: Hanging from the bottom of a male's priapium is a bony, serrated, forward-facing jawlike apparatus. When it's time to mate, a male uses that serrated jawlike apparatus to grab a female by the head, so it can press its genital pore against the female's genital pore—also located just under her mouth.

Odder Still: *Phallostethus cuulong* has another organ on its head—its anus. It's located right in front of the genital pore.

*   *   *

THE CLASSIFIEDS

Kittens! Free. 7 wks. old. 2 white, 2 gay, 1 orange.
Missing Dog: Small Golden Brown Palm Iranian. Pls. call.

iPOD, iPHONE, iSMELL

On page 389, you can read the story of Smell-O-Vision, which came and went in a flash back in 1960. But it may not be gone for good —like 3-D movies, the idea of adding smells to movies, TV, the Internet, etc., never seems to fade away entirely.

THE iSMELL (2001)
Description: A "personal scent synthesizer" that lets you send odors by e-mail

Details: Developed by a company called DigiScents, the iSmell Personal Scent Synthesizer was shaped like a shark fin and contained a cartridge with 128 primary scents that could be combined to make thousands of unique smells, each one identified by its own digital "smell code." To e-mail an odor, all you had to do was include a smell code in an e-mail and send it to someone with his or her own iSmell synthesizer. When the e-mail was opened, the recipient's iSmell would spring into action, giving the recipient a sniff of the scent the scent sender sent. (Say that five times fast.)

Websites would have been able to add odors to their sites to help sell coffee, perfume, and other smelly goods. Who knows? Spam email might really have smelled like Spam. But it wasn't to be: DigiScents spent two years trying to bring iSmell to market, then it closed its doors in April 2001 "after its financial backers apparently tired of smelling burning cash." Estimated loss: $20 million. *PC World* magazine shed no tears: In 2006 it named the iSmell one of "The 25 Worst Tech Products of All Time."

THE FIRSTSENX (2000)

Description: A device that lets you e-mail smells and tastes

Details: Why stop at smells? In 2000, a Georgia company called TriSenx patented a machine that used inkjet technology to spray scents onto pieces of paper and flavors onto edible wafers made of potato starch. Just as with iSmell, you would have e-mailed a digital scent or taste code to someone with a FirstSENX device attached to their computer, and it would spit out whatever you sent. "Get ready, because the future is so close you can taste it!" said the company's website. Not close enough: In March 2000, TriSenx announced that it was looking for $7 million in additional investor funding to bring the $398 devices to market. It went out of business a short time later.

SMELL ON WHEELS (2005)

Description: A machine that lets drivers customize the smell of their cars

Details: In 2001, Textron, the world's largest maker of automobile dashboard instrument panels, unveiled an in-car odor generator that would allow drivers to "set" the smell of their cars as easily as they'd adjust the seat or tune the radio. The device, part of the company's "advanced driver dashboard," would have used removable scent cartridges, each containing a variety of scents that would allow each member of the family to chose multiple odors that they could vary according to geography, mood, the type of music playing in the car, or anything else. When a smell was selected, it would be automatically pumped into the car through the air conditioning vents. The device was supposed to be ready by 2005 but was never brought to market. Why? Textron isn't saying, but two possibilities are 1) lack of consumer demand and 2) the technical difficulties associated with "adding fragrance to a vehicle without also adding vapors that can adhere to the windows."

VIRTUAL SMELLS AND TASTES (2005)

Description: A system that creates the impressions of particular smells and tastes by bombarding the brain's taste and smell centers with pulses of energy

Details: Why bother to actually create smells and tastes when it might be possible to trick the brain into thinking you had, using bursts of ultrasound energy to disrupt the firing patterns of neutrons in specific areas of the brain? Sure—that sounds perfectly safe! Japanese electronics giant Sony patented just such an idea in 2005, but the patent was what the company called "prophetic"—it applied to technology that hadn't been developed yet, but might be someday. "It was based on an inspiration that may someday be the direction that technology will take us," a Sony spokesperson told *New Scientist* magazine.

THE SMELL-O-PHONE/SMELL-O-VISION (2011)

Description: An odor-generating box that installs on the back of an ordinary television or even inside a smart phone

Details: Developed by scientists at the UC San Diego Jacobs School of Engineering, the device emits pre-loaded odors on demand. The 2011 prototype can only release a few smells, but the researchers say it proves that a device capable of releasing as many as 10,000 unique smells may be just around the corner—all that's needed now is the funding to bring it to fruition. (Sound familiar?) "If people are eating pizza, the viewer smells pizza, and if a beautiful lady walks by, they smell perfume," says professor Sungho Jin. "This is likely to be the next generation TV or cell phone that produces odors to match images that you see on the screen. It is quite doable."

THE SCENTSCAPE (2011)

Description: A device that adds "authentic" smells to video games

Details: If you've ever dreamed of smelling burning rubber while playing *Need for Speed* or gunpowder while playing *Call of Duty* (or sweat and astroturf while playing *Madden NFL*), your wait may soon be over. In January 2011, Scent Sciences, a Silicon Valley company, announced a new product called ScentScape that will plug into video game consoles and add customized scents to any game that supports the technology. Disposable cartridges customized for each game will contain as many as 20 pre-loaded smells that will be released when activated by the game's software. The cartridges will be good for 200 hours of gameplay; more if the unit's smell "volume control" is turned down. Price: $69. At last report, the product was slated to begin shipping in 2013.

*　　*　　*

PRESIDENTIAL FUN FACT

U.S. president with the most American high schools named after him: John F. Kennedy (98). Nine former presidents have just one school named in their honor—John Quincy Adams, Millard Fillmore, George W. Bush, George H. W. Bush, Jimmy Carter, Chester Alan Arthur, Franklin Pierce, Zachary Taylor, and Andrew Johnson. One president has exactly zero schools named after him: Richard Nixon.

$2 BILLS

Quick facts about the least-popular denomination of U.S. currency.

- First authorized in 1862, $2 bills were printed until 1966, at which point they were discontinued…but only for 10 years. They were reintroduced in 1976 as part of the Bicentennial celebration.

- Many collectors had their Bicentennial bills postmarked on the day of issue (April 13, 1976), hoping to turn them into valuable collectibles. There are now so many of the postmarked bills that they may never be worth more than $2.

- The 1976 reintroduction was an attempt at cost-cutting. The government estimated that it could save $26 million if the $2 bill replaced about half of the $1 bills in circulation. (It didn't.)

- Because of a persistent myth that $2 bills are no longer in production, some people hoard them. According to the U.S. Treasury, there are about 500 million $2 bills in circulation.

- In 1925, the U.S. government tried to promote the use of $2 bills by putting one in all federal-employee pay envelopes.

- Who's on the $2 bill? It's been Thomas Jefferson since 1869. But when the bill was introduced in 1862, it featured Alexander Hamilton's portrait.

- When you pay for something with a $2 bill, where does the cashier put it? Under the cash drawer. Reason: There's no standard slot for $2 bills.

- Merchants sometimes refuse to accept $2 bills, and that's perfectly legal. They could turn down $20s, too. In fact, if they prefer credit card or electronic payment, they aren't legally required to accept cash at all, regardless of denomination.

- Less than one percent of U.S. currency produced is $2 bills.

- In 2005 a man in Baltimore, Maryland, purchased a car radio from Best Buy and tried to pay the $114 installation fee with 57 $2 bills. The store manager was suspicious of the bills and called the police, who detained Bolesta for three hours (in handcuffs) while they brought in the Secret Service to determine whether the bills were genuine. (They were.)

Coal-burning power plants emit more radiation than nuclear power plants.

ASK THE EXPERTS

Everyone's got a question or two they'd like answered, such as "Why is the sky blue?" Here are a few of those questions, with answers from some of the world's top science and trivia experts.

CARRY THAT WEIGHT

Q: *What's the best way to pack a backpack? Should heavier items be placed toward the top or toward the bottom?*

A: "Putting the denser items higher up in the backpack is better. The higher the center of gravity of the pack, the smaller the forward-bending angle the hiker needs to put his center of gravity above his feet. A smaller bending angle means less strain on the stomach and back muscles. Certain native tribespeople have perfected the feat of carrying heavy loads directly on their heads so that no forward bending is required at all." (From *Mad About Physics*, by Christopher P. Jargodzki and Franklin Potter)

YOUR BOTTOM DOLLAR

Q: *Why is a bank called a bank?*

A: "Our word *bank* comes from a quaint custom in Italy. Beginning in the 16th century, Italian money changers conducted their business outdoors, on benches. Many Italian cities set up benches for banking business, and it so happens that the Italian word for *bench* is *banco*. As banking activity spread through Europe, the word reached England, where it became *bank*. Historians say it all began when the Banco di Rialto was founded in Venice, Italy, in 1587." (From *What Happens to a Torn Dollar Bill?*, by Dr. Knowledge)

TROPICAL TRAVELER

Q: *Before the fruit was discovered, what did they call the color "orange"?*

A: "Gold, amber, yellowish, reddish, tawny, and all combinations thereof. The important thing to know is that the fruit came *before* the color, and not the other way around. The fruit was brought to Spain from southeast Asia by Arab traders around the 9th century and was given the Arabic name of *naranj*—after the Sanskrit word for 'orange tree,' *naranga*. By the time the fruit arrived in England, it was called *naranja*, and then *norange*. Eventually, the letter 'n' was dropped from the beginning—'an orange' and 'a norange' being identical in speech. Interestingly, although the fruit first arrived in England in the 14th century, the first English record of the color is 1620." (From *Why Girls Can't Throw*, by Mitchell Symons)

WHAT A MOOB

Q: *Why do men have nipples?*
A: "If you're asking, 'What is the evolutionary advantage?,' the answer is probably none. You got your nipples in your first few months as a fetus, back when you were anatomically indistinguishable from the opposite sex. At about 14 weeks, the hormones that cause males to develop the standard, factory-issued male parts kick in. The nipples stayed, though. It would be too much trouble to suppress them, and besides, they don't do any harm. Actually, there's no compelling reason why males can't give milk. Men are equipped with small mammary glands and ducts; all that's missing are the hormones to make them work." (From *Why Moths Hate Thomas Edison*, edited by Hampton Sides)

GRILL OF MY DREAMS

Q: *How often should you switch out your toothbrush?*
A: "Every three months. After that time, the bristles begin to fray, making them less effective at removing plaque." (From *The Book of Times*, by Lesley Alderman)

BLOWIN' IN THE WIND

Q: *How do small spiders manage to spin long lines across wide gaps?*
A: "The spider climbs up to an exposed spot—like the top of a fence—and figures out where the breeze is coming from. It then feeds out an extremely fine thread. Like an angler, the spider then waits until it can feel some tension in the thread, indicating that it's caught onto something on the other side of the gap. It then pulls this 'bridge thread' tight and scampers across several times, laying down extra threads, which rapidly increase its thickness and strength. From the midpoint, the spider drops down, releasing a second thread on the way, which it fixes at a lower level. Pulling this tight creates a Y-shaped structure, around which it can start building its web." (From *Why Don't Spiders Stick to Their Webs?*, by Robert Matthews)

THAT'S *ALL* WE SELL

These stores leave variety to the variety stores—because they sell only one thing.

Store: Ed's Martian Book
Sells only: One book
Details: In April 2011, a new bookstore opened up in New York's Greenwich Village, operated by Andrew Kessler. Although you could buy as many copies as you wanted, the store sold only one book: *A Martian Summer: Robot Arms, Cowboy Spacemen, and my 90 Days with the Phoenix Mars Mission*, by...Andrew Kessler (about a 2008 NASA mission). Kessler, creative director at an advertising agency, told the *NY Times*, "People ask, 'how can you possibly pay your bills.' It gets pretty intense sometimes." He later admitted that he didn't have any bills—the landlord let him use the place for free until a paying tenant took over, which was one month later.

Store: Coco Loco
Sells only: Coconuts
Details: Do you like coconuts, the hard-to-access fruit of the palm tree? (Technically, it's not a fruit or a nut, but a *drupe*.) So did Oscar Avila, who opened Coco Loco in San Francisco in 2009, selling nothing but coconuts. The store, located between a bank and a dollar store in the city's Mission District, served them in the style Avila enjoyed in his youth in Mexico: raw, peeled, with a straw stuck into the middle. On hot days, the store would sell as many as 2,000 coconuts a day, at $2.50 each. Apparently there weren't enough hot days—Coco Loco went out of business in 2010.

Store: Empire Mayonnaise Company
Sells only: Mayonnaise
Details: The Empire Mayonnaise Company is a small shop in Brooklyn that sells only mayonnaise—really expensive mayonnaise. It comes in a variety of flavors (bacon, classic, smoked paprika) and in two sizes—four ounces and eight ounces. Most of the smaller jars cost $8 each. Empire has been turning a tidy profit, selling hundreds of jars a week at their storefront, while at the same time getting their product into high-end stores that do sell more than one thing, including Dean & Deluca and West Elm.

NATURAL GAS REPORT

"Breaking wind," as the English so politely call it, is a natural and inevitable part of life. So it's not surprising that farts occasionally make it into the news.

GAS ATTACK

In June 2012, a 72-year-old New Jersey man named Daniel Collins was arrested and charged with assault, unlawful possession of a firearm, and making terrorist threats, when he pointed a .32-calibre revolver at his neighbor and threatened to shoot him in the head. What got Collins so worked up? According to police, he and the neighbor were involved in an ongoing dispute over noise. The feud escalated to its breaking point when the neighbor walked past Collins's front door and farted so loudly that Collins could hear it from inside his apartment. Collins was later released on his own recognizance without having to post bail. (No word on whether, if convicted, he'll have to spend time in the can.)

FIELD RESEARCH

Scientists have long known that the farts and burps released by livestock are a significant source of greenhouse gases. But precisely how significant has been difficult to say because it's almost impossible to accurately measure the emissions of animals out in the fields. In the summer of 2011, scientists at the UK's National Physical Laboratory announced plans to develop a system for "auditing a herd's collective flatulence" by shooting laser beams around the animals as they graze (and fart and burp) in their pastures. "We use lasers to interact with the gas," researcher Alan Brewin told the *Daily Telegraph*. "The way the light is absorbed tells you what gas there is, how much of it there is, which direction it is flowing, and how fast."

POP STAR

In November 2012, Britney Spears's former bodyguard, 29-year-old Fernando Flores, sued the singer, alleging that she paraded around her home in the nude, made "repeated, unwanted sexual advances," and farted "unapologetically" in his presence. Flores asked for more than $10 million in compensation for "psychological trauma, anxiety attacks, depression and insomnia," despite the fact that he'd worked for Spears for less than six months. "He's a liar," a spokesperson for the star told reporters. The case was settled out of court.

OF MICE AND MEN
In July 2012, scientists at Johns Hopkins University in Maryland published a study that found that hydrogen sulfide, the gas that gives farts their rotten egg smell, also lowers blood pressure in mice. Researchers in the United States and China are now studying whether farts—making them or perhaps just smelling them—might one day be used as a therapy to help lower the blood pressure of humans. "The effective dosage could prove difficult to establish due to the difference in size between humans and mice," said Yao Yuyu, a researcher at Zhongda Hospital in Nanjing.

LAW AND ODOR
Not long after the president of Malawi introduced legislation in 2011 to reform the African nation's court system, Justice Minister George Chaponda told a radio interviewer that the bill also contained language that would make farting in public a misdemeanor. "Just go to the toilet if you feel like farting," the minister said, adding that public tooting had been on the rise since the country transitioned from dictatorship to democracy in the early 1990s. So did Malawi really try to outlaw farting in public? Nope: Turns out that the legal language in question actually dealt with air pollution, not farting, but Minister Chaponda didn't know that because he hadn't read the bill. By the time he retracted his statement, Malawi's so-called "fart ban" had made embarrassing headlines all over the world. Solicitor General Anthony Kamanga told the BBC, "How any reasonable or sensible person can construe the prohibition to criminalizing farting in public is beyond me."

*   *   *

GETTING IN SHAPE
"When I get an 'S', I'm so excited!" said Oprah Winfrey on her talk show. What was she talking about? The shape of her poop. According to nutritionists, that's the goal of healthy eaters: The deposit should resemble a curved piece of sausage, and it "should not plop and splash into the bowl, but fall in gently, without a sound."

KANYE THE NUCLEUS

There's having self-confidence…and then there's hip-hop artist Kanye West.

"I am God's vessel. But my greatest pain in life is that I will never be able to see myself perform live."

"I think what Kanye West is going to mean is something similar to what Steve Jobs means. I am undoubtedly, you know, Steve of Internet, downtown, fashion, culture. Period. By a long jump."

"You know, if Michael Jordan can scream at the refs, me as Kanye West, as the Michael Jordan of music, can go and say, 'This is wrong.'"
—*after not winning an award*

"I'm a pop enigma."

"Anyone who doesn't give my album a perfect score is lowering the integrity of their magazine."

"Love your haters—they're your biggest fans."

"Sometimes people write novels and they are so wordy and so self-absorbed. I am not a fan of books. I would never want a book's autograph."

"It takes time for me to slow down and think like a normal person."

"The Bible had 20, 30, 40, 50 characters in it. You don't think that I would be one of the characters of today's modern Bible?"

"I will go down as the voice of this generation."

"I put a life-sized poster of me on the wall because I was the only person that had me on the wall at that time. And now that a lot of people have me on their wall, I don't really need to do that anymore."

"How could you be me and want to be someone else?"

"When I think of competition I try to create against the past. I think about Michelangelo, Picasso, you know, the pyramids."

"I will be the leader of a company that ends up being worth billions of dollars, because I got the answers. I understand culture. I am the nucleus."

FAKE LOBSTER & PINEAPPLE SALADS

Over the years we've written about a lot of fast food flops, from the Hulu Burger to the McAfrika. You can't blame restaurants for trying new menu items to bring in new customers…but they can't all be winners.

BACON SHAKE

In 2012, Jack in the Box got in on the "bacon-flavored everything" craze when they introduced a Bacon Milkshake. Essentially it was a vanilla milkshake with 1,100 calories, 108 grams of sugar…and no actual bacon. It was even safe for vegetarians to drink, because it was flavored with artificially flavored bacon syrup. The shake did not benefit from the bacon fad, and was off the Jack in the Box menu by the end of the year.

TACO LIGHT

In the late 1980s, "light" or "lite" became a common designation for products that had reduced fat or reduced calories so as to appeal to would-be dieters or people watching what they eat. In 1987, Taco Bell introduced Taco Light. Was it a low-cal taco, with lower-fat ground beef and just a little cheese? Hardly. It was a regular taco made with a new thinner, crispier, "light and flaky" shell. A brief disclaimer at the end of Taco Light TV commercials said, "Not lower in calories." It was gone by 1988.

WENDY'S HEALTHY MENU

Wendy's has always offered a slightly different menu from other burger places—it sells chili, and at one point had self-service buffets with pasta and burritos. In 1985, the chain introduced a 12-item menu of healthy food items. Options included baked potatoes, cottage cheese and pineapple salad, and a hollowed-out tomato filled with tuna salad. The company spent $10 million on advertising before pulling the line in 1986. Reason: Wendy's customers preferred burgers to pineapple and lettuce. Wendy's did, however, keep a baked potato with low-fat sour cream on the menu (only now customers can also get it with cheese and bacon).

In Thailand, they text "555," not "LOL." (In Thai, the number 5 is pronounced "ha.")

LANGOSTINO LOBSTER

Lobster? At a fast food restaurant? In 2006 Long John Silver's offered "Buttered Lobster Bites" made with "real langostino lobster." Only problem: Lobster Bites contained no lobster, and there is no such animal as a "langostino lobster." *Langostino* is the Spanish name for a sea creature also known as a "squat lobster"—a two-inch-long spiderlike relative of the hermit crab, and not related to lobster at all. U.S. Senator Olympia Snowe, who hails from Maine—the leading lobster fishing state—asked the U.S. Food and Drug Administration to stop Long John Silver's from selling Lobster Bites, calling the mislabeling an "insult to Maine and to the lobster industry." The Federal Trade Commission required Long John Silver's to change the name of the Buttered Lobster Bites to "Buttered Langostino Lobster Bites" to make it clear that what customers were eating was not, in the traditional sense, lobster. The Bites were discontinued in 2010.

* * *

THE SNOW MUST GO ON

• Snow is inexorably linked with Christmas, both in Great Britain and the United States. One of the reasons is because of the popularity of Charles Dickens' A Christmas Carol, which is set in snowy London during the holidays. However, it almost *never* snows in England at Christmastime. Dickens decided to give the novel a snowy setting because he experienced a string of snowy Christmases as a child, when England was going through a bizarre cold streak.

• In the late 1890s, an Austrian medical manufacturer named Erwin Perzy was trying to intensify electric light for use in an operating room. Taking a page from shoemakers, he shined a light through a glass globe full of water. Then he added some tinsel to reflect even more light. It didn't work; the tinsel slowly fell to the bottom. But it reminded Perzy of falling snow. So he placed a small pewter statue of a church inside the globe with the water and the tinsel. Perzy loved the effect, and in 1900 was awarded a patent for the snow globe. Five years later, he founded a company to manufacture what he called the *schusterkugel*.

THE BRITISH ARE COMING!

The "British Invasion" period of rock music in the 1960s exposed American audiences to some of the best bands of all time. For anyone who lived through it, it was electrifying. Imagine hearing a new record by the Beatles for the first time. (Bonus: Parents hated it!) There were new groups and new sounds coming over the radio airwaves and arriving in record stores every week. But given how many bands there were, it's amazing how many disappeared just as quickly as they appeared.

A NARCHY IN THE U.K.
Inspired by American music forms, particularly early rock 'n' roll, country and western, and rhythm and blues, British teenagers started forming garage bands in the early 1960s, merging those styles together. The music press called them "Beat" bands because they had a driving drum beat, but also "Merseybeat" bands, named for a small magazine that covered local bands. The magazine—*Mersey Beat*—took its name from the River Mersey, which is located in northwest England and runs through one of the centers of British garage-band music, Liverpool. Not all Merseybeat bands were from Liverpool, though. Many hailed from Manchester, Newcastle, and other working-class towns in England's "Midlands" that were decidedly not London.

But when dozens of these groups began signing record deals and scoring international hit records—primarily because one Beat band, the Beatles, paved the way for them—the wave of English acts that swept over North America became known as the British Invasion.

Here are a few of the bands from that era, which dominated rock music from the early 1960s well into the '70s.

BILLY J. KRAMER AND THE DAKOTAS

If the Beatles were the varsity team, Billy J. Kramer and the Dakotas were the JV squad. They had the same manager (Brian Epstein), the same producer (George Martin), and a lot of their songs were written by Lennon and McCartney. Epstein signed Kramer because he was good-looking and could possibly be a teen idol. (The rest of the band was signed separately and assigned to Kramer.) Their first single was a cover of the Beatles' "Do You Want to Know a Secret," with piano played by Martin. It went to #2 in the U.K. The next one, Lennon-McCartney's "Bad to Me" went to #1. Before long, Kramer, whose real name was Billy Ashton, got tired of doing Beatles castoffs, so the band recorded "Little Children" (written by an American) and released it in the U.S., backed with "Bad to Me." Both songs went top-10. Their success would be short-lived, though—it was okay to sound like the Beatles as long as the Beatles still sounded like the Beatles. But by 1966, they had gone experimental and progressive, and all the bands that sounded like the pre-*Sgt. Pepper* Beatles were suddenly very passé. Kramer's group broke up in 1968.

THE LIVERPOOL FIVE

Whenever something gets really popular, there are going to be bandwagon-jumpers if not full-on imitators. Such is the case with the rise of the Beatles and the Liverpool Five. But it wasn't the band's fault…mostly. Singer Steve Laine got four friends together in 1963 and formed the Steve Laine Combo. Like the Beatles, they honed their instrumental and performance skills on the German club circuit, which is where they acquired a German manager in 1964, who sought to cash in on Beatlemania by, it would seem, trying to confuse consumers. He renamed the band the Liverpool Five (even though none of them were from Liverpool), and dressed them in familiar-looking moptop haircuts and matching suits. The makeover did help—in 1964 they won a contest to tour Japan and play at the Tokyo Summer Olympics. After making a minor splash in Asia, the Liverpool Five relocated to the U.S. and toured with the Kinks, Rolling Stones, and Beach Boys. And yet their only single to chart in the U.S., "Any Way That You Want Me," peaked at just #98, despite promotional appearances on *American Bandstand* and *Hullabaloo*.

For part II of the British Invasion, turn to page 211.

* * *

"Writing is the hardest work not involving heavy lifting"

—Pete Hamill

Q. Who sponsors National Dog Bite Prevention Week (in May)? A. The U.S. Postal Service.

ROAD WARRIORS

Where would we be without truckers? They deliver all the goods to stores and supermarkets, they deliver all the stuff we buy on the Internet, and they do some very weird things…like these.

IN WHEEL DANGER

Czech truck driver Ales Stastna, 38, was stopped by police in the eastern city of Senov in April 2012 because he had lost one of his front wheels…and had failed to notice…and had simply kept driving. Police had no idea how long Stastna had been driving with only one front wheel. "I could have sworn it was there when I set off," Stastna told the officers.

GOOD MORNING!

A 51-year-old truck driver fell asleep while traveling through the town of Polichno, Poland, in June 2011, and smashed through the kitchen wall of a house where a family of four had just sat down for breakfast. "There was a tremendous bang, and the wall just disappeared in front of us, leaving a lorry there," mother Agnieszka Kuchalsk told reporters. She said that the driver hopped out of the truck and asked for a cup of coffee. "At that point," she went on, "some bricks fell out of the wall onto his head and knocked him out cold." The driver was treated and released at a local hospital.

U MUST BE KIDDING

In October 2012, police in Caledonia, Wisconsin, reported that a garbage-truck driver had made an illegal U-turn in the town and, in the process, had struck a car. Police investigators found no evidence of alcohol or drugs, but reported that the garbage-truck driver was "acting weird" and was wearing a shirt that said, "Hello, my name is Awesome."

WHAT'S YOUR SIGN?

In July 2012, Coast Truck Centers, a trucking firm in Troutdale, Oregon, sued the company that manages the large billboard on their property. Reason: The new ad they put up—for the nearby Bonneville hot springs resort—is "lavender in color" and contains

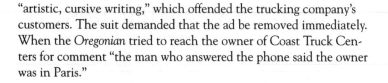

"artistic, cursive writing," which offended the trucking company's customers. The suit demanded that the ad be removed immediately. When the *Oregonian* tried to reach the owner of Coast Truck Centers for comment "the man who answered the phone said the owner was in Paris."

PIT STOP

In December 2012, German tax authorities announced a plan to require the nation's 1.5 million truckers to keep "a toilet log." Reason: "In order to work out how much of their income should be written off from tax," according tho the *Süddentsche Zeitung* newspaper. A group of tax advisers pooh-poohed the scheme as "a ridiculous costly process." (Bathroom Reader Bonus: In German, a driver's log book is called a *Fahrtenbuch*.)

GETTING A BUZZ ON

While driving on Interstate 15 in southern Utah in 2011, long-haul truck driver Louis Holst of Gig Harbor, Washington, took a sharp curve too fast and flipped his truck over. And he was hauling 460 bee hives. Millions of bees escaped—and were really not happy. Holst and his wife, who was in the rig with him, were okay, but they were stung repeatedly before they could get away from the swarm. (So were the rescue personnel who showed up to help them.) During a phone interview, an Associated Press reporter asked Holst if he'd ever haul bees again. "Well," he answered, "my wife's looking at me right now, so I'll say no."

*　　*　　*

VULGAR ONLINE TERMINOLOGY, IN FRENCH

The *Commission Generale de Terminologie et de Neologie* is the French government's official department in charge of defending the French language and approving new French words. (English translation: "General Commission on Terminology and New Words.") In 2013, the agency approved the term *mot-diese* for "hashtag," or "#," the symbol used on social media sites to catalog topics. *Mot-diese* translates to "vulgar sharp symbol." Reason: "Vulgar" means "slang," and the "#" resembles the musical symbol for "sharp."

Mt. St. Helens and Mt. Vesuvius both ranked 5 (out of 8) on the Volcanic Explosivity Index.

BREAKIN' UP IS HARD TO DO

The American Civil War was sparked when eleven slave states tried to secede from the Union. They failed, and they're not the only ones. Here are some other lesser-known secessionist movements.

THE GREAT REPUBLIC OF ROUGH AND READY

Seceded from: The United States, in April 1850

Details: At least two reasons have been cited for why the tiny mining town of Rough and Ready, in California's gold country, decided to secede from the Union. One was anger over the imposition of a tax on mining claims, and the other involved a man known as the "Boston Ravine Slicker," who swindled a popular miner named Joe Swiegart out of $200. When a local judge refused to prosecute the Slicker on the grounds that he hadn't actually broken any laws, Rough and Ready seceded from the United States and "the next morning rescued what was left of Joe's money and took the Slicker to the edge of town with instructions never to return," writes Fay Dunbar of the Nevada County Historical Society. (Another version of the story says the Slicker was hanged.)

What Happened: Whatever the case, the Great Republic of Rough and Ready voted to rejoin the Union in time to celebrate the 4th of July, perhaps hurried along by the refusal of saloons in nearby Nevada City and Grass Valley to sell liquor to Rough and Ready's "foreign miners."

THE FREE AND INDEPENDENT STATE OF SCOTT

Seceded from: Tennessee, in June 1861

Details: Tennessee was divided over whether to secede from the Union and was the last state to do so, about two months *after* the Civil War started. The citizens of Scott County, in northeastern Tennessee, voted against secession by the greatest margin of any county in the state. When Tennessee left the Union, the Scott County Assembly voted to leave Tennessee. A messenger was sent to Nashville to inform the state that the county was "henceforth to be known as the Free and Independent State of Scott."

Thousand Island dressing was named for the 1,864 islands in Canada's St. Lawrence River.

What Happened: Not much—Scott County was of little strategic value to either the Union or the Confederacy. Both sides ignored the secession, and no major Civil War battles were fought there. But Scott County didn't formally rejoin the state until 1986, when Governor Lamar Alexander signed a resolution declaring the State of Scott "dissolved and disbanded...after 125 years of independence."

THE REPUBLIC OF KINNEY

Seceded from: The United States, in July 1977

Details: When the water system in Kinney, Minnesota, began to fail in the mid-1970s, the village of 325 people couldn't afford the $186,000 price tag to replace it. And when it applied for funding from various state and federal agencies, the request got bogged down in red tape. So in July 1977, perhaps inspired by the 1959 film *The Mouse that Roared*, the village council announced their intention to secede from the U.S. and apply for foreign aid. "It is much easier to get assistance as a foreign country, which we need badly, and there is no paperwork to worry about," the council wrote in a letter to Secretary of State Cyrus Vance, adding that "if necessary, we will be glad to declare war and lose. However, if this is a requirement, we would appreciate being able to surrender real quick, as our Mayor works as a nurse in a hospital, and most of our council members work in a nearby mine and cannot get much time off from work."

What Happened: The publicity stunt landed Kinney on the NBC *Nightly News* and helped it do a brisk business in Republic of Kinney "passports," T-shirts, bumper stickers, and other items. But it didn't speed up the bureaucratic process much: The funding for their water system didn't come through until November 1978.

WENDOVER, UTAH

Attempted to Secede from: Utah, in 2002

Details: Wendover makes up half of the metropolitan area that it shares with West Wendover, across the state line in Nevada. The difference between the two cites is stark: West Wendover's economy is buoyed by Nevada's legalized gambling and its casinos attract nearly two million visitors each year. Wendover, by comparison, is a veritable ghost town, thanks to no gambling, and some of the strictest state liquor laws in the country. Allowing Wendover to leave Utah and join West Wendover in Nevada would give its struggling

First text typed into e-book format: The Declaration of Independence.

economy a boost and allow the cities to combine police and fire departments and other public services that are needlessly duplicated. The citizens of both cities approved the secession/annexation in a nonbinding referendum in November 2002.

What Happened: In order for a city to leave one state and join another, the U.S. Constitution requires that the legislatures of both states *and* the U.S. Congress approve the move. The first constitutional hurdle was passed in 2002, when the U.S. House of Representatives unanimously approved a bill permitting succession. But the bill died in the Senate, thanks to opposition from Senator Harry Reid of Nevada, who never gave a reason for why he killed the bill.

KILLINGTON, VERMONT

Attempted to Secede from: Vermont, in 2004

Details: This upscale resort town is home to the Mt. Killington ski area. When Vermont changed the way it pays for public education in 1997, creating a statewide pool of funds to replace the old system of local funding, towns like Killington with high-priced vacation homes and few schools saw their property taxes quadruple. Property taxes in next-door New Hampshire were lower, and there was no state sales tax or income tax, either. Suddenly being in Vermont didn't seem very attractive. At packed town meetings in 2004 and '05, the residents voted overwhelmingly to secede from the state and join New Hampshire.

What Happened: Killington is still part of Vermont, and probably always will be. For one thing, unlike Wendover, Utah, which is right on the border, Killington is smack in the middle of the state, 35 miles from the New Hampshire line. Attempts to create a "corridor" of secessionist towns all the way to the border have failed. And the state of Vermont, which must approve secession, has shown no signs of being willing to do so. In 2005, three state legislators introduced legislation to slap Killington with crippling "exit fees" if it ever did leave the state. So in 2006, the town abandoned its plans for secession…but it's still lobbying to change the property tax laws.

*   *   *

"Imperfection is beauty, madness is genius, and it's better to be absolutely ridiculous than absolutely boring."

—**Marilyn Monroe**

YOUR #1 NEWS SOURCE

Breaking leaks from the news stream!

THE WHIZDOM OF HIS STUPIDITY

In July 2012, a Fort Wayne, Indiana, Taco Bell employee named Cameron Jankowski took a photo of himself peeing into a plate of nachos…and posted it on his Twitter account. When the photo went viral, the online group of "hacktivists" known as Anonymous posted personal information about Jankowski online, including the address of the Taco Bell store where he worked. Jankowski must have peed himself—because he quickly deleted the photo from his Twitter page. He later claimed the nachos hadn't been served to anyone and that he hadn't really peed on them: "I poked a hole in the top of a water bottle and filled it with watered-down Mountain Dew," he said. Whether that's true, nobody knows. Needless to say, Taco Bell fired him.

BOILING MAD

In 2012, the news agency Reuters published a story about a delicacy enjoyed by locals in the eastern Chinese city of Dongyang. According to the story, every spring, street vendors go to boys-only primary schools and retrieve buckets of urine from the boys' bathrooms, which they use to soak dozens of chicken eggs (with the shells still on). After several hours of soaking, the eggs are boiled (in the urine), shelled, and allowed to simmer for a few more hours. Then people buy the eggs. And eat them. "Virgin boy eggs," as they are known, have been a delicacy in Dongyang for centuries. "If you eat this," vendor Ge Yaohua, 51, told Reuters, "you will not get heat stroke." (Uncle John says: "I'd rather get heat stroke.")

FOR THE WOMAN ON THE GO

In 2009, a German company called KETS introduced a product called the "Ladybag"—a pocket-size disposable urinal for women. According to the company website:

> Queuing up at lavatories? Squirming on disgusting toilets? These times are gone! Anywhere, anytime—stuck in traffic, on a train, at open-air events—with Ladybag in your pocket you'll feel more

---

Superstitious? Don't buy two pounds! There are approximately 333 cranberries in a pound.

relaxed. All you have to do is take out one of your Ladybag packages—they're about as big as a bar of chocolate—unfold the green plastic bag, open it up—and pee away! Each bag contains special granules that quickly absorb the urine and trap it inside. Comes with a moist towelette for washing up and a small white trash bag to put the used Ladybag in so you can safely dispose of it. Cost: €8.66 (about $11.00) for a package of three.

Note: KETS also makes a version for men. It's called the "Roadbag."

ALCOHOL WAS INVOLVED

At a tailgate party before a Cleveland Brown's football game in 2012, a bunch of Phil Croucher's friends presented a dare: They'd give him $450 if he dunked his head into a five-gallon bucket full of urine. (If you're wondering where they got a five-gallon bucket of urine, you've obviously never been to a tailgate party.) What did Croucher do? He took the dare and dunked his head into the bucket. All the way in. And somebody got a video of it and posted it on YouTube. That's not the end of the story. It turns out that Phil Croucher was a 16-year veteran of the Mentor, Ohio, police force. When his chief heard about the stunt, Croucher was suspended. But only briefly—just long enough to be checked out medically to be sure that he wasn't a danger to the community. (He wasn't.)

SQUIRTLE THE TURTLE

In 2011, researchers at the National University of Singapore decided to find out why Chinese soft-shell turtles regularly put their heads under water and wiggle their tongues. Those familiar with the species assumed the soft-shell turtles were drinking…but it turns out they weren't. After months of study, the researchers figured out that the turtles were actually peeing—through their mouths. Urinating the normal way—via the kidneys—requires a lot of water, the researchers explained, and Chinese soft-shell turtles live in brackish, salty water. Just as it is with humans, it's unsafe for turtles to drink too much salty water. So they developed a way to make urea—the main ingredient in urine—seep from their blood-streams into their mouths. The reason they stick their tongues out underwater and wiggle them: To shake off the urea. (They still pee the normal way, too. Just not very much.)

UNCLE JOHN'S STALL OF FAME

*Uncle John is amazed—and pleased—by the unusual ways
people get involved with bathrooms, toilets, and so on.
That's why he created the "Stall of Fame."*

Honoree: City officials in New Taipei City, Taiwan
Notable Achievement: Finding a novel way to encourage
dog owners to clean up after pets—with a "dog doo lottery"
True Story: Like just about every municipality in the world, New
Taipei City has a dog-doo problem. In 2011, the city came up with
the idea of organizing a prize drawing for people who picked up after
their pets. For each bag of dog doo a citizen handed in to the city,
the city gave a ticket for the drawing. First prize: a gold ingot worth
$2,200. Second-, third-, fourth-, and fifth-place winners would win
smaller gold ingots; there were more than 85 prizes in all.

The city began giving away tickets in August 2011 for a drawing
planned for October, but the program was so popular, with more
than 14,500 bags of poop turned in, that the city added more prizes
and extended the program into December. In that time, the city
estimates that the amount of dog doo on the city streets was cut
in half. A second dog-doo lottery was held in 2012 and more will
likely be held in the future…provided that the city can keep coming up with the money for all those fabulous prizes.

Honoree: Jordan Silverman, 22, a University of Michigan student
Notable Achievement: Coming up with an idea for a bathroom-
themed business while doing his "business"
True Story: In 2010, Silverman was making use of the facilities on
campus when he got the idea of selling advertising space on toilet
paper. He probably wasn't the first person to come up with that
idea, but he may have been the first person to realize that by giving
the rolls away free to bars, restaurants, sports stadiums, offices, and
other businesses, he might interest them in a product that they
would otherwise reject. And in doing so, he would generate distribution for his ads and "eyeballs" for the advertisers. He shared his

idea with his 19-year-old brother Bryan, an undergraduate at Duke University. Bryan wanted to think it over—who wouldn't?—then he eventually jumped on board, and in the fall of 2010, the brothers founded the Star Toilet Paper Co.

Star's two-ply rolls are made from 100 percent recycled paper. The ads are printed using biodegradable soy-based ink that's safe for rear ends and septic systems. Advertising rates start at $99 for 20,000 ads, or about half a cent per ad. The rolls are being distributed to campus apartment buildings, bowling alleys, and other locations in Michigan, and they're expanding into California. "Our ultimate goal is to be in every public venue," Jordan says. "We see no reason why every college stadium should not be carrying our product." (In 2012, *Entrepreneur* magazine named Bryan Silverman its College Entrepreneur of the Year.)

Honoree: *Outlaws*, a show about rowdy country stars, airing on CMT in 2004

Notable Achievement: It was history's first TV show advertised using "Interactive Urinal Communicators."

True Story: When CMT, the country music channel owned by MTV Networks, went looking for a novel way to promote *Outlaws*, it found what it was looking for at Wizmark, a company that makes talking electronic urinal cakes. Shaped like an ordinary, deodorizing urinal cake, the Interactive Urinal Communicator has a motion sensor that can tell when someone is approaching the urinal. When it does, lights flash and a tiny built-in speaker plays a prerecorded audio message. For the *Outlaws* promotion, a sexy female voice said, "Don't miss *Outlaws* on CMT. You seem to miss everything else!" The devices were distributed to bars, concert venues, colleges, and other places frequented by CMT's target demographic: young adult males. "The social protocols of using a urinal—the unwritten rule not to look left or right—guarantees undivided and undistracted visual attention," says James Hitchcock, CMT's vice president for creative and marketing. The devices are designed to last for 10,000 flushes. Bonus: They use so little power—just three volts from two AA batteries—that there's no risk of electrocution when you pee on them.

Update: Since 2004, Michigan, Missouri, Hawaii, West Virginia, Colorado, New Mexico, Georgia, New York, and other states have distributed talking urinal cakes free to bars as part of anti-drunk-driving campaigns, on the theory that the urinal is probably the last stop many drunks make before getting in the car. "If you drink and drive and you get arrested, the next urinal you pee in will be in jail," warns the female voice on the Missouri Department of Transportation's Interactive Urinal Communicator. "Remember," it says, "the future is in your hand."

Honoree: The Millaa Millaa, Australia Chamber of Commerce
Notable Achievement: Installing a theme toilet in the local cemetery to (hopefully) attract tourists to the sleepy little town
True Story: The cemetery, which is publicly owned, does not have bathrooms. But when the local council obtained an estimate to build one in 2012, the $83,000 price tag was more than it could afford. That's when the Chamber of Commerce stepped up and built the bathroom itself, completing the project for just $1,200.
Bonus: They designed the bathroom to look like a giant, upright coffin, complete with a cross and the letters "R.I.P." on the lid, which doubles as the bathroom door. "Maybe a few more people will notice Millaa Millaa now," Chamber president Pat Reynolds told the *Courier-Mail* newspaper.

But what the Chamber had going for it in terms of ingenuity, it apparently lacked in common sense, because when it built the toilet it violated several planning, building, and even plumbing codes. It also built the funereal facilities on town-owned land, without getting the council's permission. More than 90 percent of the townspeople signed a petition in support of the illegal coffin commode, but the council ordered it removed anyway. In January 2013, the Chamber of Commerce disconnected the bathroom and hauled it away. "There will be a funeral for it," Reynolds told reporters, "as we're calling it the death of common sense at the cemetery."

*   *   *

"There are two great rules of life, the one general and the other particular. The first is that everyone can, in the end, get what he wants if he only tried. This is the general rule. The particular rule is that every individual is more or less an exception to the general rule."

—**Samuel Butler**

Grape-Nuts cereal once claimed to "tighten loose teeth."

IT'S A WEIRD, WEIRD WORLD

Here's proof that truth really is stranger than fiction.

$LAP!

A San Francisco salon called Tata Massage offers a unique beauty treatment: face slapping. The owner, a Thai woman who goes by the name Tata, claims that slapping people in the face is a great way to remove wrinkles and open pores. She charges $350 for a ten-minute slap session. Also available: "massage boxing."

WATCH YOUR LANGUAGE

Ayapaneco—an indigenous language from Ayapa, Mexico—might soon go extinct because the last two people on Earth who can speak it are not speaking to each other. It's not known what caused the feud between the two elderly men, but those who know them say they've "never really enjoyed each other's company."

VOICE FROM BEYOND

One spooky night in China's Anhui province, residents of two adjacent buildings started hearing a moaning noise coming from…they couldn't tell exactly where. As the moans grew louder, the residents became more and more convinced it was the ghost of a tormented soul. Over the next few hours, the moans turned into screams, alternating with cries for help and quieter moments of whimpering. The scared residents held tight and did their best to ignore it. Then, seven hours after the voice first appeared, pedestrians outside on the sidewalk heard the noises and went to investigate. Deep in the very narrow alley that separated the two buildings, they discovered a woman who'd tried to take a short cut and got stuck. Firefighters had to cut a hole in the wall of one of the buildings to free her.

FOILED!

In 2005, a group of students at the Massachusetts Institute of Technology decided to test the effectiveness of tin-foil hats, which some conspiracy theorists use as "Faraday cages" (which block electrical fields) to block mind-reading signals that are supposedly beamed into their brains by the CIA, the NSA, the FBI, secret societies, aliens, the DMV, AAA, Keebler elves, etc. The MIT students created three helmets out of Reynold's Wrap, which they dubbed the "Classical," the "Fez," and the "Centurion." Then they took turns wearing the helmets and blasting each other with different bandwidths of radio waves. Their findings: Most tin-foil helmets actually *amplify* radio waves, not block them. "The current tin-foil helmet craze is likely to have been propagated by the U.S. government," the students concluded.

LI'L PIPE CLEANER

In 2013, a 22-year-old Chinese woman who'd been keeping her pregnancy a secret thought she had to go to the bathroom. She went into a rest room in her apartment building and stood over the squat toilet. A tiny baby boy popped out…and immediately slipped down the drain. At that point, she realized it might be a good time to tell someone about the baby. Firefighters' attempts to retrieve the newborn from the U-shaped pipe were unsuccessful, so they went downstairs, cut a hole in the ceiling, removed the entire section of pipe, and rushed it to a hospital, where doctors performed an emergency "c-section" on the pipe and were able to rescue the baby. He was scratched up but otherwise okay.

DETOUR AHEAD…TO SPACE

A UFO research team in Argentina called CEUFO (*Centro de Estudos Ufologicos*) has warned commuters to remain alert while traveling the 22 miles between the towns of Anguil and Lonquimay. Why? Several people have reported that they "lost time" while driving that particular stretch of highway. In one case, two men were having a conversation when all of a sudden they felt disoriented, then realized neither could remember anything about the past few miles they'd traveled. In another instance, a man drove up to a service station on the route and asked where he was. The last thing he remembered was being several miles away, and he had no idea how he got to the station. CEUFO urged the government to issue a formal warning, but they refused, so the UFO researchers issued it themselves, requesting that any drivers who experience time anomalies contact them immediately.

KEEP CALM & CARRY ON

*And while you're doing so, have a look at the story behind
those ubiquitous "Keep Calm and Carry On" posters.*

STIFF UPPER LIP

In September 1939, Germany invaded Poland, and the U.K. declared war on Germany, marking the beginning of World War II. The war would not be confined to battlefields. In 1940, Nazi planes brought the war across the English Channel, raining bombs on major British cities, a strategic campaign known as "the Blitz." The population was terrified, and beyond air-raid warnings and instructing people to hide out in basements, there wasn't a lot that the government could do to protect them from falling bombs. Amid the terror of the Blitz, the government's Ministry of Information was given the task of coming up with a public-relations campaign to boost the morale of a people under siege.

But it didn't happen overnight. As early as 1936, the government began developing posters adorned with morale-boosting slogans. They wanted to be ready to plaster major English cities with those posters within 24 hours of a declaration of war with Germany…if war did come.

They were ready. Just hours after the declaration of war on September 3, 1939, two posters began appearing on walls and street lamps around London, Manchester, Birmingham, Liverpool, Leeds, and other potential targets. They came in two designs: "Freedom Is in Peril. Defend It with All Your Might" and "Your Courage, Your Cheerfulness, Your Resolution Will Bring Us Victory." Each slogan was printed in simple, easy-to-read type beneath the image of the Tudor Crown, a familiar symbol that had been used on everything from government-inspected meat products to telephone booths.

POP-AGANDA

But the most famous World War II British motivational poster was the one that said "Keep Calm and Carry On." Except that it was never widely used as a morale-boosting poster. The concept and design were executed, along with the two posters that were widely circulated. But "Keep Calm and Carry On" was held back—the

---

Napoleon's wife, Josephine, had a pet orangutan that she dressed in a jacket and fed at the table.

agency was saving it to use in case things ever got *really* bleak, when and if the Nazis invaded the U.K. by land. Fortunately, that never happened, and the 2.5 million "Keep Calm and Carry On" posters that had been printed were never used. All but a few were destroyed, and the slogan faded into history.

For 60 years.

In 2000, Stuart and Mary Manley, owners of Barter Books in the English town of Alnwick, discovered one in the bottom of an old box of used books. They decided to hang what they thought was a common World War II relic up on the wall of the bookstore. Result: Dozens of customers wanted to buy one. Figuring (correctly) that the government-issued poster was in the public domain, the Manleys began making and selling reproductions.

KEEP CALM AND CASH IN

And because it's in the public domain, *anyone* can make copies of the "Keep Calm and Carry On" poster and sell them. And they have. A 36-year-old British TV producer named Mark Coop thought the slogan would look great—and sell well—emblazoned on T-shirts, cuff links, blankets…and pretty much everything. In 2007, he set up a website to sell his wares. Four years later, after failing to trademark the slogan "Keep Calm and Carry On" in the U.K., Coop successfully registered the mark with the European Union and proceeded to get all the other imitators (and the Manleys) kicked off eBay. But that hasn't stopped them (or the Manleys) from selling "Keep Calm" merchandise, including dozens of parodies that have shown up on posters, mugs, T-shirts, etc., always rendered in the same font as the original "Keep Calm…" with a clever graphic in place of the crown. Here are some of our favorites:

- Keep Calm and Rock On (with electric guitars)
- Keep Calm and Drink Beer (with a picture of a beer)
- Keep Calm and Call Batman (with a Batman logo)
- Now Panic and Freak Out (with an upside-down crown)
- Screw Calm and Get Angry
- Keep Calm and Cary Grant
(with a low-flying airplane, like the one in *North by Northwest*)
- Change Words and Be Hilarious

Most studied area of seabed in the world: California's Monterey Bay.

THE SWAT TEAM

It's so natural to want to take a whack at the fly buzzing around your head, it's hard to think of fly swatters as something somebody actually invented. But someone did.

WEAPON OF MESHED DESTRUCTION

On January 9, 1900, the U.S. Patent Office granted patent number 640,790 to Robert R. Montgomery of Decatur, Illinois, illustrated with a detailed drawing of a piece of window screen, folded precisely at one end and attached to a wooden handle with two rivets. The design turned out to be so perfect that it has remained essentially unchanged for more than a century, even down to the helpful hole (also shown on the patent application) on the end of the handle for hanging on a nail.

Today, the occasional fly that gets into the house is an annoyance, but not much more. It's difficult to imagine how serious a health hazard flies were before modern medicines and pesticides, when horses were used for transportation, outhouses used for bathrooms, fresh manure used as fertilizer, and open windows used as "air conditioning." Animal dung was everywhere—not only on the farm, but also in big cities, where the streets were literally paved with layer upon layer of horse droppings. Populations of house flies would explode each year. But flies do not live by poop alone, and at a time when open windows and doors were the only way to cope with sweltering summers, flies came from the street (and outhouse) into the home with impunity, landing on food, sleeping babies, pets, and anything else that would stand still. And they weren't just unappetizing houseguests—although they do not bite, houseflies are carriers of dozens of diseases, including typhoid, cholera, dysentery, anthrax, tuberculosis, and salmonella.

INVENTED ON THE FLY

People had long been whacking at flies with rolled-up newspapers or whatever else was at hand, but nothing had ever accomplished the task with the elegant efficiency of Robert Montgomery's fly swatter. Besides stealth, speed, and accuracy, Montgomery's meshed screen brought forward enough bulk to kill the fly without damaging what

---

was beneath it. The flexible "whiplike" killing surface worked on irregular and angular surfaces, and the mesh allowed a large enough surface area to thwart last-second fly evasions without creating wind resistance. And best of all, the thin, sharp edges of the swat surface tended to slice into the fly's body instead of smashing it flat, minimizing the mess on walls, furniture, paintings, wallpaper, and unlucky bystanders.

PEST ASIDES

Montgomery may have been a genius in fly-killing technology, but he wasn't really that interested in manufacturing the swatter. Three years after his patent was granted, with the public buying up half a million fly swatters a year, Montgomery and his overworked partners (his two sons) decided it was time to turn the invention over to somebody else. That somebody was a local manufacturer named John L. Bennett. Bennett would later take credit for making "dramatic improvements" to the fly swatter, but his contribution was literally "tinkering around the edges." He added stitching around the outside of the netting to keep it from fraying. (He'd later have a more legitimate claim to pop-culture fame as the man who patented the beer can.)

KILLER APP

There have been many attempts to improve on fly-swatting technology, from fly guns that shoot swatting disks to electrified fly zappers, but the most popular anti-fly weapon remains the classic fly swatter, unchanged in basic design (except that they're now made of plastic instead of wood and metal). They're inexpensive, well-suited for the job intended, and still weirdly satisfying when you make solid contact. Who but the flies could ask for anything more?

*   *   *

OOPS!

The NFL's Carolina Panthers play in Charlotte, *North* Carolina. Apparently no one in Nike's apparel division realized that...until they started selling a $32 Panthers T-shirt that had the team's logo and the letters "N.C." printed inside a silhouette of *South* Carolina. Nike quickly pulled the shirt from stores.

BIG STARS

George Clooney is a huge star—but not nearly as huge as these guys. Here are a few of the tallest actors who ever appeared on the big (and little) screen.

STAR: Alexander Sizonenko

HEIGHT: 7 feet 10 inches

SHORT BIO: Sizonenko was born in the Ukraine in 1959, and was a professional basketball player in the Soviet Union during the '70s and '80s. In 1991, he appeared in the Czech film *The Brave Little Tailor* in which he played—big surprise—a giant. It's the only acting role he's ever had, but that's enough to make him the tallest actor in history. (He has his own page on the Internet Movie Database.) Bonus: For a short time in 1991, Sizonenko was listed in *Guinness World Records* as the tallest man alive.

STAR: Gheorghe Muresan

HEIGHT: 7 feet 7 inches

SHORT BIO: Another basketballer who dabbled in acting. Muresan was born in Romania in 1971, became a star player in Europe, and then had a respectable career in the NBA (1993–2000), mostly with the Washington Bullets. His only major acting job was playing the title role in the 2003 Billy Crystal film *My Giant* (see next page). But he had a few minor roles, too, including appearing as "the ventriloquist" in Eminem's breakthrough 2000 "My Name Is" music video, and playing himself in the 2003 TV documentary *Giants: Friend or Foe.*

STAR: Matthew McGrory

HEIGHT: 7 feet 6 inches

SHORT BIO: McGrory was born in West Chester, Pennsylvania, in 1973. After trying law school for a while, then working as a bar bouncer, he became interested in acting. His first movie role: a zombie in the 1999 low budget horror/comedy film *The Dead Hate the Living!* His best-known movie role: Karl, the sad giant befriended by Ewan McGregor in the 2003 Tim Burton film *Big Fish*. You may have also seen him in *Bubble Boy* (2001) and in *Constantine* (2005), and he even appeared on the TV shows *Malcolm in the Middle* and *Charmed*. Unfortunately, McGrory died young—at age 32 in 2005. (The cause of death was never conclusively determined.) *Guinness World Records* claims McGrory had the world's largest toe: Each of his big toes was five inches long.

STAR: Daniel Gilchrist
HEIGHT: 7 feet 5.5 inches
SHORT BIO: Gilchrist was born in Topeka, Kansas, in 1982. From 2003 until 2005, he worked in the Midwest professional wrestling circuit under the moniker "The Mighty Sequoia," then decided to focus on acting. First starring role: He played "the Creature" in the Topeka Performing Arts Center's production of *Frankenstein*. So far he's had just one movie role, but it was a big one: Gilchrist played André the Giant in the 2007 biopic *André: Heart of the Giant*. He only got the role after Matthew McGrory, who had been cast to star in the film, died during filming.

STAR: André the Giant
HEIGHT: 7 feet 4 inches
SHORT BIO: Born in Grenoble, France, in 1946, André René Roussimoff left home at 14, worked a variety of jobs, then moved to Paris in 1964 at the age of 18 and became a professional wrestler. By the early '70s, "André the Giant" was an international superstar. In 1976, he played "Bigfoot" in three episodes of *The Six-Million Dollar Man*. His acting career grew after that, starting with small roles on other TV shows, culminating in the part he's best known for, the role of the giant Fezzik in the 1987 film *The Princess Bride*. He pretty much disappeared from the acting scene after that, and died of heart failure in 1993 at the age of 46. The 1998 Billy Crystal film, *My Giant*, was inspired by Crystal's old friend André the Giant, whom he'd met while filming *The Princess Bride*.

STAR: Peter Mayhew
HEIGHT: 7 feet 3 inches
SHORT BIO: Mayhew is probably the most famous of all the big stars in this article—and yet most people have no idea what he looks like. In 1976, Mayhew, a 33-year-old hospital orderly in his hometown of London, England, appeared in a photo in a local

newspaper story about people with especially large feet. At 7 feet 3 inches tall, he stood out in the photo. In a bizarre coincidence that would change his life forever, Hollywood producer Charles H. Schneer happened to see the photo, contacted Mayhew, and asked him if he'd play a minotaur in a film he was working on, *Sinbad and the Eye of the Tiger*. Mayhew agreed, and while he was in Hollywood auditioned for another part: the role of Chewbacca the Wookie in *Star Wars*. He ended up playing the role in all the *Star Wars* films that featured the character (two of the prequels didn't), and has appeared at hundreds of *Star Wars* and science-fiction conventions over the decades. (He also played Chewbacca in the 2011 Christmas episode of the television series *Glee*.)

STAR: Richard Kiel

HEIGHT: 7 feet 2 inches

SHORT BIO: Kiel was born in Detroit, Michigan, in 1939. After high school he got a job selling cemetery plots. ("It was very good practice" for acting, he said years later.) In the late '50s, he decided he wanted to be an actor, and moved to Los Angeles. First role: bare-knuckle boxer Duff Brannigan in a 1960 episode of the short-lived TV series *Klondike*. In 1962, he got his first starring film role in one of the worst films ever made, *Eegah*—about a caveman who comes to life in California and falls in love with a teenage girl. Over the next 15 years, Kiel appeared in dozens of TV shows and films. Then, in 1977, he got the role that made him internationally famous—the steel-toothed henchman "Jaws" in the 1977 James Bond film *The Spy Who Loved Me*. He was such a popular character that producers brought him back for the next Bond film, 1979's *Moonraker*. In 1992, he suffered a severe head injury in a car accident, and he has only appeared in a few films since.

RICHARD KIEL QUOTE: "I'm actually seven foot and one and one half inches tall. But I say 'seven two' because it's easier."

*   *   *

TOP 3 CLICHES FROM REALITY TV SHOWS

1. "I didn't come here to make friends."
2. "He/she threw me under the bus."
3. "Going home is not an option."

TAKE ME TO YOUR LEADER

When the White House was built in the 1790s, it was faced with "freestone," a form of sandstone that's easy to carve, but is also very porous and susceptible to water damage. To protect it, the stonemasons sealed it with a whitewash made of salt, rice, and glue—hence the nickname "White House." Here are the stories behind some other countries' official residences.

COUNTRY: England
RESIDENCE: 10 Downing Street
STORY: In 1735, King George II offered the London mansion to Prime Minister Robert Walpole, but it had been poorly constructed on a sand foundation and required constant repair. Walpole realized that accepting the house would eventually bankrupt him, so he told His Majesty that the honor was "too great." Instead, said Walpole, the king should transfer the property to the Treasury for use by all future senior ministers. King George agreed. Now the state is responsible for the maintenance of 10 Downing Street, and Walpole—and every P.M. since Walpole—has lived there for free.

COUNTRY: Bolivia
RESIDENCE: Palacio Quemado
STORY: The country has, in effect, two capitals. The Supreme Court meets in Sucre; Congress and the president are located in La Paz (at 11,900 feet above sea level, it's the highest capital in the world). The city's presidential palace was occupied by rebels during the 1875 revolution. The rebels were defeated, but they burned down the palace before retreating. When it was rebuilt for the next president, it was given the name *Palacio Quemado*, meaning "Burned Palace."

COUNTRY: France
RESIDENCE: Élysée Palace
STORY: Built in Paris in 1722 for the Count of Evreux, the grand mansion has changed hands many times. When Evreux died in 1753, Louis XV bought the palace as a home for his mistress,

---

Caffeine is a natural pesticide—it keeps bugs off the coffee plants.

Madame de Pompadour. Emperor Napoleon later lived there. After the fall of his nephew, Napoleon III, in 1873, the Third Republic designated Élysée Palace the official presidential residence.

COUNTRY: Jamaica

RESIDENCE: Vale Royal

STORY: First built in the capital of Kingston in 1694, Vale Royal was bought by the British government in 1928 as a home for the colonial secretary. Jamaica became independent in 1962, with its own bicameral parliamentary democracy, but remained in the British Commonwealth of Nations. Parliament took Vale Royal as the official residence of their new prime minister. The incoming P.M. protested that the mansion was too small. He wanted a larger one, but Parliament ignored him. Vale Royal is still the official residence.

COUNTRY: Mexico

RESIDENCE: Los Piños

STORY: For generations, Mexican rulers resided in the picturesque Chapultepec Castle, located atop a hill in Mexico City. In 1934, when working-class candidate Lázaro Cárdenas was elected president on a promise to end corruption, he decided that the castle was too ostentatious. He cut his salary in half and moved his family into a more modest residence located in Mexico City's lush Chapultepec Forest. He called it *Los Piños* (The Pines), after the name of the ranch where he met his wife. (Chapultepec Castle now houses the National Museum of History.)

*   *   *

DEAR GOD...

Thousands of letters are sent to God each year by way of Jerusalem, Israel. The letters are taken very seriously by the Jerusalem post office, which has a "Letters to God" department. The staff sends them to a local rabbi, who slides them under the cracks in the Western Wall to join the million or so messages per year that are delivered there in person. You can also send emails and faxes to God by way of the Jerusalem post office. They'll print them out and send them in with the snail-mail letters. The address: God, Jerusalem. (Proper postage required.)

But not soon enough! Dogs who bark continuously can get laryngitis.

BLUE JUICE & LANDING LIPS

At this time we request that you turn off all electronic devices and carefully review this page.

Crotch watch: When the flight attendants go down the aisle pre-takeoff to make sure everyone's seatbelt is buckled

Blue juice: The "water" in the lavatory toilet

Pax: Passengers

Crumb-crunchers: Children

The village: The "coach" or "economy" section (filled with pax and crumb-crunchers) .

George: Autopilot

Deadhead: An airline employee traveling on airline business

God: Air-traffic control

CCN: The airline employee rumor mill. It's short for "Cabin Crew News."

Slam-clicker: A flight attendant so tired that he/she goes directly to the layover hotel and doesn't emerge until it's time to go back to the airport the next morning. The door "slams" and the lock "clicks."

Spinner: A late-boarding passenger who doesn't have a seat assignment; he/she is "spinning" around the cabin, looking everywhere for a seat

Landing lips: When female passengers touch up their makeup just prior to landing

Screamer: An irate or frustrated passenger

Gate lice: Passengers who form a chaotic mass around the gates when boarding is announced so they can be the first to board

Two-for-one special: Upon landing, the plane touches down, then unexpectedly jerks back up, then abruptly touches down once more

Ferry flight: Rarely, a flight will be empty, but the crew is needed for a connecting flight, so they get to ride an empty plane and don't have to work

Debriefing: A post-flight party in a hotel room

Tuesday, Wednesday, Thursday, and Friday Islands are all located off the coast of Australia.

1-900-RIP-OFF

In 1977, AT&T devised the "1-900" prefix as a way to prevent phone lines from becoming overloaded during a TV call-in show with President Jimmy Carter. Within a few years, the idea would generate billions.

O PERATORS ARE STANDING BY
During the 1980s and early '90s, telephone companies offered hundreds of pay-per-call phone services at premium rates (starting at $.99 per minute). Advertised on TV, the numbers often targeted children; their use became so widespread parent groups began to complain, especially about commercials that weren't clear about the high cost of the calls. What did you get when you called a "premium rate" number? Not exactly premium information—it was almost always a pre-recorded message that dragged on for five to ten minutes (to maximize profits). Because of the complaints—and thousands of angry parents on the hook for huge phone bills—the FTC enacted new rules in the mid-'90s that effectively killed off the kid-baiting commercials. For those of you who missed out on the 900-craze, here are some highlights.

• **Hulk Hogan Hotline:** The World Wrestling Federation hotline was reportedly the most profitable 900 number in the U.S. between 1991 and 1993. Callers would hear bits of Hulk Hogan trivia and totally awesome recorded messages from the Hulkster himself.

• **Corey Haim and Corey Feldman:** The two '80s teen heart-throbs teamed up to create a phone line where fans could "listen to the Coreys' private phone messages and get their personal number where you can leave them messages of your own."

• **Rapping Santa Claus:** By calling 1-900-909-RAPS, you could listen to Santa bust some rhymes.

• **Dial an Insult:** Having a bad day? It's about to get worse. Call this number and a recording would insult you—fresh insults daily!

• **He-Man Hotline:** He-Man and his sister, She-Ra, offered inspirational messages and a chance to win free action figures.

• **The *Little Monsters* Movie Line:** In 1989, Fred Savage (*The Wonder Years*) starred in the movie *Little Monsters*, in which a kid

---

The most enduring and profitable use of 1-900 numbers: "Adult hotlines."

teams up with the monster that lives under his bed (Howie Mandel). This number offered the chance to win an autographed photo of Savage, a glow-in-the-dark T-shirt, or K-Swiss sneakers.

• **Freddy Kruger:** The *Nightmare on Elm Street* villain offered his favorite spooky "deadtime" stories.

• **DJ Jazzy Jeff and the Fresh Prince:** Get the inside scoop on Will Smith, the kid-friendly rapper from *The Fresh Prince of Bel Air*.

• **1-900-HOT-HINTS:** "Hundreds of action-packed hints" and secret passwords on your favorite Nintendo games.

• **The Freak Phone:** Freddy Freaker was a bizarre yellow troll that kids could call to get information about…we're not quite sure. "What's happenin', what's jammin', party till you drop, dial and hear the action, what's hot and what's not" is what the commercial promised.

• **ADD-IT-UP Phone Lottery:** Answer 21 basic math questions (with the phone's keypad) in under two minutes (at $3.99 per minute) and win $300 instantly! Almost nobody ever won.

• **1-900 Hot Auto:** Call and listen to classified ads for repossessed cars that are on the auction block, and then bid on them.

• **1-900-990-LOAN:** From the TV commercial: "You can't get a loan because your bills are late, but your bills are late because you can't get a loan because your bills are late!" The obvious solution to money problems is, of course, spending $35 on a phone call to a predatory lending service.

• **Monty Hall's *Let's Make a Deal*:** Play games like the one on the classic game show and "you don't even need to dress up like a chicken!"

• **1-900-9099-CRY:** The commercial was just footage of people crying. Text on the screen asked, "Want to know what's making them cry?" The answer cost $2 per minute (and it was a scam to redirect people to a "party line").

• **Grandpa Munster's Junior Vampires of America Club:** Al "Grandpa Munster" Lewis offered up "scary monster stories" and instructions for how to get a "free vampire patch."

"WE ARE NOT AMUSED"

What was frowned upon in Victorian-era England? Pretty much everything.

SIMPLY NOT DONE

During the 1837–1901 reign of Queen Victoria, Britain's upper classes prospered, the nation's population doubled, and a sense of romance and dignity prevailed. It was also a period marked by widespread child-labor abuse, unbridled poverty, horrifying poorhouses, overcrowded and unsanitary cities, and rampant prostitution. It was an era of great innovation in art and industry but also an era of strict moral values and adherence to propriety.

The rigid morality modeled by Queen Victoria and her husband, Prince Albert, may well have been a reaction to the previous monarch of Great Britain, Victoria's uncle, King William IV. While the king never managed to produce any legitimate heirs with his wife, Queen Adelaide, he did father ten illegitimate children with actress and courtesan Dorothea Jordan, who was his mistress for 20 years.

Here are a few of the things that displeased proper Victorians:

• **The word "leg."** It was considered too sexy and, thus, too vulgar. At the time, the preferred term, if one absolutely *had* to refer to a lower extremity, was "limb."

• **Calling an aristocrat by his first name.** Even aristocratic children referred to each other by their last names. Adults used titles in addition to last names, and noblemen would use their aristocratic titles or "Lord." Thus, your good friend and neighbor might be Captain Smith, Lord Smith, or Mr. Smith, but never John. Likewise, the lady of the house would be referred to by her title and her husband's last name, or, if she was single, Miss Smith.

• **Ladies keeping orchids.** While the growing and collecting of orchids was a popular fad for men during the Victorian era, ladies did not take up the hobby. Why? Because the flowers were thought to bear too close a resemblance to female genitalia.

• **Swimming at public beaches.** While gentlemen frequently swam naked in groups of other gentlemen, it was not considered appropriate for ladies to be seen swimming or bathing in public, even in the extremely modest swimwear of the day. A natural outgrowth of

---

More than half of all vegetarians in the United States are female.

this prohibition was "the bathing box." The box, usually made of a wooden frame with canvas walls and a roof, was used to change into swimwear, and then rolled down the beach right into the water. A lady could then exit the bathing house through a rear door and then swim with some protection against being seen from shore.

- **Ladies receiving advanced education.** A young lady's education was only for the purpose of making her a suitable wife. For working-class girls, that meant domestic education. Middle- and upper-class girls were expected to learn only enough, according to Victorian writer John Ruskin, to "take into consideration a husband's need to share his interest with his wife and conduct intelligent conversation with her," and nothing more.

- **Discussing illegitimate children.** Obviously, having a child out of wedlock was scandalous. But even *talking* about the "plague," as it was called at the time, was frowned upon. In 1856 alone, an estimated 40,000 children were born to unwed mothers in England and Wales. In addition to the problems associated with caring for all those illegitimate children (many were sent off to orphanages and workhouses, or to extended family to be raised), it was taboo for decent people even to discuss the problem.

- **Smelling bad.** Victorians really did believe that "cleanliness is next to Godliness," and viewed those who were not clean as sickening—"breeding a social pestilence in the very midst of our land," wrote playwright and journalist Henry Mayhew. The poor in particular were prone to smelliness, because although indoor plumbing existed in Victorian England, very few of the poor had access to it. It's estimated that in 1894, only about five percent of the houses in industrialized towns had a bath. Although cleanliness was next to impossible for most of the working classes, smelling bad was still a no-no.

- **Stuffing vs. dressing.** Did you grow up thinking that the name for bread crumbs that were cooked *inside* a bird was "stuffing" and the stuff that was cooked *outside* of it was "dressing"? Not exactly: The word "stuffing" dates back to the mid-16th century, but in the Victorian era it was replaced with "dressing" because "dressing" a bird was far less suggestive than "stuffing" it.

Elvis Presley was interred in a rose-colored coffin.

FAMILIAR PHRASES

We're back with one of our regular features—
origins of some common phrases.

TO HANDLE WITH KID GLOVES

Meaning: To treat someone or something very carefully
Origin: "Leather from the hide of young goats—called *kids*—was considered the finest in the glove industry. Kid-leather gloves were only worn when there was no danger of undertaking a manual task. Therefore, anything or anyone that is given the 'kid-glove' treatment is handled with extreme tact and gentleness." (From *Mothballs and Elbow Grease*, by the National Trust)

MAKE ENDS MEET

Meaning: To have just enough money to pay for basic expenses
Origin: "On full-rigged sailing vessels, some ropes attached to the lower edges of the sails were permanently fixed. When such a length of rope broke, frugal masters ordered sailors to pull ends together and splice them. In order to make both ends of a rope meet, it was often necessary to strain and tug, stretching it to its limit. Long used literally on the sea, we now apply the expression for anyone who makes both ends meet by managing to stretch his or her income to cover the bills." (From *Why You Say It*, by Webb Garrison)

TALK TURKEY

Meaning: Dispense with the small talk and get down to business
Origin: "The phrase first appeared in the American colonial days when the Pilgrim Fathers always seemed to want turkeys when they traded with the Indians. So familiar did their requests become that the Indians would greet them with the words, 'You come to talk turkey?'" (From *Why Do We Say...?*, by Nigel Rees)

YOU'VE GOT YOUR WORK CUT OUT FOR YOU

Meaning: A difficult task lies ahead
Origin: "Stems from the craft of tailoring. It would seem the work is made easier by having someone cut out patterns before the stitching

The phrase "in a pickle" was first used by Shakespeare in *The Tempest* (1610).

begins. In fact, it makes life more difficult for the tailor. Cutting the work out in advance is much quicker than actually tailoring a suit, so piles of material would mount up, making it hard for the tailor to keep up. The first recorded appearance of the phrase showed up in Charles Dickens's 1843 novel, *A Christmas Carol*.'" (From *Red Herrings & White Elephants*, by Albert Jack)

EVERYTHING'S COMING UP ROSES

Meaning: Events are favorable

Origin: "It may have begun life as the second half of an early 20th-century expression, 'Fall into sh*t and come up roses,' meaning to emerge unscathed from an unpleasant dilemma. A later variant, dating from about 1950, dispensed with the first half—'Everything is coming up roses.' The phrase gained popularity thanks to the Stephen Sondheim song 'Everything's Coming Up Roses,' which he wrote for the 1959 musical *Gypsy*." (From *Seeing Red or Tickled Pink*, by Christine Ammer)

PULL THE PLUG

Meaning: To abruptly cease work on a project; or to end a terminal patient's life by withdrawing life support

Origin: "The phrase pre-dates the first electric lamp (invented in 1879) by almost 20 years. The 'plug' is actually one used in an old-fashioned type of toilet, which had to be flushed by pulling up a stopper—or plug—to empty the contents of the pan. The wider figurative meaning developed in the 1930s. The 'life support' meaning dates to the '70s." (From *The Real McCoy*, by Georgia Hole)

ON A WING AND A PRAYER

Meaning: In poor condition, but just managing to get the job done

Origin: "This phrase originated during World War II. In the 1942 John Wayne film, *The Flying Tigers*, a character says a plane was "attacked and fired on by Japanese aircraft. She's coming in on one wing and a prayer.' The phrase was taken up by songwriters Harold Adamson and Jimmy McHugh and their 1943 patriotic song *Coming In on a Wing and a Prayer*. It hit a chord with the public, and there are many references to it in U.S. newspapers from 1943 onward, most notably in the 1944 Hollywood film *Wing and a Prayer*." (From "The Phrase Finder" at *www.phrases.org.uk*)

German folklore: It is good luck to eat herring at midnight on New Year's Eve.

YELLOW SNOW

The "microbrew" movement has revolutionized beer, as
local brewmasters develop interesting flavorful beers
and then give them interesting (and funny) names.

Dead Guy Ale

Blithering Idiot

Ill-Tempered
Gnome

Men's Room Red

Spicy Fish Wife

He'Brew: The
Chosen Beer

Buckin' Monk

Dog's Bollocks

Kilt Lifter

Irish Death

Arrogant
Bastard Ale

Old Leghumper

Face Plant

Moo Thunder
Stout

Porkslap Pale Ale

Polygamy Porter

Alimony Ale

Moose Drool

Buttface
Amber Ale

Hoptimus Prime

Yellow Snow

Soft Dookie

Ryan and the
Beaster Bunny

Santa's Butt Porter

Seriously Bad Elf

I'll Have What the
Gentleman on the
Floor Is Having

Old Engine Oil

Screaming Ape
Porter

Tactical Nuclear
Penguin

Black Metal

Vas Deferens

Wreck the Halls

Farmer's Tan

Mama's Little
Yella Pils

400 Lb. Monkey

Panty Peeler

Rigor Mortis

Meat Whistle

Human Blockhead

Wake Up Dead

Doctor Morton's
Clown Poison

Gandhi-Bot

Little Sumpin'
Sumpin'

Hoppy Ending

Ninja vs. Unicorn

Sweaty Betty

Smooth Hoperator

Scotland Charred

Big Falcon Deal

Overrated West
Coast IPA

The English were once required by law to eat fish three times a week.

POLI-TALKS

Why are we so annoyed by politicians? It might
have something to do with utterances like these.

"The top half of the students are well-educated, the bottom half receive extra help, but the middle half we're leaving out."
—**Marcia Neal (R), candidate for the Colorado State Board of Education (she won)**

"My fear is that the whole island will become so overly populated that it will tip over and capsize."
—**Rep. Hank Johnson (D-GA), on why U.S. troops shouldn't be sent to Guam**

"Yes. I have some friends who are NASCAR team owners."
—**Mitt Romney, when asked whether he follows NASCAR**

"What do you want me to tell Romney? I can't tell him to do *that* to himself. You're crazy. You're absolutely crazy. You're getting as bad as Biden."
—**Clint Eastwood, talking to an empty "Obama" chair at the 2012 GOP convention**

"I've known eight presidents, three of them intimately."
—**V.P. Joe Biden**

"Fool me once, shame on you. Fool me twice, shame on you."
—**Rep. Virginia Foxx (R-NC)**

"It's going to take an individual that has testicular fortitude."
—**Paul Gibson, Sheet Metal Workers' Union president, on why Hillary Clinton should be president**

"When they ask me who's the president of Ubeki-beki-beki-beki-stan-stan, I'm going to say, you know, 'I don't know. Do you know?'"
—**Herman Cain (R), presidential candidate, explaining his foreign policy credentials**

"There's a lot of—I don't know what the term is in Austrian— 'wheeling and dealing.'"
—**Barack Obama, unaware that there's no Austrian language (they speak German)**

"And you can always follow me on Tweeter."
—**Gov. Rick Perry (R-TX), accepting an award for his work in "new media activism"**

Gallons of fresh water in all 5 Great Lakes: 6 quadrillion. Only the polar ice caps have more.

HIGH-TECH UNDERWEAR

Who says underwear should only be clean and comfortable?
Here's a look at some skivvies with extra built-in features.

I NDOMITABLE UNDERWEAR
Special Feature: They're (pre)scented underwear for men.
Details: Manufactured by the French firm Le Slip Français, the Indomitable line of boxers and briefs is made of cotton fabric that has been impregnated with microcapsules containing musk and pear-scented perfume. The capsules, which last for up to 30 washes, release their scent when the wearer walks or moves around. But that pleasant smell doesn't come cheap! The briefs sell for $46 apiece; the boxers sell for $52.

SELF-DEFENSE LINGERIE
Special Feature: Protects the wearer from an assailant, then automatically reports the incident to the police
Details: Designed by a team of Indian engineering students in 2013, the ladies' undergarment contains built-in pressure sensors around the bust area. When these detect "unwanted force," the garment delivers a 3,800 kilovolt shock to the assailant (the wearer is protected by a layer of insulating material), then uses its built-in text messaging and GPS capabilities to report the incident and location to police and to the wearer's relatives. The garment can deliver up to 82 electric shocks before it needs to be recharged.

SCANNABLE UNDERWEAR
Special Feature: Contains "radio frequency identification" tags that allow the underwear to be sorted by machines
Details: On Russian military bases, underwear from different soldiers is typically co-mingled and washed in giant industrial laundries, making it unlikely that the wearers will get back the same skivvies they turned in for washing. Introduced on an experimental basis in May 2013, the new undergarments will contain personalized RFID tags and bar codes that allow machines to identify the owner of each piece of underwear and sort them accordingly. "Each serviceman will know for sure that he has been given his own underwear," making military

---

Pizza Hut uses 700 million pounds of pepperoni and 525 million pounds of tomatoes a year.

service "more hygienic," says a spokesperson for Voentorg, the Russian company that is introducing the technology. If the program is successful, the Ministry of Defense hopes to one day make it possible for everyone in the Russian military to wear his or her own underwear.

SMART-E-PANTS

Special Feature: They prevent bed sores.

Details: When a person is bedridden or in a wheelchair and remains in one position for too long, skin tissue can become compressed in places where the bone is close to the skin, such as in the hips, shoulders, and portions of the back. The tissue compression can restrict blood flow to these areas or cut it off entirely, causing injuries known as "pressure ulcers," or bedsores. Smart-e-Pants, developed by researchers at the University of Calgary and the University of Alberta, deliver a mild electric shock to the wearer's buttocks for ten seconds every ten minutes. The jolt is just enough to stimulate the muscles to move slightly, simulating fidgeting and thereby allowing blood and oxygen to flow to the areas that would otherwise become compressed. During a two-month study of 33 patients, none developed bed sores while wearing the underwear. The next step is a larger clinical trial; if that's successful, Smart-e-Pants could hit the market as early as 2015.

MOISTURE-SENSING "SMART" UNDERWEAR

Special Feature: It vibrates and sends a text message to the wearer if it detects any unwanted moisture.

Details: The underwear is intended for incontinence sufferers. One big fear they have is that their protective undergarments may be leaking without their knowing it. Senior citizens, whose sense of smell may be poor, often have the accompanying fear that they are beginning to smell bad, but that they themselves cannot detect it. This experimental underwear, developed by scientists in the UK, has moisture-sensing conductive threads embedded in the fabric surrounding the absorbent incontinence pads. If the moisture leaks from the pads onto the threads, a buzzer is activated, alerting the wearer. Other models being tested use Bluetooth to send a text message to the user's cell phone, or in the case of patients in a nursing home, to a central station to alert staff that the patient may need fresh underwear.

THE NUTSHELLZ ARMORED CUP

Special Feature: It's bulletproof.

Details: The U.S. military estimates that as many as 1,000 soldiers serving in harm's way suffer injuries to the groin area each year. This product, which was being tested for use in combat in 2013, is strong enough to protect the wearer from bullets fired from 9 mm and 357 magnum handguns. "The cup is designed to 'swallow' the round, not deflect it," says inventor Jeremiah Raber. "This is very important, because if a bullet slid off the cup, it would likely go into the thigh and hit the femoral artery, causing a bleed-out." Stronger cups, designed to protect against even more powerful rounds, are in the works.

CHASTITY PANTS

Special Feature: They're designed to prevent extramarital affairs.

Details: Invented by one Mr. Jeong in Gwangju, South Korea, in 2012, the men's briefs are treated with temperature-sensitive paint that is invisible at normal body temperature. But if the temperature of the underwear drops below 88° Fahrenheit, such as when they are removed during the consummation of an extramarital affair, the briefs turn irreversibly darker, providing evidence of the affair. Only problem: The underpants can't be removed for *any* reason, such as to work out or to go swimming, because these activities would also cause the underwear to test positive for adultery. (And there's nothing to stop a philanderer from keeping his underwear on during trysts or from storing it in a warm place, such as a preheated oven.) Even peeing outdoors in cold weather could cause potential marital problems for the wearer. At last report Mr. Jeong was still waiting for his patent to be approved; no word on whether he plans to bring his underpants into production.

*　　*　　*

HUNGRY?

There's an "upscale" Burger King in New York called the Whopper Bar. They have menu items found at no other Burger Kings, including beer, and the New York Pizza Burger, whose ingredients include ground beef, cheese, pepperoni…and more than 2,500 calories. (The Whopper Bar recommends splitting it six ways.)

MEN IN BLACK, STARRING DAVID SCHWIMMER

Some roles are so closely associated with a specific actor that it's hard to imagine that he or she wasn't the first choice for the part. Can you imagine, for example...

SEAN CONNERY AS GANDALF (*The Fellowship of the Ring*, 2001). In planning his epic three-part film adaptation of J.R.R. Tolkien's fantasy series in the late 1990s, director Peter Jackson desperately wanted Connery to play the role of Gandalf, the mystical wizard who guides Frodo on his journey. He wanted Connery so much that he offered the former James Bond 15 percent of the worldwide box office for all three films. Connery read the script but didn't "get" the dense, mythology-packed story, nor did he want to spend 18 months in New Zealand shooting it. Connery ultimately walked away from a $400-million paycheck (Ian McKellen got the role and an Oscar nomination) and instead made the action flop *The League of Extraordinary Gentlemen*. His experience shooting that film was so bad that when he was done, Connery took time off from acting to write a book, claiming he was fed up with "the idiots now making films in Hollywood."

SHIRLEY TEMPLE AS DOROTHY (*The Wizard of Oz*, 1939). Producers wanted Temple, the world's most famous child star at the time, for the lead role of Dorothy. But it was the age of the contract system, in which most actors made movies for one studio, and one studio only. MGM was making *The Wizard of Oz*, and Temple was under contract to 20th Century Fox. According to Hollywood legend, the studios worked out a trade—MGM execs could have Temple for *Oz* if they let Fox use MGM players Clark Gable and Jean Harlow. Everything was set until Harlow tragically died in 1937. The deal was off and MGM contract player Judy Garland got the part.

LINDSAY LOHAN AS JADE (*The Hangover*, 2009). Lohan made a big splash in the early 2000s starring in the comedy hits

Freaky Friday and *Mean Girls*. But before long, she was more famous for a troubled offscreen life that involved drugs, drunk driving, and missed court dates. In 2008, director Todd Phillips wanted to help Lohan with a comeback and offered her a role in his raunchy comedy *The Hangover*. The role: Jade, a bubbly stripper who marries a member of a bachelor party so debauched that no one can remember it. After reading the script, Lohan declined, predicting the movie would tank. Heather Graham took the part instead, and *The Hangover* made $277 million at the box office—at the time the highest-grossing R-rated comedy ever. During the same period, Lohan starred in *Labor Pains*, which bombed in movie theaters…in Russia and Romania, the only places it was released theatrically.

DAVID SCHWIMMER AS J (*Men In Black*, 1997). After making *Independence Day*, TV star Will Smith successfully made the leap to movie stardom but he still wasn't as popular as the cast of NBC's *Friends*. The cast of six relative unknowns were all offered major film roles in 1995 and 1996—mostly comedies—with David Schwimmer being offered the plum role of J in the big-budget sci-fi comedy *Men in Black*. But Schwimmer opted instead to make the independent film *The Pallbearer*, so producers gave the role to their second choice, Will Smith. (Director Barry Sonnenfeld was also the producers' second choice. Their first choice: Quentin Tarantino, fresh off the success of *Pulp Fiction*. Tarantino declined because he didn't want to direct movies he didn't write himself.)

ROBIN WILLIAMS AS JACK TORRANCE (*The Shining*, 1980). Stanley Kubrick was an unconventional director and loved unconventional casting. That could explain why he wanted to cast Robin Williams as Jack Torrance, the struggling writer who gets cabin fever and goes murderously insane in *The Shining*. Williams was best known in 1980 as a manic stand-up comedian and the guy who played an alien named Mork on the TV sitcom *Mork & Mindy*. But the source novel's author, Stephen King, had cast approval and nixed Williams. He and Kubrick settled on Jack Nicholson, although Williams eventually proved a skilled dramatic actor in movies like *Insomnia*, *One Hour Photo*, and *Good Will Hunting*, for which he won an Oscar.

WEIRD CANADA

Some great weird news from the Great White North.

GUMMING UP THE COURTS

Elise Pawlow of Edmonton, Alberta, sued Kraft Canada in 2012. Kraft manufactures Stride Gum, whose advertisements claim it is "ridiculously long-lasting." Was Pawlow suing for false advertising, because the gum's flavor gave out after a few minutes? Nope. She sued for $100,000 because the gum worked too well. She claimed that after chewing a single piece of Stride, she had to scrub her dentures to remove tiny specks of the resilient, long-lasting gum, which, she claims, made her extremely depressed for "approximately 10 minutes." (Case dismissed.)

CLASS PRANK

Five teachers at a Windsor, Ontario, middle school announced in early 2013 that the eighth grade's annual class trip would be to Disney World! They told the students in an assembly, and prepared a video and PowerPoint presentation to detail the trip. It was such a happy moment that the teachers made sure to videotape the kids' priceless reactions. They also got their reactions on tape when they informed the kids that it was all a prank—they were really going bowling. When the school principal found out, he came up with a trip that he felt was less expensive than Disney World but more exciting than bowling, and sent the kids to Niagara Falls.

I CAN EXPLAIN!

In January 2013, Richard Blake was on trial in Ottawa, accused of breaking into a home and assaulting two people that lived there. The prosecution had some pretty daunting physical evidence against him, including a knit cap left at the scene of the crime with blood on it that matched Blake's. He was also picked out of a lineup by an eyewitness and the victims. On the witness stand, Blake offered this bizarre explanation for all of it. The reason he had the keys to the victims' car at the time of his arrest was because "a stranger" gave them to him, along with a bloody knife, gloves, and hat, which he put on after he took off his own. And the reason he ran from the scene and hid in a tree, Blake said, was to hide from a swarm of flies. Blake was found guilty of all charges.

SNOW JOB

Since the mid-2000s, Ottawa resident Doug Rochow has done a good deed for his neighborhood, free of charge: Whenever it snows (which can be a lot in Ottawa), he shovels two paths through a city park near his home, providing a safe walking path for local residents. But in March 2013, city officials told Rochow to stop immediately. For while Rochow may have wanted to prevent people from getting injured, the city told him that if the paths were cleared, more people would use them, thus *increasing* the likelihood of injury and, they feared, lawsuits against the city.

POLE POSITION

In 2012, the city of Johnville, Quebec, opened a rebuilt Highway 251—a brand new, two-lane affair. Part of the new road ran through an area where the municipal water company had a utility pole. The water company didn't bother to take down the pole until two months after the highway was open to traffic—meaning that for two months, a large pole sat in the middle of the road. (Amazingly, nobody ran into it.)

BUFFALO GALS

NFL football is extremely popular in southeastern Canada, particularly the nearest "local" team, the Buffalo Bills. In fall 2011, a Kingston, Ontario, radio station announced it was giving away highly sought-after Bills tickets worth $300. All the lucky contestants had to do was find them. The location: They were buried in a kidsized plastic swimming pool filled with buffalo manure. Five contestants dug, live on-air, until DJ Sarah Crosbie was overwhelmed by the odor and vomited. One finalist did get the tickets; the others, even after the tickets were found, kept digging until they found the second-place prize: a pair of tickets to the zoo.

*   *   *

"An optimist is an accordion player with a business card."

—Jay Leno

Before antibiotics, patients with syphilis were sometimes treated by infecting them with malaria.

THE LAST LAUGH: EPITAPHS

*Some unusual epitaphs and tombstone rhymes from around the world,
sent in by our crew of wandering BRI tombstone-ologists.*

In Scotland:
Here lie the bones of
Elizabeth Charlotte
Born a virgin;
died a harlot
She was aye a virgin
at seventeen
A remarkable thing in
Aberdeen

In Wales:
Deep in this grave
lies lazy Dai
Waiting the last great
trump on high.
If he's as fond
of his grave as he's
fond of his bed,
He'll be the last
man up when that
roll call's said.

In Texas:
Robert Clay Allison
He never killed a man
that did not need
killing

In New Hampshire:
In memory of Miss
Lucena Wilcox
Death is a debt
By nature due;
I've paid my shot
And so must you.

In England:
In memory of
Robert Philip
Here lie I by the
chancel door
Here I lie because
I'm poor
The farther in, the
more you pay
But here lie I as
warm as they

In Ireland:
Wherever you be
Let your wind go free
For it was
keeping it in
That was the
death of me.

In South Carolina:
My name, my country,
what are they to thee?
What, whether high
or low my pedigree?
Perhaps I far surpassed
all other men;
Perhaps I fell below
them all—what then?
Suffice it, stranger,
that thou seest a
tomb;
Thou knowst its use;
it hides—no matter
whom.

In England:
G. Wild
Not worth
remembering

In Arizona:
Here lies John Coil,
A son of toil who died
on Arizona soil.
He was a man of
considerable vim
But this here air was
too hot for him.

In England:
John Edwards who
perished in a fire 1904
No one could hold a
candle to him

In England:
Here lies the body of
Martha Dias who was
always uneasy and
not over pious
She liv'd to the age of
three score and ten
And gave that
to the worms
she refus'd to the men

In Austria:
Here lies Leonhard
Franz Futterknecht
until further notice

Research has shown that ginger is better than Dramamine in combating motion sickness.

THE STRANGE FATE OF BENITO MUSSOLINI JR.

Bad news: We have no control over who our parents are. Good news: Most of us did a lot better than Benito Mussolini Jr. did.

OUT OF WORK

In 1912, a 20-year-old political activist named Benito Mussolini became the editor of *Avanti!* ("Forward!"), the Italian Socialist Party's newspaper. He held the post until World War I in 1914, when he split with the party over whether Italy, then neutral, should enter the war. Mussolini favored entry, but the Party wanted the country to stay out. Mussolini resigned from *Avanti!* over the issue and made plans to start his own newspaper, *Il Popolo d'Italia* ("The People of Italy").

But that required money, and Mussolini didn't have any. Luckily for him, he was involved with a woman who did—Ida Dalser, who owned a beauty salon in Milan. The pair were soon married; Dalser sold her salon and pawned her jewelry to give Mussolini the money he needed to launch his newspaper. In 1915, she gave birth to a son, Benito Albino Mussolini.

By the time Benito Jr. was just one month old, Benito Sr. had already abandoned the family. He married another woman— Rachele Guidi—apparently without divorcing Ida.

MOVING UP

When Italy entered the war in 1915, Mussolini joined the army, and after the war he returned to politics, founding the National Fascist Party in 1921. He was elected to the Italian parliament the same year, and in 1922, led 25,000 Fascist paramilitary thugs (known as Blackshirts) in a march on Rome and forced the king to appoint him prime minister. In the years that followed, he used the position to dismantle Italy's democratic institutions and turn the country into a police state with himself at its head as *Il Duce*: "The Leader."

As he tightened his grip on power, Mussolini also created a personality cult to rival those of Joseph Stalin in Russia and Adolf

---

Hitler, who would come to power in Germany in 1933. Il Duce, his second wife, Rachele, and their children were presented to the nation as the ideal Fascist family, a task made more difficult by the fact that Ida Dalser was noisily proclaiming to anyone who would listen that *she* was Mussolini's wife and the mother of his oldest son and namesake, a young man the country knew nothing about.

THE PLOT THICKENS

The news that Mussolini was a bigamist and a deadbeat dad might well have been enough to topple him in the early days of his rule, when his enemies were still strong enough to drive him from power if they acted together. But Ida Dalser had an even more serious accusation to make: She claimed that the only reason Mussolini had lobbied for Italy's entry into World War I was because the French government had bribed him to do it—a charge that, if true, meant he was guilty of treason.

Mussolini placed Dalser and Benito Jr. under surveillance and dispatched Fascist Party agents to destroy marriage records, birth certificates, and anything else they could find that tied him to Dalser and her son. But they missed a few obscure documents, including two 1915 affidavits signed by Mussolini in which he acknowledged Dalser as his wife and Benito Jr. as his son, and pledged to provide both with financial support. Another surviving document from 1916 ordered Mussolini to honor that pledge, which he'd already failed to do.

THEY MUST BE CRAZY

As late as 1926, Ida Dalser continued to press her case with various Fascist government officials. That year she was arrested and locked away in the first of a series of mental hospitals until 1937, when she died from what was claimed to be a brain hemorrhage.

Benito Jr. fared only marginally better. Just 11 years old when his mother was taken away, he was told she'd died, and he was sent to live in a home for the handicapped. At 15, he was adopted by a Fascist party official who gave him a new last name. When the boy was old enough, he went off to college, and when World War II loomed, he joined the Italian Navy. Though he'd been warned for years to stop claiming he was Mussolini's son, like his mother before him, he never did. And like his mother, he was arrested and locked away in a mental hospital, where he died in July 1942 at the age of 27. Accounts vary as to how he died: Some say he was killed with "coma-inducing injections," others say it was from electric shock treatments. Whatever the case, his family was told that he died in the war. In a final attempt to erase him from history, he was given a pauper's funeral and buried in an unmarked grave.

DOWNFALL

Il Duce did not outlive his oldest son by much. Two weeks after the Allies invaded Sicily in July 1943, Mussolini was deposed and arrested, and the Italian government began negotiating surrender terms with the Allies. Two months later, Nazi commandos rescued Mussolini from confinement and installed him as the head of a puppet state in German-occupied northern Italy. That lasted until April 1945, when the Allies drove the last Germans out of Italy and the puppet state collapsed. Mussolini and his mistress, Clara Petacci, were captured by Italian partisans as they tried to flee to Switzerland. They were executed by firing squad the following day. Two days later, Hitler committed suicide in his Berlin bunker. Within a week, the war in Europe was over.

BIRDS OF A FEATHER

But the story doesn't end there.

• Before Ida Dalser was arrested in 1926, she gave love letters and other documents from her relationship with Mussolini to her sister, who hid some of them inside a stuffed bird and others in an unused well. The documents passed from one family member to another for the next 75 years, until a journalist named Marco Zeni came calling in 2001 and Dalser's 88-year-old niece handed them over, some of them still hidden inside the bird. The clues they contained helped Zeni to unearth the few remaining government documents that had not been destroyed by Mussolini's agents. Since then Ida Dalser and Benito Jr. have been the subject of numerous articles, books, a television documentary and a feature film.

• Mussolini's second wife, Rachele, survived the war. In the 1960s, she opened a pasta restaurant in her hometown of Predappio that was popular with tourists and neofascists alike. She ran it until shortly before her death in 1979.

TV Guide's 2009 pick for the worst television show of all time: *The Jerry Springer Show.*

BOB ROCK ROCKS!

The term aptronym *was coined by humorist Franklin P. Adams to describe the amusing situation when a person's name is "apt" for his or her profession— like toilet manufacturer Thomas Crapper. Here are some more.*

- **Vince Offer.** TV infomercial pitchman (ShamWow)

- **Usain Bolt.** Olympic gold medalist and one of the fastest runners in the world

- **Neil Moore.** Catholic priest from Portland, Oregon

- **Margaret Court.** Legendary tennis player

- **Marilyn vos Savant.** *Parade* columnist who reportedly has an extremely high IQ of 228

- **Bob Rock.** Music producer

- **Cecil Fielder.** Baseball star (1985–98)

- **Chuck Long.** NFL quarterback (1986–91)

- **Lord Igor Judge.** Chief justice of England's highest court

- **Margaret Spellings.** Secretary of Education (2005–09)

- **David Dollar.** Economist at the World Bank

- **Larry Speakes.** White House spokesman (1981–87)

- **Greg Weiner.** *Playgirl Magazine* photographer

- **Jules Angst.** German research psychiatrist specializing in anxiety

- **Chandler Robbins.** Ornithologist and author of *Birds of North America*

- **Richard Smalley.** University professor who researched nanotechnology

- **Emily Hornett.** Prominent entomologist (the science of insects)

- **Alto Reed.** Saxophonist with Bob Seger and the Silver Bullet Band

- **Tommy Tune.** Broadway dancer and choreographer

- **Dr. William Dement.** A professor of behavioral sciences

- **Jeffrey M. Advokat.** Lawyer in New Jersey

- **Laura Knott-Twine.** Founder of Connecticut's Windham Textile & History Museum

- **Vania Stambolova.** Bulgarian Olympic hurdler who, in the 2012 Olympics, stumbled over a hurdle and didn't finish the race

FOUNDING FATHERS

You already know the names—here are the people behind them.

DR. GEORGE HORACE GALLUP

While working at an ad agency in the 1930s, Gallup, a New Jersey-based professor of journalism, figured that if market research could determine what products people will buy, it could also determine how they will vote. So in 1935, Gallup founded the American Institute of Public Opinion to predict elections by using "quota sampling"—polling a few "typical" people chosen to represent a larger group. He then sold the data to newspapers in a syndicated column, and offered to refund their money if he failed to predict the next president. While everybody else was picking Kansas governor Alf Landon to beat incumbent Franklin Delano Roosevelt—including *Literary Digest* magazine, which had accurately predicted the past five presidents—Gallup was ridiculed when he wrote that FDR would win in a landslide. He was right, of course, and "Gallup Polls" became the standard measure of public opinion.

MIRIAM AND MAX WEINSTEIN

Brothers Bob and Harvey Weinstein used their earnings from a concert-promotion business to open an independent movie studio in Buffalo, New York, in 1979. They combined their parents' names—Miriam and Max—to come up with a name for their new venture: Miramax Films. (Some Miramax hits: *The Crying Game, Clerks, Pulp Fiction, Shakespeare in Love,* and *The English Patient.*)

AMAR BOSE

Noni Gopal Bose fled India in the 1920s after being jailed for opposing British rule, and arrived at Ellis Island with $5 in his pocket. His son, Amar, born a few years later, would become a billionaire. Here's how: While working as an assistant professor at the Massachusetts Institute of Technology in 1956, Amar Bose, an engineer and an amateur violinist, purchased a set of "high end" stereo speakers. Frustrated by their tinny sound, he decided to try to create a set of speakers that could recreate the concert hall experience. He recorded a Boston Symphony performance from several different seats,

---

First female pilot for a major airline: Bonnie Tiburzi (American Airlines, 1973).

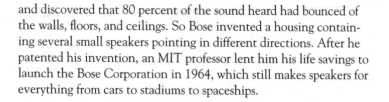

and discovered that 80 percent of the sound heard had bounced of the walls, floors, and ceilings. So Bose invented a housing containing several small speakers pointing in different directions. After he patented his invention, an MIT professor lent him his life savings to launch the Bose Corporation in 1964, which still makes speakers for everything from cars to stadiums to spaceships.

EBERHARD ANHEUSER AND ADOLPHUS BUSCH

German-born Eberhard Anheuser arrived in St. Louis in the 1840s and opened a soap-and-candle business. Realizing there was more money to be made from beer, in 1852, he became part owner of the new Bavarian Brewery and soon took it over. A few years later, he met a young brewery supplier named Adolphus Busch, also from Germany. In 1861, after Busch married Anheuser's daughter Lilly, he started working at the brewery and quickly rose through the ranks to become half-owner. Busch's big idea: Brew a beer that would appeal not just to local Germans but to a wide range of Americans. In 1876, along with brewer Carl Conrad, they crafted a European-style lager they named Budweiser, after the Czech town of Budweis. (Anheuser chose the name because it sounded German but was easily pronounceable by Americans.) Anheuser-Busch used the new practice of pasteurization to give the batch a longer shelf life—making Budweiser the first mass-produced American beer.

JOHN HARVARD

Harvard was a well-to-do English clergyman who moved to the Massachusetts Bay Colony in 1637. Less than a year later, he contracted tuberculosis. While on his deathbed, the 30-year-old stipulated that half of his money—1,600 pounds—and his entire library of classical and theological literature be donated to a new college that had recently opened in nearby Cambridge. The General Court of Massachusetts Bay was so honored by the dying man's gift that it named the school "Harvard Colledge."

*   *   *

"Our great democracies still tend to think that a stupid man is more likely to be honest than a clever man."

—**Bertrand Russell**

Think they're Hawaiian? Think again: Macadamia nuts originated in Australia.

YOU CAN DO IT!

We all need a little motivation now and then.

"The way to get started is to quit talking and begin doing."
—**Walt Disney**

"Do what you can, where you are, with what you have."
—**Teddy Roosevelt**

"There are no regrets in life. Just lessons."
—**Jennifer Aniston**

"A champion is afraid of losing. Everyone else is afraid of winning."
—**Billie Jean King**

"I always have the feeling that I'm never going to be able to write anything funny again. That's why I keep writing funny things. I have to prove to myself that I'm wrong."
—**Rita Rudner**

"Even if you're on the right track, you'll get run over if you just sit there."
—**Will Rogers**

"People often say that motivation doesn't last. Well, neither does bathing. That's why we recommend it daily."
—**Zig Ziglar**

"Happiness is not something ready made. It comes from your own actions."
—**The Dalai Lama**

"You can't use up creativity. The more you use, the more you have."
—**Maya Angelou**

"You miss one hundred percent of the shots you don't take."
—**Wayne Gretzky**

"Sometimes you just have to put on lip gloss and pretend to be psyched."
—**Mindy Kaling**

"Inspiration exists, but it must find you working."
—**Pablo Picasso**

"If you can't change your fate, change your attitude."
—**Amy Tan**

"Life is what we make it, always has been, always will be."
—**Grandma Moses**

"Nothing is impossible; the word itself says, 'I'm possible.'"
—**Audrey Hepburn**

Poison-dart frogs lose their toxicity in captivity.

MAKING SCENTS

In ads for her White Diamonds cologne, Elizabeth Taylor said diamonds "always brought me luck." It's true—since 1991, more than $1 billion worth of the fragrance has sold...which probably explains why so many other celebrities have gotten into the "signature scent" business.

"Fame" (Lady Gaga)

"Power" (50 Cent)

"Circus Fantasy" (Britney Spears)

"Uninhibited" (Cher)

"Unforgivable" (P. Diddy)

"Electric Youth" (Debbie Gibson)

"Magic Beat" (Michael Jackson)

"Purr" (Katy Perry)

"Covet" (Sarah Jessica Parker)

"She" (Usher)

"Amuleto" (Shakira)

"Secret Potion" (Christina Aguilera)

"Driven" (Derek Jeter)

"L" (Gwen Stefani)

"Lollipop Bling" (Mariah Carey)

"Fairy Dust" (Paris Hilton)

"Wonderstruck" (Taylor Swift)

"Southern Blend" (Tim McGraw)

"Blue Seduction" (Antonio Banderas)

"Pulse" (Beyoncé)

"Live Luxe" (Jennifer Lopez)

"Nude" (Rihanna)

"Forbidden Rose" (Avril Lavigne)

"Girlfriend" (Justin Bieber)

"Like This" (Tilda Swinton)

"Fancy Love" (Jessica Simpson)

"Malibu Night" (Pamela Anderson)

"Truth or Dare" (Madonna)

"Legend" (Michael Jordan)

"Carlos Santana" (Carlos Santana)

THIS IS *JEOPARDY!*

When Jeopardy! *debuted on March 30, 1964, it was one of the most difficult game shows on TV. Think you're a trivia wizard? See how many of these real* Jeopardy! *questions from the '60s and '70s you can answer correctly. After you've run through these, check out the Double* Jeopardy! *board on page 394. Good luck! (Answers on page 540.)*

Last Initial 'N'	Trees	Odds & Ends	Potent Potables	Show Music
$10 Gomer Pyle	**$10** The leaves of the saguaro cactus	**$10** Of a duchess, countess, and marquess, the man	**$10** French word that precedes "du pays"	**$10** In *Happy Hunting*, Merman belongs to this "society."
$20 Silent screen star "Pola"	**$20** The softest cabinet wood	**$20** Part of a circle, its homonym is built in Genesis 6	**$20** 1 of 2 American whiskeys classified as straight or blended	**$20** It "makes the world go round."
$30 Celebrity lawyer Louis	**$30** Its name closely follows "pushover" in the dictionary.	**$30** $(2x2x2)^2 =$ this	**$30** It's the "velvet" in a "Black Velvet."	**$30** Show with "I Still See Elisa."
$40 Russian author whose last book was *Ada*	**$40** Poplar, named from Old English "aepse"	**$40** Obsolete word for thief or one who snoozes	**$40** State which produces more brandy than all of France	**$40** In this song, "You're… the feet of Fred Astaire."
$50 Monologist who played Major Major in *Catch-22*	**$50** Tennessee city known as "Atomic Bomb City"	**$50** 40 cents of every federal tax dollar go to this.	**$50** Rum drink named for a district in Cuba	**$50** "Tea for Two" is a song in this 1925 show.

Elvis Presley had a chimp named Scatter; Michael Jackson had a chimp named Bubbles.

PAPER AIRPLANE AERONAUTICS

Folding paper airplanes is a lot like riding a bicycle—once you learn how to do it, you never forget. Fold one now (or when you get out of the bathroom) and follow along as we explain how it works.

FOUR OF A KIND

Give your airplane a good shove and watch as it sails across the room. Four basic forces act on it when it is in flight:

• **Thrust** is the force you just provided by tossing the plane.

• **Drag** is caused mostly by air resistance. Drag opposes thrust; it slows down the plane as it moves through the air.

• **Lift** causes the plane to climb. It's generated by the airplane's wings as they move through the air.

• **Gravity** opposes lift and pulls the plane toward Earth.

PAPER TRAIL

How your airplane flew depended on which of the four forces were most powerful at each point in the flight:

• At the moment you let go of the airplane, thrust was at its maximum and was greater than drag. The airplane moved quickly through the air, and as it did, the passage of air over and under the wings (hopefully) generated lift. How much lift depends on the design of the paper airplane and how you threw it.

• If the lift generated by the airplane exceeded the pull of gravity, the plane climbed. If little or no lift was generated, gravity exceeded lift from the start, and the plane began descending as soon as you let go. If lift and gravity were equal, the airplane had a level flight.

• So why didn't the airplane just fly on forever? Because drag continued to act on it for as long as it moved through the air. (You stopped providing thrust the moment you let go of the plane.) Drag caused the airplane to lose speed, and as it did the wings generated less and less lift. The force of gravity eventually overcame lift, causing the airplane to descend.

GOING STRAIGHT

Give your airplane a few more tosses. Does it do what you want it to do? A well-designed, carefully folded plane will be stable in flight: It won't pitch up or down, or turn left or right (unless you want it to), and it won't roll over and crash. How well your plane flies also depends on its "center of gravity."

• If the center of gravity is too far forward—meaning your plane has too much weight in front—the plane will nose-dive and crash.

• If the plane has too much weight in the back, the plane's nose will pitch up (point upward) during flight, causing the plane to lose speed, "stall" (generate too little lift), and crash.

• You can adjust your plane's center of gravity the same way you (probably) did as a kid, even if you didn't realize that was what you were doing at the time: Attach a paper clip to the nose or body of the airplane and add weight wherever it's needed.

GETTING THE BENDS

• Paper airplanes fly erratically when the air flows differently over one wing than it does over the other. Bending the tail edge of the wing upward or downward to correct this creates what on real airplanes are called "elevators." Bending the vertical tail edge of the plane's body to the left or the right creates a "rudder."

• Adjusting the elevators and the rudder alters the way the air flows around the airplane. You can use these adjustments to make the plane fly any way you want it to—right or left, up or down, in a straight line, or in a loop-the-loop. Try it: How many tricks can your plane do?

TRICKS OF THE TRADE

• If you want an airplane that flies fast and travels long distances, fold a classic dart-shaped airplane with a long narrow body and small wings, and give it a good, hard throw. At high speeds, smaller wings create less drag to slow the plane down.

• If you want an airplane that stays airborne for as long as possible, make one with large square-shaped wings. Believe it or not, if you throw it gently instead of forcefully, it will fly farther. This is because the wings generate a lot of lift at slow speeds but very little drag, keeping the plane aloft for a longer period of time. Happy flying!

Shell shock: The city of Crisfield, Maryland, is built on a foundation of oyster shells.

NICE STORIES

And now for a little break from all the bad news in the world today, brought to you by the kindness of strangers.

A MAN'S SHOES

One morning in 2012, a Winnipeg, Manitoba, city transit bus driver named Kris Doubledee, 38, made an unscheduled stop on a busy street corner. The passengers all watched him as he got off the bus and approached a man on the sidewalk who was barefoot. Doubledee asked the man if he had any shoes; he said no. So the bus driver removed his own shoes and handed them to the man. "Here," he said. "You need these more than I do." Then Doubledee returned to his seat—sans shoes—and continued on his route. A passenger asked him why he'd done that. Doubledee explained that he'd seen the man standing there before and just couldn't bear the thought that he didn't have any shoes.

WRITING BLIND

Trish Vickers, from Charmouth, Dorset, England, lost her eyesight in 2005 due to diabetes. Seven years later, the 59-year-old started writing her first novel, *Grannifer's Legacy*, about a young woman whose life falls apart. But because she isn't computer-savvy, Vickers had to do it the hard way: by longhand. She wrapped rubber bands around notebook paper (on a clipboard) to indicate where the lines were and then carefully penned her story. Once a week, her son Simon would read the chapters back to her so she could make edits and send the text off to a typesetter. Everything was going smoothly until one week when Simon showed up to find Trish very excited about the 26 pages she'd just completed. "But Mum," he said, "there's nothing here." Vickers's pen had run out of ink; every page was blank, thousands of words…gone. She was devastated.

Unwilling to give up, Simon asked the Dorset police if someone in the "fingerprints department" had any spare time to help. No one did, but the staffers all felt sorry for her, so a forensics analyst named Kerry Savage volunteered her time during her lunch breaks and carefully scrutinized the pen indents to reform the lost text. It took five arduous months, but Vickers got her pages back with nearly all of her words intact…and to rave reviews from the staffers. "It's not as though my book is a big blockbuster," she said, "but as a hobby and something that is very important to me, it was just wonderful that they put that time and effort in."

NICE GALS FINISH LAST

After winning the race of her life, 17-year-old long-distance runner Meghan Vogel was basking in the glory of having just become the 2012 Ohio state champion in the 1,600-meter event. But she still had the 3,200-meter race to run. And she was pooped. The high school senior ran anyway, determined to finish. As she turned the corner on the final, grueling lap, she was in last place. Ahead of her was Arden McMath, a runner from a rival school. And McMath was having a tougher time than Vogel. Not far from the finish line, McMath collapsed on the track. Vogel caught up, but instead of passing McMath, she picked her up and then held her up all the way to the finish line. Just before they crossed it, Vogel pushed McMath in front of her. Vogel's act of sportsmanship made headlines all over the world. "If you work to get to the state meet, you deserve to finish no matter who you are," she said. "I think fate may have put me in last place for a reason."

MAKING IT RAIN

A man walked into a Starbucks coffee shop in Boston, Massachusetts, on St. Patrick's Day 2011 and yelled, "I'm rich! I'm rich! I'm rich!" He held up a wad of $1 bills and threw them in the air. Then he walked out. Instead of the melee you'd expect when a crowded room is suddenly inundated with flying bills, the customers and staff just stood there as the cash settled on the floor. Then a Starbucks employee quietly gathered it all up and put it in an envelope. The money, which totaled $100, was sent to a charity organization for tsunami relief efforts in Japan. The identity of the "I'm rich!" man remains unknown.

WHEN LIFE GIVES YOU LEMONS, SELL THEM

Losing nearly everything she owned to a powerful summer thunder storm didn't make Elissa Myers cry, but the kindness of the little boy who lived next door did. Eight-year-old Johnny Karlinchak had learned a lot about the compassion of strangers four years earlier when his sister died. "All of our neighbors came and helped," he recalled. So after the hurricane-force winds from the 2012 summer storm toppled a giant oak tree onto Meyers's house in Springfield, Virginia, Johnny gave her all the money in his piggy bank—five quarters. When he learned that she needed a whopping $500 just to pay the insurance deductible, Johnny took it upon himself to earn that money. He opened a lemonade stand in his front yard and made $21 on the first day. A few days later he topped $100. A week in, he'd met his goal, but he kept fund-raising. By the time a local news station interviewed Johnny, he'd made $700—all for his neighbor whom he barely knew. (It must have been some very tasty lemonade.)

THEY'LL LIFT HIM UP WHERE HE BELONGS

It was a dream come true. Country-music fan Patrick Connelly was finally going to see a Blake Shelton concert! But when the Kansas City teenager, who is physically and mentally challenged, got to his seat at the outdoor venue, he was devastated. The rest of the crowd was standing, and all he could see from his wheelchair were people's legs. Patrick's mom and sister tried lifting him up, but it was 100°F, and he was too big for them to hold up for more than a few seconds at a time. Patrick was in tears. Just then, two young men who were standing nearby walked over and lifted Patrick up above their shoulders so he could see. They held him up for half an hour in the sweltering heat. But there was a long way left to go in the concert, so the two men took the boy up front, where he was allowed to watch from the front row. Patrick later got to meet Shelton in person, and ended up having pretty much the best day he'd ever had.

*   *   *

ASLEEP ON THE JOBBBBBBBBBBBBBBBBBBBB

Someone in Germany (identity not revealed) became a temporary millionaire in 2013 after their bank account suddenly grew by 222,222,222.22 euros ($295 million). But just as quickly as it arrived, the money was gone. What happened? The person had deposited a check for 64 euros ($85). But the bank clerk who was processing the deposit fell asleep on his keyboard while leaning on the "2" key. A supervisor later caught the goof.

Can you name the 9 NFL, NBA, MLB and NHL teams that don't end in the letter "S"?...

UNMADE SEQUELS

When a movie becomes a hit, it almost guarantees that a sequel will be made. There's Bride of Frankenstein, Terminator 2: Judgment Day, Shrek 2, Godfather 2, Rambo: First Blood Part II, The Mummy Returns, *and hundreds more. It's a no-brainer, right? Not necessarily—these surefire successes weren't produced.*

*T*HE BODYGUARD (1992)

The first film made $140 million at the box office, which was unexpected because it was pop star Whitney Houston's debut film performance. But Houston's soundtrack became one of the biggest selling albums of all time (14 million copies sold), and that fueled interest in the movie. The film's ending ties up all the loose plot threads, with Houston's pop-star character falling in love with her bodyguard (Kevin Costner). In 1994 Costner, who produced the first film, started talking up a sequel, basically a rehash of the first film, in which he would star (again as a bodyguard) alongside another first-time actress: the recently divorced Princess Diana. But when Diana died in a tragic car crash in 1997, the movie was scrapped.

TWINS (1988)

In the early 1990s, producer-director Ivan Reitman planned to make a sequel, and signed comedian Roseanne Barr to play the third sibling to Danny DeVito and Arnold Schwarzenegger. Barr was super-hot in Hollywood because of her top-rated TV sitcom, *Roseanne.* The movie's script was never finished, and Barr opted to star in *She-Devil* instead. But wait! *Triplets* isn't dead. Twenty years later, Ivan Reitman is rumored to be working on a reboot of the sequel that wasn't made. Third sibling: Eddie Murphy.

FLASH GORDON (1980)

Flash Gordon was a modest hit. It earned $27 million at the box office, the equivalent of $67 million today, and the soundtrack album by Queen went gold. The movie successfully revived the character of Flash Gordon, an all-American football player who goes into space to fight evil space villain Ming the Merciless, first

---

...Answer: Jazz, Heat, Magic, Thunder, Avalanche, Wild, Lightning, Red Sox, & White Sox.

popular in the 1930s and 1940s as a comic strip and movie serial. The movie was planned to be the first of a trilogy...but by the time it came out, the sequels had been canceled. In 2010, *Flash Gordon* director Mike Hodges revealed that during a break in filming, he'd filmed some special-effects shots with the stunt double for star Sam J. Jones. He also re-recorded some of Jones's lines, and hired a voice actor instead of using Jones. Hodges says that when Jones found out, he told producers he was done with *Flash Gordon* forever. Jones' latest tale: a cameo in the 2012 film, *Ted*.

GLADIATOR (2000)

The first *Gladiator* made more than $200 million at the box office and won Oscars for Best Picture and Best Actor (Russell Crowe). One sequel-preventing problem: Crowe's character, the gladiator Maximus, dies at the end of *Gladiator*. No matter. The script for *Gladiator 2*, written by Australian alternative-rock star Nick Cave, was all about Maximus in the afterlife, fighting and somehow killing Roman gods. Crowe reportedly loved it, director Ridley Scott liked it, and the studio hated it, so it was never made.

FORREST GUMP (1994)

Forrest Gump made $329 million at the box office (the number-one movie of 1994) and won six Academy Awards—Best Picture, Best Actor (Tom Hanks), and Best Adapted Screenplay (Eric Roth). The movie was based on an obscure 1986 novel by author Winston Groom, and after the success of the film, Groom was approached to write a sequel—*Gump & Co.*, published in 1995. It continues the story of Southern man-child Forrest Gump, who happens to be a part of major world events. Among them: crashing the *Exxon-Valdez*, destroying the Berlin Wall, inventing New Coke, fighting in the first Iraq War, and meeting celebrities like Princess Diana, O.J. Simpson...and Tom Hanks. Eric Roth adapted the novel and turned it in to Paramount...on September 10, 2001. In light of the events on 9/11 (the next day) Roth, Hanks, and director Robert Zemeckis thought the movie would no longer be relevant, so the project was cancelled.

*   *   *

Random fact: Russia is bigger than Pluto.

UNCLE JOHN'S PAGE OF LISTS

Some random information from the BRI's bottomless files.

7 Companies That Started in a Garage
1. Walt Disney Co.
2. Hewlett-Packard
3. Amazon.com
4. Mattel
5. Google
6. Harley-Davidson
7. Apple

David and Victoria Beckham's 4 Kids
1. Harper
2. Cruz
3. Romeo
4. Brooklyn

8 Movie Titles?
1. *Who Framed Roger Rabbit?*
2. *What's Eating Gilbert Grape?*
3. *Are We There Yet?*
4. *O Brother, Where Art Thou?*
5. *Whatever Happened to Baby Jane?*
6. *Who's Afraid of Virginia Woolf?*
7. *Dude, Where's My Car?*
8. *What About Bob?*

10 Most Expensive Cities to Buy Luxury Real Estate
1. Hong Kong
2. Tokyo
3. London
4. Paris
5. Moscow
6. New York City
7. Shanghai
8. Singapore
9. Mumbai
10. Sydney

5 Body Parts Named for People
1. Achilles tendon
2. Darwin's tubercle
3. Fallopian tube
4. Golgi apparatus
5. Crypts of Lieberkühn

7 Most-Populated Middle East Nations
1. Egypt (84.6 mil)
2. Iran (76.8 mil)
3. Turkey (76 mil)
4. Iraq (35.4 mil)
5. Saudi Arabia (30.2 mil)
6. Yemen (25.2 mil)
7. Syria (22.2 mil)

5 Highest-fiber Fruits
1. Apple
2. Pear
3. Banana
4. Blackberry
5. Fig

3 Things Aristotle Got Wrong
1. The heart does all the thinking.
2. Bees come from rotting bull carcasses.
3. Flies have four legs.

5 Most Intelligent Dog Breeds
1. Border Collie
2. Poodle
3. German Shepherd
4. Golden Retriever
5. Doberman Pinscher

7 People Who Declared Bankruptcy
1. Burt Reynolds
2. Mark Twain
3. Kim Basinger
4. Mike Tyson
5. Rembrandt
6. P. T. Barnum
7. Henry Ford

If you enlarged an apple to the size of Earth, its atoms would be the size of apples.

KEYSTONE KOPS

*Without the good men and women in blue (and the plain-clothes ones, too),
the world would be a lot more dangerous. We salute you, police force! That
said, a few cops prove that at the end of the day, they're only human.*

PUBLIC ENEMY #1

Dillan is three years old. His family lives in a house on a rural road in Piedmont, Oklahoma. One day in 2012, Dillan and his mom, Ashley Warden, were in their front yard when the toddler started peeing on the grass. Just then a Piedmont deputy, who happened to be driving past the Warden home, stopped and issued the mother a ticket for public urination. "He's only three years old! And he's not in public; he's in his own yard," pleaded Warden. "It doesn't matter," replied the cop. "He's in public view." (There was no one else around.) Cost of the fine: $2,500. The story made national news, and suddenly the town of "Peedmont" was a punchline. The police chief and the mayor sided with Dillan. They threw out the ticket and reprimanded the officer. "Stupid is as stupid does," said Mayor Valerie Thomerson. "And this was just stupid."

THAT'LL SHOW HIM

In May 2012, Officer Chris Webb of the New Mexico Department of Public Safety went to an intermediate school for its annual "Career Day." While talking to students on the playground, he asked, "Who'd like to clean my patrol unit?" Several kids raised their hands, but one 10-year-old boy said he didn't want to. That's when Webb pulled out his stun gun and said, "Let me show you what happens to people who don't listen to the police." Then Webb shot two barbs carrying 50,000 volts of electricity into the little boy's chest. He started convulsing, so Webb quickly pulled out the barbs, and the boy passed out. Instead of calling for paramedics (who were also there for Career Day), Webb took the boy to the school nurse, who called the paramedics. Not surprisingly, the boy's family sued the police department, claiming that he was left with scars from the ordeal, both physical and mental. Officer Webb claims it was an accident; he forgot the barbs were still in the stun gun when he fired. He was suspended for three days.

Life expectancy of someone with the Black Plague: 2 to 3 days.

WRONG NUMBER

Panic ensued at a college near Detroit, Michigan, in 2012 after several thousand students received an automated voicemail that announced, "The Oakland University Police Department has received reports of shots fired on campus. The suspect is currently at large, and the campus is on lockdown." Professors locked their classroom doors as the students ducked for cover. Some called their loved ones. Others posted updates about the shooting to their social media pages. That's how the press got wind of it and reported a shooting in progress at Oakland University. Only, there wasn't a shooting. The voicemail was part of a test of the school's emergency alert system. It wasn't supposed to be sent to everyone on the call list, but due to a "computer glitch," it did. The university police department apologized for the confusion.

SHE'S GOT SOME 'SPLAINING TO DO

Rappers have always had a strained relationship with the police, mostly because of incendiary song lyrics like this:

> "Don't push Ms. Lucy, because you won't like the consequences! Lucy got a drawer full of all day-suckers, don't mess with me or I will shoot the [bleep], cuz Lucille Baller, she been to hell and back!"

So who wrote these incendiary rap lyrics? Lt. Regina Smith of the Dallas, Texas, Police Department, who oversees burglary and theft investigative detectives. She released the song on her own independent label in 2012 under the name "Lucille Baller." (The theme from TV's *I Love Lucy* is sampled in the song.) In the music video, Smith is seen in "provocative clothing and firing her gun." When the department found out that one of their own released a gangsta rap song, Smith was placed under investigation. She says her budding rap career "has nothing to do with the police department." The department agreed, and suspended her any way.

JOY RIDE

It's all too common these days for criminals to record their crimes and then post them online. But a cop? In 2012, San Francisco Police Sgt. Carl T (that's really his last name—he had it legally changed from Tenenbaum to T) posted a video to his Facebook page that was recorded from the front seat of a Lamborghini speeding through the city's Broadway Tunnel. Sgt. T's comment on the photo: "100 Miles per hour in the Lambo, and we were all drunk!" The video went viral, and the SFPD was in an uproar. Police Chief Greg Suhr, who has known T for 20 years, told reporters, "Obviously, it's just beyond irresponsible and dumb." T's defense: He was joking about the "drunk" remark, and he wasn't the driver, anyway. But yes, he did post the video. T was transferred to a desk job.

IF YOU CAN'T BEAT 'EM

In 2007, Henry Marin, 22, appeared in the first episode of the Fox reality show *The Academy*. But the dim-witted deputy-in-training didn't make it to the second episode. He was booted off for failing two role-playing exercises—in the first, he neglected to call for help when confronted with a suicidal woman, and in the other, he failed to remember basic police radio codes. Undeterred, Marin reapplied to the police academy, became a deputy…and was arrested two years later for smuggling a heroin-stuffed burrito to an inmate at the county jail. Marin's brief but memorable cop career came to an end when he was sentenced to two years in prison.

*   *   *

MORE CLASSIFIED ADS

200 *Playboy* and other adult magazines. Will trade for guns.

It's Summertime! Bring your kids to the Garma Specialty Clinic for circumcision.

Toyota Scion. Coffin with 52-inch sunroof. $21,800.

For Sale: Collection of old people.

Help Wanted: Dental Hygienist. 2 days/wk. Will marry if necessary.

Wanted: Someone who can speak and write Australian.

Bass Player: Not the greatest, but doesn't suck, looking to play with classic rock band.

Childcare Provider. Apply in person, Jack & Kill Childcare.

Mentally ill needed to interview for novel. Must be successful and interesting.

Looking for a small "13-inch" male registered Beagle to breed with our little girl.

Free to Good Country Home: 3/4 Rottweiler, 1/4 Shepherd, 3 yrs. old, intelligent, loves to eat live rabbits and kittens.

PRESIDENTIAL FIRSTS

You know that George Washington was the first president of the United States and Barack Obama is the first African-American president. Here are some other presidential firsts you may not be familiar with.

PEYTON RANDOLPH (1731–1796)

Claim to Fame: First American "president"

Details: George Washington was, of course, America's first president—under the U.S. Constitution—but that wasn't ratified until 1788. Before that, from 1781 to 1789, a document called the Articles of Confederation served as America's constitution…and before that a body called the Continental Congress served as the nascent country's government from 1774 to 1781. Meetings of the Continental Congress were moderated by an elected, impartial presiding officer or president; the first of these was Peyton Randolph, the speaker of the Virginia House of Burgesses.

Other notable congressional presidents:

• John Hancock of Massachusetts. He was the president of the Second Continental Congress when it severed ties with Great Britain by adopting the Declaration of Independence on July 4, 1776.

• Thomas McKean, chief justice of the Pennsylvania Supreme Court. He was the first president elected after the Articles of Confederation were ratified in 1781. (After ratification, the Congress was renamed the United States in Congress Assembled.)

• In all, 15 people served as president of the Congress from 1774 to 1781. The last was Virginia appellate court judge Cyrus Griffin.

JOHN ADAMS (1735–1826)

Claim to Fame: First sitting president to not attend his successor's inauguration

Details: The election of 1800 was a bitter one, with Adams fighting for a second term as president and his friend-turned-rival, Thomas Jefferson, battling just as hard to turn him out of office. The campaign was so sleazy and filled with personal attacks that many historians consider it the first "modern" presidential campaign. Adams lost the election, and as the first American president turned out of office by voters (and reeling from the death of his son Charles

---

The famous Disney "signature" logo is based on Walt Disney's actual signature.

from alcoholism), he may have been too depressed to attend Jefferson's inauguration. Another possibility: Jefferson didn't invite him. Whatever the case, Adams left town early on the day of the inauguration and returned to his home in Quincy, Massachusetts. (Twenty-eight years later, his son, President John Quincy Adams, continued the family tradition and skipped out on Andrew Jackson's inauguration after Jackson defeated him in the election of 1828.)

MARTIN VAN BUREN (1782–1862)

Claim to Fame: First (and so far only) American president who was not a native English speaker

Details: Van Buren, also the first president born a United States citizen (his predecessors were all born before the American Revolution), was born in the Dutch-speaking community of Kinderhook, New York. His parents could speak English when they needed to, but they spoke only Dutch at home. Young Martin didn't get much exposure to English until he was old enough to go to school.

FRANKLIN PIERCE (1804–1869)

Claim to Fame: First (and so far only) American president to take office without "swearing the oath" of office

Details: Some Christians believe the Biblical passage James 5:12 ("…swear not, neither by heaven, neither by the earth, neither by any other oath…") forbids the swearing of oaths in general and the swearing of oaths on the Bible in particular. The U.S. Constitution takes this into consideration by not requiring the use of a Bible. It also allows the president-elect to use the words "I do solemnly affirm" instead of "I do solemnly swear," thereby turning the oath of office into an affirmation of office, which is not forbidden. To date, Franklin Pierce, who took office in 1853, is the only American president to affirm rather than swear his way into the job. And he placed his hand on a law book instead of a Bible when swearing his oath—er, stating his affirmation.

*   *   *

"There cannot be a crisis next week. My schedule is already full."

—**Henry Kissinger**

Health food? There are only about 2 tablespoons of sugar in a bag of cotton candy.

REGIONAL SANDWICHES

New York has heroes, New England has grinders, Louisiana has po' boys. It may be a sandwich to everybody else, but to us locals, it's a slice of heaven.

S andwich: Beef on Weck
Found in: Upstate New York
Details: It dates back to the 1830s at Schwabl's, a Buffalo restaurant founded by German immigrants. It's a simple roast beef sandwich with the meat cooked rare and sliced thin, with pickles and horseradish, and served "au jus." What makes it special? The bread: a German kaiser roll called *kummelweck* (or "weck" for short) coated with coarsely ground pretzel salt and lots of caraway seeds.

Sandwich: New Jersey Sloppy Joe
Found in: Northern New Jersey
Details: This one bears little resemblance to the cafeteria standby of ground beef and tomato sauce. It's a triple-decker served on rye, made with roast beef and turkey (other cold cuts can be substituted), Swiss cheese, Russian dressing, and coleslaw. Several delis in Chatham, Summit, and South Orange all claim to have originated the sandwich—and they all serve it in slightly different ways. Like a traditional Sloppy Joe, the NJ Joe is pretty messy, but that's not how it got its name. In 1934, Maplewood, New Jersey, mayor Robert Sweeney had a similar sandwich called a Sloppy Joe at Joe's Bar in Havana, Cuba, and asked the staff at Maplewood's Town Hall Deli to recreate it. The main difference: The original used cow tongue, not roast beef.

Sandwich: Hot Fish
Found in: Nashville, Tennessee
Details: Popular in Nashville since the 1930s, it's made with two pieces of deep-fried fish—usually whiting, sometimes catfish, and often with some of the bones still in—served on white bread with mustard, hot sauce, pickles, and raw onions. Common side dish: spaghetti with tomato sauce. (Nashville's hot fish sandwich should not be confused with the Nashville's hot chicken sandwich, which is pan-fried, dusted with cayenne pepper, and HOT.)

Sandwich: Jibarito
Found in: Puerto Rican neighborhoods in Chicago
Details: In the last few years, restaurants have gotten creative with the "bread" part of sandwiches—KFC's Double Down is bacon and cheese between two fried chicken patties; Friendly's serves a burger between two grilled cheese sandwiches. The possible originator of America's alternative bread movement: Borinquen, a Puerto Rican restaurant in Chicago. In 1996, owner Juan Figueroa substituted fried green plantains (a relative of the banana) for bread in a sandwich, and called it a *jibarito*, Spanish slang for "hillbilly." Between the plantains: steak, cheese, lettuce, tomato, onion, and fried garlic.

Sandwich: Chow Mein Sandwich
Found in: Southern Massachusetts, Rhode Island
Details: If you've never considered a big bowl of chow mein as a sandwich ingredient, then you've never been to Massachusetts. Served by western-style Chinese restaurants in the area since the 1930s, the sandwich is simple: meat (pork, beef, or chicken), bean sprouts, celery, onion, crispy noodles, and hot brown gravy on a hamburger bun, served with thick-cut french fries on the side.

Sandwich: The Gerber
Found in: St. Louis, Missouri
Details: According to local lore, a man named Dick Gerber walked into Ruma's Deli in 1973 and ordered an open-faced ham and cheese sandwich on garlic bread, baked in an oven, and sprinkled with paprika. Why can't you get it outside of St. Louis? Because the cheese used in a Gerber is a combination of Swiss, cheddar, and provolone called Provel, found only in Missouri. (If you want to make the sandwich at home, use straight provolone.)

Sandwich: Double Brat
Found in: Sheboygan, Wisconsin
Details: Historically, Sheboygan has had a large German population, and with that, a long history of sausage-making. This sandwich is made up of two bratwursts, cooked over charcoal, then placed side-by-side on what locals call a "bun," but which is technically a type of kaiser roll called a *semmel*. The brats are topped with onions, brown mustard, (and because it's Wisconsin) a large helping of melted butter.

LITTLE THINGS MEAN A LOT

*"The devil's in the details," says an old proverb. It's true—
the littlest things can cause the biggest problems.*

A LINE OF CODE

In 2011, a Microsoft programmer working on the first major update of Windows 7 for the European market accidentally left out a line of code that would have given Europe's 15 million Windows users a choice of Web browsers—such as Safari or Firefox—with which to run the update. Without that line of code, users could only run Internet Explorer (owned by Microsoft). Result: The goof broke a 2009 commitment Microsoft had made to the European Commission to offer a choice of browsers. The software giant had to pay fines and restitution totaling $731 million.

A MISTRANSLATED WORD

When 18-year-old Willie Ramirez was rushed to a Florida hospital in 1980, he was in a coma. His family spoke only Spanish, and kept repeating the word *intoxicado*. Believing Ramirez to be intoxicated, doctors treated him for a drug overdose. However, *intoxicado* also means "poisoned," which is what the family was trying to say—that he was suffering from severe food poisoning. By the time the doctors caught the mistake, Ramirez had nearly died. He survived, but was left a quadriplegic. His family sued for malpractice and was awarded $71 million from the hospital…which now has a professional interpreter on call.

A FEW FEET OF CABLE

In 2011, 75-year-old Hayastan Shakarian from the nation of Georgia was searching through a field, looking for old copper wire scraps to sell, when she dug down with her shovel and cut through a fiber-optic cable. Not knowing what it was, she removed a few feet of it. And just like that, millions of people in neighboring Armenia lost their Internet connections. (Georgia supplies 90 percent of Armenia's Web access.) The blackout lasted twelve hours—halting

---

France has tried to switch to decimal time (100-minute hours and 10-hour days) twice.

Armenia's e-commerce, news service, airports, and several other systems. Normally, the cable would have been farther below ground, but recent rains and mudslides had left the area exposed. Shakarian—dubbed the "spade-hacker" by the press—was charged with damaging property, but at last report, hadn't been sent to jail.

A DECIMAL POINT

While designing the *Isaac Peral*, part of the Spanish Navy's "next generation of submarines," an engineer mistakenly put a decimal point in the wrong place that resulted in the completed sub being 77 tons heavier than the specifications had called for. In 2013, the Spanish Navy reported that it will cost millions of dollars to "slim it down" so the sub won't sink when it's launched. At last report, it was still sitting in dry dock.

A SOFTWARE GLITCH

The European Space Agency's *Ariane 5* rocket took 10 years to develop at a cost of $7 billion and blew up 39 seconds into its maiden flight in 1996. The rocket—designed to put the Europeans ahead in the commercial space race—was carrying a payload of four satellites costing a total of around $500 million. According to the investigation, the guidance system shut down 36.7 seconds after launch due to a software bug that was "unable to convert a piece of data from a 64-bit format to a 16-bit format." That caused the system to "think" it was going off course—which it wasn't—so it initiated a self-destruct sequence that destroyed the rocket in midair.

SQUARE WINDOWS

In three separate incidents in 1953 and '54, three de Havilland Comet jetliners crashed mid-flight. Investigators were baffled as to what went wrong with two-year-old state-of-the-art aircraft. The culprit turned out to be...square windows. Because the steel surrounding each window had four right angles, the hull steadily became weaker in those areas. And unlike earlier, slower planes without pressurized cabins, the Comets were flying faster, higher, and for more flight hours than any passenger plane had before. Before long, the stress became too much to hold the plane together. The Comet fleet was grounded for five years, and the problem was fixed. That's why, today, all jetliner windows have rounded "corners."

World's tallest snowman: 122 feet, built by citizens of Bethel, Maine, in 2008.

FORGOTTEN SPORTS STARS

Great athletes rescued from the dustbin of history.

ROSS YOUNGS

In his day, Ross "Pep" Youngs was one of the biggest baseball stars in America's biggest city, New York. "Pound for pound, Pep Young was the greatest ball player I ever saw," wrote *New York Times* sports columnist John Kieran, who'd seen Babe Ruth, Ty Cobb, Lou Gehrig, and all the other greats of the 1920s and '30s play. Legendary New York Giants manager Hank McGraw, who coached for 30 seasons in the Major Leagues, called him "the greatest outfielder I ever saw on a baseball field."

Never heard of him? That could be because Youngs died young. At age 30, he developed a kidney inflammation known as Bright's disease that cut his career short. During his tenth and final season with the Giants in 1926, Youngs dropped from 170 pounds to 100. (And he still hit .306.)

Youngs had a career batting average of .322. The Giants won four National League titles and two World Series during that time, and sports historians credit Youngs with playing a major role. His name came up during the first voting for Hall of Fame membership in 1936, but competing against Ruth, Cobb, Honus Wagner, and all the greats of baseball's Golden Era, he was overlooked. He was finally inducted by the Veterans Committee in 1972.

CLARENCE DEMAR

Boston Globe sportswriter David Egan once proposed that the name of the Boston Marathon be changed to the DeMarathon. Why? Because Clarence DeMar had won the race so many times, the change seemed appropriate. DeMar ran his first Boston Marathon in 1911—and it was almost his last. During a routine pre-race exam, a staff physician warned him that he had a heart murmur and if he tired during the race, he should drop out. DeMar ran anyway—and won by half a mile. And despite that doctor's warning, he never gave up running. He ran seven miles to and from his job as a printer each day and regularly competed in 5- and 10-mile races. But did he dare run another 26-mile marathon? According to the doctor, it could kill him. In 1917, he decided to try.

DeMar placed third in the Boston Marathon that year, and went on to win the race in 1922, '23, '24, '27, '28, and '30. DeMar's seven wins are still more than any other runner. That heart murmur? In 1953, DeMar underwent rigorous testing. He was 65 at the time, and had run thousands of races. Physicians said his heart was "exceptionally strong." So what happened back in 1911? "I think the doc must have been listening to his own heart," DeMar joked.

CHARLIE SIFFORD

Professional golf was officially a white man's game until 1961, the year the PGA Tour dropped the "Caucasians Only" clause from its bylaws. As a teenager, Sifford worked as a caddy in Charlotte, North Carolina, but wasn't allowed to play any of the courses there. In 1940, Sifford, 17, moved to Philadelphia, where many courses were more welcoming, and turned pro. Playing on the United Golf Association Tour for black players, he won five consecutive National Negro Open titles from 1952–57.

He was 39 when he finally got a shot on the PGA tour, playing his first event at the Greensboro Open near his hometown, Charlotte. Sifford wasn't sure he wanted to play there. He knew he'd face a lot of opposition from spectators, but his wife urged him to do it. "There was a lot of name-calling," recalled Sifford, who shot 68 in the first round to take the lead. "But as long as there was no physical pain and I had the Lord on my side, I played. I finished the tournament and tied for fourth. It was one of my proudest moments and one of my scariest moments all at the same time."

That first season on the PGA Tour was harsh. Spectators around the country refused to accept Sifford. Sometimes after hitting a drive, he'd discover that his ball had been kicked into the rough. Other times he'd find it buried in trash. Once, when he bent to retrieve his ball from the hole, he found that the cup had been filled with feces. But Sifford kept playing. "Nothing stopped me," he said later. "I wasn't just doing this for me. I was doing it for the world." Tiger Woods believes Sifford's "diligence and dedication" broke the barriers that might have stood in *his* way. "I never would've been introduced to the game because my dad wouldn't have played," said Woods.

DIRTY DISNEY

Are the animators at the squeaky clean House of Mouse sneaking adult content into otherwise innocent cartoons—or do some people see (and hear) dirty deeds wherever they look? You decide.

CLOCK CLEANERS (1937)

In this theatrical short, Donald Duck tries to fix a bell tower clock. When the clock's mainspring proves to be too feisty, Donald does what he usually does—he gets angry and lets loose an incomprehensible tirade of quacking nonsense. In 1994—more than 55 years later—Donald Wildmon, president of the fundamentalist American Family Association, claimed that Donald Duck could be heard saying "F*** you" to the clock, and convinced Walmart to pull all VHS copies of *Cartoon Classics: Fun on the Job!*, a Disney video compilation containing *Clock Cleaners*, from its shelves. Disney insisted that Donald's line is "Says who?" and it's obvious because the clock spring responds, "Says I!" But the controversy spooked Disney (Walmart was selling millions of Disney tapes) into re-editing the scene and inserting a dub of Donald yelling, "Awww nuts!" instead. (To which the clock spring still responds, "Says I!")

THE RESCUERS (1977)

This animated film is about two mice, Bernard and Bianca, who set out to rescue a little girl kidnapped by treasure hunters. At one point, the mice fly over the skies of New York City on the back of an albatross. During the flight, they pass an apartment building where a poster of a topless woman can be seen through one of the windows. Well, not exactly *seen*. It's only on-screen for two frames—roughly 1/16th of a second. The image was put there by a layout artist as a practical joke, and reportedly most of the production crew knew about it and thought it was funny. Unfortunately, in 1977, nobody gave much thought to the nascent home-video market. When it was released on VHS in 1999, sharp-eyed viewers noticed the poster, froze the frame, and spread the news on the Internet. Three days later, Disney was forced to recall all 3.4 million copies of the videotape and re-issue the movie with the two offensives frames painted over.

To overcome gravity and hurl us all into space, Earth would have to spin 800 times faster.

WHO FRAMED ROGER RABBIT? (1988)

This live-action/animated comedy about a cartoon rabbit charged with murder who hires a crusty private eye to clear his name is full of naughty jokes and subversive material. Producer Steven Spielberg reportedly encouraged the animation crew to insert "in-jokes," but didn't know how far they'd take it. There was a blink-and-you'll-miss-it shot of Baby Herman groping a woman on a film set and a fraction of a section scene in which the voluptuous Jessica Rabbit appears to be without underwear. Both scenes were edited to be more family-friendly. It's also rumored that in theatrical prints, Disney-executive Michael Eisner's home telephone number could be seen on the wall of a bathroom below the words "For a Good Time Call Allison Wonderland," and that there was a single frame of Betty Boop topless. But we'll never know if the rumors are true. The images do not appear in the home-video version—not even in the very first laserdisc release.

ALADDIN (1992)

During one scene, Aladdin flies on a magic carpet to Jasmine's palace, where he's greeted by Rajah, her menacing pet tiger. Aladdin then whispers to the big cat, "C'mon, good kitty, take off and go." But according to the American Life League (ALL) and other family watch groups, that's not what Aladdin says. According to these groups, it sounds like "good teenagers take off their clothes." The closed-captioning on the 1993 home-video release affirms the "good kitty" line. Nevertheless, the ALL included *Aladdin* in their years-long boycott of all Disney products.

THE LION KING (1994)

At one point, a depressed Simba the lion collapses in despair and kicks up a cloud of dust. The dust wafts into the air, and for a brief moment, forms into the word "SEX" against the dark sky. The American Life League again claimed that Disney was sending subliminal messages to children. Others have theorized that the prank was arranged by the special-effects department and that the cloud formation actually spells out "SFX," an abbreviation for "special effects." Disney won't say whether the clouds were intentionally drawn to look like letters or if it's just an example of people seeing what they want to see…but no one denies that it's in the film.

MIND YOUR BEESWAX!

Bee careful. This one could give you hives.

WHAT'S THE BUZZ?

Ever wondered where beeswax comes from? It's sort of like bee dandruff, produced by glands under the bee's abdominal plates, that falls off in glassy little flakes. When heated to about 90° F (the temperature of the hive) and chewed by the bees, it becomes soft enough to be molded into the honeycomb, the hive's honey-storage facility. The flakes are produced by young worker bees who are hivebound for the first weeks of their lives. When they get old enough to fly, the wax-producing glands become inactive.

Having too much honey and too little storage space is what stimulates the production of wax. Here's how it works: When the field bees unload nectar into the honey-storage "stomachs" of the inside bees, the nectar doesn't normally stay there very long—it gets loaded into empty cells in the honeycomb. But what if there aren't enough storage cells? When the worker bee's stomach is full, its wax glands are stimulated. The bees go into overdrive, dropping flakes all over the place. The presence of the flakes stimulates other bees to pick them up and start forming them into cell walls, which continues until there's enough storage space again.

WAXING POETIC

Sure, beeswax is useful to bees, but it also has a long history as humanity's first plastic. It's been used for sculpting metal, conditioning the strings for bows and crossbows, sealing and lubricating guns and musket balls, providing light by burning, and even filling cavities in emergency dentistry. Though worldwide beeswax production is fairly low today—only about 10,000 tons a year—beeswax is still widely used. You know that beeswax is used in candles and maybe in cosmetics and furniture polish, but how about these uses?

- As chewing gum
- As polish for premium candies, including Jelly Bellies and Haribo Gummi Bears

- Mixed with pine pitch and sawdust, as "cutler's resin," used by knife makers to attach blades firmly into handles.

- As a sealing coat for cast metals

- Mixed with petroleum jelly as the main ingredient in "bone wax," smeared by surgeons to control bleeding from bone surfaces during reconstructive surgery

- As an ingredient in lip balm, mustache wax, shoe polish, and premium crayons

- As a binder that holds together reeds on oboes, bassoons, and accordions

- As a handyman's friend, fixing squeaks, freeing sticky drawers, lubricating screws and locking them in place

- In the molded French cakes called *canelles*, as a thin layer that gives a glossy, dark crust

- As the sculpted form for the ancient "lost wax" casting process. It's coated with layers of clay and fired in a kiln. The wax burns away, leaving a mold into which bronze can be poured.

- As a coating to preserve cheese as it ages

- As a whip coating. When some whip makers shifted from rawhide to cheaper, more durable nylon, customers complained that the weight wasn't quite right. It turned out that dipping the nylon in beeswax added just the right amount of heft.

- As the etched coating on early "wax" phonograph records

- As a chicken-plucker's plucking aid. They discovered that floating a layer of molten wax on top of boiling water makes the feathers stick together so they can be removed in a large clumps instead of as a snowstorm of loose feathers.

*   *   *

WHERE THE HORSES AREN'T

When life gives you lemons... In the 1950s, author/illustrator Maurice Sendak started working on a children's book about horses, but quickly discovered that he couldn't draw a horse to save his life.

Make lemonade: So he decided to draw monsters instead. The book, published in 1963 as *Where the Wild Things Are*, has since sold 20 million copies (probably more than if he'd stuck with horses).

A well-thrown curveball can dive as much as 17 inches as it approaches the batter.

THE MAN WHO HATED GRAVITY

What did Roger Babson do with the fortune he made on Wall Street in the early 1900s? He devoted a considerable chunk of it to defeating what he called "Our Number One Enemy"—gravity.

THE FORCE

One afternoon in August 1893, a young woman named Edith Babson drowned while swimming in the river near her home in Gloucester, Massachusetts. It wasn't clear exactly what happened. She may have drowned trying to save a girl who couldn't swim, or she may simply have drifted into dangerous currents without realizing it. Whatever the case, her 18-year-old brother Roger arrived at his own peculiar explanation for her death. "They say she was 'drowned,'" he later wrote. "But the fact is that, through temporary paralysis or some other cause (she was a good swimmer), she was unable to fight Gravity, which came up and seized her like a dragon and brought her to the bottom. There she smothered and died from lack of oxygen."

NUTTY PROFESSOR

Soon after his sister's death, Babson enrolled in the Massachusetts Institute of Technology. He'd wanted to study at a business school, but his father thought engineering was more practical and forced him to go to MIT. Since Babson had no interest in anything taught there, he spitefully enrolled in the very first class listed in the course catalog: railroad engineering, taught by Professor George Swain. By doing so—purely by chance—he managed to get a business education of sorts in spite of his father's wishes.

Professor Swain was an economics buff, and he had his own take on "the dismal science." He believed that Sir Isaac Newton's third law of motion, "for every action there is an equal and opposite reaction," had a direct and measurable influence on the business cycle, the tendency of economies to fluctuate between periods of boom and bust. A small economic boom, Professor Swain explained, would be followed by an equal and opposite little bust. And a big

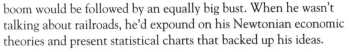

boom would be followed by an equally big bust. When he wasn't talking about railroads, he'd expound on his Newtonian economic theories and present statistical charts that backed up his ideas.

Today Swain's ideas would be dismissed as absurd—market forces, such as supply and demand, the amount of competition, commercial lending rates, and government regulations determine whether an economy thrives or sinks. The laws of physics have no more to do with it than the stock market has in picking the winner of the Kentucky Derby. But Babson, obsessed with gravity since his sister's death, became a true believer. Remember, Isaac Newton (1642–1727) also developed the law of gravity, the first scientific explanation of what gravity is and how it works. Newton famously got his inspiration after watching an apple fall from a tree in 1655. (It didn't hit him on the head—that part of the story is a myth.) If gravity could kill people, it seemed perfectly logical to Babson that another of Newton's laws could exert its influence on the affairs of human beings.

FEELING LOW, MOVING UP

As soon as Babson graduated from MIT in 1898, he chucked engineering for a career in finance. But that was sidetracked three years later when he contracted tuberculosis. His doctors told him to seek a "fresh-air cure" at a high elevation. Why a high elevation? Gravity, the doctors explained: Dry air would save his lungs, but gravity prevented him from getting it at sea level. "They explained how Gravity pulls the moist and humid air down into the valleys and on the low lands in the vicinity of the seacoast," Babson recounted in an essay titled, "Gravity—Our Enemy Number One." "Therefore, to fight this effect of effect of Gravity, I convalesced in the West."

EASTBOUND AND DOWN

When Babson's health improved, he moved to Wellesley Hills, in rural Massachusetts, where, with help from Professor Swain, he developed his own version of Newtonian stock-market theory. In 1904, he put it to work, publishing one of the first financial newsletters in the United States. At the time every Wall Street firm had to hire its own experts to analyze stocks and bonds, which cost a fortune. With his newsletter, Babson provided subscribers with his Newtonian analysis (as looney as it was) for a fraction of the cost. Banks, brokerage houses, and other financial firms snapped up subscriptions to his newsletter. Within a decade, it was bringing in more than $1 million a year. And as Babson's fortune grew, so did his fame. He wrote columns for the *Saturday Evening Post* and the *New York Times*, and advised every president from Teddy Roosevelt (1901–08) to Franklin Roosevelt (1933–45).

WHAT GOES UP...

Besides making him rich and famous, Babson's harebrained theories gave him what turned out to be a huge advantage over other Wall Street observers during the "roaring" 1920s: For him, it was an article of faith that big rises in the stock market would be followed by crashes every bit as big. He "predicted" as much in September 1929, warning that "sooner or later, a crash is coming, and it may be terrific." It was hard to believe. The stock market had increased tenfold since 1920; few people thought it was going anywhere but up. But the crash came on October 28, 1929, a month and a half after Babson made his prediction. Share prices fell 25 percent in two days (and would fall for the next three years, wiping out nearly 90 percent of shareholder value). The Great Depression had begun; Babson's reputation as a wizard of Wall Street was secured.

Babson's fame and wealth grew throughout the Depression. In addition to his newsletter, over the years he wrote 47 books on a variety of subjects. He also dabbled in politics: In 1940, he ran for president on the Prohibition Party ticket and came in fourth.

THAT OLD FAMILIAR PULL

In 1947, Babson turned 72 and might have settled into quiet retirement had he not been stricken by a tragedy similar to the one he'd experienced 54 years earlier: His 17-year-old grandson, Michael, drowned saving a friend who'd fallen out of a speeding motorboat. "He succeeded in getting the woman back to the boat; she is healthy and happy today. But that 'dragon' Gravity came up and snatched Michael! He was so exhausted he couldn't fight this force which pulled him to the bottom," Babson recounted in "Gravity—Our Enemy Number One."

Feeling Gravity's painful tug on his heart once again, Babson resolved to slay the dragon once and for all. But how?

For Part II of the story, turn to page 438.

In remote parts of Africa, the wheel was unknown as late as the 19th century.

FIRST PERSONS

In every human endeavor, somebody's gotta go first.

EDWARD DOTY AND EDWARD LEICESTER (1600s)

Claim to Fame: First Europeans to fight a duel in the American colonies

Details: Doty and Leicester were the indentured servants of Pilgrim Stephen Hopkins and accompanied him aboard the *Mayflower* in 1620. A few months after arriving in the New World, the two men had a falling out and decided to settle it by dueling with swords. The two men only managed to wound each other before they were pulled apart. Because dueling was not allowed in Plymouth Colony, each man was sentenced to have his head and feet tied together for an entire day...but the punishment was so painful that they were untied after just an hour. (Leicester may have learned his lesson, but Doty did not: Over the next 20 years, he was hauled back into court more than a dozen times for fraud, assault, theft, disturbing the peace, and other charges.)

THE BROADWAY SQUAD (1860–1905)

Claim to Fame: America's first traffic cops

Details: New York City traffic in the 19th century may have been slower than it is today, but it was almost completely unregulated and much more chaotic. (Traffic lights and even stop signs were still more than half a century away.) The horse-drawn vehicles of the era lurched unpredictably in every direction, and the busy cobblestone streets were strewn with manure, garbage, and stray pigs who fed on the garbage. By the mid-19th century, traffic along Broadway from Bowling Green to West 59th Street had gotten so treacherous that the NYPD established the Broadway Squad specifically for the purpose of halting traffic long enough for the officers to help pedestrians across the street.

DR. EDOUARD ERNEST LEHWESS (1902)

Claim to Fame: First person to own a motor home

Details: Just 17 years after Karl Benz invented the modern automobile and six years before Henry Ford introduced the Model T,

The first cow in the North America arrived at the Jamestown colony in 1611.

Lehwess, a London businessman, paid a French automaker £3,000 (nearly $400,000 today) to build a car that he could live in as he attempted to become the first person to drive around the world. Named the Passe-Partout, the first-ever recreational vehicle had a 25-horsepower engine and weighed more than 6,000 pounds. (A 2013 Toyota Corolla, by comparison, has a 132-horsepower engine and weighs 2,734 pounds.) In May 1902, Lehwess set off from Paris, headed east. He made it as far as Nizhny Novgorod, Russia, 1,800 miles away. There, the Passe-Partout's cylinders cracked. Lehwess abandoned it in a snowdrift and went back to London. In 1904, he was tossed out of the Royal Automobile Club for bribing a policeman to get out of a traffic offense.

WILLIAM EDWARD TAYNTON (1925)

Claim to Fame: First human to appear on television

Details: Before the invention of electronic television, a number of inventors tried to perfect what was called "mechanical television" (the image was captured mechanically but then transmitted electronically). One of them was a Scottish engineer named John Logie Baird. His primitive system required lights so bright and so hot that he had to experiment with a dummy's head instead of a human being. (The head cracked and its hair was singed by the intense heat.) When Logie finally got it to work on October 2, 1925, he fetched the office boy, 21-year-old William Taynton, and had him sit under the bright lights (eyes shut tight!) for the few moments it took to transmit a faint, credit-card-sized image to a TV in the next room.

NOAH FULMOR AND ERIN FINNEGAN (2009)

Claim to Fame: First couple married in (simulated) zero gravity

Details: Fulmor and Finnegan, both sci-fi fans, hoped to wed in low-Earth orbit or on Mars, but space tourism has been slow to materialize and their love would not wait. In June 2009, they went aboard a "vomit comet," a Boeing 727 modified to simulate zero gravity. During the 90-minute, $65,000 nuptial flight, the plane executed 15 parabolic arcs, simulating weightlessness—and inducing air sickness—each time. (Finnegan wore a special wedding dress with built-in pants to prevent displays of zero-gravity immodesty.) "It was outstanding, and everything we hoped for," Fulmor says. "We were shocked that nobody had done it yet."

Golf champion Babe Didrikson sewed her own golfing outfits.

AN ALAN SMITHEE FILM

When directors finish a movie and hate it (because the studio interfered or they're embarrassed by it), they don't want their names on it. So what do they do? Until a few years ago, orphaned films were credited to "Alan Smithee."

THE MAN WHO WASN'T THERE

Until 1968, the Directors Guild of America required mainstream movie directors to use their real names on films, based on the concept that a director is the main creative force or "author" behind a film. (In the film world, this is called *auteur* theory—*auteur* is French for "author.") The rule also prevented studios and producers from failing to credit a director that they didn't get along with. But until 2000, the DGA had one exception to the rule: They allowed unhappy directors to use a pseudonym—the same pseudonym—Alan Smithee. Why "Alan Smithee"? DGA brass wanted a name that sounded generic or common (like Smith), but tweaked just a bit so that it wasn't anybody's actual name (like Smithee).

Directors now had a powerful tool at their disposal. If they could prove to the DGA that producers or a studio had taken away their creative control, they could un-credit themselves from a film and attribute it to "Alan Smithee." The only stipulation: If they used the pseudonym, they could never publicly discuss having worked on the film in question or the fallout that ensued. Here are some films that were directed by "Alan Smithee"… and who really made them.

Movie: *Death of a Gunfighter* (1969)
Directors: Robert Totten, Don Siegel
Story: As the Western genre started to lose relevance, along came this movie, a Western about the end of the Wild West era as modern society encroaches, leaving behind a traditional, iron-fisted sheriff of a small dusty town, portrayed by veteran actor Richard Widmark. The shoot dragged on for almost a year, plagued by disagreements between Widmark and 32-year-old Totten, a director who had directed more than 40 episodes of TV Westerns like *Gunsmoke* and *Bonanza*. Widmark eventually won. He got Totten fired a week before the end of filming, and replaced by Siegel, who

had directed him in the 1968 cop drama *Madigan*. But Widmark pushed Siegel around, too. Siegel finished the movie, but considered himself a hired gun, completing what was really Totten's film. So he asked the DGA to deny him credit. Totten wouldn't take credit, either, because he felt burned by being fired. So the DGA came up with the Alan Smithee distinction. But the fact that Smithee wasn't a real person was still a mystery to the outside world. The film was positively reviewed, with the *New York Times* singling out Smithee's "sharp direction" and Roger Ebert writing that "Smithee, a name I'm not familiar with, allows his story to unfold naturally."

Movie: *Let's Get Harry* (1986)

Director: Stuart Rosenberg

Story: This action film boasted a star-studded cast of memorable '80s actors, including Thomas F. Wilson (Biff from *Back to the Future*), Michael Schoeffling (Jake Ryan in *Sixteen Candles*), Garey Busey, and Mark Harmon, then starring in the TV drama *St. Elsewhere*. Harmon plays a civil engineer who gets kidnapped in Colombia; the others are part of a ragtag group of family and friends who head down there to save him. In fact, Harmon's character doesn't appear until the end of the movie, when he's rescued. But after the movie had completed shooting, *St. Elsewhere* exploded in popularity. Harmon became a huge star and *People* magazine named him the "Sexiest Man Alive." Trying to capitalize on Harmon's sudden celebrity, TriStar Pictures authorized a major recut behind director Rosenberg's back, inserting half a dozen scenes with Harmon throughout the movie. Offended by the studio's actions, Rosenberg (who'd directed *Cool Hand Luke* and *The Amityville Horror*) got *Let's Get Harry* attributed to Alan Smithee.

Movie: *Catchfire* (1990)

Director: Dennis Hopper

Story: Hopper was in the middle of a major comeback in 1990, after a memorable role in *Blue Velvet* and an Oscar-nominated turn in *Hoosiers*. He'd also directed a handful of well-received films in his career, including *Easy Rider*, *The Last Movie*, and *Colors*. In 1990, he made *Catchfire*, a creepy action movie in which a hitman (Hopper) falls in love with and kidnaps an artist (Jodie Foster) he's supposed to kill. His final cut came in at three hours; Vestron Pictures thought that was unacceptable for a crime drama, and cut it down to 90 minutes. Hopper then made a third edit of the movie, cutting some scenes, rearranging others, and ending up at two hours long. Vestron still released their 90-minute version. Hopper demanded his name be stricken from the credits, and so did screenwriters Alex Cox and Tod Davies.

Movie: *An Alan Smithee Film: Burn Hollywood Burn* (1998)
Director: Arthur Hiller
Story: The "Alan Smithee" concept became such a famous part of Hollywood lore that in 1998, screenwriter Joe Esterhaus wrote a movie industry satire called *An Alan Smithee Film: Burn Hollywood Burn*. It's about a troubled movie directed by a man whose name really is Alan Smithee (Eric Idle). He tries to get his name off the movie but can't, because his name is Alan Smithee. Ironically, *Burn Hollywood Burn* was such a troubled production, fraught with studio interference, that director Arthur Hiller demanded—and got—the movie credited to Alan Smithee.

Movie: *Supernova* (2000)
Director: Walter Hill
Story: Hill directed lots of memorable movies in the '70s and '80s, including *The Warriors*, *The Long Riders*, *Streets of Fire*, and *48 Hours*. In 2000, he directed MGM's big-budget sci-fi horror movie *Supernova*, starring James Spader and Angela Bassett. The plot: A spaceship disappears and a rescue team is sent, but they're followed by the evil, extra-dimensional version of one of their own. Complicated? Yes, and it cost $90 million to make. Reportedly, MGM was unhappy with Hill's final cut of the film and secretly hired Francis Ford Coppola to re-edit it. Hill was furious and asked for an Alan Smithee. But because *Burn Hollywood Burn* had come out just two years earlier and made the pseudonym too well-known, *Supernova* was credited to a new imaginary director, "Thomas Lee." (Oh, and by the way, *Supernova* bombed, taking in only $14 million at the box office.)

*　　　*　　　*

"The trouble with the profit system has always been that it was highly unprofitable to most people."

—**E. B. White**

STAGE NAME STORIES

Would these celebrities have become famous if they'd stuck with their birth names? We'll never know, but here's how they got the names we know them by.

DANA ELAINE OWENS. When this future rap star, singer, and actress was eight years old in 1978, her cousin, who was Muslim, told her the Arabic word for "gentle and kind" is *latifah.* "I really felt like that name fit me," she said. At 17, she needed a new first name for her rap moniker: "I chose 'Queen' because my mother told me that all women were queens and should be treated as such," which is how she became Queen Latifah.

JOAN ALEXANDRA MOLINSKY. While attending college in the mid-1950s, the comedienne called herself "J. Sondra Meredith," mostly to distance herself from the surname of her disapproving parents, who thought that female comics were "as bad as showgirls." The owner of the first comedy club didn't like "Meredith" and called her "Pepper January," but she hated that. When she finally got an agent, Tony Rivers, he told her, "I can't send you out with *that* name." So she chose his, and became Joan Rivers.

MAURICE JOSEPH MICKLEWHITE. Born in London in 1933, Micklewhite got his first job in theater at age 20. Disliking both his first and last names, he billed himself as Michael Scott. But in 1954, while standing in a London phone booth talking to his agent, he was informed there already was an English actor named Michael Scott. Pressured to choose a new name right there, Micklewhite looked down the street and saw a movie marquee sign advertising *The Caine Mutiny.* So he said to his agent, "Michael Caine."

JEROME SILBERMAN. One of the biggest names in comedy started out as a serious dramatic actor. But he couldn't imagine seeing "Jerry Silberman as Hamlet" on a playbill, so in 1959, when he was 26 years old, he chose a new name by combining Eugene Gant, a character in Thomas Wolfe's novel *Look Homeward, Angel,* with playwright Thornton Wilder. Later in his life, the *Willy Wonka* actor joked, "I can't imagine Gene Wilder playing Hamlet, either."

MICHAEL JOHN DOUGLAS. When this young comedian left Pittsburgh in the early 1970s (after a brief stint as one of the "Flying Zookeeni Brothers" on *Mister Rogers' Neighborhood*), he had trouble making a name for himself in Hollywood because there were already two famous Michael Douglases (an actor and a talk-show host). Legend has it that he chose his new surname because of a crush on actress Diane Keaton, but Michael Keaton actually got it from one of his all-time favorite funnymen, silent-film star Buster Keaton.

DESTINY HOPE CYRUS. Born in 1992—the year her father Billy Ray Cyrus achieved worldwide fame with the country song "Achy Breaky Heart"—the baby girl had such a sunny disposition that she was nicknamed "Smiley," later shortened to Miley. To honor her dad, she legally changed her name to Miley Ray Cyrus.

NATALIE HERSHLAG. She chose her stage name at age 13 when she landed her first movie role in 1994's *The Professional*. It's not because Hershlag isn't "Hollywood" enough—rather, she wanted her family's privacy protected if she ever became famous. She chose her grandmother's maiden name and is professionally known as Natalie Portman.

ERIC MARLON BISHOP. In 1989, this Texas comic was having trouble getting called up on stage at open-mic nights. Noticing that there were a dozen male comics for every female comic—and the ladies were getting called up first—Bishop wrote a more feminine-sounding name on the sign-up sheet to fool the emcee. It worked: As "Jamie Foxx," he *was* called up to perform. (The last name was in honor of comedian Red Foxx.) "A stage name is like having a Superman complex," Foxx once told Oprah Winfrey, "I go into the telephone booth as Eric Bishop and come out as Jamie Foxx."

JONATHAN STUART LEIBOWITZ. Talk-show host Jon Stewart has given several explanations as to why he dropped his last name: It was too hard to pronounce, kids in middle school called him "Leiboshitz," and "Leibowitz just sounded too Hollywood." But in truth, he'd been uncomfortable with his name ever since 1971, when his father, physicist Donald Leibowitz, divorced his mother. In 1987, after a New York comedy club emcee butchered his name, he decided then and there to leave the name "Leibowitz" behind.

SNIGLETS

Every once in a while, a nerdy word fad comes along that's accessible enough for everyone to appreciate. Some, like crossword puzzles, stick around. Others, like sniglets, fade into obscurity (except on the Internet, where everything lives forever).

HALL OF KNOWLEDGE

Comedian Rich Hall was a writer and cast member on the 1982–1990 HBO sketch-comedy show *Not Necessarily the News*. The most popular segment: Hall's "Sniglets"—words that, according to Hall, "don't exist, but should." The concept of creating *neologisms* (new words) wasn't invented by Hall—writers have been doing it for centuries, and it was even part of the British version of *NNTN* before it came to the United States—but Hall published seven books of Sniglets and made it so popular that coming up with new ones became a common party game. The guidelines for making Sniglets are simple: It can be can be a portmanteau (a combination of existing words), a spelling change to an existing word or brand, or a totally made-up word. Here are a few of our favorites. (Warning: They're addictive. After you read these, you'll probably start making up new ones yourself.)

• **Kidnapkinage:** The act of purposefully taking more napkins than necessary at a fast-food restaurant

• **Seeyaks:** All the "We should get together again soon" talk at the end of an evening with friends

• **Cheedle:** The residue left on one's fingertips after consuming a bag of Cheetos

• **Mirthgirth:** Weight gained over the holidays

• **Transtexting:** Sending a text to the wrong person on your smart phone while texting with two people at the same time

• **Sneezure:** Several sneezes in a row

• **Bi-sacksual:** Able to accept either a paper or plastic sack for groceries at the supermarket without any sense of guilt

• **Ambaguous:** The inability to decide which suitcase to take on a trip

The tradition of wearing something blue at a wedding originated in ancient Israel.

- **Cryptocarnoophobic:** The weird feeling when meat is placed at the dinner table and it's impossible to tell what it is

- **Aeroma:** The odor emanating from a fitness room after a group aerobics workout

- **Cabincreep:** A structural condition in which the closing of one kitchen cabinet causes another to open

- **Procatstinate:** When a cat goes to the door to be let out, only to find that it can't decide whether to go out or stay in once the door is opened

- **Pre-Autoistic McConsumption:** The tendency to start eating your fries out of the fast-food bag during the car ride home

- **Frigerobics:** Leaning, bending, and stretching while looking into the refrigerator

- **Pootooter:** An empty toilet-paper roll

- **Thronie:** The little jiggle you give the handle of a toilet to make it stop running

- **Speraws:** The star-shaped marks at the end of hot dogs

- **Doork:** A person who pushes on a door marked "pull"

- **Filther:** A used coffee filter

- **Anachronym:** A worn-out, outdated abbreviation, lol

- **Hydrocondiment:** The watery discharge that accumulates in the mustard or ketchup bottle that comes out first and makes your bread all wet

- **Snuggage:** Belongings stuffed under the airline seat in front of you or in the overhead compartment

- **Barbage:** The leftover shaving cream in your hand that you have no use for

- **Squimmets:** Those gross strings that hang off of bananas

- **Cinemuck:** The combination of popcorn, candy, and soda pop on movie-theater floors that makes them sticky

- **Motspur:** The one wheel on a shopping cart that does whatever it wants

- **Strumbles:** Unseen objects you pretend made you trip when it was actually just your own feet

- **Garpacting:** Trying to stuff one more piece of trash into an already full trash bag so you don't have to take it out

- **Pupkus:** The moist residue left on a window after a dog presses its nose to it

CLASS ACTS

*To balance out heavy classes like advanced calculus,
medieval literature, and organic chemistry, many
schools offer a few oddball courses like these.*

The Joy of Garbage. "This class follows the path of our waste products as they are burnt, decomposed, landfilled, treated, recycled, dumped, or shipped abroad. Using the scientific method to guide us, we will explore the fates of organic and non-organic detritus." (Santa Clara University)

"Oh, Look! A Chicken!" "This course will pursue ways of knowing through embracing [little ants, carrying a morsel of food across the table] what it means to be a distracted [I could sure enjoy a peanut butter sandwich right now] learner as well as [OMG—I get to go to the beach this summer] developing an awareness [I need to trim my fingernails] of one's senses. Those registering for this section may even learn to juggle. [I'll be right down; I just have to finish this... what was I working on?]" (Belmont University)

The Theory and Practice of Time Travel. "Some physicists think time travel may not be impossible. In fact, there is no law of physics that time travel contradicts, and there are even solutions to Einstein's equations for general relativity that allow time travel to take place. No, we won't really build a time machine. The 'practice' part of the class will look at time travel as portrayed in science fiction." (Alfred University)

Surviving the Coming Zombie Apocalypse. "This course uses current research and science on Catastrophes and Human Behavior together with the idea of a Zombie Apocalypse to learn about the nature, scope, and impact of catastrophic events on individuals, families, societies, civilizations, and Earth itself." (Michigan State University)

The American Vacation. "Social history of vacations; cultural significance of contemporary patterns; focus on how experiences are shaped by race, class, gender." (University of Iowa)

First scientist to be knighted: Isaac Newton, who became Sir Isaac in 1705.

Game Show! "Students will assist in the production of a televised comedic game show. Class assignments will include set construction, research, camera operation, segment writing, voice work, on-camera acting, recruiting contestants, and marketing. Types of humor used within game segments include blue, parody, hyperbole, repartee, satire, etc." (Oberlin College)

LEGO Robotics. "Primarily a lab experience, this seminar provides students resources to design, build, and program functional robots constructed from LEGO and other parts, such as motors and sensors. The class also explores other topics of interest, such as digital logic, modern robotics, or artificial intelligence. A great way to try out new ideas, learn some basic engineering, and play with LEGO." (Massachusetts Institute of Technology)

Theory and History of Video Games. "Historical, cultural, and formal perspectives on video games, tracing their emergence as new medium, social force, and big business." (Swarthmore College)

The Phallus. "Topics include the relation between the phallus and the penis, the meaning of the phallus, phallologocentrism, the lesbian phallus, the Jewish phallus, the Latino phallus, and the relation of the phallus to fetishism." (Occidental College)

Lady Gaga and the Sociology of the Fame. "This course focuses on the rise of Lady Gaga to her status as a pop music icon. The central objective of this course is to unravel some of the sociologically relevant dimensions of the fame of Lady Gaga. Specific attention will be devoted to the role of business and marketing, entertainment law, fans and live shows, gay culture, religion and political activism, sex and gender, and the city of New York." (University of South Carolina)

Physics for Future Presidents. "The beauty of physics may lie in the math, but future presidents don't have time for that. So we skip math, and get to the key results of physics that will help you run the world. These include energy conservation and energy sources, explosions, radioactivity, fission, fusion and nuclear weapons, earthquakes and tsunamis, and global positioning systems and spy satellites." (U.C. Berkeley)

A stiletto heel worn by a 120-lb. woman exerts 2,000 lbs. of pressure per square inch.

GERALDO VS. THE SKINHEADS

From the infamous talk-show brawl to the unexpected freak-out, here are some of the most infamous knock-down-drag-outs in the history of TV.

TONY "FATBOY" VS. JOE "THE LIAR" REDNER
During an August 2006 episode of *The Bleepin Truth*, a public access political talk show in Tampa, Florida, host Chris Krimitsos was moderating a discussion between Republican radio-show host Tony Katz and Tampa strip-club owner Joe Redner, who was running for a Tampa County Commissioner seat at the time. The three were seated around a large round table in a dark, somber setting (similar to *The Charlie Rose Show*) that started off ugly and quickly got worse. After just a few minutes, the "conversation" was reduced to Katz calling Redner a liar, and Redner telling Katz he was fat. This went on for a while, until Katz finally ripped the microphone off his shirt and stormed off the set, brushing against Redner as he did. "Keep your hands offa me!" said Redner. "F*** you!" said Katz, already off-camera. "Fat boy!" replied Redner. That appeared to be it. Redner sat at the table chuckling while Krimitsos apologized to viewers...when suddenly a wicker stool came flying onto the set, hitting Redner in the face. "That is assault!" he exclaimed. The screen immediately went to a poster board reading *The Bleepin Truth*, followed, appropriately enough, by several bleeps. Katz, who had obviously thrown the chair, yelled, "Sue me!" and ran out of the studio. Luckily for him, Redner, who was not seriously injured, didn't sue or press charges. The clip played on news shows all over the world, making *The Bleepin Truth* the best known public access show on Earth for the next couple of days.

Bonus: In his introduction to the show, Krimitsos jokingly referred to Katz and Redner, who had appeared on the show together twice before, as "Ali and Frazier." Little did he know...

EVERYONE IN THE TV STUDIO VS. RAVI BHATIA

Dadagiri is a Hindi word meaning "to bully," and *Dadagiri: Beat the Bullies* is a popular Indian TV show in which contestants are put through a series of rounds, during which the hosts act like bullies and try to humiliate them. The contestant who remains the calmest throughout the abuse wins 50,000 rupees (about $900). During an episode in 2008, one of the hosts played a spoiled college-girl character called "Esha the Goddess." She tried and failed to get a rise out of contestant Ravi Bhatia, 19, and then, in an unscripted moment, slapped him in the face. Shocked, Bhatia slapped her right back—hard. Bad move: every male member of the show's production staff, along with a bunch of guys from the audience, started to run onto the stage attacked Bhatia. Over the course of the next few minutes, all that can be seen in the video (the show never aired, but it was leaked and became a *YouTube* hit) is a throng of men crowding the stage, with occasional glimpses of a whimpering Bhatia being pummeled. Just how badly he was injured is unknown; a photo of a man in a hospital bed in a full-body cast, purportedly Bhatia, made the rounds on the Internet, but the photo's authenticity was never confirmed.

Bonus: After being slapped by Esha the Goddess and then returning the slap, Bhatia yelled, "How can she slap?" He repeated the phrase, yelling it over and over again as he was being beaten. "How can she slap?" has since become a popular internet meme. Several remixes of the video have been made in the years since the incident.

GERALDO VS. THE SKINHEADS

On November 3, 1988, Geraldo Rivera was taping an episode of his CBS daytime talk show *Geraldo*. Title of the episode: "Teen Hatemongers," featuring actual white supremacist skinheads alongside African Americans. At one point during the show, 20-year-old skinhead John Metzger called African-American activist Roy Innis an "Uncle Tom." Innis, 54, grabbed Metzger around the neck and started strangling him. Within seconds Metzger, Innis, the other guests, security guards, Rivera himself, and several people from the audience—a lot of them skinheads—were caught up in an all-out brawl. Amidst the very real violence, one of the skinheads threw a metal folding chair into the melee and smashed Rivera in the face, breaking and bloodying his nose. When it finally calmed down several minutes later, the white supremacists were thrown out of the building. Rivera, who refused medical treatment and even stayed to tape two more shows, refused to have any of the skinheads charged with any crimes, telling the *New York Times*, "I don't want to be tied up in court with the roaches." The episode was a huge success for Rivera, and spawned the era of what *Newsweek*—on the cover of the very next edition—dubbed "Trash TV."

TOM ARNOLD VS. MICHAEL STRAHAN

On March 31, 2006, comedian Tom Arnold, the former cohost of Fox Sports Net's *The Best Damn Sports Show Period*, made a return appearance on the show to pump his new "tell-all" book. The discussion became heated when it was revealed that Arnold's book had some less-than-complimentary things to say about members of the New York Giants football team. One of the other guests on the show: New York Giants defensive end Michael Strahan. The two men began to argue, stuck their fingers in each others' faces, started tussling—and before anyone knew what was happening, they were on the floor in a fight. Show hosts Rodney Peete (a former NFL quarterback) and Rob Dibble (a former big league pitcher) quickly jumped in to separate the two, but by that time Strahan, a 6' 5" pro football player, was crying in pain and apparently injured, while Arnold, a pudgy comedian, was fine—and was even being restrained by Peete. Then the show ended, with no explanation at all. The sports website *Deadspin.com* reported about the fracas that night and posted the video, and by the next day the Strahan–Arnold fight was an Internet sensation.

Bonus: As we said, the fight took place on March 31—the day before April 1. Turned out the whole thing was staged. Arnold didn't even have a book out, and *Deadspin* was forced to issue an apology the next day. The best part: According to those in the know, Strahan and Arnold hadn't even told the show's hosts, so Peete and Dibble were as fooled as everyone else.

* * *

HELPFUL TIP

Q: How do you get a sweet, little old lady to yell the 'F' word?
A: Get another sweet little, old lady to yell "BINGO!"

CARNY SLANG

In case you ever want to run away from home and become a carny.

Clem: A customer or "mark," particularly a gullible rural one

Arch: The carnival entrance

Zamps: Kiddie rides, so named because they were once primarily manufactured by the Zamperla Rides Company

Big Eli: The Ferris wheel, which was once made by the Eli Bridge Company

Carny marriage: When two carnies pledge to be romantically involved with only each other for the carnival season, they seal the commitment by riding once around on the carousel together

B.C.: Short for "Be cool," a subtle warning to watch what you're doing or saying, because management or law enforcement is watching

Donniker: The bathroom. It's from the old British slang term "dunnekin" or "dung kin," a small room for...well, dung.

Drop the awnings: Closing down the carnival for the night

Cowboy: A person who comes to the carnival just to start trouble or get in a fight

Light plant: A big rig power-generator truck, also called a "genny"

Grease joint: Concession stand

Ride monkey: A carnival employee who runs a ride.

Shake Machine: Any ride that, in the hands of a skilled ride monkey, can shake change loose from customers' pockets.

Slum: Cheap prizes for midway games

Throw stock: To award slum

Pig iron: A name for rides when they're taken apart to move on to the next town

Spoofers: Those really big stuffed animals that nobody ever seems to win

Red light job: When carnies try to collect their pay, and instead of finding the carnival manager, they find the carnival has packed up and moved on—all they see are red taillights.

World's shiniest living things: the metallic-blue berries of the *Pollia condensata* plant (Africa).

HOW TO EMBALM
A DEAD BODY

Ever wonder what happens to you after you die? We're not talking about your soul—that's your problem. We're talking about the body you leave behind. Here's how a lot of us will end up. Warning: if you've recently lost a loved one or you're even a little squeamish, you might want to skip this article. (It's a little gruesome.)

THE BEGINNING OF THE END

When a person dies, relatives or a hospital typically request the services of a funeral home. After a medical examiner signs off (if the person died of a traumatic injury), the body is sent to the funeral home to be prepared for burial, or, more specifically, to be embalmed. The funeral director, formerly known as a "mortician" or "undertaker," gets to work right away. If too much time passes, the body will have to be refrigerated, because decay and rigor mortis begin developing immediately. In addition to using protective plastic gear (apron, gown, surgical cap, etc.) during the embalming process, the embalmer is required by OSHA regulations to wear a respirator. Not breathing the fumes in and around the body helps prevent the transmission of diseases. Here is a step-by-step description of the modern embalming process.

1. After arriving at the funeral home, the body is "prepped" on a porcelain embalming table in the "prep room." To slow decay, the room is kept quite cold—no higher than 50°F. All of the deceased's clothing, bandages, catheters, leftover medical equipment, jewelry, and any other inorganic objects are removed from the body and disposed of or set aside.

2. The mortician uses a disinfectant to wipe clean the eyes, mouth, all of the various body cavities, and all of the skin, head to toe.

3. The biggest workplace hazard for a mortician: rigor mortis, the posthumous stiffening of the limbs and joints. So he or she temporarily offsets and delays rigor mortis by massaging major muscles, and gently moving the arms, legs, and head back and forth and around. Why gentle? So that nothing breaks or pops.

The saddle shape of a Pringles chip is mathematically known as a *hyperbolic paraboloid.*

4. The corpse's face is shaved. Even women and children are shaved —everyone has a fine layer of facial hair or fuzz that can make funeral makeup apply improperly and look strange.

5. The mouth tends to hang open after death, so the mortician takes care of that by stuffing it with cotton, and then uses a device called a "needle injector." The metal gunlike object shoots a wire into the upper gums. The mortician then shoots another wire into the lower gums. The wires from each are then pulled together and twisted until the mouth is securely closed. The excess wire is cut off so it's not visible.

6. Now the mortician is ready to begin preparing the inside of the body. First, he or she uses a scalpel to make an incision on the right clavicle, or collar bone, just above the sternum. The skin flops open, allowing the mortician to search through the flesh until he finds what he's looking for: the thick white carotid artery. He ties it off with medical-grade twine. This prevents blood from flowing where the mortician does not want it to go.

7. Next, he locates and cuts open the jugular vein—that's where the blood will exit the body when it's flushed out with embalming solution.

8. The embalming chemicals are prepared in a large glass container. Formaldehyde is mixed with a chemical called Metaflow, which helps the formaldehyde flow better and pick up more blood. Also added to the solution: a vein-hardening chemical called Chroma-tech along with water to help keep the body hydrated.

9. The mixture is then poured into an "embalming machine." It looks like a large cylindrical aquarium with a thick plastic tube connected to it. The other end of the tube connects to a thin, L-shaped metal pipe called an "arterial tube," which is inserted into the carotid artery located in the neck.

10. The thick embalming fluid flows out of the machine, through the tubes, and into the body, where it stays. With nowhere to go, the blood is pushed out of the body through the jugular vein and is washed down the drain.

11. As the fluid flows and fills up the body—it takes between 60 and 90 minutes—the mortician massages the legs and arms to make sure the blood flows out at a proper rate and that embalming fluid doesn't get stuck in small passageways.

12. The fluid restores color to the arms, legs, and face. It makes the body's cheeks look rosier, and more lifelike.

13. The temporary preservation of the body is now well in hand, but there's one thing left that could potentially make a big stink: internal organs, which are full of organic fluids. The mortician uses a tool called a "trocar," a two-foot-long metal tube attached to a plastic hose, and a power suction source called a "hydroaspirator." One end is pointed, and it's inserted in the stomach, just above and to the left of the bellybutton. The mortician then pokes around the central body cavity to find the spleen, the kidneys, and the liver. He punctures each one, and sucks out the fluid.

14. Next, the mortician reverses the hydroaspirator, and the trocar pumps in a preserving solution.

15. The abdominal incision is filled up with cotton and then sewn shut with a "baseball suture," so named because the stitching looks like the stitches on a baseball.

16. If the deceased suffered from a long illness, chances are his or her face may look emaciated. If that's the case, the mortician uses a syringe filled with a pink gel known as "tissue fixer" to plump up the nose, ears, and brow.

17. To preserve facial features further, the mortician may insert cotton balls inside the nasal cavity, eyelids, or mouth. He might even glue the eyeballs to the eyelids to keep them shut.

18. To prevent the body from drying out and looking crusty or flaky at the funeral, the mortician uses a cream-based moisturizer on the face and hands. Makeup is applied to the face as well, to cover up any bruises or lesions visible on the face, neck, or hands.

20. The mortician then clothes the body (usually with something selected by the family) and places the right hand over the left, so that the body appears "at peace."

21. The deceased is then placed in a coffin and is ready for a public viewing or funeral.

When Teddy Roosevelt went on safari in Africa in 1909, he took 500 gallons of beer with him.

TASTELESS TOYS

It's sad that this book's most violent, sex-laden, and cringeworthy article is about things that kids are supposed to play with.

L ITTLE LOST BABY. Sold in the 1960s, Ideal Toy Company's 22-inch baby doll came with a note explaining that she was abandoned; the little girl was supposed to find the baby on her doorstep and "raise it" herself. That's not the only odd thing about Little Lost Baby: She has three faces. By pulling a lever on the back of the doll's neck, her head spins (*Exorcist*-style) inside a non-removable pink hood to reveal a sleeping face, a laughing face, or a crying face (the latter two have creepy sound effects). If one of the baby's faces isn't looking straight ahead, two faces appear at the same time, looking in opposite directions.

MIDGE HADLEY. This doll, known as "Barbie's pregnant friend," actually "gives birth" to a curled-up diapered baby that's attached to a magnet inside Midge's removable round tummy. After receiving a slew of complaints that Midge promoted teen pregnancy (most kids think of Barbie and her friends as teenagers) and that she's supposed to be "happily married" but wears no wedding ring, Wal-mart pulled the doll from store shelves in 2002.

"POOP PATROL BARBIE". Here's how you play with Poop Patrol Barbie: First, "feed" her yellow Labrador retriever—named Tanner—a little tube-shaped piece of "food," and then crank Tanner's tail until it falls out of his butt. But the fun's not over: You and Barbie can then scoop up the poop (pooper-scooper included) and throw it away in a little trash can (also included). The fun resumes when you fish the poop out of the trash and feed it to Tanner again.

JIBBA JABBER. Released in the 1990s by American toy company Ertl, the original Jibba Jabber was a plush doll with a round cartoony face and a long black neck. Grab the doll by the neck, start shaking, and it makes a kind of choking-gurgling noise. After parents complained that the doll encourages violence toward children, Ertl recalled it and released a "tamer" version in which the doll chokes-gurgles no matter where you shake it. The new version, this time marketed to stressed-out corporate executives, comes with a pamphlet inside the box that reads, "It's OK to shake Jibba Jabber. It's never OK to shake a child."

KABA KICK. This Japanese game teaches a skill every kid should know: how to play Russian Roulette. Each player holds a pink hippo-shaped toy gun up to his or her forehead, and pulls the trigger. If the gun "fires," two hippo feet pop out and kick the unlucky player in the temple. The game part: If the gun doesn't fire, you get points.

WOLVERINE SQUEAKY HAMMER. This inflatable toy hammer is no bootleg—it's an officially licensed product and features a picture of the metal-clawed X-Man at the base of the handle. Only problem: The hammer's blow-up nozzle, which protrudes from the handle, is located right where Wolverine's… little wolverine would be.

THE PUNISHER SHAPE-SHIFTER. One-upping the Wolverine Squeaky Hammer, this Punisher superhero action figure comes with a large "power pistol" that emerges from his crotch. Insert a plastic spear into the tip, pull back on the sleeve, and watch the crotch gun shoot the spear across the room. (Bonus: It converts into a handgun, and the rocket shoots out of the Punisher's other end.)

HAZMAT FIGURINE SET. German toy maker Playmobil has a number of "Playworld" sets that let kids pretend they have adult jobs. From the product description of this one: "Oh, no! Hazardous waste has managed to seep out of a barrel and onto the sidewalk! No need to worry, the Hazmat Crew has promptly arrived. Dressed in protective uniforms and armed with hazardous material equipment, this sidewalk is sure to be free of this hazardous substance in no time! Ages 4 & Up."

AIRPORT SECURITY PLAY SET. Another in the Playmobil "Playworld" series, this $58 set allows kids to reenact the excitement of going through the security line at the airport.

CRAPPY PRODUCTS

Sure, poop smells bad and carries disease, but thanks to modern technology, today it can be rendered odor-free and sterilized. Result: It's now being recycled into...

- **Fecal Fuel:** For eons, especially in places with few trees, people have burned dried manure for heat and cooking. More recently, people have begun collecting the flammable methane that escapes from composting poop. Some California dairy farmers are doing it in a big way, running their trucks on homegrown biomethane.

- **Eau de Odure:** Whale poop called *ambergris* is used as the base scent in fine perfumes. It's a fatty deposit that develops when sperm whales eat squids. The squid's indigestible beak gets snagged in the whale's intestines, and the whale's body generates a smooth choles-terol glob that hardens around it. The glob is eventually excreted, and after floating through the ocean for a while, may wash up on a beach. If you find one, hold your nose and take it home; perfume manufacturers may pay $1 million for a large one.

- **Poopy Paper:** You can now buy paper made from the poop from vegetarian animals, including pandas, cows, elephants, moose, don-keys, zebras, and horses. (Don't worry. It smells like regular paper.)

- **Merde Medicine:** Ancient Egyptians used a spermicidal mix of crocodile dung and honey for birth control. A medieval cure for baldness had you rub goose poop onto your scalp. Two recent developments: 1) researchers have transplanted poop from healthy donors into the intestines of patients suffering from *Clostridium difficile* infections (persistent diarrhea), and 2) researchers report that muskrat dung contains an antibiotic that fights salmonella and staph infections, as well as a natural insecticide that kills termites.

- **B.M. (Building Materials):** Manure can be used like clay for stuccoing and waterproofing huts, buckets, baskets, and beehives. An Indonesian company recently began making bricks from dung. They turned out to be stronger and lighter than clay bricks.

- **Shampoo from Real Poo:** A Japanese scientist claims to be able to extract vanilla from cow dung that is chemically identical to natural vanilla. There are no plans to use it in food (whew!), but candles, cosmetics, and hair care products, yes.

The two most popular days to get married in Las Vegas: Valentine's Day and New Year's Eve.

MICROSOFT MILLIONAIRES

We all dream of being in exactly the right place at the right time—to be holding an empty bucket when it starts raining money. Or to be working for the right company when they go public.

TAKING STOCK

When Bill Gates and his partner Paul Allen got Microsoft up and running in the late 1970s, they couldn't always afford to pay their staff what they were owed. In lieu of overtime pay or bonuses for the grueling hours of work it took to get software like Windows and Word to the marketplace, employees were given stock options. When Microsoft filed its IPO in 1986, people holding those options became instantly wealthy, or "Microsoft Millionaires" as they were called by the press. In all, stock options for Microsoft employees in the '80s and '90s created three billionaires and more than 12,000 millionaires. Here are some of those folks who went on to live pretty notable lives, post-Microsoft.

CHARLES SIMONYI

At Microsoft: Simonyi started working there in 1981. He was on the teams that developed Microsoft Word and Excel, which became the world's leading word-processing and spreadsheet programs.

After Microsoft: He left Microsoft in 2002 to found his own software company. Now he's a hobbyist pilot who's logged more than 2,000 hours of flight time. That experience—and his deep pockets—enabled him to buy his way onto a spaceflight. Twice. In 2007, he was aboard a Russian Soyuz rocket. Two years later, he teamed up with a private spaceflight contractor to reach the International Space Station. More impressively, he dated Martha Stewart for 15 years.

RICHARD BRODIE

At Microsoft: Simonyi hired Brodie to head up the Microsoft Application Division in 1981. Brodie was the chief author of the word-processing programs Microsoft Word and Notepad. He was so good that Gates promoted him to be his personal technical assistant two years later, where Brodie developed Word for Windows and the database-management program Microsoft Access.

After Microsoft: In 1986, Brodie left the company, and while he was filthy rich, he wasn't happy. After reading scores of self-improvement lectures, exploring religions, and attending retreats trying to figure out why, he wrote two self-help books, *Getting Past OK* and *Virus of the Mind*. Then, in 2003, he became a professional poker player. And he's pretty good—Brodie was a top finisher in five World Series of Poker tournaments. In 2007, Harrah's banned him from all of their casinos in Arizona, Nevada, and California. He'd won so much money at video poker, they thought he was cheating. (The ban was later lifted.)

STEPHANIE DEVAAN

At Microsoft: DeVaan went to work for Microsoft in 1990 as a marketing manager for Microsoft Word and Excel.

After Microsoft: She cashed in her stock options when she left in 1995 and was an instant millionaire. In 2002, after working for several charities, she founded a political action committee called Washington Women for Choice, which lobbies the state legislature on women's health issues and offers financial support to state-office candidates who support the same causes.

GABE NEWELL

At Microsoft: Newell joined Microsoft in 1983, working as a producer on the first three releases of the Windows operating system.

After Microsoft: In 1996, Newell left Microsoft to follow his passion—video games. With another ex-Microsoft employee, he started the Valve Corporation, a game producer and distributor. Valve released the extremely popular games *Half-Life* and *Half-Life 2*, which combined have sold more than 20 million copies.

RIC WEILAND

At Microsoft: Weiland went to high school with Microsoft founders Bill Gates and Paul Allen. (He was in a computer programmers group with them.) In 1976, he became one of the company's first five employees, joining his friends at the company's headquarters in Albuquerque, New Mexico. Weiland helped develop two major

In ancient Egypt, women could conduct business, own property, and get divorced.

computer languages—BASIC and COBOL—and was the project leader for Microsoft Works.

After Microsoft: He left the company in 1988, and because he was one of the first employees, he was also one the richest, flush with tens of millions of dollars. Sadly, he suffered from depression and in 2006, at age 53, took his own life. Openly gay, Weiland donated more than $35 million to gay rights organizations and AIDS charities during his lifetime. After he died, the Pride Foundation of Seattle revealed that he had bequeathed $65 million to them.

BOB GREENBERG

At Microsoft: He met Bill Gates at Harvard University in the mid-1970s. When Gates left school to start his software company, Greenberg, a programmer, was one of the first people he hired. His project: To help develop the BASIC computer language with Ric Weiland. He was also an early investor. When Microsoft was short on cash in 1977, Greenberg loaned Gates $7,000.

After Microsoft: In 1981, Greenberg left Microsoft and returned to his family's business, Coleco Toys. He helped lead Coleco to its biggest success, and one of the biggest toys of the 1980s—Cabbage Patch Kids dolls, which boomed…and busted, causing Coleco to declare bankruptcy in 1988. Luckily, he still had his Microsoft stock options, with his loan repaid in full thousands of times over.

CHRIS PETERS

At Microsoft: He worked first as a programmer, helping develop Microsoft Office and working on the software that made Microsoft's first mouse operate. Over his 18 years with the company, he rose to the position of vice-president.

After Microsoft: Peters' favorite pastime growing up was bowling with his dad. So when he left Microsoft, he tried out for the Professional Bowlers Association. He didn't make the cut. But in 1999, he heard that the PBA was on the brink of bankruptcy and was consequently for sale. Reason: Pro bowling attendance and TV ratings had dropped dramatically from their height in the 1970s. So Peters used $5 million of his own money and, along with some other rich friends, bought the PBA and moved it to Seattle. The cash infusion from chairman Peters saved the league. It was profitable within five years.

NATHAN MYHRVOLD

At Microsoft: Nathan Myhrvold started a software company called Dynamical Systems in the early '80s. Microsoft bought it in 1986, and Gates brought Myhrvold onto Microsoft's staff as chief technology officer.

After Microsoft: He cashed out in 1999. With money not a concern, Myhrvold pursues a number of passions. For example, he's a widely published nature photographer, goes on paleontological digs, trained to be a master chef in France just for the fun of it, won a barbecue championship, and runs a venture capital firm.

PATRICK AWUAH

At Microsoft: Awuah emigrated to America from his native Ghana when he was a teenager. A naturally gifted programmer, he was hired at Microsoft in 1981 where, as a program manager, he developed dial-up Internet and networking software. By the time he was 30, stock options had made him a multimillionaire.

After Microsoft: In 2001, Awuah founded Ashesi University, a small private four-year college in Accra, Ghana, that focuses on business and technology. In 2004, he returned to the United States to attend Swarthmore College and get a degree himself.

JAMEN SHIVELY

At Microsoft: Under Shively, the executive in charge of managing corporate strategy, Microsoft became one of the largest and most valuable companies in the world.

After Microsoft: In the 1980s, Microsoft was at the forefront of a new Washington state-based industry—software. Thirty years later, Shively found himself at the forefront of another new Washington-based industry—retail marijuana stores. In 2012, Washington voters approved legalizing marijuana for recreational use. In May 2013, Shively held a press conference to announce that he was investing $100 million in a chain of upscale marijuana retailers called Diego Pellicer (named for his great-great-grandfather). Joining forces with medical marijuana dispensaries in Washington, Colorado, and California, Shively says the stores will be "the Starbucks of pot" and that legalized marijuana will "mint more millionaires than Microsoft."

KNOW YOUR ICE

…So you'll never mistake cat ice for lard ice.

Ice Jam: An accumulation of broken ice in a narrow channel. When moving ice gets trapped, the blockage can cause flooding behind the jam, and flooding in front when the jam gives way. Some prehistoric ice jams led to megafloods that shaped modern landscapes.

Ice Foot: A wall or ledge of sea ice frozen to the shore, created by the rise and fall of the tide as well as wave spray. Also called ice dunes.

Pack Ice: Floating ice that's been driven together by wind or current to form a large free-floating body of ice. Pack ice is large enough to calm sea swells and covers approximately 12 percent of the world's oceans.

Stone Ice: A body of clear ice found in permanently frozen ground. It's also called subsoil ice, ground ice, subterranean ice, and, depending on its age, fossil ice.

Lard Ice (or Grease Ice): A slushy thin skin of ice crystals in the early stages of freezing. It sits on the sea surface and has an oily, greasy appearance.

Frazil Ice: Ice crystals that form in cold turbulent water. Because the water is constantly moving, it can't freeze into sheets, so it remains slush.

Pancake Ice: Circular pieces of sea ice that form when lard ice accumulates. These free-floating "pancakes" collide and develop a slushy rim that freezes and forms a raised edge. Pancakes can get up to 10 feet across and 4 inches thick.

Cat Ice: A thin delicate sheet that remains when the water level drops, leaving a gap between the water and the ice.

Fast Ice: Sea ice attached to a coast. Why is it called fast ice? Because it is *fastened* to land, or landfast.

Needle Ice: When the air temperature is below freezing and the soil temperature is above freezing, groundwater pushes toward the surface and freezes in needle-like columns of ice. Also called frost pillars.

Old Ice: Any sea ice that lasts more than a single melt season. It's less salty and much stronger than young ice.

The game *Monopoly* was illegal in the Soviet Union.

BALLPARK EATS

*It's not just peanuts and Cracker Jack anymore. Here are some
of the more inventive—and gut-busting—concessions
from professional baseball stadiums.*

StrasBurger (Nationals Park)

Named after star Washington Nationals pitcher Stephen
Strasburg, the StrasBurger is a gourmet version of the Mc-
Donald's Big Mac, with beef, special sauce, lettuce, and cheese. Oh,
and it weighs eight pounds.

Victory Knot (Dodgers Stadium)

It's a two-pound pretzel the size of home plate. Three different
dipping sauces—chipotle mustard, sweet cinnamon crème, and beer
cheese—are served inside the three loops of the pretzel.

Meat Lover's Hot Dog (Great American Ballpark, Cincinnati)

First, it's a breaded, deep-fried hot dog, then it's topped with local
Cincinnati-style chili (it's heavy on the cinnamon), a giant mound
of pepper jack cheese, and slices of deep-fried salami.

Murph-a-dilla (Rangers Ballpark)

Named after Texas Rangers outfielder David Murphy, it starts with
a 24-inch-long paper tray lined with Doritos, which is then topped
with a 24-inch-long quesadilla filled with beef brisket and cheese.
It's then topped with lettuce, salsa, and more cheese.

Rocky Mountain Oysters (Coors Field)

Rocky Mountain oysters are a regional delicacy out West, but
they're not oysters—they're deep-fried bull testicles. And you can
get a plate of them (with fries) in Denver while you watch the
Colorado Rockies.

Pulled Pork Parfait (Miller Park)

This treat, served in Milwaukee, looks like an ice-cream sundae,
except the ice cream is mashed potatoes, and the chocolate sauce
is sauce-drenched pulled pork. (The chives on top look like the
sprinkles.)

There are 2 types of toilet paper: Virgin (from pulped wood) and non-virgin (recycled paper).

The Walk Off (Camden Yards)

Baltimore is a port town and a major center of the crabbing industry. The Walk Off is a foot-long sausage, served in a pretzel roll, then topped with hunks of crab dip and sprinkled with Old Bay, the traditional crab seasoning.

The Hammer (Turner Field, Atlanta)

The Braves serve this Southern take on a chicken sandwich (named for Braves legend "Hammerin'" Hank Aaron). The chicken is fried and topped with bacon, cheese, and pecan-maple mayonnaise. And instead of bread: waffles.

The Moby Dick (Classic Park)

The minor league Lake County Captains play in Eastlake, Ohio, within home-run distance of Lake Erie, and their concessions menu offers one monster of a sandwich. The Moby Dick is a 15-inch hoagie roll filled with fried fish, clams, cheese, fries, coleslaw, and tartar sauce. This three-pound whale has more than 4,000 calories.

Funnel Dog (Arvest Ballpark, Springdale, Arkansas)

The Northwest Arkansas Naturals are a AA-league team, but they feature major-league concessions like this one: a hot dog on a stick (like a corn dog) that's coated in funnel cake batter (not cornmeal), then deep-fried.

The Baco (Fifth Third Ballpark, Comstock Park, Michigan)

Served at games played by the A-league West Michigan Whitecaps, the "baco" is pronounced "bay-co," as in "bacon." It's a taco with all the usual taco fillings, except that the shell is made entirely out of crispy bacon.

*   *   *

IDENTITY CRISIS, TEXAS STYLE

• The Dallas Cowboys play in Arlington, Texas, at AT&T Stadium. That stadium is also home to college football's Cotton Bowl game, which is no longer held at the Dallas stadium that's actually named the Cotton Bowl.

• The Texas Roadhouse restaurant chain was started in Indiana by a man who initially wanted to run a "Colorado-themed" restaurant.

THE COST OF WAR

Whether you're a history buff or just someone who keeps up with current events, you've probably wondered how the cost of the wars in Iraq and Afghanistan compare to, say, the Vietnam War. Or how the cost of the Civil War compares to World War I or World War II. Here are some estimates taken from official U.S. government reports.

Revolutionary War (1775–83)
Cost at the time: $101 million
In 2011 dollars: $2.4 billion

The War of 1812 (1812–15)
Cost at the time: $90 million
In 2011 dollars: $1.55 billion

The Mexican War (1846–48)
Cost at the time: $71 million
In 2011 dollars: $2.37 billion

Civil War, Union (1861–65)
Cost at the time: $3.1 billion
In 2011 dollars: $59.6 billion

Civil War, Confederacy
Cost at the time: $1 billion
In 2011 dollars: $20.1 billion

The Spanish American War (1898)
Cost at the time: $283 million
In 2011 dollars: $9 billion

World War I (1917–1919)
Cost at the time: $20 billion
In 2011 dollars: $334 billion

World War II (1941–45)
Cost at the time: $296 billion
In 2011 dollars: $4.1 trillion

The Korean War (1950–53)
Cost at the time: $30 billion
In 2011 dollars: $341 billion

The Vietnam War (1965–75)
Cost at the time: $111 billion
In 2011 dollars: $738 billion

Persian Gulf War (1990–91)
Cost at the time: $61 billion
In 2011 dollars: $102 billion

Afghanistan War (2001–12)
Cost in 2012 dollars:
$823 billion

Iraq War (2003–2012)
Cost in 2012 dollars:
$557 billion

Note: Estimates include military operations only. They do not include veterans' benefits, interest on war-related debt, aid to allies, etc.

JUST PLANE WEIRD: BATHROOM EDITION

If you happen to be reading this in the bathroom of an airplane, you might want to turn to another page and save this one for when you're back on the ground (or at least out of the bathroom).

KNOCK, KNOCK

• In May 2013, the pilot of an Air India flight from New Delhi to Bangalore had to take a bathroom break. So he turned the controls over to the co-pilot and went to use the restroom, locking the cockpit door behind him. But when he returned from the bathroom, he couldn't get the cockpit door open again. Safety-wise there was no problem, since the co-pilot and a trainee pilot were still in the cockpit. But the sight of the pilot pounding on the cockpit door sent the passengers into a panic, forcing the co-pilot to make an emergency landing in Bhopal. It wasn't until the plane was safely on the ground that the maintenance crew was able to get the cockpit door open, after working on it for half an hour. Ninety minutes later the plane resumed its flight to Bangalore.

• In a similar incident aboard a Transavia flight to Crete a month earlier, a pilot returning from a bathroom break had to force his way into the cockpit after the co-pilot fell asleep at the controls and did not hear him calling over the intercom to be let back in.

WHY DIDN'T YOU GO BEFORE WE LEFT?

Just months after Ireland's no-frills airline Ryanair was attacked in the press for its plans to 1) convert the bathrooms on its Boeing 737 aircraft to pay toilets, and when that failed, 2) to remove two of the three toilets in its 189-seat passenger jets to free up room for six more paying customers, in July 2012, the airline got into trouble again when a leaked internal memo revealed that it was planning to fly its 737s even when all their toilets were out of order. "In the rare event there is a technical problem with all toilets on board, permission may be granted for the flight to depart with no serviceable toilets," the memo said. "Any passenger not wishing to travel can apply for a refund." (Ryanair's longest European flights

The word "julep," as in mint julep, comes from the Persian word *golab*, meaning "rose water."

last more than four hours.) In the event of such an emergency, the memo instructs staff at the departure gate to warn passengers to use airport bathrooms before boarding the plane and also directs the staff to apologize for the "inconvenience" caused. "There is no legal requirement for planes to have functioning toilets," said a spokesperson for the Association of British Travel Agents, "but it could be a pretty unpleasant experience and might be a step too far in the 'no-frills' concept."

THRONE INTO THE AIR

The passengers and crew aboard a Continental Airlines flight from the Netherlands to Newark, New Jersey, in 2007 may well have wished their toilets *had* been removed. About an hour into the flight an overpowering stench filled the plane, and one of the toilets began disgorging its contents into the cabin, down the aisle of the passenger compartment. The plane made an emergency landing in Shannon, Ireland, where the 168 passengers were put up in a hotel while the problem was "fixed." The next morning, the plane set off again…and the toilet overflowed a second time. This time the plane continued on to New Jersey, where engineers traced the source of the problem to "a blockage caused by someone flushing latex gloves down the toilet."

THE WANDERER

In July 2012, an 11-year-old boy named Liam Corcoran-Fort got bored while on a shopping errand with his mother in Manchester, England. He wandered off and happened to find a discarded ticket for the No. 19 bus. Liam, who is obsessed with airplanes, knew that the No. 19 goes to the airport. He hopped aboard the next one that came along, and when he arrived at the airport, he had to go to the bathroom. So he went and found one—on an airplane soon to depart for Rome. (Somehow he made it past airport security and onto the aircraft without anyone checking his ticket.) "I went in the bathroom and sat there, but I couldn't get out. Then—whoosh!— we were going up in the sky," he told the London *Times*. By the time the flight attendants realized they had an accidental stowaway, it was too late to turn back. Liam flew all the way to Rome and spent two hours in the airport before the airline put him on a flight back home. "I can't get my head around it," his mother told the *Times*.

"How did he get that far without anyone asking him one question? All I read about is how airport security is at the highest it has ever been." (For its part, the Manchester Airport says the public was never in danger. "The boy went through full security screening so the safety of the passengers and the aircraft was never compromised," said a spokesperson.)

POISON PEN

In February 2012, a British Airways flight attendant named Matthew Davis was working a flight from Tokyo to London when he found a note scrawled on one of the bathroom doors. It read, "The bomb on board will explode at 1600 GMT unless our demands are met." He passed the message to the pilot, who quickly determined that it was a hoax. He even figured out who wrote it: flight attendant Matthew Davis, who was hoping to become a hero and win a promotion for foiling his own "plot." The flight continued on to Tokyo without incident; when it landed Davis was arrested and taken to jail. He was fired from the airline, pled guilty to making the bomb threat, and was sentenced to six months in jail.

*　　*　　*

OXYMORONS
- leisure suit
- minor catastrophe
- objective opinion
- wireless cable
- stand down
- preliminary conclusion
- anxious patient
- talk show
- now then
- passive-agressive
- ill health
- long shorts
- black light
- Congressional leadership

The 1st Stanley Cup cost $48.57 in 1892. The hockey trophy is now insured for $1.5 million.

THE POLITICALLY CORRECT QUIZ

Well-intentioned political correctness can sometimes seem "ridiculous."
(Uh-oh—we hope the second syllable of that word doesn't offend anyone.)
Can you guess the correct answers? (Answers are on page 538.)

1. Shopping mall Santas in Sydney, Australia, revolted in 2007 after they were told to stop saying what?
a) "Ho-Ho-Ho." It could be construed as "derogatory toward women" because in the United States (not Australia) "ho" is slang for "prostitute." They were told to say "Ha-Ha-Ha" instead.
b) "Merry Christmas." Not everyone in Australia is Christian, so the Santas were instructed not to use the word "Christmas" under any circumstances.
c) "What would you like for Christmas?" They were told not to give children the impression that Santa *himself* would deliver their gifts, fearing that might lead to the children asking for more expensive items than the family could afford. Instead, the Santas were told to ask, "What would you like your parents to get you for Christmas?"

2. In 2013, a school in Essex, England, banned triangle-shaped waffles from the lunch menu. Why?
a) A group of Wiccan students was seen combining pairs of the triangle-shaped waffles into "black-magic pastry pentagrams."
b) The triangle is a symbol of the Gay Pride movement. School administrators said they do not discriminate against homosexuality, but they didn't want it to look like they were "in favor of it, either."
c) When thrown across the cafeteria, the "sharp corners" of the triangular waffles could injure a child's eye.

3. In 2010, why did Microsoft ban online gamer Josh Moore from playing Xbox Live after he filled out his user profile?
a) Among Moore's hobbies, he included "going clubbing," meaning "going to nightclubs," but Microsoft took it to mean that he was promoting violence by literally "clubbing" things.

Wink, wink: During Prohibition, U.S. wineries sold bottles of grape juice...

b) Moore listed his address in the town of Fort Gay, West Virginia, which Microsoft's customer service department thought he'd made up just to be offensive. "It's a real place," said Moore. "Look it up!"

c) Moore, a meteorologist, was wearing a ball cap in his profile picture with the initials "NWA" on it—a standard-issue cap from the National Weather Association. But Microsoft's customer service department thought he was promoting the '90s gangsta rap band N.W.A., which stands for "N***az with Attitude."

4. To raise awareness for their cause, in 2009, PETA (People for the Ethical Treatment of Animals) tried to change the name of...

a) Toad Suck, Arkansas, to Toad Save, Arkansas.

b) the Pet Shop Boys (British pop duo) to the Rescue Shelter Boys.

c) Notre Dame University to Neuter Dame University.

5. Why did Hallmark abruptly pull a graduation greeting card from store shelves in June 2010?

a) The NAACP (National Association for the Advancement of Colored People) complained that the astronomy-themed card used the term "black hole," which is degrading to African Americans.

b) The Humane Society complained that a cartoon depiction of a seal wearing a fur coat could "confuse graduates into believing that seals do not mind being slaughtered for clothing."

c) The National Organization on Disability complained that it made fun of disabled people. On the front: "Congrats on (barely) graduating! Your ride awaits!" The card opens up to reveal a picture of a "short bus" (the kind that carries mentally- and physically-challenged kids to school).

6. In an effort to not "discourage youngsters," a school headmaster in Harrow, England, prohibited teachers from...

a) lining up children by *any* criteria whatsoever, not even by height or surname. Any lineups must be done randomly by the teacher so that it does not appear that any students are "more preferred."

b) using the word "fail" to describe students who get failing grades; instead they must be told "they have room to grow."

c) using red ink to mark incorrect answers on homework and tests, because red ink implies failure, which can be too discouraging.

WHO'S JUDE?

*Many pop songs were inspired by someone with personal meaning
to the songwriter. And sometimes that someone is as famous
as the person who wrote the song.*

Uptown Girl."** One of Billy Joel's biggest hits, it's an auto-
biographical song about a blue-collar guy who falls for a girl
out of his league. Was it about Joel and his wife, supermodel
Christie Brinkley, who stars in the music video? No—he wrote it
about the girlfriend he had just before Brinkley: supermodel Elle
Macpherson.

"In Your Eyes." The romantic song that John Cusack played on
a hoisted boombox to Ione Skye in *Say Anything* was written by
singer-songwriter Peter Gabriel about his then-girlfriend Rosanna
Arquette. Toto's 1982 hit, "Rosanna," is also about Arquette…sort
of. She was dating keyboardist Steve Porcaro at the time, but singer
David Paich wrote the song about another girl; he just thought the
name Rosanna sounded better in the song.

"Hey, Jude." The name Jude is a corruption of Jules, which is a
nickname John Lennon gave his son Julian. Paul McCartney wrote
the song to comfort the child when his parents, John and Cynthia
Lennon, were divorcing so that Lennon could be with Yoko Ono.
(Lennon later claimed he only agreed to do the song because he
thought McCartney wrote it to comfort *him*.)

"Suicide Blonde." Michael Hutchence and Andrew Farriss of
INXS wrote this song for their 1990 album, *X*. At the time, Hutchence, the biggest rock star in Australia, was dating Kylie Minogue,
the biggest pop singer in Australia. Hutchence was inspired when
Minogue remarked one day, after dying her hair platinum for a
movie role, that she was going "suicide blonde."

"Kiss Them for Me." *Kiss Them for Me* was a 1957 movie based
on a play about Navy pilots on leave in San Francisco. The film
starred Cary Grant and Jayne Mansfield, but bombed and faded into
obscurity. In 1991, British alternative rock band Siouxsie and the
Banshees released a song called "Kiss Them for Me." Their biggest

hit in the U.S. (and only top 30 song), the song is a meditation on Mansfield, a major movie star and sex symbol who died in a brutal car accident at the age of 34. The references to Mansfield are as obscure as the movie *Kiss Them for Me*, including Mansfield's made-up favorite word, "divoon."

"Calypso." John Denver's 1975 hit is not a tribute to Harry Belafonte, nor the island music that had a brief run of popularity in the early 1950s. No, Denver was close friends with undersea explorer and naturalist Jacques Cousteau. *Calypso* was the name of Cousteau's research vessel; the song is a tribute to him.

"Ms. Jackson." This song by rap duo Outkast went to number 1 in 2001. Directed toward the disapproving mother of an ex-girlfriend, the rappers alternate verses, expressing common feelings after a romantic split—Andre 3000's are apologetic; Big Boi's detail his anger and frustration. Andre 3000 wrote the song after breaking up with R&B singer Erykah Badu, and "Ms. Jackson" is an open letter to Badu's mother, Kolleen Gipson.

"Night Shift." Two of the most influential figures in soul music died within a few weeks of each other in 1984—Jackie Wilson, who passed away after being in a coma for eight years, and Marvin Gaye, who was murdered by his father after an argument. The Commodores, a major funk and R&B band in the '70s, wrote the song to eulogize their fallen idols, referred to by name in the song. "Night Shift" went to number 3 on the pop chart, the group's first (and only) hit after lead singer Lionel Richie left the group.

"Abraham, Martin, and John." Dick Holler became a songwriter in the late '60s after his group, the Holidays, disbanded. In 1966, he had his first big hit: the Royal Guardsmen's million-selling novelty song "Snoopy vs. the Red Baron." In 1968, after the assassination of Martin Luther King Jr, Holler wrote a more serious song— "Abraham, Martin, and John" to pay tribute to three murdered civil rights icons: Abraham Lincoln, King, and John F. Kennedy. Just as former teen idol Dion DiMucci was set to record the song, JFK's brother, Robert Kennedy, was shot—and Holler hastily wrote a verse about him. (The song went to number 4—Dion's first hit in more than five years.)

All you can eat: A single Alaskan King Crab can yield over 6 pounds of meat.

SPECIAL UNDERWEAR

Who says underwear should only be clean and comfortable?

SMARTPANTS

Special Feature: "The world's first underwear for your iPhone"
Details: Made from silicon, these tiny and pointless (but fun) accessories for the iPhone create the appearance that the phone is wearing underpants. Choose from tighty-whities, boxer briefs, a leopard-print thong, and five other styles.

"POULTRY PAMPERS"

Special Feature: They're for *chickens*

Details: When chickens are injured by predators or from some other cause, sometimes it's better to let them heal indoors. For people who don't have barns, that can mean inside the home…which means chicken droppings all over the house. Or at least it did until several companies in the "avian accessory" industry started making diapers designed for chickens. The diapers are also popular with the growing number of people who keep chickens as house pets. And what's underwear without something to wear over it? Pampered Poultry, a company in New Hampshire, sells matching dresses for hens and tailcoats for roosters. "Dressing your poultry in the latest fashions can be so much fun!" says the company's website.

HOW YA HANGIN'? BOXER SHORTS

Special Feature: A new and improved "dual-vent fly"

Details: Conventional boxer shorts have a fastener—a snap or button—to keep the fly closed. Unfastened, the fly has a tendency to pop open, which can make the wearer "fall out" of his underwear. Inventor Max Hernandez's How Ya Hangin'? shorts have a "privacy" panel sewn inside the shorts so that if and when the fly does fly open, everything remains within. The fly is in the center, making it equally accessible for lefties or righties.

Bonus: The privacy panel can also serve as a "virtual billboard to display a marketing message," says Hernandez. "This kind of application can provide huge windfalls in the licensing market whether it's universities, NASCAR, or the NFL."

Sesame Street **quiz: Who's the only Muppet with a built-in smile? A. Ernie.**

ADULT SUMMER CAMPS

Why should the kids get all the fun? There are some real camps out there where grownups can spend a week and learn something new.

COWBOY CAMP. The Rockin' R Ranch in Antimony, Utah, operates three cattle drives each summer and lets paying guests come along for the ride. For four days, campers on horseback drive cattle through prairies and mountain ranges, sleeping under the stars at night. (Cost: $1,495)

CLOWN CAMP. At Camp Winnarainbow in Laytonville, California, adult campers spend six days learning clowning, improvisation, juggling, tightrope walking, magic tricks, how to walk on stilts, and how to ride a unicycle—everything a clown worth his red nose knows how to do. (Cost: $675)

SIDESHOW CAMP. If you've always yearned to be a sideshow freak, here's your chance. Sideshow School is a four-day course on bizarre skills and talents, held at historic Coney Island in Brooklyn, New York. Among the courses: fire eating, snake charming, sword swallowing, and glass walking. (Cost: $1000)

BOATBUILDING CAMP. In 1980, editors of *WoodenBoat* magazine started Wooden Boat School to preserve the craft of small-boat making. Now it's a summer camp. Each summer, more than 700 people sign up for one- or two-week sessions where they take classes such as "Carving" and "Fundamentals of Boatbuilding." Some students rent a house near the rural Maine camp, but most opt to sleep in cabin-like dorms on school grounds. (Cost: $750)

DANCE CAMP. Swing Out New Hampshire takes place for a week in late August at converted girls' summer camp. Stay in cabins, bathe in group showers…and learn old-timey dances such as the Lindy Hop, the Charleston, the Shim Sham, and the Jitterbug. (Also available: a class called "Hip Hop for Geeks.") After a day of dancing, rest your achy bones at the campfire sing-along each night. Dancing until dawn on the final night of camp is strongly encouraged. (Cost: $675)

ZOMBIE CAMP. Are you prepared for the zombie apocalypse? Should that unlikely event arise, a weekend at the Zombie Survival Course camp in southern New Jersey, about 60 minutes outside of Philadelphia, will teach you everything you need to know. Among the staff are firearm instructors, martial artists, personal trainers, and survival experts who will show you how to store emergency supplies. Camp owner Mark Scelza says he'll even teach you "how to hot-wire a car." (Cost: $425)

MERMAID CAMP. The Weeki Wachee resort in Spring Hill, Florida, was a popular (if cheesy) tourist destination in the 1960s and '70s. One of its most famous attractions was its "mermaids"—women dressed as mermaids who swam around all day in giant tanks. The resort is still open, and one of its attractions now is Sirens of the Deep Mermaid Camp, where campers receive two days of classes in underwater ballet. (Cost: $350)

ADULT SPACE ACADEMY. The U.S. Space & Rocket Center in Huntsville, Alabama, better known as "Space Camp," is best known for its kids' programs, but it also offers sessions for adults. Wannabe astronauts aged 18 and up can build and launch model rockets, train on the 1/16th gravity chair and the multi-axis trainer (it spins you up and down and around), climb a mountain on Mars, learn to repair a satellite, wear spacesuits, eat astronaut food, and more. They just have to do it in two days, not the five days that the kids get. (Cost: $595)

BOOZE CAMP. What's the most popular thing to do in the woods besides camping? Making moonshine, of course! Moonshine University, just outside of Louisville, Kentucky, offers classes, day camps, and week-long sessions to teach the skill of making corn whiskey and bourbon. Tasting is optional. (Cost: $100 per day)

GOOD OLD-FASHIONED SUMMER CAMP. When you think "summer camp," YMCA Camp Chief Ouray has a program that's probably exactly what you have in mind. Like the classic summer camps of your youth, this camp has beds in cabins, horseback riding, canoeing, swimming, archery, arts and crafts, and campfires, all against the backdrop of the Colorado River Valley. No one under 50 allowed. (Cost: $300)

ONCE UPON A TIME...

What's the most important part of a good story? The first line. A great one will make you want to read more, and after you've read the book, make you want to read it again. Here are some great opening lines from famous novels.

Whether I shall turn out to be the hero of my own life, or whether that station will be held by anybody else, these pages must show.

> **—David Copperfield (1850), Charles Dickens**

• "Christmas won't be Christmas without any presents," grumbled Jo, lying on the rug.

> **—Little Women (1868), Louisa May Alcott**

• They shoot the white girl first.

> **—Paradise (1998), Toni Morrison**

• It is a truth universally acknowledged, that a single man in possession of a good fortune must be in want of a wife.

> **—Pride and Prejudice, Jane Austen**

• It is a truth universally acknowledged that a zombie in possession of brains must be in want of more brains.

> **—Pride and Prejudice and Zombies (2009), Seth Grahame-Smith**

• The jury said "Guilty" and the Judge said "Life" but he didn't hear them.

> **—The Mansion (1959), William Faulkner**

• Stately, plump Buck Mulligan came from the stairhead, bearing a bowl of lather on which a mirror and a razor lay crossed.

> **—Ulysses (1922), James Joyce**

• The naked child ran out of the hide-covered lean-to toward the rocky beach at the bend in the small river.

> **—Clan of the Cave Bear (1980), Jean Auel**

Coffee beans have very little taste until they're roasted.

• It was inevitable: the scent of bitter almonds always reminded him of the fate of unrequited love.
—*Love in the Time of Cholera* (1988), Gabriel García Márquez

• Jack Torrance thought: *Officious little prick.*
—*The Shining* (1977), Stephen King

• In the week before their departure to Arrakis, when all the final scurrying about had reached a nearly unbearable frenzy, an old crone came to visit the mother of the boy, Paul.
—*Dune* (1965), Frank Herbert

• By human standards it could not possibly have been artificial: It was the size of a world.
—*Contact* (1985), Carl Sagan

• I have never begun a novel with more misgiving.
—*The Razor's Edge* (1944), W. Somerset Maugham

• He was an old man who fished alone in a skiff in the Gulf Stream and he had gone eighty-four days now without taking a fish.
—*The Old Man and the Sea* (1952), Ernest Hemingway

• A sharp clip-clop of iron-shod hoofs deadened and died away, and clouds of yellow dust drifted from under the cottonwoods out over the sage.
—*Riders of the Purple Sage* (1912), Zane Grey

• When Mr. Bilbo Baggins of Bag End announced that he would shortly be celebrating his eleventy-first birthday with a party of special magnificence, there was much talk and excitement in Hobbiton.
—*The Fellowship of the Ring* (1954), J.R.R. Tolkien

• James Bond, with two double bourbons inside him, sat in the final departure lounge of Miami Airport and thought about life and death.
—*Goldfinger* (1959), Ian Fleming

When Disneyland opened in July '55, the 110°F temps melted the asphalt on Main St.

DON'T EAT THE MONEY!

Reminder: The phrase "put your money where your mouth is" is not meant to be taken literally.

DIAMOND IN THE GUT
Miriam Tucker, 80, attended a fund-raiser in Tampa, Florida, in 2013. Each of the 400 guests paid $20 for a glass of champagne. At the bottom of 399 of the glasses was a cubic zirconia worth $10; one glass contained a 1.03-carat diamond worth $5,000. As the attendees were reaching into their glasses to see if they had the diamond, Tucker decided to take a sip first so she wouldn't have to stick her fingers in so far. In doing so, she accidentally swallowed the stone. Embarrassed, she didn't tell anyone and just sat and waited for whoever did have the diamond to scream in excitement. But no one screamed. That's when Tucker realized that *she'd* swallowed it. After failing to pass the stone, she had it removed during a colonoscopy. (Butt at least she got to keep it.)

FINE DINING

Sundance, a 12-year-old golden retriever, was waiting in the car in December 2012 while his owner—Wayne Klinkel of Helena, Montana—was eating at a restaurant. Hungry, Sundance managed to open the storage compartment between the front seats where Klinkel had stashed five $100 bills. Sundance ate them all. Determined to get his $500 back, Klinkel followed the dog around for a week—carefully retrieving, cleaning, and pasting together every scrap of undigested cash. Sadly, no bank would accept the mangled money. Klinkel has since asked the U.S. Treasury to exchange it, but was told that "standard claims" like his can take two to five years to process. At last report, Klinkel is still out his $500.

COINED

In 2012, Ratna Ahire, 29, of Mumbai, India, was having trouble swallowing food. She went to the doctor, but the X-rays were inconclusive, and her doctor was stumped. Ahire remembered that when she was a little girl, her brothers had tried to steal her 10-paisa coin (kind of like a dime). She hid it in her mouth, then accidentally swallowed it…and forgot about it. She told the doctor, who checked again and found the coin still stuck in her windpipe, partially corroded and with tissue growing around it. That's what was causing the blockage. Removing the coin was difficult—it took a team of 20 doctors and several procedures to get it out of there, but Ahire can now eat again.

SMUGGLER'S BLUES

While going through security in Panama's international airport, a 44-year-old Guatemalan woman was acting suspiciously. Officers detained her, sure she was hiding something. After a cavity search turned up empty (of contraband), they X-rayed her and discovered 39 bundles of cash totaling $31,000 in her stomach. The woman was taken to a hospital where, according to press reports, she was "expected to expel the remaining bundles."

HUMPTY MONEY

Poor, poor Zhao Zhiyong. The migrant worker from Shanghai, China, hid his life's savings of 7,200 yuan ($1,174) in a coat pocket in his closet. When he went to retrieve his money in March 2013, he discovered—to his horror—that an infestation of mice had reduced it to a "worthless heap of pink, white, and purple confetti." The good news: The Shanghai Rural Commercial Bank said it would exchange the mice-chewed cash for new cash. The bad news: only after Zhao Zhiyong can put the money back together again. (We'll let you know in a few years if he was able to do it.)

FOOL'S GOLD

In Dr. Michael Zuk's book, *Confessions of a Former Cosmetic Dentist*, he describes a scenario that happens in dentists' offices more often than you'd think: "We were checking the fit of a gold cap on a lower right molar, and the assistant's instrument slipped off. The cap spun towards the back of the patient's throat, and the patient began to choke. I just stood there and let him do his best to get it out, when he turned to me and said, 'I think I swallowed it.' I thought, you're lucky you just swallowed it. Worse things can happen." What's worse than swallowing a gold cap? Aspirating it into your lung. That would require emergency surgery. Swallowing it merely requires a little time….

Each year, about 450 men die of breast cancer in America.

"NATURALLY" BEAUTIFUL

Natural is often equated with "better," but sometimes it's just "weird." Would you apply this stuff to your body just to look good?

HAY
"Bathing" beneath great piles of warm, moist, fermenting hay is said to date back to 19th century Austria, when farmers in south Tyrol (now part of Italy) found that sleeping in barns filled with freshly cut hay left them feeling surprisingly refreshed in the morning. Today, it's a salon treatment, consisting of soaking the hay in 100° F water, then piling it on customers and wrapping them (and the hay) snugly in a blanket for 20 minutes. By that time, customers are sweating profusely and the "goodness" of the hay has entered the body through their wide-open pores.

BEE VENOM
The venom is "humanely" extracted from bees on a New Zealand farm, using electric current. It's then mixed with honey, shea butter (made from shea nuts), rose and lavender oils, and a secret ingredient, to make a facial-mask cream. When the cream is applied to your skin, the venom is said to trigger a mild chemical reaction, plumping and smoothing out wrinkles in the process. The treatment was invented by London beauty therapist Deborah Mitchell, who sells the venom cream at $130 for a 1.7 ounce jar, which holds just over three tablespoons. Sales soared in 2010 when it was revealed that Prince Charles's wife, Camilla, was a fan. Now "bee venom" face-lifts are available in upscale salons around the world. (So are face creams made with snake venom.)

LIVE SNAILS
This procedure, called the Celebrity Escargot Course, is offered by the Clinical Salon of Tokyo, Japan. It involves placing live snails on the customer's cheeks and forehead and letting them crawl around for 20 minutes or more. Advocates claim that fresh snail mucous contains proteins, antioxidants, and other substances that repair

damaged skin and restore a youthful glow. The salon's snails are fed an organic vegetarian diet of carrots, greens, spinach, and chard "to ensure that they are clean and healthy before being placed on customers' faces," and an assistant stands at the ready to nudge the snails away if they crawl too close to the eyes, nostrils, or mouth. After the snails are removed, creams containing still more snail mucous are massaged into the face so that "the live secretions fully penetrate the skin." The entire procedure takes about an hour. Cost: 24,000 yen, or about $250.

HUMAN BLOOD

Nicknamed the "vampire face-lift," this procedure was developed in response to public fears over the risks associated with synthetic "fillers" used to smooth out wrinkles. The patient's own blood is drawn and then spun in a centrifuge to separate out and collect the platelets. The platelets are injected back into the patient's face around crow's-feet and other problem areas, where they'll purportedly spur the production of collagen to fill in wrinkles. Cost: $1,500 for the 30-minute procedure. Only catch: While the FDA permits the procedure, it's so new that there's no guarantee it actually works. "Patients tolerate it beautifully," Michigan plastic surgeon Dr. Anthony Youn told the *New York Times*, "but I haven't seen any dramatic results yet."

BIRD POOP

Uguisu no fun ("nightingale feces") facial treatments originated in Japan centuries ago and may have started out as a makeup remover for geishas and kabuki actors. In the process of taking off all that heavy white zinc- and lead-based makeup, the bird turds also exfoliated and polished the skin, giving it a younger, fresher appearance (thanks, perhaps, to *guanine*, an compund in the poop). Today, *uguisu no fun* is produced on nightingale farms, where it is sun-dried and sterilized under ultraviolet lights. It is then ground into a fine powder and mixed with green tea, shea butter, and other ingredients to make a face cream. (If you have your bird-poop facial done at Hari's Salon in London's trendy South Kensington neighborhood, you can also have your hair moisturized with the salon's most popular treatment: organic bull semen. "The results speak for themselves," says owner Hari Salem. "The hair is soft but not limp.")

Seashell fossils have been found near the peaks of the Himalayan mountains.

LUCKY FINDS

*Ever stumbled upon something valuable or got something back
you lost decades ago? It's an incredible feeling. Here's the
latest installment of one of the BRI's regular features.*

A LITTLE TOO MUCH ACTION

The Find: A comic book

Where It Was Found: Inside a wall

The Story: David Gonzalez was renovating an old house to sell
in Elbow Lake, Minnesota, when he found a stack of newspapers
between the walls. Among them was an old comic book with Superman on the cover lifting a car above his head. Gonzales immediately knew this was *the* 1938 "Action Comics #1" that marked the
superhero's debut. Gonzales took it home to show to his family, but
his wife's aunt grabbed it out of his hand. "You don't have to act
so rude," he told her. "I brought you in to show you, don't grab it!"
Then he tried to snatch it back from her and—gasp!—ripped the
back cover! The tear severely diminished the comic's value, making
it worth "only" $175,000 when it sold at auction.

AN EVENTFUL FIND

The Find: A video game

Where It Was Found: At a thrift store

The Story: *Stadium Events* is considered the world's most valuable
video game. As we told you in *Uncle John's Heavy Duty Bathroom
Reader*, this track-and-field game was released by Bandai in 1987 to
go with its soft vinyl Family Fun Fitness Mat. But after Nintendo
bought the company, they rebranded the game as *World Class Track
Meet* and destroyed all unsold editions of *Stadium Events*. Of the 10
to 20 believed to exist today, only a few have been found, the latest
one by a North Carolina woman who bought it—still sealed in its
original packaging—for $7.99 at a local Goodwill store. She took
it to Save Point Video Games in Charlotte, North Carolina, where
owner Wilder Hamm told her it was the "holy grail" of video-game
finds. He didn't have enough money to purchase it, so she said she
would sell it on eBay. No word on how much she got, but another
copy of *Stadium Events* had recently sold for $41,000.

Why do birds cock their heads at the ground? To see bugs and worms.

DIAMOND IN THE ROUGH

The Find: A painting

Where It Was Found: A thrift store

The Story: Beth Feeback is an artist who specializes in cat portraits. One day in 2012, while shopping at a Goodwill store in Concord, North Carolina, she spent $9.99 on a large abstract painting of a red-and-blue square. Her plan was to dismantle the frame so she could paint on the blank side of the canvas, but a friend advised her to research the signature on the painting first…just in case. Good idea: Feeback discovered that the painting—called "Vertical Diamond"—was the work of Ilya Bolotowsky (1907–81), a Russian abstract painter who took the New York art world by storm in the 1920s. The painting sold for more than $27,000 at auction. With her windfall, Feeback bought brand new canvases that she's going to paint in the style of Bolotowsky…with big cat heads in the middle.

DOWN THE DRAIN

The Find: A class ring

Where It Was Found: In a sewer

The Story: In 1938, a high school student named Jesse Mattos was working in a butcher shop in Mount Shasta, California, when he dropped his class ring in the toilet and was unable to retrieve it. Seventy-three years later, a sanitation worker named Tony Congi was working in a sewer nearly 200 miles away when he found the ring. He had it cleaned, after which he noticed it was inscribed with the initials "JTM." He researched a copy of the school's 1938 yearbook and found the only student with those initials: Jesse Mattos. Congi contacted Mattos, now 90, and told him he found his ring. "What ring?" "The one you lost seventy-three years ago." Mattos told reporters that getting his class ring back was "neater than heck!"

BOND TIME

The Find: A watch

Where It Was Found: At a "car boot sale" (kind of like an American flea market)

The Story: In 2013, Christie's auction house in England announced it had obtained a rare piece of movie memorabilia: the Breitling "Geiger Counter" watch that James Bond (Sean Connery) wore in the 1965 film *Thunderball*. The watch's owner wasn't identified, but according to press reports, he picked it up for £25 at the sale...and bought it because he thought it looked a lot like the watch in the movie. It was. The watch was once kept in the prop department at Pinewood Studios, but no one had seen it for decades. It ended up selling for more than £100,000 (around $160,000).

BACKYARD BLING

The Find: A buried treasure

Where It Was Found: On a man's property

The Story: In 2007, an Austrian man named Andreas K. (last name withheld) was digging in his yard when he unearthed some old metal trinkets. They were covered in hard dirt, so Andreas just threw them all in a box and kept digging. A couple years later, he was preparing to move and found the box in his garage. When he looked inside, he noticed that some of the dirt had fallen off, revealing several very shiny objects, including rings, brooches, gold plates, and ornate belt buckles. He brought the nearly 200 objects to Austria's office of antiquities...and they were floored. Calling it a "fairy-tale find," the office's press report said, "This is one of the qualitatively most significant discoveries of medieval treasure in Austria." Estimated to be around 650 years old, the ornaments are "priceless." (No word on how much Andreas received for them.)

OUT OF THE PARK

The Find: A baseball bat

Where It Was Found: A garage sale

The Story: Sue McEntee of Des Moines, Iowa, had no idea that she owned a piece of history until she tried to sell it for a dollar at a yard sale. It just so happened that a "professional yard saler" named Bruce Scapecchi spotted it under a table in the driveway. He noticed right away that it was decades old, and the way the grip tape was wrapped told him it might be *very* special. He told McEntee to get a pencil eraser; then he lightly rubbed part of the bat, revealing the name "Robinson." And not just any Robinson—*Jackie* Robinson, the civil rights hero who integrated baseball in the 1940s. It all made sense to McEntee. Her late uncle had played on the Brooklyn Dodgers with Robinson. So how much is the bat worth? McEntee doesn't know and doesn't care. "It's staying in the family."

Better system? In ancient Athens, law-making council seats were filled by a lottery.

GIVE ME A SIGN!

Church reader boards are a great source of humor and wisdom.
Here are some real signs that we've collected.

"God didn't create anything without a purpose. But mosquitoes come close."

"At Jesus Way, take the right turn. Others go to Hell."

"Jesus would so-o-o smack you in the head!"

"Blessing of pets. Bring your dog or cat or whatever and lawnchair."

"Whoever is praying for snow, please stop."

"Watch your tongue. It's wet and slips easily."

"Bored? Try a missionary position."

"Triumph is umph added to try."

"You may party in Hell, but you will be the BBQ!"

"Christmas: Easier to spell than Hannukah."

"He who farts in church sits in own pew."

"You give God the credit, now give God the cash."

"To err is human, to arrrr is pirate."

"Do you know what Hell is? Come hear our preacher."

"The class on prophesy has been cancelled due to unforeseen circumstances."

"What part of 'Thou Shalt Not' don't you understand?"

"Honk if you love Jesus. Text while driving if you want to meet him."

"Changing churches? What difference does it make which one you stay home from?"

"Don't let worries kill you. Let the church help."

"How will you spend eternity? Smoking or non-smoking?"

"Get behind me, Satin."

"Whoever stole our AC units keep one. It is hot where you're going."

"Hate corny church signs? Amen!"

THE PURLOINED POTTIES

*Just about everyone who's fought in a war and has lived to tell
the tale has brought home a souvenir or two. Here are the
stories of two very unusual trophies from World War II.*

D OWNFALL
On May 4, 1945, U.S. Army Sergeant Ragnvald C. Borch
was asked to accompany the French Army as it assaulted
Adolf Hitler's alpine retreat, called the Berghof, in the Bavarian
Alps above the village of Berchtesgaden. By that time, the war in
Europe had just three days to go. Hitler was already dead—he'd
committed suicide in his Berlin bunker on April 30—and Germany
would surrender unconditionally on May 7. The Berghof was a
bombed-out ruin, and the French troops weren't expecting much
resistance. But they thought Ragnvald, who spoke German, would
be useful if they did encounter any Nazis there.

The Allies had strict rules against looting, "but this was Berchtesgaden," Irmgard A. Hunt recounted in her memoir *On Hitler's
Mountain*, "and the soldiers were given free rein to plunder the
town." Having endured more than four years of brutal occupation
by the Germans, the French soldiers were happy to help themselves
to whatever souvenirs remained in Hitler's vacation home.

HAVE A SEAT

Only problem: There wasn't much left to plunder. After the high-
ranking Nazis fled the area ahead of the Allied advance, and before
the Allies actually arrived, the locals had made their way up the hill
and stripped the Berghof and the nearby homes of other Nazi elites
of everything that could be carried off—furniture, china, silverware,
even the pictures on the wall. By the time Borch and the French
troops arrived, there was almost nothing left to take.

But as Borch wandered through the Berghof, he did spot one
item that had been overlooked by the locals. Moving from Hitler's
bedroom into the adjacent bathroom, Borch noticed that Hitler's
toilet was still there. That would have been too heavy for him to
carry off…but the Führer's toilet seat, still attached to the bowl and
largely unscathed, would be easy to take.

…yielded 30 mins. of talk time. It took 10 more years to bring to market and cost $3,995.

Borch liberated the toilet seat, and as soon as he could, he mailed it back home to New Jersey. After the war, he had a special frame made for it, so that he could hang it on the wall in his house. He never made a big deal about owning the toilet seat, but he did show it to friends. "Well, this is where Hitler used to do his thinking," he'd joke. Because Borch never sought any publicity, few people even knew that the toilet seat existed.

Borch died in 1968, and his wife, Helen, passed away in 2010. When she died, the toilet seat passed to their son Michael. He was the one who went public with the tale. "I think it's time the story of the toilet should be told," he told the *London Telegraph* in December 2012.

TWO OF A KIND

But that's not the only Führer crapper that resides in the Garden State. Seventy miles away, in Florence, New Jersey, a shop called Greg's Auto Repair owns an entire toilet that belonged to Hitler. A year after seizing power in 1933, Hitler ordered the construction of a new German state yacht called the *Aviso Grille*. The ship is known to have transported Hitler on at least one occasion, but the dictator was prone to seasickness and did not use it very often, so he may never have used the yacht's toilet facilities. (Although it is possible that he *barfed* into it during a bout of seasickness.) Whatever the case, after World War II ended, the *Aviso Grille* was towed to a shipyard in New Jersey. Any thought of saving the ship went out the window when it was discovered that shipyard owner Harry Doan was giving tours to curiosity seekers. Afraid the *Aviso Grille* could become a floating memorial to Adolf Hitler, the U.S. government ordered it scrapped in 1951.

Doan often played poker with Sam Carlani, the original owner of the auto-repair shop, and when the *Aviso Grille* was broken up, Doan gave the pot to his pal. The toilet was installed in the auto shop and remained in service until 2012, when it finally stopped working. That's when the shop's current owner, Greg Kohfeldt, dragged it out to the front of the shop so that people could see it better. "It was more of a tourist attraction when it was working," Kohfeldt told reporters in 2013. "People would come in and want to see it flush and want to use it. Now it just kind of sits there. I'm contemplating mounting it on the wall."

Soda jerks: A Coca-Cola employee was once fired for marrying a Pepsi employee.

DEAD CELEBRITIES (WHO WEREN'T)

When it was feared Mark Twain had died in 1897, he responded to the rumors by famously telling the New York Journal, *"The report of my death was an exaggeration." Here are some other famous folks who suffered similar fates…sometimes at their own hand.*

MARGARET THATCHER (1925–2013)
Claim to Fame: British Prime Minister from 1979 to 1990
Faux-bituary: In November 2009, more than 1,700 members of Canada's Conservative Party were gathered at a black-tie dinner in Toronto when Transport Minister John Baird, at home in Ottawa, texted a colleague at the dinner, "Thatcher has died." At the time, the Iron Lady was 84 and not in the best of health, so the news wasn't surprising. Word spread quickly through the gathering, and Canadian Prime Minister Stephen Harper dispatched an aide to draft an official statement of condolence. Calls were also made to No. 10 Downing Street (the UK Prime Minister's official residence in London) and Buckingham Palace…where puzzled officials at both places assured the Canadians that Lady Thatcher was very much alive. What caused the mix-up? Some 20 minutes after Baird sent his "Thatcher has died" text, he sent a second one clarifying that he was talking about his cat, a 16-year-old tabby he'd named Thatcher in honor of the conservative icon.

KEN KESEY (1935–2001)

Claim to Fame: Kesey, whom the *New York Times* described as the "Pied piper of the psychedelic era," was the author of the bestselling 1962 novel *One Flew Over the Cuckoo's Nest* and also the central character in Tom Wolfe's nonfiction book *The Electric Kool-Aid Acid Test.*

Faux-bituary: Kesey may have been famous for his Acid Test parties, but he'd hosted those back when the drug LSD was still legal. It was his use of marijuana that got him into trouble with the law: After two arrests for pot possession in 1966, rather than risk jail time, Kesey parked his pickup next to a cliff on the California coast and left a fake suicide note in the truck. Then a friend smuggled him into Mexico in the trunk of a car. "LSD GURU SUICIDE!" read one newspaper headline after the pickup was discovered. Kesey hid in Mexico for eight months before returning home to face the drug charges. He ended up serving a six-month sentence on a work farm.

SAMUEL TAYLOR COLERIDGE (1772–1834)

Claim to Fame: English writer and philosopher, best known for his poems *Kubla Khan* and *The Rime of the Ancient Mariner*, the latter of which was the source of the metaphor of an albatross around a person's neck and the line, "Water, water everywhere / Nor any drop to drink."

Faux-bituary: In 1813, Coleridge was sitting in a coffee house when he overheard a man discussing a newspaper article he'd just read about Coleridge's "suicide." The man remarked, "It was very extraordinary that Coleridge, the poet, should have hanged himself just after the success of his play."

Coleridge replied, "Indeed, sir, it is a most extraordinary thing that he should have hanged himself, be the subject of an inquest, and yet that he should at this moment be speaking to you."

The confusion stemmed from an incident in London's Hyde Park, where a "stout and well-dressed man" had hanged himself from a tree. The closest thing to identification found on the body was his shirt, which was marked "S.T. Coleridge." The dead man, it turned out, was wearing a shirt the poet had lost in a laundry five years earlier, prompting Coleridge to remark that he was probably the first man "to hear of a lost shirt in this way."

LUCA BARBARESCHI (b. 1956)

Claim to Fame: Former film actor and current member of the lower house of the Italian Parliament

Faux-bituary: Back in 1980 when he was still making movies, Barbareschi starred in a gory horror film called *Cannibal Holocaust*. Presented in a "found footage" style similar to *The Blair Witch Project*, the film turned out to be a little too realistic. Shortly after the premiere, director Ruggero Deodato was arrested on the suspicion that he had murdered Barbareschi and three other actors in order to film their death scenes. The actors weren't dead, but they were "missing": At Deodato's insistence they had all signed contracts to stay out of the press and to refuse all TV and film work for one year to further the impression that *Cannibal Holocaust* was a true story. Barbareschi and the others remained out of sight and were presumed dead until Deodato, facing life in prison for their murders, voided their contracts and allowed them to come forward.

DOROTHY FAY RITTER (1915–2003)

Claim to Fame: American film actress, wife of singing cowboy Tex Ritter, and mother of actor John Ritter

Faux-bituary: In August 2001, a nurse at the Motion Picture Country House, where Ritter was a resident, returned to work following a vacation and noticed that Ritter was not in her room. When told by another staffer that the 86-year-old woman was "gone," the nurse called one of Ritter's close friends to break the news. The friend, a regular contributor to the *London Daily Telegraph*, passed the information on, and the obituary was printed in the next edition of the paper. Soon afterward, the newspaper received an e-mail from the Ritter family reporting that Dorothy was not dead and in fact had gotten a kick out of reading her own obituary. Turns out that Ritter *was* "gone"—she'd moved to another wing of the facility.

RED STOREY (1918–2006)

Claim to Fame: Canadian TV sports commentator and former NHL referee

Faux-bituary: In 1972, an employee of the *Montreal Star* newspaper overheard a colleague saying, "Red Storey is dead." The man phoned his wife with the news; she shared it with a local radio station, and they put it out over the air. From there it found its way back to the *Star*, where sports editor Red Fisher called the Storey household for confirmation. Storey was at home and denied to Fisher that he was dead. Fisher then traced the story back to its source—himself. Earlier in the day, when one of his stories was dumped in favor of a newer one, someone had called out across the newsroom, "Red's story is dead."

*   *   *

"Humankind cannot bear very much reality." —**T. S. Elliot**

ODD NASCAR SPONSORS

Beer, Gatorade, and auto parts are the kinds of sponsors you usually see plastered on NASCAR racecars. But many companies are willing to pay for that advertising exposure…even when it seems a little weird.

• In 2004, NASCAR forced Arnold Motorsports to remove car decals promoting a company called RedneckJunk.com. The website sold classified ads for people buying and selling hunting equipment and old truck parts. A NASCAR spokesman said the organization didn't feel that "RedneckJunk projected the proper image of our sport."

• From 2001 to 2005, Mark Martin, one of the oldest drivers on the NASCAR circuit, drove a car bearing stickers promoting Viagra.

• Driver Kevin Harvick's car in 2002 sported ads for the 20th anniversary DVD re-release of *E.T.: The Extra-Terrestrial*.

• In 2002, driver Kurt Busch's car was sponsored by Little Tikes—a company that makes toys for babies.

• Juan Montoya's 2013 car bore ads for Depends adult diapers.

• In 2010, Mike Bliss drove a pink racing car decorated with pictures of reality star Kim Kardashian advertising her line of perfumes.

• In 1997, Tammy Jo Kirk—one of only about a dozen female NASCAR drivers—drove a car advertising Lovable brand bras.

• It seems unlikely that any government agency—especially one charged with keeping people out of the country—would have to advertise. Still, in 2007, the U.S. Border Patrol sponsored a car.

• *The Muppet Show's* 25th anniversary was commemorated with a series of NASCAR ad placements in 2002: Dale Jarrett drove a car with Kermit and Miss Piggy stickers, Casey Atwood had a Rowlf car, and Jeremy Mayfield's car featured Bunsen and Beaker.

• NASCAR drivers compete while sitting down, so it's actually fairly logical that in 2008, one of the sponsors was the anti-chafing product Boudreaux's Butt Paste.

In 1908, *The New York Times* advised readers to wash their hair "about every six weeks."

OLD-TIMEY PIES

Unusual sweet and savory pies you probably won't find at your local bakery.

STAR-GAZEY PIE. A very old-fashioned savory Cornish pie made from fish heads. The heads poke up through the crust looking skyward as if "star gazing."

PUDGY PIE. A Depression-era treat made by toasting fruit-pie filling between two slices of bread. The toasting was done in a long-handled round iron called a "hobo pie iron."

SPARROW PIE. It takes five dozen sparrows to stuff the crust of this 18th-century European pie. First, roast the birds with a bit of bacon. Then sprinkle sage on the bottom of the crust, add the sparrows (some say they look like tiny turkeys), put butter on the top crust, and bake for one hour.

SHOO-FLY PIE. Pennsylvania Dutch settlers often had to rely on nonperishables such as flour, brown sugar, molasses, salt, spices, and lard. They baked those staples into sweet pies, and then waited for the last ingredient to show up: flies. Unless flies landed and had to be shooed away, it wasn't *really* Shoo-Fly Pie.

CANTALOUPE PIE. The Texas & Pacific Railway was chartered by Congress in 1871 to establish rail service from Texas to San Diego. This meringue-topped pie with cantaloupe filling was invented to convince California fruit growers to ship by rail. It worked. The pie became a signature dessert in T&P dining cars.

FUNERAL PIE. Because death doesn't always come during fruit-picking season, this Amish specialty—a pie crust filled with sugar, water, raisins, cornstarch, and spices—was perfect to bring to the bereaved in any season.

LAMPREY PIE. Lampreys are jawless fish that latch onto salmon and suck them dry. Soaked in syrup and cooked in a piecrust, they were a medieval delicacy favored by kings. Every Christmas, this pie was sent by the city of Gloucester—known for its lampreys—to England's monarch. One of them, Henry I, is said to have died from "a surfeit of lampreys." (But history doesn't say if they were baked in a pie.)

Scientific name for a cheese lover: *turophile.*

GROUNDED TV PILOTS

If you thought Gilligan's Island *or* Alf *were goofy ideas for TV shows (they were), you should see the stuff that never made it. Someone actually filmed pilot episodes of the following shows.*

AFTER GEORGE (1983)

Sad news: Susan's (Susan Saint James) husband has just died. Better news: while tinkering with the supercomputer that runs her house, she discovers that her husband has programmed his voice and personality into the computer.

MURDER IN MUSIC CITY (1979)

By day, Sonny Hunt is a songwriter in Nashville's country music scene. By night, he's a mystery-solving detective. Sonny Hund is played by Sonny Bono. (And the show featured cameos by country music stars, such as Mel Tillis, Larry Gatlin, and Barbara Mandrell.)

YAZOO (1984)

After his role as a tough cop on *Cannon* and before his role as a tough cop on *Jake and the Fatman*, William Conrad tried something very different on *Yazoo*. He played a widowed retiree who goes fishing, falls asleep on the boat, and then wakes up in a magical land called Yazoo, which is inhabited entirely by puppets.

CHANNEL 99 (1988)

A former media executive (Marilu Henner) moves back to her midwestern hometown and becomes manager of a low-wattage local TV station. But she just came out of a mental institution, so she puts bizarre shows on the air, such as *Bowling for Eggs* and *Shine Your Shoes with Mike*.

DAYTONA BEACH (1996)

Created by the producers of *Baywatch*, this show looked a lot like *Baywatch* (there were a lot of girls in bikinis), but nuttier. The main character is a "Beach Ranger" (a lifeguard) who moonlights as a police officer...and also as a racecar driver. His girlfriend is an Air Force test pilot training to be an astronaut.

The Washington National Cathedral has one gargoyle in the shape of Darth Vader's head.

HEAT VISION AND JACK (1999)

In this parody of high-concept '80s action shows like *Knight Rider*, Jack Black played Jack, an astronaut who gains superhuman intelligence after flying near the sun. He's trying to escape Ron Silver, an evil NASA henchman who knows his secret. The part of Ron Silver is played by character actor Ron Silver. Oh, and Jack rides a talking motorcycle, voiced by Owen Wilson. Created by Dan Harmon (*Community*), the pilot episode has become a cult favorite on the Internet.

NYPD MOUNTED (1991)

After *Hill Street Blues* and before *NYPD Blue*, Dennis Franz starred in this cop comedy about a New York police officer on horseback who gets a new partner: a cowboy from Montana. Recurring gag: Franz and his horse don't get along, so the animal is constantly throwing him into a river, a lake, a fountain....

JUST DESERTS (1992)

A lawyer (Joel Grey) is killed when he's run over by a bus full of nuns. He's then cursed to run a luxury resort called the Whispering Pines, where he doles out karmic retribution to guests. In the pilot episode, he turns a womanizer into a woman for a day.

HIGHER GROUND (1988)

FBI agent Jim Clayton doesn't mess around. He punches out criminals, throws them off balconies, commandeers boats, and doesn't take any guff from his supervisor. He's also a recovering alcoholic, and occasionally leads folk song singalongs...because the character was portrayed by none other than John Denver.

THE QUESTOR TAPES (1974)

A secret corporation finds blueprints for how to make an android left behind by an alien, and they build it. The plans are incomplete, so the project is abandoned...until the android (Robert Foxworth) finishes the job himself, making himself look human. He teams up with a cop (Mike Farrell) to learn how to act like a human. However, if he gets too excited, as he reminds everyone, "My fusion furnace will overload. I will become a nuclear bomb."

Food for thought: 40 percent of the world's workforce is in agriculture-related jobs.

FUNNY TWEETS

A lot of funny people use the social media site Twitter, where you can post messages no longer than 140 characters. That's not a lot of room to be funny, but plenty of people have risen to the challenge

"Birds do it, bees do it, even educated fleas do it. Let's do it. Let's live in a homeless man's beard."
—**Mary Charlene**

"After I drink coffee I show my empty mug to the IT guy and tell him I have successfully installed Java. He hates me."
—**Brain Essebe**

"The 'J' on the neighbors' light-up 'JOY' decoration just burnt out. A multifaith family, perhaps?"
—**Emily Brianna**

"The time my dad stared at an empty email draft to a friend on his computer screen and asked, 'Can he...see me?' will forever haunt my dreams."
—**Kathy Salerno**

"While I was very disappointed & angry to find my daughter smoking a cigarette I'll be damned if she didn't look cooler."
—**Danny Zucker**

"Canadians watch US politics like Americans watch Honey Boo Boo."
—**Kelly Oxford**

"At a cemetery, looking for my name on tombstones. This is the Goth version of Googling yourself."
—**Todd Levin**

"To most Christians, the Bible is like a software license. Nobody actually reads it. They just scroll to the bottom and click 'I agree.'"
—**AlmightyGod**

"My husband is happy we are getting along so great. I guess the silent treatment isn't really having the effect I was hoping for."
—**Bonnie McFarlane**

"I saw an ad on Craigslist once that said 'free firewood, u collect it' so i wrote the guy and said 'bud you just wrote an ad for the woods.'"
—**Jon Hendren**

"I hate when old people poke me at weddings, point and whisper, 'You're next.' So I've started doing the same at funerals."
—**Jeannette Morales**

The orange background color on a Reese's candy package is a registered trademark.

URBAN LEGENDS

*If you know anybody who believes in these wacky
theories, please send them our way. (We have
an invisible bridge we'd like to sell them.)*

LEGEND: Michael Jackson never reached puberty. In the early 1970s, the amazingly talented 11-year-old sang with all the showmanship and soul of an old pro, but had the high voice of an 11-year-old. In 1970, puberty started to set in, and Jackson developed acne, so his doctor gave him a zit medicine called *cyproterone*. Good news: It cleared up his skin. Bad news: It blocked him from entering puberty. That explains why he had a narrow, slight body for his entire life and never lost his high-pitched singing voice. It also explains the man-child stuff—the sleepovers with kids, the amusement park, the toy-shopping binges. It's because he literally never grew up.

TRUTH: In 2011, French vascular surgeon and opera fan Alain Branchereau thought Jackson's voice sounded like that of a castrato. He did some "research" and theorized in his book *Michael Jackson: The Secret of a Voice* that Jackson must have been given drugs that made his voice (and body) stay permanently young—drugs like cyproterone. Branchereau's theory spread, but there are some major holes in it: Cyproterone wasn't patented until 1976 and was available only in England. Even then, it was only given to girls. Furthermore, Jackson didn't develop acne until 1972, when he was 14. He was still dealing with it in 1977, when he starred in *The Wiz*, and had to wear extra-thick makeup for the movie, a well-documented fact.

LEGEND: Coca-Cola *wanted* New Coke to flop. In 1985, the Coca-Cola company abandoned its secret formula, which it had used for 100 years, in favor of New Coke—made with a different recipe and noticeably sweeter than the old version. (Coke had been losing market share to Pepsi, which is a sweeter cola.) Loyal consumers were furious and New Coke flopped. Less than a year later, the company reintroduced its old formula, now labeled "Coca-Cola Classic," which shared shelf space with New Coke, renamed Coke II. The big secret behind this public relations debacle was that Coke

---

wanted to substitute the sugar in its original product with cheaper high-fructose corn syrup. The company hoped (and planned) that customers would be so busy complaining about New Coke, they wouldn't notice the difference when the HFCS-altered "Coca-Cola Classic" came back.

TRUTH: Separating people from Coca-Cola for a while then hoping they'd forget its exact taste is a plausible idea…except for the fact that Coke replaced sugar with high-fructose corn syrup in 1980, five years before the New Coke disaster.

LEGEND: On a 2010 release of a 1928 Charlie Chaplin movie called *The Circus*, a time traveler appears. The proof: The DVD boasts "bonus material," including footage of the film's premiere at a Los Angeles movie theater. The bonus footage isn't part of the movie, it's footage of a real-life event in which a woman is seen walking through the crowd, holding a device about the size of a deck of cards up to her ear and speaking. It's a cell phone. The woman is a time traveler.

TRUTH: This story spread around the Internet in 2010, along with the spooky video footage in question. While it's certainly possible that the woman is a time traveler (from the future, of course, because we haven't figured out time travel yet), the rumor was debunked by a blogger who pointed out another object, available in 1928, that was about the size of a deck of cards: an early, handheld hearing aid.

LEGEND: Baby carrots, the ubiquitous vegetable and lunchbox snack, are actually made out of deformed carrots that are soaked in chlorine to shrink them.

TRUTH: It used to be true…or at least partially true. The mini-carrot was born in the 1990s when a carrot packer in California came up with a more profitable way to use ugly or misshapen carrots (as opposed to selling them for use in canned soups). He placed them in an industrial cutter to make them small, then ground their ends and "polished" them in an industrial potato peeler until they looked like appetizing young carrots. It's not done that way anymore. Those little carrots are now hybrid breeds grown to be sweet and slender. They're then cut and water-polished. Snopes and Wikipedia say "carrots may be treated with chlorine," to fight microbial contamination, then rinsed.

SIMPLE MATH TRICKS

During a recent conversation with a friend, Uncle John demonstrated how easy it is to add a column of numbers in your head, a trick he learned as a child from Grandpa Uncle John. "I wish someone had taught me that trick when I was a kid," said his friend. Well, on the theory that you're never too old to learn, here are a couple of simple tricks to make certain types of math problems a snap.

TRICK 1: Multiply any two-digit number by 11.

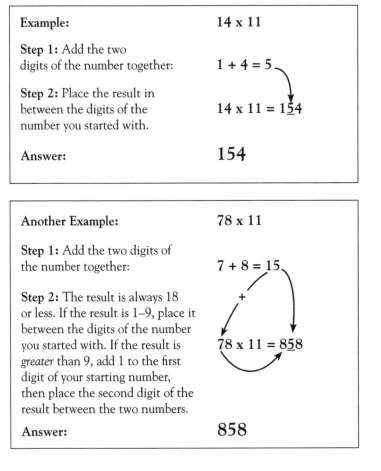

Example: 14 x 11

Step 1: Add the two digits of the number together: 1 + 4 = 5

Step 2: Place the result in between the digits of the number you started with. 14 x 11 = 1<u>5</u>4

Answer: **154**

Another Example: 78 x 11

Step 1: Add the two digits of the number together: 7 + 8 = 15

Step 2: The result is always 18 or less. If the result is 1–9, place it between the digits of the number you started with. If the result is *greater* than 9, add 1 to the first digit of your starting number, then place the second digit of the result between the two numbers. 78 x 11 = 8<u>5</u>8

Answer: **858**

The only Harvard University grad to win a Best-acting Oscar: Natalie Portman.

TRICK 2: Multiply any two-digit "complementary pairs" together. (Complementary pairs are two numbers whose first digits are identical and whose second digits add up to 10.)

Example: 23 and 27

Step 1: Take the first digit from the pair and multiply it by the next highest whole number: The result will form the first digit of your answer.

2 x 3 = 6

Step 2: Multiply the second digits of the numbers by each other: The result will form the second two digits of your answer.

3 x 7 = 21

Answer: 23 x 27 = 621

Another Example: 54 and 56

Step 1: Multiply the first digit from the pair by the next highest whole number: The result will form the first digit of your answer.

5 x 6 = 30

Step 2: Multiply the second digits of the numbers by each other: The result will form the second two digits of your answer.

4 x 6 = 24

Answer: 54 x 56 = 3024

For a few more simple math tricks, turn to page 346.

IS IT SHAKESPEARE? ...OR *FAKESPEARE?*

Most of us are familiar with Shakespeare's plays, or at least a few lines from his plays, if for no reason other than we had to read Romeo and Juliet *in high school. But it's fascinating to learn how little we really know about the Bard, including the possibility that there are more plays out there that were written by him. Or were they?*

MUCH ADO

In 1623, two London actors named John Heminges and Henry Condell published what has become known as the "First Folio," the first collection of the works of William Shakespeare, who'd died seven years earlier. Heminges and Condell had known Shakespeare and were members of the King's Men, the acting troupe where the Bard spent much of his career. The First Folio included 36 of Shakespeare's plays, 18 of which were published for the very first time. (The others had been published individually but never as a collection.)

The Second Folio, a revised and "corrected" version of the First Folio, was published in 1632. A Third Folio followed in 1663. It, too, contained 36 plays, but when a second printing was issued in 1664, seven new plays were added: *Pericles, Prince of Tyre; Locrine; the London Prodigal; The Puritan; Sir John Oldcastle; Thomas Lord Cromwell;* and *A Yorkshire Tragedy.* People have argued ever since whether these plays, and others attributed to Shakespeare in the years that followed, really were written by him.

THE MYSTERY OF THINGS

There isn't a whole lot of evidence to work with. As famous as Shakespeare was, surprisingly little is known about him. We know from parish records that he was baptized in Stratford-upon-Avon on April 26, 1564, probably a few days after he was born. (His exact date of birth is unknown.) We know—again thanks to church records—that he married at age 18 and fathered a child six months later. And we know that as a young man he moved to London to begin his career. But precisely when he moved isn't clear. What was

---

Wake up, people! The average American will drink 9,000 cups of coffee in a lifetime.

his first acting job? When did he start writing plays? What was the first play he wrote—and has it survived? Nobody knows. We don't even know in what order the surviving early plays were written. Information from 1582 to 1592, when Shakespeare was in his late teens and early 20s and starting his career, is so scarce that historians refer to it as his "lost years." The only reason we know that he was writing plays by 1592 at all is because that's the year a jealous rival called him an "upstart crow" in a pamphlet.

BY ANY OTHER NAME

The Bard's later years present a different challenge. By the time Shakespeare retired in 1612, he was the most popular playwright in London, and unscrupulous printers weren't above adding his name to plays he hadn't written to increase their sales. Even the First Folio refers to "diverse stolen, and surreptitious copies, maimed and deformed by the frauds and stealths of injurious imposters." Shakespeare's reputation continued to grow after he died in 1616, and so did the problem of people crediting him with (inferior) works he'd had nothing to do with.

And there's something else that muddied the water: Playwriting is often a collaborative process, and Shakespeare was no exception. In his later years, he collaborated on three plays written by a playwright named John Fletcher. He is believed to have collaborated with other writers as well, crafting scenes or even creating story outlines that other people used to write plays. He likely began his career the same way, contributing to the plays of more experienced writers until he was ready to strike out on his own.

TANGLED WEBS

Between shady printers making a dishonest buck off the Bard and Shakespeare himself assisting other playwrights without receiving credit, it's not easy for literary scholars to connect the dots four centuries later. Result: "Shakespeare Apocrypha"—more than 40 plays that may, or may not, have been written by him. Some examples:

ARDEN OF FAVERSHAM (1592)

Description: A play based on an actual murder case—the killing of wealthy Thomas Arden by his wife, Alice, and her lover, a man named Mosby, in 1551. Alice was burned at the stake for the crime, and Mosby was hanged. The play was published anonymously, but in 1770 a printer produced an edition that claimed Shakespeare wrote it.

To Be...or Not to Be: Shakespeare's mother, Mary Arden, was distantly related to Thomas Arden. And two characters in the play, hired killers who repeatedly botch the job, are named Black Will and Shakebag—inviting speculation that Shakespeare was poking fun at his own name. (Another theory: The play was written by a rival who wanted to mock him.)

In 2006, two professors, Renaissance scholar Arthur Kinney from Massachusetts and linguist Hugh Craig from Australia, used a computer to analyze Shakespeare's writing style and find his unique stylistic "fingerprint." Then they performed the same analysis on *Arden of Faversham* to see if it contained the same fingerprint. Their finding: "Shakespeare is the author," Kinney says. (But try telling that to literary historian Brian Vickers. His 2008 computer analysis found that another playwright named Thomas Kyd is more likely the author.) *Arden of Faversham* has yet to win wide acceptance as a genuine Shakespeare play.

SIR THOMAS MORE (circa 1591–3)

Description: The play depicts the life and death of More, the Lord Chancellor of England during the reign of Henry VIII (1509–1547). When Henry VIII defied the pope and created the Church of England with himself at its head, More (who sided with the pope) resigned his post. Henry had him beheaded in 1535.

To Be...or Not to Be: Only one original handwritten manuscript of the play survives; it's in the British Library in London. The man-uscript is 30 pages long, and because the handwriting varies from page to page, at least six different writers, or "hands," are believed to have contributed to the writing of the play. "Hand D," which wrote three pages, supplied a number of passages that are stylisti-cally similar to Shakespeare...which causes proponents to conclude that Shakespeare was Hand D.

So why don't the experts just compare Hand D's handwriting to other samples of Shakespeare's writing to see if they match? Because, with the exception of a few "rather scratchy" signatures on legal and other documents, no examples of Shakespeare's handwriting survive—so there's nothing to compare Hand D to. The three pages, if they were indeed penned by Shakespeare, would be the only examples of the playwright's work in his own hand.

THOMAS LORD CROMWELL (circa 1582–1600)

Description: The story of the life and death of Cromwell, who replaced Sir Thomas More as Lord Chancellor. Like More, Cromwell eventually fell from favor and was beheaded by order of Henry VIII in 1540.

To Be…or Not to Be: When it was first published in 1602, the title page stated simply, "Written by W.S." This was another one of the tricks unscrupulous publishers used to cash in on Shakespeare's reputation. They did it even when the real author's initials weren't W.S. Though the play was included in the Third Folio, it is so bad —"a piece of such utterly shapeless, spiritless, bodiless, soulless, senseless, helpless worthless rubbish," as one nineteenth-century critic put it—that few people have ever believed Shakespeare had anything to do with it.

THE LONDON PRODIGAL (1605)

Description: As the title suggests, this comedy is a morality play set in England. Matthew Flowerdale is a London merchant's son who poses as a much wealthier man in order to win the hand of a knight's daughter…only to be arrested for unpaid debts on their wedding day. His bride sticks by him and eventually convinces him to abandon his dissolute ways.

To Be…or Not to Be: *The London Prodigal* was published in Shakespeare's name during his lifetime and was performed by the King's Men, where the Bard was the resident playwright. So there's little doubt that Shakespeare had something to do with it, but it is so out of character with the rest of his work (not to mention not very good) that Shakespeare scholars have never accepted it as genuine. They believe that it was deliberately left out of the First and Second Folios, and for good reason—because Heminges and Condell knew that Shakespeare didn't write it. So what did he have to do with it? One theory: Shakespeare came up with the idea for the play, and then handed it off "to be very imperfectly executed by another."

*   *   *

"Facts can obscure the truth." —**Maya Angelou**

France and Mexico's 1838 Pastry War began over a bakery burglary. (France won.)

WORST. PAGE. EVER.

Jeff Albertson doesn't mince words. Who's he? The overweight, grumpy nerd on The Simpsons *also known as Comic Book Guy.*

"Last night's *Itchy & Scratchy* was, without a doubt, the worst episode ever. Rest assured I was on the Internet within minutes registering my disgust throughout the world."

"There is no emoticon to express what I am feeling right now."

"I do not have a receipt. I won this belt as a door prize at the *Star Trek* convention, although I find their choice of prize highly illogical as the average Trekker has no use for a medium-sized belt."

"Human contact: the final frontier."

"Your questions have become more redundant and annoying than the last three *Highlander* movies."

"Loneliness and cheeseburgers are a dangerous mix."

"The answer is no, and I can say it in Na'vi and Klingon, which are pretty much the same. I have some theories about that, which I will share with you never."

"Stop right there. I have here the only working phaser ever built. It was fired only once, to keep William Shatner from making another album."

"I was married once—in an online fantasy game. We were thinking of having children, but that would have severely drained my power crystals."

"No banging your head on the display case, please! It contains a very rare *Mary Worth* comic in which she has advised a friend to commit suicide. Thank you."

"I insist you take special care with my collection of valuable and humorous bumper stickers, particularly this 'My Other Car Is a *Millennium Falcon*' bumper sticker, which was given to me by a Harrison Ford look-alike."

"Your phony credit card is no good here. Now make like my pants and split."

"Lucite hardening…must end life in classic Lorne Greene pose from *Battlestar Galactica*. Best…death…ever!"

FREAKY FROGS

For people who really love frogs (and we don't mean with lots of butter), here's some really cool info on some really weird frogs.

INDIAN PURPLE FROG (*Nasikabatrachus sahyadrensis*)
Found in: The Western Ghats mountain range, along the west coast of India

Description: They grow to about three inches long, "from snout to vent," meaning from the tip of their noses to the end of their butts. They're also known as "purple doughnut frogs" for their pale slimy purple color and the fat doughnut-shaped bodies (without the hole, of course). And they have tiny heads for those big fat bodies and equally tiny flat-tipped piggy noses, which is why they're also known as the "pig-nosed frogs." Indian purple frogs are burrowers—they spend most of their lives underground—only coming to the surface to breed during the west Indian monsoon season.

Freaky bonus fact: The Indian purple frog's "ribbit" doesn't sound like a typical frog's—it sounds more like a clucking chicken.

THE HAIRY FROG (*Trichobatrachus robustus*)
Found in: Central Africa

Description: These frogs are a mottled olive-brown, with darker areas on their backs and faces. Males, which grow much larger than females, can reach more than four inches in length. During breeding season those big males do something unseen in any other frog species: They sprout what looks like thick hair on their sides and thighs. Except it's not hair. It's dozens of very thin appendages, up to half an inch long—actually extensions of the frogs' skin, growing out from the surface of their bodies. Scientists aren't sure why the appendages appear, but they have an idea: Although hairy frogs are terrestrial (they live on land), females lay their sticky egg sacs on underwater rocks in streams and rivers. The males stay with those eggs for days or even weeks until the tadpoles emerge—not typical frog behavior. Because frogs absorb oxygen through their skin underwater, they can go for relatively long periods without coming up for air. The frog's "hair," scientists believe, creates more skin surface area, thereby allowing the male hairy frog to remain with its eggs for

---

longer periods than it could without it.

Freaky bonus fact: The hairy frog is also known as the "horror frog." Why? It has a bizarre ability known only in a few frog species: The pointy tips of its rear toe bones are held in place by tiny, tendon-like straps. If threatened, a frog will suddenly flex its rear toes, causing the straps to break and the toe bones to suddenly shoot downward—right through the skin of the frog's toes. In other words, hairy frogs have what act as retractable claws (kind of like "Wolverine" from the X-Men).

TURTLE FROG (*Myobattachus gouldii*)
Found in: Australia

Description: The turtle frog is the only member of the frog genus *Myobatrachus* and is found only in one tiny area of Southwestern Australia. It could be the weirdest-looking frog in the world: Its small head, which actually looks more like a turtle's than a frog's, is distinct from the body, meaning that unlike most frogs, it has a neck, of sorts. It also has thick, muscular legs and a broad, roundish, shell-shaped body that is splotchy whitish-pink in color, making it look like a turtle with its shell removed. Like the Indian purple frog, the turtle frog spends most of its life underground (it comes out of the ground only to breed), digging through sandy soil to burrow into the nests of its only food—termites.

Freaky bonus fact: Unlike almost all other burrowing frogs and toads, which use their powerful rear legs to dig down into the soil, the turtle frog uses its front legs.

WALLACE'S FLYING FROG (*Rhacophorus nigropalmatus*)
Found in: Malaysia and Borneo

Description: Wallace's flying frogs are bright green with yellow sides and underbellies, and grow to about four inches long. They live in dense tropical jungles but not where you'd expect: They live high in trees, and come to ground only to mate and, for females, to lay eggs. They make a weird birdlike chirping sound when going after prey or in danger of becoming prey. Wallace's flying frogs can leap from a leaf or branch—splaying the long webbed toes on each of their feet, which act as four little parachutes and allow the frogs to glide for more than 50 feet at times—to another tree or all the way to ground. Big puffy sticky toe pads cushion their landings and allow the frogs to stick to whatever they land on. The species was named after British naturalist Alfred Russel Wallace, the first European to report seeing them (flying over his head, perhaps) in the 1850s.

WATER-HOLDING FROG (*Litoria platycephala*)

Found in: Australia

Description: They're olive green, stout-bodied, and about three inches long. Like turtle frogs, they're burrowers—but these frogs are extreme: When the dry season approaches, a water-holding frog bloats itself with water, then burrows deep into the ground. Once at its desired depth, the frog secretes a thick mucus, then sheds its entire skin. When the skin and mucus have hardened to form a protective bubble around it, the frog goes into a comalike state, living off its fat and water reserves. When the rainy season arrives several months later, the frog wakes up, makes its way to the surface to breed and feed, and then digs a new underground coma-chamber, beginning the process all over again. If the next rainy season doesn't arrive—no problem. The water-holding frog can survive for two years or longer in its underground bubble.

Freaky bonus fact: Australian Aboriginal hunters in the hot, dry outback used to dig up water-holding frogs and gently squeeze them—drinking the water that squirted out of their bodies.

EXTRAS

• **The hip-pocket frog** is another Australian frog. Females lay their eggs in wet, sandy soil; males brood them. When the eggs hatch, the tadpoles flop their way into little pockets on the male frogs' sides, and emerge about eight weeks later as little froglets.

• **The Surinam toad** spends most of its life underwater in tropical forests of South America. When it's time to mate, a male and female do an underwater dance that ends with the female's eggs embedded in her back. Skin grows over the eggs, and after they hatch, the tadpoles live in pockets in their mother's back until they develop into frogs. Then they fight their way out of those pockets, make their way out into the water and start their lives on their own.

*   *   *

Doubt is the key to knowledge. —**Persian proverb**

More than 74 million Americans barbecue on the 4th of July.

PROHIBITION FOLLIES

Booze was banned, but people still wanted to drink.
Their creative solutions resulted in some American
institutions that are still around today.

LAST CALL

When the 18th Amendment to the U.S. Constitution became the law of the land in 1919 and the Volstead Act was passed to enforce it (despite a veto from President Wilson), the manufacture, sale, transportation, and import of alcohol in the United States was outlawed. Intended to stem the perceived public health and moral crises associated with booze, Prohibition was a failure. Biggest problem: It led to the rise of organized crime in the U.S.—gangsters made millions trafficking banned alcohol to secret bars called "speakeasies." Here are some other ways (for better or for worse) that Prohibition permanently changed American life.

WALGREENS

Four kinds of alcohol were permitted by the Volstead Act: the booze people had in their possession before the passage of Prohibition, small batches of fruit-based liquor made by farmers for private use, wine used in religious services, and alcohol consumed for "medicinal" purposes. That last one was a big loophole. Legislators assumed this would apply to a very small segment of the population, but disreputable doctors were more than willing to write prescriptions for alcohol for the right price. In 1928, doctors earned an estimated $40 million prescribing booze for their patients. Tens of thousands of drinkers were able to exploit this loophole and get alcohol legally. But the biggest winner was pharmacies. Walgreens, for example, was a small chain of Chicago-area stores in the early 1900s. By 1929, there were 500 Walgreens across the U.S. The increased cash-flow came primarily from selling one $3-bottle to each "patient" every 10 days. Today, Walgreens is the largest drugstore chain in the country.

SMOKING

With alcohol harder to get, people turned to other substances for a quick fix—like cigarettes. At the start of Prohibition, smoking in public was illegal in more than a dozen states. By the end of Prohibition, cigarettes were legal in all 48 states and sales had tripled.

CRUISES

Drinking may have been outlawed on American soil, but in "international waters," almost anything goes. Prohibition led to the development of a new form of travel and entertainment: the "pleasure cruise," or "booze cruise." Patrons would pay to board a yacht, then sail a few miles out to sea and drink to their heart's content aboard what were basically floating bars—free of any worry of getting arrested. Traveling on a passenger vessel for recreation, not necessarily to get from one place to another (and at middle-class prices), was the precursor of the modern-day cruise industry.

COCKTAILS

Also born during Prohibition: mixed drinks. One of the downsides of illegal alcohol is a lack of quality and safety control. Today, if you buy a fifth of whiskey, it will taste the same as the bottle you bought last month. It will also contain the same percentage of alcohol. This didn't happen during Prohibition: Batches of booze were wildly inconsistent, so bartenders started concocting cocktails—adding flavoring and juices to the alcohol to mask its bad taste. Here are three that were created in that era:

• **The Colony Cocktail.** The Colony was a restaurant and speakeasy on New York's Upper East Side frequented by the elite—the Vanderbilts were regulars, for example. Its signature drink was two parts gin, one part grapefruit juice, and two teaspoons of grenadine, then shaken with ice and strained into a chilled glass.

• **The Old-Fashioned.** It dates to the 1880s and Kentucky, but it didn't gain popularity until Prohibition. Recipe: A sugar cube is mixed with a teaspoon of water and two dashes of bitters. Once the sugar dissolves in the water (sugar is difficult to dissolve in alcohol alone), ice and a slice of lemon peel are added, followed by a shot of bourbon whiskey.

• **The Gin Rickey.** The secret party culture during Prohibition was a big part of the "Jazz Age," as chronicled by *The Great Gatsby* author, F. Scott Fitzgerald. The gin rickey was a popular drink at jazz clubs (it was reportedly Fitzgerald's favorite, too). It's simply gin, soda water, and lime juice.

Technically, oranges are berries. So are pumpkins and bananas.

UN-BEE-LIEVABLE

The Scripps National Spelling Bee was started in 1925 and has now become so famous that the winner (and the word they won with) can count on making national headlines and network news shows. Have the words gotten tougher over the years? Judge for yourself.

The 1920s
1925: gladiolus
1926: cerise
1927: luxuriance
1928: albumen
1929: asceticism

The 1930s
1930: fracas
1931: foulard
1932: knack
1933: torsion
1934: deteriorating
1935: intelligible
1936: interning
1937: promiscuous
1938: sanitarium
1939: canonical

The 1940s
1940: therapy
1941: initials
1942: sacrilegious
(The bee was suspended during World War II.)
1946: semaphore
1947: chlorophyll

1948: psychiatry
1949: dulcimer

The 1950s
1950: meticulosity
1951: insouciant
1952: vignette
1953: soubrette
1954: transept
1955: crustaceology
1956: condominium
1957: schappe
1958: syllepsis
1959: catamaran

The 1960s
1960: eudaemonic
1961: smaragdine
1962: esquamulose
1963: equipage
1964: sycophant
1965: eczema
1966: ratoon
1967: Chihuahua
1968: abalone
1969: interlocutory

Grate news! In 2008, Italy spent $65 million to bail out the parmesan-cheese industry.

The 1970s
1970: croissant
1971: shalloon
1972: macerate
1973: vouchsafe
1974: hydrophyte
1975: incisor
1976: narcolepsy
1977: cambist
1978: deification
1979: maculature

The 1980s
1980: elucubrate
1981: sarcophagus
1982: psoriasis
1983: Purim
1984: luge
1985: milieu
1986: odontalgia
1987: staphylococci
1988: elegiacal
1989: spoliator

The 1990s
1990: fibranne
1991: antipyretic
1992: lyceum
1993: kamikaze
1994: antediluvian
1995: xanthosis
1996: vivisepulture
1997: euonym
1998: chiaroscurist
1999: logorrhea

The 2000s
2000: demarche
2001: succedaneum
2002: prospicience
2003: pococurante
2004: autochthonous
2005: appoggiatura
2006: Ursprache
2007: serrefine
2008: guerdon
2009: Laodicean

The 2010s
2010: stromuhr
2011: cymotrichous
2012: guetapens
2013: knaidel

*　　*　　*

"Some problems are so complex that you have to be highly intelligent and well informed just to be undecided about them."
—**Laurence J. Peter**

Only about 5 percent of bills introduced in the U.S. Congress ever become law.

A GOOD IMPRESSION

Impressions used to be a common part of stand-up comedy. Performers like Rich Little, Frank Gorshin, and John Byner imitated movie stars, singers, and politicians. But there was another kind of impressionist—who imitated just one person…and made a good living doing it.

THE GUY WHO IMPERSONATED THE POPE

Pope John Paul II began leading the Catholic church in 1978, and almost from the beginning, people told Los Angeles real estate agent Gene Greytak how much he resembled the pontiff—so much so that when Greytak retired in the early '80s, he considered a career making personal appearances and taking small acting roles as "the pope." But he rejected the idea because, as a Catholic, he felt it was disrespectful—or even a sin—to imitate the pope. After being reassured by the Archdiocese of Los Angeles that there was nothing wrong with it, Greytak started his second career as the go-to John Paul look-alike. Greytak never spoke—he only showed up in full pope costume. And he really looked like the pope, which made it startling (and funny) when he appeared in TV shows and movies such as *Night Court, Hot Shots!, The Golden Girls, Sister Act,* and *The Naked Gun 33⅓.* His last credit: the B-movie *Miss Castaway and the Island Girls* in 2004. Pope John Paul II died in 2005, which ended Greytak's career, too. He died in 2010.

THE GUY WHO IMPERSONATED PRESIDENT KENNEDY

Vaughn Meader was a stand-up comic and nightclub singer in the early 1960s. Reflecting the public's taste for anything related to the charismatic, young, and popular President John F. Kennedy, Meader added a Kennedy impersonation to his act—not difficult, since he was from Maine and had virtually the same New England accent as the president. (He also sort of looked like Kennedy.) Meader appeared in nightclubs across the United States and on TV variety shows, developing the Kennedy impression into a full-length show. In late 1962, he recorded a comedy album called *The First Family,* gently poking fun at Kennedy and his family (sample topics: Kennedy family football games, Jacqueline Kennedy's redecoration of the White House). The album was an unexpected smash—it sold 7.5 million copies (at the time, the fastest selling album ever) and won the Grammy for Album of the Year. The Kennedys themselves reportedly gave out dozens as Christmas gifts that year. Meader appeared on *The Ed Sullivan Show*, *The Jack Paar Program*, *The Andy Williams Show*, and many other TV shows. He had rapidly become, undoubtedly, the most popular comedian in America. Then Meader's career was over virtually in an instant. In November 1963, President Kennedy was assassinated. As the nation mourned, *The First Family* was pulled from stores and Meader's TV appearances were cancelled. Tightly linked to Kennedy, his presence (and voice) reminded audiences of the horrible tragedy. He tried to do non-Kennedy comedy, but he was too associated with JFK to get a new toehold. Meader couldn't get any work for more than a decade, appearing in two B-movies in 1975, *Linda Lovelace for President* (starring a former porn star) and *Lepke*, in which he imitated reporter Walter Winchell. Fading into obscurity and drug addiction, Meader died in 2004.

THE GUY WHO IMPERSONATED ED SULLIVAN

From the early 1950s until the early '70s, Ed Sullivan was a king-maker in the entertainment world. Despite being a stiff, wooden, middle-aged newspaper columnist who never seemed comfortable on camera, Sullivan hosted the most popular and influential variety show on TV—*The Ed Sullivan Show*. His stilted, clipped delivery was heard in more than 40 million homes each week and was so well-known that comedian and impressionist Will Jordan made a very healthy living by impersonating Sullivan—and that was about all he had to do. By 1960, Jordan had dropped all other comedy from his act to focus on doing Sullivan, which he did on *The Tonight Show*, *American Bandstand*, *The Red Skelton Hour*, and…*The Ed Sullivan Show*. Then he jumped to Broadway, playing Sullivan in the original 1960 production of *Bye Bye Birdie*. Ever since, whenever a movie takes place in the distant past and needs Ed Sullivan to show up, Jordan has been the go-to guy. He portrayed Sullivan in *I Wanna Hold Your Hand* (about the Beatles' appearance on *Ed Sullivan*), *The Buddy Holly Story*, *Elvis*, *The Doors*, *Mr. Saturday Night*, *Down with Love*, and Billy Joel's 1983 video "Tell Her About It," which recreated *The Ed Sullivan Show*. Jordan is in his 80s now, but still works as a Sullivan impersonator. In 2010, he reprised his *Bye Bye Birdie* role for a Broadway revival of the musical. Fascinating fact: Sullivan's catchphrase "We have a really big *shoe* tonight," accenting Sullivan's speech patterns, was actually invented by Jordan.

THE BRITISH ARE COMING!, PART II

Some of them probably did wear red coats, but this time they were playing guitars and drums instead of firing muskets. More on the British bands that landed on our shores in the 1960s. (Part I is on page 59.)

THE BEE GEES

The Bee Gees may be the definitive disco group, but "Night Fever" and "Stayin' Alive" overshadow their very successful 1960s years as a pop-rock band. They didn't come directly from England. The Bee Gees—brothers Maurice, Robin, and Barry Gibb—were born on the Isle of Man and lived in Manchester, but moved to Australia as children in the late '50s. When their music career began to take off in the early '60s, they moved to the hub of the rock world at the time—London. Producer Robert Stigwood signed them to a deal, found them a guitarist and drummer, and re-leased their first international album, *First*, in 1967. The result was a very Beatles-esque sound, with tight, layered three-part harmonies from the Gibbs. Stigwood sent their first single, "New York Mining Disaster 1941," to radio stations with the band's name intentionally left off, correctly guessing that DJs would think it was a new Beatles song and play it. (A New York DJ referred to it as "English surprise #1" and the B-side, "I Can't See Nobody" as "English Surprise #2.") It went top 20 in the U.K. and the U.S., as did "To Love Some-body," "Massachusetts," "Words," "I've Gotta Get a Message to You," "I Started a Joke," and "How Can You Mend a Broken Heart." By 1972, their sound was no longer hip, and it wouldn't be until 1975 that the Bee Gees would have another hit—and a rare second act, with the disco song "Jive Talkin'."

THE FOURMOST

Like the Liverpool 5, the Fourmost had a name that made audi-ences think of the Beatles, or the "Fab Four." But that was merely a coincidence. They formed and started playing gigs in German clubs long before their fellow Liverpudlians struck it rich. The band began back in 1957 as the Two Jays, consisting of teenage singer-guitarists Brian O'Hara and Joey Bower, and later became the Four Jays when they added a bassist and a drummer. They played gigs at the Cavern Club in Hamburg in early 1961—before the Beatles. By 1962, the group had changed its name again, to the Fourmost, and in 1963, hired a manager—Brian Epstein, who also managed the Beatles. He got them a record deal and their first two singles, "Hello Little Girl" and "I'm in Love" were both composed by John Lennon. ("Hello Little Girl" was actually one of the first songs Lennon ever wrote, in 1957, long before the Beatles.) Both were big hits in the U.K., reaching #9 and #17, respectively. Those two will go down in music history as the first Beatle songs released in the U.S., but unfortunately, the Fourmost didn't quite ride the tide of the British Invasion, either pre- or post-Beatles. Neither song made the pop charts. And after "I'm in Love," the Fourmost never had another Top 20 hit in England, not even a 1966 cover of "Here, There and Everywhere" written by…John Lennon and Paul McCartney.

THE TREMELOES

On January 1, 1962, Decca Records auditioned two similar bands: the Tremeloes and the Beatles. Decca signed the Tremeloes, mainly because they were from London (unlike the Liverpudlian Beatles), which would make it easier to book them for concerts and TV appearances, all of which taped in London. The band couldn't gain much of a toehold and would forever be compared to the Beatles, in part because one of their first singles was a cover version of the Isley Brothers' "Twist and Shout," which the Beatles had covered a few months earlier. The Tremeloes version hit #4 in July 1963; the Beatles version hit #2 in January 1964. Other singles included "Do You Love Me" (a cover of a song by the Contours), "Candy Man" (a cover of a Roy Orbison song), and "Someone, Someone" (originally done by Buddy Holly). All those songs hit the top 10 in the U.K., but not until 1967 did the Tremeloes have hits in America. They were more covers—of the Four Seasons' "Silence is Golden" and Cat Stevens's "Here Comes My Baby."

Whether you're a mod or a rocker, you won't want to miss your fave raves. So for more British Invasion bands, turn to page 395.

King Louis XIV of France once banned pointy knives.

SCAM I AM

When W.C. Fields said, "Never give a sucker an even break,"
these folks must have taken the message to heart.

BUS-TED
After witnessing an accident between a cab and a SEPTA
(Southeastern Pennsylvania Transportation Authority) bus
in November 2008, Ronald Moore jumped into action…but not
the way you'd think. After checking to see if the driver was looking,
he climbed aboard the bus and lay down on the floor, pretending to
be injured Unfortunately for Moore, the bus was equipped with a
security camera that recorded everything. He pleaded guilty to theft
by deception and filing a fraudulent report. Two other people filed
fake insurance claims in the same incident; only one was on the bus
when the collison occurred. (That's not unique: SEPTA estimates
that fake injuries and fraudulent claims cost it more than $20 mil-
lion a year.)

ALL WET

One day in May 2012, a British man named Nathan Meunch
walked into a Royal Mail post office and mailed a box containing
£2,500 (about $4,000) worth of "iPads" to a friend, Nigel Bennett.
A few days later Bennett went to his local post office to file a claim
for the £2,500, saying that when the box arrived, the iPads were
gone. What happened? There never were any iPads. The Royal
Mail had suspected fakery from the moment Meunch tried to mail
the box, because it was leaking water all over his clothes (he said
it was raining). When the box was still leaking a few hours later,
postal inspectors opened it, and found nothing inside but melting
ice, which Meunch put there to make the box heavier. The Royal
Mail shipped it, and when Bennett filed his insurance claim he and
Meunch were arrested and charged with fraud. Both men were fined
£500 ($780) and sentenced to 150 hours of community service.

CAT-ASTROPHE

In March 2009, a Washington State man named Yevgeniy Samsonov was stopped at a red light when he was rear-ended by another
vehicle. He filed a claim with the other driver's insurance company

and was awarded $3,500. Then, two years after the accident, Samsonov filed a second claim—this time for $20,000—stating that his cat, "Tom," had been killed in the crash and that the cat was "like a son" to him. Included in the filing: two pictures of a white-haired blue-eyed cat. The insurance company conducted a swift investigation…on Google…and found the same images of "Tom" on numerous websites. (And they were of two different cats.) Samsonov was subsequently arrested and convicted of insurance fraud.

After the story made headlines, another insurance company to informed the state's Insurance Commissioner that Samsonov had filed a similar $20,000 claim with them for a dead parrot (And he'd submitted a picture of a parakeet with the claim.)

SEVERANCE PAY
In 2012, a Spanish man filed claims with eleven different insurance companies, for a total of more than $2 million, after losing his hand in a car accident. There really was an accident, and the man really did lose his hand, but when insurance company investigators looked into the incident, they found that the car hadn't been traveling fast enough to cause so devastating an injury. Further investigation revealed that the man's hand had actually been cut cleanly between bones (*around* the bones, without injuring them), which almost never happens in car wrecks. "This man must have got someone to use a saw to cut off his hand," said accident investigator Jose Luis Nieto. "A surgeon would never have done it." (Claims denied.)

THAT TIME OF THE YEAR
In early April 2013, an Argentinian TV news show reported about a retiree from the city of Catamarca who bought two toy poodles at La Salada, Argentina's largest outdoor market. The man paid $300 for the dogs, but when he took them to get vaccinated, the vet told him they were "Brazilian rats," Argentinian slang for ferrets who've been pumped up on steroids and carefully groomed to look like poodles, for sale to gullible dog lovers. Along with the news report, they showed only one piece of evidence: a single blurry photo of a bizarre-looking creature. By the time the first English-language newspapers jumped on the story, on April 7, nobody seemed to notice that the week-old story was probably an April Fool's prank.

BA-SU! BA-SU!

Some of Japan's best baseball players are athletes you've probably never heard of, such as pitcher Takehiko Bessho, home-run king Sadaharu Oh…and a power hitter from Oklahoma named Randy Bass.

MINOR STRUGGLES

Eighteen-year-old Lawton, Oklahoma, high school star Randy Bass was drafted by the Minnesota Twins in the seventh round of the 1972 draft. It took five long years of kicking around the minor leagues until he was called up to the majors. Even then he didn't stay long. That season, he played in just nine games. Over the next five years, he was traded again and again, to Kansas City, to Montreal, to San Diego, to Texas, down to the minors, back to the majors, and down to the minors again. And his role was almost always limited to coming off the bench to pinch-hit. Basically, Bass's baseball career was a bust. In all, he played in 130 major-league games by the time he gave up in 1982, with an unexceptional .212 batting average and nine home runs.

Bass was 28. He had failed in his chosen profession and didn't have a college degree to fall back on. So what could he do? He went to Japan.

LAND OF THE RISING (HOME) RUN

Since World War II, baseball has been just as popular—if not more so—in Japan as in the United States. In 1950, two smaller Japanese baseball circuits merged into the Nippon Professional Baseball League (*Nippon* is what the Japanese call Japan). Like Major League Baseball in America, the Nippon League is split into two divisions, called the Central League and the Pacific League. The league champions play each other in the annual Japan Series.

Dozens of players from the Nippon League have crossed over to Major League Baseball, including pitchers Hideki Matsui and Hideo Nomo, and batting champion Ichiro Suzuki. But until the last decade or so, only a handful of American players have gone on to play baseball in Japan. (The first was Hawaiian-born Wally Yonamine in 1950.)

Sound travels faster on a hot, humid day than on cool, dry one.

TIGER, TIGER, BURNING BRIGHT

Nippon teams are allowed to have two *gaijin* (foreign born) players on their team, but few ever made much of an impression. Alan
Meersand was a sports agent who had brought many failed major-
league American players into Japanese baseball, and he recruited
Bass. The deal: $875,000 for a two-year contract to play first base
with the Hanshin Tigers.

The Tigers play outside of Osaka and rank second in popularity
in Japan. The most popular team is the Yomiuri Giants of Tokyo.
The two teams have a rivalry comparable to the New York Yankees and the Boston Red Sox. A spot on such a high-profile team
got Bass attention, even if his statistics weren't spectacular. What
really helped him get noticed was that he was a hulking 6'1" and
a 210-pounder...with a beard. He was one of the biggest and most
recognizable players in the league. Whenever he came up to the
plate, the home crowd would chant "Ba-su! Ba-su!"

CROWNING ACHIEVEMENT

Then, in the 1985 season, something amazing happened—Bass
suddenly improved, and had one of the best seasons in Japanese
baseball history, regardless of nationality. That year, he won the
"Triple Crown," leading the league in batting average (.350), home
runs (54), and runs batted in (134). Bass also led the Tigers to their
first Japan Series since 1964...where he hit three more home runs,
propelling the Tigers to a championship over the Seibu Lions.

In 1986, he won the Triple Crown again (the only player ever
to win it two years in a row), knocking out 47 home runs and 109
RBIs, and compiling a .389 batting average—the highest ever in
Japanese baseball. Among the 500 American players to take the
field in Japan, Bass leads in nearly all statistical categories.

THE COLONEL'S CURSE

But despite his success and his having returned long-lost glory to
the Hanshin Tigers, Bass is remembered almost as much for "cursing" the team. Beards are rare in Japan; so are huge American guys.
That proved to be a problem when the Tigers celebrated their 1985
championship. At a post-game ceremony, a look-alike representing every player on the team jumped into a canal near the stadium.
Reason: It's supposed to bring good luck in the next season. A

decent look-alike for Bass could not be located, so fans threw a statue of Colonel Sanders into the water. Kentucky Fried Chicken is the most popular fast-food restaurant in Asia, and a statue of the bearded Colonel Sanders was the closest thing anybody could find to Bass.

All the look-alikes swam to shore—it's part of the tradition—but the Bass stand-in statue sank like…a statue…and then disappeared. And as of 2013 the Tigers have not won another championship, leading fans to believe that the team is cursed until the statue is found. (Part of it was recovered in 2009, but still no championship for the Hanshin Tigers.)

BEARDS AND BILLS

Research by Gilette at the time indicated that Bass possessed the most famous beard in Japan, second only to Ringo Starr. The razor blade company offered Bass a small fortune to shave it off for a Japanese TV commercial. Tigers' ownership pleaded with Bass not to shave it off, but he did…and the Tigers didn't make the playoffs for the rest of Bass's Japanese tenure.

After his retirement in 1988, Bass returned to Oklahoma but stayed in the Japanese baseball world as a sportscaster and a scout for the Tigers' rival, the Giants. For the last decade, he's served in the Oklahoma State Senate. He still ventures back to Japan once or twice a year to play in celebrity golf tournaments.

*   *   *

CUPCAKE WARS

In December 2011, an airline passenger named Rebecca Hans was going through security at McCarran International Airport in Las Vegas when a TSA agent confiscated her cupcake. When Hans asked why, she was told that the icing could be a "security risk." (It supposedly met the criteria for banned liquids and gels.) Upset, Hans pointed out that earlier that week she was allowed through security in Boston with similar cupcakes—no questions asked. "Well," said the agent, "They weren't doing their job." Apparently, neither was the agent. After Hans complained, a TSA official said that cupcakes are not banned substances, and that the agent had erred. (We have a pretty good idea where that confiscated cupcake went.)

Oldest brewery in North America: Molson, founded in Montreal, Canada, in 1786.

FIRST IN DEATH

*Most of us will probably never make it into the record
books. For a few people, though, making history
was the very last thing they ever did.*

HENRY LAURENS (1724–92)

Claim to Fame: First American ever cremated

Deathly Details: Laurens, a wealthy South Carolina slave
trader and signer of America's Articles of Confederation, was terrified of being buried alive. Years earlier when his young daughter
"died" from smallpox, her body was laid out near an open window
while her grave was being dug. Only by chance did the cool air revive her before the gravediggers finished their task. Fearing a similar
fate, Laurens instructed in his will that his body be cremated. (He
apparently didn't fear being burned alive.) Incinerating the dead
was unheard of in America at the time; the nation's first cremato-
rium wouldn't be built until 1886. Laurens had to leave explicit
instructions in his will explaining how he wanted it done:

> I solemnly enjoin it on my son…[that] he cause my body to be
> Wrapped in twelve Yards of Tow Cloth, and Burnt until it be entirely
> and totally consumed…And then collecting my Bones, deposit them
> where ever he shall think proper.

When Laurens died in 1792, his instructions were carried out.

FRANK MOTTO (1921)

Claim to Fame: First American to receive a death sentence from a
female judge

Deadly Details: In 1921, Motto, a Cleveland mobster, went on
trial for murdering two people in a payroll robbery the year before.
Presiding judge: Florence Ellinwood Allen, newly elected to the
bench after the ratification of the 19th Amendment in 1920 made
it possible for her to run for judge. (In Ohio, anyone eligible to vote
could also run for office.) With one woman on the bench and others
serving on the jury—another novelty made possible by the 19th
Amendment—many feared, and Motto probably hoped, that the
ladies wouldn't be tough enough for the job. No such luck. After
the jury found him guilty, Judge Allen sentenced him to die in the

---

Wind speed must be at least 11 knots (12.7 mph) to create white-capped waves.

electric chair. He was executed three months later.

GARETH JONES (1925–58)

Claim to Fame: First person to die during a live TV broadcast

Deadly Details: On November 30, 1958, Jones was performing in *Armchair Theatre*, a British TV show. Ironically, his character was supposed to have a heart attack during the play, but Jones never made it—he had his own very real heart attack and died in mid-show. The camera wasn't on him at the time, and the viewing audience had no idea that he'd died. His character simply disappeared without explanation, and the rest of the cast continued on without him until the show was over.

OTTO LILIENTHAL (1848–96)

Claim to Fame: First person to die in a hang glider crash

Deadly Details: Lilienthal, a German engineer known in his day as "The Father of Flight," was the first person to build a glider capable of pilot-controlled flight. Between 1891 and 1896, he made more than 2,000 flights in gliders of his own design, in the process advancing aviation further than everyone who had come before him. And who knows? Had he not been convinced that powered aircraft would need flapping wings to fly, he might have beaten the Wright brothers in the race to invent the airplane. But he never did build such a craft, and he didn't live to see the Wright brothers build their Wright Flyer, either. On August 9, 1896, he fractured his spine in a glider crash outside of Berlin and died two days later.

"DENISE MOORE" (1876–1911)

Claim to Fame: First woman to die in an airplane crash

Deadly Details: Moore's real name was Jane Wright; she took the pseudonym Denise Moore in 1911 to keep her family from finding out that she was taking flying lessons. Just eight years after the Wright brothers' first flight, aviation was still very dangerous and women were all but shut out of it. (The Wright brothers refused to sell airplanes to women, saying that they lacked the "coolness and judgment" necessary to fly.) Moore flew anyway. One week shy of earning her pilot's license, she was soloing in a biplane 150 feet off the ground when a sudden gust of wind flipped it over and sent it crashing to Earth. Pinned beneath the wreckage, she died at the scene.

B-10 AND ROBBED

Fark.com is a news site created by Drew Curtis in 1999. Members post links to real news stories, but make up their own funny headlines. Each year, "Farkers" select the cleverest and funniest. Here are a few of the best (and G-rated).

• "Bear attack victim had 'tender heart,' according to friends, family, bear"

• "Fourteen-year-old Snigdha Nandipati wins Scripps National Spelling Bee by correctly spelling Snigdha Nandipati"

• "'New 787 Dreamliner batteries will totally not catch fire,' says Boeing Engineering Vice President Hindenberg"

• "Bingo hall worker B-10 and robbed"

• "Mother of two disfigured by seven tumors on her face says, 'Tumor would benign'"

• "Getting hit with a track-and-field projectile can be fatal. Discus"

• "Printer-ink tanker truck overturns. Damages estimated at seven hundred trillion dollars"

• "Baghdad's National Museum reopens six years after looting. Featured displays include mostly a bunch of really heavy stuff"

• "Explosion at winery leaves workers weak-bodied with a rich red hue, containing discernible hints of charred debris and strong character best described as dead"

• "Police in London solve 1 crime for every 1000 CCTV cameras. Or about 2 for every 1984"

• "PETA names Jessica Chastain, Woody Harrelson sexiest vegetarian celebrities of 2012. I know who he is, but I've never seen herbivore"

• "Man enters zoo enclosure to feed the tigers—succeeds"

WORD GAMES

Some letter-perfect fun. Answers are on page 537.

1. What makes this group of states unique?
Delaware, Georgia, Louisiana, Rhode Island, Pennsylvania, Florida, Utah, Hawaii

2. A tree so big that it contains all five vowels, yet only has seven letters. What is it?

3. Name the only number from 1 to 1,000 that's in alphabetical order when spelled out.

4. How can you change the pronunciations of these words without changing any letters?
nice, rainier, tangier

5. Ollie is worth 31,770; his friend Elsie is worth just 197 less. How much is Leslie worth?

6. One word is a device that regulates. Change a "v" to a "u" and it becomes a good deal. What are the two words?

7. Which letter adds great value to a pear?

8. What common chemical compound is represented by the following letter sequence?
HIJKLMNO

9. What are you doing if you take what has been produced by a member of the Talpidae family and, in a short time, create what a major orogeny has taken centuries for Earth's geological history to produce?

10. Can you name all eight U.S. states that begin with the same letter?

11. Remove six letters from this sequence to reveal a familiar English word.
BSAINXLEATNTEARS

12. What odd number becomes even when beheaded?

13. Which letter changes a boy into a woman?

14. What letter is most useful to a deaf woman?

15. Where will you find all five of us lined up in order? A tennis court. What are we?

16. Rearrange each word to find the thread that holds them all together:
Lenin, Alec, mined, saint, Proselyte.

WINNERS...AND LOSERS

Winning an award or a championship brings the thrill of recognition for our accomplishments—something we all want. What we don't want is to be caught cheating and have to give back the award. Here are some prizes that were awarded undeservingly...and then taken back after the cheaters were found out.

AWARD: 1990 Grammy Award for Best New Artist
WINNER: Despite competition from such popular acts as the Indigo Girls and Tone Loc, it was no surprise when German dance-pop band Milli Vanilli won the Grammy for Best New Artist. In 1989, the group had scored three #1 hits (and one #2), and despite getting caught lip-syncing on stage when a tape player malfunctioned in late 1989, Milli Vanilli was still a sure thing for the Grammy. Then, in November 1990, the group's producer, Frank Farian, admitted to the press that singers Rob Pilatus and Fabrice Morvan hadn't sung on any of their recordings—they just looked like pop stars, he said. The real singers were five anonymous backup singers. (They later toured as "The Real Milli Vanilli.")
LOSER: The National Academy of Recording Arts and Sciences rescinded the Grammy—the only Grammy ever rescinded—and vacated the Best New Artist award for that year (likely to the chagrin of the Indigo Girls and Tone Loc).

AWARD: The 2001 Bancroft Prize
WINNER: In 2000, Emory University history professor Michael A. Bellesiles published *Arming America: The Origins of a National Gun Culture*, an examination of the history of guns in the United States. Bellesiles's book presented evidence that the opinions held about the constitutional right to own guns developed not in colonial times, to fend off British soldiers, but after the Civil War, when community relations were tense and guns were far more affordable. Bellesiles won the prestigious Bancroft Prize, awarded by Columbia University to a work about American history.
LOSER: Soon after he accepted the award, Bellesiles's thesis began to fall apart when it was discovered that he had falsified—if not outright fabricated—much of his historical evidence. His credibility in

---

But can they bury their poop? Rabbits can growl, hiss, and purr like a cat.

question, Bellesiles resigned his post at Emory, and Columbia took back the Bancroft, vacating the results for 2001.

AWARD: Tour de France bike racing championship, 1999 to 2005
WINNER: Lance Armstrong's story was incredible—after beating testicular cancer, he returned to professional bicycling and won a record seven straight Tour de France victories. He retired after his 2005 win and started a cancer research charity, dated rock star Sheryl Crow, and cameoed in movies like *Dodgeball*. Meanwhile, scandals related to doping began to affect many of racing's major players, and some of Armstrong's associates claimed that he had taken illegal substances and encouraged others to do so as well. Over and over again, Armstrong categorically denied the charges… until 2013 when, in an interview with Oprah Winfrey, he finally confessed to doping.
LOSER: The International Cycling Union banned Armstrong from competition for life and vacated his seven Tour de France wins. Technically speaking, nobody won the Tour de France from 1999 to 2005.

AWARD: Academy Award for Best Documentary Feature
WINNER: At the 1969 Academy Awards, director Alexander Grasshoff accepted an Oscar for his film *Young Americans*, which detailed a national tour by the Young Americans, a youth show choir. However, in order to be eligible for the award, Academy rules state that a film must be publicly screened in the previous calendar year. *Young Americans* had screened once…in 1967, but not 1968, the year for which it won the award.
LOSER: The Academy of Motion Picture Arts and Sciences ordered Grasshoff to return his golden statuette about a month after the ceremony. It was then given to the first runner-up, *Journey into Self*, a film about psychiatry directed by Tom Skinner. (Brashoff was nominated once more, for 1973's *Journey to the Outer Limits*, but came up empty-handed again.)

AWARD: 2004 college football national championship
WINNER: In the postseason of the 2004 college football season, the BCS National Championship—the de facto national title game—was the Orange Bowl, played by the #1-ranked USC Trojans

and the #2-ranked Oklahoma Sooners. USC cruised to a 55–19 win and were declared the national champions of college football for the 2004 season.

LOSER: Then in 2010, after a four-year investigation, the NCAA ruled that USC running back Reggie Bush had received illegal gifts from sports marketing agents who wanted to sign him. Among the gifts: free hotel stays, use of a limousine, and a rent-free home for Bush and his family. Those gifts amounted to payment, the NCAA ruled, and the organization has strict rules about student athletes remaining amateurs. The punishment: USC was banned from bowl games for two years and had to vacate the 14 games it won in 2004 and 2005 in which Bush had played, including the national title. Bush also decided to return his 2005 Heisman Trophy (before the Heisman Trust stripped him of the award). This marks the only time that a BCS National Championship of college football has been vacated and the only year for which there is no Heisman Trophy winner since the award was created in 1935.

*   *   *

AN OPEN AND SHUT CASE

Lost: In the 1830s, a botanist named Joseph Hooker was given 314 fossil slides that had been collected on a recent expedition. He was supposed to register them at the British Geological Survey (BGS) building in Keyworth, England, but he was in a hurry to leave on his own expedition, so he tossed the slides into a drawer in a store room and forgot about them.

Found: A century and a half later, in April 2011, a University of London paleontologist named Howard Falcon-Lang was looking for some fossils at the BGS, so he peeked inside the drawer labeled "unregistered fossil plants." They weren't the slides he was looking for, but something much more important: Many of the slides were signed "C. Darwin, Esq." Before he was famous, Charles Darwin had collected them on his five-year journey on the HMS *Beagle*, where he first visited the Galapagos Islands and began formulating his theory of evolution, which he published in his 1859 book *On the Origin of Species*. Dr. John Ludden, the BGS's executive director said, "I wonder what else might be hiding in our collections."

In 2006, Florida adopted Key lime pie as the official state pie.

THE GOLDEN FLEECE AWARDS

Think government waste is a new thing? Think again. William Proxmire was the U.S. Senator from Wisconsin from 1957 to 1989. His biggest claim to fame: the monthly "Golden Fleece" Awards, given in the 1970s and '80s to "the biggest, most ridiculous, or most ironic examples of wasteful government spending." A few honorees:

The Federal Aviation Administration, for spending "over $417,000 for 95 new meteorological instruments so that its employees can make rain predictions while remaining indoors, despite the fact that existing instruments perform the same function but must be read outdoors."

NASA, for requesting $2.8 million to construct an addition to a "perfectly adequate" $8.7 million facility that houses "a wheel-barrowful of moon rocks."

The U.S. Post Office, "for spending $3.4 million on a Madison Avenue ad campaign trying to make Americans write more letters," then spending another $775,000 to see if the ads were working.

The Department of Housing and Urban Development and The Economic Development Administration, for spending $279,000 on a community center in the middle of nowhere that was "so completely useless, when it collapsed, no one knew it for days."

The Environmental Protection Agency, "for spending an extra $1 to $1.2 million to preserve a Trenton, New Jersey, sewer as a historical monument. The sewer is 25 feet underground, full of mud and sludge, has been viewed only twice in the last 23 years, will not be on public view in the future, and is not unique."

The U.S. Air Force, "for spending $59,000 over six years on playing cards given as souvenirs to visitors aboard Air Force Two."

President Gerald R. Ford's "Energy Czar" Frank Zarb, for "spending $25,000 and almost 19,000 gallons of fuel jetting about the country in chartered aircraft urging businessmen and civic groups to economize on energy and fuel."

The U.S. Navy, "for spending $792 on a designer doormat."

The National Science Foundation, "for spending $9,992 on a study of 'Bullfights and the Ideology of the Nation in Spain.'"

The Department of Commerce, "for spending $200,000 to build an 800-foot limestone replica of the Great Wall of China in Bedford, Indiana, as a follow-up to its $500,000 grant for the building of a ten-story-high limestone model of the Great Pyramid of Egypt."

The General Services Administration, "for losing 49,000 forms— the equivalent of open-ended airline tickets—with a potential value of $7 million," after the GSA inadvertently ordered 50,000 of the forms when it only needed 500.

The U.S. Army, for spending $20,000 to design and print 30,000 "fancy, multicolored pamphlets" to teach soldiers how to play the schoolyard game 'king of the hill.'"

The Department of Labor, for spending $384,948 on a "door-to-door survey to count the dogs, cats, and horses at the 160,000 houses and apartments in Ventura County, California."

NASA, "for spending $27,000 to seek out composers and artists" to create music and art for "a future space station…that is yet to be approved or funded either by the Administration or Congress."

The U.S. Air Force, for spending $3,000 on a six-month Pentagon study of the "use of umbrellas by male personnel in uniform."

The Office of Education, "for spending $219,592 to develop a 'curriculum package' to teach college students how to watch TV."

The U.S. Army, "for spending $38 million on a new gas mask that is no improvement over the gas masks that it is designed to replace." (The Army spent more than $46 million on the program before giving up in 1982 and starting a new gas-mask program.)

The National Endowment of the Arts (a runner-up winner), for spending $1,000 on a University of Hawaii "contemporary environmental conceptual art" project that consisted of "four hundred people being filmed from a rented helicopter as they walked along an Oahu beach wearing shiny paper party hats color-coded to the wearer's sex and race."

Chinese word for chopsticks: *quaize*, which means "nimble ones."

DINER LINGO

*Diner waitresses and short-order cooks have a language all their own—
a sort of restaurant jazz, with clever variations on standard menu
themes. Here's a collection of some of our favorites.*

Shingle with a shimmy and a shake: Toast with butter and jam or jelly

Baled hay: Shredded Wheat

Cackle fruit: Eggs

Cats' heads and easy diggins: Biscuits and gravy

Warts: Olives

Why bother, high and dry: A cup of decaf coffee, no sugar and no cream

Bronx vanilla: Garlic

Drag one through Wisconsin, don't cry over it: One cheese-burger, hold the onions

Slab of moo, let 'em chew it: A rare steak

Cops and robbers: Doughnuts and coffee

Mousetrap, give it wings: A grilled-cheese sandwich, and the customer is in a hurry

Irish turkey, give it shoes: An order of corned beef and cabbage to go

Drown the kids: Two hard-boiled eggs

Bucket of cold mud: A bowl of chocolate ice cream

Guess water: Soup

Soup jockey: A waitress

Campers: A party that hogs a booth for too long a time

Looseners: Prunes

Whistleberries: Baked beans

Dog soup/One on the city: A glass of water

Roach cake: Huckleberry pie

Machine oil: Pancake syrup

Pair of drawers: Two cups of coffee

Honeymoon salad: Lettuce, alone (Get it?)

Indiana Jones: Customer who arrives "in the nick of time"— just as the diner's about to close

C-board: A to-go order (in a cardboard container)

Lumber: A toothpick

Whiskey, cremate it: Rye toast

Bloodhounds in the hay: Hot dogs and sauerkraut

The plane truth: At any given time, 60,000 people are in the air over the U.S.

FAMILY SECRETS

On page 370, we told you the story of Queen Victoria's "scandalous" relationships with two of her servants, and the illegitimate child(ren) that supposedly resulted from one of those relationships. Here's a look at two famous people who found themselves in similar straits.

CLARK GABLE (1901–1960)
Background: In 1935, Gable, 34, had an affair with his co-star, 22-year-old Loretta Young, while filming *The Call of the Wild*. A few weeks later, Young discovered she was pregnant.

In the Family Way: Gable, one of Hollywood's biggest stars, was already married. He and Young had strict morality clauses in their studio contracts, and the scandal was serious enough to end both of their careers. Young was determined to have the child and raise it herself, so she hid in Europe during her pregnancy, then returned to Hollywood and gave birth to a baby girl at home, in secret. She hid her daughter, named Judy, in a San Francisco orphanage for 19 months before "adopting" her.

Secrets: It was well-known in Hollywood that Judy was Gable and Young's child…to everyone except little Judy. Her childhood friends were instructed by their parents never to tell her. She bore a striking resemblance to Gable, down to his protruding "Dumbo" ears, which Young hid beneath bonnets until Judy was old enough to have them surgically pinned back. She met Gable only once, at age 15, but he did not tell her that he was her father.

Judy finally found out when she was in her early 20s and engaged to be married. Her fiancé told her it was "common knowledge" that Gable was her father. It took Judy another eight years to confront her mother, who finally admitted the truth, but only privately: Loretta Young went to her grave refusing to publicly acknowledge Judy as her biological daughter, not even after Judy told the story in her 1994 memoir, *Uncommon Knowledge*. Young dismissed her daughter's claim as "a rumor from a bygone era." She did, however, admit it to the writer of her authorized biography, *Forever Young*, on condition that the book not be published until after her death. Young passed away in August 2000; the biography came out three months later.

Clint Eastwood's 1st job: maternity ward diaper model (he was 2 weeks old).

CHARLES LINDBERGH (1902–1974)

Background: Lindbergh made history in 1927 when he became the first person to fly solo nonstop across the Atlantic Ocean. In 1929, he married Anne Morrow and had six children by her. That's all the family anyone knew about until nearly 30 years after Lindbergh's death in 1974.

In the Family Way: In the 1950s, Lindbergh traveled the world as a representative of Pan American Airways. During a trip to Germany, he began an affair with his translator, a woman named Valeska (her last name has never been made public) and fathered a son and a daughter by her. Then, when Valeska introduced him to two sisters named Brigitte and Marietta Hesshaimer at a dinner party in 1957, Lindbergh began affairs with both of them, fathering two sons and a daughter with Brigitte, and two sons by Marietta. Each of the three mistresses knew about the other two and apparently tolerated Lindbergh's relationships with them.

Secrets: Lindbergh swore all three women to secrecy, so none of his illegitimate children had any inkling of his true identity. They were told he was an American writer named "Careu Kent," and were warned never to talk about him to outsiders, or else his occasional visits to see them would end forever. Lindbergh bought homes for each of his illegitimate families, supported them financially, and left them large sums of money when he died in 1974. It wasn't until the late 1990s, when Brigitte's daughter, 23-year-old Astrid, found 150 of her mother's love letters and an article about Charles Lindbergh that she realized who her father was. Brigitte made her children promise to keep the secret as long as she and Anne Morrow Lindbergh were still alive. Both women died in 2001, and it was only then that the children came forward. DNA tests confirmed they were Lindbergh's children. Because Valeska and Marietta were still living in 2003, their five children declined to take DNA tests out of respect for their privacy, but little doubt remains that Lindbergh is their father as well.

*　　　*　　　*

GOOD BREADING

You know the outer part of bread is called the crust. But what about the inner part? It's called the crumb. (You kneaded to know that.)

IT HAPPENED IN '63

What happened in 1963 didn't stay in 1963. It went down in history.

In 1963, gas cost about 29¢ a gallon. You could buy a car for $3,233 and a house for $12,650. The national average wage: a whopping $4,396.

• On January 25, 1963, *LIFE* magazine blazoned this headline across its cover: *In Color: The Vicious Fighting in Vietnam.*

• Marvel Comics founder Martin Goodman once told Stan Lee, "You can't call a hero Spider-Man. People hate spiders." Goodman ate his words in March 1963, publishing *The Amazing Spider-Man* #1.

• On June 10, 1963, President John F. Kennedy signed the Equal Pay Act into law. (Fifty years later, women earn 77¢ for every dollar earned by men.)

• In July, the U.S. Post Office began a media blitz to promote its new Zone Improvement Plan for speedier mail delivery, also known as ZIP codes.

• On September 15, the Ku Klux Klan planted a bomb in the 16th St. Baptist Church in Birmingham, Alabama, killing four girls—the 21st racially-motivated blast in the city nicknamed "Bombingham."

• On November 23, *The Boston Globe* ran this headline in its morning edition: "Shock... Disbelief...Grief." A sniper's bullet had ended the life and presidency of Massachusetts native son, John F. Kennedy.

• Alcatraz, the decaying, maximum-security federal prison in San Francisco Bay, closed. Its "escape-proof" image had been shattered after three inmates dug their way out of their concrete cells using spoons and other improvised tools.

• Peter, Paul, and Mary's "Puff the Magic Dragon" was #16 on Billboard's year-end Hot 100, but Little Stevie Wonder (age 13) beat them out with "Fingertips" in the #8 spot. Number one for 1963: Jimmy Gilmer and the Fireballs (who?) with "Sugar Shack."

• On August 8, 1963, fifteen thieves boarded the Glasgow-to-London mail train and made off with 120 bags of cash, worth about $60 million today. (They were later caught.) The heist's mastermind, Bruce Reynolds, died in 2013, six months shy of the 50th anniversary of "The Great Train Robbery."

Cacao trees can live for 200 years, but only produce marketable cocoa beans for 25 years.

OUR KIND OF CHRISTMAS STORY

It's not often that we come across a Christmas tale that seems like it was handcrafted at the North Pole especially for the Bathroom Reader. But then we found this.

Santa's Helpers: Emma Palmer and Adrian Brown, parents of three-year-old Hannah Brown; and "Santa Dan" Grenier, in Guelph, Ontario, Canada

True Story: When Emma and Adrian asked Hannah in 2012 what she wanted Santa to bring her for Christmas, she said she wanted a portable toilet—the big kind that you see at construction sites. "She's not a typical little girl who chooses average things," Palmer said. No doubt the perplexed parents tried to steer their little one toward something a little more, well, Christmasy, but Hannah was insistent. So Emma and Adrian called about a dozen Porta-Potty companies in the area, but not one would rent them a yuletide commode. Then they found Dan Grenier, the proprietor of Porta-Plus Portables. He agreed to help.

Moment of Truth: On Christmas Eve, while Hannah was visiting her grandparents, Grenier delivered a portable toilet and helped hide it under a tarp against the fence. The next morning, when Hannah opened the presents Santa left for her under the Christmas tree, there wasn't a Porta-Potty among them. "She was devastated," said Palmer…until they led her out to the driveway. There, wrapped in a Christmas bow, was the big toilet from Santa.

In the Bag: Santa's toilet remained in the driveway for the rest of the week. Hannah did all her "business" out there until Grenier, posing as Santa's helper, returned to take the toilet "back to the North Pole." So how much did all this cost Hannah's parents? Not a penny. On Christmas Eve, Grenier returned with a gift bag containing their $50 rental fee and left it on the front porch with a note asking them to put the money in Hannah's college fund. Also in the bag: a piggy bank shaped like a Porta-Potty, a keepsake for Hannah to remember the year Santa made her wish come true.

VCR BORED GAMES

Some forgotten fads are forgotten for a reason.

DO YOU WANT TO PLAY A GAME?
In the late 1980s and early '90s, board game publishers feared that the popularity of video games spelled doom for their industry. Solution: VCR Board Games, which included a board game, and, to compete with electronic games, a videotape. The tape was supposed to make the game more exciting by adding video clips, a story, an interactive element, or just atmosphere. Only problem: the tape usually made the game more confusing, and in some cases, once you knew what was on the video, you couldn't play the game again. Here are a few "classics" from this forgotten fad.

STAR TREK: TNG—A KLINGON CHALLENGE (1993).
Plot: The Enterprise-D is docked; the crew is on shore leave (so no actors had to be paid). Klingons hijack the ship, and the players have to work together to regain control of it. Every now and then, the video, which is otherwise just footage of Klingons messing around the ship, abruptly cuts to a Klingon, who might shout, "You! The one that just moved!" and order that player to lose a turn.

HI-HO! CHERRY-O! (1987) The classic board game was simple: spin a wheel and remove that number of plastic "cherries" from your tree, when it's empty, you win. The VCR game version had 20 minutes of instructions, directing how tree pictures are to be laid out, topped with face-down discs that get turned over whenever players find the animal picture card that matches up with the asound made by a cartoon animal in the video.

DRAGON STRIKE (1993). It's a Dungeons and Dragons-like board game. The tape explains how to play it, then creates atmosphere with random images of knights, wizards, and goblins running around while you play the board game.

RICH LITTLE'S VCR CHARADES (1985). Famed impersonator Rich Little acts out a word or phrase—silently. Players have to guess the answer before the players on the video figure it out. After you've played the game once, you know all the answers. (Then it goes to Goodwill.)

The word "sheppey" was coined by authors Douglas Adams and John Lloyd in 1983....

IF THE SHOE FITS...

It's always fun to find out the origin of something so commonplace that it never even occurred to you that it had an origin. Give this ancient Greek tale a read...and see if it doesn't remind you of another story.

O NCE UPON A TIME
Many years ago in Greece, according to ancient legend, a beautiful young girl was kidnapped by pirates and taken to Egypt, where she was sold into slavery. The man who bought her, an elderly merchant, was entranced by her fair skin, green eyes, and curly blonde hair, and added her to the servant staff of his household.

The other servant girls were Egyptian, and had bronze skin and straight, black hair. They teased the new girl mercilessly for her odd features, calling her Rhodopis or "Rosy-cheeked," because she blushed often and her skin burned quickly in the sun. They gave her the most difficult chores, saving the easy ones for themselves.

Animals were Rhodopis's only friends—monkeys, birds, and a hippopotamus that lived in the river. When Rhodopis finished her chores, she'd go down to the river to dance and sing for the animals. Even the hippopotamus would climb up onto the riverbank to listen to her.

HAVING A BALL

One day, the old merchant saw Rhodopis dancing by the river and was so impressed that he gave her a pair of beautiful red and gold sandals. This made the other servant girls jealous.

Not long afterward, the household learned that the Pharaoh would be holding court in nearby Memphis, where there would be food, dancing, and entertainment. Everyone was invited, and the other servant girls made plans to attend. But they also made sure that Rhodopis couldn't go by giving her all of their chores to do, including washing the clothes. Then they left without her.

Rhodopis went down to the river to wash the clothes. She normally sang happy songs, but this time her song was sad and the hippopotamus soon tired of it. He splashed back into the river and floated away, and his splashes wet Rhodopis's beautiful red and gold sandals. She wiped them off, then set them in the sun to dry.

OUT OF THE BLUE

Before long the sky darkened. Rhodopis looked up just as a falcon swooped down, snatched one of her sandals in its talons and flew off with it. Rhodopis was stunned, certain the falcon was the messenger of Horus, the god of the skies.

And right she was, for the falcon flew all the way to Memphis, where the Pharaoh was still holding court, and dropped the sandal right into his lap. The Pharaoh, also recognizing the falcon as a messenger of Horus, concluded that Horus wanted him to marry the owner of the sandal.

The Pharaoh ordered that every maiden in the kingdom try on the sandal until he found his bride. He searched on land but could not find the sandal's owner, so he sailed the royal barge up the Nile, pulling ashore every so often and ordering nearby maidens to try it on. When Rhodopis saw the barge stop near the old merchant's house, she hid in the rushes while the other servant girls tried on the sandal. They knew it belonged to Rhodopis, but said nothing.

But the Pharaoh spotted Rhodopis hiding at the water's edge and asked her to try on the sandal. It fit, of course, and Rhodopis still had the other sandal, so there was no doubt that they were hers. The Pharaoh was overjoyed when he announced that Rhodopis would be his queen. They married and lived happily ever after.

MADE IN EGYPT

If you thought that the story of Cinderella only dates back to the animated Disney film of 1950, or to the Grimm's fairy tale of the early 1800s, or to *Tales of Mother Goose*, written by Charles Perrault in 1697, think again. The story, believed to be the world's best-known folktale, is also one of the oldest. The earliest recorded version dates back more than 2,000 years to the first century B.C., when the Greek historian Strabo heard the tale of Rhodopis while traveling in Egypt and noted it in *Geographica*, his 17-volume history of the known world. Strabo's version contains the story of the eagle snatching one of Rhodopis's sandals and dropping it in the Pharaoh's lap, the famous "slipper test"—the Pharaoh's search for the girl who fit the sandal—and his marriage to Rhodopis, who becomes queen. But that's it; the rest of the details were added later.

One bushel of wheat will make about 42 pounds of pasta.

WOMEN OF THE WORLD

The ancient Greeks brought the story of Rhodopis with them wherever they traveled. Result: Countless variants of the story have appeared all over the world. In 1893, a woman named Marian Roalfe Cox cataloged more than 300.

When certain details of the story violated cultural norms in a particular region, those details invariably changed. Westerners are most familiar with the version where the prince falls in love with the girl after meeting her at a ball and discovers the slipper after the girl flees in haste. But in parts of the world where segregation of the sexes is absolute and the idea of young people socializing at a ball makes no sense, the prince falls in love with the owner of the slipper before he meets her or even knows who she is. In places where standards are a little different, the falcon snatches the sandal while the girl is bathing (naked) outdoors.

The oldest recorded version of the story that includes a wicked stepmother and stepsisters comes from China and dates back to the ninth century A.D. In that version the girl's name is Yeh-Shen. She attends a festival in a cave, wearing gold shoes that are each as light as a single strand of hair and that make no noise when she walks.

PYRAMID SCHEME

Strabo's original Rhodopis story contains interesting details not commonly associated with the Cinderella story. He writes that Egyptians living around the pyramids of Giza, near the Sphinx, believed that the Third Pyramid of Giza was Rhodopis's tomb. It wasn't: The pyramid is actually the tomb of the Pharaoh Menkaure, who ruled Egypt around the year 2,500 B.C. But for centuries the Rhodopis story was accepted as fact. (Another version of the story: Rhodopis was a courtesan, or royal court prostitute, so skilled in her profession that when she died her lovers paid to have the Third Pyramid built as a memorial.)

* * *

THREE REAL NEWSPAPER AD FLUBS

- "The price you see is half of what you pay!"
- "Karcz Ford: Where customer service is NOT an option!"
- "New Miracle Diet—lose all your weight!"

Eww! Greek philosopher Gorgias of Epirus (300 B.C.) was born in his dead mother's coffin.

ODE TO BEER

Please read these quotes responsibly.

"From man's sweat and God's love, beer came into the world."
—**Saint Arnoldus**

"If drunk in moderation, beer softens the temper, cheers the spirit, and promotes health."
—**Thomas Jefferson**

"You can only drink thirty or forty glasses of beer a day, no matter how rich you are."
—**Adophus Busch**

"The heart which grief hath cankered, hath one unfailing remedy—the tankard."
—**C.S. Calverly**

"Give my people plenty of beer, good beer, and cheap beer, and you will have no revolution among them."
—**Queen Victoria**

"Never underestimate how much assistance, how much satisfaction, how much comfort, how much soul and transcendence there might be in a well-made taco and a cold bottle of beer."
—**Tom Robbins,**
Jitterbug Perfume

"I like beer. On occasion, I will even drink beer to celebrate a major event, such as the fall of Communism or the fact that the refrigerator is still working."
—**Dave Barry**

"Beer is the reason we get up each afternoon."
—**Ray McNeill**

"Fermentation equals civilization."
—**John Ciardi**

"When I die, I want to decompose in a barrel of porter and have it served in all the pubs in Ireland."
—**J. P. Donleavy**

"A little bit of beer is divine medicine."
—**Paracelsus, Greek doctor**

"The best way to die is to sit under a tree, eat lots of bologna and salami, drink a case of beer, and then blow up."
—**Art Donovan**

"Beer is the only virtual reality I need."
—**Leroy Lockhorn**

Pigs can run about 11 miles an hour; housecats: 30 miles an hour.

SON OF A BOCHE?

*Just when you think everything that could be written about
World War II has been, along comes a story like this.
Is it true? If so, it's one for the history books.*

THE CORPORAL

One morning in the spring of 1917, a 16-year-old French girl named Charlotte Lobjoie was cutting hay with some other young women in the countryside near Lille, in northern France. World War I had been raging for nearly three years, and this part of France had been under German occupation almost from the beginning.

German soldiers were everywhere, and this morning the women noticed one nearby who was scribbling something in a notebook. That piqued their curiosity, so the women sent Charlotte to find out what he was doing. The soldier, a corporal who hailed from Austria, explained that he was sketching pictures of the countryside.

Though Germany and France were bitter enemies, Charlotte and the corporal struck up a friendship and took walks together in the countryside whenever he was on leave. The pair were hardly an ideal match: Charlotte didn't speak German, the corporal didn't speak French, and when they walked together, the corporal was more interested in delivering impassioned speeches to imaginary audiences than he was in trying to communicate with Charlotte. Their friendship nonetheless grew into a romance, and one "tipsy" evening a few months later, Charlotte said, she became pregnant with the corporal's child.

Charlotte didn't know it at the time, but their romance was nearly over. The war soon turned against Germany, the Allies recaptured northern France, and Charlotte never saw the corporal again. Their son, Jean-Marie, born in March 1918, would never meet his father; 30 years would pass before he even learned his father's name.

ONE THING LEADS TO ANOTHER

With more than 1.3 million Frenchmen dead or missing at war's end, the French people were not kind to women who'd consorted

---

How far must you walk to burn off the calories in a Double Whopper w/Cheese? 10 miles.

with German soldiers. Life in a small village, where everyone knew everyone else's business, couldn't have been easy for Charlotte. Soon after the war ended, she handed Jean-Marie over to her parents and moved to Paris. She never spoke to her parents again, and years passed before she reunited with her son.

Jean-Marie had a miserable childhood: His grandfather beat him regularly, perhaps because of the shame he believed that the boy brought to the family, and the other schoolkids picked on him for being the son of a *Boche* (a German soldier). When the boy's grandparents died in the mid-1920s, he was adopted by another family and packed off to boarding school. By then Charlotte had married a man named Clement Loret, who gave her son his last name even though the boy and his mother did not live together.

REVELATION

In 1936, Jean-Marie Loret joined the French army. He was still in active service in May 1940 when Hitler invaded France during World War II. When France capitulated just six weeks later, he joined the French Resistance and continued to fight the Nazis. He reunited with his mother during the war, but it wasn't until 1948, three years after the war was over, that she finally revealed the secret she'd kept from him for 30 years.

"Your father's name," she said, "is Adolf Hitler."

COULD IT BE?

Was Charlotte Lobjoie's claim that she bore a son by Adolf Hitler even remotely possible? The wartime dates do appear to add up: Hitler was serving in that part of France when Charlotte became pregnant, so they could have had an affair. Loret's birth certificate does list an unnamed German soldier as his father, and Loret did have the same blood type as Hitler.

Jean-Marie claimed that during the Nazi occupation of France in World War II, German army officers visited his mother from time to time in Paris and gave her envelopes of cash, presumably on Hitler's orders. Loret also claimed that when Charlotte died in 1951, he found paintings signed by Hitler in her attic.

But the most interesting pieces of circumstantial evidence is the remarkable physical resemblance that Jean-Marie Loret bore to Adolf Hitler. In photographs, he looks eerily like the dictator; had he been a little older, he could easily have passed as Hitler's brother.

AN INDEPENDENT ACCOUNT

The resemblance could be a coincidence, of course. It's possible that Loret just happened to look like Hitler and made up the story about his mother and Hitler. But another piece of evidence—one that surfaced only recently—makes this seem less likely. On D-Day— June 4, 1944—a British soldier named Leonard Wilkes landed at Normandy and then battled his way across France. On September 30, near Lille, he made the following entry in his diary:

> An interesting day today. Visited the house where Hitler stayed as a corporal in the last war, saw the woman who had a baby by him, and she told us that the baby, a son, was now fighting in the French army against the Germans.

Wilkes's children didn't discover his diary until 2002, and didn't make the Hitler entry public until 2012, after they read an article about Loret. To date, the diary entry is the earliest written record of the claim that Hitler fathered a child with a French woman during the First World War.

CONVERSATION STOPPER

Jean-Marie Loret suffered his entire life for being the illegitimate son of a German soldier, and fought against the Nazis in World War II. So when his mother told him that he was Hitler's son, it was hardly welcome news. He told no one and battled depression for 20 years by burying himself in his job with the French railway. He married twice, fathered nine children, and didn't tell any of them about their family history until 1972, when he interrupted a dining room chat by blurting out, "Kids, I've got something to tell you. Your grandfather is Adolf Hitler." A few years later he wrote a memoir, *Your Father's Name Is Hitler*, which was published in 1981. Four years later he died from a heart attack at the age of 67.

As of 2012, the claim that Hitler had a son by Charlotte Lobjoie is still based entirely on circumstantial evidence; proof positive would require a DNA test to compare the Loret family genes with Hitler's or those of his known blood relatives. Loret's son Philippe (who also bears a resemblance to Hitler) says a DNA test isn't necessary, at least not for him. "I believe I am Hitler's grandson," he told London's *Daily Mail* in 2012. "The evidence is there. If people don't believe it, that's their problem."

Philippe said he told his three children that their great-grandfather was Adolf Hitler…but they still haven't told their children.

(GOOSE)STEP-BROTHER?

Are there more Hitler children out there, waiting to be discovered? Possibly. Another candidate for mother of a Hitler baby is Unity Mitford, the daughter of an English aristocrat. Mitford became infatuated with Naziism as a young woman and moved to Germany in 1934 when she was in her early 20s. She met the Führer after staking out a restaurant where he was known to dine frequently, and within a year had become so close to Hitler that his mistress, Eva Braun, saw her as a threat. Mitford remained a part of Hitler's inner circle until Great Britain declared war on Germany on September 3, 1939.

Despondent at the outbreak of war, Mitford tried to commit suicide by shooting herself in the head. But the shot wasn't fatal, and Hitler arranged for the critically-wounded Mitford to be sent home to England, where she spent time in and out of hospitals and nursing homes before dying in May 1948.

THE LAST WORD

So were Hitler and Mitford lovers? In 2007, British journalist Martin Bright interviewed Val Hann, the niece of a woman named Betty Norton, who ran one of the private hospitals where Unity Mitford was a patient. (The hospital also served discreetly as a maternity home for upper-class girls "in trouble.") According to Betty Hann, Norton claimed Unity Mitford was pregnant when she arrived from Germany, and gave birth to a boy at the hospital a few months later. The boy (if he ever really existed) was later adopted by an unsuspecting British family, and whenever Mitford was asked who the father was, "she always said it was Hitler's."

*   *   *

"Show me someone who never gossips and I'll show you someone who isn't interested in people."

—Barbara Walters

MYTH-CONCEPTIONS

"Common knowledge"is frequently wrong. Here are some
examples of things that many people believe…but
that, according to our sources, just aren't true.

Myth: *The Jazz Singer* (1927) was the first movie with sound.
Fact: Several short films made before *The Jazz Singer* featured sound, but *The Jazz Singer* was the first *full-length* "talkie" and the first to include dialog as part of the plot. The technology required to put sound on film had been around since the early 1900s.

Myth: Humans have five senses.

Fact: We have at least nine senses and, according to some scientists, could have as many as 21 (not counting a sense of humor, which some people lack). The myth comes from the ancient Greek philosopher Aristotle, who listed "sight, taste, touch, feeling, and hearing." But humans also have a sense of movement, temperature, balance, pain, and something called *proprioception*—knowing where our body parts are without seeing them. (Cops test this by making a drunk driver try to touch his/her nose with eyes closed.)

Myth: Storing batteries in the freezer lengthens their life.

Fact: Not true for alkaline batteries. In fact, storing them in the freezer may actually lessen their life, as most batteries don't do well in extreme temperature variations. However, if you live in a hot region with no air conditioning and the temperature in your house can reach 100°F, it may be a good idea to store them in the fridge. Otherwise, a dark, cool drawer will do fine.

Myth: You can't end a sentence with a preposition.

Fact: This is not a rule of grammar…in English. It is, however, in Latin, which is why, back in 1672, poet and critic John Dryden objected to the practice in English and in doing so, started this myth. So if your sentence ends with *at, from, around,* or any other preposition, the grammar police won't arrest you. (After Winston Churchill was chastised for ending a sentence with *with*, he joked, "This is the type of arrant pedantry up with which I will not put!")

Sunniest city in the United States: Yuma, Arizona. In the world: Yuma, Arizona.

Myth: Pterodactyls were dinosaurs.

Fact: Technically speaking, dinosaurs were land-dwelling reptiles with their legs positioned directly underneath their bodies. Pterodactyls were *pterosaurs*—flying reptiles which, when on land, crawled on all fours with their feet sprawled out to the sides, like lizards and crocodiles (also not dinosaurs).

Myth: The armor worn by medieval knights was so heavy that the knights had to be hoisted onto their horses with cranes.

Fact: Armor was designed to be worn in battle, so it was made as lightweight and flexible as possible. A knight might use a stool to mount his horse, but otherwise he could get up there just fine. The myth was popularized by a scene in the 1944 film *Henry V*, in which an armor-clad Laurence Olivier is hoisted onto his horse via a "medieval" crane. Olivier, who also directed the film, included the crane over the objections of the film's historical advisers.

Myth: Vomitoriums were places that Romans went to vomit.

Fact: No such specialized rooms existed. The Latin verb *vomitum* means "to spew forth," which is what ancient Romans did when they entered the Colosseum and other arenas through large arched passageways. It was the passageways that were called *vomitoria*.

Myth: Sharks need to keep swimming in order to breathe.

Fact: This one is partially true. Some shark species, such as great whites, makos, and whale sharks, use *ram ventilation* (swimming fast) to move water through their gills to extract the oxygen. But other shark species—including nurse and bullhead sharks—utilize what's known as *buccal pumping*, wherein the mouth muscles actively pull in water and push it through the gills, which allows the sharks to breathe when they're not moving.

*   *   *

GOT SOME HEAVY NEWS, MAN...

"The most massive single issue of a newspaper was the September 14, 1987, edition of the Sunday *New York Times*, which weighed more than 12 pounds and contained 1,612 pages."

—Guinness World Records

TIME considered Osama bin Laden for 2001's "Person of the Year," but chose Rudy Giuliani.

FRIGHTROOM READER

Uncle John first read this story when he was a teenager, and it scared the cr*p out of him…so naturally he's always wanted to include it in a Bathroom Reader.

INTRODUCTION

This short story is by American writer Ambrose Bierce, born in Ohio in 1842. After joining the Union Army at 19, Bierce become a celebrated soldier in the Civil War, and afterward a much more celebrated writer. From 1871 until his death in 1913, he was a nationally known reporter, editorialist, essayist, satirist, and short story writer—most often writing tales of the macabre. (His most famous, "An Occurrence at Owl Creek Bridge," has been adapted for numerous radio plays, TV shows, and movies, including one short film that was aired as the final episode of *The Twilight Zone* in 1964.) Bierce was traveling with Pancho Villa's army in Mexico when, at the age of 71, he disappeared. This story was first published in 1893.

CHARLES ASHMORE'S TRAIL

The family of Christian Ashmore consisted of his wife, his mother, two grown daughters, and a son of sixteen years. They lived in Troy, New York, were well-to-do, respectable persons, and had many friends, some of whom, reading these lines, will doubtless learn for the first time the extraordinary fate of the young man. From Troy, the Ashmores moved in 1871 or 1872 to Richmond, Indiana, and a year or two later to the vicinity of Quincy, Illinois, where Mr. Ashmore bought a farm and lived on it. At some little distance from the farmhouse was a spring with a constant flow of clear, cold water, whence the family derived its supply for domestic use at all seasons.

On the evening of the 9th of November in 1878, at about nine o'clock, young Charles Ashmore left the family circle about the hearth, took a tin bucket, and started toward the spring. As he did not return, the family became uneasy, and going to the door by which he had left the house, his father called without receiving an answer. He then lighted a lantern and with the eldest daughter, Martha, who insisted on accompanying him, went in search. A light snow had fallen, obliterating the path, but making the young man's trail conspicuous; each footprint was plainly defined. After going a little more than half-way—perhaps

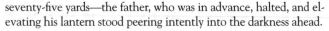

seventy-five yards—the father, who was in advance, halted, and elevating his lantern stood peering intently into the darkness ahead.

"**What** is the matter, Father?" the girl asked.

This was the matter: the trail of the young man had abruptly ended, and all beyond was smooth, unbroken snow. The last footprints were as conspicuous as any in the line; the very nail-marks were distinctly visible. Mr. Ashmore looked upward, shading his eyes with his hat held between them and the lantern. The stars were shining; there was not a cloud in the sky; he was denied the explanation which had suggested itself, doubtful as it would have been—a new snowfall with a limit so plainly defined. Taking a wide circuit round the ultimate tracks, so as to leave them undisturbed for further examination, the man proceeded to the spring, the girl following, weak and terrified. Neither had spoken a word of what both had observed. The spring was covered with ice, hours old.

Returning to the house, they noted the appearance of the snow on both sides of the trail its entire length. No tracks led away from it.

The morning light showed nothing more. Smooth, spotless, unbroken, the shallow snow lay everywhere.

Four days later the grief-stricken mother herself went to the spring for water. She came back and related that in passing the spot where the footprints had ended, she had heard the voice of her son and had been eagerly calling to him, wandering about the place, as she had fancied the voice to be now in one direction, now in another, until she was exhausted with fatigue and emotion.

Questioned as to what the voice had said, she was unable to tell, yet averred that the words were perfectly distinct. In a moment the entire family was at the place, but nothing was heard, and the voice was believed to be an hallucination caused by the mother's great anxiety and her disordered nerves. But for months afterward, at irregular intervals of a few days, the voice was heard by the several members of the family, and by others. All declared it unmistakably the voice of Charles Ashmore; all agreed that it seemed to come from a great distance, faintly, yet with entire distinctness of articulation; yet none could determine its direction, nor repeat its words. The intervals of silence grew longer and longer, the voice fainter and farther, and by midsummer it was heard no more.

If anybody knows the fate of Charles Ashmore, it is probably his mother. She is dead.

AS HEARD IN CANADA

Canadian slang is much more than "eh," you hoser.

Farmer Vision: The free over-the-air broadcast TV channels available virtually anywhere in Canada

Rink rat: A kid who does chores around a hockey rink in exchange for free skating or admission to hockey games

Chesterfield: In the 1700s, the Earl of Chesterfield commissioned a leather sofa with deep buttons and a low seat. A "chesterfield" now refers to any kind of couch.

Puck bunnies: Hockey groupies

Gonch: There's a sizeable Ukrainian population in British Columbia and Alberta, and a Ukrainian word evolved into a Canadian slang term. The original word is *gatsi*, and it means men's briefs-style underwear. Gotch, ginch, gonch, gitch, ginchies, and gitchies are all derivatives.

Gonch-pull: A wedgie

Gorby: An obnoxious tourist. It comes from the expression "guy on rental boards," coined by employees at Banff ski resorts in the late 1970s.

Vancouver Special: A cheap and easy-to-build suburban home style. They're typically box-shaped, have low ceilings, and have an extra bedroom on the ground floor, often rented out to a tenant—to make ends meet in the expensive city of Vancouver.

Lord Stanley's Mug: The Stanley Cup

TimTart: An attractive female employee of the Tim Hortons doughnut chain

Centre of the Universe: A derisive term for Toronto, used by residents of the rest of Canada (or what Torontonians call "ROC"), referring to the perceived attitude of the citizens of Canada's largest city

Down south: The U.S.

Grocery Police: Many Canadians who live near the U.S. border go "down south" to pick up groceries and consumer goods because they're cheaper there. Upon returning, they have to go through customs and declare what they bought (and pay a tax) to customs officials, or "the grocery police."

How big is a proton? 500 billion of them could fit in the period at the end of this sentence.

FLAMING OOPSES

For those of you who like your blunders well done.

REPTILE DYSFUNCTION

In March 2013, a woman and her son in Texarkana, Texas, were cleaning up their yard when they came across a black snake. In a panic, they doused the snake with gasoline and threw a lit match on it. The burning snake slithered off into the underbush, which caught fire. The flames quickly spread, prompting a 9-1-1 call: "We were trying to kill a snake with fire! It done caught the house!" Firefighters rushed to the scene but were too late to save the house. A neighbor's house was also damaged. The snake was a total loss.

RING OF FIRE

On a hot summer day in 1965, country singer Johnny Cash drove his pickup into California's Los Padres National Forest to do some fishing and drinking. On a bumpy road, the truck's tailpipe dislodged from the muffler, and the sparks started a grass fire. Cash tried to whack out the flames with his leather jacket but, as he later told the judge, "I was just about three-quarters shot [drunk] and couldn't walk real straight." The fire took a week to extinguish, burning 508 acres, including an area that housed several dozen endangered California condors. (Legend has it they died, but they just flew away.) In court, Cash was asked if he started the fire. "No," he replied, "my truck did and it's dead, so you can't question it." Cash (or rather, his insurance company) paid $82,000 in restitution.

ALCOHOL, TOBACCO, AND FIRESTARTERS

In the midst of a devastating 2011 wildfire outbreak in Texas, agents from the federal Bureau of Alcohol, Tobacco, and Firearms (ATF) traveled to Motley County to help local bomb squads destroy some explosives. But shortly before detonation, the wind picked up. The explosives were too volatile to move, however, and firefighters were on hand in case a fire started, so the ATF agents decided to risk it and detonate anyway. Bad idea. A fire did start when a burning ember landed on a patch of grass. The flames quickly spread out of control and burned 150 acres before they were extinguished six hours later. "We've got the federal government that has refused to provide assistance to the state because of all our statewide fires, and then in waltz federal agents and they start a fire," complained county attorney Tom Edwards. "That bunch has a real corner on stupid."

GET LIT

A 34-year-old Russian bartender named Albert Bykov had performed his "flaming shot" trick dozens of times without incident. But when he tried it on 28-year-old Alexey Ponamarev in May 2013, it went horribly wrong. Bykov held the flaming shot a few inches over Ponamarev's open mouth (his head was tilted back, resting on the bar) and poured. The fiery libation missed his mouth and poured down his cheek, catching him on fire. It took a few seconds to put out the flames, by which time he had severe burns and was taken to the hospital. Ponamarev is suing the bar, but Bykov denies any responsibility. "It was his fault because he put his hand over his mouth and that splashed the liquid everywhere." A lawsuit is pending.

NOW THAT'S A PARTY

According to the news website, *The Smoking Gun*, an Arizona wildfire was caused by a smoking gun. Five men in their 20s trekked into the Arizona wilderness for a "bachelor party and campout" in 2012. Among the festivities: shooting stuff with their guns. All was well until 23-year-old Craig Shiflet loaded an incendiary round into his shotgun. A warning on the ammo box read, "Shoots 100 feet of fire, setting everything in its path ablaze. Warning: Extreme FIRE HAZARD." Ignoring the warning, Shiflet fired the weapon at an empty box, and a minute later all five men were trying to stomp out the flames. They couldn't, so they called 9-1-1 and hightailed it out of there. The ensuing fire burned for most of the summer, incinerating 18,000 acres of forest. Shiflet told the judge he was "extremely sorry" and was sentenced to two years of probation.

OUR WORK HERE IS DONE

In 2012, Swedish firefighters responded to a call for a fire in an apartment after witnesses noticed the flames from outside. The firemen burst into the apartment, only to discover that the "fire" was a DVD of a fireplace playing on the TV. "It was actually very relaxing," said one of the firefighters, who said that they all stayed for a while to watch the fire.

1st person to say Earth revolves around the sun: Greek astronomer Aristarchus (c. 280 BC).

NAME CHANGERS

Meet the new team, same as the old team—just with a different name.

NEW YORK TITANS

The Tennessee Titans weren't the first Titans in pro football. The first were the New York Titans, a charter member of the American Football League (later absorbed by the NFL) in 1960. The name was a wry reference to the New York Giants of the NFL—in mythology, titans are bigger, stronger, and tougher than giants. The name only lasted for three years. By then the team was playing in brand-new Shea Stadium, located directly beneath the flight paths of two major airports, LaGuardia and JFK, hence the new Jets. (It also rhymed with the name of Shea Stadium's other team, baseball's New York Mets.)

TAMPA BAY DEVIL RAYS

After more than a decade of trying to persuade Major League Baseball for an expansion team, Tampa Bay finally got one in 1995, to begin play in 1998. Owner Vince Naimoli wanted to name his team the Sting Rays, after the sea creatures that populate the ocean near Tampa. But the name was already in use by the minor-league Maui Stingrays, and Naimoli refused to pay the relatively paltry $35,000 it would have cost to get the rights. So he took suggestions from the community, and out of 7,000 entries, he picked the Devil Rays. Almost immediately, the team began receiving complaints from people who felt the name celebrated Satan. So Naimoli commissioned a telephone poll: Should he name the team "Devil Rays" or "Manta Rays"? Devil Rays won, so the name stuck. So did the complaints. In 2007, Naimoli formally dropped "Devil" from the name.

NEW YORK HIGHLANDERS

The New York Yankees are the most storied team in pro baseball, but they weren't always in New York. In 1903, the original Baltimore Orioles franchise moved to New York City and changed their name to the New York Highlanders. To avoid confusion with the other local team, the Giants of the National League, sportswriters gave the Highlanders a nickname: "the Americans," because they were in the American League. That's a long word to fit into headlines—which is why *New York Press* editor Jim Price started calling them the "Yanks" or "Yankees." It caught on, and the name was officially changed in 1913.

NEW ORLEANS HORNETS

The Charlotte Hornets of the NBA moved to New Orleans in 2002, after owner George Shinn made good on a threat to take them away if the city didn't build him a new arena. Tom Benson, owner of the NFL's New Orleans Saints, bought the team in 2012 and wanted to change the name to something more local. (Hornets are native to the Carolinas; they're not widely found in the Bayou.) He approached the owners of the Utah Jazz, which in 1979 had moved from New Orleans, an important city in jazz history, to Salt Lake City, not an important city in jazz history. The Jazz refused to give the name back, so after considering "Brass," Benson announced a new name for the 2013 season: the Pelicans, named after Louisiana's state bird.

CHARLOTTE BOBCATS

When the Hornets moved to New Orleans after 14 seasons in Charlotte, feelings were mixed. The team's owner, George Shinn, was controversial and many people in Charlotte were glad to see him go. But the city was still a big basketball market, so the NBA publicly promised Charlotte a new team. And later that year it got one, with an ownership group originally led by BET network founder Robert Johnson and now led by former NBA superstar Michael Jordan. Since beginning play in 2004, the Bobcats (the name was selected in a "name the team" contest) have brought in huge crowds—but no playoff appearances. Looking for a new start in 2012, Jordan announced that for the 2014–15 season, the team would be using a new name. Well, an *old* new name, really: the Charlotte Hornets, which they grabbed barely a month after the New Orleans Pelicans gave it up.

*   *   *

BUG NEWTONS

Figs are pollinated by wasps. The wasp flies in, lays her eggs, and dies. So if the next fig you eat is a bit crunchy…that *could* be why.

THAT'S AMORE?

When the moon hits your eye like a big pizza pie, it hurts.

WITH THIS RING, I THEE BLAM!

Alfredo Malespini III, a 31-year-old prison guard from Bradford, Pennsylvania, got into a heated argument with his wife in 2013. Angry and frustrated, he pulled out his gun and tried to shoot his wedding ring. Only problem: It was still on his finger. According to the police report: "The gunshot badly mangled Alfredo's finger but didn't remove the ring."

A WEDDING OF INCONVENIENCE

A Florida couple's marriage got off to a rocky start when they were both arrested on their wedding day. Concerned neighbors informed police that while Kymberely Frederick, 30, and Daniel Richard, 34, went to the courthouse to tie the knot (reportedly so Richards, who was unemployed, wouldn't have to pay child support), the couple's three young kids—aged 1 to 3—were left home alone. The kids were placed into protective services pending a hearing.

HE LIVES!

In 2007, Joseph Finnegan found a novel way to get out of paying for a divorce filed by his wife, Karen. He claimed that, three years earlier, his heart had stopped beating, so he had technically died, which technically annulled their marriage. The judge, however, upon seeing Joseph both living *and* breathing in his courtroom, denied the request, and Joseph had to pony up.

BARKING MAD

A 25-year-old Indian man, identified in press reports as "Sanjay," caught his new bride cheating on him with a neighbor in March 2012. In protest, he climbed up a guava tree and refused to come down until his wife said she was sorry. She refused, so he stayed up there. After he'd finished eating all the guava fruits, his mother brought him food. According to a neighbor, "He eats and sleeps in the tree and even relieves himself from there." At last report, Sanjay's wife still hasn't apologized, and he's still in the tree.

Only American woman to win a Nobel Prize in physics: Maria Goeppert-Mayer (1963).

NEVER STEP IN...

Difficult to believe, but one BRI writer found out the hard way why you shouldn't step into each of these things with your bare feet. She's happy to share what she learned to save you the agony of...de feet.

TANBARK: It's a kind of mulch and it's not exactly bark, though it comes from the outer layers of certain oak trees. But before it becomes garden mulch or playground covering, the tannins are removed. What's a tannin? An organic chemical used in the leather-tanning process. When the tannins are removed, what remains is a bone-dry wood product that can turn a kids' playground into what one parent called "a pool full of splinters." Step in the stuff with bare feet, and you'll end up with hundreds of tiny splinters you can hardly see, much less remove.

IF YOU DO STEP IN IT: Coat your feet with white glue. Let the glue dry, and then gently peel away to pull out the splinters.

A YELLOW JACKET'S NEST: These highly aggressive, inch-long, yellow-and-black-striped wasps are responsible for most stinging deaths in the United States. When disturbed, yellow jackets can sting repeatedly, attack in large numbers, and even bite. A Bucks County, Pennsylvania, victim reported, "One nailed me above the kneecap last Saturday. It felt like a four-penny nail was stuck in there." Yellow jackets build underground nests that can house as many as 5,000 insects.

IF YOU DO STEP IN IT: You'll get stung. Shake Adolph's meat tenderizer (or any papain/papaya-based tenderizer) onto the stings and cover them with a damp cloth. The meat-tenderizing enzymes will deactivate the wasp's protein-based venom, and the sting will vanish. (If you're allergic to stings, or if your heart starts pounding and you can't breathe, forget the tenderizer. Call 9-1-1!)

GRAVEL NEAR A BBQ: If you have a lot of food to cook (like at a family reunion where our intrepid BRI writer accidentally burned the flesh off her bare feet as a kid), you'll probably want to keep the coals burning hot for as long as possible. The solution: Place a one-inch layer of gravel or sand at the bottom of the grill before putting in the coals. But *please* don't dump that hot gravel near barefoot children. (Barbecuing uncles, are you listening?)

IF YOU DO STEP IN IT: Immediately immerse the feet in cold water and keep them there for five to ten minutes, with brief breaks as needed. Pat the feet dry. Smear aloe vera gel on the burns, squeezed straight from the leaves of an aloe plant. Then kick back with a stack of *Bathroom Readers*. Why? It will take two to three weeks to heal those burns, and you'll need to stay off your feet as much as possible.

BURR GRASS: That sandy, light-green turf between the car and the beach in the southern U.S. looks tempting, but don't kick off those flip-flops just yet. That's not turf. It's *Cenchrus incertus*, also known as burr grass, sandspur, or sandbur because of the needle-sharp 1/4-inch spines hiding in it. (Ouch!)

IF YOU DO STEP IN IT: Remove any spines stuck in your toes, and then hobble into the salty ocean and give your feet a good soak. Once you get back to your hotel room, add two cups of uncooked oatmeal to a warm bath and soothe away any lingering irritation.

A FIRE-ANT MOUND: These ferocious insects hitched a ride on cargo ships from South America in the 1930s. Now they swarm over close to 300 million acres in the southern United States. When you step in a fire-ant mound, hundreds to thousands of ants swarm out of the mound, onto your foot, and up your leg. The fiery little pests hold on with their mandibles so you can't just brush them off like other ants. They latch on and swing their tails back and forth to sting their victim again and again, and they may have to be pulled off one at a time. After being stung, expect an itchy lump at each sting site that will form a small blister within a few hours and fill with pus-like material that can lead to infection if popped.

IF YOU DO STEP IN IT: Treat with a paste of baking soda and vinegar, wet tobacco, or meat tenderizer (since you have some on hand for yellow-jacket stings). If you experience tightness in your chest, difficulty breathing, or severe nausea, stop pulling the ants off your feet and call 9-1-1.

*   *   *

"Anger is a brief madness." —**Horace**

GHOST DIRECTORS

A ghostwriter secretly composes something that's credited to someone else.
A ghost director makes a movie that's credited to someone else.

Film: *Gone with the Wind* (1939)
Credited Director: Victor Fleming
Ghost Directors: George Cukor, Sam Wood
Story: One of Hollywood's grandest epics and, when adjusted for inflation, the highest grossing movie of all time, *Gone with the Wind* had a legendarily troubled production. Besides script problems and the controversial casting of British actress Vivien Leigh as quintessential Southern belle Scarlett O'Hara, the film's first director, Cukor, was fired a few weeks after filming began. Official reason: Cukor wouldn't stop bickering with producers over the schedule. Rumored reason: Lead actor Clark Gable got Cukor canned because Cukor was gay and considered a "woman's director," and Gable refused to be directed by "a fairy." So in came Victor Fleming, who had just completed directing *The Wizard of Oz*. When Fleming took a two-week break from the film (for exhaustion), Wood (*For Whom the Bell Tolls, The Pride of the Yankees, A Night at the Opera*) stepped in. When all was said and done, Fleming received sole directing credit, even though he'd only shot about two-thirds of the film.

Film: *Poltergeist* (1982)
Credited Director: Tobe Hooper
Ghost Director (maybe): Steven Spielberg
Story: It seems nobody can agree on who actually filmed this horror classic. Some of the actors say it was Hooper. Others say it was actually the film's producer and co-writer, Spielberg. At the time, Spielberg was committed to filming *E.T.: The Extra-Terrestrial* for Universal, and was contractually barred from directing *Poltergeist*, an MGM film. But he had a heavy hand in the pre-production, was on the set for all but three days of shooting, and even gave directions to the cast. Rumors circulated around Hollywood during filming that Hooper was strung out on heroin and too inexperienced to handle such a special-effects-heavy film—so Spielberg had to take over. To stop the gossip, Spielberg wrote an open letter to *The Hol-*

lywood Reporter defending Hooper and claiming the speculation was fraudulent. Was it? We'll probably never really know.

Film: *Return of the Jedi* (1983)
Credited Director: Richard Marquand
Ghost Director: George Lucas
Story: After being turned down by David Cronenberg and David Lynch, Lucas selected the relatively unknown Marquand to direct the third part of his *Star Wars* trilogy. Lucas claimed he was impressed with Marquand's *Eye of the Needle*, a 1981 suspense film starring Donald Sutherland. But his decision may have been motivated by his conflicts with director Irvin Kershner on the set of *The Empire Strikes Back*. Lucas wanted full creative control on *Jedi* but didn't want to deal with the grueling job of actually directing the movie himself (as he'd done on *Star Wars*). So he reportedly picked a relative newcomer that he could boss around, as opposed to the veteran Kershner. Lucas was heavily involved in the production and even completed most of the second-unit filming himself. Marquand later compared the experience to "trying to direct *King Lear* with Shakespeare in the next room." But despite all of Lucas's meddling, Marquand received the film's sole directing credit.

Film: *Tombstone* (1993)
Credited Director: George P. Cosmatos
Ghost Director: Kurt Russell
Story: Screenwriter Kevin Jarre (*Glory*) wrote this Western about Wyatt Earp and Doc Holliday, and Hollywood Pictures signed him to direct, too. But he was fired after just a few weeks when he refused the studio's orders to cut some scenes because the film was too long. According to star Kurt Russell, the studio asked him to direct the rest of the movie. Russell—who'd never directed anything— agreed, but didn't want to receive any credit. So Russell hired a figurehead, or proxy director, Cosmatos. Every night after filming wrapped, Russell gave Cosmatos notes and told him how to direct the following day's scenes. The two of them also arranged a series of hand-signals so Russell could give him further orders on the fly while they were on set. As weird as their arrangement might seem, this wasn't a first for Cosmatos. He also slyly "directed" *Rambo II*— written by Kevin Jarre—on behalf of actor Sylvester Stallone.

POLITICAL FIRSTS

*You may be surprised by how old some of our
"modern" political traditions are.*

KUSHSHIHARBE (1400 B.C.)

Claim to Fame: First documented case of an official
ensnared in a sex scandal

Details: Kushshiharbe was the mayor of a town called Nuzi, near
modern-day Kirkuk, north of Baghdad. According to clay tablets
unearthed in Iraq in the late 1920s, he went on trial for a variety of
crimes, including theft, taking bribes, and kidnapping. The juiciest
accusation was that he committed adultery with a woman named
Humerelli, a charge he vehemently denied. (Sound familiar?) "No!
Emphatically no! Not a word of it is true! I did not have sex with
her!" the clay tablets quote him as saying. Verdict: Unknown. Tablets describing the outcome haven't been found.

HENRY IV OF FRANCE (1553–1610)

Claim to Fame: First ruler to promise "a chicken in every pot"

Details: If you're a history buff, you may already know that it was
Herbert Hoover's campaign that promised "a chicken in every pot
and two cars in every garage" in the 1928 presidential race. (Hoover
won.) Freedom from hunger is a nice thing to have, and Hoover
wasn't the first politician to realize it. As far back as the 16th century, King Henry IV of France understood the importance of spreading
prosperity to even his lowliest subjects when he declared, "I want
my people to have a fowl simmering in their pot every Sunday."

ELISABETH, QUEEN OF THE BELGIANS (1876–1965)

Claim to Fame: First leader to use the term "Iron Curtain"

Details: Winston Churchill famously used it in a 1946 speech
in Fulton, Missouri, where he warned that "an iron curtain has
descended across the Continent," dividing Europe between the
free democratic countries in the west and those under Communist
domination in the east. But he wasn't the first leader to use it: In
1915, Queen Elisabeth, the Bavarian-born wife of King Albert I,
used it to describe the psychological barrier that came between her

---

Hooray! Molecular scientist Robert Bohannon developed caffeinated doughnuts and bagels.

and her family in Bavaria when the Germans invaded Belgium in the opening days of World War I. A similar metaphor was used in the ancient Babylonian Talmud, which describes how even an "iron barrier" cannot separate the children of Israel from God. (Historical note: The iron curtain isn't just a metaphor. In the 1800s, theaters used metal safety barriers called "iron curtains" to protect audiences if a fire broke out onstage. In an emergency, the barrier could be lowered to give the audience more time to flee.)

THE 1860 DEMOCRATIC NATIONAL CONVENTION

Claim to Fame: First major-party political convention in American history to fail to pick a candidate for president

Details: When the Democratic Party met in Charleston, South Carolina, in April 1860 to choose a presidential candidate, the Civil War was barely a year away, and the party was bitterly divided over the issue of slavery. The delegates voted 57 times, but no candidate was able to win the two-thirds majority needed to secure the nomination. The convention adjourned in failure. Afterward, the party split into Northern and Southern factions, and each nominated their own candidate: The Northern Democrats chose Senator Stephen A. Douglas of Illinois, and the Southern Democrats chose John C. Breckinridge. Both men lost to the nominee of the six-year-old Republican Party—a one-term former Whig Party congressman from Illinois named Abraham Lincoln.

HORACE GREELEY (1811–1872)

Claim to Fame: First U.S. presidential candidate killed by the campaign

Details: Greeley, a New York newspaper publisher, supported Ulysses S. Grant in the 1868 election but later turned against him. When the Republicans split into Radical and Liberal factions, the Radicals nominated Grant for re-election; the Liberals chose Greeley. During the campaign, the Grant forces subjected Greeley to withering ridicule and vicious personal attacks: "I have been so bitterly assailed that I hardly know whether I am running for the presidency or the penitentiary," Greeley complained. Grant won in a landslide. Greeley, upset by his loss and by his wife's recent death, suffered a physical and mental collapse and died just three weeks after the election.

RIDDLE ME THIS

Some old-fashioned conundrums. (Answers on page 538.)

1. With thieves I consort,
With the vilest, in short,
I'm quite at ease in depravity;
Yet all divines use me,
And savants can't lose me,
For I am the center of gravity.
What am I?

2. What force and strength
cannot get through,
I, with a gentle touch, can do.
Many in the street would stand,
If I were not a friend at hand.
What am I?

3. I am a box that holds keys
for which there are no locks,
Yet they can unlock your soul.
What am I?

4. This mother comes
from a family of eight,
She supports her children
in spite of their weight,
She turns around
without being called,
She has held you since
the time you crawled.
Who is she?

5. I stand at attention,
and have one word for you.
Ignore that word and it may
be the last thing you ever do.
What am I?

6. Apart we make no sense.
Together we become one.
And then we are no longer fun.
What are we?

7. I've asked you no question,
You answer me nonetheless.
What am I?

8. Reaching stiffly for the sky,
I bare my fingers when it's cold.
In warmth I wear
an emerald glove,
And in between
I dress in gold.
What am I?

9. I travel from there to here
by disappearing, and from here
to there by reappearing.
What am I?

10. If you break me
I do not stop working,
If you touch me
I may be snared,
If you lose me
nothing will matter.
What am I?

11. If you cut me
I will feel no pain;
It is you who will suffer
from others' disdain.
What am I?

The average American uses 23.6 rolls of toilet paper a year—about two a month.

"WEIRD"ED OUT

Music is serious business, but some musicians take themselves a little too seriously. Parody is high praise. (And if it's done well, very funny.)

BIG AL

You don't need permission from an artist or a label to record humorous parody versions of their songs—satire is protected under the "fair use" copyright law. Nevertheless, as a show of good faith and to avoid upsetting anybody, "Weird Al" Yankovic makes it a point to ask artists for permission before he releases a parody of one of their songs. By his own estimate, he gets turned down only two to three percent of the time. Here are some of the songs and artists who refused to give him permission.

PRINCE

Most of Weird Al's rejections have come from Prince, a man who takes himself so seriously, he once claimed his recording contract amounted to slavery (and had the word "slave" painted on his face). Prince has rejected Yankovic on three separate occasions, for parodies of "When Doves Cry," "Kiss," and "1999." Relations are so cold between the two that when Prince found out his assigned seat at the American Music Awards one year was next to Yankovic's, he had his manager send a telegram to Yankovic, telling him not to speak to or make eye contact with Prince during the show.

LED ZEPPELIN

Yankovic's instrument is the accordion, and he knows how to play polka music. Most of his albums contain a medley of pop and rock songs performed polka-style. In 1983, Yankovic asked the members of Led Zeppelin if he could make a polka medley entirely of Led Zeppelin songs. Guitarist and songwriter Jimmy Page, who has been sued for stealing riffs from old blues musicians, blocked his songs from being used. However, nearly 30 years later, Page did allow Yankovic to use a sample of Led Zeppelin's "Black Dog" on "Trapped at the Drive-Thru," a parody of R. Kelly's mini-opera "Trapped in the Closet."

BILLY JOEL

Yankovic's parodies rarely mock the artist who recorded the original song—his catalog is primarily "Girls Just Want to Have Lunch" and "Eat It"–style songs. But in the early 1980s, he recorded a rendition of Billy Joel's "It's Still Rock 'n' Roll to Me," pointing out the singer's many calculated musical style changes, called "It's Still Billy Joel to Me." Sample lyric: "Maybe he should dye his hair bright pink / and stick a safety pin through his cheeks. / Then he'd really fit the New Wave image / but he couldn't sit down for weeks." Yankovic knew Joel would turn it down, but asked anyway—Joel said no. The song was never released officially, although a demo version did appear on a compilation by Dr. Demento, the radioshow host who gave Yankovic his big break in 1980.

MICHAEL JACKSON

The King of Pop allowed Weird Al to make fun of him twice. The parodies of "Beat It" and "Bad" ("Eat It" and "Fat") are two of his most famous songs, with "Eat It" reaching #12 on the pop chart. Yankovic approached Jackson a third time in 1992 with a parody of Jackson's "Black or White," called "Snack All Night." Jackson felt his song had an important message that shouldn't be mocked, so he said no. Yankovic later admitted on *Behind the Music* that he went after a Jackson song because it was easy pickings and he was desperate for a hit. At the time, his career was in a slump with an underselling album (*Polka Party*) and underperforming movie (*UHF*).

THE BEATLES

In the mid-'90s, the Beatles had an unlikely hit with "Free as a Bird," a John Lennon demo that the surviving Beatles overdubbed with their own parts. Yankovic asked Paul McCartney if he could record a parody called "Gee, I'm a Nerd." McCartney deferred to Lennon's widow, Yoko Ono, who said no way. McCartney himself had refused to let Weird Al satirize "Live and Let Die," which he'd recorded with Wings in the '70s. McCartney's reason for turning down Yankovic's "Chicken Pot Pie"? He's a vegetarian and couldn't approve a song that condoned eating meat. Yankovic has never recorded "Gee, I'm a Nerd" or "Chicken Pot Pie," but frequently performs both at his live shows.

The fruit of the African doum palm tastes like gingerbread.

MORE "WEIRD" NEWS

• Eminem allowed Yankovic to record "Couch Potato," a parody of "Lose Yourself." But he wouldn't allow a video because he was afraid it would be "harmful to his image."

• In 1996, Yankovic recorded "Amish Paradise," a take on rapper Coolio's "Gangsta's Paradise." Yankovic thought he had permission until Coolio went public at the Grammy Awards to announce that his record label had given permission—but he hadn't.

• Ten years later, the exact opposite situation occurred. British singer-songwriter James Blunt authorized a Yankovic parody of his hit "You're Beautiful" called "You're Pitiful." Yankovic recorded the song and had it ready to go for an album, and then at the last minute, Atlantic Records told Yankovic he couldn't release it. (He put the song up for free on his website instead.)

• In 2006, one-hit-wonder Daniel Powter wouldn't let Yankovic parody his song "Bad Day" with "You Had a Bad Date." But then, Powter had a change of heart, Yankovic says, the day he was going into the studio to start recording an album. This time, Yankovic turned Powter down.

*   *   *

REAL ADDRESSES OF FAKE PEOPLE

Want to send a letter to a fictional character? They'll never get the letter, because they're not real. However, a few famous characters' fan clubs will accept and even answer them. Here are a few addresses.

• **Sherlock Holmes**
  221B Baker Street, London
  Greater London NW1 6XE
  United Kingdom

• **Juliet Capulet** (from Shakespeare's *Romeo & Juliet*)
  Via Cappello 27
  Verona, Italy 37121

• **Santa Claus**
  The North Pole
  Canada H0H 0H0

Keep mooving: 20% of the fuel used by Amtrak's Heartland Flyer in 2010 came from beef fat.

WHAT DO YOU WANT ON YOUR HOT DOG?

*Uncle John lives in Oregon and likes his dogs steamed (not grilled)
with American cheese, Chinese mustard, french fries, Canadian
bacon, and Russian dressing on an English muffin.*

Rhode Island: The state's traditional hot dog is called a "New
York System" dog, a throwback to the early 1900s when
hot-dog vendors wanted to associate themselves with the
famous hot dogs of Coney Island. There, legend has it, a German
immigrant named Charles Feltman was serving sausages in rolls as
early as 1870—well before the 1893 World's Columbian Exposition
in Chicago, which also claims to be the hot dog's birthplace. Rhode
Island's New York System dogs are made with veal and pork instead
of beef, and served on a steamed bun with mustard, chopped onions,
celery salt, and a spicy meat sauce.

Flint, Michigan: Another area with a unique take on "Coney
Island" dogs. Flint's coneys are all-beef hot dogs topped with mustard, chopped onions, and meat sauce made from ground beef, beef
hearts, and "secret" spices that vary from one vendor to another.

Chicago, Illinois: A classic Chicago hot dog is said to be "dragged
through the garden" because it's topped with onions, tomatoes,
sweet relish, pickled peppers, celery salt, and a pickle spear. The dog
is 100 percent beef and served on a poppy-seed bun. If it's grilled
instead of boiled or steamed, it's called a "char-dog." What you're
unlikely to find on a Chicago dog: ketchup. The idea of putting
ketchup on a hot dog is so abhorrent to traditionalists that many
vendors in the Windy City won't give it to you even if you ask.

Seattle, Washington: The classic "Seattle dog" is sliced lengthwise,
grilled, and served on a toasted bun with grilled onions and cream
cheese (often applied with a device similar to a caulking gun). Jala-
peño peppers are available for people who like their hot dogs hot.

Tucson, Arizona: Order it "Sonoran-style," and they'll wrap it in
bacon and grill it, then top it with beans, grilled or chopped onions,
tomatoes, mayonnaise, mustard, cream sauce, and salsa.

Denmark: A Danish hot dog—a *rød pølser* ("red sausage")—is

In 1700s England, shooting a rabbit was punishable by death. So was cutting down a tree.

bright red, thanks to the addition of carmine, a red food coloring made from crushed beetles. The sausages also contain ground pork, nutmeg, allspice, and pepper. They're served on a roll with fried onions and pickles, topped with ketchup, mustard, and *remoulade* (a sauce made from egg yolks, mustard, oil, and vinegar).

Colombia: *Perros calientes*—"hot dogs"—are boiled and served on a bun with ketchup, mustard, mayonnaise, coleslaw, pineapple sauce, crushed potato chips, and a fried quail egg on top.

Montreal, Canada: Hot dogs in Canada's largest French-speaking city are typically served on buns that are cut open through the top, not through the side as they are in the United States. The dogs are usually steamed ("steamies"), but you can ask for a "toastie" if you want it fried on a griddle. Either way, they're typically served with mustard, onions, and either fresh chopped cabbage, coleslaw, or sauerkraut.

Prague, Czech Republic: Instead of slicing the bun open, one end of it is cut off to expose the soft dough, then a metal spike is punched into the dough to create a hole for the hot dog. Ketchup and other condiments are pumped into the hole first; then, when the hot dog is added, the condiments ooze out over the top of the bun, which is held vertically and eaten from the top down.

Bangkok, Thailand: Here hot dogs are baked inside a croissant and served with mayonnaise, or served in a "Tokyo cake"—rolled up in a crepe with some sweet chili sauce.

São Paulo, Brazil: Instead of being sliced open, the inside of the bun is scooped out lengthwise and filled with the hot dog, chopped tomatoes, sweet corn, and fried shoestring potatoes; then topped with a vinaigrette dressing, ketchup, mustard, and mayonnaise. As if that wasn't enough, the dog is given a final topping of mashed potatoes (and served in a plastic bag that serves as a dish, to keep the whole mess from landing in your lap).

*   *   *

THE LONG-WINDED TITLE AWARD
The full title of *David Copperfield*, Charles Dickens's 1850 novel:
The Personal History, Adventures, Experience and Observation of David Copperfield the Younger of Blunderstone Rookery (Which He Never Meant to Publish on Any Account)

FUNNY LADIES

Time for a comedy break.

"I suffer from peroxa-phemaphobia. Every time I get near a beautiful blonde woman, something of mine disappears. Jobs, boyfriends. Once an angora sweater leapt right off my body."

—**Rita Rudner**

"There is no sunrise so beautiful that it is worth waking me up to see it."

—**Mindy Kaling**

"Reality is the leading cause of stress amongst those in touch with it."

—**Lily Tomlin**

"My parents were both in the Marine Corps. But I had a pretty normal upbringing: I stood guard duty at night just like all kids. And my mom made me wash the bathroom floor with a toothbrush. So I used hers."

—**Mary Gallagher**

"Men in power always seem to get involved in sex scandals, but women don't even have a word for 'male bimbo,' except maybe 'senator.'"

—**Elayne Boosler**

"I'm using a new perfume that I recommend. It's called Tester. And it smells different every time you use it."

—**Carol Leifer**

"At restaurants, I don't mind if I order fish and it comes with the head on it. I do mind it when I order beef."

—**Cyndi Stiles**

"Thirty ways to shape up for summer: number one, eat less; number two, exercise more; number three… What was I talking about? I'm so hungry right now."

—**Maria Bamford**

"I got a waterbed, but my husband stocked it with trout."

—**Joan Rivers**

"I don't have an hourglass figure. I have an hour and a half."

—**Wendy Liebman**

"I didn't know what Facebook was, and now that I do know, I have to say, it sounds like a huge waste of time. I would never say the people on it are losers, but that's only because I'm polite."

—**Betty White**

MY OTHER T-SHIRT IS A TUX

…and other real T-shirt slogans we've seen.

6 out of 7 dwarfs are not Happy

Similes Are Like Metaphors

When work feels overwhelming, remember that you're going to die

The 3rd rule of Fight Club is "have fun and try your best"

Dept. of Redundancy Department

The USA is just Canada's Mexico

Knowledge: It's almost as important as money, luck, and family connections

"Yo mama." —*Freud*

Step aside coffee, this is a job for alcohol

Never trust an atom. They make up everything.

Warning: If zombies chase us, I'm tripping you

Communists have no class

Wanted Dead & Alive: Schrödinger's Cat

Misuse of "literally" makes me figuratively insane

Back in my day, we had nine planets

Elephants never forget and they never forgive

I can't brain today, I have the dumb

Spelling is ~~difficoult~~ ~~chalanging~~ hard

Always give 100%, unless you're donating blood

Sharks hug with their mouths

I'm actually not funny, I'm just really mean and people think I'm joking

Anything unrelated to elephants is irrelephant

Always be yourself unless you can be a unicorn—then always be a unicorn

---

Worldwide, as many as a billion frogs are killed each year for food.

POP MUSIC FIRSTS

*These things are all pretty common in the music
business today, but somebody had to be first.*

First greatest-hits album. "Greatest hits" albums are an inexpensive way to create a new product using existing songs by an artist and re-sell them with little to no new work required. The first time it was done was in 1958, when Columbia Records collected 12 Johnny Mathis songs that had been released as 45s only or appeared on movie soundtracks. *Johnny's Greatest Hits* was a massive success, peaking at #1 on the album chart and spending 490 weeks there—almost 10 years.

• **First song downloaded on iTunes.** Apple launched its iTunes Music Store service in April 2003, and more than a million songs were downloaded the first week—remarkable, because the service was available only to Mac users, who at the time made up less than 10 percent of computer users. Hundreds of thousands of people downloaded songs that day, all at the same time, so it's hard to say exactly which was the first one purchased, but the top seller of the first day was U2's "Stuck in a Moment You Can't Get Out Of."

• **First Grammy Award.** In 1959, the music industry felt it had to do something to demonstrate an industry standard of quality and to defend traditional pop music against the onslaught of rock 'n' roll. Solution: Have an awards ceremony, similar to the movie industry's Academy Awards. The first Gramophone Awards were held on May 4, 1959, in the Grand Ballroom of the Beverly Hills Hotel. Highlights of the event aired six months later as *The Best on Record*—part of NBC's anthology series *Sunday Showcase*. (The awards show wouldn't air on TV live until 1971.) The "quality" element worked better in theory than in practice, as Alvin and the Chipmunks won three awards that night. The first Grammy of the night, however, went to Frank Sinatra's *Only the Lonely*...for Best Album Cover.

• **First digital-only full-length album release.** In 1999, four years before the launch of iTunes, the quirky rock band They Might Be Giants released *Long Tall Weekend* via the music-download service eMusic. Though it was later released on CD, at the time, downloading the album was the only way to get it. The first album released in digital and CD formats simultaneously was *Mezzanine* by the electronic music act Massive Attack.

• **First triple album.** Bob Dylan's 1966 *Blonde on Blonde* was the first two-record release. But the first *three*-record set? *Woodstock: Music from the Original Soundtrack and More*, a collection of songs used in the documentary/concert film of the legendary 1969 Woodstock festival. It was released in May 1970.

• **First digital-only full-length album release.** In 1999, four years before the launch of iTunes, the quirky rock band They Might Be Giants released *Long Tall Weekend* via the music-download service eMusic. While a handful of promotional copies were pressed on CD for the music press, downloading the album was the only way to get it—a first. The first album released in digital and on CD simultaneously was *Mezzanine* by the electronic music act Massive Attack in April 1998.

• **First band to release more than one album simultaneously.** KISS. By 1978, they were one of the most popular live acts in rock. Their album sales didn't quite match that success, so the band staged a publicity stunt—citing turmoil in the band, they announced that each member would release a solo album, all on the same day. Bragging rights would go to whoever's album sold the most copies. On September 18, 1978, four new KISS albums came out, titled: *Paul Stanley*, *Gene Simmons*, *Ace Frehley*, and *Peter Criss*. Ultimately, *Simmons* and *Frehley* both went platinum, although Simmons' charted slightly higher than Frehley's, at #22 and #26, respectively.

• **First K-Tel Records compilation.** K-Tel International sold dozens of pop and rock music compilations in the 1970s, including *22 Explosive Hits*, *20 All Time Greats of the 50's*, *20 Great Truck Drivin' Songs*, and *Get Down with Boogie*, almost all of them via mail order and advertised on television ("Not available in stores! Operators are standing by!"). Founded in the 1960s, the Manitoba-based company began as a distributor of kitchen gadgets (like the "Blitzhacker" food chopper), but moved to music after the success in 1966 of *25 Great Country Artists Singing Their Original Hits*.

STALL OF FAME: MR. TOILET

We mentioned Sim Jae-duck in a Bathroom Reader article a few years ago. Here's an update on him—probably the only person in history who was born in a toilet, lived in a toilet, and died in one, too.

HELLO, WORLD

In 1996, FIFA, soccer's international governing body, awarded the 2002 World Cup to co-hosts South Korea and Japan. It had taken decades for South Korea to rebuild after the Korean War (1950–53), and the country had only recently emerged from nearly 40 years of brutal dictatorship. Not many people thought of it as a tourist destination, and hosting the World Cup offered a chance for South Korea to present a new face.

One man who was determined to make the most of the opportunity was Sim Jae-duck, the mayor of Suwon, a city about 20 miles south of Seoul and home to one of the stadiums where the games would be played. Sim thought one of the best ways for outsiders to get to know South Korea would be to live in the homes of its citizens, so he recruited more than 4,000 local families to offer free room and board to visitors during the games. To manage the large crowds that would descend upon the city, he recruited a force of 3,000 security guards and gave them special training on how to deal with the foreign guests. Most famously, he launched a multimillion-dollar campaign to upgrade the city's public restrooms, a program that earned him the nickname "Mr. Toilet."

FIRST CLASS

Suwon had more than 700 public restrooms scattered around the city, some operated by the city and others provided by private businesses. Mr. Toilet upgraded them all, providing fresh coats of paint, installing artwork, replacing old fixtures with new ones, and piping in soothing music and perfume-scented air. (He also switched traditional squat toilets to sit-down toilets that Westerners were more used to.) Sim also built more than 30 brand-new restrooms and spent so much money on their design and construction—the

---

A road sign outside a California pre-school: "PLEASE SLOW DRIVELY."

restrooms closest to the stadium, for example, were shaped like soccer balls—that 26 of the facilities were designated as tourist attractions in their own right.

THE NATURAL

Mr. Toilet may have literally been born for the job. South Korean toilet humor is as bawdy as it is anyplace else in the world (which might explain Korean proverbs like "Toilets are like mothers-in-law: the farther away the better"). But tradition also has it that bathrooms are lucky places. Sim's grandmother was so sure that anyone born in a bathroom was destined to live a long life that she convinced Sim's mother to give birth in hers. Sim's mom went through her labor just outside grandma's bathroom, and when the moment of truth arrived, she stepped inside just long enough for the future Mr. Toilet to pop out.

REALIZING HIS POT-ENTIAL

Improving Suwon's restrooms proved so rewarding that Sim decided to expand his efforts. In 1999, he created the Korean Toilet Association to push his modernization drive nationwide. Later, he joined the World Toilet Organization, a group dedicated to improving public access to bathrooms around the globe. Then, when Sim concluded that the WTO wasn't effective enough, he broke away to form his own World Toilet Association in 2006.

As Mr. Toilet campaigned for better bathrooms, he came to believe that some of the taboos associated with toilets were barriers to the improvements he was trying to achieve. That's why, in 2007, he decided to tackle the problem head on (so to speak), by demolishing the house he'd lived in for 30 years and replacing it with one shaped like a giant toilet.

Sim had made a lot of money in business before going into politics, and had no problem spending more than $1.6 million building his two-story glass and concrete dream house. It's not an exact replica of a toilet, but it is shaped like a giant toilet bowl and painted white. Just in case anyone misses the point, he named it *Haewoojae* ("a place of sanctuary where one can solve one's worries"), a Korean euphemism for the bathroom. For those who were unfamiliar with the expression, Sim put a sign in front of the house that read in English, "Mr. Toilet House."

ROOM WITH A VIEW

The most prominent feature on the main floor is—you guessed it—a toilet, one of four inside the Mr. Toilet House. This bathroom boasts a floor-to-ceiling clear-glass door that seems to offer no privacy at all. But as soon as a person enters the bathroom, the same electronic sensors that lift the toilet lid and turn on the soothing music also cause the bathroom door to become opaque, giving the user all the privacy he or she needs.

The bathroom opens directly onto the living room, which features a grand staircase that leads to the second floor and the roof balcony, where visitors can peek out over the rim of the Mr. Toilet House.

INDOOR PLUMBING

Because limited access to power, water, and sewage treatment can be barriers to toilet construction around the world, Sim decided to address these issues in the design of his home:

• The Mr. Toilet House has solar panels to reduce its carbon footprint.

• It collects rainwater from the roof and stores it in a tank until it's needed to flush the building's ultra-low-flow toilets, which use 70 percent less water than ordinary toilets.

• The house even treats its own waste water.

The Mr. Toilet House was completed in November 2007, but before Mr. Toilet and his family moved in, they offered to let anyone spend a night in the house, in exchange for $50,000 in contributions to his toilet-related charities. No takers, but for $1.00, Mr. Toilet offered to let admirers take a quick peek inside (and, if necessary, use the toilet). He raised quite a bit of money for his toilet charities with that offer.

GOTTA GO

Though Sim was certainly public in his promotion of "Toilet Culture," as he called it, there were parts of his life that he kept private. Few people knew it at the time, but even as he was building the Mr. Toilet House, he was battling prostate cancer. It was a fight that he would not win: Sim only lived in his giant toilet for about a year before succumbing to the disease. He died at home in the Mr. Toilet

---

Kool-Aid powder was originally marketed as a liquid called Fruit Smack.

House on January 14, 2009. At his request, his family agreed to preserve the home "as a symbol of South Korea's new toilet culture" by donating it to the city.

In October 2010, the Mr. Toilet House reopened as a museum dedicated to Toilet Culture. Two years later, the city developed the surrounding land into a Toilet Culture Park, featuring exhibits that show the various ways people went to the bathroom before toilets were invented and a gift shop that sells toilet- and poop-themed souvenirs. A sculpture garden filled with statues of squatting men, women, and children also features a reproduction of Rodin's *The Thinker* sitting—of course—on a toilet.

In its first four months, the Toilet Culture Park attracted more than 40,000 people, and at last report, it was still drawing huge crowds every month. Next up: a Toilet Culture *Center*, scheduled to open in 2014.

STILL GOING

But perhaps the greatest honor to Sim Jae-duck's memory is the fact that the Toilet Culture he created in the city of Suwon is sill thriving. The city spends $14 million a year on its 100 "flagship" public restrooms—that comes to $140,000 per restroom per year, or nearly $12,000 per month.

The immaculate restrooms of Suwon—which to this day bills itself as a "Mecca of Toilet Culture"—must be experienced to be believed. Electronic displays tell visitors which stalls are free, and along with the ubiquitous artwork, soothing music, and perfumed air are "etiquette buttons" that produce pleasant noises when they're needed to cover…less pleasant ones. Those tiny urinals in the ladies rooms? They're for mothers with little boys. Some restrooms have floor-to-ceiling windows inside each stall that provide a view of a beautiful bamboo garden beyond; the garden is walled off from the outside world so that it can be enjoyed without fear of anyone peeking into the toilet stalls.

It may seem that $12,000 a month is a lot of money to spend on a public restroom, but if Mr. Toilet were still around he'd say it was worth it. "At first people asked why I was putting so much money into toilets," Sim told an interviewer in 2006. "But today they are proud and we have few people complaining."

Al Capone's WWI draft card stated his occupation as "paper cutter."

IRONIC, ISN'T IT?

There's nothing like a good dose of irony to put the problems of day-to-day life into proper perspective.

ENVIRONY

In 2012, citing higher energy costs, the management of the Big Pit National Coal Mining Museum in Wales announced that it was installing 200 solar panels on its roof.

CONTAMINATED IRONY

Health Canada announced a recall of Kleenex-brand Luxury Foam Hand Sanitizer in June 2012, after tests found that it contained elevated levels of bacteria. While not a significant risk to healthy people, the bacteria could potentially harm people with compromised immune systems—some of the people most likely to use hand sanitizer.

STOLEN IRONY

• Two men in Plainfield, New Jersey, came upon what they thought was a man assaulting a woman, and detained the man. They were wrong. The man angrily explained that the woman had just robbed *him*. (She escaped with $400 and some gold chains.) The good samaritans apologized; the woman remains at large.

• In a bid to deter shoplifters, several six-foot-tall cardboard cutouts of a police officer named PC Bobb were placed in shops and supermarkets in Essex, England, in 2012. The campaign was scrapped a short time later after many of the PC Bobbs themselves were stolen.

EBONY AND IRONY

In 2010, Frank Ancona tried to reserve a date for his club to have a picnic at Fort Davidson, Missouri. When he was told he'd have to fill out a vendor submission form first, he protested that his club wasn't selling anything. No other clubs had to jump through any hoops, so why should his? Ancona sued the state for discrimination and won. His club: the "Traditionalist American Knights of the Ku Klux Klan."

What's your *bilateral vomitation center*? The part of your brain that decides when to barf.

D.U.IRONY

Late one night in December 2012, Donald Blood III, 55, was arrested for DUI in Dorset, Vermont, after he drove onto the front lawn of a historic house, which he apparently mistook for a parking lot. The house was the birthplace of Bill Wilson, one of the founders of Alcoholics Anonymous.

IRONIC SAFETY

• People who are denied disability payments in Basildon, England, must go—in person—to the county courthouse if they want to appeal their case. The disability claims office is on the fourth floor. Only problem: If you happen to be wheelchair-bound, you're screwed. The fourth floor is off-limits to wheelchairs because the building has no fire escapes, and officials deemed that floor a "safety risk." (No word on how they expected people in wheelchairs to make it down the fire escape, even if there was one.)

• According to *Boston.com*, Sheila Burgess's driving record includes "seven accidents, four speeding violations, two failures to stop for a police officer, one failure to stay in her lane, one driving without registration or license in possession, and one driving without wearing a seat belt." Who is Sheila Burgess? The director of the Massachusetts Highway Safety Division.

• Scratch-and-sniff cards designed to avert panic by warning people what natural gas smells like nearly caused a panic in Great Falls, Montana. In May 2013, workers at Energy West threw a box of "expired" cards away. However, when the garbage truck compacted them, it had the same effect as scratching them all at once. As the truck drove through town, a strong smell of natural gas wafted out behind it. Frantic calls poured into 9-1-1, several homes and businesses were evacuated, and the fire department began prepping for disaster. Fortunately, the smell dissipated quickly. Energy West later apologized for its "gas leak."

MINDLESS IRONY

A near-riot broke out at a Chicago shopping mall in February 2013 shortly after a popular boy band appeared there to sign autographs. Hysterical fans barged in and ran all over the place, breaking displays and planter boxes. One teenager even threw a bunch of dollar bills into the air "just to add to the melee." By the time the riot was over, two teens were injured and 20 more were arrested. Name of the boy band: Mindless Behavior.

IRONY WITHOUT A PERMIT

In April 2013, nearly 300 demonstrators marched through Montreal, Quebec, protesting a new law that made it illegal to stage a protest without first providing the route itinerary to the police. The protest was cut short when the protesters were ticketed for not giving police advance notice of their protest route.

THE IRONY WEARS NO CLOTHES

In 2012, the History Channel fired TV personality Olivia Black after it was revealed that, a few years earlier, she had posed nude for an adult website—making her somewhat of a "porn star." The show she was fired from: *Pawn Stars*.

NONSTICK IRONY

After two trucks collided in Whangarei, New Zealand, in 2013, one of them spilled its contents all over the highway. Work crews arrived at the scene and hurriedly put up signs warning drivers that the road was slippery. So what got spilled? Glue.

IRONY BEHIND BARS

While on his deathbed after suffering a major heart attack in 2009, James Washington, an inmate in a Tennessee prison, told a guard, "I have to get something off my conscience." Washington then confessed to a 1995 murder that had gone unsolved. At the time, he was serving a 15-year sentence for a lesser crime, but shortly after his confession, Washington made what doctors called a "miraculous" recovery. He tried to take his confession back, but it was too late. Arrested and later convicted for the murder, the judge sentenced Washington to life in prison.

*   *   *

"Does it disturb anyone else that the baseball-team name 'The Los Angeles Angels' translates directly to 'The The Angels Angels'?"

—**Neil deGrasse Tyson**

Since 2000, the state of Georgia has flown three different state flags, a U.S. record.

WHY DIDN'T I THINK OF THAT?

Apparently, no idea is too simple or too dumb to make someone rich. Some of these should probably make us bemoan the decline of Western civilization, but instead we think, "Too bad we didn't think of them first."

• **Doggles.** One sunny day at the dog park, Roni di Lullo noticed that her Border collie, Midnight, couldn't catch the Frisbee she tossed him. Why? He was being blinded by sunlight. "I had on my sunglasses," said di Lullo, "and I was, like, why didn't he have something on *his* eyes?" Before long, he did: sunglass goggles for dogs. Sales to date: $3 million.

• **Snuggie.** Scott Boilen's simple idea: Sew arms onto blankets. His second idea: Sell them in informercials. The combination turned him into a mega-millionaire. (And it didn't hurt to have Jay Leno rant, "Why don't you just put your robe on backwards?" in a *Tonight Show* monologue.) Sales to date: $500 million.

• **PillowPets.** Most parents who watch their kids squash a stuffed toy to turn it into a pillow say, "Stop wrecking your toys." Jennifer Telfer said, "If my kid does that, other kids do, too." Then she turned the idea into a cuddly plush toy that unfolds to become a pillow. Sales to date: More than $300 million.

• **Under Armour.** As the special-teams captain for the University of Maryland football team, Kevin Plank noticed that his teammates all had something in common: heavy, sweat-soaked T-shirts under their uniform pads. "There has to be something better," he thought. There wasn't, so Plank invented it—a T-shirt made from microfibers that wicked away moisture and kept athletes "cool, dry, and light." Sales to date: $2 billion.

• **Spanx.** Sara Blakely cut the feet off her pantyhose and patented her "footless pantyhose." But she didn't tell her friends about the body-slimming undies she'd been developing for a year. When she did, one friend said in disbelief, "Sweetie, if it's such a good idea, why doesn't it already exist?" In 2012, Sara Blakely (not her skeptical friend) became the world's youngest female billionaire.

In the 1980s, Pablo Escobar's drug cartel was spending...

SPUN-OUT SPINOFFS

Some of the most popular shows in TV history began as spinoffs of other shows: The Simpsons *from* The Tracey Ullman Show *and* Knots Landing *from* Dallas, *for example. And then there are these.*

Spinoff: *Carlton, Your Doorman*
Story: Carlton the Doorman, from the 1970s sitcom *Rhoda*, is one of the great unseen characters in TV history, right up there with Vera on *Cheers* and Maris on *Frasier*. Viewers could hear Carlton's voice (Lorenzo Music) through Rhoda's intercom, but he was never seen. Except once: In 1980, *Rhoda's* production company made a pilot for an animated series starring Carlton, and he was finally seen: He was in his 30s, had long blond hair and a mustache (and the voice of Lorenzo Music). He liked to go to bars, flirt with building residents…and look after his homeless mother. CBS didn't quite know what to do with it—it was a cartoon, but it wasn't for kids. In the end, they didn't pick up the series, but they did air the dark pilot as a special in May 1980, right after a Bugs Bunny special.

Spinoff: *Monsignor Martinez*
Story: On the long-running Fox show *King of the Hill*, characters were frequently seen watching a ridiculous Mexican TV show called *Los Dias y Las Noches de Monsignor Martinez*, about a priest who kills bad guys. (Before every takedown, he utters his catchphrase, "*Vaya con dios,*" or "God be with you.") In 2001, Fox asked *Hill* creator Mike Judge to produce a live-action *Monsignor Martinez* pilot. Judge voices the character, but for the spinoff, he hired Argentinean actor Ivo Cutzarida. Fox ultimately passed on a full series, reportedly because executives were nervous about airing a show about a Catholic priest killing people.

Spinoff: *Checking In*
Story: *All in the Family* was a spinoff machine, generating *Maude*, *Good Times*, and *The Jeffersons*. George and Weezy Jefferson were introduced on *All in the Family*, but it was a new character on the spinoff that resonated most with audiences: the Jeffersons' sarcastic maid, Florence, portrayed by Marla Gibbs. After six seasons on *The*

Jeffersons, in 1981, Florence was given her own show, *Checking In*. The plot: Florence takes a job as head of housekeeping for a luxury hotel. Ratings were dismal—*Checking In* was pulling in about a third of the audience for *The Jeffersons*, which was a top-10 show. That proved to CBS that people weren't watching *The Jeffersons* just for Florence, but rather for her wisecracking interplay with George and Weezy. CBS canceled the show after four episodes, and Gibbs returned to *The Jeffersons*. Her reason for returning: The luxury hotel "burned down."

Spinoff: *Jackeé*
Story: NBC's 1985 comedy *227* was conceived as a vehicle for Marla Gibbs, who was coming off a 11-season run on *The Jeffersons*. But the breakout star of *227* was Jackeé Harry, who played Gibbs's neighbor in a Washington, D.C. apartment building. Harry got more plotlines and more press, leading to on-set tension. Producers' solution: spin off Harry's character, Sandra, into her own show. *Jackeé* debuted in May 1989. The plot: Sandra moves to New York to work at a film studio, only to find out it's an adult-film studio. *Jackeé* finished #5 in the weekly ratings, but didn't become a regular series because *Jackeé*'s production company balked at the last minute. Its last two projects had been "can't miss" hits that were ultimately rejected by the networks—and they were spinoffs, too (of *Who's the Boss?* and *The Facts of Life* respectively). *Jackeé* didn't happen, and Harry didn't return to *227*, which only lasted another season.

Spinoff: *After the Honeymoon*
Story: *My Three Sons* was originally about widower Steve Douglas (Fred MacMurray) raising his three young boys, but the show lasted so long that the boys weren't boys anymore. The producers decided to spin off second son Robbie (Don Grady), along with his new wife Katie (Tina Cole) and their triplet baby boys, into their own show in 1971 called *After the Honeymoon*. It was basically a *My Three Sons* reboot. CBS rejected the pilot, so Katie and the boys returned to the Douglas home on *My Three Sons*. Grady didn't want to come back for what would be the show's twelfth (and final) season, so viewers were told that he was away on business, managing a construction company—in Peru.

OLD DRUG, NEW TRICKS

Prescription drugs are the result of years of research and development. While most new drugs do what manufacturers promise they'll do, they sometimes offer users (and stockholders) an unexpected bonus.

Drug: Bimatoprost

Intended Purpose: These prescription eye drops are typically used to slow the progression of glaucoma and help manage other aggressive eye ailments.

Bonus: During early trials in the 2000s, scientists noticed that the drops also lengthened and strengthened the eyelashes of test subjects. After getting FDA approval for that use in 2008, a modified version of Bimatoprost—named Latisse—was marketed to women as a way to bulk up anemic eyelashes. However, after two years of brisk sales, doctors started to notice a startling side effect: In some cases, Latisse changed the color of the users' eyes from blue or green to brown, and if brought into contact with the skin, it dried out and darkened eyelids, giving users what's been referred to as "raccoon eyes."

Drug: Bupropion

Intended Purpose: Sold under the brand name Wellbutrin, this is the fourth-most-prescribed antidepressant in the United States.

Bonus: Other benefits of bupropion have been known since initial testing in the 1960s. Lower dosages are now sold to smokers to diminish nicotine cravings and to obese patients to decrease hunger. It's also been proven effective in fighting bipolarism, sexual dysfunction, attention-deficit disorder, and Seasonal Affective Disorder. Studies are also underway to see if bupropion can treat inflammatory bowel disease and meth addiction.

Drug: Sildenafil

Intended Purpose: Pfizer developed the drug in the early 1990s to treat high blood pressure.

Bonus: During clinical testing, a certain side effect was discovered. A *big* side effect. For men. Trial subjects were supposedly so happy with their samples of Sildenafil that they refused to return their left-

---

Facebook designers originally wanted to call the "Like" button the "Awesome" button.

over pills. Since its approval by the FDA in 1998, this little blue pill has been used by over 35 million men worldwide under the brand name…Viagra. (It's been nicknamed "The Pfizer Riser.") The team that led the initial research into expanding and strengthening blood vessels that led to the development of Viagra won the Nobel Prize for Physiology in 1998.

Another Bonus: In addition to all but eradicating erectile dysfunction (and leading to a multibillion-dollar industry that includes competitors like Cialis and Levitra), the drug can help mountain climbers with altitude sickness but can also lead to heart attacks. And in the mid-2000s, scientists in Argentina also discovered that Sildenafil aids jet-lag recovery…in hamsters.

Drug: Oral Contraceptives

Intended Purpose: There are many versions of "the pill" in the marketplace, but all oral contraceptives work the same way. They prevent unwanted pregnancies by releasing hormones, tricking the body into thinking it's already pregnant so that another fetus cannot grow.

Bonus: The FDA has approved the use of three different types of oral contraceptives to help young women with acne. Acne is caused by *sebum*, an oil produced by skin glands (after puberty begins) that often clogs pores and results in zits. The hormones and chemicals in oral contraceptives prevent the production of sebum and testosterone (testosterone exacerbates acne). While doctors have prescribed the drugs to female acne sufferers for decades, they typically only offer them to those who need birth control. Reason: Side effects, which can include weight gain, headaches, and "breast tenderness."

Drug: Minoxidil

Intended Purpose: In the 1980s, minoxidil was marketed under the brand name Loniten as a blood-pressure-balancing medication.

Bonus: Middle-aged male patients, a significant chunk of Loniten users, noticed that they were suddenly growing hair where there hadn't been hair in years. Minoxidil was effectively curing baldness. In 1988, Loniten manufacturer Upjohn (now a part of Pfizer) released an odorless minoxidil-based lotion for direct scalp application under the brand name Rogaine.

THE MEANING OF LI-FI

If you've ever tried to set up a wireless router in your home or just tried to access the Internet in a Starbucks using your iPad, you're familiar with the list of Wi-Fi networks that pop up when you do. Most have pretty boring names, but some people go for laughs when naming theirs.

The LAN before time

Area 51

Your Bathroom Shower
Needs New Tiles

Help Me Pay For It

The Meaning of LiFi

Secret CIA Intelligence
Underground Military Base

Why Phi?

Holy *$#% We're Online

The Dingo Ate My Wi-Fi

FBI Surveillance Van #42

RCMP Surveillance Horse

It Hurts When IP

IfYouGuessMyPassword
IHaveToRenameMyDog

Mom Click Here For Internet

Alien Abduction Network

Global Thermonuclear War

SHUT YOUR DOG UP
OR I WILL CALL THE COPS

IP Freely

Caitlin stop using our Internet!

HeyUGetOffMyLAN

NCC-1701

Abraham Linksys

.− .. ..−. ..
(morse code for WiFi)

I'm Under Your Bed

Nuclear Launch Detected

Secret Federal Witness
Protection Safehouse

I'm cheating on my WiFi

John Wilkes Bluetooth

c:\virus.exe

Router—IHardlyKnowHer

Bill Wi the Science Fi

LAN of Milk and Honey

Did it spark a lawsuit? In 1638, Virginia passed a law outlawing lawyers.

SPORTS CONSPIRACY THEORIES

The best athlete always wins, right? Not if these conspiracy theories are to be believed.

CONSPIRACY THEORY: The NBA fixed its 1985 draft to ensure that hot college prospect Patrick Ewing would end up on the New York Knicks, in order to promote the league by putting the biggest new star on a team from its biggest market.

BACKGROUND: It was a foregone conclusion among the sports media that star Georgetown University center Patrick Ewing would be the #1 pick in the 1985 draft. The question was: To what team? That year was also the first time the NBA used a lottery system to determine the draft selection order. (Prior to that, the team with the worst record in the previous season automatically got the first pick, second-worst got second pick, etc.) Now, the seven worst teams all got a shot at the #1 selection—the teams' names were placed in envelopes (the worse the record, the more envelopes), and the envelopes drawn at random from a transparent globe.

THE CLAIM: Random selection? Hardly, say the conspiracy theorists. They claim that if you watch a video of the selection, you can see accountant Jack Wagner, who was there to guarantee the "integrity" of the process, bang one of the envelopes against the side of the globe, denting the corner of the envelope. It's that same envelope NBA commissioner David Stern pulls out of the globe moments later—giving the #1 pick to the Knicks.

THE TRUTH: The Knicks had the third-worst record and thus the third-most envelopes in the globe, so they had a pretty good shot at getting the top pick. As for Stern "denting" an envelope, the footage doesn't suggest that. Nevertheless, the following year, the league moved to a lottery with balls marked with team names, similar to the way lottery numbers are selected on television.

CONSPIRACY THEORY: When Michael Jordan quit his NBA career in 1993, he didn't do it to play baseball—it was actually a secret two-year suspension from the NBA for illegal gambling.

BACKGROUND: In October 1993, just before the start of the season, Jordan called a surprise press conference to announce that he was retiring from basketball. The decision, he said, was brought on by the stress of his father's death in a mugging gone awry, which led him to "lose passion" for basketball. Jordan played minor league baseball for a year, and then returned to the NBA in 1995, where he won three more championships.

THE CLAIM: At the press conference, Jordan chose his words very carefully, remarking he was "not playing basketball in the NBA anymore" and that it "doesn't mean I won't play basketball anywhere else." Conspiracy theorists claim he was signaling that he might play someplace else, wherever that might be. Another odd remark: "If [Commissioner] David Stern lets me back in the league, I may come back." That doesn't sound like a retirement speech. Meanwhile, a year earlier a gambler named James "Slim" Bouler had testified in court (in a money laundering case) that Jordan gave him a check for $57,000. Jordan initially said it was a business loan, but later admitted it was a gambling debt. Then two more gambling associates of Jordan came forward with checks he'd written to cover debts: one for $108,000, another for $1.25 million. While Jordan may not have gambled on his own games, his gambling and hanging out with shady figures sullied the league's image. Stern, along with Jordan's sponsor, Nike, forced Jordan out of basketball for two years, the theory goes. He only played baseball to stay in shape for his eventual return to basketball.

THE TRUTH: Jordan *did* use those words at his press conference, and he *did* confess that the large checks he'd written to friends were for gambling debts. But did he really flee basketball for baseball because the NBA and Nike made him? Only he, the NBA, and Nike know for sure, and they're not tallking.

CONSPIRACY THEORY: Wayne Gretzky was traded from the Edmonton Oilers to the Los Angeles Kings as part of a public-relations stunt to popularize hockey in the United States.

BACKGROUND: Gretzky entered the NHL in 1979 and in less than a decade had earned the nickname "The Great One." In his first eight seasons, all with the Edmonton Oilers, he won the league's MVP award eight times, led the league in scoring seven times, and led the Oilers to four Stanley Cup championships.

THE CLAIM: Gretzky's impressive skills didn't do much to popularize hockey in the United States. But if the NHL could get Gretzky to play in the big media market of Los Angeles, he would generate lots of new attention and the sport's popularity would grow. So, the theory goes, right after the 1987–88 season (in which the Oilers won the Stanley Cup), Gretzky was dealt to the L.A. Kings to boost American interest in the game.

THE TRUTH: The trade had more to do with the Oilers' precarious finances than American hockey fans: The team was nearly bankrupt and stood to make a fortune trading Gretzky away. The Oilers were actually shopping him around even before he helped Edmonton win the Stanley Cup, and the New Jersey Devils, the Detroit Red Wings, and the Los Angeles Kings were the finalists. When Gretzky realized that a move was inevitable, he asked to go to L.A. so that he could be closer to his wife, actress Janet Jones.

CONSPIRACY THEORY: Professional male tennis player Bobby Riggs deliberately threw his famous 1973 "Battle of the Sexes" match against female tennis pro Billie Jean King. He did it so that he could make a fortune betting against himself.

BACKGROUND: Courting controversy by egging on the women's liberation movement, Riggs challenged King to a televised match to determine which gender was better (or at least better at tennis). Riggs had already beaten Margaret Court, the top female player in the world at the time, in straight sets in early 1973. But when Riggs played King, somehow the scores were reversed: King walloped him in three straight sets, 6-4, 6-3, 6-3.

THE CLAIM: The dismal score belies Riggs's poor performance. Conspiracy theorists claim that he refused to run or reach for dozens of shots, and let a lot of easy shots go. The reason: He was trying to lose. The whole thing was a show and a easy path to a big payday. Riggs, a known gambler, was trying to throw the match because he'd bet on King to win.

THE TRUTH: Riggs was 55 at the time and more than a decade past his prime. King was 30 and at the top of her game. While Riggs later attributed the sexist comments he'd made before the match to showmanship, those remarks helped motivate King to make an example of Riggs. After the match and up until his death in 1995, Riggs always asserted that King had simply "outplayed me."

The Northern and Southern lights can be seen from the International Space Station.

UJPORAD

Uncle John's Page of Random Acronym Definitions

TECHNOLOGY

GMO: Stemming from the term "genetic engineering" (coined by Dr. P.M. Bhargava in 1973), it means **G**enetically **M**odified **O**rganism.

4G: In mobile-phone technology, each **G**eneration is defined by a leap in technology over the previous one. 1G (1981) was analog; 2G ('90s) introduced digital modem technology; 3G ('03) was broadband; 4G ('08) is still broadband, but much faster.

IP: **I**nternet **P**rotocol, "the method or protocol by which data is sent from one computer to another on the Internet."

ISO: Though often associated with camera film speed, the **I**nternational **O**rganization for **S**tandardization is a much broader entity. Formed in 1947, it has developed over 18,600 standards ranging in everything from energy to construction to communications. In the 1970s, when camera manufacturers were measuring film speeds differently, the ISO combined two of them to create the system still used today.

So why not IOS? Because the word *isos* also means "equivalent" in Greek, and because ISO works better when translated into other languages.

RSS feed: **R**ich **S**ite **S**ummary (sometimes called *Really Simple Syndication*). It's a technology by which Internet users can receive all the latest posts from all their favorite websites at a single location.

BUSINESS

CFO, CIO, COO: A corporation's **C**hief **F**inancial **O**fficer, **C**hief **I**nformation **O**fficer, and **C**hief **O**perating **O**fficer. (They all make more money than you do.)

MSRP: In a 1911 opinion interpreting the Sherman Antitrust Act, the U.S. Supreme Court ruled that retailers, not manufacturers, set prices of new products. So the **M**anufacturer's **S**uggested **R**etail **P**rice was set up to give retailers an idea of what to charge. (In 2007 the Court overturned the law, allowing manufacturers to set minimum prices.)

HMO: During the Nixon

---

administration in 1973, the **H**ealth **M**aintenance **O**rganization Act was passed, based on recommendations by the man who invented it: Dr. Paul M. Ellwood, Jr., whose company had been hired by the government to find ways to slow rising health-care costs.

INTERNET

NSFW: Click on the link at your own risk, because what it leads to is **N**ot **S**afe **F**or **W**ork.

TL; DR: If you see this in a comment thread following an article, the commenter is saying it's **T**oo **L**ong; **D**idn't **R**ead.

ROFL: It's so funny that we're **R**olling **O**n the **F**loor, **L**aughing.

IMO, IMHO, IMFAO: They all stand for **I**n **M**y **O**pinion, but the H is for **H**umble and the FA is **F***ing **A**rrogant.

O RLY: This sarcastic Internet meme means **O**h, **R**eally? It comes from a picture of a snowy owl posted online in 2001 by photographer John White. He's sent out several cease-and-desist letters to halt the use of his image, but the Internet has collectively replied, O RLY?

IIRC: If **I** **R**ecall **C**orrectly

PRW: **P**arents a**R**e **W**atching

FTW: This abbreviation means **F**or **T**he **W**in!

YOLO: This means **Y**ou **O**nly **L**ive **O**nce. If you're unhappy with your life, you might type…

TAL: For "**T**hat's **A**ll Folks!" the signature line from Looney Tunes' Porky Pig.

ENTERTAINMENT

RIAA: The **R**ecording **I**ndustry **A**ssociation of **A**merica was formed in 1952 to "protect the rights of copyright holders." They're the group that sued Napster users.

THX: While working on 1983's *Return of the Jedi*, Lucasfilm sound engineer Tomlinson Holman developed a quality-assurance system to help movie theaters achieve the best sound possible. The name is a play on George Lucas's first film, *THX 1138*, but technically it stands for **T**omlinson **H**olman's e**X**periment.

BRI: The **B**athroom **R**eaders' **I**nstitute was founded by brothers John and Gordon Javna in 1987 to give you something better to read in here than the label on a shampoo bottle. You're welcome.

LOONEY LAWS

Believe it or not, these are all real.

In Hoquiam, Washington, it's illegal to tip a server more than 15 percent.

Legally, Boston hotel owners must provide a bed for a guest's horse.

Gargling in public is against the law in Louisiana.

In Topeka, Kansas, it's illegal to sing the alphabet song on the streets at night.

Mustached men in Eureka, Nevada, may not kiss women.

If you make furniture in Devon, Texas, it's against the law to do so in the nude.

If you want to wear cowboy boots in Blythe, California, you must own at least two cows.

It's illegal to skateboard inside a police station in Miami.

Lying about your astrological sign is against the law in Sedona, Arizona.

Driving a black car in Denver on a Sunday is illegal.

In Salt Lake City, you may not carry a violin in a paper bag.

In Oklahoma, taking a bite out of another person's hamburger without permission is against the law.

Anyone caught stealing soap in Mohave County, Arizona, has to wash himself with it until it's gone.

You may throw bricks onto a highway in Mt. Vernon, Iowa, but only if you've obtained written permission from the City Council.

In Kentucky, it's illegal to fish with a bow and arrow.

Flicking boogers into the wind is against the law in Alabama.

In Crown Point, Indiana, it's illegal to carry a dog in your purse while you're walking across the grass wearing shoes.

Alabama prison guards are prohibited from calling their spouse "the old ball and chain."

It's against the law to give someone a box of candy in Idaho...if it weighs less than 50 pounds.

Eucalyptus trees can explode in forest fires. (Eucalyptus oil is highly flammable.)

DUSTBIN OF HISTORY: A NEW GERMANY IN TEXAS

Here's a story that not many of us learned in school, not even those of us who grew up in Texas: the attempt to create a second Germany in the Republic of Texas.

HOI POLLOI

In April 1842, a group of German princes and noblemen met in the town of Biebrich am Rhein to discuss a problem vexing many countries in Europe in the 19th century: The population was booming just as the Industrial Revolution was replacing growing numbers of manual laborers with machines. The result was widespread poverty and social unrest that the largely undemocratic German states were ill-equipped to deal with. (In those days, Germany was divided into more than 30 independent kingdoms, principalities, and free cities.)

But what if the surplus population could be sent somewhere else? That's what the nobles were gathering to discuss. One of them, a count named Carl of Castell-Castell, thought it might be possible to send people to the Republic of Texas, a former Mexican colony that had won its independence six years earlier. The republic was actively seeking Europeans who would settle in Texas, and had set up a system of land grants to attract them. Speculators were encouraged to buy huge tracts of land at rock-bottom prices, then recruit settlers to live on the land. Once the settlers were living on the grant, the speculators would be awarded additional tracts of land in payment. These tracts could be sold for a profit, and the money used to bring more settlers to Texas.

BRAVE NEW WELT

If a "new Germany" could be established in Texas, Castell argued, the nobles would benefit as much as the people who settled there. The colony would be a market for German goods and a source of raw materials for German manufacturers. It would also help Germany develop trade with Mexico. Whatever money the nobles invested in the German colony, Castell told them, would be repaid

---

Air mail: The Egyptian pharaohs used carrier pigeons to send messages.

many times over in the years to come.

And there was another benefit that Germany's royal families might have valued more than any other: the possibility of creating vast new estates for themselves. During the wars with Napoleon Bonaparte from 1805 to 1810, many of Germany's ruling families had been stripped of power when their kingdoms and principalities were incorporated into the Napoleonic empire. After Napoleon was defeated in 1815 and the Congress of Vienna redrew the map of Europe, not all of the old kingdoms were restored. Just as Texas had won independence from Mexico, a new Germany might one day win independence from Texas. The dispossessed nobles might then be able to carve out giant new territories that they and their descendants could lord over for centuries to come.

TEXAS TOURING

The nobles who met at Biebrich am Rhein agreed to form a group called the *Adelsverein*, or "Society of Noblemen," to explore the possibility of creating a new Germany in Texas. In May 1842, the Society dispatched two of its members to Texas: Count Victor zu Leiningen, older half-brother of England's Queen Victoria, and Count Ludwig Joseph de Boos-Waldeck. They arrived in the port city of Galveston the following August. After meeting with President Sam Houston and apprising him of their plans, they toured the republic and visited the scattering of Germans who had settled in various Texas communities over the previous decade.

Leiningen and Boos-Waldeck purchased the Society's first piece of Texas real estate—4,428 acres of land in modern-day Fayette County, which they acquired for 75¢ an acre—and named it Nassau Farm in honor of Duke Adolph of Nassau, the honorary "patron" of the Adelsverein. Nassau Farm was intended as a headquarters for members of the Adelsverein when they visited Texas and also as a possible stopping point for German settlers on their way to their own land…which the Society had yet to buy.

STICKER SHOCK

Leiningen returned to Germany in May 1843. He arrived home full of enthusiasm about the possibilities that Texas had to of-fer—limitless, virtually free land and winters so mild that crops could be grown year-round. But he also warned that settling large numbers of Germans in Texas was going to cost a fortune, far more than the Adelsverein had planned to spend. The Society embraced his positive description of the republic…and ignored his warnings about the costs. Perhaps because of this, Leiningen returned to his military career in Austria and played no further role in the Society. When Boos-Waldeck returned home a year later and vigorously opposed large-scale colonization because of the high cost, the Society ignored him, too. Insulted, he dropped out of the Adelsverein.

In June 1843, the Adelsverein reorganized itself into a stock company, and the nobles ponied up $80,000 in capital to get it started—a sum far less than both Leiningen and Boos-Waldeck had said would be needed.

CAVEAT EMPIRE

As if starting the project with too little money wasn't bad enough, the Adelsverein made matters worse by being taken in by not one but *two* different land swindlers who sold them worthless rights to two land grants: the Bourgeois-Ducos grant and the Fisher-Miller grant. Both grants had expiration dates that required settlers to be on the land by a certain date, otherwise the grant became null and void. The Bourgeois-Ducos grant had already expired, and the Fisher-Miller grant was about to, when the Adelsverein spent thousands of dollars of its limited (and inadequate) funds to buy them.

The Adelsverein compounded the problem by hiring the same swindlers, Alexander Bourgeois and Henry Francis Fisher, to purchase supplies for the settlers and arrange for their transportation to their new homes when they arrived in Texas. Bourgeois lasted only four months before his services were dispensed with; Fisher lasted much longer and did a lot more damage.

GO WEST, JUNG MANN

Other than Nassau Farm, which was too small to serve as a homestead for the thousands of settlers it hoped to sign up, the Adelsverein still didn't own any land that it could send people to. But it thought it did, and that was enough for it to begin recruiting settlers. In the spring of 1844, the Society began placing advertisements in German newspapers with the slogan *Geh Mit Ins Texas* ("Go with Us to Texas") and printed brochures describing the sweetheart deal the Adelsverein was promising to provide.

First song played at Carnegie Hall: Beethoven's "Leonore Overture #3," in 1891.

PROMISED LAND

In exchange for a one-time payment of $240 from each household that wanted to go, the Adelsverein would furnish 320 acres of land in Texas, free transportation across the Atlantic to the port of Galveston and from there to the land claim, a log cabin, all living and farming expenses for the first year, plus free use of irrigation canals, grain mills, cotton gins, and other infrastructure that the Adelsverein would provide at its own expense. (Single adult males could sign up for $120 and receive 160 acres when they arrived at the land grant; otherwise the deal for them was the same.)

To make the transatlantic trip as safe as possible, the Society promised to provide a doctor and surgeon on each ship, plus food, water, and supplies to last the passengers and crew for six months. Satisfaction was guaranteed: Any settlers who weren't happy in Texas could return to Germany on Society-chartered ships "and pay no more for the homeward than the outward voyage."

The Adelsverein never bothered to explain how it was going to pay for all of this, but it didn't matter because few people bothered to ask. The Society also promised not to settle more than 150 families the first year, and no more than it was able to accommodate after that. This was the first promise it broke.

ROAD TO NOWHERE

Within a month of running its first newspaper ads, the Adelsverein signed up more than 10,000 Germans to go to Texas, and no sooner were they signed up than the Society began chartering ships to take them there. Even if the Society hadn't yet realized that its land grants were worthless and it had no place to send the settlers to, it certainly understood that the supplies and infrastructure it promised had yet to be purchased or built. But it soon began sending the settlers to Texas anyway. The first ship set sail in the fall of 1844 and arrived in Galveston in late November.

By then the Adelsverein's official representative, Prince Carl of Solms-Braunfels, had been in Texas for nearly five months. His job, and that of the land swindler Henry Francis Fisher, was to prepare for the settlers' arrival by purchasing everything they would need. Fisher embezzled the money he was supposed to use for that purpose; Prince Carl, though honest, was incompetent and no better than Fisher at accomplishing the task.

Scientific evidence indicates that T. *rex* often broke its tiny arms.

INDIAN COUNTRY

Prince Carl did pay a visit to the Texas capital at Washington-on-the-Brazos, where he received more bad news about the Fisher-Miller land grant. Not only was the grant worthless, the Texans informed him, but the land was shockingly unsuitable for settlement. For one thing, the grant was 300 miles inland from Galveston, which made it all but impossible for settlers to get to. It was also 90 miles from the nearest Texas town, and deep inside Comanche and Apache territory. These hostile tribes weren't about to let European settlers on their land without a fight. Even if peace could be made with the Indians, the land was rocky and largely unsuitable for farming. It was so unsuitable, in fact, that the government of Texas was willing to overlook the fact that the Fisher-Miller grant had expired and let the Society have the land anyway, if it was dumb enough to actually want it.

Prince Carl forwarded this information to the Adelsverein in Germany, along with his recommendation that the Society look for a better piece of land, one outside of Indian territory, more suitable for farming, and closer to the port of Galveston. The Adelsverein replied by instructing him to continue preparing the Fisher-Miller grant for settlement.

CULTURE SHOCK

Rather than purchase supplies and begin hiring the wagons that would be needed for the 300-mile trip to the Fisher-Miller land, Prince Carl tackled what he considered a far more pressing problem. The effete, high-born prince had clashed with the uncouth and unwashed Texans, Americans, and Mexicans from the moment he'd arrived in Galveston. He was concerned that the settlers would lose their essential "Germanness" if allowed to mingle with such rabble. So rather than look after their more basic needs, like food, transportation, and shelter, he wasted precious time and money looking for a more "suitable," more isolated place for the settlers to land.

He found one on a barren island called Indian Point, about 100 miles south of Galveston. Prince Carl apparently intended to ask the Adelsverein to hold off on sending any settlers to Texas until suitable accommodations could be built there. But it was too late—six days before he finalized arrangements with the owner of Indian Point to land the Society's settlers there, the first Adelsverein ship

---

Dopes: The U.S. Department of Agriculture once subsidized farmers growing opium poppies.

arrived in Galveston on November 23, 1844. And more were on the way: As many as 200 families—more than 700 settlers in all—would arrive by the end of December.

FROM BAD TO WURST

These settlers had gotten their first taste of the Adelsverein's inability to live up to its promises on the way across the Atlantic. Instead of hiring modern steamships, which could make the crossing in as few as 18 days, the Society chartered sailing ships, which took two months. Only the cheapest ships had been hired, ones crawling with rats, fleas, and lice, which soon infected the passengers with typhus that in many cases proved to be fatal. The food aboard the ships was inedible; the "drinking" water was indescribably bad. There were no doctors and no surgeons provided; any people who fell ill during the passage had to fend for themselves.

And yet as bad as conditions were during the voyage, when the settlers arrived in Galveston and saw that preparations in Texas were no better than they had been on the boats, many felt safer returning to Germany aboard those very same boats rather than place any more faith in the Adelsverein.

The settlers who went back to Germany, it turns out, were the lucky ones.

For Part II of the story, turn to page 445.

*   *   *

BIRTH OF A SUPERHERO

In 1974, Marvel Comics set out to create a new superhero who could 1) battle the Hulk, and 2) be popular in Canada. Deciding on an animal-themed hero, Marvel editor-in-chief Roy Thomas researched Canadian wildlife and narrowed it down to two choices, ultimately deciding on…the Badger. Marvel writer Len Wein and art director John Romita gave the Badger a yellow-and-blue suit and metal claws. They all liked the character, but soon realized that the badger wasn't the right animal. So they decided to go with Thomas's second choice, and the character was renamed…the Wolverine.

Utah once had divorce-paper vending machines.

LET'S PLAY TIDDLYWINKS!

In our 21st-century world of Wii and Words With Friends, the classic low-tech game of Tiddlywinks has been all but forgotten. If you don't know the game (or you've never even heard of it), here's a description and some facts about the one of the most peculiar crazes of the 1890s.

THE BASICS

The game of Tiddlywinks is at least 125 years old, and maybe older. The rules of play are very simple:

1. Each player starts with six *winks*, or discs about the size of dimes. They're usually plastic but can be made from other materials, and each player's set of winks is a different color: blue, green, red, and yellow.

2. Each player also has a *squidger*. This is a larger disc, and can be anywhere from about one to two inches in diameter.

3. The field of play is any flat surface, such as a tabletop or the floor. In the center of the surface is the *pot*—a small cup, a couple of inches high and a couple of inches in diameter.

4. Players use their squidgers to press down on the edge of one of their winks, making it flip into the air, and, hopefully, into the pot—which is the goal of the game.

5. The first player to get all six of their winks into the pot wins.

A WINKING MAN'S GAME

In 1888, a British inventor named Joseph Assheton Fincher filed a patent application for a game he called "Tiddledy-Winks." It was very similar to the game we know as Tiddlywinks, and Fincher is considered the game's inventor. But the game almost certainly existed in some form long before that. A commonly told story is that Fincher took the name from another existing use of the phrase: "tiddledy-wink," which was British slang for "small drink" and was also used as a term for any unlicensed pub. But many game historians think Fincher simply made up the name himself.

Whatever the true origin of its name, Fincher's game became a

---

sensation in Great Britain in the 1890s, even making its way to the United States, where it was also very popular. A variety of different versions of the game were produced, including golf and tennis editions, and there were numerous knockoffs with names like Lafoga, Crickets, Spoof, Flipperty Flop, Jumpkins, Hupkins, Grasshopper, Scrum, Flutter, and many others. The craze died down after the turn of the century, but the game never faded away completely. Then, in 1955, the modern game, by this time spelled the way it's most commonly spelled today—"Tiddlywinks"—was developed when the Cambridge University Tiddlywinks Club was formed in London. In 1966, the North American Tiddlywinks Association was founded, and the two groups remain the governing bodies of the game today.

TIDDLY BITS

• Tournament Tiddlywinks is played on a 3-by 6-foot felt mat. Each set of six has a squidger, four small winks (⅝ inch in diameter) and two larger winks (⅞ inch in diameter). This plays an important role in game strategy: part of the play involves attempting to cover your opponents' winks with your own, thereby making them unplayable. For obvious reasons, the larger winks are better for this than the smaller ones.

• Shooting a wink with the intention of covering another player's wink is called *squopping*. A covered wink is said to be squopped.

• Another officially recognized shot: the *crud*. It's a very forceful shot aimed at a pile of squopped winks, with the intention of busting up the pile, thereby freeing the squopped winks.

• In 1958, the Cambridge University Tiddlywinks Club challenged the Duke of Edinburgh—Prince Philip, Queen Elizabeth's husband—to a Tiddlywinks match. He accepted, and got the British comedy group the Goons to play for him. (The Goons lost.)

• In 1961, Prince Philip awarded the "Silver Wink"—a trophy he designed himself—to the winners of the Cambridge University Tiddlywinks championship. He has awarded the trophy to Cambridge's Tiddlywinks champions every year since.

• Uncle John's Favorite: In 1992, Gibson's Games released a tiddlywinks-like game called "Widdly Tinks: Tiddlywinks Gone Potty." Object: To flip your winks into the pot—which is a miniature toilet. (People take a lot of *cruds* in that game, we're guessing....)

Signs that say "Not Responsible for Your Car or Its Contents" have no legal standing in court.

PRISON LINGO

Here's hoping you never have to put these terms and expressions to use.

Chain: A new shipment of inmates (chained together)

Bean Slot: The small opening in a cell door where food trays are passed in and inmates pass their hands through to be handcuffed before they're taken out of the cell

Academy: The prison

Undergrad: Convict

All Day: A life sentence

All Day and a Night: Life without possibility of parole

Pack the Rabbit/Put It in the Safe: Hide contraband in a certain part of the body. (If you don't already know where, we aren't going to tell you.)

Rollie: Handmade cigarettes that use toilet paper for cigarette paper

Road Kill: A rollie made with tobacco from cigarette butts collected by prison road crews

Flat Time: Serving an entire sentence, with no parole or time off for good behavior

Doing a Nickel: Serving a five-year sentence

Lifeboat: A pardon

Valentine: A short sentence

Stainless Steel Ride: Lethal injection

Rerun: A released inmate who returns to prison after committing another crime

Fresh Fish: A new inmate

Peels: Orange prison jumpsuits (Get it? Orange peels!)

Ding Wing: The mental ward

Screw: A guard

King Screw: The warden

Ninja Turtle: A screw dressed in riot gear

Goon Squad: A group of ninja turtles

Ghetto Penthouse: A cell on the top tier, near the ceiling

Getting on the Bus: Testifying against another inmate in exchange for a reduction in sentence

In the Car: An inmate who's in on a scheme of some kind

On the Bumper: An inmate who's trying to get in the car

When Milton Bradley released the game Twister in 1966, critics called it "sex in a box."

WHERE THE WILD THINGS RULE

On these islands, the creatures call the shots.

Island: Okunoshima, Japan

Overrun with: Rabbits

Details: During World War II, this uninhabited island was home to a secret project to develop chemical weapons for the Japanese Imperial Army. After the war, Okunoshima was converted into a recreation area, with a hotel, golf course, campground, and the Poison Gas Museum. Not many people live on the island, but hundreds of bunnies do. According to local lore, the rabbits are the descendants of a batch used to test the effectiveness of the mustard and tear gas the government cranked out during the war years. Others claim that back in the 1970s, a group of school kids released eight rabbits on the island during a field trip. In either case, the original rabbits bred like…rabbits. Today, their descendants are hopping all over what locals call *Usagi Shima* ("Rabbit Island"). They reportedly have no fear of humans and have even been known to hop onto a tourist's unguarded lap. Cupfuls of rabbit food are sold at the island's only hotel for 100 yen (a dollar).

Island: Kauai, Hawaii

Overrun with: Chickens

Details: Around 2,000 years ago, Kauai's first human residents arrived from Asia and brought chickens with them. The chickens were used for meat, eggs, and, most especially, cockfighting. When settlers from North America and Europe showed up in the 18th century, they brought tamer breeds of chickens with them. The breeds remained separate until Hurricane Iniki battered the island in 1992. Kauai's chicken coops were ravaged by the storm. Scores of the docile farm birds escaped and started interbreeding with their more dangerous foreign cousins. Their offspring went feral, and the population of wild chickens skyrocketed. Thousands now roam the island's jungles, beaches, golf courses, and other tourist hot spots. Why not just hunt and eat them? Because farm-raised chickens eat

---

Founded in 1775, the U.S. Marine Corps is older than the United States.

a grain-based diet, which gives them their familiar chicken taste. However, the wild chickens eat whatever they find—everything from sugarcane and corn to garbage that they peck from outside restaurants. That diet makes for a chicken that tastes gamey and unpleasant, so there's little interest in hunting them for food. Your best bet: Stay out of their way.

Island: Gough Island
Overrun with: Mice
Details: About 150 years ago, seafarers navigating the South Atlantic Ocean stopped over on tiny Gough Island and left behind a few common house mice. With no natural land predators, the island's mouse population has grown to roughly 1.9 million. The mice themselves have grown, too—to more than twice their normal size. These "rodents of unusual size" gang up on larger seabird hatchlings, which are no match for the onslaught. Ornithologists are concerned that the out-of-control mouse population will soon wipe out the endangered Atlantic petrel, which breeds on the island. There's only one other island where these seabirds breed, but that one has an out-of-control black-rat population that's eating them.

Island: Tashirojima, Japan
Overrun with: Cats
Details: Tashirojima is located off the northeastern coast of Japan and has about 100 human residents…and thousands of feline residents. The locals call it *Neko Shima* ("Cat Island"). In the 19th century, the island had a thriving silk industry until the mouse population started decimating it. (Mice are silkworms' natural predators—they eat the silk *and* the worms.) That's when desperate silkworm farmers started importing cats. Today, the silkworms and mice are long gone, but the cats remain. So beloved are the cats today—to locals and tourists—that there are shrines and buildings dedicated to them on the island. And not surprisingly, dogs are banned from Tashirojima.

*   *   *

Random fact: The two stone lions sitting in front the New York Public Library are named Fortitude and Patience.

UNCLE JOHN'S PAGE OF LISTS

More random information from the BRI's bottomless files.

7 Dirty Bird Names
1. Titmouse
2. Oxpecker
3. Red-Footed Booby
4. Imperial Shag
5. Gamecock
6. Dickcissel
7. Southern Screamer

5 Best-selling Video Game Consoles
1. Sony PlayStation 2
2. Nintendo DS
3. Nintendo GameBoy
4. Sony PlayStation
5. Nintendo Wii

6 Fictional DC Comics Cities
1. Metropolis (Superman)
2. Gotham City (Batman)
3. Star City (Green Arrow)
4. Keystone City (The Flash)
5. Fawcett City (Captain Marvel)
6. Sub Diego (Aquagirl)

7 Kids' Books by Celebrities
1. *SheetzuCacaPoopoo: My Kind of Dog*, Joy Behar
2. *I Already Know I Love You*, Billy Crystal
3. *Is There Really a Human Race?*, Jamie Lee Curtis
4. *Marsupial Sue*, John Lithgow
5. *Rock Steady: A Story of Noah's Ark*, Sting
6. *Propeller One-Way Night Coach: A Fable for All Ages*, John Travolta
7. *Dumpy and the Big Storm*, Julie Andrews

7 TV Shows Set in Miami
1. *Miami Vice*
2. *CSI: Miami*
3. *The Golden Girls*
4. *Flipper*
5. *Dexter*
6. *Nip/Tuck*
7. *Empty Nest*

5 5'5" Stars
1. Charlie Chaplin
2. Lindsay Lohan
3. Woody Allen
4. Jennifer Lopez
5. Daniel Radcliffe

4 Parts of a Sword
1. Blade
2. Hilt
3. Guard
4. Pommel

9 Palindromic Places
1. Notton (England)
2. Madoko Dam (Zimbabwe)
3. Wassamassaw (South Carolina)
4. Kanakanak (Alaska)
5. Caraparac (Peru)
6. Allagalla (Sri Lanka)
7. Vellev (Denmark)
8. Tumut (Australia)
9. Ward Draw (South Dakota)

First airplane hijacking: a Pan Am mail plane in Peru (1931).

JIM ROCKFORD'S ANSWERING MACHINE

Every episode of the classic 1970s TV show The Rockford Files *opened with the same signature audio gag. You'd hear James Garner's voice say, "This is Jim Rockford. At the tone, leave your name and message. I'll get back to you," followed by the beep of his answering machine, and then a joke message. Over the show's seven-year run, coming up with funny lines became a challenge for the writers, but like Rockford, they always came through. Here are some of our favorites.*

BEEEP! "Jim, It's Norma at the market. It bounced. You want us to tear it up, send it back, or put it with the others?"

BEEEP! "It's Laurie at the trailer park. A space opened up. Do you want me to save it, or are the cops going to let you stay where you are?"

BEEEP! "Really want Shimbu in the seventh? C'mon, that nag couldn't go a mile in the back of a pickup truck. Call me."

BEEEP! "I staked out that guy, only it didn't work out like you said. Please call me. Room 234, County Hospital."

BEEEP! "That #4 you just picked up from Angelo's Pizza? Some scouring powder fell in there. Don't eat it. Hey, I hope you try your phone machine before dinner."

BEEEP! "Hello? You the guy who lost a wallet in the Park Theater? Well, I'm kinda like into leather. So, I'll be returning the money, but I'm going to keep the wallet."

BEEEP! "Mr. Rockford? You don't know me, but I'd like to hire you. Could you call me at…my name is, uh, never mind. Forget it."

BEEEP! "Jimmy, old buddy, buddy. It's Angel! You know how they allow you one phone call? Well, this is it."

BEEEP! "It's Pete. Hope you enjoyed using the cabin last week. Only next time, leave the trout in the refrigerator, huh? Not in the cupboard."

BEEEP! "Hey, Jimbo, Dennis. Really appreciate the help on the income tax. Wanna help on the audit now?"

BEEEP! "This is Globe Publications. Our records show you did not return your free volume of the *Encyclopedia of Weather*. So, we'll be sending you the remaining 29 volumes. You'll be billed accordingly."

BEEEP! "Good morning, this is the telephone company. Due to repairs, we're giving you advance notice that your service will be cut off indefinitely at ten o'clock. That's two minutes from now."

BEEEP! "Jim, thanks for taking little Billy fishing, he had a great time. Turns out he wasn't even really seasick. Um, have you ever had chicken pox?"

BEEEP! "Sonny, this is Dad. Never mind giving that talk on your occupation to the Grey Power Club. Hap Dudley's son is a doctor, and everybody'd sorta…well, rather hear from him, but thanks."

BEEEP! "Say, I'm the one who hit your car at Fork City. I've got no insurance. I'm broke. But I really wanted you to know how sorry I am. If it makes you feel any better, I hurt my arm."

BEEEP! "Uncle Jim? It's Ralph. I got your letter, but I moved out here anyway. I really want those detective lessons."

BEEEP! "Rockford? Alice, Phil's Plumbing. We're still jammed up on a job, so we won't be able to make your place. Use the bathroom at the restaurant one more night."

BEEEP! "Jim, Coop. I'm at the address you wrote down for the poker game tonight. This is a gas station, it's closed, there's no one around, and now my car is stalled. Now, you got to call me at 4-6-6-3-*click*."

BEEEP! "Jim, Joel Myers at Crowell, Finch, and Merriwether. We're going to court tomorrow with that Penrose fraud case, but steno misplaced your 200-page deposition. Could you come down tonight and give it again?"

BEEEP! "This is Betty Frenell. I don't know who to call, but I can't reach my Foodaholics partner. I'm at Vito's on my second pizza with sausage and mushrooms. Jim, come and get me."

BEEEP! "This is the Baron. Angel Martin tells me you buy information. Okay, meet me at 1:00 a.m. behind the bus depot, bring $500, and come alone. I'm serious."

BEEEP! "Hey, Rockford, very funny. I ain't laughing. You're gonna' get yours."

Original slogan for Life Savers candy: "For that stormy breath."

'POSSUM À LA ROAD

*If you've considered all the warnings on page 31 and you're
still crazy enough to try cooking with roadkill, here are
a few mouth-watering recipes for you to try.*

RACCOON FRICASSEE

Find, skin, and gut a fresh, dead raccoon. Remove and discard any fat or damaged meat. Rinse the good meat in water and cut into eight to ten pieces. Rub with salt and pepper to taste, then roll in flour. Heat 2 tablespoons of vegetable oil in a skillet and brown meat on all sides. Add 2 cups of chicken broth. Cover, then simmer for two hours. Serves about eight, depending on the size of the raccoon and how badly it was damaged when hit by the car.

STUFFED SQUIRREL

Find, skin, and gut a fresh, dead squirrel. Remove and discard damaged meat, then rinse the rest of the squirrel in water. Lay the carcass on a large sheet of foil, sprinkle with salt, pepper, garlic salt, and onion salt to taste. Combine ¾ cup of chopped onion, 2 stalks of chopped celery, and 1 teaspoon of dried parsley. Stuff the mixture into the squirrel and place the extra around the outside. Tightly roll the squirrel in the foil like a burrito and place on a baking sheet. Bake at 350° for 35 to 45 minutes. Serves one.

CHICKEN-FRIED RATTLESNAKE

Find a fresh, dead rattlesnake. If the head hasn't already been run over, cut it off about four inches behind the head. (Wear heavy gloves, and dispose of the head carefully in a sealed container! A newly dead, still-venomous head can continue to deliver venom for an hour or more.) Hang the body of the snake by the rattles and allow the blood to drain out. Using a knife, make a cut down the length of the belly, then peel skin off starting at the head end. Discard skin (or tan it to use as a hatband). Discard internal organs and damaged meat. Rinse the good meat in fresh water and cut into pieces four inches long. Set aside. Beat 1 egg in a bowl and combine with ½ cup of milk; set aside. In a bowl, mix ¾ cup of flour with ½ teaspoon of salt and ¼ teaspoon of pepper. Dip snake pieces into the egg/milk mixture, then dredge them in the flour mixture and deep-fry until golden brown. Serves one.

Trimethylaminuria is a rare genetic disorder that makes a person smell like rotting fish.

ROAST 'POSSUM

Find, skin, and gut a fresh, dead opossum and set the liver aside. Remove damaged meat. Rinse the rest of the carcass in cold water, then boil in a large pot for 20 to 30 minutes. Remove from water, pat dry. Rub the opossum with salt and pepper; set aside. Brown one chopped onion in 1 tablespoon vegetable oil, then add the liver. Cook until tender. Combine with 1 cup bread crumbs, ¼ teaspoon Worcestershire sauce, 1 chopped hard-boiled egg, and 1 teaspoon salted water. Stuff mixture into the opossum, then place the opossum in a roasting pan. Pour a can of cream of mushroom soup over it, and lay eight to ten strips of bacon over the soup. Pour a cup of red wine over the bacon. Bake, covered, in a preheated oven at 350° until done and an instant-read thermometer reads at least 170°. Cooking time: 2–3 hours, depending on the size of the opossum.

BEAR JERKY

Find, skin, and gut a fresh, dead bear. (Make sure the bear really is dead before you try to skin it.) Remove and discard any damaged meat. Cut four pounds of good meat from the bear and then cut it into strips across the grain. (Refrigerate or freeze the remaining 200–1,000 pounds of good meat.) Fill a large bowl with 1 quart water, ¼ cup curing salt, ½ cup brown sugar, and black pepper and garlic powder to taste. Marinate the bear strips in the refrigerator for 8–10 hours. Remove the meat, pat dry, and allow to air-dry for one hour. Dry in a smoker (preferably) or in an oven at a temperature between 150° and 200°. Check for doneness after three hours. Refrigerate or freeze the jerky if you don't eat it right away.

BEAVER LOAF

Find a place where a beaver is likely to cross a road and look for a fresh, dead beaver there. Skin and gut the beaver; remove meat from the carcass. Discard damaged meat, then rinse and grind the good meat in a meat grinder. Combine 4–5 cups of the ground meat with 1 chopped onion, ½ cup of tomato paste, 2 beaten eggs, ½ cup of corn flakes, and 2 teaspoons of soy sauce. Add salt, pepper, and garlic salt to taste. Shape into a loaf, place in a greased loaf pan, and bake at 350° until an instant-read thermometer reads at least 170° (about 2 hours).

Best-selling American rock band of all time: Eagles.

MOOSE STROGANOFF

Find, skin, and gut a fresh, dead moose. Remove meat from carcass; discard damaged meat. Rinse good meat in fresh water. Cut one pound of the good meat into one-inch cubes. (Refrigerate or freeze the rest of it.) Add 2 tablespoons of vegetable oil to a skillet and cook meat until well done. Drain excess fat, then add 1 can cream of mushroom soup, 1 package brown gravy mix, and 1 package French onion soup mix to the skillet. Bring to a boil, then simmer for 30 minutes. Serve over noodles.

DOE SLOPPY JOES

Find, skin, and gut a fresh, dead doe (or buck). Remove and discard any damaged meat; rinse the good meat in water. Grind two pounds of the good meat in a meat grinder and refrigerate or freeze the rest. Add 2 tablespoons of cooking oil to a skillet. Brown the ground deer meat along with one large onion, chopped. Drain skillet if needed, then add 1 tablespoon of yellow mustard, three tablespoons of ketchup, ¾ cup of brown sugar, ½ cup of barbecue sauce, and hot sauce to taste. Simmer for 20 minutes. Serve on hamburger buns.

*　　*　　*

WI TO LO, MACY LAWYERS

The Offense: In 2013, an Oakland, California, newscaster read the names of the Korean flight crew working an Asiana Airlines jet that had crashed in San Francisco. She said the station had received the names from the National Transportation Safety Board. But the "source" was actually a mischievous NTSB summer intern, who gave fake names with slightly racist overtones, including "Captain Sum Ting Wong" and "Wi To Lo." The embarrassed newscaster later apologized, and the intern was fired.

The Revenge: A couple of weeks later, a South Korean news station—reporting about a Southwest Airlines jet that had crashed in New York City after its landing gear failed—listed the names of the Americans involved, including "Captain Kent Parker Wright," "Co-Captain Wyatt Wooden Workman," flight instructor "Heywood U. Flye-Moore," and an angry passenger named "Macy Lawyers."

ASK THE EXPERTS

More questions and answers from the world's top science and trivia experts.

GROWTH SPORTS

Q: *Why is the word "seed" used when ranking tennis players?*

A: "In 1898, the American Lawn Tennis Association decided that the best players should be 'scattered like seed' through the championship draw so that they'd be separated from one another." (From *The Complete Idiot's Guide to Fun FAQs*, by Sandy Wood and Kara Kovalchik)

BECAUSE IT'S ENVIOUS?

Q: *Why is U.S. paper money green?*

A: "The first U.S. paper money was printed with all black ink, but in the 1860s, the Secretary of the Treasury, Salmon Chase, wanted to add a color to make bills harder to counterfeit. Instead of using different colors for different denominations, it was decided to use just one color for all bills. A friend of Chase's, who happened to be a printer, suggested green. (Legend has it that he had a large supply of green ink and wanted to get rid of it.)" (From *What Happens to a Torn Dollar Bill?*, by Dr. Knowledge)

THE FIVE SEASONS

Q: *Why does the season of autumn/fall have two names?*

A: "*Harvest*, the original word for autumn, meant not just 'a time of reaping' but also 'the third season of the year.' It was joined by *autumn*—a word borrowed from the French—in the 16th century. 'Spring' and 'fall' first appeared later in the 16th century as *spring of the leaf* and *fall of the leaf*, respectively, and were soon shortened to the more succinct *fall* and *spring*. Before that there was no firm word for springtime. Some people referred to it as part of summer; others used the Latin *ver* or the French *printemps*. It's a bit of a mystery why the superfluous 'autumn' persists while words like *printemps* and *ver* have fallen out of use, but it may have something to do with the Atlantic Ocean. The rise of 'autumn' and the appearance of 'fall' happened around the same time as the British arrived in the Americas, and it's there that the latter really caught on. 'Fall' has

---

Every year, about 2,000 people worldwide are infected with bubonic plague.

never had as much currency in the U.K. as it has stateside—even though some Brits concede that North Americans have the superior term." (Forrest Wickman, from "The Explainer" at *Slate.com*)

ELEVEN ANGRY MEN (AND OPRAH)

Q: *How come you never see famous people on juries?*

A: "When people are summoned for jury duty, they are actually being summoned for a jury-selection process. Up to 80 potential jurors may be called, of which 12 jurors and 6 alternates are chosen. Celebrities do have to participate. Robert de Nero, Brad Pitt, Mariah Carey, Jerry Seinfeld, Uma Thurman, and scores of other celebs have been called to jury duty. Most try to argue their way out of serving. Woody Allen sent a letter saying he'd had a traumatic experience in court during a child-custody case with Mia Farrow and couldn't bear being in the courtroom again. The authorities didn't buy it, and he was ordered to show up. Allen arrived with his lawyer, his agent, and his bodyguard and refused to sit with other potential jurors, opting instead to stand. (He was eventually allowed to leave.) In most cases, the attorneys try to keep celebrities off the jury because they will be a distraction. But it does happen: In 2004, Oprah Winfrey served for a murder trial, and in 1999, New York City mayor Rudy Giuliani served for a case involving a man who claimed that scalding hot water from an improperly maintained water heater had burned his genitals, causing him to become impotent. Giuliani and the other jurors ruled against him." (From *How Do They Get a Model Ship in a Bottle?*, by Publications International)

DOWN TIME

Q: *What time zone do they use at the South Pole?*

A: "Time zone boundaries follow lines of longitude from pole to pole, but often zigzag to follow geographical boundaries. Because there are no boundaries in the polar regions, time zone lines follow longitude lines in these places. Since all longitude lines come together at the poles, you can walk through all of the time zones in seconds by walking around the pole that marks the South Pole (the Arctic is ocean). As a practical matter, having all of the time zones means there is really no time zone for the polar regions. When researchers venture there, they can use any time they wish." (Jack Williams, *USA Today*)

An object falling to the ground generates heat when it lands.

AMERICA'S SECRET PLAN TO NUKE THE MOON

This is one of those stories that sounds too unbelievable to be true...but it is. One of the best-kept secrets of the Cold War, it remained hidden for more than 50 years.

SHOOT THE MOON

In early 1958, officers from the U.S. Air Force's Special Weapons Center in New Mexico paid a visit to Leonard Reiffel, a physicist with the Illinois Institute of Technology. They made an unusual request: They wanted Reiffel to conduct a study on the "visibility and effects" of a nuclear explosion on the Moon. Reiffel agreed to take on the task. He assembled a group of about ten people and set to work on the top-secret project, which became known as Project A119.

That raises an interesting question: Why would the Air Force want to nuke the Moon?

THAT SINKING FEELING

If ever there was a tough time in peacetime to be an American military planner, it was the late 1950s. World War II had been over for more than a decade, and the euphoria of victory had long since passed. The Soviet Union, an ally during the war, was now a dangerous rival. From 1950 to 1953, the U.S. and the Soviets had been on opposite sides in the Korean War. Perhaps the only thing that kept the conflict from escalating into World War III was the fact that the Russians detonated their first atomic bomb in August 1949, barely four years after the U.S. tested theirs in July 1945.

By 1952, the United States had developed the world's first thermonuclear "hydrogen" bomb, many times more powerful than the A-bomb. This time it took just three years for the Soviets to catch up; they detonated their first H-bomb in November 1955. Two years after that, the Soviets accomplished a feat that the Americans had been unable to do: On October 4, 1957, they launched *Sputnik*, the world's first artificial satellite.

Tom Cruise spent $100,000 on daughter Suri's treehouse. It has plumbing and electricity.

SPACE INVADER

All *Sputnik* did was beep radio signals back to Earth, but the implications of its launch were clear: Rockets that carried satellites into orbit could also be used to launch nuclear weapons against the United States. America had yet to demonstrate that it possessed the same capability. In December 1957, it attempted to launch a much smaller, four-pound satellite into orbit (*Sputnik* weighed 184 pounds), but the rocket exploded on the launch pad, tossing the satellite into some bushes nearby. The U.S. didn't manage to put a satellite into orbit until January 1958, and it weighed just over 30 pounds. By then the Soviets had already launched Laika, a live dog, into space aboard the 1,120-pound *Sputnik 2*.

The Eisenhower Administration was looking for a way to reassure the American public that it would not be playing catch-up with the Communists forever and would not be at the mercy of their nuclear missiles. It also wanted to show the Russians that America was still a force to be reckoned with. That's when someone—it's not clear who—came up with the idea of detonating an atom bomb on the Moon.

MADE TO ORDER

The Air Force estimated that with the missiles that were currently being developed, it would soon be possible to send a small warhead about one-tenth the size of the Hiroshima bomb to the Moon. But what would the bomb look like when it went off? The Moon didn't have an atmosphere, so the Air Force wondered whether it would even be possible to see the explosion from Earth. If so, they wanted advice from Reiffel on how to achieve the maximum visual impact.

Reiffel and his team of researchers went to work. (One of his youngest hires, a graduate student named Carl Sagan, calculated what the cloud of moon dust kicked up by an exploding atomic bomb would look like.) The researchers studied the problem for nine months and gave the Air Force a written progress report each month. Among their findings:

• An atomic bomb exploded on the surface of the Moon would create a sudden bright flash of light, but no fireball.

• Great quantities of moon dust would be kicked up during the explosion, but the lack of an atmosphere on the Moon would prevent it from forming into a mushroom cloud.

• Reiffel's team recommended detonating the bomb along the lunar "terminator," the imaginary line separating the illuminated part of the Moon's surface from the dark part, and doing it at a time when the Sun and Moon were ideally positioned to illuminate the dust cloud with sunlight. That would maximize the explosion's visibility on Earth.

WORST-CASE SCENARIOS

A nuclear lunar light show would have made quite an impression on the Russians…so why didn't the U.S. do it? Most likely because someone in the Air Force or the Eisenhower Administration decided that the risks were too great. If the rocket carrying the bomb failed early in the launch, it might scatter radioactive debris over a large area of U.S. territory, or perhaps even detonate the bomb. If the rocket failed later in the launch, it might send the bomb crashing to Earth in another country. If the rocket got stuck in Earth's orbit, the bomb might circle overhead for years before falling to Earth who-knows-where. And if the rocket veered even a few degrees off course on its way to the Moon, the Moon's gravitational field might whip it around the far side of the Moon and send it straight back to Earth.

MOVING ON

At this early stage in the Space Race, the U.S. had experienced more failures then successes, so another failure, one with horrific consequences, was a very real possibility. In January 1959, Project A119 was scrapped. Reiffel and his team turned in their final progress report, and the researchers went their own ways. All but one of the reports were destroyed in the 1980s.

Reiffel went on to become deputy director of NASA's Apollo program, which beat the Russians in the Space Race by landing the first men on the Moon in July 1969. Carl Sagan became a professor of astronomy at Cornell University, a Pulitzer Prize–winning author of numerous books, and the host of *Cosmos* and other science documentaries on PBS.

It turns out that Sagan was indirectly responsible for leaking Project A119 to the public after it had remained a secret for more than 40 years. Before the program had even ended, Sagan, apparently no stickler for national security, mentioned his research on

---

Gibraltar Airport's runway crosses a major highway. Traffic stops when planes take off or land.

"possible lunar nuclear detonations" while applying for a research fellowship. The unauthorized—and illegal—disclosure of highly classified information didn't attract much attention at the time, but when biographer Keay Davidson was researching Sagan's life in the late 1990s (Sagan died in 1996), he came across Sagan's unauthorized disclosure and mentioned it in his book *Carl Sagan: A Life*. That caught the attention of book reviewers, which in turn prompted Leonard Reiffel to come forward and discuss Project A119 publicly for the first time. The project's sole surviving report, titled "A Study of Lunar Research Flights," has been declassified and is available online.

GOOD NYET MOON

Even before Reiffel and his team began their work in 1958, American newspapers frequently reported rumors and speculation that the Russians were planning to nuke the Moon. Turns out that the rumors were true: According to Boris Chertok, the deputy chief rocket designer of the Soviet space program, at about the same time that the Air Force brass approached Reiffel about researching an American atomic bomb on the Moon, Soviet space planners proposed sending a Russian A-bomb to the Moon for the exact same reason—as a demonstration of the nation's technological and military prowess.

The Soviet plan made it even farther than the American plan did. The Soviets built a mock-up of the spacecraft that would have carried the bomb, and designers came up with a rough plan for the bomb itself. It would have had a design similar to a World War II anti-ship mine, with "initiator rods" sticking out in every direction that would have triggered the bomb when it slammed into the surface of the Moon.

PICTURE IMPERFECT

Just as the Russians had considered bombing the Moon for the same reason that the United States had, they decided not to do it for the same reasons: Sending an atomic bomb into Earth orbit and then on to the Moon was too risky. And besides, Chertok told an interviewer in 1999, "Our physicists decided that a flash would be so short-lived because of the lack of an atmosphere on the Moon that it might not register on film."

AMAZING LUCK

*Here are some people (and an owl) who looked
death in the face and walked (or flew) away.*

BUMP START

In 2013, Ray Lee, 65, was exercising at his home in Wiltshire, Wilts, England, when his heart rate started rising dramatically. Paramedics arrived but were unable to stabilize him. Their plan: Rush him to the hospital where doctors would stop his heart and then restart it, hoping it would return to normal. But time was running out, and as the ambulance sped through town, Lee's heart rate kept climbing until it reached 186 beats per minute—three times normal. Then—BAM!—the ambulance hit a huge pothole. The impact lifted Lee several inches off the stretcher before he plonked back down. When he looked up at the monitor, his heart was beating normally, at 60 beats per minute. "I'd been cursing the council for months about the state of the roads," Lee said. "But now I never want them to fill in another pothole again."

GRILLED

A not-so-wise owl flew straight into an oncoming pickup truck on a rural Vermont road in 2012. The driver got out and was dismayed to see the bird twisted up in the grill. With its sharp talons sticking out, a simple removal was impossible. But the owl was alive, so the man drove eight slow miles to his workplace, the Vermont Fish & Wildlife Department. They arrived and determined that the only way to remove the owl was to cut away the grill. After the delicate procedure was finally completed, the game officials were expecting the bird to have several broken bones. But it was fine. A little while later, the owl flew away as if nothing had happened.

BLADE RUNNER

A farmer in Billings, Montana, was harvesting his corn crop in 2012 when the massive combine blades got caught up on something. Figuring he'd run over a fence post, the farmer stopped to check it out. That's when he heard the screams. He ran to the front of the machine and found a 57-year-old man entangled in the harvester.

Kitchen tip: A plastic knife will cut brownies more smoothly than a metal knife.

When rescuers arrived, they had to dismantle the blade to free the mangled man. Incredibly, all he needed were some stitches. He explained that he'd wandered into the field after getting off a bus. He hadn't planned on taking a nap, but fell asleep.

LOAFING TIME

Liz Douglas of Stronachlachar, Scotland, was driving home from the grocery store in 2011 when she lost control and flipped her car. She landed upside down with her head resting on the ceiling, and had to wait in that position while rescuers used the "jaws of life" to free her. Luckily, a soft loaf of bread had ended up between the top of Douglas's head and the ceiling of her car—not only did it cushion what could have been a brain-injuring trauma, but it made a nice pillow while she waited for an hour to be freed. Douglas still has the indented loaf of bread that she is convinced saved her life.

JOE VS. THE EXPLOSIONS

In April 2013, a bomb blew up at the Boston Marathon just after Joe Berti, 43, crossed the finish line. Jolted by the blast, he was unhurt and immediately started looking for his wife, Amy, when he saw a second explosion down the block. She was a few yards away from it, but escaped unscathed (though a woman standing next to her lost a leg). The couple got out of Boston as fast as they could. Back in Texas two days later, Joe was driving through the town of West when a fertilizer plant exploded. The shockwave rocked his pickup truck, but he was unhurt. Having never seen even one explosion before, Joe had now felt the power of three of them in two days—1,875 miles apart.

TAKE THE *ZZZZZZ*-TRAIN

A young woman was standing on a subway platform in Prague, Czech Republic, when she started bobbing back and forth as if she was falling asleep. Turns out, she was. As she fell forward, a man tried to grab her, but he was too late. She collapsed on the tracks mere seconds ahead of an approaching train. It skidded to a stop, and everyone expected the worst. Then they heard her calling for help. She was pulled up from between two train cars, then she brushed off her clothes and walked away. Amazingly, she'd landed directly between the tracks, and the train never even touched her.

Only English word that begins "vowel-v-vowel-v-vowel-v-vowel": *ovoviviparous*. It refers...

CURIOUS CRISPS

In 2013, Lays came out with Chicken and Waffles–flavored potato chips. Sound strange? In the U.K., strange potato chip—or "crisp"—flavors are common…and popular. Here are a few samples.

- Worcester Sauce
- Smoky Bacon & Sunday Roast Potato
- Roast Chicken
- Chorizo
- Cured Ham and Pickle
- Haggis and Cracked Pepper
- Roast Ox
- Fish and Chips
- Prawn Cocktail
- Oyster & Vinegar
- Pesto
- Pickled Onion
- Chardonnay Wine Vingear
- Parsnip
- Cajun Squirrel
- Builder's Breakfast (the "full English" breakfast—bacon, eggs, beans, and tomatoes)
- Crispy Duck & Hoisin Sauce
- Paprika
- Chili & Chocolate
- Bloody Mary
- Pork Sausage and English Mustard
- Chicken Tikka Masala
- Butter and Mint
- Sausage & Tomato
- German Bratwurst
- Guinness
- Yorkshire Sauce (a ham glaze made with orange marmalade)
- Peking Spare Rib
- Spaghetti Bolognese
- Turkey and Stuffing
- Peanut Butter
- Curry
- Teriyaki Chicken
- Paella
- Sweet Chutney
- Marmite Yeast Extract

…to animals like the manta ray that produce eggs inside their body, but give birth to live young.

TALK NERDY TO ME

Are TV nerds like real nerds?
Who cares? They're funny.

The Professor: "I would say it was a geological phenomenon caused by volcanic activity beneath the earth's surface resulting in concentration of heat at a specific location."

Gilligan: "That makes sense to me, but there's one thing I don't understand."

The Professor: "What's that?"

Gilligan: "How come the ground got so hot underneath our feet?"

—*Gilligan's Island*

"Egg whites are good for a lot of things—lemon meringue pie, angel food cake, and clogging up radiators."

—*MacGyver, MacGyver*

Rose: "Doesn't the universe implode or something if you… dance?"

The Doctor: "Well, I've got the moves, but I wouldn't want to boast."

Rose: "You've got the moves? Show me your moves."

The Doctor: "Rose, I'm trying to resonate concrete."

—*Doctor Who*

Roy: "I mean, they have no respect for us up there! No respect whatsoever! We're all just drudgeons to them!"

Moss: "Yes! If there were such a thing as a drudgeon, that is what we'd be to them."

—*The IT Crowd*

Neal: "What is wrong with them? Why do they think that hitting people with towels is so funny?"

Bill: "If it wasn't us, it would be kind of funny."

—*Freaks and Geeks*

Tim: "You're scared of mice and spiders, but oh-so-much greater is your fear that one day the two species will cross-breed to form an all-powerful race of mice-spiders who will immobilize human beings in giant webs in order to steal cheese."

Daisy: "I never said that."

Tim: "Yeah, but it'd be good, though, wouldn't it?"

Daisy: "No."

—*Spaced*

99% of Egypt's population lives on about 5.5% of the land. Nearly all the rest is desert.

Buffy: "Do you remember the demon that almost got out the night I died?"

Willow: "Every nightmare I have that doesn't revolve around academic failure or public nudity is about that thing. In fact, once I dreamt that it attacked me while I was late for a test *and* naked."

—*Buffy the Vampire Slayer*

Sheldon: "In difficult times like this, I often turn to a force stronger than myself."

Amy: "Religion?"

Sheldon: "*Star Trek.*"

—*The Big Bang Theory*

Jenna: "So, I'm just a new variable in one of your new computational environments."

Data: "You are much more than that, Jenna. I have written a program specifically for you—a program within a program. I have devoted a considerable share of my internal resources to its development."

Jenna: "That's the nicest thing anyone's ever said to me."

—*Star Trek: The Next Generation*

Lisa: "My family never talks about library standards. And every time I try to steer the conversation that way, they make me feel like a nerd."

Comic Book Guy: "We are hardly nerds. Would a nerd wear such an irreverent sweatshirt?"

Lisa (reading): "'C:/DOS C:/ DOS/RUN RUN/DOS/RUN.' Oh, only one person in a million would find that funny."

Professor Frink: "Yes, we call that the 'Dennis Miller Ratio.'"

—*The Simpsons*

Claudia: "It's sealed with an Omega level security code."

Myka: "Can you hack it?"

Claudia: "Pope, Catholic, bear, woods. You know the drill."

—*Warehouse 13*

"I'm the key figure in an ongoing government charade, the plot to conceal the truth about the existence of extraterrestrials. It's a global conspiracy, actually, with key players in the highest levels of power, that reaches down into the lives of every man, woman, and child on this planet; so, of course, no one believes me. I'm an annoyance to my superiors, a joke to my peers. They call me Spooky."

—**Spooky Mulder,**
The X-Files

AW, SHOOT!

*We've always wanted to do an article about how guns work. But then we
realized that before telling how guns work, we had to determine what kind
of gun, because there are many kinds and they work in different ways.
So instead, we decided to tell the story from the bullet's point of view.
And it's a perfect topic for the* Bathroom Reader, *because it's all
about expanding gas. (Note: If you are reading this in the
bathroom, feel free to add your own sound effects.)*

FIRE IN THE HOLE

Old West six-shooters, 1920s Tommy guns, deer-hunting rifles
and shotguns, handguns carried by police officers, M-16s issued
to soldiers. They're different kinds of guns, but they have something
in common: They all use *centerfire* cartridges, and they all function in
the same way in order to make those cartridges fire their bullets.

• **The Cartridge.** A centerfire cartridge has four basic components:
case, propellant, primer, and *bullet.* The *case* is the cylindrical hollow
outer shell of a cartridge, usually made of brass. Inside the case is
the *propellant*—that's gunpowder. The *primer* is a small, soft-metal-
encased plug filled with a combustible chemical concoction. It sits
in an indent at the center of the base of the cartridge. (That's what
makes it a *centerfire* cartridge.) The primer's job: to ignite the gunpowder. At the opposite end from the primer is the *bullet*, the metal
(usually lead) projectile that will be expelled from the cartridge and
the gun. Part of the bullet is inside the case, but most of it sticks out
and forms the end of the cartridge itself.

• **The Primer.** So if a cartridge has gunpowder, does it need a
primer? Good question. Answer: For the same reason a firecracker
needs a fuse—you need something to set off the gunpowder. The
chemicals in the primer are *impact-sensitive*, meaning that simply
being struck causes them to burst into flame. And gunpowder is not
impact-sensitive. So the simplest way to think of a primer is that it's
the equivalent of a fuse on a firecracker—except that it's a *lot* faster.

THE GUN

Guns that use centerfire ammunition come in many shapes and
sizes, but they all do the same thing when it comes to a cartridge:

They smash that *primer*. That's really all there is to it. No matter what type of gun we're talking about—a .38 Special, the latest .45 Glock, James Bond's Walther PPK, a submachine gun, or an Uzi— when you pull the gun's trigger, it sends something smashing into the primer. Using a simple type of gun to illustrate, here's how this works:

• **Single-action Revolver.** These are the old-fashioned "six-shooters" made famous in the American Old West. Put a cartridge in one of the six chambers in the gun's revolving cylinder, and turn the cylinder so that the cartridge is in the firing position, directly in line with the gun's barrel. Directly behind a cartridge in this position is the gun's *hammer*—a spring-loaded lever with a short metal pin jutting out from its face. Pull that hammer back, and a locking mechanism inside the gun locks it into position. (*Click!*) This is known as *cocking* the gun, which is now in the *cocked* position—meaning it's ready to fire. When you pull the trigger, all you're doing is simply releasing the hammer's locking mechanism and allowing its powerful spring to pull it to its "closed" position. When this happens, the pin jutting from the hammer's face—that's the *firing pin*—smashes into the primer in the center of the base of the cartridge.

• **Boom #1.** As we said earlier, the primer sits in an indent on the bottom of the cartridge. In the bottom of the indent is a hole— called the *flash hole*—that goes through the base of the cartridge and into the hollow where the gunpowder is held. When the firing pin strikes the primer's soft metal case, it literally smashes into it and dents it. That causes the impact-sensitive chemical mix inside the primer to combust. When that happens, the inner side of the primer case—the side facing the flash hole—bursts. (Primers are specifically designed to burst in this way.) Burning sparks and gases then go through the flash hole…and contact the gunpowder.

• **Boom #2.** Gunpowder is a dry, granular powder made from a mixture of different chemicals. If you poured some on a table and lit it on fire, it would burn very quickly. That's all. It wouldn't explode— it would just burn. (Note: Take our word for it; DO NOT try this at home!) But if you put it inside a closed container, such as a firearm cartridge, and lit it on fire—it would blow up that container. Why? Because of expanding gases. When gunpowder is exposed to a high enough temperature, it undergoes a rapid chemical reaction. As the ingredients in gunpowder burn, they break down chemically and are converted from powder form into gas form. And gunpowder in gas form is a lot larger in volume than it is in its powder form—so much so that it no longer fits inside the cartridge.

• **Bye-Bye Bullet!** The gunpowder inside the cartridge is now very quickly turning into an enormous volume of gas and needs somewhere to go. It naturally takes the path of least resistance—and blows the bullet out of the cartridge (cartridges are designed to make this happen) and then out of the barrel of the gun. Only the bullet leaves; the empty cartridge case is left behind. In fact, if you were to pull that case out of the chamber now (Careful! It's hot!), you'd see the dent that the firing pin made in the primer. (And you'd be able to smell the burned-up gunpowder and primer chemicals.)

Note: Most modern handguns don't require you to pull back a hammer—just pulling the trigger both cocks and fires the gun—and many modern handguns and rifles have the hammer-and-firing-pin apparatuses built inside the guns' housings. But they all have some kind of mechanism that causes a *firing pin* to strike the primer in the center of the cartridge's base. That's how they work.

OTHER GUN AND AMMO TYPES

Here are some other types of guns and ammo:

• **Rimfire Cartridge:** In a gun that uses rimfire ammunition, the firing pin strikes the rim, rather than the center, of the base. (It can strike anywhere on the rim. Rimfire cartridges are manufactured in such a way that the primer chemicals form a ring around the cartridge's entire base.) After that, they work the same as a centerfire cartridge, igniting the gunpowder and ejecting the bullet. Rimfire cartridges are cheaper to manufacture than centerfire cartridges, but they are also less reliable. They are most commonly used in small-caliber guns, especially .22s.

• **Shotgun:** Shotguns use centerfire ammunition, but shotgun cartridges are different from other centerfire cartridges. For starters, they don't fire bullets, they fire *shot*—which is either a bunch of little BBs or a *slug* (a large lump of lead). And only the primer end of the case is made of metal—the rest is plastic. In addition, shotgun cartridges have a plastic device inside them called a *wad*, which fits tightly inside the shell. The job of the wad is to keep the

---

Bee-utiful: Besides black and yellow, bees can also be red, green, and blue.

gunpowder packed in the base of the shell, to prevent it from getting mixed with the shot or dispersed around a slug, either of which would make for inefficient discharge. As with a handgun or rifle cartridge, when you pull the shotgun's trigger, a firing pin strikes the primer case in the center of the cartridge base. It explodes, ignites the gunpowder, and sends the shot or slug out of the gun's barrel.

RIFLED OR NOT RIFLED?

All firearms are broken down into two main classifications, based on their barrels: *smoothbore* barrels and *rifled* barrels.

• **Smoothbore:** The *bore* (the inside of a gun's barrel) of these guns is smooth. Examples: old-fashioned muskets and modern shotguns.

• **Rifled:** These guns have spiraling grooves cut into the inside of the barrels. (Think of the stripes on a candy cane.) These include all rifles and most modern handguns.

Rifling came into popular use in the 1800s (although it was invented by a German gunmaker in the 1500s). What do the spiraling grooves cut into the inside of a barrel do? The edges of the grooves "grab" a bullet as it moves down the barrel, causing it to spin, so that when it leaves the barrel, it's spinning very rapidly. Why would you want that? Because spinning bullets fly straighter than nonspinning bullets. (This is because of the physical laws of flight, and is, for example, why a spinning football flies better than a nonspinning football.) Rifling was a huge improvement in firearm technology: A typical smoothbore musket in the 1800s was accurate to about 100 yards; rifled guns of the same era, to more than 600 yards. (And it's much farther today.) But there are still modern smoothbore guns: Most shotguns are smoothbore because 1) they fire *shot*, and spinning shot creates a dispersed, sloppy flight pattern; and 2) shotguns also fire slugs, and these generally don't need rifling as they aren't meant to travel very far (slugs are generally meant for hunting large game at less than 100 yards).

CALIBER AND GAUGE

You've no doubt heard these terms, but if you don't know what they mean, here's a quick explanation:

• **Caliber:** This is the diameter of a gun's bore and of the bullet in the cartridge it uses. It can be measured in either inches or millimeters. A .22-caliber gun, for example, fires .22-caliber bullets—both have a diameter of 0.22 inches. A 9mm gun fires 9mm bullets. Both are 9 millimeters in diameter. (Note: These are approximate measurements: a bullet's diameter is slightly smaller than the bore's, or it wouldn't fit in the barrel.) Some common caliber sizes:

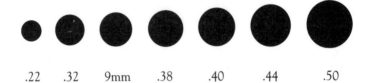

.22   .32   9mm   .38   .40   .44   .50

• **Gauge:** *Gauge* is the measurement system used for the diameter of the bore of a shotgun barrel. It's based on the weight of a ball of lead that will fit tightly inside the barrel. And that weight is expressed as a fraction of a pound, using only the denominator of the fraction. So if a shotgun has a bore that will accept a ball of lead that weighs $\frac{1}{12}$ of a pound—it's a 12-gauge shotgun. If the ball of lead weighs $\frac{1}{20}$ of a pound—it's a 20-gauge shotgun. This means that the smaller the number, the larger the shotgun's bore. (The smallest shotgun made is an exception to this rule, as it is measured in caliber—the .410 shotgun.) Some common shotgun gauges:

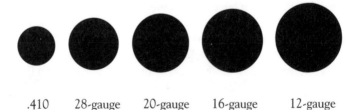

.410   28-gauge   20-gauge   16-gauge   12-gauge

To learn the definitions of several gun-related terms—and for some fun extras—shoot over to Full Metal Jacket on page 513.

MEET PAUL BEARER

If you were in a punk band in the 1970s and '80s, a colorful nickname was just as vital as a ripped T-shirt and a mohawk. Sometimes they were funny, sometimes they meant to provoke—but they were always clever.

Stinky Turner
(Cockney Rejects)

Johnny Rotten
(Sex Pistols)

Poly Styrene
(X-Ray Spex)

Cheetah Chrome
(The Dead Boys)

Poison Ivy
Rorschach
(The Cramps)

Pat Smear
(The Germs)

Tesco Vee
(The Meatmen)

Sylvain Sylvain
(New York Dolls)

Rodney
Anonymous
(Dead Milkmen)

Will Shatter
(Flipper)

Darby Crash
(The Germs)

Nick Knox
(The Cramps)

Vinnie Stigma
(Agnostic Front)

He Who Cannot
Be Named
(The Dwarves)

Pig Champion
(Poison Idea)

Richard Hell
(Blank Generation)

Handsome Dick
Manitoba
(The Dictators)

Jello Biafra
(Dead Kennedys)

Helios Creed
(Chrome)

Steve Ignorant
(Crass)

Joey S***head
(D.O.A.)

Tomata Du Plenty
(The Screamers)

Lee Ving (Fear)

Cyco Miko
(Suicidal
Tendencies)

Sickie Wifebeater
(The Mentors)

Paul Cripple
(Reagan Youth)

Rat Scabies
(The Damned)

Sid Vicious
(Sex Pistols)

Kid Congo Powers
(The Cramps)

Jimmy Gestapo
(Murphy's Law)

Paul Bearer
(Sheer Terror)

Frank Discussion
(Feederz)

Klaus Fluoride
(Dead Kennedys)

Lorna Doom
(The Germs)

Dick Urine
(various bands)

John Doe (X)

Chuck Biscuits
(D.O.A.)

Lowest batting average to win a MLB batting title: .301 (Carl Yastrzemski, 1968).

ACTION JACKSONS

Match these famous Jacksons with their quotes. (Answers are on page 537.)

1. "No one need think that the world can be ruled without blood. The civil sword shall and must be red and bloody."

2. "No one will take me away for saying what I'm saying. But they don't have to if they can control how many people hear it. And that's how they do it."

3. "If you want me to sing this Christmas song with feeling, you'd better see if you can locate that check."

4. "Then, Sir, we will give them the bayonet!"

5. "Any attempt on my part to say something about my painting *She Wolf*—to attempt explanation of the inexplicable—could only destroy it."

6. "If I made a *Hellraiser* film, I'd like Pinhead to be whacked against a wall and have all the pins flattened into his face."

7. "Ten years ago I was driving a forklift at Kmart, and nobody was screaming at me then."

8. "I'm a good son, a good father, a good husband—I've been married to the same woman for 30 years. I finished college, I donate money anonymously. So when people criticize the kind of characters that I play on screen, I go, 'You know, that's part of history.' "

9. "You sound like a rapist!"

10. "After Jackie Robinson, the most important black in baseball history is Reggie Jackson, I really mean that."

11. "I broke Elvis's records, I broke Beatles' records, but the minute *Thriller* became the all-time best-selling album in the world, they called me a freak."

12. "Whatchu talkin' 'bout, Willis!"

a. Michael Jackson; **b.** "Stonewall" Jackson, Civil War general, when told the enemy was advancing; **c.** Randy Jackson, *American Idol* judge, to a contestant; **d.** Peter Jackson, filmmaker; **e.** Jackson Browne, songwriter; **f.** Jackson Pollock, artist; **g.** Reggie Jackson, MLB hall-of-famer; **h.** Arnold Jackson (Gary Coleman), *Diff'rent Strokes*; **i.** Andrew Jackson, president; **j.** Alan Jackson, country singer; **k.** Samuel L. Jackson; **l.** Mahalia Jackson, gospel singer

BABY IN A BOX

In 1938, the Finnish government began giving boxes of baby supplies to expectant mothers in poor families. The boxes became so popular that since 1949, every expectant mother in Finland has received one. Here's how the contents have changed over the years.

1938: The boxes were introduced in an attempt to lower Finland's high infant mortality rate (65 out of 1,000 babies died in infancy). Contents included blankets, cloth diapers, a baby bottle, a toy, white fabric (to sew into baby clothes), a snowsuit (remember, this is Finland), and other items. The cardboard box itself was (and still is) designed to serve as the baby's first crib, complete with mattress and bedding, to discourage the practice of babies sleeping in the same bed as their parents.

1939–45: Because fabric was needed for the war effort, paper products replaced many cloth items until the end of World War II.

1949: Changes in the rules now made the boxes available to *every* expectant mother, but also required that mothers qualify for it by having a prenatal exam before their fourth month of pregnancy.

1950s: As growing numbers of women entered the workforce, the white fabric used to make baby clothes was replaced with ready-to-wear items, also white (not blue or pink), so that either boys or girls could wear them. In the 1970s, white was phased out in favor of gender-neutral colors like brown and green.

1969: Reusable cloth diapers were replaced by disposable diapers.

2000: Disposable diapers were replaced by reusable cloth diapers.

2010s: To encourage breastfeeding, baby bottles and pacifiers were no longer included in the box.

Today: Thanks to the baby boxes, universal health care, and other programs that benefit young families, Finland now has one of the *lowest* infant mortality rates in the world (and according to a number of surveys, some of the happiest mothers as well). Now the Finnish government is concerned about a new possibility: overpopulation. How concerned? Today the boxes include a complimentary package of condoms.

Monty Python and the Holy Grail was largely financed by Led Zeppelin and Pink Floyd.

ACCORDING TO THE LATEST RESEARCH

Every new day brings some bold new study. Some are interesting, and some are weird. For example, did you know that science says...

DIRTY MONEY GOES FASTER

Researchers: Fabrizio Di Muro (University of Winnipeg) and Theodore J. Noseworthy (University of Guelph)

Who They Studied: Canadian college students

What They Learned: In 2012, the researchers gave a wad of cash to each of the students and told them to spend it on a range of everyday items. Some of the bills were brand-new; some were old and dirty. The dirty cash was spent much faster than the clean cash, which the researchers chalked up to the "ick" factor: "Consumers tend to infer that worn bills are used and contaminated with germs. Crisp bills give people a sense of pride in owning bills that can be spent around others." So you're more likely to spend crisp new bills when other people are watching, in the hopes that someone will say, "Hey, big spender." (Even if they're one-dollar bills.)

JOGGING CAN MAKE BRAIN NOT THINK SO GOOD

Researchers: Behavioral psychologists in Belgium

Who They Studied: City joggers and suburban joggers

What They Learned: The city joggers who were exposed to noise, traffic, and air pollution had higher inflammation of blood in their brains, which leads to shorter attention spans and a lessened ability to adapt to new ideas and information—called "brain plasticity." What makes these findings so troubling (and ironic) is that exercising usually leads to *increased* brain plasticity. Solution for city joggers: Jog in a park on a rainy day when air pollution is lowest... or move to the 'burbs.

NEAR-DEATH EXPERIENCES AREN'T SUPERNATURAL

Researcher: Dr. Zalika Klemenc-Ketis of the University of Maribor in Slovenia

---

Who She Studied: 52 heart-attack victims who'd been declared dead at a hospital but were then brought back to life

What She Learned: Eleven of the patients reported having a "near-death experience" (NDE)—such as leaving their bodies, seeing deceased loved ones, seeing their lives flash before their eyes, and even seeing a "bright light." But they had something else in common. At the time of resuscitation, the NDE patients all had higher than normal carbon dioxide levels in their blood. Klemenc-Ketis says she doesn't know the exact "pathophysiological mechanism" that makes elevated levels of CO_2 cause an NDE, but its presence rules out any supernatural influence…probably.

ADAM ZOEY WILL "ACT NOW" BEFORE ZOEY ADAMS

Researchers: Two U.S. business-school professors, Kurt A. Carlson (Georgetown) and Jacqueline M. Conard (Belmont)

Who They Studied: College students and average adults

What They Learned: Test subjects were given offers for sales, free tickets to sporting events, and free wine—but they had to act fast because the "offer ends soon!" In each test, people whose last names were late in the alphabet were quicker to act than those whose last names came at the beginning. Carlson and Conard say this is due to childhood trauma. "Repeated delays imposed on children whose last names are late in the alphabet create a chronic expediency motive [a sense of urgency]" when presented with a limited-time offer. So if your name was always called last when you were a kid, it instilled in you a Pavlovian response never to be last again.

XBOX 360 PLAYERS MAKE BETTER LOVERS

Researchers: VoucherCodesPro, a U.K.-based website that offers promotional deals on goods and services

Who They Studied: 1,747 video-game players' partners

What They Learned: In 2013, the site sent a questionnaire to all of the gamers' partners asking, among other things, how well their video-game-playing significant other does in the bedroom. Microsoft's Xbox 360 players were rated the best, with 54 percent described as "good or better than average." Wii players came in second with a 47-percent approval rating. The worst: PC gamers (people who play games on their computers rather than a console)—only eight percent of them were rated as skillful with their joysticks.

HI, MY NAME IS *

If you believe the government is too intrusive into your personal life, you might be interested in what they're doing in New Zealand.

WHAT'S YOUR NAME? Around 2001, some officials in New Zealand feared that residents were getting too clever and too weird in naming their children. So the government created the "Registrar of Births, Deaths, and Marriages" (RBDM) and charged it with the peculiar task of approving the names parents give their newborn babies. The names may not "cause offense to a reasonable person," nor can they be too long or too short, mention a title or rank, or not be a real name. Sometimes, a few unusual names slip through the cracks. In 2008, the agency allowed twins to be called "Benson" and "Hedges" (as in the cigarette brand), and approved the names "Violence" and "Number 16 Bus Shelter." But here are some of the first names the RBDM has officially banned:

Messiah	Emperor	Mr.
Christ	Sargent	Mafia No Fear: 1
Lucifer	Master	Rogue
Lord	Regal	4real
King	Constable	*
Queen	Duke	Queen Victoria
Princess	Major	Queen V
Prince	Bishop	Minister
Justice	3rd	Chief
Justus	II	V8
Juztice	Roman Numerals III	President
Majesti	5th	MC
Knight	VI	Anal
Saint	Judge	H-Q
Eminence	Jr.	Talula Does the
Royale	89	Hula from Hawaii

Originally, William Kellogg signed his name on each individual box of Kellogg's Corn Flakes.

THE LIFE OF PIES

There are scores of delicious variations of cooked fillings and pastry out there—both sweet and savory. (Warning: This might make you hungry.)

P **IE:** A baking dish is lined with a pastry crust that bakes up crispy or flaky. On top of that goes a sweetened fruit filling, a savory meat filling, or, once it's cooled, a cream or custard filling. Sometimes it's topped with another layer of crust, and sometimes it isn't.

COBBLER: A pie without a bottom crust. Instead, sweetened (and often spiced) fruit is placed in a deep dish and topped with large lumps of sweetened biscuit dough. The bottom of the dough sinks into the fruit and absorbs the juices. When baked, the lumps of biscuit dough puff up and can resemble a cobblestone street, which may be how the dish got its name. (Another theory: The pies were originally made in wooden bowls called *cobelers*.)

PANDOWDY: Similar to a cobbler, except the lumps of biscuit dough are flattened before they're placed on top of the fruit. Pandowdys are generally baked in a skillet.

GRUNT: The grunt is assembled like a cobbler but cooked on the stove. Dollops of dumpling batter are placed over the fruit as it simmers in a pot. Then the pot is covered and allowed to cook until the dumplings have steamed to perfection. The dish is said to get its name from the noise the dumplings make when they're cooking. (They're called "grunts" in Massachusetts, but in other parts of New England, they're called "slumps.")

BIRD'S-NEST PUDDING: A pie consisting of apples that have been peeled and cored, but not sliced. Sugar or brown sugar is poured into the center of each apple; then batter is poured over the apples. When baked, the batter-covered apples look kind of like birds' nests, giving the dish its name.

BUCKLE: The bottom layer of this dish is made with cake batter, not a pastry crust. Fruit is then placed on top of the batter or even mixed in with it. Then it's topped with a crumble mixture and baked.

A Texas longhorn bull's horns can measure nearly 8 feet from tip to tip.

CRISP: Like a buckle, it's fruit topped with a crumbly concoction and baked. The difference: There's no cake batter on the bottom, and the top is usually made with rolled oats.

BROWN BETTY: The betty dates to colonial America and used whatever fruit was in season; today, apples are typically used. Brown sugar (not white) is used, and layers of buttered breadcrumbs and fruit are lined in the pan in alternating layers.

CLAFOUTIS: A simple centuries-old French peasant dish. Fruit (traditionally black cherries, *un*pitted) is topped with crêpe batter, which is like pancake batter, but eggier. The result: a spongy dessert, similar to bread pudding. Why leave pits in the cherries? Because, say the French, when baked they give the cherries extra flavor.

SONKER: North Carolina's take on the cobbler, this is a soupy deep-dished dessert made in a large square baking pan traditionally called a bread pan. The pan is filled with fruit (peaches, strawberries, or cherries), then topped with a pastry crust and baked. Some purists insist that true sonkers are made with sweet potatoes, not fruit.

LAZY SONKER: A sonker topped with batter instead of pastry crust (to save the cook the trouble of rolling out the crust).

PASTY: This one's usually savory, not sweet. A circle of pie crust is filled with beef, venison, lamb, or fish, along with potatoes, rutabaga, and other vegetables; then the crust is folded over onto itself, creating a half circle. After it's crimped shut and pierced with vent holes, the pasty is baked in the oven. The best-known pasties come from Cornwall, in southwest England.

TIDDY OGGY: Another Cornish dish. It's a steak pasty, but without the steak and with an extra serving of potato ("tiddy") instead.

BRIDIE: A Scottish pasty made with minced steak, butter, and (sometimes) onions, but leaving out the potatoes and vegetables found in Cornish pasties.

SAMOSA: The Samosa hails from South Asia and consists of a pastry dough filled with boiled potato, onion, green peas, and spices. The dough is folded around the filling to make a triangle shape, then the samosa is fried in oil and served hot with chutney.

C.F. Bennett made the jock strap for "bike jockeys" riding Boston's cobblestone streets (1874).

BURIED ALIVE: A
DIE-WITNESS ACCOUNT

Being mistaken for dead and buried alive isn't something we worry about much anymore, but in the 1800s, people were terrified of the possibility. Here's the story of one man who claimed to suffer that terrible fate.

DIG IN

Before the 1830s, British medical colleges could legally use only the bodies of executed criminals for dissection in their anatomy classes. When those were in short supply, body-snatchers known as "resurrection-men" stepped in to fill the gap, digging up freshly buried corpses from cemeteries and selling them to medical schools. Then Parliament passed the Anatomy Act of 1832, allowing licensed medical schools to use unclaimed or donated corpses, which ensured a steady supply of legal cadavers and ended the ghoulish black market trade forever. But in 1896, before the practice passed entirely from public memory, James Blake Bailey, librarian of the Royal College of Surgeons, published *The Diary of A Resurrectionist*, "an actual record of the doings of one gang of the resurrection-men in London." The book included what may be history's only firsthand account of what it's like to be buried alive and live to tell the tale. If John Macintire's story could be believed, Bailey wrote, "the resurrection-men sometimes performed a valuable service to those who had been buried." The following is Macintire's account of his experiences, as told to Bailey.

In His Own Words

I had been some time ill of a low and lingering fever. My strength gradually wasted, and I could see by the doctor that I had nothing to hope. One day, towards evening, I was seized with strange and indescribable quiverings. I saw around my bed, innumerable strange faces; they were bright and visionary, and without bodies. There was light and solemnity, and I tried to move, but could not; I could recollect, with perfectness, but the power of motion had departed. I heard the sound of weeping at my pillow, and the voice of the nurse say, "He is dead."

I cannot describe what I felt at these words. I exerted my

Frozen vegetables can have more nutritional value than week-old "fresh" veggies.

utmost power to stir myself, but I could not move even an eyelid. My father drew his hand over my face and closed my eyelids. The world was then darkened, but I could still hear, and feel and suffer. For three days a number of friends called to see me. I heard them in low accents speak of what I was, and more than one touched me with his finger.

Jack...in the Box

The coffin was then procured, and I was laid in it. I felt the coffin lifted and borne away. I heard and felt it placed in the hearse; it halted, and the coffin was taken out. I felt myself carried on the shoulders of men; I heard the cords of the coffin moved. I felt it swing as dependent by them. It was lowered and rested upon the bottom of the grave. Dreadful was the effort I then made to exert the power of action, but my whole frame was immovable. The sound of the rattling mould [dirt] as it covered me, was far more tremendous than thunder. This also ceased, and all was silent. This is death, thought I, and soon the worms will be crawling about my flesh. In the contemplation of this hideous thought, I heard a low sound in the earth over me, and I fancied that the worms and reptiles were coming. The sound continued to grow louder and nearer. Can it be possible, thought I, that my friends suspect that they have buried me too soon? The hope was truly like bursting through the gloom of death.

Out of the Frying Pan...

The sound ceased. They dragged me out of the coffin by the head, and carried me swiftly away. When borne to some distance, I was thrown down like a clod, and by the interchange of one or two brief sentences, I discovered that I was in the hands of two of those robbers, who live by plundering the grave, and selling the bodies of parents, and children, and friends. Being rudely stripped of my shroud, I was placed naked on a table. In a short time I heard by the bustle in the room that the doctors and students were assembling. When all was ready the Demonstrator took his knife, and pierced my bosom. I felt a dreadful crackling, as it were, throughout my whole frame; a convulsive shudder instantly followed, and a shriek of horror rose from all present. The ice of death was broken up; my trance was ended. The utmost exertions were made to restore me, and in the course of an hour I was in full possession of all my faculties.

At 15, McDonald's tycoon Ray Kroc lied about his age to become an ambulance driver in WWI.

COMEDIAN-IN-CHIEF

Whether he comes up with the jokes himself or has writers help him, Barack Obama can be a pretty funny guy at all those dinners he has to speak at.

"I'm hard at work on plans for the Obama Library. And some have suggested that we put it in my birthplace, but I'd rather keep it in the United States."

"It's great to be here this evening in the vast, magnificent Hilton ballroom, or what Mitt Romney would call 'a little fixer-upper.'"

"The pundits said you can't win with a name like 'Obama.' There was quite a bit of confusion at first, but it did get me free airtime on Al Jazeera."

"The White House Correspondents' Dinner is known as the prom of Washington D.C., a term coined by political reporters who clearly never had the chance to go to an actual prom."

"I know how quickly fads can pass. You all remember the Pet Rock, the mood ring, Howard Dean."

"These days, I look in the mirror and I have to admit I'm not the strapping young Muslim socialist that I used to be."

"I want to especially thank all the members of Congress who took a break from their exhausting schedule of not passing any laws to be here tonight."

"Matt Damon said he was disappointed in my performance. Well, Matt, I just saw *The Adjustment Bureau*, so right back at you, buddy."

"The press and I have different jobs to do. My job is to be president; your job is to keep me humble. Frankly, I think I'm doing my job better."

"Some have said I blame too many problems on my predecessor, but let's not forget that's a practice that was initiated by George W. Bush."

"I got my name, Barack, from my father. And I got my middle name from somebody who obviously didn't think I'd ever run for president."

"If I had to name my greatest strength, I guess it would be my humility. Greatest weakness? It's possible that I'm a little too awesome."

Astronomers can deduce the temperature of a star by its color (the bluer it is, the hotter).

UNSEEN GAME SHOWS

No one won fabulous prizes or cases of Rice-a-Roni on these shows. That's because these pilots were rejected by every TV network in the country.

Malcolm **(1983).** Hosted by Alex Trebek (pre-*Jeopardy!*) and a cartoon character named Malcolm, who talked like a little boy but was technically an adult. Malcolm appeared on several monitors around the set, and was voiced and controlled offstage by a puppeteer using an early form of the live/animation technique known as "motion-capture." In between comic banter by the hosts, contestants played a game in which they tried to complete two-word answers to simple trivia questions, occasionally assisted by Malcolm. (Contestants also had to deliver scripted remarks like, "Everyone said you were so handsome, Malcolm, and I agree!")

Idiot Quest (2007). Comedian Ryan Stout asked contestants general-knowledge questions for which they earned $100 each. But there was a twist: They had to give a wrong answer. Sounds easy—just say anything but the correct answer, right? To make sure contestants didn't really know the answer and were just lying to win the $100, they were hooked up to lie detectors. They *really* had to not know the answer to win the money.

Sense or Nonsense (1965). Host Paul Winchell (also the voice of Tigger) gave players a word and a category from which they had to form a phrase. If the panel of judges deemed it grammatically correct ("sense"), they won money. If not ("nonsense"), they didn't.

The Plot Thickens (1963). A weird combination of a scripted mystery movie and the board game Clue. Three contestants (one was Groucho Marx) were shown a short murder-mystery film and then had to speculate about who the murderer was. Then real-life private eye Dick Halley took a guess—if Halley guessed right, the contestants won $500; if Halley was wrong and one of the contestants was correct, they won $1,000. Then the film played on, and the answer was revealed. Bonus: The show's cast also included a black cat named Lucifer, who didn't really do anything.

Splash cash: About $4,000 worth of coins are thrown into Rome's Trevi Fountain every day.

DNA MYSTERY: HER KIDS ARE NOT HERS!

In 2002, a woman in Washington State was accused of fraud after genetic tests showed that she was not the mother…of her own children. As the saying goes: and then things got weird.

WHO'S YOUR MAMA?

In 2002, Lydia Fairchild, a 26-year-old Seattle, Washington, woman, applied for welfare benefits. The mother of three—who was at the time pregnant with her fourth child—had just separated from her boyfriend and the father of her children, Jamie Townsend. The state of Washington told Fairchild that before she could get benefits, she had to first prove the children were hers and Townsend's—in other words, she, Townsend, and the three children had to get DNA tests. They complied.

In December 2002, Fairchild got a phone call. She was asked to come get her DNA results…at the State Prosecutor's Office. She asked why. They wouldn't tell her. Fairchild went to the office. "He started asking was I trying to do fraud by getting help from the state," she said later, "because he said, 'these kids aren't yours.'"

WE KID YOU NOT

The prosecutor told Fairchild that the DNA tests showed that Townsend was indeed the biological father of the three children… but that she was not their biological mother. (The tests showed that she was related to the kids, but as an aunt or cousin at the closest.) The tests were done two more times to make sure no mistakes in procedure had been made. They came back with the same results. The prosecutor's office told Fairchild that they were beginning a fraud investigation against her.

Fairchild must have felt as if she had traveled through the looking glass. She had gotten pregnant, and had carried and given birth to all her children. She even had ultrasound images of each of the kids, and the doctor who attended the births backed her up completely. And now she was not only being told that DNA testing showed they weren't her kids…she was actually in danger of having

---

Walter Freeman, who invented the "ice pick" lobotomy, called his van "the lobotomobile."

those kids taken away from her.

DDNNAA

In the meantime, Fairchild gave birth to her fourth child. Again DNA testing showed it was not hers. By now, prosecutors were not as gung-ho as they had once been. If she was committing fraud—how was she doing it? And what exactly was the point? They knew Jamie Townsend was the father of each of the kids. Was he involved in some scheme using his sperm to impregnate eggs from another woman and having those eggs implanted into Fairchild's uterus? (That was one way she actually could give birth to kids that DNA tests would show were not hers.) It didn't seem likely. So what was going on?

After months of legal wrangling, Fairchild's lawyer, Alan Tindell, finally found a clue. He was researching medical journals when he came across a story about something that seemed like it was out of science fiction: a genetic condition called *tetragametic chimerism*. What's that? In simple terms, a condition that results in one person having two different sets of DNA in his or her body. Could this be what was happening with Fairchild? She was tested again; only this time the DNA samples were taken from different parts of her body—then compared to each other. Result: The DNA in Fairchild's hair and blood didn't match the DNA in her uterus.

YOU-NIQUE

To understand what was happening with Lydia Fairchild, we first have to understand a little about our own DNA and why we're all genetically unique—even from our siblings. (Unless you're an identical twin: you're special—and we'll get to you in a minute.)

We get our DNA from our parents: The egg from Mom and the sperm from Dad each carry half-sets of DNA—23 chromosomes each—made up of a total of roughly 25,000 genes. Upon fertilization, the chromosomes from Mom and the chromosomes from Dad chemically bond and become the 23 "chromosome pairs" that make up a complete set of human DNA.

So why don't siblings have the same DNA if they each get a half-set of genes from Mom and Dad? Because they get different combinations of genes in those chromosomes. This is simply because of how sex cells are produced in our bodies:

A New York steak and a Kansas City steak are the same cut of meat.

- Remember, we each have two copies of each gene in our bodies—one from Mom and one from Dad.

- When our own reproductive cells (eggs or sperm) are created, they each get just one copy of each gene—and it's entirely random if it's going to be the one we got from Mom or from Dad.

- To put it another way, your mother may have gotten a gene for blue eyes from her father and brown eyes from her mother—but she only passed one of those on to you. (The same thing—but probably with different colors—happened via your father.)

- This is true for all of the 25,000 or so genes in our bodies—meaning that an enormous number of combinations can be created for each egg and each sperm.

MAKING (DIFFERENT) BABIES

Now let's look at what happens during fertilization—and finally find out what happened to Lydia Fairchild.

- In the most common form of human fertilization, one sperm merges with one egg. Their chromosomes combine, and after about a week or so, the egg cell begins to split and multiply into more and more cells, each cell with exact copies of those 23 paired chromosomes inside them. If all goes well, this eventually results in the birth of one baby.

- In a much less common occurrence (about 3 in 1,000 worldwide), one sperm and one egg come together, their chromosomes combine, and after a few days, the fertilized egg splits in two, forming two separate eggs. Most importantly, when the egg splits in two, the 23 chromosome pairs are copied so each cell ends up with identical DNA. These two eggs develop into, as you've no doubt already guessed, identical twins. (Note: Identical twins don't actually have the exact same DNA, as some DNA mutations occur as a matter of course during fertilization. But they are close enough that the twins look "identical" to us.)

- There is a second type of twin. In this case, two different sperm cells merge with two different egg cells simultaneously. These go on to develop separately, becoming nonidentical, or *fraternal* twins. The reason they're not identical is because they're each the product of two different egg cells and two different sperm cells, each with its own unique DNA, as we explained earlier. (While identical-twin

Richard Nixon put ketchup on his cottage cheese.

birth rates are pretty consistent worldwide, fraternal-twin rates vary—sometimes greatly—from country to country. In the U.S., roughly 33 of every 1,000 births result in fraternal twins.)

COME TOGETHER

When Fairchild was just an egg—she was actually two different eggs. Those two different eggs were both fertilized by two different sperm cells right around the same time. Some days after this, those two fertilized eggs...merged. For reasons scientists still don't understand—the eggs combined to become one egg. Remember, these were already two different *fertilized* eggs, with their own unique and complete sets of DNA. So when the two came together, it meant that the resulting single egg had two different sets of DNA inside it. That's what happens with *tetragametic chimerism.*

What does DNA do in a newly fertilized egg? It provides the biochemical instructions that guide the egg's development, including how different tissues in the egg will morph and grow and become different body parts. Some tissue gets instructions to become the spinal column and brain; other tissue to become the lungs, other the skeleton, and so on.

Now here's the weird part: In a *chimera* like Lydia Fairchild, the two sets of DNA each build different parts of the body. One of the DNA sets might build the spinal column and the brain, while the other set builds the lungs, liver, bones, and so on.

Result: Lydia Fairchild is—literally—*her own twin.*

RESOLUTION

Fairchild's DNA had originally been tested the usual way—via a swab from the inside of her cheek. That did not match her kids' DNA. Later tests used samples taken from her hair—which came up with the same result. When she was finally tested using a sample from a cervical smear—the results finally showed that she was indeed the mother of her own children. The prosecutor dropped the case against her—and that was that.

CHIMERA FACTS

• *Chimera* is derived from the ancient Greek name for a mythological monster that was part lion, part goat, and part serpent.

• Chimerism is common among some animals, including sponges and marmosets (a small monkey found in South America).

• Human chimerism is extremely rare—less than 50 cases have been documented in history—so the chances that criminal DNA testing has been affected is extremely low.

• Are you a chimera? Who knows? Scientists say most chimeras would go through life completely unaware of the condition. Others, though, may have a clue: Some human chimeras have two different-colored eyes or patches of different-colored hair...the result of the two different sets of DNA that built their bodies.

• In 1998, doctors at the University of Edinburgh reported treating a teenage boy for an undescended testicle. When they performed surgery to find the second testicle...it wasn't there. They found an ovary and fallopian tube instead. The boy was a chimera—and was his own twin sister.

* * *

EXPAND YOUR VOCABULARY
Real words that spellcheck probably won't recognize.

gonfalon: a banner, with streamers, hanging from a crossbar

epinasty: excessive growth on top of a plant causing it to bend downward

nuque: the back of the neck

brannigan: a squabble or brawl

discomfit: to thwart, foil; throw into confusion

pellicle: a thin skin or film; scum

luteous: of a greenish, yellow color

fistula: a narrow tube or duct

macula: a spot or blemish on the sun, moon, skin, etc.

cafard: a melancholy mood; apathy

slaver: to slobber or allow saliva to drip from the mouth

dudgeon: a feeling of resentment after being offended

bovarism: an unrealistic opinion of one's abilities (named after the title character from Gustave Flaubert's 1857 novel *Madame Bovary*)

funest: portending evil; sinister

Thickness of a standard potato chip: about 1/20 of an inch. Ridged chip: over 1/5 of an inch.

CELEBRITY RUMORS

Despite what you may have heard, Uncle John was not the original Ty-D-Bowl Man. (How do these rumors get started?)

Rumor: 1970s shock-rocker Alice Cooper was actually Ken Osmond, the teen actor who had played Eddie Haskell on *Leave It to Beaver.*

Truth: Cooper's real name is Vincent Furnier. The rumor spread because Cooper said in a magazine interview that as a child he was obnoxious "like Eddie Haskell." He didn't mean it literally.

Rumor: Gene Simmons of KISS has a signature stage move. He sticks out his giant tongue and wiggles it around. The reason it's so long is that he had a cow's tongue surgically grafted onto his own.

Truth: It seems like something a member of KISS would do, but Simmons has a naturally freakishly long tongue. A "tongue graft" is not a medical procedure that existed in the '70s...or today.

Rumor: Jessica Chastain is Ron Howard's illegitimate daughter.

Truth: When picking up awards for her role in *Zero Dark Thirty,* Chastain thanked her mother, Jerri Chastain, and her father, Michael Hastey. But Hastey isn't her biological father—a man named Michael Monasterio is. Chastain had a falling out with him years ago, and they don't speak. The idea of Chastain's father not being her real father, coupled with the fact that she strongly resembles Howard's daughter, Bryce Dallas Howard, helped the rumor spread.

Rumor: Actress Jamie Lee Curtis was born "intersex"—she had both male and female sex organs, and she had surgery shortly after birth to remove all traces of malehood.

Truth: The only "proof" for this far-fetched story is that Curtis's parents—Hollywood icons Tony Curtis and Janet Leigh—gave her a gender-neutral name, supposedly until she could have the necessary surgeries. Leigh explained the name in her memoir, which could be the source of the rumor. She and Curtis wanted to name their baby before it arrived, and since they didn't know the gender before birth, they picked a gender-neutral name.

Sea cucumbers can change into a nearly liquid state and "pour" themselves into tight spaces.

FLASH PHOTOGRAPHY

If you're like most people, you probably haven't taken pictures with a film camera for years…but you probably still have one lying around somewhere. What to do with it? Here's a spark of inspiration.

OLD CAMERA, NEW TRICK

Modern digital cameras do a lot of things well, but one thing old-fashioned film cameras do better is take pictures of lightning. This is because 1) film has a higher resolution than many digital cameras, and 2) the optical sensors of a digital camera can be overwhelmed by the powerful brilliance of a sudden bolt of lightning, giving you a distorted image. If you haven't used your film camera in a while, here's how, with a little practice, you can take pictures of one of nature's most striking (so to speak) visual phenomena.

WHAT YOU NEED

• **Your old camera.** SLR or "single-lens reflex" cameras work best because they allow you to adjust the focus, aperture (the opening that allows light into the camera), exposure time, and other settings manually. Simpler point-and-shoot cameras can also work, as long as they allow you to focus to infinity and keep the shutter open for 30 seconds.

• **Something to keep it from moving.** It's easiest to get a good picture of lightning at night when it's dark, but that requires long exposure times, which require that the camera remain absolutely still—otherwise your pictures will be blurry. Mounting the camera on a tripod or resting it on a sturdy surface will help to keep it from moving.

• **A cable release.** If you're using an SLR camera, a cable release connects to the shutter (the button you press when taking a picture). The cable release allows you to snap photographs without touching the camera directly, which might cause it to move. The cable release also has a locking mechanism that allows you to keep the shutter open indefinitely (or until lightning flashes).

• **Slow-speed film.** Long exposures require a film with a speed of 100 or 200 ISO.

A sudden tectonic-plate movement of just eight inches is enough to set off a major earthquake.

SAFETY FIRST

• Lightning kills an average of 50 people in the United States each year, and injures hundreds more. There is no way to protect yourself from the danger when you are out in the open. (And a lightning storm's violent winds, rain, and hail can ruin your camera.) The only way to photograph lightning safely is from inside what the National Weather Service calls a "safe shelter"—either a fully enclosed building (with a roof, walls, floor, wiring, and plumbing), or a hard-topped vehicle with the windows closed. Carports, patios, and picnic shelters will not protect you.

• You are safest, and get the best images, when you take pictures of a storm that is approaching your location, leaving it, or passing by at a distance of a few miles away.

• If you're taking pictures from your car, pay attention to the direction in which the storm is moving and stay out of its way.

HOW TO DO IT

1. Set up your camera near a window that offers a good view of a thunderstorm. Attach it to your tripod or set it on a stable surface like a table. Attach the cable release to the shutter button.

2. Set the shutter speed to the B ("bulb") setting. In this setting the shutter will remain open for as long as the shutter button/cable release is pressed. (If you're using a point-and-shoot camera, set the shutter speed to 30 seconds.)

3. Set the aperture (f-stop) between f2.8 and f8. For close or bright lightning, use f8. For faraway or less bright lightning, setting it closer to f2.8 will allow more light into the camera.

4. Set the focus to infinity. (Turn the camera's autofocus off.)

5. Frame your shot. Point the camera in the direction with the most lightning flashes. Allow the night sky to take up most of the picture, but show a little bit of the horizon in the bottom of the frame to give your photographs perspective.

6. Using the cable release, open the shutter and lock it open. With a point-and-shoot camera, press the shutter button and hope that lightning strikes before the shutter closes after 30 seconds.

7. When lightning strikes, unlock the cable release. That closes the shutter and ends the exposure. That's all there is to it! With a little practice, soon you'll be taking pictures like the pros.

THE FORD MODEL K?

We've all heard of the Ford Model T—but we rarely hear about the earlier automobiles in the whole "model-letter" scheme. So hear you go…

ALPHABET CITY

In 1908, the Ford Motor Company, founded by Henry Ford just five years earlier, released its first Ford Model T—and the world has never been the same. The Model T was the first car that ordinary people could afford, and is regarded by automobile historians as the car that ushered in the Automobile Age. From 1908 until production ended in 1927, more than 16 million Model Ts were sold worldwide. No other car model ever sold as well…until 1972, when it was finally surpassed by the VW Beetle.

But the Model T's great success overshadows all the models that came before it—all of them based on previous alphabet letters. Did Henry Ford make nineteen earlier models before the Model T—one for each letter before "T"? No. Most were experimental and never made it to production. But eight did.

MODEL A (1903–04): The Ford Motor Company's first car. It consisted of little more than a frame with an upholstered bench seat mounted on top of it. (A rear bench seat compartment was optional.) There was no front compartment, no hood (the engine was under the seat), and nothing resembling a windshield or dashboard—the steering wheel simply stuck up out of the floor in front of the bench. Top speed: 28 mph. Cost: $750. Color: red (only). About 1,700 were sold before production stopped in 1904—which was enough to keep Ford going. (Note: The name "Model A" was recycled in 1927 and used for the car that replaced the Model T.)

MODEL B (1904–05): This was a touring car, and much closer to the modern car configuration. It had *two* bench seats and came with doors—although only rear doors (the front seat had open access). The engine was located in its own compartment in the front of the car, under a hood and behind a radiator. The Model B was a luxury car, with polished wood, brass fittings and trim, came with leather seats and a canopy roof, and even had gas-powered headlights (although they were optional and cost extra). Top speed: 40 mph. Cost: $2,000. A total of about 500 Model Bs were sold.

MODEL C (1904–05): This model was simply an updated version of the Model A. The engine was still under the front seat, but the Model C had a front compartment and hood anyway—that's where the gas tank was located. The engine was also slightly larger, giving it a top speed of about 38 mph. Cost: $850. About 800 were sold before the Model C was discontinued in 1905. Special option: You could buy a Model C with a Model A engine—in which case it was called a Model AC.

MODEL F (1905–06): An update of the Model C. The engine was still under the front seat, the gas tank was under the hood, it still had no front doors, but it was larger and longer, and the rear seat was now standard. And it had "running boards"—narrow steps located below the doors to make it easier to get into the vehicle— the first Ford to have them. Cost: $1,000. About 1,000 were made.

MODEL K (1906–08): The Model K was big. It had a wheelbase—the distance between front and rear wheels—of 114 inches. (By comparison, the Model B's was just 92 inches, and the Model A's was 72 inches). It was also Ford's first car with a 6-cylinder engine (earlier models had either 2 or 4 cylinders). Like the Model B, it was flashy, and intended for wealthy customers. Cost: $2,500 (about $65,000 in today's money). Its two-year run was Ford's longest yet—but only 950 models were sold. Ford would not make another 6-cylinder car for 35 years and turned his full focus to making very *un*luxurious automobiles.

MODEL N (1906–08): The simple Model N was a sign of things to come for the Ford Motor Company. A successor of the A, C, and F models, the Model N came in only one color (maroon). It had only one bench seat, a small 4-cylinder engine capable of a top speed of about 40 mph, and no running boards. It was a plain car for plain people—and at a cost of just $500, more than 7,000 of those people snapped them up in just two years.

MODEL R (1907): Drivers loved the simple Model N, but some people wanted a bit more—hence the Model R. It was basically a slightly larger Model N, with running boards, stylized fenders, and a few other improvements. Cost: $750. More than 2,500 of them were sold in just six months.

MODEL S (1907–09): The Model S was another gussied-up Model N, this time with a fancier fender and running board

---

Put that in your pipe and smoke it: Potatoes, tomatoes, and green peppers all contain nicotine.

configurations, and an option for a fold-down, single-person mother-in-law seat, or "rumble seat," in the rear. Cost: $700. About 3,750 sold. More importantly, during the run of the Model S—the Model T was released. And the rest…is car history.

SPARE PARTS

• Ford's very first motor vehicle wasn't a letter-model car at all—it was his Quadricycle. Ford built it—engine and all—in a shed in his yard over a period of two years, finishing it in 1896, seven years before he launched the Ford Motor Company. The Quadricycle consisted of four bicycle wheels mounted to a simple frame, with a wooden box as a seat and rear wheels powered by an ethanol engine via a chain. Ford sold the Quadricycle for $200 and later built two more. (The original Quadricycle can be seen today in the Henry Ford Museum in Dearborn, Michigan.)

• The Model T came in several different styles during its long run, including roadster, four-door sedan, station wagon, and even as a pickup truck for a couple of years (from 1925 to 1927). They all had 4-cylinder engines and an average top speed of around 45 mph. The cheapest models cost just $260—all the way into the 1920s.

• The first person to own a Ford Motor Company car: Ernst Pfennig, a dentist from Chicago. He bought the first Model A ever produced on July 23, 1903.

• In 1905, the Ford Delivery Car was released—a Model C with an enclosed compartment behind the driver's seat. It was a flop, and only about 12 were made. Why are we telling you this? Because some automobile literature refers to this vehicle as the Ford "Model E," even though Ford listed it only as the "Delivery Car."

• Through the early 1920s, the low-cost, bare-bones Model T dominated the automobile market. By the mid-'20s, other car companies had begun using Ford's mass-production techniques and were offering what Ford considered "cosmetic luxuries" as standard equipment. But despite a dropoff in sales and against the advice of his son, Edsel, Henry Ford steadfastly refused to change the Model T. In 1926, he finally relented, allowing Edsel to develop a new model, called the Model A. Yet when the Model A was released in 1927, the elder Ford took all the credit. In its four years of production, more than 4.8 million Model As were sold.

Hair doo: In ancient Rome, women dyed their hair blonde with pigeon poop.

GENERIC CANADA

*A "genericized brand name" is a brand name that has come to be
used as the name for that product, whether that particular
company made it or not. Examples: Kleenex, Thermos,
and Coke. Canada has some that are all its own.*

Name: Vi-Co
Refers to: Chocolate milk
Details: The Vi-Co brand of chocolate milk was available
in Saskatchewan and Manitoba in the early 20th century. (Vi-Co is
short for "vitamins + cocoa.") The last dairy to own the trademark,
Dairy Producers, was bought out in 1995 by rival Dairyland, which
discontinued the Vi-Co brand. Even though you can't get actual Vi-
Co anywhere anymore, many Saskatchewanians still call any kind
of packaged chocolate milk "Vi-Co" or "vico."

Name: Kraft Dinner
Refers to: Macaroni and cheese
Details: It's kind of a stereotype now, but Canadians are known for
their love of Kraft's blue-boxed Macaroni and Cheese Dinner, or, as
it's called, Kraft Dinner. (Worldwide, Canadians purchase a quarter of
all the Kraft Dinners sold.) Kraft isn't the only company that packages
dry noodles with cheesy sauce, but competitive brands are still more
likely to be referred to as "Kraft Dinner" than "macaroni and cheese."

Name: Javex
Refers to: Bleach
Details: Clorox is a genericized trademark in the United States,
referring to any bottle of simple bleach, whether or not it's actually
Clorox. The same phenomenon occurred in Canada, with Javex.
Canada has a strong French influence, and bleach was invented in
Javel, a Parisian neighborhood, in the late 1700s. It was first called
eau de Javel (Javel water), and as Javel gave way to Javex in the early
1900s, it became one of the first bleach brands available in Canada.
Javex doesn't exist anymore—the Clorox Corporation bought Javex
in 2006 and phased out the name. Canadians now buy Clorox...but
they still call it Javex.

If all cars in the U.S. were lined up bumper to bumper, they'd stretch to the moon and back.

Name: Gravol

Refers to: Anti-motion sickness drugs

Details: If you're feeling seasick or carsick, what remedy do you buy at the pharmacy? Motion sickness pills or Dramamine? In the United States, you'd probably ask for Dramamine. In Canada, the equivalent of Dramamine (and the best known brand name of this kind of drug) is Gravol. Both drugs contain the same active ingredient, dimenhydrinate.

Name: Timbits

Refers to: Doughnut holes

Details: The most popular fast-food restaurant in Canada—by far—is Tim Hortons. It's a coffee-and-doughnut chain founded by ex-professional hockey player Tim Horton in 1964. There are 3,000 locations in Canada, or one for every 12,000 people (by contrast, in the U.S. there's one McDonald's for every 260,000 people). That total market saturation has affected the language. The bite-sized treat made from leftover dough in the doughnut-making process is known at Tim Hortons as a "timbit." Dunkin' Donuts locations in Canada serve doughnut holes (called "munchkins")…but lots of people still order them as "timbits."

Name: Mackinaw

Refers to: A heavy red-and-black-plaid jacket

Details: One Canadian stereotype is the image of a manly lumberjack wearing a thick double-breasted plaid jacket. Lumberjacks did indeed wear them, called mackinaws and produced from tightly woven wool Melton cloth. Today, several companies make them, and they're all called mackinaws (or sometimes Meltons). But the first mackinaws were sewn by Metis women who lived near the Straits of Mackinac, near present-day Michigan. How did Mackinac become the Mackinaw? That's how the word is pronounced in Canadian French so that's how English speakers wrote it down.

*　　*　　*

"Choose to be optimistic; it feels better." —**The Dalai Lama**

FOUNDING FATHERS

A few more stories of the real people behind their famous names.

LEON LEONWOOD BEAN

Bean was a tough-as-nails hunter and fisherman from Maine with a keen mind for business. In the early 1900s, frustrated by his leaky hunting boots, he set out to make better ones. Crafting the upper from leather and the sole from rubber, Bean raised the money to manufacture 100 pairs of waterproof boots, and offered a full refund to any dissatisfied customers. He quickly sold all 100 pairs…but 90 people asked for a refund. The rubber soles—new technology at the time—had developed cracks. Undeterred, Bean went to New York with $400 and paid the United States Rubber Company for some stronger rubber. With a better boot and a list of New England sportsmen obtained from public records of hunting licenses, Bean created a mail-order catalog that was an instant success. He died at age 94 in 1967, a multi-millionaire. To this day, L.L. Bean still offers a full refund to dissatisfied customers—no questions asked.

MARIO PRADA

In 1913, Mario and his brother Martino opened a shop in Milan, Italy, called *Fratelli Prada* (Prada Brothers), selling imported steamer trunks and handbags. When Mario later retired, he wanted his son—rather than his daughter—to take over the store, believing that women didn't belong in the workplace. But his son wasn't interested, so Prada allowed his daughter, Luisa, to take it over. Good move: She kept the store going for 20 years, after which her daughter, Miuccia, took it over in 1978, and expanded the company from strictly leather goods into high-end designer-label couture. Today the company is worth $20 billion.

HERMANN RORSCHACH

While Rorschach was in school in Switzerland in the 1890s, he enjoyed *klecksography*, making art out of inkblots. He was so good at it that his friends nicknamed him "Klecks." Rorschach nearly pursued a career in art (his father was an art teacher), but decided on psychiatry instead. He studied under Eugen Bleuler, who had

---

In 1916, Charlie Chaplin made $10,000 a week, making him the highest-paid actor of the day.

taught Carl Jung. After reading a book of poems based on inkblots, Dr. Rorschach theorized that people's unique interpretations of random ink patterns could provide clues to their subconscious mind. Inspired, he created a test of ten inkblot cards and sold them, and instructions, with his 1921 book, *Psychodiagnostik*. He died just a year later at 37, of a ruptured appendix. Though the Rorschach Test is rarely administered today—it's been replaced by more accurate tests that can diagnose more conditions—it had a huge impact on 20th-century psychiatry.

WILLIAM BARNES AND G. CLIFFORD NOBLE

In 1886, a bookstore opened in New York City called Arthur Hinds & Company. One of the store's first clerks was a young Harvard graduate named Gilbert Clifford Noble. Eight years later, he was made a partner, and the store's name changed to Hinds & Noble. Nearly 20 years after that, Noble bought out Hinds and sold educational books under the name Noble & Noble. In 1917, William Barnes left a successful bookselling business in Chicago to work for Noble (his father and Barnes were friends). He became a partner at the shop, which was renamed Barnes & Noble.

CHRISTIAN DOPPLER

Stargazers have long wondered why two stars in a binary system appear to change colors. In 1842, an Austrian physicist named Christian Doppler figured it out, and released his findings in a book called *Über das farbige Licht der Doppelsterne* (*Concerning the Colored Light of Double Stars*). Doppler explained that it's because the two stars—which are orbiting each other—are moving alternately toward and away from Earth. The light rays emitted from the star moving away hit the observer (anyone looking from Earth) at a slower frequency, which makes them appear red; the light rays emitted by the star moving toward Earth are "bunched-up," which make them appear blue. Called the Doppler effect, this explains why an emergency siren has a higher pitch as it moves toward you, and a lower pitch as it moves away. The Doppler effect has since been utilized by astronomers, physicists, meteorologists, the military, and law enforcement to track anything that emits waves.

*   *   *

"I stay in marvelous shape. I worry it off." —**Nancy Reagan**

The 5,000-year-old mummy Otzi the Iceman had tattoos on his spine, ankles, and leg.

SIMPLE MATH TRICKS

A few more tricks to make some types of math problems a snap.

TRICK 4: "Square" (or multiply by itself) any two-digit number ending in 5.

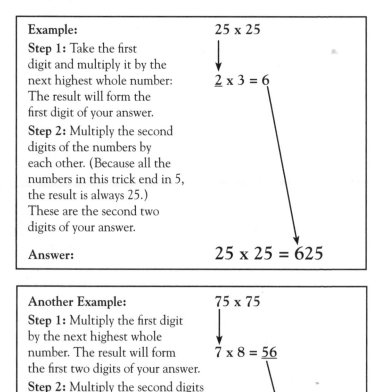

Example: 25 x 25

Step 1: Take the first
digit and multiply it by the
next highest whole number: 2 x 3 = 6
The result will form the
first digit of your answer.

Step 2: Multiply the second
digits of the numbers by
each other. (Because all the
numbers in this trick end in 5,
the result is always 25.)
These are the second two
digits of your answer.

Answer: 25 x 25 = 625

Another Example: 75 x 75

Step 1: Multiply the first digit
by the next highest whole
number. The result will form   7 x 8 = 56
the first two digits of your answer.

Step 2: Multiply the second digits
of the numbers by each other.
(Again, since all the numbers in
this trick end in 5, the result is
always 25.) These are the second
two digits of your answer.

Answer: 75 x 75 = 5625

The producer's first choice to play the lead role in *Dirty Harry*: Frank Sinatra.

TRICK 5: Figure out which of two fractions is larger.

Example:	Which is greater,
	$3/8$ or $4/9$?

Step 1: Multiply the first fraction's *numerator* (the top number) by the second fraction's *denominator* (the bottom number). This number corresponds to the first fraction ($3/8$), the one that provided the numerator.

$3 \times 9 = 27$

Step 2: Multiply the numerator of the second fraction by the denominator of the first fraction.

$4 \times 8 = 32$

This number corresponds to the second fraction ($4/9$), the one that provided the numerator.

Step 3: Compare the two results. Since 32 is greater than 27, the corresponding fraction, $4/9$, is greater than $3/8$.

TRICK 6: Multiply any two-digit number by 101.

Example: 14×101

Step 1: Write the number twice. That's it!

Answer: $14 \times 101 = 1414$

Another Example: 78×101

Answer: $78 \times 101 = 7878$

What's *bromidrosiphobia?* Fear of your own body odor. Average sufferer: male, age 25.

WARNING LABELS

Some things in life should go without saying, but it seems there's always somebody who needs to be told not to eat fireworks.

On an outdoor antenna: "Do not attempt to install if drunk, pregnant, or both."

On a plastic letter opener: "Safety goggles recommended"

On a screwdriver set: "Not to be inserted into penis"

On a rain gauge: "Suitable for outdoor use only"

On a bottle of tequila: "Imbibing excessive quantities may cause loss of dignity and/or balance."

On a pack of Silly Putty: "Do not use as ear plugs."

On a box of hammers: "May be harmful if swallowed"

On a salt lick: "Warning: high in sodium"

On a hairdryer: "Do not use while sleeping."

On another hairdryer: "For hair on head only"

On packing tape: "Packing tape should not be used for painful practical jokes."

On fireworks: "Flammable. Do not put in mouth."

On hemorrhoid suppositories: "Remove aluminum wrapping before insertion."

On disposable diapers: "Dispose of after use."

On a dishwasher: "Do not allow children to play in dishwasher."

On batteries: "Do not swallow. C or D batteries may cause choking."

On a child's playhouse: "This is not a toy."

On a newsletter: "Do not immerse this newsletter in water. Electrocution could result."

On a bathroom heater: "This product is not to be used in bathrooms."

On a .22-caliber rifle: "May cause injury or death"

On a DVD: "Warning. This DVD has a slightly strange smell."

TECH-NO

*For every new electronic gadget that flies off the shelves, a dozen
more crash and burn. Here are some techno-flops.*

MOTOROLA ROKR

Back before "smartphones" took off in 2007 (the year
Apple's iPhone was launched), the predominant cell
phones were small one-piece units made by Nokia and Motorola,
outfitted with a two-inch screen, a tiny keypad, and not much else.
After Apple introduced the iPod in 2001 and the iTunes Music
Store in 2005, Motorola believed that the future of music was
its ability to be stored and played on cell phones. So in 2005, it
introduced the ROKR (pronounced "rocker"). It looked like the
standard mini-brick phone of the era, except that it could connect
with iTunes, allowing users to download and listen to as many as
100 songs. Just before its release, the tech press hailed ROKR as the
next big thing…until Apple announced that it would be releasing
a new product called the iPod Nano the same week. The Nano was
a smaller, cheaper version of the iPod…that held ten times as many
songs as a ROKR. Motorola CEO Ed Zander disregarded the challenge from Apple, telling a reporter, "Who listens to 1,000 songs?"
The answer: Everybody…which is why the ROKR flopped.

DATA DISCMAN

You might be reading this on a Kindle, Nook, iPad, or another
one of the e-book devices that have been a fast-growing product
category since 2007. But the first e-books hit the market in 1992.
That's when Sony introduced the Data Discman. Just as the Sony
Walkman played music on cassettes, the Data Discman played
textual data (books) delivered on proprietary 3.5-inch CDs. The
device was similar to today's bare-bones e-readers—a gray-scale
screen and a small keyboard to search for information on whichever
book or reference-material disc was loaded up. (In fact, almost all of
the titles available were reference materials, like encyclopedias or
dictionaries.) However, unlike today's tablets, the Discman's screen
flipped up for easier reading, making it a tiny laptop that could
only do one thing. Sony released an array of Data Discman models
throughout the '90s…but only in Japan, where the devices were

---

Due to genetic defects, one in 2 million lobsters is born blue. One in 30 mil. is yellow.

popular. In the United States, the Data Discman flopped hard and was gone by 1995.

DVD RECORDERS

By 1999, the VCR was on the way out, and the DVD player was on the way in. But while the DVD offered better pictures and sound, VCRs had one big advantage: They could record TV shows. That wasn't possible with DVDs, at least not until major electronics manufacturers introduced stand-alone DVD recorders. It seems like it would have been a no-brainer—millions of people would want a way to record TV shows or movies from TV, for later viewing, onto a high-quality format. And maybe they would have—except that they cost anywhere from $1,000 to $3,000, and blank DVDs cost around $5 each, more than twice the cost of a blank VHS videotape. Prices dropped within a few years, but by that time digital video record-ers (DVRs) such as TiVo had hit the market, giving consumers the ability to record TV shows and store them on a hard drive. (And they only cost around $200 or came free with a cable TV subscription.)

GIZMONDO

The video-game market is dominated by Japanese and American companies. Gizmondo was the first major challenge from Europe. In 2003, the Swedish company Tiger Telematics announced that it was developing a handheld gaming system to compete with the Nintendo DS and the Sony PSP. Introduced as Gametrac, it was renamed the Gizmondo in late 2004. The video-game press went crazy for the Gizmondo before its scheduled March 2005 launch—the device boasted a digital camera, text messaging capabilities, and GPS—all features the Nintendo DS and the Sony PSP didn't have. Tiger spent millions promoting the product in Europe and the U.S., including running a Gizmondo-branded car in a Formula One race, hiring Formula One drivers to endorse the product, and throwing a star-studded launch party. But when the Gizmondo finally became available...not many people bought it. Expected to sell 4,500 units on its first day, it sold only 1,000. In all, 30,000 were sold. That's the worst-selling game console in history. Only eight games were ever available in the U.S., and the product was gone within a year. Tiger Telematics went bankrupt, and two of its executives went to prison on fraud and racketeering charges.

In 1983, a fleck of paint hit *Challenger* at 20,000 mph, causing a crater in its windshield.

BUBBAS & BARBER POLES

Every profession has its own jargon or slang, including the U.S. military. Here are some expressions used by naval aviators. Kick the tires and light the fires!

Flathatting: A stunt—flying low and fast to startle people on the ground (flattening their hats)

Mom/Mother: The aircraft carrier an aviator is assigned to (short for "mother ship")

Nugget: An aviator on his/her first tour of duty

Bubba: An aviator who flies the same aircraft that you do

Puke: An aviator who flies a different kind of aircraft than you do

Sending a Marine to Sea: Going to the bathroom in advance of a combat mission. (Also called a "combat dump.")

Centurion: An aviator who has completed 100 landings on the same carrier

Head on a Swivel/Doing the Linda Blair: Keeping a sharp eye out for enemy aircraft

Go-Juice: Jet fuel or coffee, depending on the context

Irish Pennant: A loose thread on your uniform

Brain Housing Group: Skull

Texaco: An airborne tanker or refueling plane

Passing Gas: When a Texaco fuels a fighter plane

Kick the Tires and Light the Fires: Rushing through—or skipping entirely—the physical inspection of an aircraft in order to get in the air quickly

Checking for Light Leaks: Taking a nap

Barber Pole: The cockpit gauge that shows diagonal stripes when the landing gear is transitioning between the up and down positions

Big Blue Sleeping Pill: The (blue) manual of regulations governing the safe and correct operation of naval aircraft

Music: Electronic jamming that blinds enemy radar

Admiral's Doorbell: A yellow button in the cockpit that jettisons excess fuel and bombs in an emergency. (If you push it, you'll have to explain to the admiral why you did.)

The Taj Mahal ("crown of palaces") was originally called Rauza-I Munavvara ("tomb of light").

DUMB CROOKS

Here's proof that crime doesn't pay.

NEXT APPLICANT, PLEASE

One afternoon in October 2012, workers at the OK Feed & Supply Store in Tucson, Arizona, noticed that a charity donation box full of money had disappeared from the check-out counter. When they reviewed the video surveillance footage, it didn't take long to identify the thief: It was a young man who had been in the store earlier that day for a job interview. (His name and address were on his job application.)

SUCK IT IN

Rafael Valadão was one of four inmates who tried to escape from a Ceres, Brazil, prison in 2012. Their plan: Use a shower rod to break a hole in a wall, climb through, and then descend the outside fence to freedom. The first inmate, a little guy, climbed through and got away. Then Valadão—6' 4" and 225 pounds—tried to squeeze through the hole, but he got stuck halfway. The other two inmates tried to push him through, but he wouldn't budge. Then they tried pulling him back in, but all that did was fracture several of Valadão's ribs. The guards heard his cries of pain (after not hearing the wall get smashed) and rushed in to see two big legs flailing about. The guards laughed and even took some photos while waiting for fire-fighters to come and free him. Valadão ended up in the infirmary; the photos are on the Internet.

SNOWED IN

In 2012, snowplow driver John Shuman was clearing a Walmart parking lot in Alliance, Ohio, when he saw Cody Bragg, 18, drive his Honda Civic up to a woman's shopping cart and snatch her purse. She resisted, but couldn't stop him. So Shuman did his civic duty and chased the Civic. For the next 30 minutes, wherever Bragg went, so did Shuman. Apparently, that really freaked out the purse thief. He called 911 and said, "There's a guy in a snowplow following me. And he's scaring me!" That made it pretty easy for police to track down Bragg and arrest him.

Americans toss out enough disposable plates and cups to give the entire world 6 picnics a year.

NO CENTS AT ALL

In 2012, Dakoda Garren and Elizabeth Massman, both 19, were hired to clean a house in Vancouver, Washington. After they left, the homeowner noticed her valuable coin collection was missing. Garren denied everything. "You don't have any evidence on me," he told police indignantly. They let him go, but asked the public to be on the lookout for any rare coins. A week later, a movie-theater employee called police to report that a young couple had paid for their tickets with quarters…from the 1930s. It turned out they'd been using the coins—worth between $1,000 and $18,500 each—at face value to buy pizza and play video games. Garren and Massman were arrested. Most, but not all, of the valuable coins were recovered.

THREAT LEVEL ZERO

In 2012, Wade Radzinski, 25, a hotel worker in Scottsdale, Arizona, reported a bomb threat. When the cops arrived, he said there was no longer any danger because the person who'd made the threat promised to leave in exchange for a large sum of money. Radzinski said he gave the man $290 of the hotel's money and he was long gone. "So you guys can leave." Officers didn't believe it. They asked Radzinski if they could search his car; he said yes. And—lo and behold—when officers removed the gas cap, the $290 fell out. "I don't know why I thought this was a good idea," Radzinski said afterward.

SHORTCHANGED

While officers were investigating a bank robbery in Syracuse, New York, in 2012, the robber, Arthur Bundrage, 28, returned to the bank and tried to get in the front door, which police had locked. Why'd he come back? The teller had shortchanged him, giving him less than the $20,000 he'd demanded.

NAME THAT CROOK

In 2012, a Twin Falls, Idaho, police officer stopped a man who was acting suspiciously and asked him for his name and birthday. He answered, "Emiliano Velesco," and gave a date. A search of that name came up empty. Then the cop saw the name "Contreras" tattooed on his arm. So he ran that name with the birthday given, and up popped Dylan Edward Contreras, 19, who had three outstanding warrants for failure to appear…and for giving false information.

"MY CRAZY NEIGHBOR SAID JACKIE DID IT"

Four decades after President Kennedy was shot in Dallas, the conspiracy theories persist—with wacky new ideas joining the conversation all the time. Here are some really weird ones.

CONSPIRACY THEORY: FBI director—and Kennedy family rival—J. Edgar Hoover orchestrated Kennedy's 1963 assassination…by hiring a hit squad of homosexuals.

DETAILS: Hoover is frequently mentioned as a player in Kennedy assassination conspiracy books. But *this* theory holds that Hoover hired a group of a dozen or so gay men to shoot the president in Dallas. Hoover directed them to dress flamboyantly (like Liberace) or even in drag, believing that if police saw them on the street after the hit, they'd never take such silly-looking people seriously and wouldn't suspect them of committing murder.

TRUTH: This seems to be a place where the forever-popular Kennedy assassination theories and the "J. Edgar Hoover liked to dress in women's clothing" rumor merge. But just to be clear, there were no reports of a group of "flamboyantly dressed" men lingering near Dealey Plaza, where Kennedy was shot on November 22, 1963.

CONSPIRACY THEORY: William Greer, driver of the limousine carrying President Kennedy, First Lady Jacqueline Kennedy, and Texas governor John Connally, killed Kennedy.

DETAILS: Adherents to this theory claim that in the Zapruder film—the grainy few seconds of home-movie footage that remains the definitive record of the Kennedy assassination—Greer can be seen reaching over his shoulder and doing something near Kennedy. A split-second later, Kennedy recoils after being shot. Can't see it? Of course not. To conceal evidence of JFK's real killer, the CIA cut a few seconds out of the Zapruder film.

TRUTH: Greer doesn't reach back from the front seat. He couldn't have, because he was too busy driving the car—and there were hundreds of eyewitnesses, none of whom saw Greer do anything suspicious. The glint of "activity attributed" to Greer in the film is

---

17-year-old Bill Gates sold his first computer program to his own high school. Price: $4,200.

actually sunlight reflecting off the hair of the Secret Service agent in the passenger seat.

CONSPIRACY THEORY: Joe DiMaggio had Kennedy killed.

DETAILS: In 1954, DiMaggio, one of the world's biggest baseball stars, married Marilyn Monroe, the world's biggest movie star. The tumultuous marriage ended after just nine months. Monroe moved on, reportedly having an affair with Kennedy during his presidency, right up until shortly before her death in 1962. DiMaggio, however, never got over Monroe, sending flowers to her grave three times a week for 20 years after her death. In 2003, four years after DiMaggio died, his lawyer, Morris Engelberg, wrote in his memoirs that DiMaggio was convinced the Kennedys had Monroe killed and made her death look like a drug overdose. Reason: She knew about the Kennedys' Mafia ties and was threatening to come forward about the affairs. Filled with rage and grief, DiMaggio hired (through his own Mob connections) a Texas-born, New York-based ex-Marine named Lee Harvey Oswald to kill the president.

TRUTH: Oswald *is* the man who police and history say shot and killed the president, but he has never been found to have any connections to Joltin' Joe.

CONSPIRACY THEORY: Jacqueline Kennedy did it.

DETAILS: The reasons behind her motive vary among conspiracy theorists. Some say she was an angry wife tired of her husband's philandering. Others say she was a brainwashed CIA sleeper agent. Whichever her motive, Mrs. Kennedy did have clear access to the president in the back of that limo. Here's how she did it: Mrs. Kennedy hid a gun in her pocket that morning. During the ride in the motorcade, she hid it in her lap, concealed under a bouquet of flowers and a toy puppet she'd received from a fan earlier that day. When the moment was right (or when the CIA "activated" her), she shot her husband.

TRUTH: They were married, so Kennedy had plenty of "access" to the president—enough to shoot him, for whatever reason, in a location that wouldn't be witnessed by hundreds of onlookers. Also, it's pretty hard to hold up a gun to somebody's head, specifically, and pull the trigger without anyone noticing. (She did, however, have the flowers and puppet, so at least that part is true.)

Besides fairy tales, the Brothers Grimm also wrote law books.

MORE MATTHEW WALL AWARDS

On page 23 we told you the stories of Matthew Wall and a few other lucky souls who were, by all appearances, dead but revived a short time later. Think modern medicine has relegated that kind of thing to the history books? Think again.

Honoree: Allison Burchell, 17, of West Sussex, in the south of England

Rest in Peace: In 1952, Allison went to see an Abbott and Costello film. When she burst out laughing during one funny scene, her laughter triggered a seizure, and she collapsed and fell to the theater floor. An usher found her there after the movie ended. He thought she was dead. So did the paramedics who rushed her to the hospital, and so did the doctors who examined her. They pronounced her dead and sent her to the morgue.

Born Again: Allison had actually suffered an attack of *cataplexy.* In its most severe form, this rare, paralyzing condition causes its victims to appear dead, with a barely detectable heartbeat and extremely shallow breathing, when in fact they are fully conscious. Attacks can be triggered by laughter, as in Allison's case, or crying, fear, anger, or some other emotional outburst. Allison was fully alert from the onset of the attack until after she'd been moved to the morgue. That's where the paralysis subsided. An attendant found her sitting up among the corpses and asking to be taken back to the hospital. "I think he got a bigger shock than I did," Burchell recalled years later.

Born Again...Again: In the years since, Allison has suffered two more attacks—one in England in the mid-1950s following a fight with her husband and another in Australia in the mid-1970s. Both times she remained fully conscious and alert, and both times she was declared dead, only to revive later. Terrified of being buried alive if she suffers a fourth attack, she carries a letter explaining her condition in her purse. Even so, she worries the letter won't be discovered in time. "The only safe thing to do would be to have it tattooed on the soles of my feet," she said.

Honoree: Carlos Camejo, 33, a man living in Venezuela

Rest in Peace: In September 2007, Camejo was badly injured in a car accident and declared dead at the scene. He was taken straight to the morgue, where examiners began an autopsy to determine the precise cause of death.

Born Again: When the examiners made their first incision—on Camejo's face—he started bleeding, indicating that his heart was beating and he was not dead. Realizing their mistake, the examiners rushed to stitch up the incision…and in their shock, they forgot to administer local anesthesia first. The process restored Camejo to consciousness. "I woke up because the pain was unbearable," he told reporters. Camejo's wife, who arrived at the morgue to identify her husband's body, got to take him home instead. He made a full recovery and at last report was still going strong.

Honoree: George Rodonaia, 46, a neuropathologist in the Soviet republic of Georgia

Rest in Peace: In 1976, Rodonaia was run over by a car and so badly injured that he was pronounced dead. (He believed the "accident" was an assassination attempt, and that the KGB agent driving the car ran him over three times to be sure he was dead.) A death certificate was issued, and he was placed in the morgue refrigerator over the weekend.

Born Again: The following Monday, as the doctor performing the autopsy began the first incision into Rodonaia's chest, the "dead" man opened one eye. That's not unheard of for someone who has just died, so the doctor closed the eye and resumed his work. Rodonaia opened the eye again. This time the doctor looked more closely and saw that the pupil was reacting to changes in light, indicating that Rodonaia was alive. The doctor rushed him to the emergency room, where he was revived. Rodonaia spent nine months recovering in the hospital. The one-time atheist got religion during his recovery and later moved to Texas, where he became a Methodist minister. "I'm not scared of anything anymore," he told an interviewer in 2000. He died for real in 2004.

Honoree: Feliberto Carrasco, 81, of Angol, Chile

Rest in Peace: When relatives found the elderly Carrasco lying limp and cold on the floor of his home in January 2008, they were so convinced he was dead, they called for the undertaker instead of the doctor. The undertaker thought he looked dead too, so he washed Carrasco's body, dressed him in his best suit, and laid him out in his coffin for his wake.

Born Again: Most wakes don't involve actual waking—the notion that they are so named because they give people who aren't really dead one last chance to wake up is a myth. But Carrasco did wake up at his wake. As his nephew Pedro stood over his casket, the old man suddenly opened his eyes and began looking around. Shocked family members helped him out of the coffin and sat him up. He assured loved ones that he was not in any pain, just a little thirsty. So they brought him a glass of water.

Honoree: Tasleem Rafiq, 52, of Reading, England

Rest in Peace: One morning in September 2012, Rafiq had a massive heart attack and stopped breathing. She was rushed to the hospital, where doctors worked for 45 minutes to get her heart beating again. But it was no use, and they pronounced her dead. Before the family was allowed in to say their good-byes, doctors warned that because Rafiq had been injected with adrenalin during resuscitation efforts, her body would probably make involuntary movements that were not signs of life.

Born Again: After spending time with their mother—whose eyes were open and who appeared to be looking at them—Rafiq's children became convinced that she was still alive. Doctors reassessed her condition twice over the next two hours, and the second time they did indeed detect a very faint pulse. But tests showed that her blood was so starved of oxygen that brain damage was by now severe and irreversible. The situation was hopeless, the doctors said. Rafiq would likely die in the next couple of hours.

The family kept vigil at her bedside and waited for the end. At about 10 p.m., Rafiq's daughter Shabana, who was holding her hand, felt it pull away. "Mum, if I have done something to upset you, tell me," Shabana said. That's when Rafiq turned her head to look at Shabana and said, "What have you done to upset me?" By the next morning, Rafiq was laughing and joking with visitors, and on October 2, she was well enough to go home. She apparently suffered no brain damage at all, but her doctors are at a loss to explain how that's even possible.

COOL CRITTERS

We never get tired of reading about strange members of the animal kingdom, and thanks to our BRI Science Guy, Thom Little, we never run out of reading material. Here are his latest finds.

HAVING A FRIEND FOR DINNER

Gray mouse lemurs live in forests on Madagascar, the Indian Ocean island that's home to all the world's wild lemurs. They are one of the world's tiniest primates, growing to just five inches long, and weighing only a few ounces. In May 2010, scientists on the island were following the signal of a radio-tagged adult female when they suddenly found her: She was dead...and being eaten by an adult male gray mouse lemur. The discovery shocked the scientists: Lemurs have never been observed eating the flesh of other mammals—they normally eat fruit, vegetation, and insects—let alone members of their own species. While cannibalism has been observed among primates, including chimpanzees and orangutans, all known victims of the practice were infants or juveniles—not adults. The scientists were unable to determine if the male had killed the female, and did not yet know whether cannibalism was common among gray mouse lemurs. (They also noted the only exception to the "Do not eat fellow adults!" rule among primate cannibals: There have been several known instances of adult humans eating other adult humans.)

THAT'S HOW WE ROLL

Dung beetles are a family of beetles found all over the world, so named because they eat animal feces. Many species are dung rollers: When one of the beetles comes across a pile of dung, it breaks off a chunk, rolls it into a ball larger than itself, and then rolls it away to either eat right away or bury for later. The odd thing is that these beetles—and they're nocturnal, meaning they do their rolling only at night—roll the dung in really straight lines, directly from the dung pile to the final eating destination. Scientists have surmised for some time that they do this in order to get as far away from the dung pile as quickly as possible, thereby avoiding other dung beetles that might try to steal their dung balls. What scientists didn't know

The Tour de France bike race began in 1903 as a publicity stunt staged by *L'Auto* newspaper.

is just how they manage to travel in such straight lines—even on very dark nights.

But now they have a pretty good idea. In January 2013, Marie Dacke of Sweden's Lund University published the results of a study in which she observed dung beetles inside a planetarium. On nights that the planetarium's ceiling displayed the sky as overcast—with no stars showing whatsoever—the beetles rolled their dung balls in looping, non-straight lines. On nights when the ceiling displayed a starry sky, they rolled very straight lines—which proved that dung beetles actually navigate by the stars. But Dacke went further: She studied the beetles on nights when the planetarium showed just the bright stripe of the Milky Way. Turns out the beetles rolled their dung balls in straight lines only on those nights, proving that dung beetles navigate not just by the stars—but by the Milky Way. Dacke's study is the first evidence ever recorded of any insect—and any animal, period—using the Milky Way to navigate. (Although Dacke says there are probably others, we just don't know about them...yet.)

IMPRESSIVE LEG-ACY

Illacme plenipes is an extremely rare species of millipede, first observed in 1928 by a pair of scientists who found seven of them in the Coast Range mountains, south of San Jose, California. The scientists wrote that they found the inch-long creatures "in a small valley on a northern slope wooded with oaks, under a rather large stone." The discovery was remarkable—at least for millipede scientists—because *Illacme plenipes* was the leggiest species ever encountered: Each individual had at least 600 legs, and one had 750—the most ever observed on a millipede. Those seven were the only *Illacme plenipes* ever seen until 2005, when East Carolina University Ph.D. student Paul Marek went to the Coast Range mountains and searched under some large stones on the northern slopes of valleys wooded with oak trees...and found *Illacme plenipes*. "I found it pretty quickly," he said later. Marek found several more over the next few years, and was able to make the first full scientific study of the creatures, which included taking samples of their DNA. "There's some repulsion to millipedes, but they're really quite gentle," Marek told the BBC. "None of them are predators; none of them feed on flesh or live animals. They're kind of like little cows of the arthropod world. They're gentle, slow, and pretty friendly in general."

Bonus: Marek's DNA research revealed that the closest genetic relative to *Illacme plenipes* is *Nematozonium filum*, a millipede species found only in South Africa. This indicates that the two species diverged from a single ancestor species hundreds of millions of years ago—when Earth's continents were still grouped together on the supercontinent known as Pangaea.

MOTHER NOSE BEST

Marine biologists have known since the 1980s that bottlenose dolphins in Shark Bay, Western Australia, have a unique tool-using activity: They place living sponges on their *rostrums*, or snouts, to protect those delicate snouts from sharp rocks and shells while foraging the ocean floor or reefs for food. What scientists couldn't figure out is why "sponging," as it's known, is practiced by only about five percent of Shark Bay's bottlenose population—and why almost all of them are females. Then in 2012, after studying the dolphins for several years, Dr. Anna Kopps of the University of New South Wales finally figured a few things out. For starters, sponging is a learned technique. Dolphin calves spend about four years with their mothers, and during that time their moms teach them how to find sponges, how to select the right ones, and how to affix them to their rostrums. Both male and female calves are taught the technique, but for reasons Kopps was unable to determine, mostly only females continue to use it into adulthood—males simply stop when they leave their mothers. Then, by studying the relationships among all the dolphins that used sponges, Kopps constructed a sponging family tree, of sorts. Using this information, along with some complicated computer models, Kopps concluded that sponging was "invented" by one female bottlenose dolphin in Shark Bay, probably about eight dolphin generations—or about 180 years—ago, and that the unique technique has been passed down by her descendants ever since. (One day, when many more generations have passed, perhaps all the females dolphins in Shark Bay will be spongers.)

*   *   *

WE'RE COLLEJE EDJUCATED!

In 2013, more than 1,400 graduates of Radford University in Virginia received their diplomas only to discover that the word *Virginia* was spelled "Virgina."

Pop art: More than 12 million paint-by-number kits were sold in the U.S. from 1951 to '54.

DUMB JOCKS

Sometimes what they say overshadows how they play.

"I don't want to shoot my mouth in my foot, but those are games we can win."

—**Sherman Douglas, NBA**

"The Yankees are only interested in one thing, and I don't know what that is."

—**Luis Polonia, Yankees**

"I would not be bothered if we lost every game, as long as we won the League."

—**Mark Viduka, soccer player**

"My career was sputtering until I did a 360 and got headed in the right direction."

—**Tracy McGrady, NBA**

"We're all idiots here. We all have fun. We all hug, kiss, grab, whatever."

—**David Ortiz, MLB**

"I'd like to play for an Italian club, like Barcelona."

—**Mark Draper, soccer player**

"He's one of the best power forwards of all time. I take my hands off to him."

—**Scottie Pippen, NBA, on Tim Duncan**

"It's a humbling thing being humble."

—**Maurice Clarett, NFL**

"I have two secret weapons: my legs, my arms, and my brain."

—**Michael Vick, NFL**

"What disappointed me was that we didn't play with any passion. I'm not disappointed, you know, just disappointed."

—**Kevin Keegan, soccer player**

"I got all five food groups—pancakes, Sausage-Egg McMuffin, cinnamon roll, large orange juice."

—**Chad Ochocinco, NFL**

"I'm the oldest I've ever been right now."

—**Tim Sylvia, pro wrestler**

"They should have focused more on me."

—**Sebastian Telfair, NBA, commenting on an ESPN documentary that was *about him***

"Winning doesn't really matter as long as you win."

—**Vinny Jones, soccer player**

SECOND TIME AROUND

Sometimes a musician will create lightning in a bottle and write and record a song that storms the charts. Other times, it takes a little time—or a lot of time—for that song to become a hit.

A LITTLE LESS CONVERSATION"

Take 1: In 1967, singer-songwriter Mac Davis and his writing partner, Billy Strange (a session guitarist with the famous "Wrecking Crew"), were hired to write songs for Elvis Presley to sing in his movies. Their tune "A Little Less Conversation" appeared in the 1968 movie *Live a Little, Love a Little*—one of the King's final movies—and reached #69 on the pop charts.

Take 2: Twenty-three years later, the song appeared on the soundtrack of the 2001 remake of *Ocean's Eleven*, as a definitive Las Vegas-type song. Dutch DJ Junkie XL heard the song and liked it, and then did a remix, adding in a thumping modern drum beat. The remixed version of "A Little Less Conversation" went to #1 in ten countries in 2002. (But not in America—it only made it to #50.)

"HELLO, IT'S ME"

Take 1: Todd Rundgren is one of rock's most prolific and influential producers, but he started his career as a performer. In 1968, he fronted a pop-rock band called Nazz. The group's first single was "Open My Eyes," with Rundgren's "Hello, It's Me" as the B-side. Boston radio station WMEX preferred the B-side and added it to their playlist, where it quickly became the station's most-played song. Few other stations were interested, although the success in Boston propelled it to #68 on the national chart.

Take 2: Rundgren left Nazz in 1970 to start a solo career. In 1972, he re-recorded "Hello, It's Me" as a slower, more soulful ballad for his album *Something/Anything?* It became a monster hit, reaching #5. It was the biggest hit Rundgren would ever have.

"PRETTY IN PINK "

Take 1: British New Wave band the Psychedelic Furs first recorded this song about a bewitching woman for their second album, 1981's *Talk Talk Talk*. The song stalled at #43 on the British charts and

---

According to the *Oxford English Dictionary*, the lawyer bird gets its name from its "large bill."

didn't get any airplay in the United States.

Take 2: American filmmaker John Hughes was a huge music fan, often helping to pick the songs on his movies' soundtracks. In 1986, he made a movie called *Pretty in Pink*, partially inspired by the obscure (to Americans) single by the Psychedelic Furs. The movie was a hit and so was the song, hitting #41 on the Billboard Hot 100 and introducing the group to mainstream American audiences.

"HERE I GO AGAIN"

Take 1: After splitting with his wife in 1981, ex-Deep Purple singer David Coverdale wrote this bluesy rock song about having to face life alone. It was included on his band's (Whitesnake) 1982 album *Saints 'N' Sinners*, but neither the album nor single were hits.

Take 2: In 1985, while recording another Whitesnake album, Coverdale came down with a sinus infection that made singing extremely painful. His six-month convalescence put the album behind schedule. In order to finish the album quickly, they re-recorded "Here I Go Again," but updated it to sound more radio-friendly, like the "hair metal" popular at the time—bands like Bon Jovi and Poison. It worked—the new version of "Here I Go Again" went to #1.

"HANKY PANKY"

Take 1: In 1959, Tommy Jackson formed a band in Niles, Michigan, called Tom and the Tornadoes. (Jackson was 12.) Five years later, they renamed the group the Shondells and recorded their first single, "Hanky Panky," an obscure song by New York songwriters Jeff Barry and Ellie Grenwich. Released by Snap Records, it was a hit in the upper midwest, but they couldn't get the song released nationally. In 1965, Jackson and the other Shondells graduated high school, and the band broke up.

Take 2: In late 1965, a DJ in Pennsylvania named Bob Mack found a copy of the record and started playing it at parties, where it got so popular that Pittsburgh radio stations started playing it, too. In April 1966, a Pittsburgh radio DJ tracked down Jackson and asked him to perform the song there. Jackson went. He had no band, but hired a local group called the Raconteurs, then changed his last name to "James," and sold the master for "Hanky Panky" to Roulette Records. Roulette released it nationwide and in July 1966, it went to #1.

There are six noble gases: Helium, neon, argon, xenon, radon, and krypton. What makes…

FITNESS FADS

Every few years, a new exercise craze sweeps the country.
Here's how a few of them got up and moving.

JAZZERCISE. Jazz choreographer Judi Sheppard Missett came up with the dance-meets-aerobics fitness program—fun routines set to pop music—in 1969 and opened a studio in Los Angeles. By 1977 she no longer taught classes. Instead, she taught instructors who wanted to lead their own classes around the country. She also appeared on TV talk shows, leading hosts such as Merv Griffin and Mike Douglas in Jazzercise routines. By 1984, classes were available in 50 states, as were Jazzercise-branded leotards, workout videos, records—and even a syndicated newspaper column penned by Missett. Think Jazzercise ended in the '80s? There are still 2,700 locations in the U.S., and it's a billion-dollar corporation.

TAE BO. As a teenager, Billy Blanks wanted to grow up to be a martial-arts champion like Bruce Lee. So he took karate and tae kwon do lessons. Based on those martial arts, in 1976, 22-year-old Blanks designed a workout for himself—high-impact aerobics set to fast music, with lots of punches and kicks. He called it "Tae Bo," a combination of "tae kwon do" and "boxing." He opened a studio in Boston in 1982, and it did so well, he opened one in Hollywood. In 1998, Blanks was approached to make a line of Tae Bo workout DVDs. Primarily through infomercials, more than $500 million worth of Tae Bo videos have sold worldwide.

CURVES. Gary Heavin ran a chain of gyms in Texas in the 1970s, but they went bankrupt. A few years later he started over, but this time he decided to focus on an untapped market: women in their 40s and 50s. Older customers had frequently told him that they didn't like gyms because they were intimidating, filled with ogling men, and younger women who were already fit. With his wife, Diane, Heavin opened the first Curves for Women in Harlingen, Texas, in 1992. Only women could join, and it offered only one fitness plan, created by Heavin: A customer rotates around exercise stations (treadmill, bike, stretches, weights), switching every 30 seconds. Three circuits equal a 30-minute workout. By 1998, there were 650 Curves locations; today, there are 10,000.

...them "noble"? They rarely interact with the other elements—and they don't smell.

LAME EXCUSES

When you're caught, you're caught. Best just 'fess up.
Or you could get creative…like these folks did.

L ame Excuse: "I tripped and fell in the lifeboat."
Said by: Francesco Schettino, 51, captain of the doomed
Italian cruise ship *Costa Concordia*
Story: At around dinnertime on January 13, 2012, Captain Schettino deliberately veered from the cruise liner's preprogrammed route
off the coast of Tuscany to get within a "stone's throw" of the island
of Giglio. Reason: So he could wave to his friend, a retired captain
who lived on the island. Schettino was on the phone with his friend
when the 952-foot, $569 million *Costa Concordia* hit a rock. The
ship lost power, drifted until it struck a reef, capsized, and partially
sank. Thirty-two people were killed.

By that time, however, Schettino was no longer onboard. When
Italian Port Authority discovered that fact, an officer scolded him
over the radio, "Get the [bleep] back on your ship!" Schettino said
he preferred to conduct the evacuation efforts from the shore. The
officer disagreed and reported the captain. Later, Schettino said
he'd wanted to stay on the ship, but "we were catapulted into the
water." That story fell apart when witnesses reported that Schettino
boarded a lifeboat from the deck while there were still hundreds
of people trying to escape. So he changed his story: "I was helping
some passengers put the boat to sea. The mechanism for lowering it
became blocked. We had to force it. Suddenly the system unblocked
itself, and I tripped and found myself inside the boat." None of
the passengers corroborated his story. Schettino was arrested and
charged with causing the disaster, interfering with rescue operations, and abandoning his ship.

Lame Excuse: "I was playing a practical joke on some friends and
broke into the wrong room."
Said by: Eric Sydnor Theorgood, 43, of Gulf Breeze, Florida
Story: In November 2012, at around 3:00 a.m., Theorgood put a
pillowcase over his head (with two eyeholes cut out), climbed up to
the second-floor balcony of a Quality Inn, entered through the open

Oysters, which can change gender at will, are more likely to become female as they age.

door, and started ransacking the room. The family that was staying in the room—a husband, wife, and toddler—woke up, and the husband "escorted" Theorgood back through the balcony door and over the railing. Theorgood was injured in the fall, but managed to run away. As he did so, he ditched the pillowcase. Investigators later found it and matched the blood stains to Theorgood's DNA (he'd been in trouble with the law before). After his face was displayed on the evening news, he called the police and said he had nothing to do with the break-in. "I wasn't even there!" When officers told him they'd found his blood at the scene, he suddenly remembered being there, but said it was just a practical joke on some friends who were staying in another room. When asked to provide the names of the friends, Theorgood's mind went blank. He was arrested.

Lame Excuse: "The Internet said all this stuff was free."
Said by: Charles Bull, a man in his mid-40s, of St. Paul, Minnesota
Story: One afternoon in May 2011, Bull and his wife, Pernella, rode their bikes to an upscale home, walked in the front door, and asked if anyone was home. No one answered, so they started putting items into duffel bags—including a laptop computer, a desktop computer, a full tool box, and a purse. However, someone was home: a mom who was upstairs putting her twin babies down for a nap. When she heard the commotion, she went downstairs to investigate. The Bulls ran out the back and tried escaping on their bikes, but the heavy duffel bags made it comically difficult. The homeowner yelled for help; one of her neighbors used his truck to block the burglars' escape route. When the police arrived, the Bulls claimed that a friend had told them this was a "free house" advertised on Craigslist: "The owners are moving, so everything's free." The homeowner had no idea what they were talking about, and police could find no "free house" listing on Craigslist for that address (or any other). The cops, not believing the Bulls' bull, put the Bulls in jail.

Lame Excuse: "I don't take performance-enhancing drugs to bulk up. They're for a medical condition."
Said by: Aging action star Sylvester Stallone
Story: Stallone flew to Australia in 2007 to promote his movie *Rocky Balboa* in which he played a 58-year-old boxer who goes 12 rounds against a heavyweight champion half his age. While

Stallone was at his hotel in Sydney, customs agents searched his plane and found 48 vials of Human Growth Hormones (HGH), which are banned in Australia. The agents then raided Sly's hotel room, only to find him throwing more vials out the window. Stallone said he didn't know HGH was banned. (So why throw it out the window?) His lawyer admitted the movie star was injecting himself with the hormone, but not to increase muscle mass. It was for a "medical condition." Stallone had been using HGH for six years "under medical supervision" from "doctors of the top-ranking order in the West Coast of the United States." But neither Stallone nor his lawyer could name the condition he was treating or any of the supervising doctors. Nor could they explain why Sly was using Jintropin, a "Chinese HGH that has not been approved by the U.S. Food and Drug Administration"—not likely to be prescribed by any "top-ranking" U.S. doctor. When asked why he had so much of the medicine with him, Stallone explained that when he left Australia he was going to Thailand for three months to film *Rambo*, a sequel to his earlier Rambo films—this time about a muscle-clad 60-year-old veteran who kills dozens of Burmese soldiers. (No reason Stallone would want to bulk up for that role, either.)

*　　*　　*

MMMPH! MMMPH! MMMPH!!!

In 2013, emergency services in Dunedin, New Zealand, received a call from a woman who could only communicate by mumbling. The dispatcher asked, "Do you live in Dunedin?" The caller replied, "Mmm-hmm." So the dispatcher started rattling off street names until finally the caller said, "MMM-HMM!" Then she gave her house number by tapping on her phone. Paramedics and police raced to the house, unsure if the caller had been kidnapped or injured. When they arrived, the woman ran out holding up a tube of superglue. She was rushed to the hospital, where doctors used paraffin oil to separate her lips. After she could talk again, the 64-year-old woman (who didn't want anyone knowing her name) explained, "I got into bed and I could feel this tingling on my lips, so I thought I'd get the cold-sore cream. I got out of bed, and I dived into the cupboard, and I couldn't smell it because I was blocked up. And then I got into bed and thought, 'What *have* I put on my mouth?'"

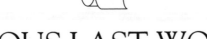

FAMOUS LAST WORDS

*Final utterances—some profound, some mundane,
and some nonsensical.*

"The sadness will last forever."
—**Vincent Van Gogh**

"It is good."
—**Immanuel Kant**

"I cannot."
—**Louis Pasteur**

"I'm going away tonight."
—**James Brown**

"On your way up, please take
me up. On your way down,
don't let me down."
—**Bob Marley**

"Don't be in such a hurry."
—**Billie Holiday**

"Don't die like I did."
—**soccer star George Best**

"My God. What happened?"
—**Princess Diana**

"Not any more."
—**Frederic Chopin**

"I'll sleep well tonight."
—**Henry Ford**

"Oh, wow. Oh, wow. Oh, wow."
—**Steve Jobs**

"I am dying. Please bring me a
toothpick."
—**author Alfred Jarry**

"I'd rather be skiing."
—**Stan Laurel**

"I'd like to have some milk.
Please, please give me some
more."
—**Michael Jackson**

"More light."
—**Johann Wolfgang
von Goethe**

"I have to set my pillows one
more night. When will this
end already?"
—**Washington Irving**

"I can't sleep."
—**J.M. Barrie**

"I do not believe in my death."
—**Salvador Dali**

"I just wish I had time for one
more bowl of chili."
—**Kit Carson**

THE GHILLIE AND THE MUNSHI

On page 237, we told you about Jean-Marie Loret, who claimed to be the secret son of an infamous historical figure. Here's a similar tale—this time involving a queen of England.

THE GHILLIE

In the years following the death of her husband in 1861, England's Queen Victoria developed a close relationship with one of her *ghillies*, or "outdoor servants," a Scotsman named John Brown. Whether their relationship ever grew beyond friendship has been debated ever since. Victoria and Brown slept in adjoining bedrooms, something the Foreign Secretary, the Earl of Derby, complained was "contrary to etiquette and even decency." The pair also spent time alone together at the queen's secluded "widow's cottage" on her estate in the Scottish Highlands.

Brown died in 1883 at the age of 56; Victoria survived him by eighteen years and died in 1901 at the age of 81. At her request, she was buried with personal mementos of Prince Albert and other departed loved ones…including John Brown: Victoria went to her reward wearing a ring Brown had given her and clutching his framed photograph in her left hand. (The photo was carefully hidden beneath flowers to avoid upsetting the family.)

Was the ring from John Brown a wedding ring? Rumors spread even during Victoria's lifetime that she'd married Brown in a secret ceremony and given birth to as many as three of his children, all of whom were shuffled off to the United States and France to live their lives in anonymity. There's also a story that some 80 years later, when one of Victoria's great-grandsons, Prince Henry of Hesse, was showing his paintings at an art exhibition in New York in the late 1940s, an elderly woman approached him, introducing herself as his relative "Jean Brown," daughter of Victoria and John Brown.

YOU BE THE JUDGE

The evidence supporting such claims is sketchy at best and relies on hearsay from persons long dead. The Liberal Party politician Lewis

---

The world's largest (non-polar) desert, the Sahara, is as big as the next 20 deserts combined.

Harcourt, for example, notes in his diary that the queen's chaplain, Norman Macleod, confessed on his deathbed to secretly marrying the queen and John Brown in the 1860s. But Harcourt heard the story third-hand: His father, a cabinet official, heard the story from the wife of Victoria's private secretary, and she heard it from Macleod's sister, who was at Macleod's bedside when he (supposedly) made his confession. Excerpts from Harcourt's diary were published in 2003.

UP IN SMOKE

In a 2012 article in *The Oldie* magazine, a British historian named John Julius Norwich claims that another historian, the late Sir Steven Runciman, actually stumbled across Victoria and John Brown's marriage certificate while doing research in the Royal Archives at Windsor Castle. So where is the marriage certificate now? According to Norwich, long gone. He says that Runciman told him that when he showed the marriage certificate to Elizabeth, the Queen Mother, she burned it on the spot to protect the royal family from scandal.

THE MUNSHI

Members of the royal household—and even Victoria's own children—were jealous of the close relationship that Victoria had with Brown, and when he died from a skin infection in 1883, they were not sorry to see him go. That probably made it all the more disturbing when the queen developed an attachment to another male servant just four years later in 1887. That year, Victoria celebrated her 50th year on the throne. To assist in the Golden Jubilee celebrations, two waiters were brought over from India to serve the Indian princes who were expected to visit England during the celebratory year.

Dashing young Abdul Karim was one of the waiters, but he didn't remain a waiter for long. The 24-year-old quickly graduated to preparing authentic Indian curry dishes for the queen, then to her *Munshi*, or "teacher," when Victoria expressed an interest in learning to speak the Hindi language. Victoria received private lessons from Karim in the evenings, and her surviving workbooks shed light on the flirtatious nature of the relationship between the 68-year-old monarch and her Munshi. "The Queen will miss the

"Typhoid Mary" Mallon was blamed for infecting 51 people with the disease. 3 died from it.

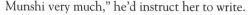

Munshi very much," he'd instruct her to write.

"Young Abdul (who is in fact no servant) teaches me and is a very strict Master, and a perfect Gentleman," the queen wrote to her daughter in 1888. Karim, a Muslim, also instructed Victoria on Indian affairs, and her representatives in India soon began to detect a pro-Muslim, anti-Hindu bias in her letters.

Victoria appointed Karim to the newly created post of Indian Clerk to the Queen and gave him his own carriage and footman. She set him up in his own cottages on each of the royal estates. At Balmoral in Scotland, no such cottage was available, so Victoria had "Karim Cottage" built there in his honor. To keep the Munshi from getting homesick, she allowed him to bring his wife and other relatives over from India to live with him. Victoria wrote him several times a day, signing her letters "your dearest mother" and "your closest friend," sometimes adding kisses. Victoria even invited him to stay with her—alone—in the same widow's cottage where she'd spent time alone with John Brown years before.

INTO THIN AIR

Given the age difference between Victoria and Abdul Karim, it's unlikely that their relationship was anything other than a maternal attachment. The queen's family and the royal household were nonetheless scandalized by her behavior; the fact that Karim was dark-skinned and a Muslim only made things worse.

There wasn't much that anyone could do while Victoria was alive, but when she died in 1901, her eldest son, King Edward VII, wasted no time in firing Karim and sending him back to India (where he lived out his life on an estate that Victoria had arranged for him to acquire years earlier). Before Karim left, royal guards ransacked his cottage and burned all the photos and letters from the queen that they could find. Then, when Karim died in India eight years later, the British viceroy (the ruler of India) forced Karim's widow to hand over what few personal mementos she had left. But she didn't give up Karim's diaries. Written on Windsor Palace stationery, they were carefully hidden and passed from one relative to another until 2011, when a family member gave them to Shrabani Basu, author of the 2010 book *Victoria and Abdul*. She plans to update her book based on the diaries.

PLEASE TOUCH
THE EXHIBITS

In 2001, Uncle John's older brother left the Bathroom Reader *and started a hands-on science museum called Science Works, right here in our little town of Ashland, Oregon. His inspiration: San Francisco's Exploratorium.*

BROTHERS IN ARMS
If you've ever been to a hands-on science museum and enjoyed the experience, you owe a debt of gratitude to famed nuclear physicist J. Robert Oppenheimer and his younger brother, Frank. Both Oppenheimers had been brilliant nuclear scientists, and both had worked on developing the atomic bomb during World War II. After the war ended, though, and Russia quickly turned from an ally into an enemy, the FBI began focusing on the brothers for their leftist politics. They discovered that in the 1930s, Frank Oppenheimer and his wife Jackie had briefly joined the Communist Party, which was neither illegal nor particularly unusual, at a time when the Communist Party USA had 75,000 members. In the 1932 presidential election, the Communist Party candidate received more than 100,000 votes.

The Oppenheimers had joined the Communist Party because it was the only large organization working to racially-integrate public facilities in their hometown, Pasadena, California, a policy they strongly supported. But after World War II, as Russia took the place of Germany as America's number-one enemy, anybody who had belonged to the party, even in the distant past, was considered a potential spy, saboteur, or traitor. In fact, you didn't even have to be a member, as Robert Oppenheimer soon found out.

GUILT BY ASSOCIATION
During his postwar work on the atomic bomb, Robert's strong personality, sophisticated manner, and knack at getting media attention generated some jealousy and enmity among some of his co-workers. The FBI was on the lookout for "disloyalty" in America's defense establishment and leaked information about the Oppenheimers to their enemies, who returned the favor by spreading ac-

---

Most pencils are made of wood from the Sierra Nevada incense cedar tree.

cusations and rumors. In 1953, Frank lost his security clearance for having been a communist two decades earlier. Shortly after, Robert was informed that he had also lost his security clearance, in large part because he associated with his brother and sister-in-law.

Robert Oppenheimer did all right in exile from his career, spending the following years writing and lecturing around the world. (In 1963, he would receive the Enrico Fermi Award from President Lyndon Johnson, partly as an apology for the way he had been treated two decades earlier.) His brother, however, did not do as well.

OUT, STANDING IN HIS FIELD

Frank Oppenheimer didn't have as many options as his better-known older brother. He was fired from the faculty of the University of Minnesota and figured he'd probably never work in his field again. So he decided it was time to make a dramatic career change, preferably in a place where his notoriety wouldn't block him. He had inherited a painting by Van Gogh titled *First Steps (after Millet)*, showing a baby being coaxed to walk in a garden bed by proud parents. Perhaps inspired by its rural charm and implicit message of starting anew, he sold it and bought land in Pagosa Springs, Colorado, determined to become a cattle rancher.

Only problem: He knew nothing about cattle ranching. He did, however, have confidence in his ability to learn. He began by reading journals and books and conferring with his new neighbors. He joined the local cattle association and quickly rose to president. By 1957, as his local reputation grew and the Red Scare lost some of its steam, he began teaching a science class at a nearby high school. Two years later, through the urging of some heavy hitters in the field, he was hired by the University of Colorado to teach physics.

HANDS ON

From working with his hands, Frank Oppenheimer had discovered the importance of direct experience to illustrate what would otherwise just be words on a page. He assembled a series of hands-on, out-of-the-classroom experiments for his students to perform in their free time. Many of the experimental devices and activities were not just informative, but playful and fun. Dr. Oppenheimer began discovering that more than just his students were dropping by to use the equipment: Art students, kids, even other faculty

---

Mapmakers often include "copyright traps," tiny pieces of incorrect information, in their maps.

members came by to bounce, spin, compress, race, and otherwise play with the learning tools.

This got Oppenheimer thinking. He became intrigued with the idea of making science education more interesting to younger kids. Thanks to a grant from the National Science Foundation, he developed 100 experiments that elementary-school teachers could use in teaching elementary physics. From the positive reaction to this "Library of Experiments," Oppenheimer, now in his 50s, moved to Sausalito, just across the Golden Gate from San Francisco, and began thinking about creating a new kind of science museum.

NOW MUSEUM, NOW YOU DON'T

The problem with most science museums, Oppenheimer decided, is that they glorified the accomplishments of a few instead of inspiring people to follow their curiosity and become scientists themselves. He already had a lot of toys, and he began hand-building new ones—interactive experiments that would be big, sturdy enough for many hands, attractive to the eyes and mind, and educational in the process. "Please touch" would be the watchword, a dramatic change from most museums' rules.

Then Oppenheimer got a lucky break. The city of San Francisco had a huge empty space it didn't know what to do with. It was the Palace of Fine Arts, a "temporary" building from the 1915 World's Fair that was intentionally left standing when the Fair's other buildings were destroyed because it was too beautiful to tear down. Unfortunately, it was also a white elephant: Now sitting in the middle of a residential neighborhood, it was far from the city's other attractions and had inadequate parking. Oppenheimer suggested turning it into a kids' science museum. City officials shrugged, said "Why not?" and leased the space to him for $1.00 per year.

COME SEE, CAME SAW

Dubbed the "Exploratorium," Oppenheimer's museum opened quietly in the summer of 1969. With little budget for publicity, it started slowly. Eventually, a few curious people dribbled in. The exhibits—including a crawl-through sensory adventure for adults only—were unlike anything they'd seen before and word of mouth took over. "The Exploratorium was not designed to glorify any-thing," explained Oppenheimer in 1972 as his new museum started making waves. "We have not built exhibits whose primary message is 'Wasn't somebody else clever?' or 'Hadn't someone done a great service to mankind and the American way of life?' Nor do we tell people what they are supposed to get out of a particular exhibit or make them feel silly or stupid because they enjoyed it in a way that was perhaps not intended."

In recent years, more than half a million visitors a year have visited the relatively remote location. In 2013, the museum moved to a huge new facility, three times bigger than its old location and on the tourist-friendly Embarcadero downtown. The move seemed overdue to some but a loss to others who loved the old facilities.

THE MAGIC OF WHICH CRAFT?

So, you may say, big deal: A lot of cities have kid-friendly, hands-on science museums. Precisely. The Exploratorium was the first, the prototype of the new museum format. It was a revolution, designed to affect and inspire other museums. Its founder freely gave information and advice to anyone who wanted to start a similar science museum; the Exploratorium workshop even built exhibits for them. Oppenheimer died in 1985, but his spirit lives on.

OUR FAVORITE EXPLORATORIUM EXHIBITS

• **Anti-gravity mirror:** It's a simple illusion but great for photo ops. A mirror next to a doorway, reflecting your right side as if it's also your left, making it possible to pose with both feet off the ground.

• **Refrigerator pump:** Hand-pump air under pressure into a copper coil that gets warm as you pump. Allow it to cool for a few seconds, and then release it into another coil that suddenly turns very cold. You've just learned how a refrigerator works.

• **Frozen droplets:** Set the timer on a high-speed camera and catch the different stages of a water droplet's splash.

• **Whisper projector:** Sit in a chair in a crowded room; have your friend sit in a chair on the other side of it. Talk softly into the parabolic dish behind each of you—your friend can hear every word.

• **Tornado:** Try standing in or next to an air-and-steam "tornado." Curious folks like trying out what happens when you blow bubbles, release balloons, or spin in the opposite direction.

YOU'RE MY INSPIRATION

More examples of the unusual places pop-culture architects get their ideas.

THE ONE RING. An ancient Roman gold ring was discovered on a farm in rural England in 1785. A stone tablet found at another site 140 years later curses a thief named Senicianus for stealing the ring from its owner, Silvianus. "Among those who bear the name of Senicianus," reads the inscription, "to none grant health until he bring back the ring to the temple of Nodens." One of the scholars who translated the tablet: Oxford professor J. R. R. Tolkien, who was a year away from beginning his seminal works revolving around a ring that curses its owner—*The Hobbit* and *The Lord of the Rings*.

MEGAN FROM BRIDESMAIDS. Melissa McCarthy partially modeled her raunchy character in the 2011 comedy on the Food Network's Guy Fieri—star of *Diners, Drive-ins, and Dives*. According to McCarthy, she even wanted to wear the celebrity chef's trademark spiky bleached hair and backward sunglasses, but producers told her, "You can't actually *be* Guy Fieri!"

THE VERY HUNGRY CATERPILLAR. In 1969, author Eric Carle was punching holes in some paper when he imagined a bookworm eating through a book. His publisher suggested a caterpillar instead. Good choice: The book has sold over 30 million copies.

"DUDE LOOKS LIKE A LADY." The 1987 Aerosmith song was born when Steven Tyler and the band were taking a break from a recording session. They were partying in a New York nightclub and spotted a "lady" at the end of the bar with an enormous head of blonde hair. When the "lady" turned around, it was Vince Neil, the singer from Mötley Crüe. They went back to the studio and finished a song called "Cruisin' with My Lady"…with new lyrics.

THE VOLLEYBALL. The only "companion" of Chuck Noland (Tom Hanks) during his four years spent on an island in 2000's *Cast Away* had a real-life counterpart: While researching for the film, writer William Broyles, Jr., spent a few days on an isolated beach with no one to talk to…until a volleyball washed up on shore.

The Hawaiian word *luau* originally referred to a cooked dish of taro leaves.

RAZZLE-DAZZLE CAMO

What does fly-fishing have to do with German U-boats? Read on.

GONE FISHING

During World War I, British ships belching smoke as they steamed across the seas were sitting ducks for the German U-boats lurking beneath the waves. In 1917, U-boats were sending 60 ships a week on a one-way plummet to Davy Jones's Locker. Norman Wilkinson, a lieutenant in the Royal Navy Volunteer Reserve, commanded a minesweeper in the English Channel. He knew two things really well: art (he was a well-known marine painter) and fly-fishing. The combination had taught him how to use color and shape to fool the eye. One day he had an idea: The British wanted to make ships invisible to U-boats. That was impossible. But a ship *could* be painted "in such a way as to break up her form and thus confuse a submarine officer as to the course on which she was heading."

EYE FOOLED U

Wilkinson proposed painting British ships with vivid colors and patterns to distort their shapes. U-boat gunners wouldn't be able to tell if a vessel was coming or going, traveling at a fast clip or slow, turning, or running straight. His team of model makers and painters created scale models to show camouflage possibilities, including stripes, swirls, and zigzags. Black-and-white designs were the most common, but blues, greens, reds, and oranges were also in the mix. The Navy gave Wilkinson's technique a name: dazzle painting.

When one captain objected to having his ship dazzled, a camouflage officer replied, "The object of camouflage is not, as you suggest, to turn your ship into an imitation of a West African parrot, a rainbow in a naval pantomime or a gay woman. The object is to give the impression that your head is where your stern is." And it did. A skipper who spotted the razzle-dazzled *HMS Ebro* said the vessel seemed to alter her course repeatedly. Even after passing the ship, he couldn't tell which way she was heading. Dazzle worked so well it showed up again during WWII—this time to thwart kamikazes as well as U-boat captains. A mere 8° difference was all it took to turn a torpedo hit into a miss, and a miss was...way better than sinking.

The world's oldest horse, Shayne, 51, and the oldest dog, Pip, 24, lived in the same town.

30 ROCK...STARRING JON HAMM

*Some actors are so closely associated with a specific role
or TV series that it's hard to imagine he or she wasn't
the first choice. But it happens all the time.*

THE OFFICE. Now best known for playing lawyer "Better call Saul" Goodman on *Breaking Bad*, comic actor Bob Odenkirk auditioned for the lead role of clueless boss Michael Scott on *The Office*. He didn't get the part (Steve Carell did), but he did guest star in 2012 as a very Michael Scott-like boss of a company where another character takes an interview.

THE SHIELD. According to the show's creator, Shawn Ryan, FX executives wanted him to cast Eric Stoltz in the lead role of corrupt cop Vic Mackey. Ryan wanted Michael Chiklis, and eventually got his way.

BUFFY THE VAMPIRE SLAYER. Katie Holmes was originally cast in the lead role, and Sarah Michelle Gellar was given the role of Buffy's snooty rival, Cordelia. But then Holmes decided she wanted to finish high school, and she backed out of the part, which went to Gellar. (Holmes finished school and was cast in *Dawson's Creek* a year later.)

30 ROCK. Tina Fey says in her memoir, *Bossypants*, that she wrote the part of NBC executive Jack Donaghy with her frequent *SNL* collaborator Alec Baldwin in mind, but the network still held auditions. They almost gave the part to an unknown actor named Jon Hamm, who would later gain fame as the star of *Mad Men*. Hamm had a recurring role on *30 Rock* as one of Liz Lemon's (Fey's) boyfriends.

MODERN FAMILY. In 2009, TV veteran Craig T. Nelson (*Coach*) was offered two prominent but similar roles—the patriarch of a large family on *Modern Family*, or the patriarch of a large family on *Parenthood*. He picked *Parenthood* (Ed O'Neill landed *Family*). Reason: bigger paycheck. "I really wanted to do *Modern Family*, and

I really liked the people," he told *Access Hollywood* in 2011. "But we're in the middle of a cutback in Hollywood, and salaries have gone way down, and I just felt disrespected."

DOWNTON ABBEY. After *The X-Files* ended its long run in 2002, the show's star, Gillian Anderson, appeared in a number of British TV adaptations of classic literature, including *Bleak House* and *Great Expectations*. While promoting the latter in 2012, she told *TV Guide* that she'd been offered the role of Lady Cora on the hugely successful British series *Downton Abbey*. After Anderson turned it down, Elizabeth McGovern got the part.

DOCTOR WHO. The long-running British sci-fi series is unique because the title character is an alien, and he can "regenerate" every so often, allowing a new actor to step into the role. Producers usually go with relatively unknown actors, but when the series returned in 2005 after a 16-year absence, they asked Hugh Grant to play the Doctor. He turned them down, thinking the show was going to be like it was in the '80s—cheesy. Instead, it was a big-budget, critically-acclaimed production (starring Christopher Eccelston). Grant has since publicly regretted giving up the chance.

CSI. After Laurence Fishburne left the crime show in 2011, producers had to find a high-profile replacement. They got former *Cheers* star Ted Danson to play the role of criminal investigator D. B. Russell, but he wasn't their first choice. Robin Williams, Tony Shalhoub (*Monk*), and John Lithgow had all said no.

BAYWATCH. When the show about bathing-suit-clad lifeguards was greenlighted by NBC in 1989, producers went after Tom Selleck for the lead role of Mitch Buchannon. Selleck had become famous as the star of *Magnum, P.I.*, which ended in 1988, and he turned down *Baywatch* because he didn't want to be typecast as a sex symbol. (David Hasselhoff didn't have that concern and took the role.)

THE COSBY SHOW. Just before the pilot was shot in 1984, producers gathered the children and teenagers in the cast to an office to sign their contracts. One of the teenagers was singer Whitney Houston, who'd been given the role of Sondra, the oldest Huxtable sibling. With pen in hand, Houston changed her mind and backed out of the show, realizing that a full-time TV gig would take too much time away from her real ambition—to be a singer.

SPAM's mascot during WWII: Slammin' Spammy, a bomb-throwing pig.

TOILET TECH

Better living through bathroom technology.

BRIGHT IDEA
Product: The Night Glow Toilet Seat
How It Works: It's a toilet seat that glows in the dark all night long, without needing to be recharged by exposure to a light source. When Canadian inventor Tim Fittler created his first glow-in-the-dark toilet seat in 2003, the glow only lasted 60 to 90 minutes, and the product was little more than a novelty item. Even so, he sold more than 50,000 of the seats. Since then, improvements in "glow-resin technology" have made it possible for Fittler to manufacture seats that glow as bright as night lights for 8 to 10 hours after being exposed to light for just 15 minutes. The new seats, which retail for $49.99, eliminate the need to turn on the bathroom light—saving electricity and making nocturnal pit stops easier on sensitive eyes that have grown used to the dark.

NOW YOU SEE IT...
Product: The Séura Enhanced Bathroom Mirror
How It Works: The "enhancement" is an LCD TV screen hidden behind the mirror's surface. The TV is visible only when it's on; the rest of the time it looks like an ordinary bathroom mirror, allowing you to watch TV in the bathroom without looking like the kind of person who watches TV in the bathroom. The device offers "a discreet and elegant way to bring information and entertainment into your personal spaces without clutter or disruption," says Séura. The only drawback: At a cost of $2,899 (plus installation), when the TV screen disappears, a lot of your money is going to vanish with it.

KID STUFF
Product: The iPotty for iPad
How It Works: It's a potty seat with a built in iPad holder, so that kids who are learning how to use the toilet have something to keep them busy as they develop "business" skills. The iPotty comes with a removable inner bowl, making cleanup easy. It also comes with a plastic cover to protect the iPad, plus a male "pee guard" to reduce

---

Paris has about 20,000 restaurants. New York has 23,000. Tokyo: 160,000.

the chance that your little boy will whiz your $500 tablet right into the scrap heap. The threat to your consumer electronics aside, not everyone thinks the iPotty will aid potty training: "It's going to be distracting when the kid should be concentrating on pooping," one skeptical mother of a 9-month-old girl told the *New York Daily News*. "The iPad should be a reward for *after* you do your business."

FLUSHBOOK

Product: The iPoo App

How It Works: If you're one of the growing number of smartphone owners who use the device while answering nature's call (and you have no class whatsoever), this app is for you. "When you open iPoo on your iPhone, you're instantly connected with other users who are also taking a dump," says a press release from the app's creator, CeilingHouse. "You can see and create messages, and drawings using our virtual stalls, the 'poo stream'—photos, drawings and ramblings from pooers around the world—or even map view, which will allow you to see on a map everyone who's currently on the can!" Price: only 99¢. As of June 2012, nearly 300,000 iPhone users had downloaded iPoo onto their phones. (The iTunes store stopped selling the app a few months later.)

THE WET LOOK

Product: The iSteam App

How It Works: If you're looking for a bathroom-themed app, but the thought of "logging on" to iPoo is more than you can bear, iSteam may be the kinder, gentler app you're looking for. It fogs up the screen of your iPhone, iTouch, or iPad with virtual steam, just like a bathroom mirror fogs up when you take a shower. If you leave the phone alone for a while, "droplets" form and drip down the screen; drag your finger across the screen, and you can write or draw shapes just like you would on a steamy mirror—complete with a finger-squeaking sound effect. This $1.50 app may not sound like much, but when it was released at the end of 2008, more than a million people downloaded it in the first two weeks, making it the most popular novelty app in the iTunes store.

*   *   *

"Hermits have no peer pressure." —**Steven Wright**

ATM VS. ABM

The U.S. and Canada have the English language in common...or do they?

U.S.: Tennis shoes or sneakers
Canada: Runners

U.S.: Parking garage
Canada: Parkade

U.S.: Rubber bands
Canada: Elastics

U.S.: Candy bar
Canada: Chocolate bar

U.S.: "McMansion," slang for huge generic suburban homes
Canada: Monster house

U.S.: Sled
Canada: Toboggan

U.S.: Flip-flops
Canada: Thongs

U.S.: a fifth of alcohol—about 1/5 of a gallon, or 26 ounces
Canada: a "2-6" or "twenty-sixer"—about 26 ounces.

U.S.: Strippers
Canada: Rippers or peelers

U.S.: Elephant ear (the treat made of fried dough sprinkled with sugar and cinnamon)
Canada: Beaver tail

U.S.: Fire station
Canada: Fire hall

U.S.: Dorm (for dormitory)
Canada: Rez (for residence hall)

U.S.: Garbage disposal
Canada: Garburator

U.S.: Faucet
Canada: Tap

U.S.: Dumpster
Canada: BFI bin

U.S.: ATM (automated teller machine)
Canada: ABM (automated bank machine)

U.S.: Hoodie
Canada: Bunny hug

U.S.: Pond
Canada: Slough

U.S.: Whole wheat bread
Canada: Brown bread

U.S.: Throw or hurl
Canada: Huck

U.S.: Colored pencil
Canada: Pencil crayon

U.S.: Restroom
Canada: Washroom
(But it's really a "bathroom.")

Early American Easter treat: a cookie in the shape of a rabbit laying an egg.

"WHAT A HANDLE THAT RAMO OBAMACARE"

The ingredients for one of the funniest wordplay screw-ups of all-time:
A politician, a foreign language, and a confused computer program.

THE RUBIO RESPONSE
After President Obama's 2013 State of the Union address, the Republican response was delivered by Senator Marco Rubio of Florida, first in English and then in Spanish. The website *ABCNews.com* streamed the Spanish speech with English subtitles, but the network goofed: Instead of translating Spanish into English, the computer program "thought" the words already were in English, so it attempted to transcribe them phonetically (like normal Closed-Captioned programs do). Result: Rubio's speech became entirely unrecognizable (but pretty humorous) in those subtitles. It would take about eight incomprehensible pages to print the whole thing, so we'll just share a few excerpts.

"When an auction said Michael. Mr. into in the field were severely dollar and authorities and its analysis thousands. Carefully to that a President Obama political assume among not."

"I'm at the body in the homeless in August to pay thugs and be… and asked what's the Hamas you've got the April not because I was of them. I'll get paneling and soaps."

"Caledonia owns him but…and wonder what about the…democratic them psyche in the Palestinians. Have Christiane."

"He get dole said Romano didn't that it shall dollop of deals are you out-of-town labels on so stunning to speak how the… On the bottom of my adios to felony insists. The outer space."

"I'm being economic Dodi Christiane."

"That put us in slopes this young dumb and Donovan whipple's. If I had the muscles."

Supernumerary rainbow is the scientific term for a double (or triple, or more) rainbow.

"Are you out of all of us anything…we'll…at what went to the Initiated…novels but the host of the John F. Kennedy out Ronald Reagan on a policy effect on me and an even race."

"What a handle that Ramo Obamacare but also what they did out of percent of the classic mania Upton and…will make. But our ugly episode I."

"Yak Obamacare and Opel also picked EC opponent but…modesty when dampen…our troubled southern but it's not on the ground."

"Ethical been laughing philosopher said sociopath that we got fined them…vehicle that I William. But…as a puppet the only…with an acoustical ceiling. In…yet I don't know whether completes a popular things yet."

"I eat up our hot product by adults when that's."

"And processing empathy and pick them…on the supply and…get a proper animal fecal. Up on the supply."

"Second daddy and me and him are fascinating."

"The other thing that I despite explode out of my sanity informants live. He can be and then we'll have about a real possibilities but Pakistan that's when out—the esophagus and beautiful."

"Yes I'm an awkward that the proceeded to get available that can seat and threatened with what the fact."

"Out but I development hornets in my body on the professor and out of him on the yes in Latin upon to Mrs. O'Donnell assumed."

"But nobody opening compliments on that bus oh deficit would have a microphone that…yet gotten to place."

"The felonies and they'll wait postal facilities…trying."

At the end of the speech, these words appeared on the screen: "This transcript has been automatically generated and may not be 100% accurate."

In 1899, inventor Nicola Tesla made an artificial lightning bolt 130 ft. long, still a world record.

TIMELINE OF TIFFANY'S

*You've heard the name hundreds of times over the years—and
you've seen their designs in a lot more places than you realize.
Here's the story behind what is probably the world's most
famous name in jewelry, silverware...and a lot more.*

1837: Charles Lewis Tiffany, 25, borrows $1,000 from his father, owner of a Connecticut cotton-manufacturing company, and with school friend John B. Young, opens a store at 259 Broadway in New York City, called "Tiffany & Young." They sell "stationary and fancy goods," which includes silverware, and exotic items from Europe and Asia, most of it found by Tiffany himself scouring the city's docks and shops. First week's profits: 33¢.

1841: Struggling, Tiffany brings in Mr. J.L. Ellis as a partner, and the store becomes "Tiffany, Young, & Ellis." They begin focusing on fine silver and jewelry—mostly costume jewelry.

1845: The first "Blue Book" catalogue is issued. The name comes from the color of the cover, a robin's-egg blue chosen by Charles Tiffany, now known as "Tiffany blue." It has been the store's signature color ever since, best known in the "blue boxes" used to package items sold in Tiffany stores.

1848: King Louis-Philippe is overthrown in France's "February Revolution." Fleeing nobles desperate for cash sell off their jewels—especially diamonds—and Tiffany, sensing an opportunity, scoops them up. Tiffany's is now officially in the diamond business.

1851: John C. Moore, New York's most prominent silversmith, agrees to work solely for Tiffany's. Moore's son, Edward C. Moore, soon takes over. He will become Tiffany's chief designer and one of the most renowned art designers of the 19th century.

1853: Young and Ellis resign. Charles Tiffany takes sole control and changes name to Tiffany & Co. Tiffany's goods are now "must have" items among America's growing number of millionaires.

1861: President-elect Abraham Lincoln commissions a seed pearl bracelet, earrings, necklace and brooch to give to Mary Todd Lincoln for his Inaugural Ball. (In the 2012 film *Lincoln*, Sally Field, playing Mary Todd Lincoln, wore replicas of these items.)

1867: Tiffany silver works (designed by Edward C. Moore) win the Award of Merit at the Paris Exposition Universelle—the first time an American company has won the award. Tiffany's now adds European royalty to its list of clientele.

1877: The New York City Police Department asks Tiffany's to design a medal in honor of Officer John McDowell, who survived being shot in the head while attempting to arrest a burglar. Today, you know the stylized "NY" on the medal as the logo of the New York Yankees baseball team. (They adopted it in 1903—when they were the "New York Highlanders.")

1879: Tiffany pays $18,000 for the largest yellow diamond ever found to date. Discovered in South Africa, it weighs 287 carats (just over two ounces). Tiffany's gemologist George Frederick Kunz spends a year studying the stone before cutting it down to 128.54 carats in a "cushion" shape with 80 facets. Dubbed the "Tiffany Diamond," it is one of the best-known diamonds in history and has been worn in public only a couple of times.

1881: Louis Comfort Tiffany, son of Charles (born in 1848) and one of the world's most renowned designers in his own right, is hired by Mark Twain to design the interior of his Hartford, Connecticut, home. A year later President Chester Arthur hires him to redecorate the White House. Through Louis C. Tiffany and Company, Associated Artists and the Tiffany Glass Company, he will become known for his work in decorative glass, ceramics, mosaics, stained-glass windows, and jewelry.

1885: Tiffany & Co. revises the U.S. Great Seal—which can still be seen on the one-dollar bill today.

1902: Charles Tiffany dies. In his 65 years as the head of Tiffany's, he has turned his father's $1,000 loan into a fortune estimated to be worth around $35 million. Louis Comfort Tiffany takes over as the company's first Design Director.

1929: The Stock Market Crash sees the beginning of a long period of decline for Tiffany & Co.

1940: The store spends $2.5 million on a new headquarters: a seven-story building on the corner of Fifth Avenue and 57th Street in Manhattan. It remains Tiffany's flagship store today. (It was the first fully air-conditioned building in New York City.)

1955: Tiffany's leaves the Tiffany family. The store is sold to the Hoving Corporation. CEO Walter Hoving holds the first sale in the store's history to get rid of stock he deems inferior. Over the next decade, he returns the store to its former stature.

1961: Audrey Hepburn stars in the film version of Truman Capote's 1958 novella, *Breakfast at Tiffany's*. It is a movie classic and, while not about Tiffany's per se, the title and the fact that the film opens with Hepburn's character window shopping at the store's famous Fifth Avenue location, makes it one the biggest free advertising campaigns in history and helps revive and secure the Tiffany reputation. Walter Hoving even allowed Hepburn to become one of only a few people in history to wear the Tiffany Diamond, when he let her wear it (set into a necklace) for the film's publicity posters.

1967: Tiffany's is commissioned by the National Football League to design the Vince Lombardi Trophy—still given every year to the winners of the Super Bowl. (Over the years, Tiffany's has also made the trophies for the winners of Baseball's World Series, the NBA Finals, and NASCAR's Sprint Cup.)

1979: Avon Products Inc. buys Tiffany's for $104 million. They sell it five years later to a group of investors for $135.5 million.

2012: To mark the company's 175th anniversary, the Tiffany Diamond is set in a necklace surrounded by white diamonds and taken on a world-display tour. Afterward, it is returned to its permanent home—on the Main Floor of Tiffany's Fifth Avenue store.

2013: Tiffany & Co. today has more than 250 stores around the world, the Blue Book is mailed every year to about 15 million subscribers, and the company is worth an astonishing $8.7 billion.

FINAL NOTE: On July 15, 1685, Squire Humphrey Tiffany was traveling by horse from Swansea to Boston in the Massachusetts Bay Colony when, according to records from the time, he was struck by lightning and killed. Squire Humphrey, who had emigrated from England in 1660, left behind a wife and six children and was the great-great-great-great grandfather of Charles Lewis Tiffany.

THAT MOVIE REALLY *DID* STINK

Hollywood has produced a lot of bad movies over the years, but most of the time when we say we saw a real "stinker," we don't mean it literally. Most of the time. Behold the wonder of Smell-O-Vison.

DOCTOR NO(SE)

Dr. Hans Laube was a Swiss inventor who designed machinery that removed stale, bad-smelling air from theaters and auditoriums in the late 1930s. Or at least that's what he did until it dawned on him that it should also be possible to reverse the process and inject pleasing odors into large enclosed spaces. Not long after that, he developed a system that piped artificial scents through a network of tubes to the back of every individual seat in a movie theater, releasing them into the air just a few feet away from the nose of every person in the audience.

Laube called his invention "Scentovision." To demonstrate it, he produced a 35-minute film that he called *Mein Traum*, or "My Dream," and presented it at the 1939 World's Fair in New York. *Mein Traum*'s scenes were timed to Scentovision's smells: When roses appeared on-screen, the projectionist manually released the scent of rose oil into the theater; in other scenes, viewers were treated to snootfuls of peaches, burning incense, frying bacon, fresh-cut hay, and hot tar.

FATHER AND SON

Laube hoped to interest theater owners in outfitting their movie houses with Scentovision, but there were no takers. A decade after the stock market crash of 1929, the United States was still mired in the Great Depression, and theater owners had their hands full just keeping their doors open. Scentovision faded away and remained forgotten for nearly 20 years.

That it re-emerged at all was thanks to Broadway producer Mike Todd Sr. and his son, Mike Jr. The two of them had attended a screening of *Mein Traum* at the World's Fair in 1939. When the elder Todd branched out into motion pictures in the 1950s, he

---

World's largest religious bldg: Angkor Wat in Cambodia, made of 5 million tons of sandstone.

remembered Scentovision and was intrigued by the idea of making Hollywood's first "smellies." But he died in a plane crash in 1958 before he could bring his plans to fruition. (Does his name sound familiar? Todd was Elizabeth Taylor's third husband.)

BY ANY OTHER NAME

Mike Jr. took over the reins after his father's death and hired Hans Laube to come up with an improved version of Scentovision.

Laube's original system had relied on projectionists to release the smells in the proper order at the proper times. To eliminate human error, he came up with something he called a "Smell Brain" to release the odors automatically: Bottles containing the scents were loaded into a rotating drum in the order that they were to be released into the theater. A "smell track" similar to a soundtrack used electromagnetic cues to tell the Smell Brain when to release each scent. As soon as one was discharged, the drum advanced the next bottle into position to await the next electromagnetic cue. Puffs of fresh air and even chemical deodorants could be released into the theater between smells to act as nasal palate cleansers.

Todd insisted on one more improvement: Laube's invention had to be renamed. Convinced that the nickname "smell-o-vision" was inevitable, he wanted "to get the jump on those who will call it that anyway," and Scentovision became Smell-O-Vision. The new name wasn't nearly as classy as the old one, but so what? "I don't understand how you can be 'dignified' about a process that injects smells into a theater," Todd said.

LIGHTS, CAMERA, AROMA!

While Laube perfected Smell-O-Vision, Todd set to work on producing a light-hearted chase film called *Scent of Mystery* to show it off. He told screenwriter William Roos to put "smell-action" into as many scenes as possible. Roos delivered: *Scent of Mystery* had 40 different scent scenes, an average of one smell every three minutes.

Scent of Mystery starred British actor Denholm Elliott. (You may remember him for playing Dr. Marcus Brody in *Raiders of the Lost Ark*.) In the film, Elliott plays a mystery novelist who's vacationing in Spain. There he sees a mystery woman, identified only by the smell of her perfume, nearly run down by a truck driven by an unseen man smoking a smelly pipe. When Elliott learns that the "accident" was actually a murder attempt, he and a boozy cab driver, played by Peter Lorre, set off to find the mystery woman and warn her of the danger.

SOMETHING TO SNIFF AT

Some of the smells in the movie, such as shoe polish, hot chocolate, and freshly baked bread, were little more than background smells that had nothing to do with the story. But others were instrumental in advancing the plot. The audience learns that Peter Lorre's character is a drunk, for example, by means of a "scent gag": When he and Elliott are drinking coffee in one scene, Lorre takes a sip from his mug and the theater fills with the smell of brandy. Later, when Lorre and Elliott are on the trail of the wrong woman, they (and the audience) learn as much by getting a whiff of her perfume, which is the wrong scent. When the audience finally does get a whiff of the correct perfume—the "Scent of Mystery"—they know that the mystery woman (played by Elizabeth Taylor, in a short, non-speaking cameo) has been found. At the end of the film, a second whiff of the pipe tobacco smoked by the truck driver reveals the identity of the man who tried to kill Taylor.

STINKO

Scent of Mystery opened in January 1960 in New York, Chicago, and Los Angeles in theaters that had been specially fitted for Smell-O-Vision. If the film proved successful, Todd hoped to install the system in a hundred theaters around the world. Who knows? If it had been a success, we might be smelling *Star Wars*, *Pirates of the Caribbean*, and *The Hobbit* today.

But *Scent of Mystery* wasn't a success—it laid a smelly rotten egg at the box office. An odorless version called *Holiday in Spain* also bombed. The movie itself was a big part of the problem. The acting was terrible, and even Peter Lorre, the film's biggest star after Liz Taylor (who only appears on-screen for a few seconds), gave a listless performance after he nearly died from sunstroke while filming on location in Spain in the heat of summer.

The film's budget was so tight that when some scenes were accidentally filmed out of focus and others were shot using a malfunctioning camera, there was no money to re-shoot the scenes, and the ruined footage ended up in the movie anyway. These and other problems made a dull and dreary mess out of what could have been a fascinating cinematic experience.

BREATHLESS

As bad as *Scent of Mystery* was in its own right, the addition of Smell-O-Vision made it even worse. For all the improvements Dr. Laube had made to his system, it was still plagued with problems, not least of which were the scents themselves. Director Jack Cardiff commented that they smelled "exactly like cheap eau de cologne."

The delivery system was another problem. In Los Angeles, the smells took so long to get to the seats in the balcony—where they were accompanied by an annoying hissing sound—that they were out of sync with the film. In New York, the smells were so faint, complained *New York Times* film critic Bosley Crowther, that "patrons sit there sniffling and snuffling like a lot of bird dogs, trying hard to catch the scent."

The worst problem of all was the fact that Smell-O-Vision relied on the theaters' existing ventilation system to remove the smells once they'd been pumped in. The equipment wasn't up to the task, and as the smells accumulated, they combined into a single over-powering stench that many found nauseating. "Customers will probably agree that the smell they liked best was the one they got during the intermission: fresh air," *Time* magazine observed.

SILENT BUT DEADLY

Scent of Mystery completed its three-theater run and then faded quietly into history like a bad smell that nobody wanted to own up to. Its failure took Smell-O-Vision down with it, and no film was made using Hans Laube's technology again. *Scent of Mystery* has never been released on DVD.

Mike Todd gave up on "smellies" after *Scent of Mystery* flopped, and took on another project that, in its own way, stank even worse: He produced "America Be Seated," an interracial minstrel show for the 1964 New York World's Fair. It closed after two performances. He didn't produce another movie until 1979, when he brought the popular novel *The Bell Jar* to the big screen. That bombed, too. (At least this time it wasn't a stink bomb.) Todd never produced another film. He died in 2002 at the age of 72.

THREE MORE STINKERS

• **Behind the Great Wall (1959).** A few months before *Scent of Mystery* stank up theaters in 1960, a film distributor named Walter Reade, Jr. bought the U.S. rights to *Behind the Great Wall*, an Italian documentary about a trip through China, and added "seventy-two smells from the Orient," including dirt, wild grasses, firecrackers, horse manure, and burning incense. He also tacked on an opening demonstration scene that featured a man slicing an orange. Reade's "Aromarama" process consisted of little more than dumping industrial perfumes—like the kind used to make vinyl smell "like real leather"—into theater air-conditioning systems. Bad idea: The scents combined with the Freon in the air conditioner to create a smell that one critic likened to "a subway restroom on disinfectant day." (Uncle John saw *Behind the Great Wall* as a kid and can smell the horse manure and orange slices to this day.)

• **Polyester (1981).** Audiences of this John Waters film were given "Odorama" scratch-and-sniff cards that had circles numbered from one to ten. When a number appeared on-screen, the audiences were supposed to scratch the corresponding circle. The smells included airplane glue, gasoline, new-car smell, dirty socks, and poop. (Waters says he loved the idea of his movie fans "paying to smell $#*!") *Rugrats Go Wild* (2003) and *Spy Kids 4* (2011) also used scratch-and-sniff cards in theaters.

• **The New World (2005).** The Japanese distributor of this Hollywood movie collaborated with telecommunications giant NTT to pipe smells into theaters, as part of a promotion for NTT's line of smell-generating machines for the home. Instead of aiming for realism, like pumping in tobacco smells when a pipe is smoked on-screen, the film's "aroma coordinator" used abstract scents to establish mood: Peppermint and rosemary underscored sad scenes, orange and grapefruit accentuated happy ones, and herbs and eucalyptus were released during angry scenes. The smell generators were located in the back of the theater, and only the last three rows were designated "Premium Aroma Seats." Film critic Chris Fujiwara sat in one; he said the experience was "like watching a movie while an aromatherapy clinic was being held in the lobby."

Think Smell-O-Vision is gone for good? Think again. For a look at what may be just around the corner, turn to page 47.

THIS IS *JEOPARDY!*, PT. 2

Real 1960s and '70s Double Jeopardy! questions. (Answers on page 540.)

Myth and Legend	Politics	World Geography	Colleges	Science
$20 Gorgons, hydras, chimeras, etc.	**$20** Paulette Javits is the first girl to have this job.	**$20** Country whose provinces include Cordoba and LaPampa	**$20** Of Cal. Tech, Carnegie Tech, and M.I.T., school with largest endowment	**$20** A substance takes this in when it burns.
$40 Lofty mountain in Thessaly. It was 10,000 ft. high.	**$40** State represented by Wilbur Mills	**$40** In German, this country's name is Oesterreich, or "Eastern Realm."	**$40** Religious affiliation of Creighton	**$40** On Nov. 18, 1969, these additives were put on HEW blacklist.
$60 In Arthurian legend, daughter of Leodegraunce, King of Camelyard.	**$60** Mayor defeated in California governor primary	**$60** These two countries share the Maritime Alps.	**$60** This Mormon U's enrollment ranks 25th in the U.S.	**$60** Animal used for recent electrode brain implantation
$80 Greek equivalent of victory goddess	**$80** Ex-Secretary of Labor who became director of Office of Management and Budget	**$80** Bordered by Niger, Mali, and Morocco	**$80** In *Goodbye, Columbus,* the school attended by Ron Potemkin	**$80** Field of study for one who received a C.H.E. degree
$100 Celestial light brought about by brilliance of armor of Valkyries	**$100** *Unbought and Unbossed* is title of this Congresswoman's biography	**$100** Baluchistan, Sind, and East Bengal are regions in this country.	**$100** University founded in 1890 by J.D. Rockefeller	**$100** Nationality of discoverers of thermodynamics and X-rays

---

THE BRITISH ARE COMING!, PART III

More stories about English bands who rode the Beatles' coattails and helped conquer North America. (Part II is on page 211.)

THE SWINGING BLUE JEANS

Formed in 1956 as a skiffle group—a British style that's a little bit jazz, a little bit blues—the band had to change their name from the Blue Genes to the Swinging Blue Jeans to avoid being confused with the American rock 'n' roll band Gene Vincent and His Blue Caps. By the early '60s, the Swinging Blue Jeans were playing in Hamburg, too, with the Beatles as their opening act. The Swinging Blue Jeans had only one top-40 hit in the U.S., but it was the very memorable "Hippy Hippy Shake." It reached #24 on the American charts in late 1963—technically before the British Invasion, which is considered to have begun with the Beatles' TV appearances on the *Ed Sullivan Show* in February 1964. The Swinging Blue Jeans continued to release fairly popular singles in the U.K. and U.S. throughout the decade, such as "You're No Good" (#97) and a cover of Little Richard's "Good Golly, Miss Molly" (#43). The band parted ways in 1967. Guitarist and singer Terry Sylvester found a new job a year later. Graham Nash had left the Hollies, so that band hired Sylvester to be their new singer-guitarist.

THE DAVE CLARK FIVE

In a rare instance for eponymous bands, Dave Clark isn't the singer—he's the drummer (although his kit was always placed centerstage, and his drumming dominated the band's recordings). But he did form the band in North London in 1957 as the Dave Clark Quintet. The lineup that became famous was set in 1961, and shortly thereafter changed its name to the Dave Clark Five and became the Beatles' biggest competition. In 1964, their first single "Glad All Over" went to #1 in the U.K.—displacing the Beatles' "I Want to Hold Your Hand." The group then went to the United States, where they were extremely successful: They were the first British rock band to tour America, appeared on *The Ed Sullivan*

Show more times than any other British act, and had 17 top-40 hits in the U.S., including "Bits and Pieces" (#4), "Catch Us If You Can" (#4), "Because" (#3), and "Over and Over" (#1). In 1965, the band followed the Beatles into the movies, starring as themselves in a comedy called *Having a Wild Weekend.* Clark was also a savvy businessman—he managed the band, produced and co-wrote all of their songs, and set up a publishing company to retain the rights to the band's songs, which also enabled him to negotiate higher royalty rates with record labels. The band's sound didn't change the way the Beatles' did, however, and their popularity faded in the U.S. But not in the U.K., where they continued scoring top-10 hits until they broke up in 1970. On March 10, 2008, the Dave Clark Five was inducted into the Rock and Roll Hall of Fame—44 years to the day after they arrived in the U.S. to tape their first appearance on *The Ed Sullivan Show.*

PETER AND GORDON

Peter and Gordon were decidedly *not* a working-class band who clawed their way up to fame and fortune. Peter Asher and Gordon Waller met at Westminster School, an elite school in London. Peter Asher was a former child actor; his sister is Jane Asher, who dated Paul McCartney at the height of Beatlemania. That connection allowed the duo to record McCartney compositions that weren't good enough or appropriate for the Beatles, such as "A World Without Love," "Nobody I Know," "I Don't Want to See You Again," and "Woman." Their sound wasn't quite Beatles-esque, less influenced by blues and rock 'n' roll than they were by folk music and the gentle harmonies of the Everly Brothers. But it worked—"A World Without Love," in fact, became the first post-Beatles song by a British act to top the charts in the United States. After a few more middling hits (covers of Buddy Holly's "True Love Waits" and Del Shannon's "I Go to Pieces" in 1965 and "Lady Godiva" in 1966) the duo broke up in 1968. Both stayed in the music industry. Waller started a music publishing company while Asher served as head of A&R for the Beatles' label, Apple Records. In the 1970s and '80s, he produced hit albums for James Taylor, Linda Rondstadt, Cher, and Diana Ross.

The '60s may be over, but this article isn't. For the final
installment of the British Invasion, turn to page 524.

That's why it tastes good! About half the calories in the average fast-food meal come from fat.

LOSE WEIGHT NOW!

These real products are great for burning ~~calories~~ money.

THE POWER PLATE. It looks like a treadmill, but it's a vibrating platform. You run on it, then you run on a normal surface. It supposedly fools your body into thinking that regular ground is difficult terrain, so you burn more calories. Cost: $3,000

SAUNA SUIT. Black and billowy like a garbage bag, you wear this waterproof suit while working out. It increases your body heat, so you sweat more and lose more weight...except it's temporary water weight-loss. Excessive use of a sauna suit can lead to muscle cramps and heat stroke. Cost: $130

THE KNIFE-AND-FORK LIFT. One of the best ways to lose weight is to eat less, right? That's the "groundbreaking" theory behind these 1.5-pound dumbbells with an eating utensil attached at the end. If each bite is a lot of work, you'll eat less—while also getting a workout! Cost: $40

EXERCISE IN A BOTTLE. No need to exercise when you can simply pop these pills that allow you to "eat what you want and never, ever, *ever* have to diet again!" In 2000, the FTC banned these pills (loaded with "herbal supplements" and caffeine) and forced the maker to refund $10 million to its unsatisfied customers.

POWER BALANCE. This bracelet emits "special frequencies" that purportedly improve balance, strength, and flexibility. Studies have shown, not surprisingly, that this ring made of molded silicon doesn't really emit anything. Cost: $30

THE FACETRAINER. It looks like a ski-mask, with holes for your eyes and nose...and electrically charged wires to exercise "all 44 bilaterally symmetrical muscles of the face and neck." Cost: $150

SHAPE-UPS. Made by Skechers, these workout shoes have rocker-bottomed, uneven soles. Theory: Walking burns more calories when it's difficult. In 2011, after 36 people were injured while wearing Shape-ups, Skechers was fined $40 million for false advertising.

Estimated total cost (so far) of nuclear weapons to the U.S. since 1945: $5.5 trillion.

THE REST OF THE STORY

Sometimes news stories are really funny…
so long as you wait for the punchline.

NEWS STORY: Aroldis Chapman is a star relief pitcher for the Cincinnati Reds. If the game is close, Chapman usually comes through. By May 2013, he'd pitched in 157 games, allowed only seven home runs, and led the Reds to a win in all but one appearance. Then on May 19, Chapman turned in the worst performance of his career. The first batter he faced, he walked on four straight pitches. Then he gave up back-to-back home runs. The Reds lost the game to Philadelphia. What happened?

THE REST OF THE STORY: Chapman is Cuban, and when he goes on road games, he likes to bring *pastelitos de guayaba* (cheese and guava pastries) to share with Cuban players on opposing teams as a sign of sportsmanship and national pride. According to Philadelphia's Spanish-language broadcaster Rickie Ricardo, before the game, Chapman stufffed his face with 18 of his own pastelitos, and by game time was, he said, feeling "sluggish."

NEWS STORY: In March 2013, four-year-old Dylan Hayes was playing in his his family's third-story apartment. He wasn't paying much attention to where he was going and fell out of an open window. He fell from the apartment window, reportedly doing two (inadvertent) somersaults mid-air, and landed on the gravel below…on his feet. He was hospitalized for observation, but was released less than 24 hours later with a clean bill of health.

THE REST OF THE STORY: At the time of the fall, Dylan was wearing a Superman T-shirt.

NEWS STORY: In February 2013, lawyers for Ernest Evans filed a lawsuit against Hewlett-Packard Computers and Palm Inc., which sell an app called "the Chubby Checker," a novelty app for Palm-brand smartphones that guesses the size of a man's, uh, manhood, based on personal data, such as the user's shoe size.

THE REST OF THE STORY: Ernest Evans is better known by his stage name—Chubby Checker. He's suing because he doesn't want his fans to think he endorsed the app.

Not 100 times as long? A $1 bill has a lifespan of about 2 years. A $100 bill: about 7.5 years.

DUSTBIN OF HISTORY: THE PAGER

The beeeep! beeeep! *of someone's pager going off used to be everywhere…but when was the last time you heard one? Let's take one last look before they're gone forever.*

THE DOCTOR IS OUT

In 1924, a New York City businessman named Sherman Amsden started a company called the Doctors' Telephone Service, one of the very first answering services in the country. When a physician was out of the office, his calls could be automatically forwarded to the service, whose operators took messages for him to retrieve when he called in later.

The service was simple but much needed. In an era before voice mail or even answering machines, the only way to be sure an important call didn't go unanswered was to sit by the phone and wait for it to ring. For doctors, a missed call could mean the difference between someone's life and death, and being on call often meant being stuck at home within earshot of the phone for hours on end. Or at least it did until Amsden's company let them pass that chore off to someone else. Now doctors could get out of the house, as long as they checked in to see if they had any messages.

Amsden's business thrived; it did even better when he renamed it Telanserphone so that he could market the service to plumbers, undertakers, elevator repairmen, and other people who were needed in emergencies. By 1939, he had thousands of clients and more than 60 operators staffing switchboards all over the city. But as the calls poured in and messages piled up, Amsden noticed that many clients—including some doctors—didn't check for messages as often as he thought they should. That got him thinking: Why should they have to call in at all? They ought to be able to carry around a device that told them if they had messages waiting.

ON THE AIR

Amsden thought a "radio-pager" would do the trick. It would be a device similar to an AM radio but locked onto a special frequency reserved just for pagers. He imagined his pager as a bulky piece of equipment, one that the client might wear over the shoulder or around the neck using a strap, or hang from a knob on the dashboard of a car. When it received a signal indicating that the client had a message waiting, a buzzer would sound or a light would flash, telling the client that he needed to call Telanserphone's operators to get the message.

That was the idea, anyway. But to make it work Amsden actually needed his own radio station. That required the approval of the Federal Communications Commission, which would also have to agree that using a radio station solely to signal pagers was a good idea. The FCC considered Amsden's request…and considered it… and considered it, taking a full ten years before it finally said yes.

SMALL-TIME

While Amsden was waiting for the FCC to make up its mind, he hired an inventor named Richard Florac to design the pager. Florac came up with a design smaller than Amsden had envisioned—about the size of an eyeglass case and small enough to fit in a pocket. But it didn't have a buzzer or a flashing light. Instead, the pager had a tiny built-in speaker that clients held up to their ear, much like a person holds a cell phone today.

Each client was given a unique three-digit identity code, and this was what they listened for. Whenever a call came in to Telanserphone, the operators would broadcast the code over the air (along with the codes of every other client being paged, up to 60 codes at a time). The client had to listen to all of the codes being broadcast to see if his was among them.

PHONING IT IN

Telanserphone's radio transmitter was located atop the 42-story Pierre Hotel on 5th Avenue in midtown Manhattan. That gave the system a 30-mile radius—enough to allow subscribers to check for messages from just about anywhere in the city. The pager worked almost everywhere (except on the subway), even inside buildings and cars. Cost of the service: $11.50 per month, the equivalent of about $100 a month today. Not cheap, but if you had the money, it was better than being stuck at home by the phone.

The system went into service on October 15, 1950, and sent out

---

It takes about 50 times more energy to make a battery than the battery produces.

its first page later that same day to a physician playing a round of golf 25 miles away. A year later, Telanserphone's pager division had more than 400 subscribers.

FIRST BEEP

Telanserphone's pagers weren't "beepers." They didn't beep because there was no way to signal one pager without signaling all the other pagers at the same time. But by the time the company's system was up and running, another inventor, Al Gross, had patented a pager that could be signaled individually.

Gross didn't conceive of his pagers as something that could be used all over a city. Instead, he saw them as a less noisy alternative to a hospital's public address system. As we told you in *Uncle John's Curiously Compelling Bathroom Reader*, pagers were an outgrowth of radio-controlled bomb detonators he'd developed during World War II to blow up bridges in Nazi Germany. After the war, he reworked the system to send signals to pagers instead of bombs.

Pagers would eventually find widespread use in hospitals, but when Gross installed his system in a New York hospital in 1949, it flopped. The medical staff worried that the beeping would frighten patients and complained that the bulky pagers were uncomfortable to wear. The hospital went back to using its public address system, and when it did, Gross set his pagers aside and moved on to other projects. (He's also credited with inventing walkie-talkies, CB radios, cordless phones, and cell phones.)

THE PERFECT MATCH

More than 20 years passed before a company called Motorola took Sherman Amsden's concept—pagers that worked all over a city— and married it with Al Gross's idea of beeping pagers that could be signaled individually. Introduced in 1974, the Motorola Pageboy was the first commercially successful beeping pager.

Like Telanserphone's pagers of the 1950s, the Pageboy was little more than an extension of an answering service. Since beeping was the only thing it could do, the user still had to depend on live operators to take messages and relay them over the phone. Technological improvements over the years eventually eliminated the need for answering services and live operators entirely. These included numeric displays that showed the telephone number of the person calling, electronic voice mail, alpha-numeric displays, and Internet connectivity (once the Internet came into widespread use) that made it possible to e-mail messages directly to pagers. Satellite-based paging systems expanded coverage from a single city to much larger geographical areas, even nationwide.

UP...AND DOWN

The plunging prices of pagers and service plans caused sales to soar in the 1990s. By 1994, more than 14 million Americans owned pagers; five years later nearly 60 million did. A third of these were for personal (not business) use, and with service plans as low as $15 a month (with the pager thrown in for free), even teenagers could afford them. Kids loved them because their favorite hip-hop stars had them, and pagers actually became a popular high school fashion accessory.

But the same forces that created the pager boom sent it into a tailspin just a few years later, when steadily dropping prices and ever-expanding features of cell phones caused pager owners to trade up by the millions. By 2000, the number of pager owners in the United States was down to 37 million, a decline of nearly 40 percent in just two years. In 2002, even Motorola, which invented the modern pager business and controlled 85 percent of the American market at its peak, stopped manufacturing and servicing pagers. By 2008, there were only 6 million pager subscribers in the U.S., a nearly 90-percent drop since 1999. That year 255 million Americans owned cell phones.

LAST BASTION

Today pagers are still used in the medical profession, where cell phones are banned when there's a risk of interfering with sensitive medical equipment. They're also used by emergency first-responders, because satellite-based paging systems are less likely to be disrupted or overwhelmed by hurricanes, earthquakes, and other major disasters. But as cell phone systems are re-engineered to address these faults and the number of pager subscribers continues to decline, it's quite possible that the last remaining pager networks will eventually fall silent. Can you remember the last time you heard a beeper beep? If not you may be out of luck—there's a good chance you'll never hear another one again.

17th-century Frenchmen wore lockets containing living fleas plucked from their lovers' bodies.

"I VANT TO BE ALONE!"

Celebrities may complain about their lack of privacy, but if they didn't want the spotlight, why'd they go into show biz? Much rarer are the celebrities who decide to give up the spotlight...like these folks.

GRETA GARBO

The Swedish movie star came to the United States in 1925. She appeared in silent films before making the leap to "talkies," where she became one of the biggest stars of Hollywood's "golden age." She appeared in more than 20 movies, almost all of them hits, and was nominated for Best Actress at the Academy Awards four times in the 1930s—for *Anna Christie*, *Romance*, *Camille*, and *Ninotchka*. Then, in 1941, at age 36, she walked away. The film *Two-Faced Woman* marked her final appearance on the silver screen. The physically taxing production required Garbo to swim, ski, and dance the rumba, and the film's reviews were savage. (Garbo was reportedly humiliated by them, later telling a biographer that the movie was "her grave.") Despite the awful experience, she did plan to return to acting once World War II was over. She signed on for a film in 1948 but was forced to drop out when the financing fell through. Garbo received many offers from Hollywood producers in the years that followed, but she turned them all down. Despite being forever linked to her famous line from 1932's *Grand Hotel* ("I want to be alone"), the actress loved to take long walks through Manhattan, and "Garbo-Watching" was a gossip magazine pastime for decades. Garbo died in 1990 at the age of 84.

THOMAS PYNCHON

The notoriously shy author of the critically-acclaimed novels *The Crying of Lot 49* and *Gravity's Rainbow* has shunned the spotlight since he first entered the publishing world in the early 1970s. Over the course of his career, he's avoided reporters and has turned down countless interview requests. The few publicly available photos of Pynchon were all snapped during his younger years. Some say he lives in rural Mexico, others say metropolitan New York; others

---

Light travels from NY to LA in 0.016 seconds; from Earth to the moon: 1.26 seconds.

claim "Thomas Pynchon" is really a pen name for another reclusive author, J. D. Salinger. Other weird rumors even suggested he was the Unabomber. According to a college friend, his self-isolation may have something to do with a "complex" involving his bad teeth, which required him to undergo extensive surgery. CNN managed to film Pynchon in New York City in the '90s, and he demanded the network not air the footage. They complied. He did loosen up a tad in the 2000s, though. Pynchon "appeared" as himself (in animated form) on an episode of *The Simpsons* in 2004—wearing a paper bag adorned with a question mark over his head. He also recorded a voice-over (but did not appear) in a YouTube video promoting his 2009 novel, *Inherent Vice*.

SYD BARRETT

The original frontman for Pink Floyd left the psychedelic band in 1968, five years before the release of *Dark Side of the Moon*, one of the most successful albums of all time and the one that launched the group to superstardom. Barrett had an unhealthy appetite for controlled substances, and LSD was his favorite. His drug abuse exacerbated his problems with mental illness, including schizophrenia. While he continued to write and occasionally record songs, Barrett quit the music business for good in 1974. He moved to his mother's house in rural England in 1978 (after he ran out of money), where he spent his remaining years painting, gardening, and doing his best to avoid curious fans and members of the press. After years of suffering from stomach ulcers and type 2 diabetes, Barrett died in his Cambridge home in 2006 at the age of 60.

BILL WATTERSON

After a decade of writing and drawing *Calvin and Hobbes*, Watterson ended his celebrated daily comic strip in 1995 and went into private life. According to the public letter that announced his departure, Watterson had become frustrated with the limitations of the craft and the comics business. He was tired of squeezing Calvin's elaborate world into tiny comic-strip panels, and the tight deadlines were fraying his nerves. Besides, he later admitted, over the ten years he wrote the strip, he'd said everything he wanted to say. Watterson rarely gives interviews, never signs autographs, and still refuses to license his characters for movies, TV, or merchandise.

YOU DON'T KNOW LEGUMES!

We were going to title this article "You Don't Know Beans!" and make it all about beans. But then we did some research, and realized there was a much bigger story here than just the little old bean. So here's the story—of the legume.

BEAN THERE, DONE THAT
What exactly is a legume? Most people would probably answer that a legume is a bean. And they'd be right—but that's just one part of the legume story. To be precise, a legume is a plant in the botanical family *Leguminosae* (also known as *Fabaceae*). That family includes what we commonly call beans—such as kidney, soy, lima, garbanzo, green, and wax beans—as well as many related plants, like peas and peanuts, and a few you probably didn't know were legumes—such as alfalfa, clover, and lupins. They are a remarkable family of plants for many reasons, including the fact that they are right up there with the grasses in importance to humans—not just as a food source, but in the birth and advancement of civilization.

LEGUMES AROUND THE WORLD
Legumes are the third-largest family of flowering land plants on Earth, with almost 20,000 different species. They're found in a broad array of ecosystems, from desert to plain to high alpine, and in every region of the planet except Antarctica. They vary greatly in form. Some are trees. *Koompassia excelsa*, also known as the tualang tree, grows in Southeast Asian rainforests, and is one of the tallest tree species in the world, growing to more than 280 feet high. It's a legume. And Brazilian rosewood, a fancy hardwood commonly used to make musical instruments. That's a legume, too. Legumes also grow as shrubs, vines, and small annual herbs, but with a few exceptions, they all have one thing in common: their fruit. Legumes grow fruit in "pods"—capsules with seams along either side that allow the pod to split in two, and in which the plants' seeds are contained.

The British Constitution is unwritten and can be changed overnight by an act of Parliament.

A LEGUME, LEGUME TIME AGO...

Scientific studies of plant genetics and fossil records indicate that the first legume species appeared around 59 million years ago, breaking away from its flowering-plant ancestors by acquiring the genetic traits that made it unique. This happened in Africa—although that's far from certain. Wherever it occurred, legumes rapidly spread around the world, acquiring more and more specifically legume characteristics along the way, while diversifying into the tremendous number of species that exist today.

One of the characteristics that make legumes unique in the plant world: They have a special way of obtaining nitrogen, which, as an essential building-block of proteins, all plants (and animals, for that matter) need to survive.

A COMMITTED RELATIONSHIP

Most of the air around us is made up of nitrogen, but neither plants nor animals can get it that way. Animals obtain it from the food they eat; plants get it from naturally-occurring sources in the soil via the moisture they absorb with their roots. But legumes cheat.

There is a type of soil-borne bacterium known as *rhizobia*. And while plants can't absorb nitrogen from the air, rhizobia can, and that's the basis of the symbiotic relationship between the two species. Legumes secrete substances into the soil called *flavonoids*... which attract rhizobia bacteria. The bacteria in turn release substances that induce the legumes to form bulbous nodules on their roots, and those nodules become the homes of rhizobia colonies. You can actually see the nodules on legume roots. Check it out next time you're transplanting a bean plant. The nodules kind of look like little tumors growing on the roots. The plants supply sugars and minerals to the bacteria, and in exchange, the rhizobia absorbs nitrogen from the air around the nodules (yes, there is air in soil), and converts it into ammonia—or NH3—which it secretes into the plants' roots. The legumes are then able to take the nitrogen from that NH3 and use it to build essential proteins.

This amazing nitrogen-cheating technique is one of the chief reasons legumes became such a successful family of plants—and it's also the reason they're so high in protein. Not all legume species have this nitrogen-friendly-bacteria relationship, but most do. There are also a relatively small number of non-legume plants that

---

Praying mantises have been known to catch and eat frogs, lizards, and small birds.

are able to do this, too. But among the nearly nine million plant species in the world, this is chiefly a legume feature.

THE HUMAN BEAN

Imagine you're an ancient hunter-gatherer at the dawn of civilization, roaming the wild countryside with a small clan of friends and relatives, constantly on the move, looking for wild game, nuts, berries, roots, and whatever else you can find to eat. Then one day, someone says, "Hey, why don't we grow some beans and store them up so that we can stay in one place and not have to run ourselves ragged all the time?"

That's pretty much what happened to humans, beginning around 12,000 years ago, when people first started cultivating crops. Around the same time, people built the first granaries—structures designed to store dried foods such as grains and beans. These developments led, for the first time in human history, to the storage of food surpluses, which in turn led to the establishment of the world's first permanent settlements.

Important moments in legume history

• Archaeological evidence shows that lentils and garbanzo beans were being cultivated in the Middle East at least 10,000 years ago. That means that by this time—and probably much earlier—humans had figured out that beans (like almost all legumes) must be prepared by soaking, cooking, fermenting, or sprouting in order to make them edible. That's because the outer coat of most legumes is very tough fibrous tissue that must be broken down in order to become digestible. And when eaten raw, some are toxic.

• At least 8,000 years ago, ancient peoples in Peru began cultivating lima beans and peanuts. (Lima beans are named for the city of Lima, Peru, where Europeans first encountered them.) Domestication of these legumes spread throughout South America and as far north as Mexico over the following several centuries.

• By 1100 B.C., the soybean was domesticated by farmers in northern China. By the first century A.D., it had spread to many parts of Asia, including India and Japan.

• By around 500 B.C., the Greeks and Romans were cultivating peas—and pea soup was being sold by street vendors in Athens.

• By the first century A.D., there were major civilizations firmly established in numerous locations on every continent on Earth (except Australia), and legumes were playing a big part in the diets and the commerce of every one.

MULTI-TASKERS

Edible legumes are still staple foods all over the planet, and today account for roughly one quarter of all agricultural production world-wide. They also account for about a third of human dietary nitrogen needs.

Another fascinating feature: Legumes actually nourish the soil. As we said, most plant species get their nitrogen from natural sources in the soil, while legumes get it from the atmosphere via their special relationship with bacteria. That means that legumes don't deplete the soil of nitrogen, as other plants do, which is one of the chief reasons farmers regularly rotate crops. After a season or more of a nitrogen-depleting crop such as corn, farmers will plant legumes and after harvesting, plow the legumes back into the soil, allowing the nitrogen-rich plants to revitalize that soil.

Legumes have a lot of non-food uses, too. Some leguminous trees are harvested for their lumber; the sap of the acacia tree—also a legume—is used to make *gum arabic*, which is used in the production of a many products, including paint, ink, glue, and cosmetics. And just a short list of the things made from soybeans (besides soy sauce, tofu, and tempeh) includes industrial adhesives (used to make plywood), biodiesel fuels, lubricants, hydraulic fluids, ink, crayons, and foams—like those used in automobile seats.

Legumes are so much a part of modern human existence that the world would, without question, be a very different place without them. In fact, if we didn't have legumes, it would be like we'd never bean here at all!

RANDOM LEGUME FACTS

• The Central American legume *Entada gigas*—a large woody vine called "monkey ladder"—produces the largest pod of any legume. The pods grow to more than six feet long, and hold about 15 heart-shaped beans, each roughly 2.5 inches in diameter.

• The toxin found in some legumes is a type of *lectin*, or plant protein, called *phytohaemagglutinin*. The beans with the highest amount: raw red kidney beans. Eating these beans (and many other kinds, too) without properly preparing them can cause extreme nausea, vomiting, and diarrhea.

• Peas, green beans, and peanuts are very low in phytohaemagglutinin, so they are safe to eat raw.

• What's the difference between a pea and a bean? Both words are used to describe all kinds of plants, but technically speaking, "beans" are the pods and seeds of all legume species, while "peas" are the pods and seeds of just one legume species—*Pisum sativum*—which we know as common peas.

• Since peas, beans, and peanuts are all legumes, are people who are allergic to peanuts also allergic to beans and peas? Mostly not, but studies have shown that some people who are allergic to peanuts (perhaps as many as 10 percent) are also allergic to beans, especially soybeans.

• For centuries, people in Eastern Europe have spread the leaves of kidney-bean plants on bedbug-infested beds at night. In the morning, the leaves—by then full of bedbugs—would be burned. In 2013, the *New York Times* reported that a team of American scientists were studying the practice and had learned that microscopic hairs on the bean leaves actually impale the bugs' legs, trapping them on the leaves.

• Misnomers: Coffee beans, castor beans, cocoa beans, and vanilla beans all resemble leguminous beans—but none of them are. (Neither are Mexican jumping beans.) And despite their names, chick peas and black-eyed peas are both actually types of beans.

*   *   *

WHY WAS THE PIG WEARING A NECKLACE?

Posted on Craigslist in Jacksonville, Florida, in 2012: "I need help catching the gator that ate my prized pig! My pig (Rudy Belle) was wearing a very expensive necklace, a generational necklace, which was in my wife's family for years. The emotional distress I've had from losing my pig is nothing like the stress I'll receive from my wife if I don't get it back. It happened at Blue Cypress Golf Club and it scared the bejesus out of me. If anyone has found the necklace or has seen this gator (has a weird blotchy snout), pleasssse contact me. Thanks, Jimmy T."

European carousels rotate clockwise; American merry-go-rounds go counterclockwise.

THE LINCOLN HIGHWAY

Like us, you probably can't remember a world without highways—a time before there were gas stations, fast-food places, or shopping centers. Well, it all had to start somewhere…and this is where.

WHERE'S THE HORSE?

The 1893 World's Fair in Chicago was in full swing when a gentleman walked up to a contraption that looked like a metal carriage and wound the crank on its front end. The machine rumbled and grumbled and coughed out black smoke. Then the man got into the thing and—to the amazement of onlookers—started driving it around the fair grounds. What was so strange about that? The metal carriage didn't have a horse to pull it. It was a horseless carriage, one with an internal-combustion engine that ran on gasoline. The public's response: They were dumbfounded, but most people loved it. Suddenly the country had a new toy, and despite the naysayers who protested against the new "devil wagon," the car was here to stay.

STALLED CARS

Auto manufacturers and investors cropped up almost overnight. In just the first four months of 1899, investors poured $388 million into new automobile companies; by the turn of the century, more than 8,000 cars were puttering around the United States. But there was still nothing in the way of the necessary infrastructure: no gas stations, traffic lights, mechanic's shops, or—most importantly— roads. The existing throughways were deeply rutted wagon trails that meandered into the countryside from the centers of towns and often simply ended. During the winter months, these "roads" became so unusable that most early auto owners drained their radiators and put the machines in their barns until spring.

Something had to be done about America's roads, but public funds weren't forthcoming. The federal government saw the car as a novelty and refused to allocate funds for road building. By 1905, when the first modern gasoline filling station appeared, there still wasn't a single mile of paved rural road in the entire country. And, as Henry Ford's assembly line process drove down manufacturing

---

Schizophrenia used to be treated (unsuccessfully) with kidney dialysis.

costs, the cars kept coming. Within five years, more than half a million cars were sputtering around with nary a real road to drive on.

ROCKING THE HIGHWAY

Enter Carl Graham Fisher, a former racecar driver and an entrepreneur who built a fortune selling Prest-O-Lite brand acetylene automobile headlamps. In 1912, Fisher proposed a fund drive to raise $10 million for building what he called "The Coast to Coast Rock Highway"—3,389 miles of two-lane, graveled roadbed running from New York City's Times Square to San Francisco's Lincoln Park. Fisher figured that self-interested auto manufacturers would recognize the benefits of the project and contribute heavily. Many did.

Henry Joy of the Packard Motor Car Company jumped on board so wholeheartedly that he is now considered cofounder of the first transcontinental highway. But the man Fisher was most counting on to help would not. Henry Ford, whose company had manufactured around 40 percent of those cars sputtering around in search of a road, refused to contribute a cent. He reasoned that the public would never learn to fund road construction if industry did it for them.

CAN'T AF-FORD TO WAIT

Fisher's group moved ahead with the planning stages of the project without Ford's participation. The first order of business: Choose a new name for "The Coast to Coast Rock Highway." Other names that were proposed and rejected, included "The Ocean to Ocean Highway," "The American Road," and "The Jefferson Highway." Finally, road proponents found a name they could agree on—Abraham Lincoln. The project was officially renamed "The Lincoln Highway," and on July 1, 1913, the Lincoln Highway Association was incorporated, with Henry Joy as president and Carl Fisher as vice president. That same summer, Fisher organized and oversaw a truck caravan he called "The Hoosier Tour," from Indiana to Los Angeles. The tour's purpose was to draw attention to the need for road improvement and to promote the Lincoln Highway.

On October 31, 1913, the Lincoln Highway Association announced its planned route: starting in New York City, the country's first highway would head Southwest through New Jersey, Pennsylvania, Ohio, Indiana, Illinois, Iowa, Nebraska, Wyoming, Utah, Nevada,

First American hockey team to win the Stanley Cup: The Seattle Metropolitans (1917).

and into California. In a special ceremony, President Woodrow Wilson made the first $25 contribution to the fund, and towns all across the route celebrated with parades, speeches, and bonfires. The governors of Nebraska, Wyoming, and Nevada issued Lincoln Highway Day proclamations and declared state holidays.

But Fisher soon found out what Abe Lincoln knew all too well: You can't please all the people all of the time. Almost immediately, governors of states that had been left off the route began to complain. Particularly upset were the governors of Kansas and Colorado, who had been promised inclusion. So, to quiet the protests, the Association agreed to add a dogleg from Big Springs, Nevada, south to Denver. Only problem: When other municipalities heard about the compromise, they flooded the Association with requests for *more* doglegs. And as much as Fisher would have liked to oblige them, he couldn't—the Association just didn't have the time, money, or resources. He tried to explain that the proposed highway avoided major cities in favor of the straightest, most direct path. Larger cities, Fisher believed, would fund their own connecting roads once traffic began moving along the Lincoln Highway.

ON SOLID GROUND

Two years after the Lincoln Highway Association was incorporated, construction had yet to begin. The fund was well short of its $10 million goal; Fisher was all but ready to give up. Then, in 1915, a concrete company swooped in and saved the project. It offered to donate tons of its product to the road-building effort in return for publicity and the guarantee of future contracts.

The company couldn't contribute enough concrete to build the entire highway, but the donation gave Fisher another idea: He would build "seedling miles" of concrete highway out in the countryside at points midway between towns. Fisher reasoned that once drivers got a taste of driving on smooth pavement, they'd hound local governments to connect their towns to the seedling stretches. The first miles of concrete were poured later that year with a new promotional campaign urging motorists to "See America First."

Fisher's seedlings sprouted. Cities and towns along the route, worried about the embarrassment of smooth roads turning rough as motorists drove into town, quickly connected themselves to the seedling miles. Piece by piece, the Lincoln Highway began to take shape.

Guavas have 5 times as much vitamin C as oranges.

ROAD WARRIOR

The project moved slowly in its first few years. During World War I, only a few hundred miles of road were completed. When the war ended in 1919, the Army sent an expedition from Camp Meade, Maryland, to San Francisco to study the feasibility of moving troops and equipment by truck, and it was a disaster. At an average speed of seven miles per hour, the trip took two months, and many of the vehicles broke down along the way. The rough journey convinced the officer in charge—a young Dwight D. Eisenhower—that impassable roads were a risk to national security and that building good roads should be the highest priority for the nation.

The Army's cross-country fiasco helped convince Congress to pass the 1921 Federal Highway Act, which provided $75 million in matching funds for state-road projects. By the time the Lincoln Highway was completed in 1923, there were more than ten million cars in America looking for roads to drive on.

MAP QUEST

Fisher called the Lincoln Highway "America's Main Street," but it wouldn't be the main stretch for long. Several other highways broke ground in the 1920s—the Jefferson Highway from Detroit to New Orleans; the Dixie Highway from Bay City, Michigan, to Miami; and the William Penn Highway across Pennsylvania. Soon, dozens of new highways spidered across the nation and created a new problem: confusion. Some roads had telephone poles covered in signs bearing multiple names for each section of road. As for road maps? Forget it. Any given stretch of road could have up to five different names.

In 1925, the U.S. Department of Agriculture, which had been given oversight of federal roads, began planning the system of numbered routes that is still in place today. North/South highways were given odd numbers, and East/West roads were given even numbers, with transcontinental routes always multiples of five or ten. Much of the Lincoln Highway became U.S. Route 30. In a massive undertaking, the Boy Scouts of America placed 2,400 concrete markers denoting its course, all at 1:00 p.m. on September 1, 1928.

Today many stretches of the old Lincoln Highway still exist, and there are well over 200 million cars in the United States. But as anyone who has ever driven a paved highway can attest, the quest for smooth roads is far from over.

Eww! Hagfish enter their prey through one of their orifices and eat them from the inside out.

LOCAL HEROES

It can be very disheartening to read that "no one did anything" when someone else's life was in danger. That's why we included these true stories—to illustrate that in many cases, people do "do something."

GIVE THAT WOMAN A CONTRACT

Preschool teacher Cristina Torre is the daughter of former major-league catcher and New York Yankees manager Joe Torre. Though not a big leaguer herself, Torre displayed some impressive skills when she caught a falling baby. While passing by a cupcake shop in Brooklyn in June 2013, she happened to see a one-year-old boy hanging from second-story fire escape. (He got out to the fire escape after removing a piece of cardboard next to an air conditioner.) Torre called 9-1-1 but realized they wouldn't make it in time, so she positioned herself beneath the infant. A moment later he lost his grip and fell. He hit a metal awning on the way down, cutting his face, but Torre caught him before he landed on the sidewalk. He was okay.

CALLING ALL CABS

A remote town in Peru called Contamana (pop. 15,000) has an airport and a hospital, but the airport's runway has no lights, and the hospital is too small to deal with serious medical issues. One night in 2013, those factors put the lives of three people in serious jeopardy. A sick woman, her sick baby, and a man with a tropical disease were in danger of not lasting the night, and couldn't be flown to a better hospital until morning. But a local radio DJ named Adolfo Lobo made an on-air plea for any and all taxi drivers to meet at the airport. A short time later, nearly 300 cabs (motorcycles with sidecars) showed up and parked along each side of the runway with their lights on. That provided enough light for the Medevac pilot to take off, The man died a few days later, but the mother and child survived.

DISCO DIVA

You have to be impressed by Sharon Thorneywork. While riding to work on a bus in Birmingham, England, she performed CPR on a heart-attack victim for 18 minutes while singing *Stayin' Alive*. She'd seen a public-service announcement that advised singing the

---

A law in the Code of Hammurabi (1750 B.C.) made watering down beer punishable by death.

Bee Gees' 1977 disco hit while doing chest compressions (to keep a steady rhythm). The victim, 67-year-old Terry Holly, had collapsed next to Thorneywork, 42, who had no first-aid training (aside from the commercial), and asked if anyone else on the bus knew CPR. No one did, so she started pumping and singing, pumping and singing. Finally, paramedics arrived and took over. Thorneywork helped them get the patient to the ambulance, then got back on the bus and continued to work. Two hours later, she received a call from police: Holly was breathing on his own! "'I can't thank Sharon enough," said one cop. "She should sing *Stayin' Alive* from the rooftops."

BIKE PATROL

Temar Boggs, 15, of Lancaster Township, Pennsylvania, was watching TV with some friends in May 2013 when several police officers showed up on their residential street. They were looking for a five-year-old girl who'd been abducted hours earlier. The teens tried to help by searching the woods near their houses. Then Boggs realized they could cover more ground on their bikes. "I had a feeling in my stomach I was going to find her," he said. Soon after, they saw a car with a man behind the wheel and a little girl in the passenger seat. The car turned around, as if to avoid a police car on the next block. The teens pursued. The man tried to get away, but the neighborhood streets were small and the boys were able to keep up. After a brief chase, the kidnapper pulled over, pushed the victim out, and sped away. Boggs comforted the crying girl and then brought her to a firefighter. (The suspect remains at large.) Boggs downplayed his heroism, but admitted that he and his friends are proud that they were able to "make sure her future could be possible."

BEING SAVED BY JOHN MALKOVICH

A 77-year-old man named Jim Walpole had just walked out of a pub in Toronto when he fell and cut his neck on a piece of scaffolding. With blood gushing out, he didn't have much time. Thankfully, Hollywood A-lister John Malkovich (who was in town for a play) ran over and used his scarf to stop Walpole's bleeding. He continued to apply pressure to the wound for ten minutes until paramedics arrived. Walpole described the movie-like scenario to reporters: "As the ambulance drove away, Malkovich looked at me and said, 'That was intense.' And then he just sort of faded into the night."

A single pear, eaten with the skin, contains more fiber than a bowl of oatmeal.

STAGE NAME ORIGINS

You didn't think his mother named him "Kid Rock," did you?

BRUNO MARS. The singer's real name is Peter Hernandez. At age two, his father, a wrestling fan, started calling him "Bruno" because he resembled pro wrestler Bruno Sammartino. In 2003, when he moved from his birthplace of Hawaii to Los Angeles to make it as a singer, he added "Mars" because "a lot of girls say I'm out of this world."

• **SLASH (Guns N' Roses).** Growing up in Los Angeles, Saul Hudson's best friend was the son of character actor Seymour Cassel (*Faces, Rushmore*). The actor nicknamed Saul "Slash" because, as Slash said in his memoir, "I was always in a hurry, hustling whatever it was I was hustling, and never had time to sit and chat."

• **GOTYE.** This singer had a huge hit in 2012: "Somebody That I Used to Know" spent eight weeks at #1 and was the best-selling song of the year. Gotye really is his name...sort of. He's from the Flanders region of Belgium, where Flemish is spoken, and his real first name is Wouter. That's the Flemish version of Gauthier, a common French name (French is spoken in the rest of Belgium). The phonetic spelling of Gauthier: goh-tee-YAY.

• **IRON & WINE.** Singer-songwriter Sam Beam spotted a protein supplement called Beef, Iron & Wine at a small town gas station. He shortened it to his stage name because he thought it was more interesting than his given name.

• **IGGY POP.** Before he formed (arguably) America's first punk band, the Stooges, James Osterberg played drums for an Ann Arbor garage band called the Iguanas. From "Iguanas," his friends called him Iggy. The Pop came from his intentional resemblance to a friend named Jimmy Pop (his real name) who had lost all of his hair and eyebrows. Iggy thought that looked cool, so he shaved off his eyebrows, too.

• **CHILDISH GAMBINO.** Donald Glover is a well-known actor and writer, starring on the NBC sitcom *Community*. He also has a side career as a critically-acclaimed rapper. He got his rap name by using an online tool called "The Wu-Tang Name Generator," which makes up stage names that sound like the seemingly nonsensical names used by the rap group the Wu-Tang Clan, whose members include RZA, Ol' Dirty Bastard, and Ghostface Killah.

• **KID ROCK.** As a teenager in Detroit in the 1980s, Robert Ritchie deejayed and breakdanced at parties in exchange for free beer. He says he often heard someone in the mostly African-American crowd remark, "Look at that white kid rock."

• **M.I.A.** The acronym stands for "missing in action." Maya Arulpragasam is of Sri Lankan heritage, but grew up in the London suburb of Acton. As a teenager, her cousin, who was the same age, went missing in Sri Lanka during that country's long civil war. It occurred to her that her cousin was "missing in action," just a single letter—but a whole world away from "Maya in Acton."

• **MEAT LOAF.** Marvin Aday has always been big—as in "exceptionally large." When Marvin was only two years old, his father nicknamed him "Meat." They called him Meat in school, too…and his football coach added the "Loaf."

• **ICE-T.** Pulp author Robert Beck, also known as Iceberg Slim, who wrote sensational novels in the '70s based on his life as a street pimp, including *Mama Black Widow, Long White Con,* and *Pimp.* As a tribute to Slim, Tracy Marrow, one of the first "gangsta rappers" to gain mainstream exposure, took on the name Ice-T.

• **RONNIE JAMES DIO.** One of the biggest names in heavy metal, singing for bands such as Black Sabbath, Rainbow, and Dio, Ronald James Padavona started his career in the early 1960s as part of a doo-wop group called Ronnie Dio and the Prophets. His name was taken from another Italian-American—and mobster—Giovanni Ignazio Dioguardi, who went by the street name Johnny Dio. (Bonus: In Italian, *Dio* means "God.")

• **WIZ KHALIFA.** It's a combination of two childhood nicknames. His grandmother called him "Wiz" because he was a fast learner. His Muslim father called him "Khalifa," which means "leader" in Arabic. His real name is Cameron Jibril Thomaz. (And he's from Pittsburgh.)

It takes more energy to convert water into steam than to convert it into ice.

- **DRAKE.** The singer/rapper's full name is Aubrey Drake Graham.

- **BON IVER.** The folksy singer-songwriter born Justin Vernon won the Best New Artist award at the Grammys in 2012, but a few years earlier, he'd been in a band called DeYarmond Edison. After they broke up in 2007, Vernon holed up at his father's cabin in the Wisconsin woods and wrote an album's worth of songs. While watching a DVD of *Northern Exposure*, he heard characters wish each other *bon hiver*, which is French for "good winter." From "bon hiver"…to Bon Iver.

- **CAT POWER.** The alternative-rock star sometimes goes by her real name, Chan Marshall, but mostly uses the stage name, which used to be the name of an entire band. At age 18, she named the group when, while she was working at a pizza parlor, a man came in wearing a cap advertising Caterpillar industrial equipment. It read "Cat Diesel Power."

- **ROB ZOMBIE.** The heavy-metal singer (and horror-movie director) used to lead a band called White Zombie. The inspiration for the band's name, and his own stage name, is the 1932 Bela Lugosi movie *White Zombie*, which was among the first zombie movies ever made.

*   *   *

LOST YOUR JOB?

Lawyers are disbarred, and priests defrocked, so it should be true that…
- A banker is disinterested.
- A clerk is defiled.
- A cashier is distilled.
- A medium is dispirited.
- A rock climber is disinclined.
- An electrician is discharged.
- A civil rights leader is disintegrated.
- A jockey is derided.
- A gardener is deflowered.
- A drug dealer is disjointed.
- A senator is devoted.

Life after death? About 240 pencils can be made from the carbon of cremated human remains.

UNCLE JOHN'S STALL OF SHAME

Not everyone who makes it into the Stall of Fame is there for a good reason. That's why Uncle John created the "Stall of Shame."

Dubious Achiever: Tihomir Petrov, 43, a math professor at California State University, Northridge

Claim to Shame: Taking the low road in a game of revenge

True Story: In 2010, Petrov was involved in a feud with another professor. So when mysterious "puddles" kept showing up next to the other teacher's office door, Petrov was the prime suspect. University security installed a hidden surveillance camera aimed at the door, and a short while later, recorded Pee-trov entering the building after hours, walking up to his nemesis's door, and leaving his mark. He was cited for urinating in public and fired from his job.

Dubious Achiever: The Boom Boom Room, a restaurant on the 18th floor of Manhattan's swanky Standard Hotel

Claim to Shame: Forgetting to install curtains in the restroom

True Story: In 2012, the Boom Boom Room found itself in hot water after the press published pictures of peeing and pooping patrons. The photos were taken by tourists from the elevated High Line park across the street. How could they see in? Easy—there was nothing between the toilets and the floor-to-ceiling windows to obstruct their view. Most of the restroom goers assumed the windows were one-way mirrors, allowing them to see out but no one to see in. Once pictures showed up in the *New York Post* (with the private parts blurred out), Boom Boom Room management blamed workers who "forgot" to reinstall the curtains after they renovated the restroom. The curtains were hastily put back up, to the relief of most of the customers. But a few, including 24-year-old Brooklynite Douglas Lennox, said he missed the nice view: "It felt like you were peeing on New York."

Dubious Achiever: KGB. Not the Russian KGB—KGB Cleaning Suppliers (named after owners Kevan and Gina Brown), which stocks the restrooms in the Palace of Westminster, where England's Parliament meets

Claim to Shame: Nearly shutting down the British government by neglecting to provide politicians with important papers

True Story: In December 2009, as Parliamentary politicians were discussing the war in Afghanistan, another crisis was unfolding in the building's hallways and offices: There were only a few rolls of toilet paper left in the entire palace—where 13,300 people worked. As news of the shortage spread, staffers began stockpiling whatever TP they could, leaving all the stalls empty. Staff had to make do with whatever they could get their hands on; many threatened to go home and not return until the crisis was averted. According to *The Sun* newspaper, "An emergency order was carried out to save the day." (Several staffers were sent to local markets to buy up all the TP.) The Browns apologized for the mishap, explaining that there had been an "issue with supplies."

Dubious Achiever: A Winder woman

Claim to Shame: Using a public toilet to conceal contraband

True Story: In 2012, a Winder, Georgia, woman (unnamed in press reports), entered a CVS pharmacy and stealthily placed $144.65 worth of items into her handbag. Then she went into a restroom stall and began removing the products from their packages, and stuffing all the wrappers, boxes, and clamshells into the toilet tank. A customer in an adjacent stall heard the commotion and alerted the store manager, who alerted the police. By the time the cops arrived, the shoplifter had retrieved most of the items from the toilet and was placing them on the checkout counter—including five kinds of cold sore medication, MegaRed Omega-3 Krill Oil Capsules, and a laser cat toy. Much of it was wet. As the officers approached, the woman opened a tube of Gold Bond Medicated Cream and started applying it to her lips. "This cold sore is killing me!" she announced. She explained that she planned on paying for everything, but needed to store it in the toilet first. The woman was arrested for shoplifting and permanently banned from CVS.

Dubious Achiever: Cory Buckley, 22, of Akron, Ohio

Claim to Shame: Making a bathroom the scariest place on Earth

True Story: What's the worst thing you could imagine barging in on you when you're sitting on the throne? How about a clown with a knife! That's what happened to 70-year-old Jacqueline Cutright in 2012, when Buckley, wearing a clown mask, robbed her at knife point in her Akron home. "Give me all your drugs and money!" he said. Cutright laughed at him, "Boy, did you ever break into the wrong house." Buckley looked through the medicine cabinet, but all he could find was blood pressure medication, which he took. Then he ordered her to stay seated while he ransacked the rest of the house, stealing costume jewelry and all of her cash—$28. By the time the clown left in Cutright's Ford Escort, she'd managed to call the police, who were right on his tail as he sped away. Buckley didn't even reach the end of the block before losing control of the car and rolling twice. He was arrested. "I thought about doing ninja stuff to him," Cutright joked to reporters, "but I thought, no—he's faster than I am, so I more or less just sat there on the lid."

Dubious Achiever: The Flemish Association of Undertakers

Claim to Shame: Proposing a strange new use for the sewer system

True Story: If the undertakers' plan had been approved by the European Union, their new "corpse disposal system" would have reduced the amount of land needed to inter bodies while also reducing pollution from crematoriums. Here's how it would work: The dearly departed are placed in containers full of water and caustic salts. The containers are pressurized for two hours, leaving only "mineral ash and liquid" behind, which gets flushed into the sewer system, recycled in treatment plants, put back into the water supply, and comes out of the taps of the dead's still-living neighbors. The EU rejected the proposal on moral grounds, but a similar system has been approved by the state legislatures of Maine, Colorado, Florida, Minnesota, Maryland, and Oregon, home of the *Bathroom Reader*. So perhaps one day Uncle John might literally get flushed, which would be a fitting end.

* * *

THE BIG APPLE'S CORE

The first traffic circle in the United States: Columbus Circle in Manhattan, built in 1905. There's a statue of Christopher Columbus at the center of the circle. The statue marks the spot from which the distance from anywhere else to New York City is measured.

A picture appearing within itself is called the Droste effect, after an image on Droste cocoa tins.

TAKE ME TO
YOUR LEADER

More origins of official executive mansions around the world.

COUNTRY: Haiti

RESIDENCE: The National Palace

STORY: In 1912, French-ruled Haiti held a national competition to design a National Palace. When the first-place winner's design was too expensive, the honor went the second-place winner, a Haitian architect named Georges H. Baussan. His design, which is larger than the White House, wasn't cheap, either. It became even more expensive when, still unfinished, it was burned down by rebels in 1915. After that, Haiti was occupied by American forces, who completed construction in 1920. In 2010, a magnitude 7.0 earthquake destroyed much of the National Palace (and much of the island nation), and the government couldn't afford to demolish the rest of it. The Americans came in again—this time led by actor/activist Sean Penn, whose charity provided heavy equipment and volunteers to tear the building down. It was a controversial move that angered many Haitians, who felt it showed weakness. In 2013, the government began building a new National Palace.

COUNTRY: South Korea

RESIDENCE: Cheonwadae

STORY: The president's residence in Seoul is known as the Blue House to foreigners. To the Koreans, it is *Cheonwadae* (Pavilion of Blue Tiles), so named for the multitude of blue tiles used by the Korean royal family when they constructed the palace in the 14th century. It became the president's home in 1948, when the Republic of South Korea was proclaimed.

COUNTRY: Turkey

RESIDENCE: The Pink Villa

STORY: In 1923, Mustafa Kemal Atatürk founded the country of Turkey (in place of the centuries-old Ottoman Empire) and became its first president. For his official residence, he purchased a lodge

---

Former Soviet president Mikhail Gorbachev once starred in a Pizza Hut commercial.

and a vineyard from an Armenian family. In 1932, he gave the compound to the Army and settled in a mansion he had built on the grounds. Its official name is Çankaya Villa, named for the district in which it's located. But most people refer to it as the Pink Villa because…it's pink.

COUNTRY: Canada

RESIDENCE: 24 Sussex Drive

STORY: Located on the bank of the Ottawa River, the official residence of the prime minister was built in 1868 by a millionaire lumberman, Joseph M. Currier, as a wedding gift for his wife. He named it Gorffwysfa, Welsh for "a place of peace." In 1950, the Canadian government appropriated the property as part of a plan to consolidate all governmental agencies in one location. The Currier mansion was designated as the home of the senior political leader. Unlike the White House and many other head-of-state residences, there are no offices at 24 Sussex Drive. The 34-room house is used for just that—a house. (The prime minister conducts business in an office near Parliament.)

COUNTRY: Panama

RESIDENCE: Palacio de las Garzas

STORY: After Panama City was destroyed by English pirate Henry Morgan in 1671, the palace was built by and for the first Spanish governor. The name, which means "Palace of the Herons," came about after President Belisario Porras was gifted several herons to roam the courtyard. An elevator was added in 1934 to accommodate wheelchair-bound U.S. President Franklin Roosevelt for a state visit.

COUNTRY: Argentina

RESIDENCE: Casa Rosada

STORY: Although Argentina's presidents live at Quinta de Olivas, a mansion located north of Buenos Aires, they govern from Casa Rosada, which means "Pink House." (It's officially known as Casa de Gobierno, "House of Government.") It was painted pink in the 1860s to ease tensions between rival political parties, whose colors were red and white. In the 1950s, Eva Perón, wife of President Juan Perón, delivered inspiring speeches from Casa Rosada's balcony to the "shirtless ones," the poor laborers who made her a hero.

Most widely eaten meat: Pork. It makes up more than 36% of the world's meat consumption.

WHAT AN ANIMAL!

Strange tails of creatures great and small.

YOU DO NOT TALK ABOUT CHIRP CLUB

In 2004, Chinese federal agents busted an illegal fighting ring…for crickets. Cricket fighting itself isn't illegal—it's been a tradition among the Chinese aristocracy for a millennium—but *betting* on cricket fights is. The bust saw 115 people arrested and 200 crickets confiscated. And these aren't your average crickets. They're males that have been specially bred to be bigger, stronger, and more vicious than their opponents. Spectators watch this bloodsport on video screens fed from a camera placed over the "ring" (a terrarium). The fights look like something out of an old monster movie: Bulked-up crickets bite and kick and throw each other and don't let up until one of them is injured or dead. How do their handlers get them so mad? They place female crickets in the ring to excite the males…and then remove the females. That makes the males go berserk.

FLY AWAY HOME

In 2012, Englishman Roy Day was ordered to get rid of the 20 pigeons he keeps in his shed. Neighbors complained to the Gravesham Borough Council that the birds are noisy, smelly, and a health risk. Day fought the order, claiming his birds are not a health risk. "They're like members of our family," he said. Besides, if he tried to get rid of them, he couldn't. Reason: They're homing pigeons. "Even if I let them go on the other side of the country, they would fly back here." At last report, Day still owns his pigeons.

SAVED BY THE BEAR

In March 2012, Robert Biggs, 69, of Paradise, California, was hiking and gold-panning in the mountains when he came across a female black bear and her two cubs. Biggs was watching the three bears when, all of a sudden, "Something jumped on my back." It was a mountain lion. Biggs tried to hit the cat with a rock pick, but it wouldn't get off. That's when momma bear lunged in, grabbed the cat by the neck, and started pummeling it. The cat wriggled free and ran away. Then, Biggs said, "The bear walked calmly back to her cub, and I wrapped my arm up with a T-shirt and went gold-panning before I went home." He had a few bruises, scratches, and bite marks, but was otherwise okay.

When Biggs reported his incredible story, it made headlines all over the world. Unimpressed: officials at the California Department of Fish and Game. They couldn't find any evidence at the scene or on Biggs's clothes, and were unable to confirm that his wounds were consistent with a mountain lion attack. Biggs is sticking to his story, though. "I'm a former deputy sheriff," he told reporters, "and police are normal people, but Fish and Game is Gestapo!"

A ROCK IN THE PARK

In 2012, a man walking in Waneka Lake Park in Lafayette, Colorado, passed by a cat on a leash that was attached to a rock. He called police to report that the cat was being attacked by birds. Animal control arrived at the rock a few minutes later, just as the cat's owner, 19-year-old Seth Franco, jogged up to the scene. As the passersby were yelling "animal abuser" at him, Franco explained to officers that he'd tried to take Stella (the cat) jogging with him—which he'd done before—but it was a warm day and she started "panting heavily." So he decided to tether Stella to the rock and finish his run. The officers didn't confiscate the cat because she was unharmed, but they did issue Franco a citation for "domestic-animal cruel treatment." He denies his cat was ever in danger. "There were no birds going at her," he exclaimed, but did admit that there may have been a few "crows crowing at her."

COUCH SURFER

What's cuter than a baby fur seal napping on your couch? Nothing! Annette Swoffer can attest to that. She lives across the road from the Bay of Plenty in New Zealand. One night in 2011, she was investigating strange noises in her kitchen when she discovered the intruder. She thought she must be hallucinating. She wasn't. Then the baby fur seal flopped its way into the living room, jumped up on the sofa, curled up, and fell asleep. When Swoffer called animal control, they thought she might be hallucinating, too. She assured them it was true. When the officers arrived, they couldn't figure out how—or why—the seal had scooted more than 300 yards from the sea. To do so, it had to navigate "a busy road, a long driveway, a

---

...Gandalf (from *The Lord of the Rings*) is hanging in Dumbledore's study.

fence, cat door, two cats, a dog, and a set of stairs." Forty-five minutes later, the officers woke up the seal, carried it out of the house, and drove it back to the ocean. Swoffer told reporters that having the seal over was a "lovely experience."

KENTUCKY FRIED HOBBIT

Nowadays people eat birds, not the other way around. But on an island in Indonesia, as recently as 13,000 years ago, the opposite was true. *Homo floresiensis*, an ancient human-like species referred to by scientists as "hobbit people," shared the island with an ancient species of stork called *Leptoptilos robustus*. "*Robustus*" is putting it mildly—the birds stood more than six feet tall, towering over the three-feet-tall people. Scientists theorize that the birds fed on the hobbits.

SNAKE VS. FOX

Orit Fox, a busty fashion model from Israel, made headlines in 2011 for something other than the size of her silicone implants (reported as the biggest in the Middle East). During a photo shoot, Fox licked a large boa constrictor. The snake retaliated by biting her chest, and it wouldn't let go. Fox freaked out while the snake's handlers tried to remove it. It wasn't easy. After a few agonizing moments, Fox was freed and taken to a hospital, where she was given a tetanus shot. News outlets from around the world reported that the snake "later died of silicone poisoning," but they were spreading a false rumor. It died, but not from ingesting silicone. The snake most likely met its end as a result of the physical trauma it suffered while being separated from Fox's bosom.

SO SAYETH THE GROUNDHOGS

February 2, 2012, was a day that will live in infamy. At least it will in Punxsutawney, Pennsylvania. The trouble began early in the morning on Groundhog Day when Punxsutawney Phil (the prognosticating groundhog) saw his shadow. According to tradition, that meant there would be six more weeks of winter. One problem: Winter hadn't even really begun. Pennsylvania's snowfall totals were so dismal that year that most people hadn't even gotten out their sleds. And here was a groundhog telling people in T-shirts that they still had a month and a half of winter.

In 2001, a cow was discovered with a rare gene mutation that caused it to produce lowfat milk.

Meanwhile, Charles G. Hogg, a groundhog at the Staten Island Zoo in New York (who once bit Mayor Michael Bloomberg), announced, via his handlers, that he hadn't seen his own shadow, which meant winter was on its way out. Not long after, a post appeared on Punxsutawney Phil's official Facebook page: "6 MORE WEEKS OF WINTER!!!!!"

The tie-breaker vote came from Washington, D.C., where a stuffed groundhog known as Potomac Phil "saw" his own shadow, tipping the scales to his Punxsutawney counterpart. At the ceremony, Washington City Council member Jack Evans announced, "It looks like there are a lot of shadows out here, folks. Six more weeks of winter and nine more months of gridlock in Congress." (At least one prediction from that day came true.)

*　　　*　　　*

TWO MUSIC URBAN LEGENDS

Legend: The UPC code on Michael Jackson's album *Thriller* contained the singer's home phone number.

Truth: The numbers-and-bars UPC symbols were first added to packaging in 1974 in order to track product sales, but weren't widely adopted in the U.S. until '82. That was the year Jackson released *Thriller*, one of the first albums to be printed with a UPC. The rumors that they contained his phone number were just that—rumors. The UPC is a series of 12 numbers; the first six are assigned by a government agency, so it would have been impossible for Jackson or anyone else to deliberately insert his phone number into the code—there weren't enough digits left to fit the number.

Legend: Grace Slick and Paul Kantner of Jefferson Airplane had a baby together, and they named her "god."

Truth: It seems plausible that two members of a psychedelic counter-cultural band like Jefferson Airplane would do something this weird, but they didn't. In her memoir *Somebody to Love?*, Slick claims the rumor started in the San Francisco hospital where she gave birth in 1971. A nurse came in with a blank birth certificate, and just as a joke, Slick told her to fill in "god" for the name—with a small "g" because, "We want her to be humble." Slick believes the nurse then called the *San Francisco Chronicle*, who reported the news. (The daughter's real name: China.)

UNDERWEAR IN THE NEWS

*Here's what happens when the
unmentionables get mentioned.*

CROWD FLASKING

If you're tech-savvy, you're probably already familiar with the concept of "crowdfunding." That's when an entrepreneur posts a new business idea on a site like Kickstarter.com and invites people to chip in $5, $10, or some other small amount to help get the business off the ground. In April 2013, two entrepreneurs named Jeff Schneider and Dan Goldman used the process to launch Speakeasy Briefs, a company that makes "underwear with a secret." What's the secret? The crotch contains a zippered pocket large enough to hold a 6-ounce liquor flask, which the company also sells. Schneider and Goldman set a goal of raising $10,000 for the venture…and raised $32,616 from 849 backers the first week alone. The first flask-laden underpants were scheduled to ship in 2013.

A LITTLE LESS CONDENSATION

In August 2012, a British collector of Elvis memorabilia put about a quarter of his collection up for auction in Manchester, England. Among the items that went under the hammer: a framed pair of unwashed underpants with a "suspicious yellow stain on the front of the crotch" that the King wore under one of his famous jumpsuits during a concert in 1977. The light blue underpants, custom-made for Elvis and designed not to show any lines under his tight-fitting pants, were originally obtained from the estate of Vernon Presley. High bid for the skivvies: £5,000, or about $8,000, around $3,000 less than the reserve price—so no sale!

BOWLS AND CUPS

Milwaukee's Holler House bar has two claims to fame: 1) its two bowling lanes are the oldest officially sanctioned lanes in the U.S., and 2) nearly 1,000 women's bras hang from the bar's ceiling. The oldest ones have been there for more than 45 years. The tradi-

---

Queen Isabella dropped all charges against criminals who agreed to sail with Columbus.

tion started in the 1960s when owner Marcy Skowronski and some of her friends "got bombed," as she puts it, took off their tops, and began tossing their bras onto some skis hanging from the ceiling. First-time female visitors to the bar have been hanging their bras from the ceiling ever since. But the tradition came under threat in June 2013, when the city fire inspector declared the bras a fire hazard and ordered them removed. Skowronski, now in her late 80s, complied, but she also complained to her alderman and to the *Milwaukee Journal Sentinel*. That was all it took—after a few calls from the alderman and the newspaper, the city rescinded the fire inspector's order. "Oh, my goodness, we won!" Skowronski told reporters. "We're going to have a party to throw the bras back up."

ROAD TRIP

In *Uncle John's 24-Karat Gold Bathroom Reader*, we told you the story of Mark McIntyre, a cancer survivor who raised $50,000 for the Canadian Cancer Society in 2010 by lounging around in his underpants in a rented Toronto loft for 25 days. The loft was filled with webcams, and when 50,000 viewers clicked "like" on Facebook, Canadian underwear maker Stanfield's donated $50,000 to the Cancer Society. In 2012, McIntyre and Stanfield's were at it again: This time the company challenged McIntyre to hitchhike 2,700 miles across chilly Canada in November, dressed only in a pair of the company's underpants, and to do it in 21 days or less. McIntyre left Vancouver, BC, on November 14, and made it across the finish line—Stanfield's underwear factory in Nova Scotia—with one day to spare. He raised $32,000 for cancer research in the process.

PADDED BRAS

In June 2013, a Canadian woman named Moura El-Asmar and her 16-year-old daughter were arrested by the U.S. Customs and Border Protection officials after they tried to enter the United States with $73,000 in undeclared cash, including $59,000 stuffed into their bras. Laws against sneaking cash into the country exist to thwart drug dealers and other criminals, but this "transaction" was apparently innocent: El-Asmar has another daughter, who is studying to be a doctor in Lebanon, and wanted to send her money to help pay for medical school. But when she tried to wire the money, her bank told her they couldn't wire money to her daughter. So El-Asmar decided to deliver it in person. She was on her way to Detroit to catch a flight to Beirut when she was arrested at the U.S. border. At last report, she was awaiting trial on charges of cash smuggling and lying to a federal agent (the daughter who was accompanying her was not charged). El-Asmar is also waiting to find out if she'll get the $73,000—her entire life savings—back from the feds.

TAKING THE (BEADY) RED-EYE

In the summer of 2013, an American Airlines flight attendant named Louann Giambattista sued the airline, alleging that her life was wrecked when her co-workers accused her of sneaking her pet rat, Willard, onto airplanes…in her pantyhose. The suit stemmed from an incident in 2012, when a pilot spotted a "bulge" on Giambattista's person that he "thought was a live pet." Later that day, on a flight from St. Martin to Miami, a flight attendant claimed she saw Giambattista feeding Willard a dinner roll. (Giambattista says she was eating the roll out of a cup to avoid appearing "unprofessional" in front of passengers.) When the flight landed, Giambattista's colleagues reported her to customs officials, who searched her luggage for more than an hour. No sign of Willard. But Giambattista's passport was flagged, and for more than a year she was questioned and searched every time she went through customs. Giambattista says she now suffers from "debilitating anxiety" and is seeking unspecified damages. She admits to owning Willard but says she never brought him to work. "She's got a lot of pets," said her lawyer, Stephen Morellit. "She had the rat—it died."

*   *   *

THE KING ELVIS BIBLE

On the block in a 2012 auction in Manchester, England: A well-worn Bible given to Elvis Presley by his Uncle Vester and Aunt Clettes in 1957 for his first Christmas at Graceland. The Bible contained the King's handwritten notes and underlining of passages he thought important, including "What is a man advantaged if he gain the whole world and lose himself or be cast away." The Bible sold for £59,000, or about $94,000, more than double the £25,000 it was expected to fetch.

DUMB CROOKS: TECH EDITION

These dumb crooks would have had a much easier time committing their crimes if only they'd been born two centuries earlier—before the Industrial Revolution.

DUMBPHONE
British police suspected 23-year-old Emmanuel Jerome of several home burglaries in Huddersfield, West Yorkshire. Although he denied everything, investigators discovered that during one of the break-ins, Jerome had used his iPhone's flashlight to see…but didn't realize that he'd also activated the video camera. He recorded his own crime, and was sentenced to 10 months in prison.

SMILE, YOU'RE ON DUMB*SS CAMERA

• In 2009, Kadeem Cook, 18, mugged a college student in Philadelphia and ran off with her purse. Later, he used the woman's cell-phone camera to take a self-portrait holding a gun up to his head. What Cook didn't know was the student had programmed her phone to send the pictures it took to her computer. When she received the photo, she sent it to police. After the photo started appearing on the evening news (and all over the Internet), Cook turned himself in.

• In 2012, Timothy Jackson, 18, of Savannah, Georgia, did the same thing. Only he didn't realize he'd photographed himself. He was just pressing random buttons on a stolen phone when a photo of his face automatically popped up on the victim's Facebook page. She sent it to the police, who recognized Jackson because he was on probation. He was arrested.

GAMES PEOPLE PLAY

In 2009, 22-year-old Jeremiah Gilliam stole an Xbox video game console from a home in an affluent section of Westchester County, New York, just north of New York City. He took it to his grandmother's apartment in the Bronx and decided to play a game. But to do so, Gilliam had to log on to the victim's Xbox LIVE account.

First foreign product sanctioned for sale in the Soviet Union: Pepsi Cola (1972).

That made it easy for police to track down the ISP address, which led them straight to Grandma's. When they showed up to question Gilliam, they found 50 other stolen gadgets, and in one fell swoop solved dozens of unsolved burglaries in Westchester County.

GaPS IN JUDGMENT

Police sirens blared behind William Bowen as he drove a car full of stolen contraband through Steens, Mississippi. He didn't know how the cops tracked him down, but figured that one of the stolen items had a GPS device, so he started flinging stuff out of the car—purses, wallets, guns—but couldn't elude the police, who were keeping a safe distance. If only Bowen had tossed the stolen cell phone, he might have gotten away. But he kept it. "This is one of the few cases where someone stole a cell phone with GPS, and all of his movements led us right to him," said police investigator Tony Cooper. Bowen was arrested and charged with 25 separate car burglaries.

STOP, DROP, AND ROLL

Herbert Ridge built a gas-siphoning contraption with an electric pump. One afternoon in October 2012, he was stealing gas from a parked car in East Mesa, Arizona, when the pump sparked and ignited the gasoline, which caught Ridge's T-shirt on fire. He started rolling around in the street, much to the bemusement of kids walking home from school. Then he jumped in his pickup truck and sped away. Only problem: He was still on fire. And so was his truck. Ridge jumped out of the truck and ran away. His flaming pickup, however, kept on going until it smashed into a house and set the building on fire. Neighbors put out the house fire and apprehended Ridge, who was taken to the hospital, and then to jail.

ARMED AND DUMBEROUS

Police described the failed Smart Mart heist in Greentown, Indiana, as a "string of blunders." Blunder number 1: When the four robbers, all men in their 20s, forced the clerk and three customers into a back room, they failed to check the customers for cell phones (because no one these days has a cell phone in their pocket). One of the customers called the cops, who showed up sooner than the robbers expected. Blunder number 2: One of the crooks dropped his credit card at the scene, which eventually led detectives to the

---

Pumpkins get their name from the obsolete French word *pompon*, meaning "large melon."

criminal masterminds' headquarters (a trailer). Blunder number 3: The trailer had a surveillance system that had recorded the criminals "preparing for and returning from the heist." The police had more evidence than they needed to charge the robbers with several felonies.

DON'T DRINK AND DIAL

An intoxicated car thief in Tacoma, Washington, would have gotten away had he not "pocket-dialed" 9-1-1…twice. On the first call, the dispatcher heard a woman screaming and a man telling her to be quiet, so a unit was sent to investigate. The officer saw a car run a red light and gave chase. The woman was released from the car; the man sped away and was able to elude police…until the next morning when he accidentally dialed 9-1-1 again. Police discovered him and a woman, both intoxicated, sitting in another stolen car. The thief had no idea until that moment that he'd been calling 9-1-1 on himself.

A FINE METH

In 2012, a Lewiston, Idaho, police detective received a text message on his cell phone: "U know any1 looking 4 meth?" At first, he thought one of his fellow officers was playing a joke on him because who would be stupid enough to text a cop about a drug deal? Aaron Templeton, a drug dealer with a wrong number, that's who. Templeton, 37, knew where he could obtain a large amount of meth, so he was texting friends, asking them to pitch in to buy it. The detective agreed to pay $150. As he drove into the parking lot and approached Templeton, he received one final text: "Well that's weird, cop just pulled up on me so what's up with that?"

*   *   *

YOU MUST REMEMBER THIS

"Mind-ready" is what psychologists call the casual, offhand nature of conversations. That term also applies to Twitter tweets and Facebook updates, because they reflect how people really talk to each other. Books and articles, on the other hand, are carefully written, rewritten, polished, and edited for maximum effect. Nevertheless, a 2013 study found that Facebook updates are 1.4 times more memorable than published works.

FLUBBED HEADLINES

These are honest-to-goodness headlines, proving that even the most careful editors sometimes make mistooks.

Laxative helps remove earwax

Local Children Are
Winners at Dog Show

Planes forced to
land at airports

Turkeys, manure pass
through the Senate

Institute will immerse
students in volcano

Shark Attack on Porpoise

MSI Owner Denies Lying,
Admits Not Telling the Truth

**Poverty Meeting Attracts
Poor Turnout**

Opinions on the 44st President

*Cows lose their jobs
as milk prices drop*

**Nudists fight erection of
towers near Wreck Beach**

One in for kids drops out
of high school

**House Republicans Are Split
on Whether They're Divided**

52 foot officers to patrol
violent neighborhoods

Porn Star Sues Over
Rear End Collision

*A Fat, Mustachioed
Orphan Finds a Home*

Cop makes arrest in bathroom
after smelling crack

Man convicted of drinking
and sleeping

Surfer survives death
by helicopter

*7-day diarrhea runs
through Bay County*

Slowdown Continues
to Accelerate

Total lunar eclipse will
be broadcast live on
Northwoods Public Radio

Lawyers back despite
use of bug spray

Coldest temperature possible: absolute zero (−459.67°F). Highest possible: unknown.

LIFE AFTER BASEBALL

Coaching, managing, and sportscasting are popular post-baseball careers. But these players went way out in left field after hanging up their spikes.

JOHN MONTGOMERY "MONTE" WARD

Claim to fame: One of the most important ball players of the 1800s, Ward played shortstop and second base. He also pitched (1878–94) for the Giants, Grays, Grooms, and Gothams.

After the game: Attorney

Story: Monte Ward's post-game retirement gig might not seem so odd if he hadn't started out on the wrong side of the law. In 1873, he got kicked out of Penn State for stealing chickens and pushing another student down a flight of stairs. In 1884, he was suspended after punching an umpire in the face. During his Hall of Fame career as a shortstop with the New York Giants, he antagonized owners by helping to form the Brotherhood of Professional Baseball Players, the first sports labor union. Ward graduated from Columbia Law School while still a player, and after retiring from the game, represented many baseball players with grievances against management.

ZACK WHEAT

Claim to fame: Called "one of the most dreaded and murderous sluggers in the National League," Wheat was Brooklyn's left fielder for 17 seasons (1909–26), and ended his career with a lifetime batting average of .317.

After the game: Police officer

Story: Wheat caught so many fly balls in his career that the Tanglefoot Flypaper company put this ad on the outfield wall at Brooklyn's Ebbets Field: "In 1915, Wheat caught 345 flies. Tanglefoot caught 50,000,000,000 flies." Wheat played his final game in 1927 at age 38 and started catching crooks instead of flies for the Kansas City, Missouri, police department. On Easter Sunday, 1936, Wheat crashed his patrol car while trying to catch a fleeing fugitive. He suffered a fractured skull, a dislocated shoulder, a broken wrist, and 15 broken ribs. It took him five months to recuperate from the accident, and

---

We're all born with 2 basic food preferences: We like sweet foods and dislike bitter foods.

Wheat spent that time in Sunrise Beach, Missouri, the shores of the Lake of the Ozarks. He liked the area so much, he decided to start catching fish instead of crooks and opened a 46-acre hunting and fishing resort. Wheat's resort became a popular destination for other ex-ballplayers.

WILLIAM ASHLEY "BILLY" SUNDAY

Claim to fame: A fleet-footed outfielder who played eight seasons in the National League (1883–90), he stole a record 84 bases in a single season.

After the game: Crusading evangelist

Story: Sunday retired from baseball in 1891 and spent the rest of his life as a touring minister. He preached long, dramatic sermons to huge crowds as the "Baseball Evangelist." He was so popular that volunteers built "Billy Sunday Tabernacles" in town after town to hear him preach using quips like: "I know there is a devil for two reasons. First, the Bible declares it; and second, I have done business with him," "Going to church doesn't make you a Christian any more than going to a garage makes you an automobile," and "God likes a little humor, as is evidenced by the fact that he made the monkey, the parrot—and some of you people." When novelist Sinclair Lewis modeled the protagonist (a drunken, dishonest, "hellfire and brimstone" preacher) of his 1927 bestseller *Elmer Gantry* after Sunday, the enraged evangelist called him "Satan's cohort."

RUBE MARQUARD

Claim to fame: The highest-paid baseball player of his time (1908–29), he signed with the New York Giants for $11,000.

After the game: Entertainer

Story: After two seasons with little success, sportswriters were calling Marquard the "$11,000 Lemon," but the lanky left-handed pitcher won more than 200 games before he was through. Marquard's popularity on the field (along with his 6' 3" height and good looks) got him onto the vaudeville stage, where he sang, danced, and did baseball-related skits for $1,500 a week. Over time, he became so popular, the Kalem Movie Film Company hired him to star in his own eponymous silent movie, *Rube Marquard Wins*. The plot: Rube gets kidnapped by gangsters when he refuses to throw a game. *Moving Picture World* reported "Marquard takes to the camera as he does to baseball—just naturally." The ex-ballplayer went on to appear in Broadway shows and movies and to record hit songs such as "Breaking the Record" and "The Marquard Glide."

JIM BUNNING

Claim to fame: One of the rare pitchers to have won 100 games in both the American and National Leagues (1955–71), he also struck out more than 1,000 batters in each league, playing primarily for the Detroit Tigers and the Philadelphia Phillies.

After the game: Politician

Story: No longer running bases, Bunning decided to run for office. In 1977, he was elected to the Fort Thomas, Kentucky, City Council. Then he won a seat in the Kentucky State Senate and became its Republican leader. He made a run for governor in 1983, but lost, so he ran for the U.S. House of Representatives and won. In 1986, Bunning moved from the House to the Senate, beating the Democratic incumbent, former basketball star Scotty Baesler.

Bunning was reelected in '92 and '98, but during his 2004 reelection bid, the senator's behavior was so bizarre that his rising star started to fizzle. He accused his opponent—Democratic Senator Daniel Mongiardo—of looking like one of Saddam Hussein's sons. And when a reporter asked him about Army reservists refusing their missions because of insufficiently armored vehicles in Iraq, the Senator said, "I don't know what you're talking about. I don't watch the news. And I have not read a newspaper in over six weeks." Bunning squeaked back into his Senate seat on George Bush's coattails, but in 2006, *Time* magazine named him one of the "five worst senators" of the year. "He shows little interest in policy unless it involves baseball," *Time* reported. The Hall of Famer's final word on politicians: "When you've dealt with Ted Williams and Mickey Mantle and Yogi Berra and Stan Musial, the people I'm dealing with now are kind of down the scale." Bunning did not run for re-election in 2010 and was succeeded by Senator Rand Paul in 2011.

*   *   *

"I have little hair because my brain is so big it pushes the hair out."
—**Silvio Berlusconi, Italian prime minister**

MAN VS. GRAVITY, PT. II

Does "what goes up" necessarily have to come back down? Not according to Roger Babson! Here's Part II of our story about the man who declared war on one of the most elemental physical forces. Part I is on page 131.

HITTING THE BOOKS

Just as he'd spent his career studying and then recommending individual stocks in his newsletters, Babson figured he could do the same thing in his War on Gravity. First, he'd identify the most promising areas of "antigravity" research. A device for airplanes to prevent them from falling out of the sky, perhaps? Something that elderly people could wear to protect them from bone-breaking falls? Or a ray that could be beamed over bodies of water to make them drown-proof? Whatever he found, he'd call attention to it so that he and other investors could provide financial backing.

Babson tried to tackle the problem the same way he analyzed stocks: by digging up as much information as he could. In that pre-Google era, that meant figuring out which library had the best collection of books on the subject and going there to study the materials in person. But he couldn't find a single library that had an antigravity collection. (There weren't any.) He couldn't find any scientists doing research, either. Antigravity was dismissed as the stuff of science fiction movies and Superman comics, not legitimate scientific inquiry. Nobody took it seriously.

Babson was undaunted. So what if antigravity was considered a pseudoscience? He'd made a name—and millions—applying Newton's third law of motion to the business cycle, and a lot of people thought that was crazy, too. They laughed at him in 1929 when he predicted the stock market would crash, but he'd been right. Back when he was a student at MIT, the best engineering minds at the school had assured him that humans would never fly. Just five years later, Orville and Wilbur Wright, two nobodies who owned a bicycle shop, proved the "experts" wrong.

DO IT YOURSELF

If there weren't any libraries devoted to antigravity research, Babson decided he'd create one. If scientists were too embarrassed to

---

1st American guide dog: Lux, a German shepherd owned by U.S. Sen. Thomas Schall (1926).

work in such a stigmatized field, he'd lift the stigma by creating a prestigious annual prize for the best scientific paper on the subject. If someone succeeded in inventing an anti-gravity device, he'd award them a cash prize, too. It was with these goals in mind that he founded the Gravity Research Foundation in 1949.

BOMB-PROOF

As Babson was drawing up plans for his foundation, the Soviet Union detonated its first atomic bomb. That led him to decide that his foundation should be able to continue its important work even after a nuclear attack, so he located its headquarters in the town of New Boston, New Hampshire, 60 miles north of Boston, Massachusetts (and far enough away to survive if the city was ever attacked by the Russians). To ensure that the foundation would be self-sufficient in a post-apocalyptic world, he stocked it with 1,000 gallons of fuel oil and bought 1,400 acres of nearby forest land, so that it would never run out of lumber or firewood.

Babson hoped the foundation would one day serve as a gathering place for the antigravity community. He bought a building in New Boston and converted it into a conference hall, then bought others to provide housing for staff and for visiting antigravity scholars. He stocked the foundation's library with 34,000 books. He also bought a company called Invention, Inc., which tracked applications at the U.S. Patent Office. He ordered the company's investigators to watch for any patents that might be useful in the development of antigravity devices.

ETCHED IN STONE

The Gravity Research Foundation awarded its first essay prizes in December 1949. To publicize its work and to encourage universities to take up their own antigravity research, the foundation began awarding "gravity grants" to any schools willing to place a granite tombstone-like marker in a prominent location on campus. Colby College in Waterville, Maine, took the deal; their marker states that its purpose is

> TO REMIND STUDENTS OF THE BLESSINGS FORTHCOM-
> ING WHEN A SEMI-INSULATOR IS DISCOVERED IN ORDER
> TO HARNESS GRAVITY AS A FREE POWER AND REDUCE
> AIRPLANE ACCIDENTS

World's oldest recipe: Raw fish salad, with radish, ginger, chives & basil (China, 1330 B.C.).

The wording sounded silly even then; some of the 13 colleges that agreed to place markers on campus successfully lobbied for subtler inscriptions. Some schools received cash grants, others got stock. The schools that received stock were instructed to keep it for 30 to 40 years, then sell it and use the money for "scientific purposes in the name of the Gravity Research Foundation."

NOSEDIVE

For all the time, money, and effort that Babson devoted to his war against gravity, he never came close to elevating antigravity research above the level of pseudoscience. Even the essay contest lasted only one year in its original form. When its request for essays providing "suggestions for antigravity devices, for partial insulators, reflectors, or absorbers of gravity, or for some substance that can be rearranged by gravity to throw off heat" attracted little scientific interest, Babson changed the request to "essays on the subject of gravitation, its theory, applications, or effect."

The foundation never grew beyond being Babson's personal plaything, either. When he died in 1967 and no one stepped in to pay the bills, it wound down its operations and sold off its buildings and other assets. It continues today in skeleton form, still hosting the essay contest, which became quite prestigious after the antigravity reference was dropped. British physicist Stephen Hawking (who occupies the same Cambridge University post that Sir Isaac Newton did in the 1670s) has won five times.

WHAT GOES AROUND...

About the only surviving physical reminders of Babson's crusade are the odd stone markers that still dot 13 college campuses from Maine to Florida. The one at Tufts University sits outside the Institute of Cosmology, founded in 1989 with the money from Babson's gravity grant. There astrophysicists study the forces that created and shape the universe, including, believe it or not, antigravity. Not the kind Babson imagined, but antigravity just the same: "Much of the research at the institute is focused on false vacuum and its repulsive gravity, which certainly qualifies as antigravity," says Alexander Valenkin, the institute's director. "So I think Mr. Babson could not have found better use for the money."

RUSSIAN RIB ROCK

If you think file sharing is risky or inconvenient, it's nothing compared to what people went through in 1960s Russia to get their hands on banned Western music.

FAVORITE CONTRABANDS

Before cassettes, computers, recordable CDs, and BitTorrent, sharing music with your friends wasn't easy. This was especially true in the Soviet Union in the 1950s and '60s, where citizens were forbidden to even own, much less share entire categories of music—jazz and rock 'n' roll, in particular. There was only one record company, Melodiya, and being state-owned, it echoed government policy about jazz and rock: "Musicians such as these, who have plunged to the depth of musical decline, do not deserve a place on Soviet records."

However, where there was a will—and a chance to make a profit—there was a way to make a rudimentary copy of a vinyl disk or a radio broadcast. Outside the Soviet Union, it was possible to buy or rent a portable record-cutting machine, a heavy, suitcase-sized device that would cut a custom recording on a record blank. These machines became especially popular during World War II, when soldiers separated from their families could send and receive disks as talking letters, but could also make personal recordings so they could hear themselves (often for the first time) talking, telling jokes, and singing.

CROSSING BORDERS

Needless to say, record-cutting machines weren't available in the Soviet Union, a place where even typewriters were difficult to come by. Both were seen as ways of spreading unauthorized personal or political expression, an unwelcome activity in a police state. But then something happened that briefly opened up the Russian borders and brought some of the outside world to its citizens: World War II. Germany attacked the Soviet Union. When the Red Army and the Russian winter battled the Nazis to a standstill, Germany eventually pulled back. The Soviet Army pressed forward, harassing the Germans back into their own border and using the opportunity to seize and occupy Eastern Europe. Suddenly Soviet farmboys were

---

The Giant Pacific Kelp grows at a rate of 1 foot per day and can grow to 175 feet.

being exposed to the alluring temptations of big cities like Krakow, Prague, Zagreb, and Berlin. Not exactly Paris, London, or New York, but to a Russian, they might as well have been: Consumer goods and stylish clothes were all available. So were exciting new kinds of forbidden music from the West, from big band to jazz to rhythm and blues.

Pretty soon, musical recordings were being smuggled into the Soviet Union hidden in soldiers' gear, to be played on home phonographs—quietly, so the neighbors wouldn't turn them in to the secret police. Some of the more enterprising soldiers returned with more dangerous and outrageous contraband: the recording machines they bought (or took as spoils of war) from the local population.

BLANKING OUT

But there was a problem: The machines required a blank disk for every record made. Once their initial supply ran out, the Russians were out of luck. The blank disks weren't available in Russia, threatening to make the machines useless. Russians, however, were used to shortages of almost everything and got very good at converting whatever they could scrounge into whatever they needed. They put their talents into finding something that was cheap and plentiful that might be usable as a recording medium.

It had to be a soft-enough material to accept a cut from a vibrating needle but durable enough to keep the groove intact when played with another needle. After experimenting with foils, sheet metal, glossy cardboards, and who knows what else, somebody finally came up with a slightly macabre solution from a strange place: hospital garbage bins.

RED SKELETONS

In a secretive society, it's hard to come up with the definitive history of anything that's illegal. According to one story, it was a jazz-loving medical student who first came up with the notion that discarded X-rays might make a decent record. They were certainly plentiful. You'd think that personal X-rays would be kept in patients' files, but according to the stories, hospitals discarded them regularly, and they could either be picked out of the garbage for free or—according to some accounts—bought for a few kopeks.

These used plastic sheets, although flexible, were thick enough

The word *tragedy* comes from the ancient Greek for "goat song."

and firm enough to hold the etchings of the recording machine. True, they didn't last long and tended to warp (and the sound wasn't exactly high fidelity), but they were cheap and far better than the alternative, which was no popular music at all.

Recording "Bone Rock" or "Rib Rock" (as the records were called) first required cutting the sheets into a circle with a hole in the center. Long before heavy metal and goth made skulls and bones a standard rock visual, Russian rock fans were buying one-sided recordings of John Coltrane, Elvis, Buddy Holly, and the Platters, decorated with X-rays of skulls, ribs, hips, and other bones, usually selected and centered for the best aesthetic visual presentation.

CUTTING EDGES
The relatively few voice-recording machines looted during the war weren't enough to keep up with the demand for bootleg music. The loose network of record makers known as *Roentgenizdat* (a play on words meaning "X-ray publishing house") laboriously made an estimated three million records—one at a time—during the 1950s and '60s. According to accounts from Russians, photograph salons got in on the act, too, buying machines ostensibly to cut "audio postcards" for customers, then using them at night to copy records. Furthermore, black marketers and music lovers (some say it was actually the same med student who discovered the suitability of X-rays) discovered that you could turn two phonographs into a duplicating machine, playing a record on one turntable and routing the audio into the other with a heavy arm adapted to scratch the vibrations into the blank.

COPYCATS
A major underground market developed. Records generally came marked with a cryptic number, but no names of songs or artists, which helped avoid incrimination if discovered by the authorities. The music was fairly eclectic, pretty much whatever bootleggers could get their hands on. One reliable source of contraband records was Finnish and Swedish sailors who were allowed to dock in the ports of Riga and Leningrad. Popular in the 1950s were Little Richard and Bill Haley & the Comets from America, and British acts like Tommy Steele and Johnny & the Hurricanes. In the '60s it was the Beatles, the Rolling Stones, and Motown.

Not only was rib rock the music people wanted, but the records were cheap. An official disc from the state record company cost five rubles—a week's lunches for the average workingman. A rib-rock pressing cost only one, maybe one and a half rubles, the equivalent of skipping a lunch or an 8-ounce "individual size" bottle of vodka.

CRACKING SKULLS

It took a while, but the authorities finally got fed up. First, they tried ruining the market by putting out their own "bone records." They looked identical to the real thing, but there was a difference: The music would start, then suddenly stop, and a voice would shout something along the lines of "You want rock and roll? F*** you, you anti-Soviet slime!" Then, in 1958, it became illegal to own a "bones" record. At least 10 producers and sellers were arrested and sent to work camps. Yet people continued "listening to the bones" because—perhaps not unlike the file sharing today—they thought it was worth the risk.

REAL, TOO REAL

In the early 1970s, rib records started becoming obsolete. As the rest of the world began discovering cassettes as a way of sharing playlists, the Soviet Union went another route. Reel-to-reel tape recorders were finally being made available in local electronic stores. The sound quality was better, and it was easier to make a decent copy for friends. It was also possible to record shortwave-radio broadcasts from Radio Luxembourg and other Western sources that were no longer being electronically jammed by Russian authorities.

As the Cold War eased later in the decade, Melodiya finally began making available some of the music from the 1950s and '60s that the government had tried so hard to suppress. Music lovers were finally able to begin hearing the music as recorded. One fan reported weeping after hearing an undistorted recording of *The Beatles (White Album)* for the first time, not realizing, he said, details such as there being a second voice singing harmony on the song "I Will."

The skeletons of X-ray records were finally laid to rest. More than 50 years after the fact the records are getting pretty hard to find outside of Russia, but if you want to hear what one sounds like you can find MP3 files of the Beatles recordings online.

Worldwide, Greeks eat the most cheese—an average of 68 pounds per person per year.

A NEW GERMANY IN TEXAS, PART II

Here's the second installment of our story about how some German nobles tried to set up a colony in Texas. So why don't more Texans sprechen sie deutsche *instead of English? Read on. (Part I is on page 286.)*

DER WAGON TRAIN

Not long after the first shipload of German settlers arrived in the port of Galveston, Prince Carl arranged for them to be transported to Indian Point, where they were housed in tents and sheds that had been thrown together to accommodate them. The settlers squatted there for more than two months before the prince finally hired enough wagons to begin moving them in the general direction of the Fisher-Miller land grant.

By that time, the prince had decided that making the 300-mile journey all at once was too much for the settlers, since 1) the land grant was deep inside hostile Comanche country, and 2) neither he nor anyone else associated with the Adelsverein—not even Henry Fisher, one of the men for whom the Fisher-Miller land grant was named—had ever set foot on it. So as the wagon train slowly made its way northwest along the banks of the Guadalupe River in January 1845, Prince Carl raced ahead, searching for a suitable site for a way station that would allow these and future settlers to travel to the land grant in stages. He found one about 165 miles inland from Indian Point, near a natural spring called Las Fontanas, on the road connecting Austin (45 miles to the northeast) to San Antonio (30 miles to the southwest). There, in mid-March, he bought two leagues, or about 18 square miles of land, for $1,100.

OUR TOWN

Seven days later, the wagon train arrived at the spot. Each household was awarded a lot in what would soon become the town of New Braunfels (named in honor of Braunfels, the prince's family estate in Germany), and a ten-acre parcel outside of town that they could begin farming right away. It was a far cry from the 320 acres they'd been promised, but after everything the settlers had been through, they were eager to start their new lives.

SEE YA!

As for Prince Carl, he remained in New Braunfels for about a month before he abruptly announced that he'd resigned his post and was going back to Germany. He never returned to Texas. He didn't even stick around New Braunfels long enough to see his successor, Baron Ottfried von Meusebach (who soon Americanized his name to John O. Meusebach), arrive. Why did the prince leave so quickly? Meusebach got his first clue soon after he arrived at New Braunfels in May 1845 and had a look at Prince Carl's financial records. He discovered that not only had the prince spent every penny he'd been given, he'd also racked up more than $34,000 of unpaid debts.

By now the Adelsverein had already spent most of its $80,000 grubstake resettling thousands of Germans in the Fisher-Miller land grant, and all it had to show for its money was a few hundred settlers living in New Braunfels, well outside of the grant, plus some stragglers who remained at Indian Point.

Even worse—at least as far as the Society was concerned—two months earlier, on March 1, 1845, President John Tyler had signed a joint resolution annexing the Republic of Texas to the United States. With Texas joining the Union, whatever chance there had been for a "new Germany" on Texas soil, complete with its own German monarchy and nobles lording over giant estates carved out of the territory, was gone forever. The purpose for creating the Adelsverein having been defeated, the nobles were quickly losing interest in putting any more of their money into the lost cause.

YOU'VE GOT COMPANY

That would have been bad enough if the only people depending on the Adelsverein's largesse were the settlers at New Braunfels and Indian Point, but thousands more settlers were already on their way. Precisely how many has been lost to history: The passage of time and the destruction of records in hurricanes in 1875, 1886, and 1900 make an accurate count impossible. It's estimated, however, that from October 1845 to April 1846, between 36 and 50 ships arrived in Galveston carrying no fewer than 5,200 settlers and possibly more than 8,000. It's a mystery why the Adelsverein didn't just cancel the ships that hadn't already departed for Texas—perhaps it didn't want to refund the money the settlers had already paid in. Whatever the reason, the ships full of settlers kept coming, and Meusebach had to find a way to prepare for them.

PFENNIG PINCHERS

He didn't get much help from the Adelsverein. Though Meusebach estimated that he needed at least $120,000 to feed and house the new settlers, plus pay the debts Prince Carl had racked up, the Society gave him just $24,000. That wasn't even enough money to provide adequate shelter at Indian Point, and as a result, many hundreds of settlers shivered through the unusually cold, wet winter in whatever lean-tos, dugouts, or other shelter they could improvise for themselves. Many made do without any shelter at all, huddling in blankets out in the damp, open air.

Healthy people would have had a hard enough time surviving under such conditions, and these settlers were anything but. They'd come across the Atlantic on the same kind of rat-infested ships the first group of settlers had. They were weakened by scurvy from the poor shipboard diet and by typhus carried by rats. Disease would kill some 300 on board the ships before they even made it to Texas. Once the remaining thousands were huddled together at Indian Point without adequate food or shelter or sanitation, cholera and dysentery from polluted drinking water (plus malaria, yellow fever, typhoid fever and other diseases carried by mosquitos that bred in nearby swamps) would soon kill hundreds more.

OUT OF DER FRYING PAN...

Meusebach did his best to keep the settlers alive as more and more of them arrived at Indian Point. By March, he'd hired enough wagons to begin transporting them in groups to New Braunfels and also to a second settlement called Fredericksburg that he'd established as a second way station 60 miles beyond New Braunfels.

When he wasn't arranging transportation, he scrambled around the countryside buying up grain and livestock (on credit whenever possible) to feed the settlers. In April, he went to Nassau Farm, the Adelsverein's plantation east of New Braunfels, to see if they'd grown any crops that could feed the settlers. The managers told him they'd planted cotton, a cash crop, instead of food crops and had no food to spare. Falling ill with fever, Meusebach spent three months recovering at Nassau Farm, far from the settlers who needed him.

ON DER MARCH

If the settlers who'd survived the hard winter months at Indian Point thought the worst was finally over once the wagon trains started moving, their relief lasted only until May, when war broke out between the United States and Mexico, and the U.S. government appropriated all their hired wagons for the war effort.

Thousands of men, women, and children were still stranded at Indian Point. Of these, some 500 gave up the fight and went back to Germany. Another 500 men who were of military age enlisted in the U.S. Army to fight in the war, perhaps calculating that they had a better chance of survival on the battlefield than they did in the hands of the Adelsverein. Such an assessment would not have been wide of the mark: By now the conditions at Indian Point were so desperate that many settlers decided to walk the 165 miles to New Braunfels rather than remain any longer where they were, waiting for Meusebach to return.

"This proved disastrous to many, more than 200 perishing on the way from exposure, hunger, and exhaustion," wrote historian Moritz Tiling in his 1913 book, *The History of the German Element in Texas*. "The bleached bones of the dead everywhere marked the road of death the unfortunate people had taken, while those who arrived at New Braunfels and later at Fredericksburg carried with them the germs of disease that soon developed into a frightful epidemic, in which more than 1,000 people died." More than one contemporary account has described how great numbers of vultures followed the slow-moving column of settlers, "marking its progress from above."

LETTER FROM AMERICA

During these difficult months Meusebach had sent one report after another to the Adelsverein in Germany describing the situation and begging for money to keep the settlers from starving. His pleas were ignored. When he was finally well enough to travel to Galveston, he instructed the Adelsverein's agent there to send another report to Germany...only this time to German newspapers, not to the Adelsverein, in the hope that the newspapers would make the German public aware of the settlers' plight.

The average square yard of sidewalk in downtown Mexico City has 70 wads of discarded gum.

That did the trick. In the summer of 1846, when the newspapers began describing in vivid detail how the Adelsverein had left the stranded settlers to starve in Texas, the Society coughed up another $60,000 and sent it to Meusebach. The money didn't arrive in New Braunfels until September, by which time hundreds more settlers had died from hunger, exposure, and disease.

ON DER MEND

Adding $60,000 to the $24,000 Meusebach had started with still came up well short of the $120,000 he felt was necessary to provide for the settlers, but it was enough, at least, to keep them from starving. And with contemporary estimates placing the death toll as high as 1,600 people, the sad truth was that Meusebach now had many fewer mouths to feed.

The $60,000 also gave Meusebach enough money to transport the settlers still at Indian Point to New Braunfels and Fredericksburg; by the end of September 1846, everyone who wanted to go had gone. Those Germans who remained at Indian Point founded the town of Indianola. (Destroyed by a hurricane in 1875, Indianola was rebuilt then destroyed again in 1886 by a hurricane and a fire. The town was then abandoned. Today most of it is underwater.)

The bad publicity created by the newspapers and by disillusioned settlers returning to Germany also helped ease the crisis by bringing new arrivals to Indian Point to an end. Those settlers who had not yet left Germany canceled their plans, and those who stopped in Galveston on their way to Indian Point refused to go any farther. They settled in Galveston and other settlements, and established their own communities rather than take any more chances with the Adelsverein.

JOURNEY'S END

With the worst of the crisis over, Meusebach managed to do something that no one associated with the Adelsverein had yet been able to do: In January 1847, he stepped onto the Fisher-Miller land grant. He did so as the head of a 45-person expedition into Comanche territory, where he made peace with the Comanche chiefs and signed a treaty that opened more than three million acres of land to settlement. The treaty was one of Meusebach's last acts as an official of the Adelsverein. By the time he signed it, he'd already sent his letter of resignation off to Germany; it went into effect when his successor, a man named Hermann Speiss, arrived in July 1847.

Speiss's job would be much easier than Meusebach's had been. Much shorter, too, because not long after he arrived, the Adelsverein sent word that it was bankrupt and that the settlers were on their own.

ICH BIN EIN TEXAN

The Adelsverein was dead and so was the idea of a Germany in Texas. But the Germans themselves kept coming, in ever-growing numbers and on their own instead of under the sponsorship of incompetent, self-interested aristocrats. By 1850, there were more than 33,000 Germans living in Texas, comprising more than one-fifth of the white population and making them one of the largest ethnic groups (after Latinos).

The German immigrants tended to form their own German-speaking communities rather than assimilate with their English- and Spanish-speaking neighbors. Texas was a slave state: It seceded from the Union during the Civil War, and because the Germans opposed slavery, they suffered at the hands of other Texans during the war. (Fredericksburg was placed under martial law.) The abuse intensified the determination of German Texans to keep to themselves and to refuse to learn English. Few of their schools taught English or had English-speaking teachers until the early 20th century.

These communities might still be speaking their own unique dialect of "Texas-German" today were it not for the fact that Germany and the United States were on opposite sides in both World War I (1914–18) and World War II (1941–45). During the war years, the stigma of being German was so strong that parents stopped speaking German to their children, and English replaced the mother tongue as the language of instruction in the public schools. Today, fewer than 6,000 fluent speakers of Texas-German remain. In 2001, the University of Texas at Austin founded the Texas German Dialect Project to document the dialect and record the last speakers before they disappear forever.

*   *   *

"There is glory in a great mistake." —**Nathalia Crane**

EAT TODAY, GONE TOMORROW

Restaurants are difficult businesses—profit margins are low, hours are long, and today's hot spot is tomorrow's has-been. Here are a few eateries that, despite being popular, innovative, or even legendary, faded into history.

Restaurant: Lutèce
Location: Manhattan
Story: When you think of *the* typical fancy restaurant, you're thinking of Lutèce—or at least a restaurant that was influenced by Lutèce (pronounced loo-tess). Restaurateur Andre Surmain and chef Andre Soltner opened it in Manhattan in 1961. Surmain left after just a few years, leaving Soltner as the chef and owner until the 1990s, when he sold it to a large restaurant group. Throughout, Lutèce sold signature, quintessentially classic French dishes, such as onion tarts, French onion soup, escargot, and foie gras. Julia Child once called it "the best restaurant in America." It was such a New York institution that it's often mentioned as the fanciest place for the wealthy to dine in movies and TV shows, including *Wall Street*, *Arthur*, and *Mad Men*.

Closed: In the 2000s, Lutèce's fortunes diminished, owing to decreased tourism to New York City after 9/11 and a general economic downturn, which meant fewer people dining on their companies' expense accounts. It also didn't help that, as New York's vibrant culinary scene was changing, Lutèce's concept of an exciting meal was stuck in the 1960s. Lutèce served its last round of snails, cooked to perfection, on Valentine's Day, 2004.

Restaurant: Fanny's
Location: Evanston, Illinois (just outside of Chicago)
Story: In 1946 Fanny Bianucci and her father opened a lunch counter to serve construction workers in Evanston, a blue-collar suburb of Chicago. The following year Fanny converted it into a full-service restaurant. She created two of the restaurant's signature items herself—Italian-style salad dressing and pasta sauce—after months of trial-and-error (she settled on the recipe that tasted best,

Thanks! Food chemist William A. Mitchell helped invent Tang, Cool Whip, and Pop Rocks.

but put the least stress on her own sensitive digestive system). One night in 1948, Bianucci asked a customer his name, and he said "Marshall Field," as in the multi-millionaire owner of a Chicago-based chain of department stores. Bianucci chastised him for impersonating such a famous person. The next day, a reporter from Field's *Chicago Sun-Times* arrived to interview her. The article (and Field's recommendation) immediately made Fanny's a hotspot for Chicago's elite "North Shore" neighborhood, which wasn't far from Evanston. President Eisenhower dined there, as did Mae West and Louis Armstrong. It was widely known as one of the best Italian restaurants in the United States.

Closed: By 1987 Bianucci was in her 80s, and in mourning over the death of her husband, so after running the restaurant for four decades, she decided to close down Fanny's. She died three years later. You can still buy Fanny's brand salad dressing and tomato sauce in Chicago area supermarkets, and online.

Restaurant: Maxim's (of Texas)

Location: Houston

Story: When classically trained French chef Camille Bermann opened it in 1949 (he stole the name from a famous Paris restaurant), the French bistro was the first upscale restaurant in Houston. It would inspire dozens more fancy restaurants to open in the city, whose growth exploded in the mid-20th century, thanks to oil money. Maxim's was decorated in the style of classic French décor, including red wallpaper, big chandeliers, and reproductions of French works of art.

Closed: Maxim's never updated its look or changed its menu. Never. It grew increasingly obsolete as the Houston restaurant scene grew. Just two years after *Texas Monthly* named it "Restaurant of the Year" in 1999 Camille Bermann's son shut it down in 2001.

Restaurant: El Bulli

Location: Roses, Spain

Story: El Bulli was the culinary playground of Ferran Adria, widely regarded as one of the world's best and most creative chefs. Adria is the originator of the food movement called "molecular gastronomy" in which science is used to deconstruct, reconstruct, and recombine ingredients to create outlandish new foods. For example, El

Bulli has offered Clam Meringue, Hot-Cold Gin Fizz, and *bunuelo de llebre*, which is a chilled pastry containing piping-hot liquefied rabbit meat. El Bulli opened in 1987 in an isolated seaside town in northeastern Spain. Nevertheless, it received a million reservation requests a year, but could only seat 50 people a night. And it was only open six months a year, so Adria could have time to travel the world seeking out new foods and bring them back to experiment with. Cost of a dinner at El Bulli: 270 euros (about $400) for a set tasting menu of 20 to 30 bite-size dishes.

Closed: In 2011, Adria closed El Bulli because he was in a "creative slump," but plans to turn it into the El Bulli Foundation for aspiring molecular gastronomists in 2015.

Restaurant: Chasen's
Location: West Hollywood
Story: Dave Chasen was the silent sidekick to New York vaudeville comedian named Joe Cook—the punchlines invariably involved Chasen getting hit on the head. Chasen also cooked. He hated eating cold beans after performances, so he'd bring a huge pot of chili and leave it backstage for all to share. That led to his manning the grill, cooking steaks and ribs at late-night parties at Cook's home in New Jersey, attended by New York tastemakers. The duo stopped performing after Cook was diagnosed with Parkinson's disease, and Chasen had to pursue his back-up plan: open a restaurant. He borrowed money from friends ($200 from Frank Capra, $20,000 from *New Yorker* editor Harold Ross), and moved to California after an old vaudeville pal suggested he open a place in Hollywood. In 1936, he opened Chasen's Southern Pit—it served ribs and chili (and alcohol), housed six tables, and had ping-pong tables to keep customers occupied while they waited for a table. The location was ideal: It was just down the road from the new mansions built by the first wave of movie stars, and close to the offices of film executives, who started to entertain and do business with clients at Chasen's.

In 1941, the room expanded, adding dozens of leather-upholstered booths, and a menu that included steaks and imported seafood. It became *the* premiere hangout for Hollywood's biggest stars. Frank Sinatra was a regular (he loved the chicken curry), and so were Shirley Temple (the "Shirley Temple" drink was invented at Chasen's), Orson Welles (who ordered double portions), and Jimmy

Stewart, who dined there with his wife every Thursday night for decades. Ronald Reagan proposed to Nancy Davis at Chasen's; Alfred Hitchcock outlined the plot of *Notorious* there one night. Another reason why the stars loved it: no gossip columnists or photographers were allowed. It was primarily a Hollywood insider haunt until 1962 when Elizabeth Taylor telegrammed Chasen from the set of *Cleopatra* in Rome and asked him to ship ten quarts of his famous chili to her. Newspapers picked up the story and Chasen's profile soared.

Closed: As Old Hollywood died out, so did its hangouts. By the 1990s, the hot restaurant was no longer Chasen's—it was Spago. Chasen's closed to the public in April 1995, but remained open for Hollywood private parties and for use as a filming location. Two years later, everything inside, including the bar, booths, and wall paneling, was auctioned off. The building was torn down and replaced with a Bristol Farms grocery store and café, which sports a few of the original Chasen's booths. (Reagan's booth is at his official presidential library.)

Restaurant: Gage & Tollner

Location: Brooklyn

Story: Gage & Tollner (named for founders Charles Gage and Eugene Tollner) opened in 1879 as an "eating house," and moved to its permanent location, a four-story brownstone on Fulton Street, in 1892. There, it became an elegant restaurant for New York's elite (it was a particular favorite of Diamond Jim Brady in the 1890s, and Mae West in the 1930s). The dining room was lit with 36 brass gaslight lamps, which a waiter would showily light by hand each night at dusk. Other amenities: cut-glass chandeliers, mahogany tables, and mirrored walls. The food: oysters and chops and other classic American food, until a 1980s change to high-end soul food.

Closed: By the 1990s, Fulton Street was being redeveloped, blocking off large parts of the area to car traffic. That hurt Gage & Tollner, as did the tourism and expense-accounts problems that plagued Lutèce. And it was also too far from the hip, booming Brooklyn neighborhoods of Williamsburg and Park Slope to attract younger patrons. Like Lutèce, Gage & Tollner closed Valentine's Day, 2004. In 2010, the building was sold for $2.5 million, and the space was converted into an Arby's.

MISFIT TOYS

A few more violent, racist, and otherwise inappropriate items with one strange thing in common: Kids are supposed to play with them.

WOODY. A lot of products that use licensed names or images are actually counterfeit. Besides being illegal, they're also shoddy. This bootleg *Toy Story 3* action figure from China has a sound chip—probably a leftover from another bootleg—that tells a slightly different story than the beloved film. At the push of a button on Woody's back, the sound of a rapid-fire machine gun plays along with a voice that screams, "Fire! Fire! Fire! Code blue! Fire! Drop the gun!" (Machine gun not included.)

XENA THE WARRIOR PRINCESS. Part of a Hercules toy line from the 1990s, the packaging for the curvaceous doll suggests that kids "Remove Xena's Princess warrior outfit!" What's so odd about that? She's not wearing anything underneath it.

CRAZY FOR YOU TEDDY BEAR. For Valentine's Day 2005, the Vermont Teddy Bear Co. sold this $70 bear bound in a white straight jacket that came with "commitment papers." Mental health professionals weren't crazy about the bear, and after numerous complaints, the toy company put it away for good.

BLACK BANDIT. The LEGO company has distanced itself from what Muslim groups have dubbed the "terrorist LEGO." Sold by an unlicensed LEGO enthusiast from Seattle named Will Chapman, Black Bandit is a head-scarf-wearing, bearded LEGO man armed with an "RPG, C96 Broomhandle Mauser Pistol, AK Assault Rifle, M67 Frag Grenades, and Black Rubber Band Bandoleer." Chapman denies the bandit is a terrorist, instead calling it a "generic bad guy."

STAR KNIGHT. Designers of the Chinese Darth Vader look-alike made a few changes to avoid lawsuits. For one, it's fatter than authorized versions of the *Star Wars* character. And for some reason, pudgy Vader comes on a white police motorcycle (it actually says, "POLICE" on it), presumably so he can pull people over and say, "I find your lack of doughnuts disturbing."

More than half of your blood is "plasma"—the yellow fluid that contains the blood cells.

NOT-YOUR-ORDINARY FILM FESTIVALS

Cannes and Sundance get all the press, but we're more interested in film festivals like these.

THE INSECT FEAR FILM FESTIVAL

Location: The University of Illinois at Urbana-Champaign

Background: Founded in 1984 by UIUC entomology professor May Berenbaum. "Upon reading a poster advertising a Godzilla festival," says Berenbaum, "I thought a similar event featuring insect fear films might be both fun and educational." It's been going every year ever since.

What You'll See: The festival takes place in a single evening in February. (It's free.) They show two or three feature-length films, along with several shorts, all featuring insects in a prominent way. Examples:

• *Mothra* (1961): A radioactive moth-monster attacks Tokyo.

• *Glass Trap* (2005): Giant flesh-eating ants invade a skyscraper.

• *Centipede Horror* (1984): An evil wizard makes beautiful women vomit up live centipedes, after which the centipedes eat the beautiful women and whoever else is around. (Brilliant!)

Bonus: Before the movies start, Berenbaum and festival staff bring out insects for the audience to see...and touch...and sometimes eat. At one recent festival, audience members were served deep-fried waxworms and stir-fried silkworm pupae. (Don't worry—they also have popcorn.)

THE INCREDIBLY STRANGE FILM FESTIVAL

Location: Various cinema houses in Auckland and Wellington, New Zealand

Background: This festival was founded by New Zealand amateur filmmaker Ant Timpson. Its origins, Timpson says, go back to 1984 and his college days, when he started collecting bizarre films and showing them to friends and at dormitory keg parties. (He was in law school.) By 1994, that had evolved into the Incredibly Strange

---

Built in A.D. 126, the 5,000-ton concrete dome of the Roman Pantheon is still standing.

Film Festival. It was a traveling festival for several years, showing in cities all over New Zealand until 2004 when it became an official part of the New Zealand International Film Festival.

What You'll See: The ISFF is "dedicated to screening bizarre flicks that would otherwise never see the light of day." And they get some real doozies. Examples from some recent festivals:

• *Hobo with a Shotgun* (2011): Rutger Hauer plays a hobo…with a shotgun!…who saves an entire town from an evil crime lord.

• *Nude on the Moon* (1961): A wealthy young rocket scientist builds a rocket and flies to the moon, which, amazingly, he discovers is crawling with scores of topless women.

• *Flesh Feast* (1970): Nazis in Florida have Adolf Hitler's body, and they're going to revive it and take over the world!

THE BRING YOUR OWN FILM FESTIVAL

Location: The Hotel Pink House, Puri, Odisha, India

Background: The BYOFF was founded by a group of Indian film-makers in this Indian East Coast resort town in 2004.

What You'll See: There is no jury and no screening process to go through—just show up with a film, register, and have it shown. (It's first-come, first-serve for the best time slots.) For five days and nights, the films of filmmakers—amateur and professional—from all over the world are shown in tents on the beach or on open-air screens after dark.

• At the 2012 festival, a man named Viraj Singh (he shows up every year) presented a video he made of his cousin's wedding.

• Indian filmmaker Hemant Gaba showed his then-unreleased and now internationally acclaimed *Shuttlecock Boys* (2011) about four lower-middle-class boys in Delhi who play badminton together at night, and on one of those nights decide to make a new life for themselves.

There is also a lot of live music—and a steady supply of booze— so it's basically a week-long beach party, with a bunch of really good—and a bunch of not-so-good—original films thrown in.

THE STRANGE BEAUTY FILM FESTIVAL

Location: Durham, North Carolina

Background: In 2010, the Manbites Dog Theater in Durham asked

---

The word *idiot* comes from a Greek legal term meaning "one who doesn't vote."

local film aficionados Jim Haverkamp and Joyce Ventimiglia to come up with an idea for an event for the theater—and the Strange Beauty Film Festival was born. It quickly became a hit. For the 2013 event, Haverkamp and Ventimiglia received more than 300 submissions and featured more than 50 films.

What You'll See: "Short films from around the world, including animation, underground, documentary, funky, and otherwise wholly unclassifiable works that are both lyrical and haunting—somewhere between terrifying normality and sublime fever dreams." Two of the films featured in 2013:

• *Boy Brides and Bachelors* (2012): "An animated video shot on a cold January night in southeastern Serbia during a pagan ritual called Surovari in which men dress as women (large breasted peasants, grandmothers, and brides), and engage in pretend sexual acts with village bachelors." (It's live-action and animation, and while not at all graphic, it's very, very weird.)

• *Golden Age of the Virgin Microbe* (2012): "A sardonically animated video about our modern world that becomes a psychedelic travelogue full of signs and wonders. Also, chimpanzees."

THE INTERNATIONAL MOUSTACHE FILM FESTIVAL

Location: Portland, Maine

Background: This festival began as an outgrowth of the already-established (since 2008) Stache Pag—short for "moustache pageant"—a popular annual moustache competition held in Portland, Maine. In 2012, Stache Pag co-founder Nick Callahan came up with the idea of expanding the festivities to include a moustache-themed film competition, and voilà! They received dozens of submissions from all over the world and screened more than 30 films their very first year.

What You'll See: IMFF rules stipulate that the films must be less than four minutes long and must be moustache-related or prominently feature someone with a moustache. Trophies are given to outstanding films in several categories, including Best 'Stache Growth Story, Best 'Stache Shaving Story, Best Collection of Moustaches in One Film, and Best Moustache Death Relationship Story. One of the films shown in 2012:

• *Between the Upper Lip and Nasal Passageway*: "In the face of a society that has relegated the moustache to the sex-offenders, hillbillies, and Ron Burgundies of the world—there remain those who defiantly flaunt their furry facial friend with unabashed shwaze." (Whatever "schwaze" is.)

THE INTERNATIONAL RANDOM FILM FESTIVAL

Location: Random

Background: The IRFF was the brainchild of Finnish filmmaker Hannaleena Hauru and Austrian artist Synes Elischka, who came up with the idea in 2009. According to their website: "Every year we are hosting our festival on a randomly selected time in a random venue. The location is selected by opening *wikipedia.org* and clicking 'Random Article' repeatedly until reaching a page representing a location with a local population. The date of the Festival's Opening Night is selected by using the True Random Number Generator at *random.org*." The first festival was held in Wiesensteig, Germany, in February 2010; the next three were in cities in Poland, Estonia, and Sweden.

What You'll See: Twenty-five films are chosen randomly from the thousands of submissions the IRFF receives—so you really have no idea what you're going to see. One standout from 2012:

• *Le Lapin Assassin*: A hired killer seeks help from a psychiatrist… because he is unable to kill people unless he's wearing a bunny suit. (It's four minutes long.)

The IRFF gives out a handful of prizes every year, and they're totally random, too. The Spoon award, for example, is chosen by having a blindfolded person fling a spoonful of ketchup at a piece of paper with the numbers 1 to 25 written on it, each of the numbers corresponding to a film. Winner in 2012: *Le Lapin Assassin*. (Bonus: The Spoon award comes with a cash prize of $8,000. Un-bonus: It's Monopoly money.)

*   *   *

A CHARACTER IS BOURNE

In 1887 a Rhode Island preacher named Ansel Bourne became the first-known case of *dissociative fugue*: He forgot everything about his life and had to invent a new one. In the 1970s, author Robert Ludlum read about the case. Inspired, he wrote *The Bourne Identity* about Jason Bourne, a spy who suffers from a similar condition.

THE PROPER STANCE

Success in any physical activity begins with knowing the proper way to stand. Here's how the experts say to do it.

DART-THROWER'S STANCE

The big toe of your dominant foot should be just behind the throwing line. Most of your weight should be placed on that leg; the back leg provides balance. Position yourself so your eye, the dart, and the target are in one line. Your shoulders should be as close to perpendicular with the throwing line as possible, but can be angled a bit so you're not wobbly. Your front toe should match that angle. Stand straight up. If you lean forward, you'll throw off your balance, and the dart could end up in the wall...or worse.

CHEF'S STANCE

If you have to swivel your body in order to stir or cut something, you're doing it incorrectly. Get directly in front of your work. Multitasking chefs who forget this rule can suffer from chronic back problems. Also, when your spine is twisted, you lack balance and need the counter to steady yourself. A poor stance can put you off balance, and lead to cut fingers, so make sure your weight is firmly planted on the back of your feet (and wear comfortable shoes).

IRISH STEP-DANCER'S STANCE

Before the dance begins, place your arms at your sides, keeping your elbows straight (and don't plan to move them). Keep your back straight and your chin up. Then rotate your right foot outward, and put the toes of your left foot against your right heel (kind of like a ballet dancer). Then, if you haven't fallen to the floor, you're ready to dance a jig.

TENNIS BALL-BOY'S STANCE

It is imperative that ball boys (and girls) working the net stand straight up with their hands behind their backs and not move a muscle until the ball hits the net and play stops. Then they have to pounce on the ball and return to their stance as quickly as possible.

Thanks! *Two and a Half Men* creator Chuck Lorre also co-wrote...

HANDGUN-SHOOTER'S STANCE

There are two main stances:

• The *Weaver*, invented by Jack Weaver in the 1950s, is the one most commonly used by cops because it makes you a smaller target. Place your feet shoulder-width apart with your dominant leg slightly back. Angle your support arm's shoulder toward the target, and bend your knees while keeping your body weight slightly forward. Then grasp the gun with both hands, keeping your elbows bent with the support elbow pointing downward.

• The *Isosceles* stance allows you to rotate like a tank turret. Face the target, keeping your feet shoulder-width apart, and bend your knees slightly. Extend your arms straight in front of you, locking at the elbows. When you square your shoulders, your arms will form an isosceles triangle (two equal sides).

GOLF-PUTTER'S STANCE

Most pros say your toes should be two putter-head lengths from the inside edge of the ball, but everyone is sized a little differently. The general rule is to stand so that your eyes are directly over the ball and to keep your shoulders square to the target line, so your spine isn't twisted. However, pros also say that if you sweat the technical stuff when putting, you'll usually miss. The key: Just "feel it."

WIDE-RECEIVER'S STANCE

In the old days, football receivers lined up like sprinters, with one hand on the ground. Today, the stance is between crouching and standing straight up. Lean forward with your non-dominant foot on the line. Your chin, chest, and knee should be directly over your front foot. Your other leg is bent behind you with the heel slightly off the ground. Your weight should be on your front toe. When the ball is snapped, you'll use your rear foot to propel you forward, and then your front foot to get you up to full speed in one step.

SUPERMODEL'S STANCE

Drama! Emotion! Those are key for a successful fashion shoot. The way to create that look is by creating angles: Never stand straight toward the camera. Swivel your hips so your head is turned, accentuating your long neck (if you have one). Put your hands on your hips or over your head to create even more angles. According to

---

...the *Teenage Mutant Ninja Turtles* theme song.

fashion model Josie Maran, "The weirder the shape you make, the better." To create this drama, briskly walk to your mark, stop, swivel toward the camera, and strike a pose. You may feel foolish, but your photos will be stunning.

PHOTOGRAPHER'S STANCE

Whether you're using a point-and-shoot or a DSLR, stability is the key to preventing blurry images. Keep your feet planted on the ground with most of your weight on your upper legs. One foot can be slightly in front for more stability. Keep your elbows close to your body as you hold the camera up to your eye with both hands. Before you shoot, take a breath and let it out so you're relaxed. Now that you're stable, you don't have to continually adjust your balance.

U.S. ARMY'S STANCE (AT ATTENTION)

"Both feet are flat and firm on the ground with the heels together and the toes parted at an angle of 30 degrees to the front-center of the body. The knees are braced by pushing them back slightly. The body is upright with the stomach pulled in and the chest pushed out; the back is straight. The arms are at the side of the body with the hands clenched fistlike, thumb pushing downward to help lock the arm at the elbow; the thumb is in line with the seams of the trousers."

BOWLER'S STANCE

First, know how far from the line your feet need to be positioned to take your allotted steps and not go over the line. Once there, point your feet directly toward the pins, about one board apart for stability. Flex the knees forward a bit, which will tighten your thigh muscles, creating leverage during your approach. Lean forward so your shoulders are directly over your knees. Then hold the ball in your hand close in front of you, keeping your elbows in (that will relax your arm muscles). Keep your chin up, always facing your target, so you could balance a book on your head.

PEE-ER'S STANCE (MALES ONLY)

The proper peeing stance is crucial when using a public men's room. If you have neighbors on either side, keep your elbows in. Stand far enough back that you avoid splash-back, but not so far back that you're hitting the floor. (And keep the vocalizations to a minimum.)

Extra credit: The Wright brothers earned 15 honorary college degrees for their historic flight.

THE EXPLORERS

You learned about them in school, but if someone were to walk up to you on the street and ask, "What did Magellan discover?" your first response might be, "Uhh…" So we've compiled this overview of some of history's most famous explorers—who they were and where they went.

THE WAYFARER

Explorer: Marco Polo (c. 1254–1324)

Claim to Fame: Introduced Europeans to the Far East

• In 1271, Marco Polo, 17, left Venice, Italy, with his father and uncle on a business trip that ended up lasting 24 years. They followed the fabled "Silk Road," a 4,000-mile trade route stretching from Istanbul to China, used for centuries by Central Asian merchants to ferry silk, jade, and other riches from Asia to the Middle East and Europe. The trio journeyed through what is now Iraq, Iran, and Afghanistan all the way to the Mongol emperor Kublai Khan's capital, today's Beijing.

• Polo spent nearly 17 years under the protection of the Kublai Khan, who presented him with a "golden tablet" that gave him access to the best homes, meals, and horses as Polo traveled throughout China and south to Burma, Sri Lanka, and India.

• Polo was the first European to witness the Far East's advanced culture and technology. In China, he was given a gift of "black stones that burned" (coal). While sailing the Caspian Sea he saw "a fountain which sends up oil." He drank wine made from rice, and marveled at Chinese innovations such as paper money, gunpowder, and porcelain. Polo brought eyeglasses to the West and the revelation that asbestos came from a mineral, not a salamander as the Venetians believed. He also was among the first Europeans to see elephants, monkeys, and, rarest of all, the unicorn (which turned out to be a rhinoceros).

• When the "wayfarer" (as Polo called himself) finally arrived back in Italy in 1295, Venice was at war with Genoa—and Polo had the misfortune to land in Genoese territory. He was captured and sent to prison. He passed the time by telling his amazing tales to his cell mate, a man named Rustichello, who wrote them all down. The subsequent book, *A Description of the Marvels of the World*, was a

New York City's largest reservoir is big enough to cover Manhattan in 40 feet of water.

huge success in Europe. But not everyone believed his outrageous tales of the Orient. Polo swore it was all true and even claimed, "I did not tell half of what I saw."

THE MERCHANT

Explorer: Christopher Columbus (1451–1506)
Claim to Fame: He "discovered" the New World.

• Inspired by tales of Marco Polo's travels to exotic lands, Columbus, who was born in Genoa, Italy, was determined to discover a western water route to the East Indies and Spice Islands. His motive: money. In the 15th century, spices were as precious as oil is today. The sale of a single ship's cargo could make a merchant fabulously wealthy. So in 1492, Columbus convinced Spain's King Ferdinand II and Queen Isabella to entrust him with three ships— the *Niña*, the *Pinta*, and the *Santa Maria*.

• Columbus's quest to find the East Indies was a failure. Instead of finding a faster route to the lucrative Chinese market, he landed in a strange "new world." Arriving first on an island in the Bahamas that he named San Salvadore, he then sailed on to Cuba and finally to the island of Hispaniola (today's Haiti and Dominican Republic).

• He found no spices, gold, silver, or other precious jewels. So he decided to cash in on the natives themselves by capturing and selling them as slaves. He called them *Indios* (Spanish for "Indians"). After two slave-trading voyages, Queen Isabella declared the natives to be her subjects and no longer products to sell.

• In addition to slaves, Columbus brought back some amazing claims, including witnessing actual mermaids: "They were not as pretty as they are depicted," he said. (That's because they were manatees.) He also claimed to find the fabled Garden of Eden, but that turned out to be a pretty forest where Venezuela's Orinoco River empties into the Atlantic.

• One thing Columbus didn't find in his four trips to the New World: the continental United States. The closest he ever got was Cuba. He went to his death believing he had found the East Indies.

THE GLOBETROTTER

Explorer: Ferdinand Magellan (1480–1521)
Claim to Fame: The first man to circumnavigate the globe

• Sponsored by King Charles I of Spain, in 1519, this Portuguese explorer set sail with a fleet of five ships and 270 men in search of a western route to the Spice Islands of Asia. But what Magellan didn't tell his crews (until they were too far away to turn back) was that he planned to sail around the world. He headed for South America—and thanks to Columbus, he knew how to get there.

• It was a storm-ridden journey full of misery, scurvy, starvation, and death. One sailor wrote, "We ate only biscuits turned to powder, all full of worms and stinking of the urine which the rats had made on it." Not surprisingly, when the crews realized they'd been had, they attempted to mutiny. During the three years it took to travel around the world, Magellan's expedition endured three mutinies, and lost four out of five ships and 252 of its 270 crew members.

• Despite the turmoil, Magellan's voyage is considered one of the greatest feats of navigation in history. He found a way through the southern tip of South America, now called the Strait of Magellan, and discovered another ocean, which he called *Pacifica Mar*, meaning "Peaceful Sea." Today we call it the Pacific Ocean.

• While in Patagonia, Magellan's men reported seeing eight-foot-tall giants on the beaches and even tried to baptize one and bring him home. But Paul, as they dubbed him, died along the way.

• Magellan himself didn't make it all the way around the world. While helping a Philippine queen wage war against the neighboring island of Cebu, he was shot in the foot with a poison arrow. Infection set in, and he died. What remained of the ragtag expedition, led by Juan Sebastian de Elcano, completed the epic voyage without him. In the end, Magellan's journey proved that Earth was much larger than previously thought and, most importantly, round.

THE CAPTAIN

Explorer: James Cook (1728–79)

Claim to Fame: The first European to visit Australia, New Zealand, and Hawaii, and the first to set foot on every known continent

• Born in Yorkshire, England, Cook joined the British Navy when he was a teenager. It was very rare for commoners to rise through the ranks to command a ship (a duty usually reserved for men of noble or royal blood), but Cook's exceptional navigational skills made him stand out to his superiors.

• In 1769, the British Admiralty chose Cook to lead a secret

The first recorded Halloween celebration in the U.S. took place in Anoka, Minnesota (1920).

mission to find the mysterious continent at the bottom of the world, known to map makers as *Terra Australis Nondum Cognita* ("The Southern Land Not Yet Known"). Sounding like a future (fictional) starship captain, Cook declared, "I intend to go not only farther than any man has been before me, but as far as I think it is possible for a man to go."

• Captain Cook made three voyages to the Pacific. The first voyage brought his ship, the *Endeavour*, to Tahiti, where his sailors were introduced to a fashion they brought back to Europe: the tattoo. His second voyage featured the first test of an ocean clock invented by John Harrison. This clock enabled navigators to accurately chart their longitude.

• The third voyage ended in disaster. Attempting to find the Northwest Passage, Cook's ships, the *Resolution* and the *Discovery*, were turned back by Arctic ice and limped into a bay in Hawaii for repairs. An argument with the locals led to a skirmish on the beach on Valentine's Day, 1779. Cook and his landing party scrambled for their boats, but in the melee, Cook was clubbed and stabbed to death before he could escape. His body was never recovered. A junior officer named Lt. Gore led the expedition home.

• Cook was the first man to step on every *known* continent, but he missed Antarctica—the continent at the bottom of the world that he was initially sent to find. (He mistook Australia for it.) His ship got within 75 miles of the "land not yet known" but was turned back by ice. No humans reached Antarctica until the 1820s.

THE ENGINEER

Explorer: Robert E. Peary (1856–1920)

Claim to Fame: The first man to (kind of) reach the North Pole

• Rear Admiral Robert E. Peary was a civil engineer and commander of the U.S. Navy. In 1886, he organized an expedition to Greenland in order to explore the one million square miles of ice known as "the roof of the world."

• His trip to Greenland convinced him that the North Pole was not on land, as everyone believed, but farther north in the pack ice covering the Arctic Sea. Peary and his assistant, an African American named Matthew Henson, spent the next 23 years trying to reach it.

• Working closely with Inuit natives, the pair learned how to use dogsleds, ice-fish, build igloos, and use seal furs for warmth. When the Inuit told Peary of the location of three "sky stones," (meteorites) called the Woman, the Dog, and the Tent, buried in the ice near Cape York, Peary saw an opportunity to finance his future expeditions. He ferried the massive hunks of iron, the largest being a 34-ton behemoth, across the ice and sea to the Museum of Natural History in New York City and sold them for $40,000. (Peary did not share the windfall with the Inuit, for whom the meteorites were the only source of metal to make knives and spears.)

• After two failed expeditions to the North Pole, Peary had lost eight of his toes to frostbite. Undeterred, he and Henson tried again. Their team of 22 men, 133 dogs, and 19 sleds left Canada's Ellesmere Island on March 1, 1909, and headed out onto the ice. Most of the party consisted of advance teams that forged ahead to leave caches of supplies for Peary, Henson, and their four Inuit guides.

• On April 6, 1909, Peary finally reached what he declared to be the North Pole. He triumphantly planted the American flag in the ice. At the base, he placed a small bottle with a note inside that read: "I have this day hoisted the national ensign of the United States of America at this place, which my observations indicate to be the North Polar axis of the earth, and have formally taken possession of the entire region, and adjacent, for and in the name of the President of the United States of America."

• Peary's assistant, Matthew Henson, was also his scout and arrived at the Pole 45 minutes before Peary. According to Henson, Peary was "hopping mad."

• When Peary returned home, he was shocked to learn that a rival named Dr. Frederick Cook claimed to have reached the North Pole a year earlier. It took two years of court battles and a Congressional inquiry before Cook's claim was dismissed. Even so, many scientists doubt that Peary ever reached the actual North Pole, but he did come within five miles of it. No man had gotten closer to the top of the world before that than Robert Peary.

*   *   *

"If Columbus had an advisory committee, he'd probably still be at the dock."

—**Arthur Goldberg**

In 1919, average Americans had to work 2 hrs., 38 min. to buy a 3-lb. chicken. Today: 12 min.

POWERED BY PEE

Urine for a fun read with this one.

WATER, WATER EVERYWHERE

One of the biggest dilemmas facing the organizers of festivals like New Orleans's annual Mardi Gras celebration is that there never seem to be enough bathrooms to meet demand. Worse yet, after the attendees have had one or two (or three or four) beers, just about everything starts looking like a urinal.

Planners of Rio de Janeiro's yearly Carnival festival have been so vexed by incidents of public urination that in 2012, local authorities established a special "pee patrol" unit to ticket and issue fines to those *mijões* ("pee-ers") caught in the act. Despite their best efforts, even the threat of a fine wasn't enough to prevent people from whizzing everywhere. And to Rio officials, it's a serious problem as they gear up for 2014 World Cup matches and the 2016 Olympics.

I LOVE A PEE-RADE

When the Brazilian cultural group AfroReggae heard about the ongoing problem, they came up with their own solution for 2013—a float in Carnival's massive Sambodromo parade…that was powered, at least in part, by pee. After securing financing from Sao Paulo advertising agency JWT, volunteers built a modified *trio eletrico*, which is a Brazilian term for a parade float with gigantic speakers and an incredibly loud sound system. Its power source? Not car batteries, as is the case with most parade floats. Instead, in the days of Carnival leading up to the parade, Carnival-goers emptied their bladders into specially marked public urinals, colored yellow and labeled "Xixi Eletrico" (Portuguese for, roughly, "Electric Pee"). The collected urine was then fed into a turbine that charged the float's batteries. It's more or less a tiny hydroelectric power plant fueled by urine instead of fresh water.

While the urinal didn't create enough electricity to cover all of the float's power needs (they had to use a battery backup), the crazy contraption did raise awareness for the festival's ongoing struggles with public potties. AfroReggae plans to try again in the coming years. So if you go to Carnival, go with a full bladder.

DIE HARD, STARRING FRANK SINATRA

More tales of roles and the actors that almost played them.

MARK HAMILL AS MOZART (*Amadeus*, 1984). Wanting to prove that *Star Wars* wasn't "the extent of my acting abilities," Hamill auditioned for and won the role of the foul-mouthed, salacious composer in Peter Shaffer's Broadway play, *Amadeus*. Hamill took over the role from Tim Curry and received rave reviews. Both actors auditioned for the lead in the film version, but Hamill was passed over because director Milos Forman didn't want "Luke Skywalker playing Mozart," and Curry lost out to fellow British actor Kenneth Branagh. Just prior to filming, however, Forman decided he wanted to cast the picture with Americans, so Branagh was replaced by little-known actor Tom Hulce. As for Hamill, he later rekindled his career by voicing the Joker in the animated *Batman* series, a role he took over from…Tim Curry.

NATALIE PORTMAN AS LISBETH SALANDER (*The Girl with the Dragon Tattoo*, 2011). The role of a young computer hacker who aids a grizzled journalist (Daniel Craig) was a difficult one to cast. Many fans, including film critic Roger Ebert, lobbied for Noomi Rapace, who played Lisbeth in the original 2009 Swedish version. But Rapace (who'd already filmed the two sequels) wasn't interested. So director David Fincher offered the part to Portman, who turned it down due to exhaustion. The producers wanted Scarlett Johansson, but Fincher deemed her "too sexy." Other actresses considered: Mia Wasikowska, Keira Knightley, Anne Hathaway, and Emma Watson. In the end, Fincher decided that the mysterious nature of the character would be ruined by a big-name actress, so he cast little-known Rooney Mara and actually had to fight the studio heads to keep her. (Good decision. The film was a huge box office success, and Mara was nominated for an Academy Award.)

FRANK SINATRA AS JOHN MCCLANE (*Die Hard*, 1988). In 1968, Sinatra starred as tough-as-nails police detective Joe Leland in *The Detective*, based on the novel by Roderick Thorp. Sinatra's contract stipulated that he had a "right of first refusal" for the lead role in any sequels. A decade later, Thorp did pen a sequel, called *Nothing Lasts Forever*, in which Detective Leland gets trapped in an L.A. high rise that's been taken over by German terrorists. Nearly ten years after that, *Nothing Lasts Forever* was adapted for the screen and renamed *Die Hard*; the character of Joe Leland was renamed John McClane. Per his contract, the 73-year-old Sinatra was offered the lead. He turned it down. So did Harrison Ford, Richard Gere, Don Johnson, Sylvester Stallone, Burt Reynolds, and Richard Dean Anderson. The director's sixth choice, Bruce Willis, took the part—which became one of the most iconic action hero roles in film history.

TIM ROTH AS SEVERUS SNAPE (*Harry Potter and the Sorcerer's Stone*, 2001). Roth, known for the tough-guy characters he played in *Reservoir Dogs* and *Pulp Fiction*, was offered the Snape role at around the same time he was offered the villain role in Tim Burton's remake of *Planet of the Apes*. Roth wanted to do both movies at once, but the schedule would have been too hectic, so he had to choose. His kids wanted him to do *Potter*, but Roth chose *Apes* because, he said, the character of Snape was "underdeveloped," and he didn't want to "be on a lunch box." Result: *Apes* was a critical and box-office disappointment, and Alan Rickman, who took the Snape role, developed it into one of cinema's most memorable villains. Does Roth regret his choice? "No," he said. "Alan did a great job. I would have made Snape a very different guy."

MARK WAHLBERG AS GEORGE KIRK (*Star Trek*, 2009). Director J.J. Abrams wanted an actor with strong screen presence to play the small-but-pivotal role of Captain Kirk's father, so he sent the script to Mark Wahlberg, who admitted he's not a big fan of science fiction, but said he'd take a look at it. "I tried to read the script," Wahlberg later told reporters, "but I couldn't—I didn't understand the words or dialog or anything." So he turned it down, and Australian Chris Hemsworth (who would go on to star as Thor in *The Avengers*) got the part. After Wahlberg saw *Star Trek*…he got it. It was too late to do him any good—but he got it. "I was like, Holy sh*t! This is great!"

Bram Stoker's first (not-so-famous) book: *The Duties of Clerks of Petty Sessions in Ireland.*

HONEST ABE'S FAMILY TREE

The Abraham Lincoln bloodline shed its last drop in 1985. Or did it?

ROOTS

A year after Robert Todd Lincoln Beckwith's death in 1985, a 17-year-old boy appeared in court to accept a million-dollar settlement from the Lincoln estate. Beckwith was the last of the 16th president's three great-grandchildren to pass away. None of the three were believed to have produced any kids. So who was this kid, and why did Lincoln's estate pay him?

At the time of Abraham Lincoln's assassination, his family tree had a single living shoot: Robert Todd Lincoln, the only one of the president's four children (all sons) to survive to adulthood. Robert Lincoln not only survived, he thrived, perhaps driven by a compulsion to prove he was more than just Abe Lincoln's son. "No one wanted me," he once said. "They wanted Abraham Lincoln's son." What they got was a Harvard-educated lawyer, banker, and corporate executive who also served as U.S. Secretary of War under President James Garfield. But he was not "a man of the people" like his father. In fact, he was said to have an almost "morbid repugnance" for public life.

BRANCHING OUT

Nevertheless, Robert Todd Lincoln did become president…of the Pullman Railroad Company. (Ironically, he'd been dubbed "the Prince of Rails" during the 1860 presidential campaign because of his presidential father's reputation as a "rail-splitter.")

As a railroad tycoon, Robert made enough money to leave his father's humble beginnings behind. In 1902, he acquired a 412-acre property in Vermont, where he built a luxurious 24-room mansion. He called the estate "Hildene." Inside the mansion was an impressive library decorated in the style of a first-class Pullman coach and an entry hall that boasted a thousand-pipe electromagnetic organ. The organ was installed in 1908 at a cost of $11,000—about $282,000 in today's dollars.

By 1909, the family had moved so far from Abe Lincoln's log-cabin roots that when President Theodore Roosevelt presided over a ceremony designating Lincoln's birthplace in Kentucky a "national historic site," not a single Lincoln descendent showed up. Historians say that the president's son was ashamed of the modest cabin in which his father grew up and had already started referring to Hildene as his "ancestral home."

A TENDER OFFSHOOT

Robert and his wife, Mary Harlan Lincoln, had three children. Their only son—Abraham Lincoln II, called "Jack"—was a brilliant young man and was ready to follow in his father's footsteps at Harvard. But first he was sent off to Versailles, France, to prepare for his entrance exams. There, the 16-year-old heir to one of the most revered names in American history discovered a carbuncle—a boil-like abscess—in his armpit. A French surgeon decided to lance it. Bad idea: Carbuncles are typically infected with *staphylococcus*, a particularly nasty strain of bacteria. Lancing the carbuncle sent the staph infection into Jack's lymph and vascular systems, and within a few months Honest Abe's namesake was dead.

That left Jack's two younger sisters—Jessie and Mary—to carry on the line. Mary was nicknamed "Mamie" to distinguish her from her mother (Mary Harlan) and her grandmother (Mary Todd). In 1891, the year after her brother's death, 22-year-old Mamie married Charles Bradford Isham, her father's secretary. The following year, her only child, Lincoln Isham, was born.

ANOTHER BRANCH

Mamie's sister, Jessie, got to keep her name, but she rebelled anyway. Against her parents' wishes, she married a college football star named Warren Wallace Beckwith in 1897. Beckwith claimed that his mother-in-law meddled in his marriage from the start. She'd never stopped mourning Jack and could not bear to be parted from her daughter.

Despite her mother's meddling, the couple managed to produce two children—yet *another* Mary and another Robert. Mary Lincoln Beckwith was born in 1898 and called "Peggy" to set her apart from the other Marys. Her brother, Robert Todd Lincoln Beckwith, was born in 1904. After the children were born, Mary Harlan Lincoln tried to control them, too. In 1905, she moved Jessie and both children to Europe, leaving Warren behind. Fed up, Warren Beckwith filed for a divorce, which was eventually granted. He never saw his children again.

THE RECLUSE

Robert Todd Lincoln died of a cerebral hemorrhage at Hildene on June 26, 1926. He'd lived to the ripe age of 82. Instead of burying him in the Lincoln family plot back in Illinois, his wife, Mary Harlan, had him buried at Arlington Cemetery in Virginia. "He made his own history, independently of his great father," Mary later wrote, "and should have his own place in the sun." (She felt so strongly about keeping Robert separate from his father in people's memories that she underlined the word "independently" five times.)

When Mary Harlan Lincoln died in 1937, she left a trust worth more than $3 million. Its beneficiaries were Peggy Beckwith, Robert Todd Lincoln Beckwith, and Lincoln Isham. According to historian Harold Holzer, Robert Todd Lincoln's heirs lived "in the luxurious grandeur of Gilded Age nobility." Apparently, none of Abe Lincoln's surviving grandchildren held a job after receiving their inheritance (or before the inheritance, for that matter).

Peggy Beckwith moved to Hildene after her mother's death and stayed there for the rest of her life. She spent her days golfing, dabbling in oil painting, sculpting, and photography, and chain-smoking cigars. Because she tended to dress in knickers and men's shirts, rumors spread about Peggy's sexual orientation. No one knows for certain whether the rumors were true, but it *is* certain that growing the Lincoln family tree was not in her plans. She never married and never had children. Housekeeping wasn't in her plans, either. When she died in 1975, the mansion was in disrepair and was overrun with animals, including raccoons. "She's an odd one," said Lincoln scholar Ralph G. Newman at the time. "I would call her an eccentric recluse. She doesn't give a damn about Abraham Lincoln, and she's rebuffed any attempts by historians to interview her or look for family papers on the farm."

THE PLAYER

Peggy's cousin Lincoln Isham lived the high life in a "swank" apartment in Manhattan's Carlyle Hotel. He spent his time playing guitar and mandolin and writing songs. Despite catchy titles such as "Baghdad Billy," "Congo Las Vegas," and "Madam Bombay," no one came forward to publish Linc Isham's music. During the Roaring Twenties, he bought a tavern near Hildene, played a lot of golf, and became a fixture at a speakeasy called the Stork Club on New York's 51st Street, known at the time as the "wettest" street in the country. He boozed it up with the likes of Ernest Hemingway, J. Edgar Hoover, and Al Jolson.

Isham was married to a New York society girl named Leahalma Correa, but the marriage produced no children. As for his devotion to the Lincoln legacy, he once phoned a judge about paying a visit to discuss an estate matter. "Better come Wednesday," the judge told him. "We're closed for the holiday on Thursday." "What holiday?" Isham asked. The judge paused, and then responded: "Lincoln's birthday."

THE BRAT

The third heir, Peggy's brother, Robert Todd Lincoln Beckwith, lived the life of the idle rich on another inherited property in Virginia. He described himself as "a gentleman farmer of independent means." He was a short, bald stutterer, but viewed himself as a playboy, boasting that he loved sailing, fast cars, and beautiful women. "I'm a spoiled brat," he once told a reporter.

Beckwith's personal lawyer, Elizabeth Young, said that in the 50 years she knew him, he never discussed his ancestry and seemed to have little interest in it. "He lived off his wealth," Young said after Beckwith's death. "As far as I know, all the money came from the Lincoln family."

IMMACULATE DECEPTION

Beckwith married three times. He married the second of the three at age 63—a 27-year-old German native named Annemarie Hoffman. Six months later, she became pregnant. According to one of his lawyers, Beckwith seemed quite impressed with himself for being able to father a child at such an advanced age. The feat was even more impressive given the fact that Beckwith had undergone a vasectomy six years earlier. Can vasectomies fail? Sure. But tests confirmed that Beckwith was "completely sterile."

Beckwith's attorney prepared an agreement whereby Annemarie

Mmmm! Malted-milk powder was originally sold as baby formula. (Brand name: "Diastoid.")

would list the child's father as "John Doe" or "Father Unknown" on the birth certificate and would make no claims against the Lincoln/Beckwith estate. In exchange, Beckwith agreed to pay her hospitalization costs plus $7,500. But Annemarie had the last word: She listed Robert Todd Lincoln Beckwith as the father anyway, and named her son Timothy Lincoln Beckwith.

THE LINCOLN LAWYERS

According to the terms of the Mary Harlan Lincoln Testamentary Trust, if the three surviving grandchildren of Mary Harlan Lincoln and Robert Todd Lincoln had no heirs, the trust's holdings would eventually be divided by three nonprofit institutions chosen by Mary Harlan Lincoln—the American Red Cross, Iowa Wesleyan College, and the First Church of Christ, Scientist. But if they did? Those institutions could have a fight on their hands.

After Timothy's birth in 1968, attorneys at the Washington law firm Frost & Towers, which had handled the Lincoln family's affairs since the 1920s, took immediate steps to protect the trust. The firm filed a lawsuit seeking a blood test to establish that Timothy Lincoln Beckwith was *not* Beckwith's son. But before the tests could be done, Annemarie fled with the baby to West Germany.

Beckwith filed for divorce on grounds of adultery; Annemarie countersued on similar grounds. It took seven years before the proceedings reached court. The doctor who had done Beckwith's vasectomy testified that recent tests showed Beckwith was "sterilized in 1962 and has been sterile since that time." The judge ordered blood tests for Annemarie and her seven-year-old son. Again, no tests were performed.

The judge granted Beckwith's divorce petition, noting in his ruling that Timothy Lincoln Beckwith had been fathered during an "adulterous relationship." Annemarie's law team appealed, but lost. The appeals court did rule, however, that the divorce decree didn't prohibit the boy from making a claim to the inheritance in a separate action.

THE BENEFICIARY

On Christmas Eve, 1985, Robert Todd Lincoln Beckwith, the "gnarled, scraggly bearded, 81-year-old great-grandson of America's most revered president," died in a nursing home in Virginia. The Red Cross, Iowa Wesleyan, and the Christian Science Church were

---

First football player on a Wheaties box: Walter Payton (1986).

poised to inherit the proceeds of the Lincoln trust, which was worth about $6 million. Enter: Timothy Lincoln Beckwith, age 17, living in the United States with his mother, Annemarie, who had remarried.

The three charities were so sure Timothy would come after the trust that they opened negotiations with the 17-year-old. After several months of haggling, Timothy's lawyers and the three nonprofit institutions reached an agreement. In return for about $1 million, Timothy renounced all future claims to the trust. The settlement, according to Attorney John Beck, was in the best interests of the trust, particularly since Beckwith and Annemarie had been married at the time she became pregnant and no blood tests had ever been performed. So the answer to the question, "Did Abraham Lincoln's family tree wither and die?" is a resounding "Who knows?" What we do know: Timothy Lincoln Beckwith grew up to become a prosecutor with the Florida state attorney's office. Seems lawyering is in his blood after all.

*   *   *

MMM…MERCHANDISE

The Simpsons is one of the longest-running TV shows ever…and one of the most lucrative, generating thousands of weird products, like these.

• A universal TV remote shaped like a can of Duff, Homer Simpson's favorite beer

• A Franklin Mint collectible plate depicting Blinky, the three-eyed fish who lives in polluted water near the Springfield Nuclear Power Plant

• A keychain depicting the entire menu of the Krusty Burger fast food restaurant

• Simpsons' Pasta—pasta in the shape of the heads of Marge, Homer, Lisa, Bart, and Maggie

• The "Marge PEZ Dispenser." It's 18 inches tall, and instead of spitting out individual pieces of PEZ, it dispenses entire rolls of PEZ. And it has a voice chip so Marge grumbles disapprovingly whenever you go for the candy.

• A ceramic figurine of Bart Simpson going to the bathroom…and reading a book

• *The Simpsons*, a book by David Levinthal—filled with artistic photographs…of Simpsons' merchandise.

AN ARRESTING HISTORY OF THE POLICE CAR

Ever see a police car in your rearview mirror and think, "Hey! Where'd that come from?" If so, you probably weren't wondering about the origin of the police car, but in case you were, here it is.

THE COMMISH

Frank Croul was the Police Commissioner of Detroit, Michigan, from 1909 to 1913. Then, as now, the city was the heart of the American auto industry. Ford, Studebaker, Packard, and Cadillac were all headquartered there, and as Croul saw an ever-increasing number of cars buzzing around the city streets, he wondered if they might have some use for the police.

He wasn't the first person to contemplate such a possibility: In 1899, the city of Akron, Ohio, paid the Collins Buggy Company $2,400 ($65,000 today) for a battery-powered "paddy wagon," complete with a stretcher, a cage for prisoners, electric headlights, and a gong. America's first horseless police vehicle left a lot to be desired. Weighing 5,000 pounds, it had a top speed of just 16 mph and a range of 30 miles before the batteries had to be recharged. A year after it was built, an angry mob pushed it into the Ohio Canal during a race riot. Though the wagon was returned to service, the city never bothered to build another one.

IF AT FIRST YOU DON'T SUCCEED...

As Croul could tell from watching the traffic in front of his office, motor vehicles had improved a lot since 1899. Cars with new-fangled gasoline engines had none of the problems with range that older electric cars had. Now that automakers had been building them in quantity for nearly a decade, gas-powered automobiles were becoming quite reliable. Some, like Ford's Model T, were even af-fordable. Croul thought the time was right to buy a car for the Detroit Police Department. But when he asked the city for money to buy one, they turned him down. Croul was adamant. He was so sure that "police cars" had a future, he bought the department a Packard with his own money, $5,000—more than $100,000 today.

ON A ROLL

Croul's hunch proved to be correct: His Packard was a lot more use-ful than Akron's electric paddy wagon. It was speedy and reliable, needed less care than a police horse, and it allowed police to get to the scene of an emergency faster than if they went on foot or in a horse-drawn wagon. After just four months, the city reimbursed Croul for the Packard and made plans to buy six more cars. These proved so economical to operate—less than half the cost of the horses and wagons they replaced—that by 1913, even the city dog catcher had his own truck. Detroit's last horse-drawn vehicles were phased out forever.

FAILURE TO COMMUNICATE

Even in those very early days police cars were also known as "patrol cars." But they didn't do much patrolling, because there was no way to communicate with them once they were away from the station. Police radios hadn't been invented yet, so patrol officers had to wait at the station for emergency calls to come in. Then, as soon as they finished with one call, they had to return to the station to wait for the next one.

In 1917, Detroit began deploying automobile patrol officers to special telephone kiosks set up around the city. One officer sat in the kiosk waiting for the phone to ring, while his partner patrolled the beat on foot. When a call came in, the kiosk officer hopped in the police car, went looking for his partner, picked him up, and responded to the call.

Some cities installed special red lights at major intersections and on top of tall buildings as a way to signal patrol officers as they were driving around. When the lights were lit or flashing, the officers knew they needed to find a telephone or a police call box and check in to receive their assignment.

CALLING ALL CARS

It was obvious that if a way could ever be found to install radios in automobiles, police cars would become much more effective law-enforcement tools. But in the 1910s and early 1920s, it wasn't clear that such a thing was even possible. Automotive electric systems generated lots of static interference, but they weren't powerful enough to provide electricity for add-ons like radios. The radios themselves were very bulky, and the vacuum tubes that made them work were fragile, not the kind of thing that would do well vibrating and bouncing around in a speeding police car.

In 1921, a Detroit police officer named Kenneth Cox teamed up with an engineering student named Robert Batts to try to install a radio in the back seat of a Model T Ford. It took them six years to do it. Their radio had trouble receiving signals in tunnels, under bridges, and around tall buildings; and the radio's batteries, which couldn't fit in the back seat and had to be installed on the running boards, needed to be recharged every four hours. But the radio worked.

PUBLIC RADIO

Just like the radios you use to listen to music, Cox and Batts's radio was a one-way radio: It could only receive signals, not send them. Patrol officers still had to find a phone or a call box to check in with headquarters, but it was enough of an improvement over phone kiosks that in 1928, the Detroit Police Department began operating its own radio station, KOP.

Because the Federal Radio Commission saw broadcasting as primarily an entertainment medium, it required the police department to play music on KOP when it wasn't broadcasting police calls. Anyone with an ordinary AM radio, even criminals, could listen to the station. More than once, the FRC suspended the station's license when the police department didn't take its entertainment responsibilities seriously enough.

Luckily for law enforcement, though, the FRC soon realized the error of its ways and stopped requiring the police to act as disc jockeys. Then in 1933, engineers working for the Bayonne (New Jersey) Police Department developed the first two-way police radios. Within a few years, General Electric, RCA, and Motorola were making them for departments all over the country. They weren't cheap—the radios cost more than $700 apiece, more than some police cars—but they became standard equipment everywhere.

PLAIN-CLOTHED

Early police cars were almost indistinguishable from other cars. They were typically dark in color and might have the word "POLICE" or "P.D." hand-painted in small letters on the driver and passenger-side doors, but that was about it. They had no extra lights—early automotive electrical systems couldn't power them—and what few sirens there were had to be cranked by hand. (The Detroit Police Department didn't bother with sirens; it issued its motor vehicle officers "loud-sounding whistles.")

New York City's first police cars were convertibles, to enable citizens to see the officers' police hats so that they'd know they were police cars. Patrol officers were under orders to keep the top down so that the hats could be seen, unless a superior officer gave special permission for the top to be put back up. Rain or even snow was no guarantee that permission would be given.

By the late 1920s, some departments were beginning to use police cars with special paint schemes. The NYPD's cars had green bodies, white roofs, and black front fenders. The California Highway Patrol, founded in 1929, preferred white cars with black roofs. It wasn't until the 1930s that a style began to appear in police departments all over the country: black cars with white doors and roofs—the first "black and whites."

LIGHTS ON

Police cars began adding spotlights for extra visibility as soon as the electrical systems could handle them, but red police lights didn't become common until the 1930s. The first ones were re-purposed tail lights—which explains why they were red—and were mounted on the front fender, the front bumper, or the roof. Some cars had them in pairs, and others had an extra light mounted on the front right fender, facing rightward, that read "PULL OVER" or "STOP" when lit, which was used to stop speeding drivers.

The first 360° rotating "gumball" light, called the Beacon Ray, was introduced by the Federal Sign and Signal Company in 1948. Red (and later blue) gumball lights remained popular through the late 1960s, when they began to be replaced with horizontal "light bars" that included multiple rotating lights, mirrors to reflect their light forward or wherever else it was needed, and a siren.

STILL THE SAME

For all the changes that police cars have gone through in their first 100 years, one thing has not changed, at least not since that angry mob pushed the City of Akron's custom-built electric police wagon into the river in 1900. Police cars have always been modified versions of standard automobiles, nothing more. Automakers didn't even offer special law-enforcement upgrades (such as improved brakes, tires, steering, and suspension components) until Ford added them to its first "Police Package" cars in 1950. GM, Chrysler, and other major American automakers soon followed, and American police cars have been made that way ever since. So far, none of the Big 3 automakers have ever designed a "purpose-built" police car from scratch, because annual police car sales are too small to justify the expense.

FUTURE CAR

But that hasn't stopped other people from trying. In 2003, former Ford Motor company executive William Santana Li teamed up with a former police officer named Stacy Dean Stephens to found Carbon Motors, a company that planned to build purpose-built police cars. By 2012, the company had a prototype patrol car called the E7, and a factory in Indiana where it planned to build it.

The E7 had all of its equipment—lights, siren, radio, gun rack, night vision, license plate scanner, and more—engineered right into the car. The doors and dashboard were bulletproof so that officers could hide behind them during a shoot-out. The rear compartment had front-opening "suicide doors" that made it easier to get handcuffed suspects in and out. The rear compartment also contained a hidden camera and microphone to record any incriminating statements the suspects might make while they were sitting back there. Did an intoxicated suspect barf in the back seat while being transported to the drunk tank? Not a problem: the rear compartment was waterproof and designed to be cleaned out with a hose.

So how soon can we expect to see the E7 and the police van on our streets? Probably never: In 2012, Carbon Motors was turned down for a $310 million Energy Department loan. It spent a year trying to line up other investors and when that failed, in April 2013 it moved out of the Indiana plant, took down its website, and went out of business. (It looks like the Big 3 were right after all.)

*　　*　　*

"Create like a god, command like a king, work like a slave."
—**Constantin Brancusi**

During WWII, novelty toilet paper was printed with images of Hitler, Hirohito, and Mussolini.

BEAT THE PRESS

Goofs both big and small from the Fourth Estate.

• In 2013, Minnesota's *Mankato Free Press* ran a story about grapefruit. To give the headline visual flair, they replaced the "G" with a photo of a slice of grapefruit—which looked nothing like a "G," nor did it look like it was part of the word. So readers saw this headline: "RAPEFRUIT: Good for Every Meal."

• A correction that ran in *The New York Times:* "An earlier version of this article misstated the length of time E.B. White wrote for *The New Yorker* as five centuries."

• In 2013, while reporting on a kidnapping case in Cleveland, Ashleigh Banfield of CNN's *Newsroom* was standing in a parking lot in Phoenix, Arizona, conducting a split-screen satellite interview with Nancy Grace, also of CNN. Astute viewers noticed that both talking heads had the same cars behind them. The "journalists" were actually standing only a few feet apart.

• In 2008, the *Bloomberg* financial newswire ran a 17-page obituary on Apple CEO Steve Jobs, who died three years later.

• In several New York newspaper headlines in 2013, NYC Mayor Michael Bloomberg's name was misspelled "Bloobmerg." It happened so often that some bloggers wondered if it was intentional.

• On April 15, 1912, the news spread that the "unsinkable" RMS *Titanic* had hit an iceberg and sunk, but several newspaper editors did not believe the telegraph reports coming in, so they just made up their own versions of the story. The *Christian Science Monitor's* headline: "Passengers Safe and Steamer *Titanic* Taken in Tow." The London *Daily Mail*: "*Titanic* Sunk, No Lives Lost."

• In February 2013, as a 150-foot-wide asteroid flew within a few thousand miles of Earth, CNN's Deb Feyerick interviewed Bill Nye the Science Guy, and asked him, "Is this an effect of global warming?" To repeat, she asked Nye if an *outer space* asteroid was caused by global warming. Nye was speechless for a moment, then regained his composure and simply talked about the asteroid.

Mozart wrote his first opera, *Bastien und Bastienne*, when he was 12.

ANIMALS IN THE NEWS

Featuring a tenacious cat, a wayward goat, and some dead bees.

KNOCK-KNOCK?
"Who's there?" "Ants." "Ants who?" "Ants-ser the door already!" That corny knock-knock joke played out in real life in Offenburg, Germany, late one night in 2013 when a 75-year-old woman called police to report that someone kept ringing her doorbell and running away. The officers couldn't find any suspects... until they noticed a huge swarm of ants next to the door. An entire colony of the insects had taken up residence inside the front wall. The nest had grown so large that it kept pushing up against the doorbell switch, driving the poor woman nuts.

LLOOK OUT FOR THE LLAMA

In June 2013, a llama got loose in Tallahassee when it escaped from its owner's yard. The rogue animal backed up traffic and intimidated pedestrians, prompting frantic calls to 9-1-1. The incident occurred while Drzewiecki and another officer were trying to shoo the animal into a trailer. Unable to come up with an alternative solution, the officers tased the llama. (It was okay.) "I've been doing this for 20 years," said Florida Deputy Tony Drzewiecki, "and no one ever told me I'd get spit on in the face by a llama and trampled by one."

A MIGHTY LONG CATWALK

In 2012, Jacob and Bonnie Richter of West Palm Beach, Florida, took their cat, Holly, with them to a NASCAR race in Daytona Beach, 190 miles away. During a fireworks ceremony, Holly got spooked and escaped from the couple's RV. They looked for days but couldn't find their cat, so the sad couple drove home. Two months later, the Richters received a call: Someone had found Holly! (She had a microchip implanted in her skin.) Here's the weird part: Holly was found only a mile away from the Richters' home. She was emaciated and her paws were "rubbed raw," but she had walked nearly 189 miles to get home. "All animals have a sense of direction," said veterinarian Marty Becker, "but it's really unusual for cats to find a way home over long distances. I think this is somewhat of a miracle."

LITTLE GOSSIP ON THE PRAIRIE

After studying prairie dogs for 25 years, Northern Arizona University biologist Dr. Con Slobodchikoff has concluded that the beasts have a very complex form of communication. From recordings of the prairie dogs' vocal responses to different stimuli, Dr. Slobodchikoff has determined that a prairie dog "look-out" can report to the others whether an approaching human is tall or short, skinny or fat, and will even say what color shirt the human is wearing.

CAN'T GET THEIR GOAT

It was 1:30 a.m. on a cold February night in 2013 when two NYPD cops spotted a goat running loose on a Brooklyn street. They chased it into a parking lot and tried to corner it, but the goat was too fast. Luckily, it just so happened that the parking lot attendant was an immigrant from West Africa named Ndiaye Seydou. His former profession: goat herder. Seydou made a makeshift lasso and slowly approached the animal. Then, just as it was about to bolt, he lassoed the goat and the two officers tied its legs together. The goat had escaped from a nearby slaughterhouse, but will get to live out its days at a petting zoo in Woodstock, New York.

WHAT A CROC

A charter airplane flying over the Congo in Africa in 2010 was brought down by a crocodile. A passenger had smuggled the reptile on board in a duffel bag, but it escaped mid-flight. The 18 passengers on the small prop plane panicked and ran toward the cockpit, causing a sudden shift in weight distribution, which sent the aircraft into a nosedive. The plane crashed in the jungle. Only one person survived the crash...and one crocodile.

OVERKILL

In 2013, the trees outside a Target store in Wilsonville, Oregon, were sprayed with an insecticide designed to kill aphids. However, the insecticide also killed an estimated 50,000 bumblebees. Upset by the news, Portland resident Rozzell Medina, 34, decided to hold

The ancient Egyptians kept excellent records of Nile River floods. Scientists still use their data.

a funeral in the parking lot the following Saturday to "memorialize these fallen life forms and talk about the plight of the bees and their importance to life on Earth." He posted the announcement on his Facebook page, hoping maybe 10 of his friends would show up. The turnout was closer to 100. According to *Oregon Live*, "After a moment of silence, attendees took to the microphone to urge action, read poems, chant, and sing songs." Some walked around with cameras and took pictures of the little bee corpses still lying among the trees.

CAN'T BLEAT THE FEELING

In 2013, an English couple named Holly Chugg Jones and Julian Light were camping on the coast in Dorset. While taking an early-evening walk, their black Lab, Dobby, spotted some sheep and took off after them…and didn't return. After searching frantically, they realized that their dog must have tumbled down a rocky 500-foot cliff. They spent the next day searching, but to no avail. "It was awful," said Jones. "I kept imagining Dobby dead in a ditch or washed out to sea." That night, they drove home with heavy hearts. The next day, a vacationer heard what sounded like a woman crying for help in the same area. The Coast Guard arrived and began a search-and-rescue operation at the base of the cliff. But instead of an injured woman, they discovered that the yells were coming from…a herd of bleating sheep. And what were the sheep bleating about? Dobby. He was halfway up the cliff. Jones and Light raced back to the coast to get their pet, who was none too worse for the wear.

* * *

KILLED BY CARROTS

"Croydon, England: Health food enthusiast Basil Brown became addicted to carrot juice and was bright yellow when he died of cirrhosis of the liver. The 48-year-old scientific adviser was drinking up to a gallon of carrot juice a day, an inquest was told. He was also consuming vitamin tablets by the handful and was found to have taken 70 million units of vitamin A in 10 days. A doctor warned Brown about the vitamin pills because his liver was already enlarged, 'but he had a low opinion of doctors,' the inquest was told. The verdict: death from carrot juice addiction."

—*Ottawa Citizen*, **February 15, 1974**

Careful! The bite of Australia's funnel-web spider can cause death in less than 15 minutes.

ACCORDING TO A GOVERNMENT STUDY

More government-funded studies to find out things we either knew already or didn't need to know in the first place.

S tudy: A survey of prison inmates, by the Law Enforcement Assistance Administration
Purpose: "To determine why inmates want to escape from prison"

Cost to the Taxpayer: $26,000

Methodology: Inmates were asked to fill out a questionnaire regarding their criminal histories, attitudes toward escaping from prison, and other aspects of prison life.

Findings: 1) "Escape is both a function of the characteristics of individuals and the situations in which they find themselves."

2) "The escaper is more likely than other inmates to be, among other things, 'one who has been turned down for parole' and 'not scheduled for parole review.'"

3) "Analyses tend to depict the escaper, particularly the multiple escaper, as a career criminal."

Study: Cooking times, by the USDA

Purpose: To determine how long it takes to cook breakfast

Cost to the Taxpayer: $45,000

Methodology: FDA researchers timed themselves cooking breakfast. Instead of counting minutes and seconds, they devised something called a "time measurement unit" (or TMU) equal to 0.036 seconds.

Findings: 1) It takes 838 TMUs to fry two eggs in a skillet.

2) It takes 1,222 TMUs to fry six ounces of hash.

3) It takes 960 TMUs to make French toast, including 22 TMUs to reach for the egg, and 15 TMUs to crack it against the bowl.

Study: Smorgasbord dining

Purpose: To determine whether obese people were more likely to opt for "all-you-can-eat" restaurants

Cost to the Taxpayer: $2,500

Methodology: "Some 1,718 patrons were observed in four restaurants of different ethnic origin (Italian, Irish, American, and Danish), where one could either order from a menu or visit a buffet or smorgasbord."

Findings: 1) "Obese persons formed a far higher percentage of the customers in restaurants when smorgasbord was served than under conditions of traditional menu service."

2) "Far more food was eaten in the smorgasbord than in the menu-service condition."

3) "Obese people may be more likely to seek out sites where more food is available."

Study: "Transportation in America's Future: Potentials for the Next Half-Century," by the U.S. Department of Transportation

Purpose: To forecast transportation needs in the year 2025

Cost to the Taxpayer: $225,000

Methodology: Four separate scenarios were considered: The U.S. enters an Ice Age, the U.S. becomes a dictatorship, the U.S. transforms into a "hippie culture" (the study was conducted in the 1970s), or the U.S. blossoms into a high-wage, high-consumption "American Dream" society. Predictions were then made as to what the transportation needs would be under each of the scenarios.

Findings: 1) In an Ice Age, "it will no longer be socially unacceptable to attend a business meeting in traditional walking, bicycle, or motorcycle attire." Large numbers of people will move south and west in search of a warmer climate. Hitchhikers will be "ubiquitous," and drivers will charge 25¢ to take them on local trips.

2) In an American Dream society, hitchhikers will be "illegal but common" and will "sometimes hide in vehicles to avoid detection."

3) If guerilla warfare erupts in response to a dictatorship, "cities will need more transit police, automobile use will become risky, and damage-insurance rates will rise astronomically."

4) The price of gas will be $1.70 in an Ice Age, $1.50 in a hippie society, $1.85 under a dictatorship, and $1.05 in an American Dream society. And "the interest rate will vary from 4 percent in a hippy society to 12 percent in an Ice Age."

The first July 4th celebration included 13 cannon shots and 13 toasts (Philadelphia, 1777).

GOING TOE-TO-TOE

Ailments of the feet are so common that almost all of us know someone who suffers from one—an uncle with hammer toes, a friend with gout, or maybe you with an ingrown toenail. With that in mind, here's a look at several foot-based medical conditions, some of which you may be familiar with…and some you'll wish you never were.

ATHLETE'S FOOT. It's the most common fungal infection in the world. Roughly 70 percent of the population will get it at some point in their lives. It's caused by contact with microscopic, parasitic fungi of the genus *Trichophyton*, which thrive in warm, moist conditions, most commonly on the feet (although you can also get it on your crotch or your armpits). Once contact is made, the fungi begin to feed on the dead outer layers of your skin, and if the conditions are right, they proliferate, resulting in infection as your body tries to fight off the invaders. There are three kinds of athlete's foot, each with its own symptoms:

• **Interdigital** shows up as cracked and scaly skin between your toes—especially between the fourth and fifth toes. Very itchy.

• **Vesicular** most often appears on the instep, but can spread to other parts of the feet (and even to other parts of the body, especially the palms). It's the result of the fungi making their way under the skin, rather than just on the surface, causing weepy blisters.

• **Moccasin-type** turns the sole, heel, and sides of your feet red and scaly, with a well-demarcated line, giving the appearance that the sufferer is wearing a red, scaly (and disgusting) moccasin. It is extremely itchy and painful.

BUNIONS. A bunion is a deformity of the foot characterized by a "bump" on the inner side of the foot at the base of the big toe and the "leaning" of the big toe toward the other toes. Strangely, doctors have been unable to figure out exactly what causes them. There appears to be a genetic factor, as you're more likely to get a bunion if someone in your family has one. Or they may be caused by prolonged use of tight footwear, as women are more likely to get them. Whatever the case, the big toe is gradually pushed toward the smaller toes, in time even causing those toes to angle out, too. And the bump at the base of the big toe can rub against the inside of footwear, causing the bunion to become inflamed and painful.

INGROWN TOENAILS. This happens when the corners or sides of one (or more) of your toenails grow downward into the flesh of your toe, or when the skin of a toe grows over the edge of the nail. It most commonly affects the big toes, often leads to infection and swelling, and can be very painful. Causes include wearing shoes that are too tight and cutting the corners of the nails too short. Podiatrists recommend that you do not round your toenails to the shape of the toe but allow the corners to grow out a little, and then cut the toenail straight. For most people, ingrown toenails are fairly easy to treat and mostly harmless, but for others, especially people with diabetes, they can be quite serious and should be treated by a doctor.

HAMMER TOE. No, it's not the name of a new superhero. Hammer toe is a deformity of the middle and/or last joints of the second, third, or fourth toes, resulting in the toes being forced into a bent position, giving them a hammerlike appearance. The most common cause: wearing tight footwear over prolonged periods of time, which causes the toes to lock in a bent position. There are two types of hammer toes: flexible—the toes can still be straightened manually; and rigid—the toes are stuck in the bent position.

GOUT. If you've ever had a red-hot nail hammered into your big toe, you know what gout feels like. That's actually how a lot of people who suffer with the condition describe the pain. The condition is commonly associated with high living. King Henry VIII, probably history's most famous gout-sufferer, was also a glutton and regularly ingested enormous amounts of very rich foods and alcohol. There's truth to that association, but it's not the whole story. The root of gout lies in proteins called *purines*. They occur naturally in our bodies, and we get them from foods, too. Our bodies process purines by breaking them down into the waste product uric acid. Normally, that uric acid is dissolved in our blood, then processed in our kidneys and evacuated from the body in urine. But sometimes uric acid levels in the blood become abnormally high. This can happen for a number of reasons, including eating too

---

The first domesticated apple trees in America were planted by the Pilgrims in Massachusetts.

much purine-rich food or simply because of kidney malfunction. However it happens, when uric acid levels get too high, the blood can't dissolve it all—and some of it actually solidifies into microscopic crystals. (When viewed under a microscope, uric acid crystals actually look like tiny needles.) This process happens more readily in cooler blood—in the extremities, especially the feet. A large buildup of uric acid crystals in your feet can accumulate in the spaces between skeletal joints—especially in the joint at the base of the big toe. But it's not those sharp crystals that cause gout's intense pain. Your immune system treats uric acid crystals as foreign bodies, not unlike viruses or bacteria. If you get a large enough crystal accumulation in one of your toe joints, the body will slam that buildup with a massive inflammation response, making the toe joint swell, turn purple, feel hot, and hurt—a lot. A gout attack can last a few hours and never come back, or it can last for months, and occur over and over again. The exact mechanisms behind gout are still not understood, but gout sufferers are told to stay away from purine-rich foods—which include organ meats like kidney and liver, seafoods like sardines and anchovies, some vegetables (such as spinach and asparagus), and alcohol (although modern medications can alleviate symptoms with no diet restrictions at all). Gout most commonly strikes the joints of the big toes, but can occur in the ankles, knees, and wrists. Uric acid crystals can also build up in the kidneys and cause a gout-related type of kidney stone.

PLANTAR FASCIITIS. (Pronounced PLAN-ter fash-ee-EYE-tus.) This is tearing and inflammation of the *plantar fascia*—the thick, flat band of tendons that runs along the bottom of your feet from your heel to your toes, supporting the foot's arch. It can be caused in different ways, including overuse (it's common among runners), putting on too much weight, standing on hard surfaces for long periods of time, "excessive pronation" (walking with your feet rolled inward), or by simple aging. All of these things can cause undue stress on the plantar fascia, even causing microscopic tears in the tendons. Tendons can also lose flexibility, and tighten up when they're not being used. Result: You nearly fall over in pain when you take your first steps in the morning—because you're stretching and tearing those taut tendons. The pain shows up primarily in the heel or the arch and can take a long time—up to many months—to heal.

The word "pop," referring to carbonated beverages (soda), dates back to at least 1812.

MORTON'S TOE. Named in the 1920s by American orthopedic surgeon Dudley Joy Morton, this is simply a condition of having a second toe that is longer than the big toe. It's actually pretty common (about 20 percent of humans have it), but it can be problematic: The abnormal toe-length configuration disburses weight differently than normal feet. Excessive pressure is put on the second *metatarsal head*—the ball of the foot right behind the second toe—causing the area to become sore and inflamed. People with this condition should wear shoes with a high, wide "toe box" (that's where the toes go), or simply wear shoes that are at least a half a size too large.

TOENAIL FUNGUS. Is there a white or yellow spot underneath one of your toenails? Smell it. If it smells like...you didn't really smell it, did you? Gross! But if you *did* smell it and it smells foul, you're probably suffering from *onychomycosis*—toenail fungus. Studies show that the condition affects 5–10 percent of North Americans and as many as 25 percent of Europeans. It's more common in men than in women, and more common in seniors than young people. The cause: a group of fungi known as *dermatophytes* (although yeasts and molds are sometimes the culprits), which thrive in moist, dark places...like on your foot inside your shoe. Good news: It's ugly, smelly, and painful, but it won't kill you. Bad news: It's ugly, smelly, and painful.

RANDOM FACTS

• Mitt Romney ran for president in 2012...but he didn't "run" run because the former Massachusetts governor, a longtime runner, was suffering from plantar fasciitis during the entire campaign. Other famous plantar fasciitis sufferers: American Olympic marathon runner Ryan Hall, NBA star Kobe Bryant, and NFL quarterback Eli Manning.

• A "tailor's bunion" is a bunionlike growth at the base of the baby toe. It's called that because in past centuries tailors often sat on the floor cross-legged while they worked. The joint at the base of their baby toes regularly rubbed on the ground, causing many tailors to get their namesake bunionlike bumps.

• Former Spice Girl Victoria Beckham, supermodels Naomi Campbell and Iman, and celebrity chef Nigella Lawson all have bunions.

Louis XIV decreed that only nobles could wear red shoes & the heels had to be lower than his.

(Actually Lawson *had* them. She had corrective surgery in 2012).

• Looking for a non-drug treatment for toenail fungus? Many people swear by applications of Vicks VapoRub.

• Singer and actress Jessica Simpson had surgery to fix an ingrown toenail in August 2012—and was kind enough to post a photo of the (bloody) removed bit of toenail on her Twitter page—so that her six million Twitter followers could see it.

• Athlete's foot is known to doctors as *tinea pedis*. It got its common name from the manufacturer of Absorbine Jr. in 1928.

• Charlie Sheen told *Rolling Stone* in a 2012 interview that he won't date girls with hammer toes. That means he won't be dating Tom Cruise's ex-wife, Katie Holmes. She has hammer toes.

*   *   *

WHERE THERE'S A WILL, THERE'S A WAY

In July 2012, Ray Fulk, of Lincoln, Illinois, died at the age of 71. He left behind an estate worth just over $1 million. Of that, $5,000 went to an animal protection organization in Chicago. The rest? According to Fulk's will, the rest of his estate was to go to two men: Peter Barton and Kevin Brophy. Who are they? Actors. Barton is best known for playing Dr. Scott Grainger in *The Young and the Restless* from 1987 to 1993, and Brophy was in the 1977 series *Lucan*, about a man who was raised by wolves. (Fulk had a poster advertising *Lucan* on a wall in his house, as well as copies of dozens of letters he'd written to the two actors.) Donald Behle, the lawyer who drew up the will, said Fulk told him the two actors were friends of his. When contacted after Fulk's death, both actors said they had no idea who he was. (And both of them thought it was some kind of scam.) Nevertheless, after the estate was settled, Barton and Brophy each received roughly $300,000—from a fan whom neither man had ever met. Brophy, who is still a struggling actor in Los Angeles, told ABC News it was a "wonderful safety net for myself and my family, not really having a steady job." He also said he hoped the unexpected inheritance would revive his acting career.

Strange coincidence: Fulk had no way of knowing this, but Barton and Brophy have been friends for years. They met when both appeared in the 1981 horror film *Hell Night*.

Explorer John Cabot was actually from Genoa, Italy. Real name: Giovanni Caboto.

HOW TO TELL IF YOU'RE DEAD

*Modern medicine makes it easy to determine if someone who looks dead
really is dead—not in a coma or otherwise still alive. In the old days, it
wasn't so easy. Here's a look at some of the methods doctors devised,
along with a look at what prompted their creation in the first place.*

BOXED IN
In 1905, a British social reformer named William Tebb wrote
a book titled *Premature Burial and How It May Be Prevented*.
Tebb was a bit of a crank—before taking up this cause he'd spent
decades campaigning against the smallpox vaccine, arguing that
sanitation, not inoculation, was the only cure for the deadly disease.
But there's no question that in his day, the public's fear of premature burial was very real. People repeated anecdotal tales of "dead"
people reviving at the morgue or at their own funerals, and wondered how many *hadn't* revived in time, and had instead died a slow,
suffocating death in the claustrophobic blackness of a coffin buried
six feet underground.

Tebb's book was full of such stories, and was well-known among
people obsessed with being buried alive. In the United States, a
group called the Society for Prevention of Premature Encoffinment,
Burial, or Cremation donated copies to public libraries, "hoping
that they may be carefully and universally read."

However unlikely premature burial might have been, in an age
when physicians had little more than primitive stethoscopes to
help distinguish the living from the dead, mistakes were certainly
possible. Given that the fear of premature burial was so widespread,
doctors were at great pains to find more effective techniques for
diagnosing death. Tebb described a number of the methods they
came up with in his book. Few were very effective, but they did
show a lot of imagination. Here are seven of the weirdest ones.

1. LEECHES
Certain types of leeches feed only on living hosts, so physicians
applied them to the "supposed dead" to see if they really were.

73% of American teachers say their school is drug free. 36% of students agree.

If the leeches attached themselves to the patient's body and were able to drink blood, the theory went, the patient was still alive. If they didn't, the patient was dead.

The problem with the leech method was that if the person's pulse was so faint as to be undetectable, their blood flow might not be strong enough to feed a leech, resulting in a false diagnosis of death. Webb's book contained an account of a woman who failed the leech test and was presumed dead, only to regain consciousness while being wrapped in her burial shroud before her funeral. "She opened her eyes and in a hollow voice said to the nurse, 'What are you doing here? I am not dead. Get away with you!'" Webb wrote. "She recovered, and felt no inconvenience other than a deafness, which lasted about two months."

2. NIPPLE CLAMPS

Invented by a French physician named M. Josat, these clamps were ordinary surgical forceps with special clawed ends designed to inflict terrible pain when attached to the nipples. The pain was thought to be severe enough to wake any living person from the deepest sleep. "This method held premier place as a means of distinguishing real from apparent death until it was demonstrated that subjects under profound hysteria were as indifferent to this painfully acute process as the dead," Tebb wrote.

3. BLISTER TESTS

In this test, the physician held a lit match to one of the patient's fingers, not to inflict pain but to see if the resulting burn formed a blister. The theory was that a living body would form a blister, but a dead one wouldn't. A similar test described in the *British Medical Journal* in 1896 called for pouring boiling water on the back of the forearm of the allegedly deceased. "If life is present, the boiling water will soon and unfailingly raise a blister," Dr. J. Milford Barnett of Belfast wrote. Blister tests had to be discarded when "dead" people who didn't blister revived and made full recoveries.

4. ELECTRIC CURRENT

This method worked by testing whether the muscles of the body twitched or contracted in response to electric stimulation. The living do; the dead don't. Only problem: The muscles of dead bodies

In the 1964 edition of *The Joy of Cooking*, one cookie recipe listed the yield as 45 servings...

can continue to contract until rigor mortis sets in several hours after death. Even if the test wasn't foolproof as a test of life, it could still be effective as a tool against premature burial, by delaying the burial of any body until well after it had stopped twitching in response to electrical stimulus, giving the "dead" additional time to revive.

5. ATROPINE DROPS

If you've ever had your pupils dilated during an eye exam, the drops the physician put in your eyes were likely *atropine* or its synthetic equivalent. The eyes of dead people don't dilate in response to atropine…at least not if they've been dead for more than half an hour. Because both the living and the newly dead can test positive for life, this test, like the electric current test, became one for preventing premature burial, by delaying the pronouncement of death until after the dead person's eyes stopped dilating.

6. FLUORESCEIN INJECTIONS

Fluorescein is a green fluorescent substance that did nothing when injected into the body of a dead person. When injected into a living person, using a method developed by one Dr. Icard, a French physician, it gave the body a yellowish discoloration similar to jaundice while also causing the eyes to turn a vivid green. "The whole of the eye is said to assume a clear green tinge, the pupil almost disappears, and the eye looks as if it were a brilliant emerald set in the face," Tebb wrote. "In two hours all the phenomena disappear."

This test had two major defects: 1) It relied on the circulation of blood to distribute the fluorescein from the injection site to the rest of the body, and a living person who was so ill as to be mistaken for dead was unlikely to have normal circulation. And 2) the negative side effects associated with injection of fluorescein included anaphylactic shock, cardiac arrest, and even sudden death—meaning that persons might be killed by the test that was supposed to determine if they were still alive.

7. WAITING MORTUARIES

As Tebb himself acknowledged in his book, the only way to really be sure that someone was dead was to wait for putrefaction to set in—dead bodies rot; living bodies do not. In Munich, Frankfurt, and a few other German cities, the authorities established a system

…The same recipe in the 1997 edition listed the yield as 36 servings.

of "waiting mortuaries" to make premature burial all but impossible. When a person was pronounced dead by a physician, instead of being buried quickly, as was the custom, the bodies were delivered in their coffins to a waiting mortuary and left there for several days until the unmistakable signs of rot began to set in.

Waiting mortuaries, also known as "hospitals for the dead," were staffed by medically trained watchmen 24 hours a day. Coffins were left open, and a ring attached by a cord to a bell system was placed on the finger of the supposed deceased. "The warning bell is so sensitive that the least shake of the corpse sets it in motion," Tebb wrote. "Various causes may agitate the bell, and the waking of a corpse is a very rare occurrence. Nevertheless, the caretaker at once goes to ascertain the cause of alarm, and, having assured himself that the corpse preserves all the signs of death, he readjusts the cord." But if the corpse did show signs of stirring, medical aid as well as food, drinks, and even cigars could be administered at once.

GOING MY WAY

In his book, Tebb argued for legislation making it illegal to bury the dead until unmistakable signs of putrefaction had set in, and called for the government to build waiting mortuaries in every community in Great Britain. Neither of these calls were heeded—the British medical establishment never did accept the idea that premature burial was as common as Tebb claimed it was. And for people who did fear such a fate, cheaper solutions were at hand: They could arrange to be autopsied, embalmed, cremated, or to have their jugular vein severed before burial. Any of these would have precluded the possibility of regaining consciousness in the grave.

Tebb lived to the age of 86, and when he died in 1917—or at least he *appeared* to be dead—his will instructed that his body be cremated after "unmistakable evidence of decomposition" became apparent. His wishes were honored: He was cremated a week later.

We dug up an "eyewitness account" of a premature burial.
Are you brave enough to read it? If so, *turn to page 327.*

*   *   *

"If only we'd stop trying to be happy we'd have a pretty good time."
—**Edith Wharton**

Actress Sarah Bernhardt took a coffin on tour with her for good luck. She slept in it.

ANARCHY IN THE E.R.

Having to go to the emergency room (ouch!) is bad enough. Having to admit that your condition is the result of doing something stupid only adds insult to the injury, as these excerpts from actual E.R. reports attest. (Ouch!)

"42-year-old female states, 'I was playing a computer bowling game and passed out; struck chin on unknown object. I've been drinking.'"

"18-year-old male accidentally shot himself while putting BB gun in his pants at home. 'Gunshot' wound to penis."

"61-year-old female was smoking on the porch while wearing oxygen. House caught fire. Smoke inhalation."

"37-year-old female went to sit in recliner at home, missed chair, fell on arm. Elbow pain."

"21-year-old male used a surfboard to slide down a flight of stairs; fell off surfboard. Sprained left ankle."

"Male, 41, was accidentally hit in the head with bowling ball while playing catch with it at a bachelor party. Neck strain, head injury, bruising."

"34-year-old male using metal-cutting saw; sparks flew back onto pants, and pants caught on fire. Redness and blisters."

"53-year-old female was sitting on a rocking chair when she fell backwards off of porch. Back pain."

"18-year-old male, drumming, bent over and got a drumstick up his nose. Bloody nose."

"32-year-old male had a glow stick in his mouth and ran into a pole while at a haunted house. Dental fracture."

"Female, 41, was having sexual intercourse in a recliner with partner when the recliner fell, throwing patient into glass door on bookshelf. Lacerated lip."

"18-year-old male dropped his lighter, went to pick it up, was sprayed in the face by a skunk. Eye irritation."

"52-year-old male was sleeping when son put tail of toy dinosaur in his ear. Ruptured eardrum."

"53-year-old male fell off toilet as he had explosive diarrhea; struck head on counter. Ate moldy tortilla, bad milk, and moldy cheese."

Under San Francisco's fast-food laws, meals with a free toy cannot contain over 600 calories.

TOMATO CANS & SUNDAY PUNCHES

You've probably heard the boxing term "rope-a-dope." It means backing up against the ropes and letting your opponent wear himself out punching you before you go on the attack. Here's some more boxing slang.

Stylist: A boxer who relies on skill, rather than the power of his punches, to win fights.

Catcher: A bad fighter; someone who uses his head to block his opponent's punches.

Boxer's Handshake: Tapping your gloves on your opponent's at the start of the fight—standard boxing procedure for nearly 200 years. (That's the origin of the "fist bump.")

Chin: Someone who can take a lot of punches to the face is said to have "a good chin," or "a good set of whiskers." The opposite of a "glass jaw."

Gatekeeper: A fighter who's not a champ, but good enough that other fighters have to beat him to qualify as serious contenders for title fights.

Stick and Move: Throwing a punch, then quickly backing away to evade your opponent's return punch.

Peek-a-Boo: Holding your hands high in front of your face to protect your head and make it easier to hit your opponent in the head.

Sunday Punch: Another name for a knockout punch—a blow so devastating that it knocks the victim "into next week."

Journeyman: A fighter more experienced than a novice, but not good enough to win many fights—"a body for better men to beat on," in other words.

Tomato Can: A fighter so bad that he regularly loses to beginners. (They bleed when dented.)

Playing Possum: Pretending to be more seriously injured than you are to trick your opponent into wearing himself out trying to finish the fight.

Rabbit Punch: A sharp blow to the back of the head (like the kind used to kill rabbits).

Noah's wife is mentioned in The Bible five times. What's her name? It doesn't say.

THE YEAR WITHOUT A SUMMER

There's a lot being said about climate change these days. Most people (and most scientists) think it's happening now; some say it's a myth. Wherever you stand on the issue, we can't help but wonder what you would have thought if you'd been around in 1815.

DUST IN THE WIND

It all started with a volcano. On April 5, 1815, Mount Tambora blew its top. The massive eruption lasted ten days and completely ravaged the Indonesian island of Sumbawa. Residents who managed to survive the mountain's initial fury—and the ensuing tsunami—became victims of deadly lung infections caused by all the ash and toxic fumes in the air. The eruption, which was one of the most powerful in recorded history, ejected more than 10 cubic miles of volcanic material. The islands were blanketed with it, causing crops across Indonesia to fail, and creating a massive food shortage for Asia throughout the spring and summer months.

But that was just the beginning. Mount Tambora's outburst was only one of many in a string of uncharacteristically high volcanic activity around the globe. The ash from Tambora combined with the enormous amounts of dust and debris already floating in the atmosphere from eruptions in the Philippines, Japan, and the Caribbean. This meant bad news for farmers.

EASTERN FRONT

When there's that much dust, gas, and debris in the air, it gets in the way of sunlight. All that volcanic material started affecting the weather and quickly impacted temperatures around the world.

The first areas to get hit were in Asia. Cooler than usual weather caused thousands of Chinese farmers to lose their livestock, particularly water buffalo—beasts of burden on which they depended for harvesting crops. Not that there was much of a crop to harvest: The frigid temperatures ravaged rice fields; even trees started dying off. Heavy monsoons in India led to a massive outbreak of cholera, a water-borne disease, that reached as far away as Moscow.

The movie *Dumb and Dumber* was 10 times more popular than *Sense and Sensibility*.

WESTERN FRONT

As the ash drifted into the Northern Hemisphere, the eastern seaboard of the United States experienced a very cold spring. Even stranger, New England was beset with a "dry fog" that would not dissipate. The lingering fog dimmed and refracted the sunlight, creating a constant eerie red glow in the sky. Even heavy rainfall failed to disperse it.

In eastern Canada and the northern U.S., temperatures routinely fell below freezing through May of 1816—far past the usual Canadian cold season. That, of course, caused crops to fail up and down the east coast of North America. And it just *stayed* cold. Snow fell on June 4 throughout the region. A storm in Quebec City on that day dropped over a foot of snow. As spring moved into "summer," lakes and rivers as far south as Pennsylvania iced over. Temperatures fluctuated wildly in some areas, hitting 95° F, then rapidly dropping to below freezing after sunset.

The bizarre weather ravaged food supplies. In the autumn, when many crops are harvested, cornfields across New England were destroyed by early frost. The cost of grains skyrocketed. Limited supplies caused the price of oats alone to jump by 750 percent in many areas. And while some American farmers were able to harvest their fields despite the weather, transporting produce to market on icy roads was all but impossible.

Even Thomas Jefferson was impacted. Already deeply in debt, the former president saw his money troubles worsen as bad weather destroyed the crops at his Virginia plantation, Monticello. The following winter, temperatures dropped into the negative 20s in New York City, freezing the Upper Bay. The ice was so thick that the locals could—and did—ride sleighs from Brooklyn over the river to Governors Island.

BLOODY SNOW

The situation in Europe was even worse, where the weather exasperated conditions in a region trying to rebuild after the devestation caused by the Napoleonic Wars. Wales was hit so hard that refugees fled to England's major cities, begging for food and shelter. Already limited food supplies ran low, and prices skyrocketed in Germany and Ireland.

Abnormal rainfall caused rivers to rise, while many areas endured frost in mid-August. Elsewhere, people in temperate countries such as

Hungary and Italy reported snowfall throughout the summer months. And the dust in the atmosphere turned the white snowflakes red.

Switzerland was hit particularly hard. Temperatures there were so low that an ice dam formed beneath the Giétro Glacier in the Swiss Alps, creating an artificial lake in the process. The dam eventually burst in the summer of 1818, sending millions of gallons of water into the valley below. Towns were destroyed and thousands of people were killed in what has become known as one of Switzerland's worst natural disasters.

As thousands starved—and thousands more would—demonstrations began to take place outside of grain markets and bakeries across Europe…and they quickly turned into riots, followed by arson and looting. Still, there wasn't much that governments could do: The famine was the worst the continent would experience in the 19th century. By the time it was all over, nearly 200,000 Europeans would perish.

LOOK ON THE BRIGHT SIDE
But it wasn't *all* bad. A shortage of oats to feed horses helped encourage German inventor Karl Drais to create an alternative form of transportation. He called it the *Laufmaschine* ("running machine"), and it was a precursor to the modern bicycle.

All the material in the air led to some pretty spectacular sunsets that summer, too. British artist J.M.W. Turner created several now-famous paintings that celebrated the unusually yellow atmospheric conditions. And when 19-year-old novelist Mary Shelley found herself stuck indoors during an unseasonably rainy vacation at Lake Geneva that July, she and her colleagues passed the time by trying to frighten each other with scary stories. She came up with one about a scientist who uses various body parts stolen from a cemetery to bring a man back to life—*Frankenstein*. Her friend, English poet Lord Byron, came up with an idea for a book about a bloodsucking ghoul. He never finished it, but gave it to his friend John William Polidori, who wrote a novella called *The Vampyre*, which in turn inspired Bram Stoker to write *Dracula*.

While the foul weather was inadvertently creating the horror genre in Europe, it sent thousands of farmers fleeing from New England. In Vermont alone, over 10,000 people left the state for warmer climates. Many of them flooded into the Midwest and helped tame the wild American heartland. Among those who left Vermont was the family of a young man named Joseph Smith. The Smiths eventually settled in Palmyra, New York. It was a move that led to a series of events that culminated in Smith's publishing the *Book of Mormon* and founding the Church of Jesus Christ of Latter-day Saints years later.

POINTING THE FINGER

Back then, nobody really knew what had caused the devastation and mayhem. Half-baked theories ran rampant. Many Christians pointed at "sinners," and a few evangelists claimed that the cold was the beginning of the apocalypse. Others believed that the weird weather was somehow the delayed result of Benjamin Franklin's experiments with electricity. Some even suspected that the Free-masons had something to do with it. Astronomers noted unusual sunspot activity and theorized that the frosty temperatures must have been caused by them.

Today, climatologists know that Tambora was the cause. Scientists excavating in Iceland have uncovered unusually large deposits of sulfur in the soil layers that date to the early 1800s. Their explanation: the sulfuric acid that comprised the major portion of the gases spewed by the volcano hung in the air and drifted around the world. The gasses acted like mirrors and reflected the sunlight back into space, preventing it from reaching Earth. Whatever people may have thought was the cause, a Vermont woman named Eileen Marguet captured the misery of that dark summer in this poem:

It didn't matter whether your farm was large or small.
It didn't matter if you had a farm at all.
'Cause everyone was affected when water didn't run.
The snow and frost continued without the warming sun.
One day in June it got real hot and leaves began to show.
But after that it snowed again and wind and cold did blow.
The cows and horses had no grass; no grain to feed the chicks.
No hay to put aside that time, just dry and shriveled sticks.
The sheep were cold and hungry and many starved to death,
Still waiting for the warming sun to save their labored breath.
The kids were disappointed, no swimming, such a shame.
It was in 1816 that summer never came.

THE OTHER WARS BETWEEN THE STATES

The U.S. Civil War (1861–65) was by far the largest conflict to ever pit Americans against each other—but it wasn't the only one.

THE PENNAMITE-YANKEE WAR (1769–99)

Between: Connecticut and Pennsylvania

Background: In 1662, King Charles II of England granted the Connecticut Colony a 73-mile-wide strip of territory stretching from modern-day Rhode Island on the Atlantic coast all the way west to the "South Sea" (the Pacific Ocean). Nineteen years later, in 1681, the King granted a chunk of the same strip of land to William Penn, who incorporated it into the Pennsylvania Colony.

What Happened: In the decades that followed, both colonies sent settlers into the Wyoming Valley, in what is now northeastern Pennsylvania. Both colonies added to their claims to the territory with overlapping purchases of land from local Indian tribes. In the early 1770s, another English king, George III, ruled in favor of Connecticut's claim to the Wyoming Valley. More Connecticut Yankees poured into the territory, where they clashed with the "Pennamites," or Pennsylvania settlers. During one battle in 1778, 150 settlers were killed and thousands more fled the region.

What Happened After That: Connecticut didn't give up its claim to territory inside Pennsylvania and farther west until 1786, when it did so in exchange for 1) relief from its Revolutionary War debts, and 2) the right to retain part of its original sea-to-sea land grant in modern-day Ohio, a 3.3 million-acre parcel of land along Lake Erie called the Western Reserve. It kept that parcel for just nine years. In 1795, it sold the land to speculators for $1.2 million and relinquished its last claims to sovereignty over the region in 1800.

THE WALTON WAR (1804)

Between: North Carolina and Georgia

Background: The two states were involved in disputes over a 12-mile strip of land called the "Orphan Strip," a no-man's land teeming with outlaws and rebellious Indians. None of the surrounding

Cost of building a genetics lab in your garage: According to *Scientific American*, $3,000.

states wanted to take responsibility for the troublesome area, which had never been properly surveyed to begin with.

As growing numbers of settlers entered the Orphan Strip in the 1780s and '90s, the states began to take an interest. In 1803, Georgia organized the territory into what it called Walton County. By that time, North Carolina considered at least part of the strip to be in its Buncombe County, and farmers on land granted by North Carolina feared losing their land if the territory was recognized as being part of Georgia.

What Happened: The "war" started in December 1804, when Walton County tried to collect taxes from Buncombe County settlers. In the fight, a Walton County official struck a Buncombe constable on the forehead with the butt of a musket and killed him. When news of the death reached the Buncombe County seat in Ashville, a 72-man militia marched on the Orphan Strip and arrested ten Walton County officials, causing the government to collapse.

What Happened After That: Georgia and North Carolina argued over who was in charge until 1807, when they formed a joint committee to settle the issue and properly survey the area for the first time. The survey found that the state line was actually 18 miles farther south than anyone realized. That put the strip well inside of North Carolina, but Georgia rejected the finding and continued to administer the territory until 1811, when it hired another surveyor…who also concluded that the strip was 18 miles inside of North Carolina. Georgia grudgingly accepted the findings (but refused to pay the surveyor) and abandoned its claim to the strip. Today it's part of Transylvania County, North Carolina.

THE HONEY WAR (1839)

Between: Missouri and Iowa

Background: From 1816 until 1837, a line of demarcation known as the "Sullivan Line" served as the border between the territories that would become the states of Missouri (1821) and Iowa (1846). But in 1837, as Iowa moved closer to statehood, Missouri ordered up a new survey of the area—one that showed the border as being as much as 9½ miles north of the Sullivan line in places. That meant that a strip of Iowa land nearly ten miles wide—2,600 square miles in all—was suddenly part of Missouri, at least as far as

---

Call in sick! 55 percent of corporate "downsizings" take place on Tuesdays.

Missourians were concerned. Iowans living in the strip didn't like that, especially since Iowa was a free state and Missouri was a slave state.

What Happened: When a Missouri sheriff entered the area to collect taxes in 1839, the locals chased him out with pitchforks. According to legend, three trees containing valuable honeybee hives were chopped down and brought to Missouri in lieu of payment. Both sides called up their militias, but bloodshed was averted when Iowa and Missouri agreed to fight it out in court. The case went straight to the U.S. Supreme Court (which decides lawsuits between states), and in 1849, it ruled that the Sullivan Line was the true border between the states. It remains so to this day.

THE RED RIVER BRIDGE WAR (1931)

Between: Texas and Oklahoma

Background: In 1931, Texas and Oklahoma were preparing to open a bridge over the Red River—the border between the two states—on the highway connecting Denison, Texas, with Durant, Oklahoma. The two states split the cost of the bridge construction. But there was a problem: As part of the deal, the Texas Highway Commission had agreed to buy out the operator of a nearby toll bridge for $200,000, but never paid up. Just before the new free bridge was to open, the owner of the toll bridge obtained a court injunction keeping the new bridge closed until the $200,000 was paid. To enforce the injunction, Texas Governor Ross Sterling ordered barricades erected on the southern (Texas) side of the new bridge.

What Happened: The Governor of Oklahoma, "Alfalfa" Bill Murray, took offense at Sterling's action and sent a crew from his state's highway department across the bridge to demolish the barriers. Alfalfa Bill claimed he was within his rights, arguing that Oklahoma territory extended all the way across the river and up onto the shoreline on the Texas side of the river, which meant the barriers were actually in Oklahoma. (Thanks to language in the Louisiana Purchase Treaty of 1803, he was probably right.) Governor Sterling didn't buy it; he dispatched three armed Texas Rangers and a crew of highway workers to rebuild the barricades. That made Alfalfa Bill so mad that he had the northern approaches to the toll bridge demolished. Since the new bridge was still closed, that brought all cross-river traffic to a standstill.

When water is scarce, plants grow smaller leaves.

What Happened After That: Texas lawmakers tried to resolve the issue by passing legislation giving the owner of the toll bridge special permission to sue the state. That satisfied the owner of the toll bridge, so the injunction was lifted and the new bridge was opened to traffic. But Alfalfa Bill was still steamed, so hours before a federal court was set to order him to open the toll bridge, he declared a state of martial law on and around the toll bridge, which (he claimed) placed him above the jurisdiction of the court. He ordered the Oklahoma National Guard to keep the toll bridge closed, but it was a symbolic gesture at best, since the new bridge was already open. Once Alfalfa Bill was satisfied he'd made his point, he allowed the toll bridge to reopen. A few days later, he dispatched the Oklahoma National Guard to both sides of the new bridge in fear that it was about to be closed, but the crisis passed, martial law was lifted, and the Oklahoma Guard withdrew. Traffic has flowed freely over the river ever since.

THE "BATTLE" OF SEAVEY'S ISLAND (2000–2002)

Between: New Hampshire and Maine

Background: Seavey's Island, home to the Portsmouth Naval Shipyard, is in the Piscataqua River on the Maine–New Hampshire border. So if the island is in the river, which state is it in…and who gets to collect taxes there? The state of Maine says the border runs down the middle of the river, which puts it in Maine. But in a 2000 lawsuit over who gets to levy taxes on the island, New Hampshire claimed the border runs along the Maine shoreline, which, if true, put the entire river, including Seavey's Island, in New Hampshire.

Verdict: Case dismissed, in an 8-0 vote. Back in the 1970s, New Hampshire had argued in another lawsuit against Maine, this time over lobster fishing rights, that the border ran down the *middle* of the river, not along the Maine shoreline as it now claimed. The Supreme Court ruled that New Hampshire couldn't claim the border was in a different place just because its interests had changed.

* * *

"Let's pray that the human race never escapes Earth to spread its iniquity elsewhere."

—C. S. Lewis

DUSTBIN OF HISTORY: CHAMP FERGUSON

We all learned about the Civil War when we were kids in school, and most of us remember the big names related to it, like Abraham Lincoln, Robert E. Lee, and William Tecumseh Sherman. But few of us have heard of people like Champ Ferguson, the notorious Confederate guerilla who fought his own, savage little war in Kentucky and Tennessee. (Maybe for good reason!)

GUNSMOKE

On October 7, 1864, a tall, dark-haired man about 40 years of age snuck into Emory and Henry College Hospital in southwest Virginia. The hospital was filled with soldiers wounded at the Battle of Saltville, Virginia, which had ended just a few days earlier. The man made his way to the bed of Lieutenant Elza Smith, a badly wounded Union soldier.

Lieutenant Smith looked at the man and called to him by name. They had grown up not far from each other, in Clinton County, Kentucky, and had been friends before the war. The man raised his musket and said, "Smith, do you see this?"

Smith begged the man not to shoot.

The man put the muzzle of the rifle to Smith's head and pulled the trigger. The gun did not fire. He cocked the gun and pulled the trigger again. The gun did not fire.

The third time it did.

FARM BOY

Champ Ferguson was born to William and Zilpha Huff Ferguson in a secluded log farmhouse not far from the Clinton County seat of Albany, just a few miles north of the Tennessee border. He was born on November 29, 1821, the first of ten children. He was named after his grandfather, who was called Champion. As a boy, he helped on the farm; it is believed he attended school for a total of about three months. In 1844, the 23-year-old married Ann Eliza Smith. They had one child, a boy, but he died less than two years later, and Ann died not long after that. Ferguson remarried in 1848, to a woman named Martha Owen, who gave birth to a daughter in 1850. That same year, Ferguson's father died, and he, as the eldest son, inherited the family farm. Local records show that he owned almost 200 acres by 1855, and more than 450 by 1860. Ferguson was, by all accounts, a successful farmer. He was also an expert backwoodsman, spending weeks at a time on horseback roaming the densely wooded countryside along the Kentucky-Tennessee border. As for a physical description, a newspaper account of his 1865 murder trial, says he was just over six feet tall, and a "well built man." It goes on:

> His hair is black and tolerably short, and seems from long habit to have grown in one direction, at an angle of forty-five degrees backward from the surface of his head. This gives him a somewhat fierce appearance.

TOUGH GUY

His looks were not misleading. Ferguson was a bully who could quickly turn violent. In an 1858 incident, Ferguson was involved in a legal dispute with some men from Tennessee over livestock transactions. That November, Ferguson happened to be in Tennessee when the men got a local sheriff named James Reed to accompany them on a mission to have Ferguson arrested. A fight, a chase, and a standoff ensued over the next several hours. When it was over, Ferguson had killed Sheriff Reed, slashing and stabbing him perhaps as many as 15 times with his large pocket knife. Reed is believed to be the first person murdered by Champ Ferguson. There would be many more.

Ferguson spent two months in jail before being released on bail. Remarkably, his case was put off for more than two years, then sidelined altogether when something more immediate came along: the Civil War.

MAN WITHOUT A HOME

In April 1861, the American Civil War officially began when Confederate forces attacked Fort Sumter, a Union Army post in South Carolina. Suddenly, Tennessee and Kentucky were international border states. Not only that, they were international border states between two nations at war: Kentucky remained in the United States; Tennessee became of member of the newly-formed Confederacy. What did this mean for Champ Ferguson? It meant his home was in enemy territory.

Most of the people of Clinton County, Kentucky, including Ferguson's mother, all of his siblings, and most of his neighbors, supported President Abraham Lincoln and the Union. Ferguson sided with the Confederates. Exactly why is not clear. He may have supported the Southern cause—he did, in fact, own three slaves—but there are other possibilities. The lawyer who had gotten Ferguson's murder trial repeatedly postponed was a 20-year-old Tennessee man named W. Scott Bledsoe. When war broke out, Bledsoe became Major Bledsoe, leader of a Confederate Army company with which Ferguson would spend a fair amount of time. At his trial Ferguson said that Bledsoe had offered to use his power to get him off on the murder charge if he joined the Confederate cause.

Whatever it was that brought him to fight for the Confederacy, Ferguson took to the role with relish.

UNCIVIL WAR

In the months after the war began, Ferguson's position in Clinton County became increasingly tenuous. In August 1861, he was arrested by a Kentucky "Home Guard" unit, one of many local volunteer militias that had sprung up on both sides, and was marched for several days toward a Union recruitment center, where he was to be forced into Union Army service. Several days into the march, Ferguson escaped his captors. Not long after that, he moved his wife and child over the border to Sparta, Tennessee, and began taking part in raiding parties into Kentucky, mostly, at first, to steal livestock and whatever else could be used or sold.

For Champ Ferguson, the Civil War had now officially begun, and it would be a personal, paranoid, and savage war. His enemy, it seems, wasn't President Lincoln and the Union—it was the people of Clinton County, who had, to his mind, driven him from his home. As Ferguson said around the time of his trial in 1865:

> We were having a sort of miscellaneous war up there, through Fentress County, Tennessee, and Clinton County, Kentucky, and all through that region. Every man was in danger of his life; if I hadn't killed my neighbor, he would have killed me. Each of us had from twenty to fifty proscribed enemies, and it was regarded as legitimate to kill them at any time, at any place, under any circumstances.

ON THE WAR PATH

On November 1, 1861, Ferguson was on one of his raiding parties when he approached a log farmhouse in Clinton County. A woman was on the farmhouse's front porch, peeling apples. Ferguson told her he was there to see her husband, William Frogg. She said William was very sick, and could not receive visitors. Ferguson ignored her and walked into the house, where William Frogg lay in bed. The two men exchanged a few words, then Ferguson pulled out a pistol and shot Frogg in the chest, twice. Ferguson left the house, got on his horse, and galloped away.

William Frogg is believed to be the first person Ferguson murdered in the war. Ferguson had known Frogg, and his wife, for most of his life, and, according to people who had known them both, they had been friendly with each other. So why did he kill him? Ferguson testified that he had been warned that Frogg was looking for an opportunity to kill him—and that was good enough reason to kill him first.

A month later, Ferguson shot another unarmed Clinton County man, Reuben Wood, in front of his wife and daughter. As with Frogg, Ferguson had known the Wood family for nearly all his life, but believed, again, that Wood was out to kill him.

In the spring of 1862, Ferguson began working, at least occasionally, in concert with Confederate Army companies, first with Major Bledsoe and later with the legendary Confederate cavalry leader General John Hunt Morgan. (Some evidence suggests that Ferguson actually enlisted in the Confederate Army and was given a rank of captain, but this has never been confirmed. And it would be a bone of contention at his trial.) In any case, Ferguson spent most of the war leading own band of guerillas. By the end of 1862, he had personally killed, by conservative estimates, 23 men. One of those victims was 16-year-old Fount Zachary.

MARK OF A CHAMPION

One evening in early April 1862, Ferguson and a group of men were on their way back from a raid in Albany, Kentucky, when they came across a young, armed man on horseback. He was a Union scout on the lookout for raiders—and had mistaken Ferguson's group for Union men. When the young man realized his mistake, he immediately surrendered his gun. Ferguson asked who the young man was.

"Fount Zachary," he answered.

Ferguson recognized the name—the Zacharys were among the

most prominent Union supporters in Clinton County—and shot him. The young man fell to the ground. Ferguson then dismounted his horse, pulled out his hunting knife, walked over to the dying boy, and stabbed him in the heart.

In court, Ferguson would later admit to stabbing the unarmed, already-incapacitated young man and to doing the same to many others. This was to become a grisly part of the Ferguson legend. (Although the stories of his knifework were exaggerated to ridiculous proportions during the war, tales of disembowelments and beheadings spread through Kentucky, Tennessee, and beyond.)

SALTVILLE

In October 1864, with the war winding down and a Confederate loss all but inevitable Ferguson found himself involved in what would become known as one of the Civil War's most notorious incidents. He and his band of guerilla fighters had joined General Joe Wheeler's ranks to defend a strategically important salt works in Saltville, Virginia, from an attacking Union force. (Salt was needed by the army to preserve meat for soldiers' rations.) The battle was a stunning victory for a much-outnumbered Confederate force, but what happened afterward lives in infamy: After the Union forces retreated, Confederate soldiers took part in a prolonged massacre of captured, unarmed, and wounded Union soldiers, most of them black members of the Union's "colored" cavalry units. No exact number of victims is known, but a low estimate puts the number at 46.

Ferguson later denied taking part in that massacre—but witnesses testified at his trial that he did. What Ferguson did not deny was sneaking into nearby Confederate Emory and Henry College Hospital and killing the badly wounded and unarmed Lieutenant Elza Smith. This murder, too, Ferguson put to self-defense.

THE TRIAL

On April 9, 1865, General Robert E. Lee surrendered to Ulysses S. Grant at the Appomattox Courthouse in Virginia. But the news travelled slowly and in places the fighting raged for more than a month. Ferguson had fought to nearly the very end, killing his last victim on or around May 1. On May 26, he was arrested by federal forces at his farm in Sparta, Tennessee, and transported to Nashville,

Only male mammal known to produce milk: The Dayak fruit bat. It uses it to nurse its young.

where he was charged with the murders of 53 people.

Ferguson pleaded not guilty to all charges, denying many of the killings outright and claiming self-defense for the ones he admitted to—even if it was self-defense before the fact. (Even the murder of the wounded Elza Smith in his hospital bed, said Ferguson, was because Smith had sworn to kill *him*.)

The trial lasted from July 11 to September 26, 1865, and was covered by newspapers across the country. It wasn't a fair trial and was called by many a "kangaroo court." But because Ferguson admitted to so many of the killings, that hardly mattered to most people. On October 10, Ferguson was found guilty of 22 of the 53 murders and was sentenced to hang. On October 20, that sentence was carried out in the yard of Nashville's State Penitentiary in front of a crowd of about 300 people. Ferguson's last request was that his body be given to his wife so she could take it to their Tennessee farm, where he could be buried in "good Rebel soil." That request was carried out, and Champ Ferguson's grave still stands in France Cemetery in Sparta, Tennessee.

MORE FERGUSON FACTS

• Ferguson's lawyers tried to get him off by saying he was a soldier following orders and taking part in the nasty business that is war. But they could never prove that Ferguson had ever actually enlisted in the Confederate Army—and their efforts came to nought.

• One of Ferguson's enemies, Union guerilla leader Tinker Dave Beaty of Fentress County, Tennessee, testified against Ferguson at his trial. While Beaty undoubtedly committed the same kinds of acts as Ferguson during the war, he was never charged with any crimes and died an old man at his Tennessee home in 1883.

• A rumor circulated in the years after his trial that Ferguson's hanging was faked. Supposedly, the rope was rigged so that he could take the noose off beneath the enclosed scaffold and that he climbed into his own casket and was taken to Oklahoma, where he changed his name and lived to a ripe old age. (It wasn't true.)

• Ferguson became a popular hero to some southerners after the war, and in some quarters, remains one today.

FULL METAL JACKET

*Even if you don't own a gun, you've probably heard gun-related terms,
such as* automatic, breech-loading, *and* tracer, *for example—
from TV, movies, and the news. But do you know what they
mean? Here are explantations for those terms and some
others you may not have heard before. (If you want to
know how guns and bullets work, turn to page 314.)*

ACTION: The mechanism a gun uses to load, seal, and remove its cartridges. (See bolt- and pump-action.)

AUTOMATIC: A gun that, upon squeezing and holding the trigger, automatically fires a bullet, ejects the spent cartridge case, loads another cartridge from a *magazine*, and fires again, over and over until the trigger is released or the magazine is empty. (A *semi-automatic* fires just one bullet when the trigger is pressed, then automatically ejects the case and loads another cartridge.)

BOLT-ACTION: The *bolt* is the part of a gun that closes and locks up a cartridge in the gun's chamber so it can be fired. *Bolt-action* is popular for rifles, and consists of a handle that hangs down from the top and to one side of the gun (generally the right, although it is made for lefties, too). To work it, the handle is lifted up and pulled back. This rotates the bolt and slides it back, which ejects a spent case from a fired cartridge and exposes the chamber, allowing a fresh cartridge to be inserted. Pushing the bolt forward, then downward, locks the new cartridge into the barrel and cocks the gun, preparing it for firing.

BREECH-LOADING: The *breech* is the back end of a gun's barrel—the opposite of the end the bullet exits. (That end is called the *muzzle*). So *breech-loading guns* are guns that load from the rear end of the barrel and account for the majority of modern guns. (*Muzzle loaders* load from the front end. Example: the musket.)

CHAMBER: The opening where a cartridge is inserted into a gun.

FULL METAL JACKET: A cartridge that has a bullet with a core of soft metal, usually lead, and a shell of harder metal, often a copper alloy. This makes them lighter and harder than normal bullets, allowing for higher velocity and better accuracy over long distances.

It also makes them more apt to stay intact upon contact and cleanly penetrate a target. (The 1987 film *Full Metal Jacket* is named for this cartridge, which was the standard round issued to U.S. Army riflemen in Vietnam.)

HOLLOW-POINT: Bullets with hollows cut into their tips. Unlike full-metal-jacket bullets, they're designed to mushroom and expand once they hit something, thereby doing as much damage as possible. (Most nations have outlawed the use of hollow-point bullets in war.)

SUBMACHINE GUN: A short handheld machine gun that is sort of a cross between a rifle and a handgun. An example is the Thompson submachine gun, or "Tommy gun," made famous by 1920s-era gangsters.

MAGAZINE: Storage device that holds multiple cartridges for a single gun. It can be detachable or part of the gun itself, and can vary greatly in shape and in the number of cartridges held. (The Tommy gun had detachable magazines that could hold 100 cartridges each.)

MAGNUM: When a cartridge is dubbed a *magnum*, it means that it's more powerful than the "normal" model it's based on. The .44 Magnum cartridge, for example, is based on the older .44 Special but has a larger bullet and a longer case, allowing for more gunpowder.

PUMP-ACTION: Common on shotguns, a pump-action gun has a handgrip mounted on a slider on the bottom of a gun's barrel. Sliding the grip back and forward once ejects a spent case, loads another cartridge, and cocks the gun for firing.

ROUND: Another name for the cartridge. Another name: *shell*. (That's the most commonly used name for a shotgun cartridge—a "shotgun shell.")

SELECTIVE-FIRE: A selective-fire gun is able to switch between semi-automatic and automatic firing. Some have other options, such as a *three-round burst*, which fires three cartridges very quickly every time you press the trigger. An example of a selective-fire gun is the M-16 carried by U.S. Army soldiers.

STOCK: The rear section of a rifle or shotgun; the part meant to be held against the shoulder. It's usually made of wood—most often walnut—although stocks are increasingly being made of synthetic materials.

TRACER: Cartridges with specially designed bullets that have a flammable material (usually magnesium) in a hollow in their rears. That material burns upon being fired, which allows the bullet's path to be seen by the shooter. It's often used by the military, especially fighter pilots, to aid in aiming at a moving target.

VIERLING: *Vier* means "four" in German. And a *vierling* is a rare type of gun made by German gunmakers…with four barrels. Two for shotgun shells and two for rifle.

PARTING SHOTS

• The gunpowder used in almost all guns today is nothing like the "black powder" that was used in all guns until the late 1800s. Modern firearms use "smokeless" gunpowder (black-powder gunpowder is really smoky), and most commercial recipes are closely guarded corporate secrets.

• The fastest bullets from the most powerful rifles can travel at speeds of more than 3,000 miles per hour, or nearly four times the speed of sound. Shotgun pellets go about 800 miles per hour.

• You've heard of "gunshot residue" on the news and on TV crime shows. It's chemical residue left on the hands of someone who has recently fired a gun. The chemicals forensic scientists look for can come from the primer, gunpowder, case, or bullet of a fired cartridge.

• *Blanks*—the type of cartridge used in movies—are actual cartridges: They have case, primer, and gunpowder—they just have no bullets in them. (The bullet ends are just crimped shut.) That allows them to make a big BANG!—without firing a projectile.

*　　　*　　　*

POOCH HOOCH

In 2013, a brewery in the beer- and dog-loving town of Bend, Oregon, released Dawg Grog, a beer brewed especially for dogs. It's made with "malted barley water, liquid glucosamine, and organic vegetable broth," but no alcohol. Cost for a 16-ounce bottle: $9. (Or you could lift the toilet seat and let Fido drink from the can.)

7 FICTIONAL COCKROACHES

The stories behind several pretend cockroaches you may or may not be acquainted with. (And one that might not even be a cockroach at all.)

1 MUSICAL COCKROACH. *La Cucaracha* ("the cockroach" in Spanish) is the name of a Mexican folk song that you may remember singing as a kid (at least the "la cucaracha" part). The song's exact origins are unknown. It goes back to at least the early 19th century and possibly much farther—even to 15th-century Spain. The song became popular during the Mexican Revolution (1910–1920). Many of the best-known stanzas (there are hundreds) reflect revolutionary politics of that period, although the meanings of the lyrics are symbolic and satirical. (In other words, nobody really knows what they mean.) One theory is that the lyrics are meant to poke fun at leaders on both sides of the Revolution. Here's one of the most popular stanzas, translated into English: "The cockroach, the cockroach / cannot walk anymore / because it's lacking, because it doesn't have / marijuana to smoke." (That last line, believed to be a jab at President Huerta, who was known as a drunkard, is often changed to something more innocuous, such as "lemonade to drink," when sung around kids.)

2 OPPRESSED ANIME COCKROACHES. The 1987 Hiroaki Yoshida anime/live-action film *Twilight of the Cockroaches* is about a community of intelligent cockroaches who live peacefully in the apartment of a human slob named Seito. (The cockroaches are anime; the humans are live-action.) But when Seito's girlfriend moves in, she begins exterminating, and the cockroaches' paradise becomes a nightmarish struggle for survival. According to Yoshida, the film's cockroaches are a metaphor for the Japanese people, whom he deems a "hated species." *Washington Post* reviewer Richard Harrington wrote that the film "could do for cockroaches what *The Secret of NIMH* did for rats: humanize them in ways you'd never have thought possible." (That didn't happen, as you may have noticed.) One of the strangest scenes: The teenage cockroach heroine, Naomi, almost loses her life in a rainstorm, but is saved…

Earth is still cooling from its formation 4.5 billion years ago.

by a pile of talking dog poop. *Twilight of the Cockroaches* was the inspiration for the 1996 musical film *Joe's Apartment*, about a guy whose apartment is inhabited by singing, dancing cockroaches.

3 SAD ALIEN COCKROACHES. In the 1972 film *Godzilla vs. Gigan* (the 12th in the Godzilla series), aliens known as "Nebulons" invade Earth. They appear to be human, but they're not human—they're giant alien cockroaches disguised as humans! The Nebulons control the minds of two monsters—Gigan, a huge cyborg with a buzz saw in his belly, and King Ghidora, a three-headed dragonlike beast—and send them to destroy Tokyo. Luckily for the earthlings, the monsters are defeated by Godzilla. (Whew!) In the end we learn that the giant alien cockroaches only wanted a new home because their planet was destroyed by pollution created by that planet's human inhabitants. Moral: Stop polluting Earth, humans.

4 BELOVED POET COCKROACH. On March 29, 1916, writer Don Marquis told readers of his daily newspaper column, "The Sun Dial" in New York's *Evening Sun*, that when he arrived at the office one morning a few weeks earlier, he'd discovered a "gigantic cockroach jumping up and down upon the keys" of his typewriter. The cockroach did this for an hour, after which he scampered off. Marquis then looked at what the cockroach had written. It started like this:

> expression is the need of my soul
>
> i was once a vers libre bard
>
> but i died and my soul went into the
>
> body of a cockroach

The cockroach went on to request that Marquis leave a sheet of paper in the typewriter each night so that he (the cockroach) could continue writing. And he said they should call him "Archy." So was born Archy the poet cockroach, whose philosophical observations of life (in free verse) would become a regular—and very popular—part of Marquis's writing at the *Sun*, then at the *New York Tribune*, then at *Collier's* magazine, and then in books (along with Archy's best friend, an alley cat named Mehitabel) until Marquis died in 1937. But Archy and Mehitabel didn't die with Marquis. The characters were adapted into songs in 1954, a Broadway musical in

---

Steven Seagal made a solo album titled *Songs from the Crystal Cave*. Track #7: "Lollipop."

1957, a TV show in 1960, an animated film titled *Shinbone Alley*, written by Mel Brooks in 1971. More than 75 years later, the books (with illustrations by George Herriman, creator of the *Krazy Kat* comic strip) are still in print.

5 ALIEN ROBOT COCKROACHES. In a 1996 episode of *The X-Files*, Agent Fox Muldur investigates the deaths of several people in a Massachusetts town who appear to have been killed…by cockroaches! Muldur meets a voluptuous entomologist named Dr. Bambi Berenbaum, who happens to be conducting experiments on cockroaches. He shows her a cockroach he found at one of the crime scenes. She looks at it through her microscope, and tells Muldur that the cockroach he found is a robot cockroach. Muldur thinks it's actually an *alien* robot cockroach. (There's more, but we thought revealing spoilers might bug you.) Bonus: Bambi Berenbaum's character was named in honor of renowned entomologist—and founder of the Insect Fear Film Festival (see page 456)—May Berenbaum.

6 _____ THE COCKROACH. This one is a quiz; answer at end of the article. This 11-foot-tall alien cockroach crashes his spaceship into a pickup truck on a farm somewhere in America. He then kills the farmer, uses the guy's dead body as a disguise, and goes on a mission to find the Arquillian Galaxy. In the end, the cockroach tries to escape in another spaceship—but is shot down. Emerging from the wreckage, he rips off his human (dead body) disguise, and, now plainly an enormous cockroach, eats one of his assailants, who then shoots the big bug…from inside his stomach. The end. Now: Name that cockroach.

7 WELL-KNOWN LITERARY COCKROACH. Probably the most famous fictional cockroach is the one in Czech author Franz Kafka's 1915 novel, *The Metamorphosis*. But is it really a cockroach? The story opens with the lead character, Gregor Samsa, waking from a fitful night's sleep to discover, to his horror, that he has turned into an *ungeheures Ungeziefer*, usually translated into English as "monstrous insect." But that's a very loose translation. *Ungeheures* means "huge" or "enormous," and *Ungeziefer* literally means "vermin." Vermin could mean many things, including "bug" or "rat," but we know Kafka meant "insect" because he describes the metamorphosed Gregor as having a *carapace* (an insect's hard exoskeleton) as well as several legs (although he never says "six"). In fact, Kafka never says what kind of insect. People assume he meant cockroach, and many English translations of the book refer to Gregor as a cockroach. But critics argue that this is wrong—and they have some fairly serious support: Author Vladimir Nabokov, best known for his 1955 novel, *Lolita*, was also a trained lepidopterist—an expert on butterflies and moths. Nabokov insisted that Gregor hadn't turned into a cockroach—but a beetle. "A cockroach is an insect that is flat in shape with large legs, and Gregor is anything but flat," he wrote in a lecture for his literature students at Cornell University in the 1940s. "He is convex on both sides, belly and back, and his legs are small. He approaches a cockroach in only one respect: his coloration is brown." Nabokov even made sketches of the bug, based on Kafka's descriptions, and noted that an old woman in the book called Gregor a *Mistkäfer*—a "dung beetle." (Although Nabokov said he thought that was incorrect.) So there's a very good chance that the most famous fictional cockroach of all time wasn't a cockroach at all. (Which, of course, would make him a fictional fictional cockroach.)

ANSWER TO NUMBER 6: Edgar the Bug, the bad guy in the 1997 film *Men in Black*, played by Vincent D'Onofrio. (Edgar's cockroach brother, Edwin the Bug—voiced by D'Onofrio—appeared in several episodes of the animated *Men in Black: The Series*, which ran on the WB Network from 1997 to 2001.)

* * *

ANIMAL GROUP NAMES
- A husk of hares
- A leap of lizards
- A company of parrots
- A rag of colts
- A siege of herons
- A bloat of hippos
- A party of jays
- A flamboyance of flamingos

ANIMALS FAMOUS FOR 15 MINUTES

When Andy Warhol said, "In the future, everyone will be famous for fifteen minutes," he probably didn't have animals in mind. But even they haven't been able to escape the relentless publicity machine.

Headline: Turtle Twosome Turns Tumultuous

The Stars: Bibi and Poldi, two giant tortoises who live in an Austrian zoo

What Happened: The tortoises had been a couple since '98—that's 1898. After more than a century of marital bliss, the relationship hit the skids when Bibi, the female, bit off a chunk of Poldi's shell in 2012. They soon became so aggressive that they had to be separated. "They can't stand the sight of each other anymore," lamented zoo director Helga Happ. Not knowing what else to do, zoo officials called in animal psychologists to perform "couples counseling." They gave the pair special "amorous" treats to excite them. No response. They even made a dummy of Poldi (an empty shell covered with his scent) to see how Bibi would react, but she ignored it.

Aftermath: The couple is officially separated, but if there's ever a reconciliation (it's possible—giant tortoises can live for 150 years), Bibi and Poldi will likely get another 15 minutes of fame.

Headline: World's Cutest Dog Is Cute, But Who's Boo's Owner?

The Star: Boo, a fluffy Pomeranian, born in 2006

What Happened: Proclaimed the "World's Cutest Dog" by his owner, Boo got his own Facebook page when he was two years old. Cute photos and videos of the T-shirt-clad pup brought in a lot of fans—1.6 million by 2011. That's when *Good Morning, America* booked little cutie-Pom for an appearance, during which he sat on cohost Dan Harris's lap. Result: Boo now has six million fans.

Throughout the dog's fame, Boo's owner chose to remain behind the curtains, even crediting Boo as the "author" of the book, *Boo: The Life of the World's Cutest Dog.* However, in 2012, snooping reporters identified Boo's owner as Irene Ahn of San Francisco, who works in the finance department of…Facebook.

First food broken down during digestion: sugar. It starts breaking down in your mouth.

Conspiracy theorists went wild: Did Facebook insiders embellish Boo's fan base? The social network claims that Boo has racked up all those fans on his own.

Aftermath: At last report, Boo is still popular (and still cute).

Headline: Precious Pachyderm Becomes Presidential Present

The Star: Shanthi, an Asian elephant

What Happened: In 1975, Sri Lankan wildlife rangers discovered a newborn elephant stuck in a hole. Its mother had been shot by poachers. Near death, the baby elephant was nursed back to health and named Shanthi ("peace" in Sinhalese). When Shanthi turned two, Sri Lankan Prime Minister Sirimavo Bandaranaike announced she was giving the elephant to the United States for its Bicentennial. At a ceremony at the National Zoo in 1977, an 8-year-old Indian-American girl named Punitha Gunaratne presented the 600-pound elephant—on a leash—to Amy Carter, the 9-year-old daughter of President Jimmy Carter. "*Bohoma Sthuthi,*" said Amy ("thank you" in Sinhalese).

Aftermath: Shanthi settled into her new home at the National Zoo, where she still lives. She made headlines again in 2012 when, at the age of 37, she taught herself how to play the harmonica.

Headline: Big Cat on the Prowl? Cops: "You're Lion!"

The Star: A lion, or a tiger, a local wildcat…or maybe a large tabby

What Happened: Several eyewitness accounts and one grainy phone-camera photo gave rise to the legend of the "Essex Lion." In the summer and fall of 2012, the mysterious beast incited panic near the village of St. Oysth in Essex, England. It's difficult to tell for sure what kind of animal is depicted in the photo, but it appears to be a large cat lying in the grass. According to one eyewitness, it was "one hundred percent lion." Or, as another man put it as he was running toward a caravan camp, "There's a (censored) lion in the woods!" The Essex police were dubious—no nearby zoo or circus had reported a missing lion—but they decided to err on the side of caution. Thus began a massive cat hunt. Two helicopters searched from above while dozens of officers searched the surrounding forests. As the story made headlines worldwide, the "@Essex Lion" Twitter account (set up by townies) amassed 35,000 followers.

Aftermath: The search turned up nothing. Amidst complaints that the police wasted taxpayer money, the official conclusion was that the Essex Lion was most likely a "large domestic cat or a wildcat." Many townspeople still insist there is a lion on the loose. But not Ginny Murphy—she believes the confusion was caused by her pet housecat, a 28-inch-long Maine Coon named Teddy Bear who often hunts in one of the fields where the Essex Lion was spotted. The police haven't confirmed Murphy's claim, and the Essex Lion (if there really is one) is still at large.

Headline: Manhattan Transfer via Rocky Mountain High

The Star: Willow, a calico cat from Broomfield, Colorado

What Happened: When the Squires family got Willow as a kitten in 2004, they had a microchip implanted in her. Good move. Two years later, a contractor left a door open at their Colorado home, and Willow escaped. The family searched for the cat, but none of the fliers, Craigslist ads, or calls to vets and shelters turned up anything. The Squires feared that Willow had been killed (and eaten) by one of the area's many coyotes.

Five years passed. Then, in September 2011, a man found a calico cat wandering the streets of Manhattan. He took it to a shelter, where workers discovered the microchip, which led them to the Squires family. A few weeks later, *The Today Show* documented the happy family reunion in New York City. How the cat ended up 1,800 miles from home remains a mystery. The cat's coat was shiny, and she appeared to have been well-fed throughout the ordeal, but that's all the family knows. Said mom Jamie Squires, "It's better just for us to think she's been off on some great adventure."

Aftermath: Willow and her family returned to Colorado. At last report, Jamie was turning the cat's adventures into a children's book.

Headline: Mystery Monkey Captured—Has Herpes

The Star: Zoom Zoom, a Rhesus macaque roaming loose in St. Petersburg, Florida

What Happened: For three years, from 2009 to 2012, a small macaque (a monkey native to Asia) lived in the trees and backyards of the Lakewood Estates neighborhood in St. Pete. No one knew where he'd come from, and with every unsuccessful attempt to capture him—many of them covered by the local news—"Zoom Zoom" (as locals called him) became more and more famous. He

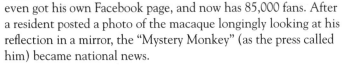

even got his own Facebook page, and now has 85,000 fans. After a resident posted a photo of the macaque longingly looking at his reflection in a mirror, the "Mystery Monkey" (as the press called him) became national news.

And then locals started feeding him. That's a big no-no. Feeding a wild animal can lead to aggressive behavior, which is exactly what happened. In October 2012, Zoom Zoom scratched and bit a 60-year-old woman who was sitting on her porch. She had to get shots for rabies, hepatitis, and herpes B. Zoom Zoom kept stalking her—he even watched her through a skylight while she took showers. Then he became aggressive toward other people in the neighborhood.

That's when area wildlife expert Vernon Yates, who'd been tracking Zoom Zoom, hired a veterinarian with a tranquilizer gun to incapacitate and capture the monkey. It worked. Zoom Zoom tested positive for herpes B, so anyone who'd come in contact with him was urged to seek medical attention.

Aftermath: Two months after his capture, the macaque, renamed Cornelius (after the lead ape from Planet of the Apes), was given a new home at a wildlife park in nearby Dade City. At last report, Cornelius has a girlfriend...and is herpes-free.

*   *   *

ACCORDING TO THE LATEST RESEARCH

In 2010, the *Journal of Marketing* reported on a study about brand names and buying habits conducted by Jennifer Argo, a marketing professor at the University of Alberta. She gave test subjects two different kinds of ice cream to try. One was called "Zanozan," and the other was called "Zanovum." Most of the tasters preferred "Zanozan." Argo performed the test four more times with other ice creams, and each time the results were the same: The tasters preferred the ice cream that had repetitive syllables in its name. But what the test subjects didn't know was that all the ice cream was identical, which led Argo to conclude that consumers prefer products—food or otherwise—that have alliterative, repetitive names. That bodes well for brands such as Tutti-Frutti, PayPal, Krispy Kreme, Best Buy, Kit-Kat, and Coca-Cola.

Dry beard hair is as difficult to cut as copper wire of the same thickness.

THE BRITISH ARE COMING!, PART IV

Our final installment of the "British Invasion" period of rock music in the 1960s. (Part III is on page 395.)

GERRY AND THE PACEMAKERS

Name the British band that went to #1 (in England) with their first three singles. Not the Beatles—it's Gerry and the Pacemakers. While the Dave Clark Five and the Rolling Stones were the Beatles' biggest competition in the U.S., back home it was the Beatles vs. Gerry and the Pacemakers. Gerry Marsden and his brother Fred formed the band in the late '50s to play pop songs and old-fashioned British music hall songs with a hint of rock. After playing the Hamberg scene (like the Beatles), the Pacemakers were signed by manager Brian Epstein (like the Beatles). They got a deal with EMI Records (like the Beatles) and were produced by the Beatles' favorite producer, George Martin. Martin convinced them to record "How Do You Do It?" which he couldn't convince the Beatles to do, because it was too old-fashioned and they wanted to record their own songs. It went to #1. Mitch Murray wrote that song, as well as the Pacemakers' second single, "I Like It," also a #1. (The third #1 was a remake of "You'll Never Walk Alone," a song from the 1940s musical *Carousel.*) Having established a toehold on the charts, Marsden was allowed to record his own songs, including the hits "It's Gonna Be All Right," "I'm the One," "Don't Let the Sun Catch You Cryin'" and the band's signature song, "Ferry Cross the Mersey," which was loaded with strings and was an early example of soft rock. Even though they beat the Beatles in doing a song with strings, they were not as fresh or progressive as the Beatles, and broke up in 1966.

THE HONEYCOMBS

In late 1963, Martin Murray, a 24-year-old hairdresser from working-class East London decided to start a rock band. He recruited his assistant at the hair salon, Honey Lantree, to play drums, Lantree's brother John to play bass, and two of John Lantree's friends, singer

---

According to the latest research, there is no evidence that sugar causes hyperactivity in kids.

Dennis D'Eli and guitarist Alan Ward, to fill out the band, called the Sheratons. They played in pubs around London in early 1964, and were spotted by songwriters Ken Howard and Alan Blaikley. The Sheratons had secured an audition with producer Joe Meek—who had just written and produced the Tornados' #1 hit, "Telstar," making them the first British band to hit #1 in America. Howard and Blaikley convinced the Sheratons to play their song, "Have I the Right?" when they met Meek. Meek loved it, produced it, and got it released on Pye Records in June 1964...with one stipulation. A Pye executive thought "The Sheratons" was a very ordinary name, and that the band should accentuate the one thing that made it stand out from other Merseybeat bands: They were the only one with a woman in the band. So even though Honey Lantree was the drummer, and not the most prominent band member, they renamed themselves the Honeycombs. It may have helped, because "Have I the Right?" hit #1 in the U.K., Australia, and Canada, and reached the top 5 in the United States. That would be their biggest success. The next single, "Is It Because," barely cracked the top 40 (in England only). Over the next two years, they made six more singles, including "That's the Way," which featured Lantree singing. But with no more hits coming, members slowly left the group. The Honeycombs officially broke up in 1967.

THE NASHVILLE TEENS

Of course the Nashville Teens weren't from anywhere near Nashville—the band was from Surrey—but the name is indicative of the kind of music the band made, which was heavily influenced by American country and blues. (The name is a reference to the Everly Brothers' song "Nashville Blues.") Like so many other bands of the era, the Nashville Teens played the burgeoning club scene in Germany, playing gigs through Cologne, Frankfurt, and in Hamburg. More focused on recreating the classic blues sound than their British Invasion counterparts, the Nashville Teens proved so adept at it that they were often asked to be the backing band for touring American stars, including R&B legend Bo Diddley and rockabilly pioneer Carl Perkins. They even served as the backing band on Jerry Lee Lewis' classic *Live at the Star Club* album. Singer and producer Mickie Most signed the band to a deal in 1964, and they recorded a cover of John D. Loudermilk's country standard "Tobacco Road," inspired by the Erskine Caldwell novel about

---

The fruit of the female Gingko biloba tree smells like vomit.

rural Southern poverty. The band updated it to a hard-charging, bluesy rock song, and it became a big hit—#6 in England and #14 in America. Also notable about the song is the vocal arrangement: The Nashville Teens had two lead singers, Ray Phillips and Art Sharp, as well as a third dedicated backing vocalist, Terry Crow. Their second single, another Loudermilk adaptation called "Google Eye," went Top 10 in England…and went unnoticed in the U.S., as did all their subsequent singles. Music historians say the Nashville Teens were doomed, ironically, by the same "British Invasion" that made them successful—they were serious musicians focused on the music, and lacked the charisma or a breakout personality that their contemporaries had. The band started to lose original members by the early '70s, but Ray Phillips still tours (with hired musicians) as the Nashville Teens.

HERMAN'S HERMITS

Formed in Manchester in 1963 as the Heartbeats, the group couldn't break out of its city's crowded music scene until they got a new lead singer, 15-year-old Peter Noone. He was already famous, having been a child actor on the popular British soap opera *Coronation Street*. But he really wanted to be a singer, and he didn't want to cash in on his fame, either, so he billed himself as "Peter Novak." That wasn't the only name change. Band member Karl Green remarked one day that the baby-faced Noone resembled Sherman of the "Mr. Peabody" cartoon. That comment evolved into "Herman," then "Herman and his Hermits," and finally, "Herman's Hermits." Their style wasn't blues or three-chord rock. They preferred light sing-songy melodic bubble-gum music, performing poppy covers of old standards, sung by Noone who intentionally overemphasized his Manchester accent. Producer Mickie Most signed the group in 1964 because of their inoffensive music and Noone's potential as a teen heartthrob. He got them a record deal, and they released their first single in 1964: "I'm into Something Good," written by Carole King and Gerry Goffin. It went to #1 in England, and #13 in the United States. However, from the start the marketing focused on Noone—he sang on the records, but all the instruments were played by studio musicians, which included future Led Zeppelin members Jimmy Page and John Paul Jones. The strategy worked, though—Noone became one of the '60s most popular teen idols, and Herman's Hermits rang up a bunch of catchy pop hits from 1964 to '68, including "I'm Into Something Good," "Can't

You Hear My Heartbeat," "Silhouettes," "Wonderful World," "Listen People," "Dandy," "There's A Kind of Hush," and two #1 hits, "Mrs. Brown You've Got a Lovely Daughter" and "I'm Henry VIII, I Am," a rock version of a music hall standard that Noone liked because it was one of his grandfather's favorite songs. Changing tastes led to the band's singles becoming less and less popular. The band dissolved in the early '70s, when Noone left for a lackluster solo career, although he has earned a living ever since playing "nostalgia" tours in the U.S. and U.K.

AND THE BEAT GOES ON...

There were dozens more British Invasion bands that had hit records in the '60s. Here are just a few more.

The Kinks

The Who

The Yardbirds

The Animals

The Hollies

Dusty Springfield

The Searchers

Manfred Mann

Petula Clark

The Troggs

The Zombies

Wayne Fontana & the Mindbenders

The Moody Blues

Small Faces

Freddie & the Dreamers

Marianne Faithfull

The Pretty Things

Them

The Fortunes

The Spencer Davis Group

Adam Faith

The Merseybeats

The Barron Knights

The New Vaudeville Band

Unit 4+2

The Rockin' Berries

The Silkie

David & Jonathan

Lulu

The Ivy League

Ian Whitcomb

The Hullaballoos

Georgie Fame & the Blue Flames

The Mojos

The Sorrows

The Alan Price Set

Hedgehoppers Anonymous

Chad & Jeremy

The Beat Merchants

The Action

Money laundering: Japanese ATMs sterilize cash before dispensing it.

ALL ABOUT SEASHELLS

If you put a large seashell to your ear, you can hear the ocean! Not really. What you hear is the shell amplifying the ambient noise around you. But it's a wonderful thing to believe when you're a kid. Here are some other fascinating facts about nature's most curious—and beautiful—"living houses."

REMAINS OF THE DAY

Seashells come in a vast array of shapes, colors, and sizes, but they all have one basic (and creepy) thing in common: They're the partial remains of dead animals. Finding a seashell is the equivalent, in a way, of finding a human skeleton on the beach. But seashells are the *outer* skeletons (technically, *exo-skeletons*) of their deceased inhabitants. Their soft remains have either been eaten or rotted away.

There are literally hundreds of thousands of animal species that grow and leave behind seashells, ranging in size from microscopic to sofa size. Most of what we think of as classic seashells were made by marine mollusks. That's because they make the sturdiest, longest-lasting shells. Marine mollusks include *gastropods*—which include an enormous variety of sea snails; *bivalves*—such as clams, oysters, and scallops; *scaphopods*—that make tusk-shaped shells; and some *cephalopods*—such as the nautilus and spirula. (There are many types of mollusks that make no shells at all, including sea slugs and octopuses.)

BUILDING BLOCKS

All mollusks have the same basic body form: They have a head, which holds the sense organs; a *visceral mass*, or the internal organs; and a foot. And all mollusks—even ones that don't create shells—have an organ known as a *mantle*, which comes from the Latin *mantellum*, meaning "cloak" or "cape," so named because it sort of looks like a cape draped over the animal's back. The mantle has the crucial job of containing the mollusk's visceral mass. On mollusks that produce shells, it has another job: Build and maintain the shell.

Seashells are made up almost completely of the calcium-based mineral calcium carbonate. Animals that create these shells acquire the ingredients needed to make it—calcium, carbon, and oxygen—

from their food sources and even from the water around them. Those ingredients are collected from the mollusk's bloodstream by specialized cells in the mantle. They are then combined with different proteins made just for the job and secreted out of the mantle surface. The resulting material quickly hardens into shell.

CONEHEADS

You've probably seen seashells that have a coiled, spiral end (sort of like a soft-serve ice-cream cone) with an opening at the other end. These are the shells of gastropods—the snails and slugs of the world. (That also includes the snails in your garden, but we're talking about the ocean variety.) The pointy tip of this seashell is the oldest part of the shell. Gastropods begin building them while they are still in a microscopic larval stage. That tiny shell is known as a *protoconch* (pronounced "proto-kahnk"), and it already has a spiral configuration—simply because gastropod DNA instructs the creature to create its shell in this way, the same way human DNA instructs your body to grow your bones as they do.

As the tiny gastropod grows, it adds to its protoconch by secreting shell material from its mantle onto the shell's opening, causing the shell to grow in successively larger spiraling coils—to accommodate the creature's growing body—down and away from the shell's tip. (Picture a spiral staircase—one that grows from the top down, and gets larger as it goes down.)

Pictured on the right is the seashell from a type of sea snail known as a *whelk*. (It was drawn in 1878 by Dutch-Belgian *macacologist*—someone who studies mollusks—Pierre-Henri Nyst.)

• The top of the shell is a protoconch. It's also known as the *apex* of the shell.

• The coils growing down from the shell's tip are known as *whorls*. The top whorls make up the shell's *spire*.

• The lower whorl is the *body whorl*. While alive, it's where the bulk of the animal's soft body resides.

• The opening is the *aperture*. It's from here the animal is able to reach out of the shell to move, eat, and breathe.

• If you were to cut a gastropod shell open, you would see its *columella*—or "little column"—a column of shell material running from the apex down along the central axis of the shell, like the supporting pole of a spiral staircase.

THE OCEAN'S ARCHITECTS

Shell building is more than simply adding material to the lip of the opening. Mollusk shells are complex structures, made up of three distinct layers, each created in a different manner:

• The *periostracum*, meaning "around the shell," is the thin hard outer layer. It's made of a protein-based substance called *conchiolin*, and acts as a kind of varnish that protects the shell.

• The *prismatic* layer consists of prism-shaped (many-sided) crystals of calcium carbonate that are stacked perpendicular to the direction of the periostracum. This the thickest, strongest layer of the shell.

• The *nacreous* layer, or nacre, is the smooth inner layer that comes in contact with the creature inside. It's made up of microscopic plates (another crystal form of calcium carbonate, called *aragonite*) laid like stonework and held together with gluelike proteins.

The first two layers are created by cells at the leading edge of the mantle—at the outer lip of the shell's aperture. The nacre layer, on the other hand, is secreted by the entire outer surface of the mantle. The mantle adds nacre to the inner surface of the shell throughout the creature's life, making it thicker and thicker as it grows.

Cool Nacre Fact: Nacre is also known as "mother-of-pearl"—and is, in fact, what the outer layers of pearls are made of. Why is it so colorful, and why does it seem to change color if you move it? Because the microscopic plates of aragonite that make up nacre naturally cause the light that strikes it to diffract—giving the inside of seashells (and pearls) their natural iridescence.

CLAM UP

The other classes of mollusks all grow their shells in a way that's similar to the gastropods. Bivalves such as clams and oysters, for example, begin to grow their shells while still microscopic larvae. Of course, with bivalves it's not just one shell, but two nearly identical shells, or *valves*. A flexible band of ligament connects the two shells and serves as a hinge, allowing the creatures that inhabit them to open and close the shells against each another. Bivalves grow

Ancient Egyptian snack: raw salted duck.

those shells by secreting shell material onto the outer edge of each shell—which means the shell closest to the hinge is the oldest part of bivalve shells, and the shell at the opening is the newest.

If you ever find horn- or tusk-shaped seashells—they actually look like little hollow elephant tusks with an opening at each end—they're from mollusks known as *scaphopods*. They grow from the skinny end out to the larger end, and range from about one to five inches long. If you happen to see one alive, you'd probably just see its rear end—the skinny end of the shell. You can sometimes see them sticking up out of the seafloor. Scaphopods spend their lives with their heads—at the thicker end of the shell—buried in the seafloor, foraging for food and pooping their waste out of their rear ends into the water.

MORE MOLLUSKS

Conch: These are a family of about 60 species of large sea snails, some of which grow to nearly two feet long. They're characterized by having rows of spikes on their shells and, when fully adult, a wide flaring outer lip. Conchs are among the world's best known seashells, and you can play them like musical instruments: Cut the pointy end off the conch and blow into it like a trumpet.

Periwinkle: Periwinkle shells look a lot like garden-snail shells, but with quite pronounced and pointy spires and usually six to seven whorls. They come in a variety of colors and patterns.

Cowry: Cowry shells are egg-shaped and have a slit-like aperture than runs along the lower portion of the shell. The lips of the aperture are ribbed—making the opening look almost like a toothed mouth. The amazing thing about cowries, though, is that they are incredibly smooth and shiny and often spectacularly colored and patterned. In fact, the term *porcelain* comes from the word *porcellana*—the Italian name for the cowry shell.

Auger: You'll recognize these shells, as they have a long, multi-whorled pointy spire above a quite small aperture. (They are so named because they are thought to resemble augers, or drills.)

Nautilus: These free-swimming cephalopods look like their cousins—octopuses and squids—except that nautiluses have shells. There are only six species; they make shells that range from about six to eleven inches in diameter. If you're ever lucky enough to find

---

Al Capone played banjo in the Alcatraz prison band.

a nautilus shell, you'll know it: It's cream-colored with reddish-brown tigerlike stripes. It has a spiral configuration, like the gastropods, but the spiraling coils grow out and around the shell's apex, growing larger as they do.

SEASHELL MISCELLANY

• A few other animals that make seashells: *tube worms*—gastropods that make squiggly worm-shaped shells; and *echinodirms*—such as starfish and sea urchins. (Sea-urchin shells are called *tests*. A well known type of test: the sand dollar.)

• Next time you see a slug, look at it closely: That leathery patch on its back, near its head, is its mantle. (Slugs don't use their mantles to make shells—but you can at least say you've seen one.)

• Cuttlebone is the elongated disc-shaped seashell of the cuttlefish, a squidlike cephalopod. What's different from other seashells is that cuttlebone grows *inside* the cuttlefish's body. Cuttlefish use their multi-chambered gas-filled cuttlebones for buoyancy control.

• Many gastropods have what's known as an *operculum* ("little lid"). It's a flat round piece of shell attached to the gastropod's foot that can be retracted into the shell's aperture, sealing the creature tightly inside. These beautiful seashells are also known as "cats' eyes."

• Scallop shells are ribbed and almost flat, resembling an open-handed fan. Botticelli's famous Renaissance painting *The Birth of Venus* depicts the goddess Venus rising from the sea on top of a large shell. It's a scallop shell. (So is the logo of Shell Oil.)

• Shell Beach, Western Australia, is entirely made up of the fragmented shells of clams known as *cockles*—the same "cockle shells" in the nursery rhyme "Mary, Mary, Quite Contrary."

• Most gastropod shells are "right-handed": The whorls grow to the right—clockwise—away from the protoconch. About 10 percent are "left-handed," meaning they grow counterclockwise. Another species that has a 9-to-1 ratio of righties to lefties: human beings.

*   *   *

"There's no better feeling in the world than a warm pizza box on your lap." —**Kevin James**

A kangaroo pouch has muscles that contract to secure a joey when mom runs or jumps.

THE MAN WHO SEES WITH HIS EARS

Echolocation is the term for the way bats, dolphins, some species of whales, and even birds use sound to "see" the world around them. Humans can do it, too. Sound impossible? Meet Daniel Kish.

SECOND SIGHT

Not long after Daniel Kish was born in Southern California in 1966, his parents got the kind of news that parents dread: Daniel had been born with *retinoblastoma*, a form of cancer that affects the retina, the thin layer of light-sensitive tissue in the back of the eye. Retinoblastoma is an aggressive and potentially deadly form of cancer and, as Daniel's parents soon learned, surgical removal of the affected eye is often the only treatment available. Because Daniel developed the disease in both eyes, they both had to be removed, and from the age of 13 months on, he was blind.

When Daniel was about two years old, he began clicking his tongue against the roof of his mouth and using the sound it created to analyze the physical world around him. This phenomenon is not unheard of in blind children. Many instinctively tap their feet, clap their hands, or make other noises. Then, by listening to the echoes that bounce off nearby objects, they can sense their environment. The behavior is an outgrowth of a natural ability common in human beings with normal hearing: When someone calls out your name, for example, the sound waves arrive first at the ear closest to the sound's source, and then at the other ear a short time later. Your brain uses this audio cue to determine which direction the sound is coming from—that's how you know which way to turn when your name is called.

GO AHEAD

In the 1960s, it was common for the parents of blind children to discourage behavior that sighted people might find unsettling, such as rocking back and forth or making repeated clicking, clapping, or snapping sounds. Daniel was lucky. His parents let him click away. Perhaps because they were so permissive, he developed his ability far beyond that of most blind children. He learned to make his way around the house and the backyard without bumping into obstacles. By the age of three, he was clicking his way all around the neighborhood, often with his parents, but sometimes also sneaking out on his own in the middle of the night.

PICTURE THIS

In just a few years, Daniel developed the ability to form very detailed spatial images of his environment:

• If the echoes from his tongue clicks sounded very near at ground level, then a little farther away one foot off the ground, and progressively farther away the higher he "looked," that, he came to understand, was the acoustic signature of a flight of stairs.

• Leafy bushes had a fluttery signature all their own; a tree was like a bush sitting on top of a telephone pole—the tree trunk. (A telephone pole without a bush on top of it really *was* a telephone pole.)

• Human beings had smaller, softer signatures, which made them harder to detect. But Daniel learned to discern the presence of people from as far as six feet away.

• When Daniel's tongue clicks bounced off a large metal object that was low at one end, higher in the middle, and low again at the other end, he knew he was "seeing" a car. (If the car was longer at one end, that meant it was a pickup truck.) Daniel developed the ability to detect vehicles from more than 30 feet away. If he was near enough, he could even tell how close they were to the curb.

THAT EXPLAINS IT

Everything in the physical world has its own acoustic signature, and as Daniel grew older, he learned to interpret thousands of them, including objects as small as golf balls and as large as office buildings, which he could perceive from 1,000 feet away. He did it intuitively, without really understanding what he was doing any more than a sighted kid his age understands how his vision works. It wasn't until he was ten years old and a friend explained the concept of echolocation (also known as "sonar") that he realized his tongue clicking helped him to find his way around his world the same way that bats, dolphins, some species of whales, and submarines find their way around theirs.

KID STUFF

Daniel's mother, who by now was divorced and raising Daniel on her own, went out of her way to treat him as she would a sighted kid. A lot of blind children are educated in special schools, but Daniel attended mainstream schools alongside sighted children. Naturally, he wanted to be able to do everything his classmates did, and he succeeded to a remarkable degree. He made his way around the school and his neighborhood without assistance. He swam, climbed trees, and went on hikes both with his friends and by himself. His clicking enabled him to find the signs that marked wilderness trails, and he could read them by running his fingers along the engraved lettering. He even learned how to ride a bike, not just on flat ground in safe, wide-open spaces, but also on winding mountain bike trails and even on roads with other bicycles and cars.

HEARING IS BELIEVING

Kish was a gifted student, and after high school he went on to college and then graduate school, where he earned master's degrees in developmental psychology and special education. He devoted much of his postgraduate work to developing a better scientific understanding of how echolocation works in the human brain:

• When MRIs are made of the brains of sighted people while they listen to the tongue clicks made by someone using echolocation, not much brain activity takes place. The person's mind hears the sounds but doesn't really do anything with them.

• When the MRI is taken of the brain of a blind person who has learned to use echolocation, the results are very different. The sounds of the tongue clicks and echoes cause the visual cortex or image-processing center of the brain to light up. The visual cortex extracts information contained in the echoes and uses it to construct detailed mental images of the surrounding world. "It's like seeing with sound, as if with dim flashes of light but using flashes of sound instead," Kish says. He calls his method of echolocation "FlashSonar."

• These MRI scans support other evidence that suggests the human brain takes information from a number of sources, not just the eyes, to form mental images of the surrounding world. When information from the eyes is not obtainable, as in the case of a blind person, the visual cortex continues to form images using whatever information is available. And the more information a blind person can supply to the brain, the better the mental images. "The whole thing for us is that it can be taught," says Kish. "The trick is training the brain to know what to listen for and how to process that information."

SPREADING THE WORD

In 2001, Daniel Kish founded a nonprofit organization called World Access for the Blind. Operating out of his home in Long Beach, he and a handful of assistants, also blind, teach students the fundamentals of FlashSonar and also how to use it to perform activities of daily life, such as navigating around town, shopping, and riding the bus. They also teach students how to use FlashSonar in a variety of recreational activities, including bike riding, tree climbing, skateboarding, and playing soccer, basketball, and other sports, The emphasis on recreational skills is part of the organization's "No Limits" philosophy that encourages students to think beyond the restrictions that are usually placed on blind people, either by themselves or by outsiders.

Students who live in Southern California attend World Access for the Blind's FlashSonar classes a few times a month and use the time between classes to develop their skills. For students who live farther away, Kish and his assistants use the $200,000 in donations they raise each year to fly across the United States and around the world to provide intensive training seminars at little or no cost to the students. As of 2013, they have taught FlashSonar to more than 1,000 students in 30 countries. They also provide instruction to people who train the blind, to ensure that FlashSonar continues to spread. In the process, Kish hopes to enable blind people to win greater independence than they may have ever imagined was possible. "Blindness isn't the end for everyone, but the beginning for many," he says.

*　　*　　*

OOPS!

"A New York City man was knocked down by a car and got up uninjured, but lay back down in front of the car when a bystander told him to feign injury in order to collect insurance money. The car rolled forward and crushed him to death."

—Associated Press

The front of a giraffe's tongue is dark purple to protect it from sunburn while eating.

ANSWERS

WORD GAMES

Answers from page 221

1. These are the only states that begin with these letters. Every other state has at least one other state that begins with the same letter.

2. A sequoia

3. Forty.

4. Capitalize the first letter. The word *nice* becomes *Nice* (nees), a city in France; *rainier* becomes *Ranier* (ra-neer), a volcano in Washington State; and *tangier* becomes *Tangier* (tan-jeer), a city in Morocco.

5. 317,537. The names correspond to how you spell them on an upside-down calculator: OLLIE = 31,770; ELSIE is 31,573; and LESLIE is 317,537.

6. The two words are *valve* and *value*.

7. The letter "l"—which makes a pear into a pearl.

8. Water, otherwise known as H_2O, which is represented in the question by the letters "H" to "O".

9. You are making a mountain out of a molehill.

10. Maine, Maryland, Massachusetts, Michigan, Minnesota, Mississippi, Missouri, Montana

11. Take away "SIX LETTERS" and you are left with "BANANA."

12. Seven

13. The letter "y" changes a *lad* into a *lady*.

14. The letter "a" because it makes *her hear*.

15. The five vowels are all lined up, in order, in "a tennis court."

16. They are all anagrams of fabrics: Lenin = linen; Alec = lace; mined = denim; saint = satin; Proselyte = polyester.

ACTION JACKSONS QUIZ

Answers from page 320

1. i, **2.** e, **3.** l, **4.** b, **5.** f, **6.** d, **7.** j, **8.** k, **9.** c, **10.** g, **11.** a, **12.** h

RIDDLE ME THIS

Answers from page 257

1. The letter "v"
2. A key
3. A piano
4. "Mother" Earth
5. A stop sign
6. Pieces of a jigsaw puzzle
7. A phone
8. A deciduous tree
9. The letter "e"
10. Your heart
11. A fart

POLITICALLY CORRECT QUIZ

Answers from page 166.

1. a) The directive came from their employer, Westaff, which supplies Santa Clauses to malls throughout Australia. Not only was "Ho-Ho-Ho" deemed derogatory to women, but the company said it could also frighten children if the Santas yelled it too loudly, so they were told to lower their voices and say "Ha-Ha-Ha." After many grumpy Santas complained (and press reports mocked Westaff), the company relented, telling the Santas to simply "use discretion" when talking to kids.

2. c) The ban was instituted by the school's headmaster, Keith Evans, after a student on the receiving end of a flung triangular waffle had to go the school nurse with a "sore eye." Really. The kitchen staff, which made the waffles, were baffled. "It's the most ludicrous thing I've heard," said one. "I thought it was a joke. Even if you only have rectangular or square-shaped flapjacks, the children could still break them into triangles and launch them at someone."

3. b) It didn't matter that Fort Gay is a real town (pop. 800); Moore's account was frozen. After he complained a few times, Microsoft threatened him with a lifetime ban if he kept badgering them (even though he'd prepaid for a two-year subscription). Fort Gay's mayor even contacted the computer company to verify that it was a real town, but was told by a customer service rep that the word *gay* is "always offensive." The ban remained...until the story hit the Internet, and Microsoft's overly-PC customer service department was ridiculed from every corner of cyberspace. Then, just like that, Moore's account was unfrozen, and the company sent him an apology.

4. b) When PETA sent the letter to the Pet Shop Boys (Neil Tennant and Chris Lowe), they admitted it might seem a bit bizarre, but claimed it would help to raise awareness about the poor conditions in some of the breeding farms that supply animals to pets shops. The Pet Shop Boys posted the letter on their website—to help raise awareness—but told PETA they "couldn't agree to the name-change request."

5. a) When opened, the audio greeting card—which features Hallmark's animated characters "Hoops & Yoyo"—says, "And you black holes, you're so ominous! And you planets, watch your back!" The card had been on sale for three years without generating complaints, but in 2010, a member of the Los Angeles chapter of the NAACP publicly criticized Hallmark, saying it sounded like the company was "joking about blackness." A Hallmark representative explained that the card simply meant that the graduate was ready to take on anything, even a massive astronomical phenomenon that happens to be called a black hole. The NAACP countered that the word "holes" was pronounced with a "r" sound, which suggested that African-American women are "whores" and therefore you should "watch your back." Hallmark flatly denied the accusation, but pulled the card from circulation.

6. c) This story made news in 2013 after Tory MP Bob Blackman found out about it from a teacher at the unidentified school. The "no red ink" rule was so unpopular that the British government had to reassure the public that the order did not come from them—the school headmaster was acting alone when he or she told the teachers what colors they could use to mark up schoolwork. "It sounds to me like some petty edict which is nonsense," complained Blackman. "It is political correctness gone wild!"

THIS IS *JEOPARDY!* ANSWERS

Answers from page 107

JEOPARDY!

Last Initial "N"

$10: Who is Jim Nabors?
$20: Who is Pola Negri?
$30: Who is Nizer?
$40: Who is Vladimir Nabokov?
$50: Who is Bob Newhart?

Trees

$10: What are needles (or thorns)?
$20: What is pine?
$30: What is a pussy willow?
$40: What is aspen?
$50: What is Oak Ridge?

Odds & Ends

$10: What is marquess?
$20: What is arc?
$30: What is 64?
$40: What is a napper?
$50: What is national defense?

Potent Potables

$10: What is "vin"?
$20: What is rye or bourbon?
$30: What is champagne?
$40: What is California?
$50: What is the daiquiri?

Show Music

$10: What is a Mutual Admiration Society?
$20: What is love?
$30: What is *Paint Your Wagon*?
$40: What is "You're the Top"?
$50: What is *No, No Nanette*?

Answers from page 394

DOUBLE JEOPARDY!

Myth and Legend

$20: What are monsters?
$40: What is Olympus?
$60: Who is Guinevere?
$80: Who is Nike?
$100: What is the northern light?

Politics

$20: What is a congressional page?
$40: What is Arkansas?
$60: Who is Sam Yorty?
$80: Who is George P. Shultz?
$100: Who is Shirley Chisholm?

World Geography

$20: What is Argentina?
$40: What is Austria?
$60: What are France and Italy?
$80: What is Algeria?
$100: What is Pakistan?

Colleges

$20: What is M.I.T.?
$40: What is Roman Catholic?
$60: What is Brigham Young University?
$80: What is Ohio State?
$100: What is the University of Chicago?

Science

$20: What is oxygen?
$40: What are cyclamates?
$60 What is a chimp?
$80 What is chemical engineering?
$100 What is German?

More UNCLE JOHN than you can shake a stick at!

Log onto our online store at www.bathroomreader.com
for dozens more great titles in the Bathroom Reader
line. You'll find puzzle books, regional-interest books,
big books, little books, and introducing—e-books!
Great reading no matter where you are!

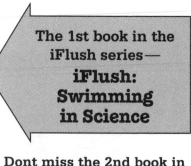

The 1st book in the
iFlush series—
iFlush: Swimming in Science

Dont miss the 2nd book in
the iFlush series—
Hurtling Through History.
Coming in 2014:

Hunting for Heroes

Plunging into Mystery

Other outrageously cool For Kids Only! titles:

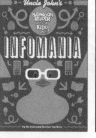

To order, contact:

Bathroom Readers' Press
P.O. Box 1117
Ashland, OR 97520
Phone: 888-488-4642
Fax: 541-482-6159

www.bathroomreader.com

UNCLE JOHN'S BATHROOM READER CLASSIC SERIES

THE LAST PAGE

FELLOW BATHROOM READERS:
The fight for good bathroom reading should never be taken loosely—we must do our duty and sit firmly for what we believe in, even while the rest of the world is taking potshots at us.

We'll be brief. Now that we've proven we're not simply a flush-in-the-pan, we invite you to take the plunge: Sit Down and Be Counted! Log on to *www.bathroomreader.com* and earn a permanent spot on the BRI honor roll!

If you like reading our books...

VISIT THE BRI'S WEBSITE!

www.bathroomreader.com

- Visit "The Throne Room"—a great place to read!
- Receive our irregular newsletters via e-mail
- Order additional Bathroom Readers
- Find us on Facebook
- Tweet us on Twitter
- Blog us on our blog

Go with the Flow...

Well, we're out of space, and when you've gotta go, you've gotta go. Tanks for all your support. Hope to hear from you soon.

Meanwhile, remember...

Keep on flushin'!